THE FALL
OF THE
DYNASTIES

THE FALL
OF THE
DYNASTIES

THE COLLAPSE OF THE OLD ORDER: 1905—1922

by Edmond Taylor

Skyhorse Publishing
A Herman Graf Book

First published in 1963

First Skyhorse Publishing edition 2015

All rights to any and all materials in copyright owned by the publisher are strictly reserved by the publisher. All inquiries should be addressed to Skyhorse Publishing, 307 West 36th Street, 11th Floor, New York, NY 10018.

Skyhorse Publishing books may be purchased in bulk at special discounts for sales promotion, corporate gifts, fund-raising, or educational purposes. Special editions can also be created to specifications. For details, contact the Special Sales Department, Skyhorse Publishing, 307 West 36th Street, 11th Floor, New York, NY 10018 or info@skyhorsepublishing.com.

Skyhorse® and Skyhorse Publishing® are registered trademarks of Skyhorse Publishing, Inc.®, a Delaware corporation.

Visit our website at www.skyhorsepublishing.com.

10 9 8 7 6 5 4 3 2 1

Library of Congress Cataloging-in-Publication Data is available on file.

Cover design by Brian Peterson
Cover illustration is of the assassination of Franz Ferdinand and was published in *Le Petit Journal* in 1914.

Print ISBN: 978-1-63450-601-4
Ebook ISBN: 978-1-5107-0051-2

Printed in the United States of America

Acknowledgments

My greatest debt—an immense one—for help on this book is to my wife, Anne V. Taylor, who in addition to offering sound criticism and encouragement at every stage of its preparation carried a large part of the burden of research and collaborated in writing several of the key chapters, notably Chapters 1, 5, 8, 11, 17, and 18. I naturally owe a particular debt for encouragement, criticism, and advice to John Gunther. I am also indebted for research and advice on several sections to Dr. Elsa Bernaut, Beata Levy, and Waverley Root, and to Eleanor Ohman, who also gave devoted secretarial assistance. I am deeply grateful to Manes Sperber for detailed and invaluable comments on the entire manuscript, and to Dr. Max Ascoli who offered several excellent suggestions for its improvement.

Contents

*Maps and Genealogical Charts
by Rafael Palacios*

CHAPTER 1

Sarajevo: The Shots That Still Ring Round the World

ONE of the last known photographs of the Archduke Francis Ferdinand of Habsburg, heir to the throne of his uncle, the octogenarian Emperor Francis Joseph of Austria-Hungary, shows him coming down the steps of the city hall in Sarajevo a few minutes after eleven on the morning of Sunday, June 28, 1914. Under the refulgent uniform topped with a plumed hat his stout body is rigid; his heavy features seem congested and his neck swollen above the tight-fitting collar; his thick, curling mustaches bristle like a wild boar's. Beside him walks his morganatic wife Sophie, the Duchess of Hohenberg, her plump face looking pinched and taut. They are just about to step into a waiting car. Both are clearly uneasy, but not yet really frightened. The local Bosnian dignitaries who line the steps, framing the doomed couple, are not frightened either; many of them are Moslems—paradoxically the only friends the Catholic Habsburgs have in this seething, semi-Oriental province, only recently freed from the Turkish yoke, but already clamoring for a Yugoslavia which has not yet been born—and they know that man does not evade his fate. The knowledge is written on their faces; the photograph catches them with their gloved hands raised to their flower-pot hats in a gesture of awe and resignation, as one salutes a funeral.

The whole scene, captured for posterity by some anonymous cameraman, stands out so vividly across the years that in looking at it one almost has the impression of reliving a personal nightmare. As in certain nightmares, incredulity wrestles with the sense of doom. Surely someone will cry out a warning before it is too late, surely someone will try to do something. In fact, someone does, but it is the wrong thing, and already it is too late. In five minutes Francis Ferdinand and Sophie will be lying unconscious in their speeding car bleeding to death from an assassin's bullets: an ancient dynasty—and with it a whole way of life—will start to topple; then another and another and another. Close to nine million men fell in World War I as a direct result of those two shots fired in a dusty Balkan town roughly half a century ago; then 15,000,000 more in a second, greater conflict implicit in the ending of the first one. The visit that the Habsburg heir and his wife paid to Sarajevo lasted only a little more than an hour—not quite the length of a normal feature film—but the drama of those 60 or 70 minutes has literally revolutionized the whole course of modern history; reconstructing it helps to understand many of the tragic dramas that humanity has witnessed since.

The view of Sarajevo as one approaches from the southwest is a lovely one. High but gently sloping mountains almost encircle it. The valley of the Miljacka, a shallow torrent that cuts the town in two, narrows at its eastern outskirts to a rugged gorge commanded by the ruined Turkish fort (*serai*) from which it takes its name. The old Moslem quarters crown the upper slopes of the natural amphitheater that rises nearly six hundred feet on both banks of the stream; the slender minarets of their hundred mosques soar like rhythmed prayer above whitewashed villas in walled, tangled gardens. The raw modern town below merely serves as a foil to their enchantment. This is Sarajevo today, and this—save for the faint scars left by Allied bombing in World War II—is how it appeared to Francis Ferdinand in the clear morning sunlight, as his open-topped car, with the gold and black fanion of the Habsburgs fluttering in the fresh mountain air, drove into town from the railroad station.

Though not a man normally sensitive to beauty, the archduke no doubt was gladdened by the scene. He demonstrated no more enthusiasm than he habitually displayed at the opera or at Court balls—a constant complaint of the artistic and pleasure-loving Viennese—but as he leaned stiffly against the leather-upholstered seat condescending to the view, his arrogant, morose face, with the sagging middle-aged jowls—he was fifty-one—seemed unusually cheerful. Francis Ferdinand had in fact every reason to be satisfied with life, and even to feel a little mellow that June morning. The ostentatious, almost provocative, military maneuvers along the Serbian border that had been the official pretext for his visit to Bosnia—he was Inspector General of the armed forces—had gone off well, at least from the Austro-Hungarian viewpoint. For once there had been no slackness—nothing like that disgraceful incident a couple of months earlier near Trieste when he had personally caught one of the sailors from his naval guard sneaking a cigarette behind a hedge (he had had the fellow put in the brig for a fortnight). Francis Ferdinand was a humorless, taciturn martinet with a mania for spit-and-polish who also took seriously the serious side of soldiering and administration; he had an almost Prussian phobia about *schlamperei*,[1] the Austrian genius for insouciant inefficiency. The royal suite in the hotel of the little spa, Ilidze, where he had spent the previous night had been quite comfortable—no *schlamperei* there, either—and Sophie, whom he had brought along with him, in violation of all protocol, had enjoyed the respectful attentions of his young staff officers. The ceremonial visit to Sarajevo, promised, for all its tedium, to be even more satisfying; its timing had a private significance that in the Archduke's mind may possibly have overshadowed the political one. June 28 was the anniversary of the most important date in his life.

Fourteen years ago on that day, Archduke Francis Ferdinand of Austria-Este (as he preferred to call himself) had married Countess Sophie Chotek, a member of a noble but comparatively obscure Czech family, and a lady-in-waiting to his cousin, the Archduchess Isabella. From the Habsburg viewpoint she might as well have been a chambermaid. "Love makes people lose all sense of dignity," Francis Joseph exclaimed when he heard the news. The old Emperor had never quite forgiven his heir for this misalliance; it had taken a whole year of stubborn negotiations to win his consent to the marriage. But even Francis Joseph could not have softened the iron writ of Habsburg House Law, the supreme code of the dynasty. At a solemn assembly of the Court and the Privy Council in the ancient Hofburg Palace in Vienna, Francis Ferdinand had been obliged to renounce all rights of rank and succession for his children before taking Sophie as his morganatic wife. He had never forgotten the humiliation. He loved Sophie enough to swallow it, but it rankled all the same. The Archduke was no royal iconoclast or bohemian; he was a snob and a pedant obsessed—despite his marriage to a commoner—with the privileges of royalty generally and with his own dynastic rights in particular.

Oddly enough, the marriage had turned out happy. When Francis Ferdinand developed tuberculosis and was written off for dead by his uncle's court—another slight he never forgave—Sophie with tireless devotion nursed him back to health. They had three children, Ernst, Max and Sophie, the last two known in the family as Maxl and Sopherl—whom the Archduke adored. Momentarily oblivious to all protocol, he enjoyed sitting on the floor to play with them, often receiving important visitors in this position —and woe to any visitor who did not instantly follow the royal example. The conjugal union of the Habsburg autocrat-to-be with the daughter of the empire's despised Slav minority seemed a model of bourgeois felicity;

[1] This defect seems to have been one of the Habsburg imperial administration rather than of the Austrian national character, properly speaking. The present-day visitor encounters little evidence of *schlamperei* in the tidy, prosperous Austrian Republic of the 1960s.

actually it was in all probability something more than that: the day they took their last ride together it was still a love match.

In fact, this graceless couple—Francis Ferdinand looking more like the typical Prussian boor of the epoch than like a Viennese gentleman; Sophie a square-faced matron well past her prime, in no way improved by the overdecorated hat and the high, tight collar of her dress—sitting side by side on the back seat of their ungainly antebellum vehicle, en route to keep their rendezvous with death, were united by an undying tenderness as romantic in its way perhaps as any in history. The smiles they exchanged as the royal cortege approached the center of town and the first scattered cries of *"Zivio"* rang out were warm and intimate. It was in part for Sophie's sake that the Archduke had organized the trip to Sarajevo, and she knew it.

In the stylized ballet of Vienna Court life, strictly regulated by an etiquette going back to the days of Maria Theresa, there was no place for Sophie. In 1906 the Emperor had given her the title of Duchess of Hohenberg and thereafter she was allowed to attend Court at the Schoenbrunn Palace, but never on the same footing as her husband. The Archduke's numerous enemies exploited every weapon in the armory of protocol to vex and humiliate her. At Court galas, for example, when etiquette called for a "ceremonial entrance," orders were issued that only half the folding door should be opened for her. Eventually Francis Ferdinand, a brooding, vindictive man, burning with ill-concealed impatience for his uncle to die and given to black fits of depression and rages so violent that Sophie sometimes feared he was going insane, set up a kind of rival Court at his Belvedere Palace on a hilltop overlooking Vienna. The great German and Magyar feudal families were but perfunctorily represented there; the Archduke particularly loathed the haughty Magyar nobles because of their independence, and surrounded himself with a paradoxical mixture of Slavs, reactionary clerics, and German Christian Socialists. This tended to split the aristocracy and officialdom of the empire into two factions without wholly solving the problem of the Duchess's rank.

Unlikely as it sounds today, this tiresome and anachronistic imbroglio played a real part in setting the stage for a world disaster. It was to punish his detractors and to atone to Sophie for all the times she had been forced to walk at the tail of some court procession while he had headed it with an Archduchess on his arm, that Francis Ferdinand in 1914 hatched up a kind of *protocol-putsch*. He would take advantage of his new office as Inspector General of the armed forces—he was appointed in 1913—to attend the forthcoming maneuvers in the recently annexed province of Bosnia-Herzegovina. While there he would pay an official visit to its capital, Sarajevo, in his military capacity rather than as heir to the throne. But of course he would have to be treated like royalty. And he would take Sophie with him—on their wedding anniversary. She would be received like the wife of an Inspector General who happened to be the royal heir—that is to say, like a queen.

The political motivations back of the Archduke's visit to Sarajevo were no less convoluted than his private ones. They were rooted both in Habsburg family history and in the complex human geography of the Danubian Basin. While these two subjects deserve fuller exploration, it is enough at this point to recall a few of their salient features. To begin with, there is the key fact that Austria-Hungary was called the Dual Monarchy because it was not a nation but two separate and theoretically sovereign nations ruled by a common King-Emperor and linked by rather sketchy joint, or imperial, administrative services (including the army). This, however, is a gross oversimplification; in many respects Austria and Hungary were less like nations than like two associated empires. In each a master race—in Austria, the Germans; in Hungary the Magyars—ruled more or less oppressively over a number of subject peoples. (Being a master race at home did not prevent the Magyars from complaining that they themselves were oppressed, or at least exploited, by the Germans throughout the Empire.) Most of the submerged nationalities belonged to the Slavic race, (though there were also many Italians and Rumanians) but they stemmed from several different branches of it, and instead of being grouped in one area they were scattered throughout Austria-Hungary along with various ethnic minorities, like the addled limps and features of the subjects in certain surrealist portraits. The Czechs lived in the part of northern Austria that had once been the independent Slavic Kingdom of Bohemia; their close kinsmen, the Slovaks, lived more to the east and therefore under the much harsher Hungarian yoke. Hungary also owned large parts of what is today Yugoslavia, and thus had an important South Slav—Serb and Croat—minority as well as the Slovak one. The Slovenes, another South Slavic people, were partly under Austrian dominion, however. The Habsburgs, as the feudal overlords of this anachronistic hodge-podge of peoples naturally, had the most trouble with their biggest and proudest vassals, the Magyars; therefore, they tended to favor certain of their Slav subjects as a sort of counterweight to Magyar ambition or stubbornness. Francis Ferdinand pushed this family tradition to extreme limits; he detested the Magyars, and whether to annoy them or for more statesmanlike reasons, constantly sought to appear as the champion of the Empire's Slavs. (The fact that he had married a Czech noblewoman naturally facilitated, and perhaps inspired, this role.) Francis Ferdinand was undoubtedly more clearsighted than most high-ranking Austrian officials in recognizing the ominously growing strength of the nationalist movement among the empire's Slav minorities, particularly among its South Slavs. At one time the Archduke apparently hoped to combat the separatist lure of the Yugoslav dream—which was being actively promoted by expansionist elements in the adjacent

BOSNIA
Also showing Racial Distribution
in Surrounding Territory

AUSTRIA

STYRIA

DANUBE R.
Vienna
Presburg
Gran
Budapest
Ödenburg
Czeged

H U N G A R Y

DANUBE R.
TISZA R.

Warasdin
Mohacs
Agram (Zagreb)
DRAVE R.
Esseg
C R O A T I A
SAVE R.
SLAVONIA
Belgrade
VRBAS R.
BOSNA R.
Banialuka
DANUBE R.
B O S N I A
DRINA R.
SAVA R.
SERBIA
Travnik
Zara
Sarajevo
DALMATIA
Spalato
Mostar
ADRIATIC
SEA
HERZEGOVINA
MONTENEGRO
Miles
0   60
Cetinje
palacios
ALBANIA

Croats and Serbians (Slavs)   Germans
Slovenes (Slavs)   Magyars
Slovaks (Slavs)   Rumanians
                                Albanians

Kingdom of Serbia—through offering the South Slavs home rule in a separate state of their own within the Empire.

Bosnia had a significant, if ambivalent, relationship to all such schemes, and it was a major factor in the general Balkan imbroglio. Vienna had administered the provinces—together with its sister province of Herzegovina —since 1877 when the native Christians (mostly Serb or Croat by race) had driven out their Turkish masters. The original legal basis for the arrangement had been a general European treaty, aimed precisely at preventing the freshly liberated territory from becoming a bone of contention among the powers, which had put it under Austro-Hungarian administration in a sort of mandate. (Juridically, Bosnia-Herzogovina remained part of the Ottoman Empire.) Then in 1908 the old Emperor's ministers had persuaded him to sign a decree formally annexing the provinces to his empire. This irresponsible act had disturbed the great powers, enraged the pepper-patriots in free Serbia—who had hoped some day to annex Bosnia-Herzegovina themselves—and inflamed the pro-Serbian or Pan-Slav nationalism of the local population. In deciding his official visit to the Bosnian capital, the Archduke no doubt felt that it would have a soothing effect locally while attracting the favorable attention of Slav nationalists elsewhere in the empire. On the one hand the visit—together with the maneuvers near the frontier—demonstrated that the empire would tolerate no nonsense either from the Serbian irredentists in Belgrade or from the South Slav secessionists within its own borders. On the other hand, it would demonstrate—somewhat more cryptically it would seem—the future Emperor's sympathy with the legitimate aspirations of loyal Slav nationalism, and his well-known love for his Slav subjects. By the same token, it would once more infuriate the Magyars.

This was how Francis Ferdinand and his wife happened to be riding together in a slow-moving open car in the heart of what was practically a zone of military occupation on the fatal Sunday. The regal-looking motorcade, the flaunting flags, the curious if rather silent crowds lining the wide avenue along the right bank of the Miljacka as the cortege turned into it— these were the Archduke's anniversary presents to Sophie.

To most of the Bosnians who turned out to greet—or simply to stare at —their presumptive future monarch and his wife, the date marked a quite different sort of anniversary. June 28—actually June 15 by the Serbian Orthodox calendar—is the Vidovdan, the Feast of St. Vitus. To the Slav peoples of the Balkan Peninsula it is a holiday unlike any other. For centuries it was a national day of mourning because it commemorates the battle of Kossovo in 1389 when the Turks destroyed the medieval kingdom of Serbia and enslaved its Christian subjects. Since 1912 it has been the symbol of a glorious resurrection—the defeat of the Turks in the first Balkan War that led to their virtual expulsion from Europe.

Like all historic anniversaries that pluck men's heartstrings with contradictory fingers, the Vidovdan looses deep, confused emotions among those who observe it: it is a day when good friends drink too much and fall to brawling, when even the stranger's most tactful word grates as if on a nerve laid bare.

Francis Ferdinand, the least tactful of men and the most intrusive of all possible strangers, knew that the date he had picked for his first visit to Sarajevo was the Vidovdan. He was *also* aware that Bosnia and the Bosnian capital had remained under the Austro-Hungarian yoke what they had been under the Turkish—hotbeds of nationalist conspiracy and terrorism (the revolutionary tradition was gloriously revived against the Nazis in World War II). Perhaps he counted on his reputation as a champion of the Slavs within the Empire to disarm hostility. Its real effect was to make him seem dangerous as well as hateful to the fanatics of Slavdom; extremists always fear a moderate adversary.

"Suicide while of unsound mind," would seem the most likely verdict on the visit to Sarajevo if Francis Ferdinand had not taken along with him the being whom he loved most in the world: his wife. Certainly he would not have exposed her if he had really believed there was danger. His fatal insensitivity to the public temper in Bosnia demonstrates how little human contact there was between the Habsburgs and their subjects. In the expressive Chinese phrase, the dynasty after ruling for six hundred years had lost the Mandate of Heaven (as the reader will see later, most of the other surviving twentieth-century dynasties had lost, or were about to lose it, too). Not only were the Habsburgs out of touch with their subjects, but communication had partly broken down between different organs of their state.

The civil authorities both in Sarajevo and in Vienna had picked up warnings of a plot against the Archduke. For a while one school of history believed that certain of these authorities, particularly those with Magyar connections, had deliberately allowed the heir to the throne to walk into a trap—perhaps had even encouraged the assassination plot. Today, with much hitherto secret evidence now available, the expert consensus is less dramatic but in one way stranger. The civilian and the military authorities of the empire were simply not speaking to each other, or at least the latter were not paying any attention to what the former said. Francis Ferdinand had not wanted to give the official Court a pretext for interfering with his plans to honor Sophie; he insisted on treating the visit as a purely military matter. His pigheadedness infuriated the Court and the joint Austro-Hungarian Ministry of Finance, which was responsible for the civil administration in Bosnia. The eighty-four-year-old Emperor disapproved so strenuously of the Archduke taking his wife to Bosnia that he had left in a huff for his summer palace at Ischl to avoid receiving the couple on their return to Vienna. The soldiers joined enthusiastically in the feud. Marshal Oskar Potiorek, the military governor of Bosnia and a superb Central European specimen of early Blimp, never reported to his nominal chief, the Finance Minister, that the visit had been arranged. Perhaps he did not trust the minister's security; in any case, he attached no importance to the stories of political unrest in his territory. "Like most soldiers in occupied countries," remarks the British historian A. J. P. Taylor, "they [Potiorek and his Staff] hardly acknowledged the local population except as cleaners in the barracks."

The end result of this bureaucratic schizophrenia was that Potiorek assumed sole responsibility for the security of the Archduke's party without having the means to assure it. Many of his soldiers and gendarmes had been drawn away to take part in the field maneuvers, and a recklessly sparse cordon held back the crowd when the royal cortege—six motorcars with the Archduke's second—entered Sarajevo shortly after 10 A.M. on the Vidovdan.

The first portent came just after the royal car passed the Bank of Austria-Hungary on the avenue bordering the Miljacka embankment.

Franz, Count Harrach, the Archduke's aide-de-camp, was in the front seat next to the chauffeur. Sophie was in the back on the right-hand side, nearest the embankment; Francis Ferdinand next to her. Opposite them sat Potiorek, a splendid self-important figure with a vacant military face. He was showing them what the army had done for the arts in Sarajevo—the newly built Austrian barracks in mustard-colored bureaucratic baroque across the river. Where his finger pointed there was a gap in the crowd on the sidewalk and standing in the gap, a tall dark young man, who, exactly at that instant, made a queer gesture with his hands. There was a small sound, no louder than cork popping from a bottle; then odd, disconnected things began to happen. Harrach thought—mistakenly—that he had heard a bullet whistle near his head. Sophie definitely felt something graze the back of her neck and put up her hand to touch it. Potiorek saw a black object float away from the young man on the embankment and land somewhere behind the royal car. The front tire of the following one blew out with a loud noise, spilling officers into the street. One of them, Lieutenant Erich von Merizzi, Potiorek's aide-de-camp, could not understand at first why his face was suddenly dripping blood. On the embankment a confused scuffle broke out in the crowd and a tall figure raised a hand to its mouth, then jumped over the parapet into the bed of the stream; many bystanders craned their necks to see what was happening to him down there among the boulders. It was close to 10:30.

In the royal car the Archduke and his wife sat very straight. Potiorek, looking over their heads, reported that a bomb had gone off; Francis Ferdinand replied, rather surprisingly, he had been expecting something of the sort. Potiorek reported further that an officer in the third car had been hurt; it seemed to be Merizzi. Francis Ferdinand said to stop the car and look after him. Nobody protested this lunatic order, which was promptly obeyed. The lead car then halted, too. Down in the bed of the Miljacka several policemen were dragging along the dark young man—who now smelled of bitter almonds and vomit—while conscientiously beating him with the flats of their swords. His name, they were soon to discover, was Nedjelko Cabrinovic and he was a nineteen-year-old printer, born in Sarajevo.

Lieutenant von Merizzi turned out to be only slightly wounded; the car with the crumpled front wheel was quickly pushed off to the curb for whatever good that might do. Puzzling over the strange sequence of events, the military experts in the royal party came up almost at once with the right explanation. The first popping sound that had seemed to jar things off their course was the fuze cap or detonator of a small bomb or hand grenade blown off when the dark young man had purposely whacked it against a lamppost. Undoubtedly it was this fragment—too light to hurt anyone—that had grazed Sophie's neck. The bomb proper, merely charged by the initial detonation, had gone off twelve seconds later, thus explaining why it had hit the wrong car. Though inexpertly handled in the present instance, the device seemed too complicated to be the handiwork of local artisans. Grenades of the type described were popular at the time in Serbia; the redoubtable *comitadjis* (Serb partisans) had found during the Balkan War that they worked nicely on Turks. The conclusion was not reassuring; Potiorek lost no time in ordering the remaining cars of the cortege to resume their route—this time at a much faster pace—and not to stop until they reached the city hall. If he had realized the true situation he would have ordered them to drive still faster, and in the opposite direction.

The brief reception by the city fathers at the *Rathaus,* a tasteless structure erected by the Austrians in the late Turkish bath style of architecture that now houses a museum of provincial handicrafts, was not a success. The mayor had hardly commenced his address of welcome when the Archduke furiously interrupted him.

"Mr. Mayor," he nearly shouted, "I come here on a visit and I get bombs thrown at me. It is outrageous."

It was only with difficulty that Francis Ferdinand was persuaded to make a short, extemporaneous speech in reply to the mayor's. The son of one of the local aldermen who was present as a child at the ceremony described its strange, oppressive atmosphere to the British novelist Rebecca West when she visited Sarajevo between the two wars, collecting material for her *Black Lamb and Grey Falcon,* one of the most magical of all travel books:

"We were all silent, not because we were impressed with him [the Archduke] for he was not at all our Bosnian idea of a hero. But we all felt awkward because we knew that when he went out he would certainly be killed . . . we knew how the people felt about him and the Austrians, and we knew that if one man had thrown a bomb and failed, another man would throw another bomb, and another after that if he should fail . . . it gave a very strange feeling to the assembly."

While the reception was going on upstairs, in the city hall, Cabrinovic, the would-be assassin, still alive despite the cyanide he had swallowed before jumping off the embankment and the subsequent beating by the police, was being questioned at the police station. He had information that could have saved the royal couple and his interrogators were not exactly gentle in trying to get it out of him, but he kept his mouth shut as long as was necessary.

Before leaving the city hall there was a huddle with Potiorek. The Archduke criticized the military governor for the inadequate protection given his party and enquired somewhat caustically if there were likely to be more attempts to assassinate him during the remainder of his visit.

Potiorek, according to a deposition he gave later, replied in pure Blimp that "I hoped not, but that in spite of all security measures one could not prevent someone standing in the vicinity of the car from attempting something similar."

According to another version, Potiorek, forgetting the deference due to royalty even exclaimed testily,

"What, do you think the streets of Sarajevo are full of assassins?"

If he actually said anything like this he was, of course, technically correct, since it was determined later that there had been only five or six or at most seven, assassins in the streets—all stationed at intervals along the embankment of the Miljacka in the quarter mile or so between the bank of Austria-Hungary and the city hall. In any event neither Potiorek nor the chief of police, who was present at the impromptu conference, at first thought it advisable to cancel the rest of the scheduled drive through the town. It was only when Francis Ferdinand insisted that before going on to the museum, which was the next scheduled stop, he wanted to visit the military hospital to enquire about von Merizzi's wounds, that Potiorek proposed evasive action. The ride to the hospital should be safe enough, he thought. It meant retracing part of the morning's itinerary along the Miljacka embankment, and that was the last place where any hypothetical assassins who might still be at large would be expecting the Archduke to appear. However, it might be advisable to drive at top speed and after visiting the hospital to cancel the rest of the program in order to punish the inhabitants of Sarajevo for the morning's outrageous events.

Nothing brings out the inevitability of the fall of the house of Austria more sharply than Francis Ferdinand's prompt, condescending acceptance of the egregious suggestion that he punish the Habsburg-hating Bosnians by depriving them of his presence. Yet it might have saved his life if it had been efficiently carried out. A new car was brought up. The Archduke and Sophie got in—she had insisted on accompanying him—while Count Harrach, shielding his royal master with his body, stood on the left-hand running board, nearest the embankment; that is the direction the bomb had come from earlier. The chief of police and the deputy mayor took their places in the lead car. The Archduke's again came second. Both lurched into gear and began to speed along the embankment, following the morning's route in reverse.

Did the heir of the Habsburgs realize that death stood waiting for him a few hundred yards away? Rebecca West, who evidently loves wild animals and dislikes Habsburgs, recalls a gruesome anecdote about him. Like his royal cousin and crony, Kaiser Wilhelm II of Germany, Francis Ferdinand was an almost psychopathic butcher of game; not long before he had boasted of having shot his three-thousandth stag. He took special pride in a new technique of shooting hares that he had worked out; the improvement consisted in placing his beaters in a pear-shaped formation that brought the hares practically to the muzzle of his gun and enabled him to slaughter record bags. Miss West suggests that in the last moments of his life Francis Ferdinand may have discovered how it felt to be a beast at bay.

Actually, the hunters of men who earlier had set up their firing line along the Miljacka embankment had given up in panic or despair by the time their intended victim left the city hall. This is one of the weirdest features of the Sarajevo drama. In a sense Francis Ferdinand and Sophie were doomed from the moment they entered the town, but their fate was merely a mathematical probability. The assassination plot was one of those inept but nonetheless deadly conspiratorial operations combining professional planning with amateur execution. The executors were six untrained youths. It was virtually certain under the circumstances that some links in the murder chain would break down, but very likely that at least one would hold. This likelihood was nearly upset. A sort of statistical miracle almost occurred at the last moment; that it finally did not was due to a countervailing factor which was itself a foreseeable probability: that same Austrian *schlamperei* which was Francis Ferdinand's particular *bête noire*.

As the lead car reached the Latin Bridge—it has a different name today —it turned right off the embankment up what was then named Francis Joseph Street—the originally scheduled itinerary for the party. Nobody had thought to tell the chauffeur that it had been changed. The Archduke's chauffeur blindly followed. Even so, the royal couple might have escaped if Potiorek had not intervened to set things right.

"Not that way, you fool," he yelled at the chauffeur. "Keep straight on."

The rattled flunky stopped so he could shift into reverse—not two yards from a slight, hollowed-eyed boy of nineteen who had just come out of a coffeehouse where he had gone to steady his nerves; his world had collapsed about him half an hour before when the grenade thrown by his friend Cabrinovic went wild and there seemed to be nothing left to live for. He had a loaded automatic pistol in his pocket that he had given up the hope of being able to use. Now, though dazed by the miraculous second chance that fate had offered him, he drew it out and remembered to aim. He could hardly have missed. The range was less than ten feet and as long as Sophie sat straight there was no obstacle between the Archduke and the killer's gun; he was at the curb on the right; Harrach was standing on the left side of the car, his useless sword dangling in his hand. It was 11:15.

The assassin fired twice. The first shot hit Francis Ferdinand, tearing through his chest and lodging against his spine. The second, aimed at Potiorek, hit Sophie in the abdomen, either because the gunman's hand swerved or because she tried to jump up and shield her husband with her body. For a few seconds both of them continued to sit straight; Potiorek thought that the assassin—grabbed by neighbors in the crowd just as he was raising the automatic to put a bullet in his own head—had missed. Then, as the chauffeur finally got the car turned in the right direction and it leaped forward, the Duchess collapsed against the Archduke. He remained upright, but a thin dark rivulet of blood stained the front of his tunic, and the corners of his mouth were red.

Up to that moment the assassination drama had seemed almost more burlesque than tragedy; it had much of the sordidness and confusion of a third-class bullfight. But good breeding helps to tidy up many a messy situation, and real love redeems almost any squalor. Francis Ferdinand and Sophie Chotek had lived out their lives in a faded, tinsel Court during one of the most tawdry epochs in human history, but in their dying they attained the dignity of tragedy.

"Sophie, Sophie, don't die; live for our children," murmured Francis Ferdinand, trying to brace her unconscious body as the car sped toward the governor's palace. Then, to a question from Harrach, he answered, "It is nothing."

Six times, in a steadily more feeble voice he repeated: "It is nothing." And so it was.

Since October 1918 Sarajevo has been part of Yugoslavia; today it is the capital of the Yugoslav People's Republic of Bosnia, and the house in front of which the Habsburg Archduke and his wife were shot is a museum dedicated to the memory of their assassins. Just opposite the curb where the royal car stopped a black marble tablet on the wall reads: HERE ON

THIS HISTORIC SPOT GAVRILO PRINCIP WAS THE ANNUNCIATOR OF LIBERTY ON THE DAY OF THE VIDOVDAN, JUNE 15 (28), 1914.

Considering everything that has happened in the world since the date of the assassination, this wording sounds a bit parochial, but the importance given Princip as an agent of destiny is not exaggerated. It is fitting that the marble tablet should mention only his name, and that the old Latin Bridge across the Miljacka is now the Princip Bridge. Not only did he fire the fatal shots himself, but—though he was only a nineteen-year-old high school student at the time—he was the moral leader, of the assassination conspiracy and its field commander. He is not just a Balkan folk hero but a twentieth-century one; by his act he ushered in a whole age of conspiracy, a time of assassins.

"I am not a criminal for I have suppressed a harmful man," Princip said at his trial.

Resolute, fearless, singleminded and ruthless, Princip was a type of political fanatic that has become only too familiar to us. The son of a peasant from a small village in Herzegovina, he had never known anything but poverty, yet from earliest childhood he burned with a thirst for education that was like a fever.

He was sickly and frail; ill health—probably tuberculosis—often kept him from school but he read voraciously and had passed all but the last-year examination in the Belgrade high school, where the scholastic system was less rigid than in Austria. Living in free Serbia exalted his ingrained anti-Austrian rebelliousness into a mystical South Slav nationalism that took the place of the Orthodox faith in which he had ceased to believe; reading Bakunin and Kropotkin planted in his mind the cult of violence and destruction. He began to think of himself as a professional terrorist and one night paid a secret visit to the tomb of a famous young Bosnian terrorist in Sarajevo so that he could solemnly pledge himself to commit a similar deed.

At first glance the whole Sarajevo plot, despite its ultimate success, looks like a schoolboy escapade that somehow turned into tragedy, a mixture of Tom Sawyer and Blackboard Jungle. Counting Princip, six persons took part in the actual killing: five Serbo-Croats from Bosnia and one Bosnian Moslem. None was more than nineteen and one was only seventeen. The genesis of the crime is steeped in adolescent romanticism. It goes back to the cafes of the Green Crown and the Golden Sturgeon in Belgrade where Bosnian exiles and *comitadji* veterans of the Balkan War used to congregate to talk politics and murder over tiny syrupy cups of Turkish coffee or glasses of fiery Serbian *slivovitz* taken to wash down mouthfuls of even more fiery Serbian onions and slices of sun-dried raw beef. Among the patrons of these two colorful establishments (which were also popular with at least two competing secret services) were three youthful Bosnian ex-patriates—really refugees from the Austrian school system: Princip,

Cabrinovic, who was then working at the Serbian state printing plant and who was to throw the bomb at the Archduke, and Trifko Grabez, the eighteen-year-old son of a Bosnian village pope. They came to hero-worship at the feet of the ex-*comitadjis* and to inflame each other's imaginations with talk of someday themselves committing an *attentat*—a spectacular act of terrorism—like those that had won undying glory to the heroes of the anti-Turkish resistance throughout the centuries. Since Bosnia was no longer under Turkish rule the *attentat* clearly had to be directed against the Austrian oppressors.

At first they had no specific target in mind. The *attentat*—any *attentat*—was an end in itself. The decision to kill Francis Ferdinand was an after-thought—or so the boys believed—inspired by a newspaper clipping announcing his visit to Sarajevo which Cabrinovic received in the spring of 1914 from some anonymous correspondent in Bosnia. Kind *comitadji* friends whom they had met at the cafe supplied them all the approved equipment for an *attentat*—bombs, pistols, phials of cyanide—and instructed them in its use. They were even provided with reduced-fare tickets to the Austro-Hungarian border—somebody seemed to think of everything—and were given letters of introduction to a couple of freedom-loving Serbian border guards who helped them slip back into Bosnia.

Before they realized it the original three had collected quite an elaborate little underground organization around themselves—seventeen persons all told. Several of them were mature and politically sophisticated Bosnian nationalists—a mysterious, rather sinister schoolteacher named Danilo Ilic became the chief organizer and recruiting agent for the conspiracy but the triggermen recruited for the most active roles were even more pathetically immature than the Belgrade trio. One of them, a boy of seventeen, having flunked a math examination, felt there was nothing left for him but suicide and joined the plot as a means of achieving it. He had been given his weapons the day before in a park, after which he joined some school friends at a cafe for an ice and boasted to them of the desperate deed he was going to do. They shrugged their shoulders.

Cabrinovic himself had a tendency to giggle at the wrong moment and was considered too "naive" to be trusted with a revolver—that was why he had a bomb. On the eve of the *attentat* he had his picture taken for posterity at a photographers and startled his girl friend by sending her flowers.

When the time came for action the schoolboy conspirators—with the exception of Princip—behaved as might have been expected. Cabrinovic at least acted, though wildly and ineffectually. Three simply panicked and ran when they heard his grenade explode. Grabez waited for a while, then rushed to his uncle's house where he hid his bomb under the toilet seat.

Only Princip kept his nerve. When he saw Cabrinovic being dragged away he toyed a moment with the idea of shooting him "so things would go no further," then killing himself. He dropped the scheme when he saw the Archduke's car speed by—too fast for a shot or a bomb—and realized that Cabrinovic had missed after all. For a while he walked around in a daze, not knowing what to do next, had his cup of coffee, and—as we have already seen—turned up by accident on the very spot where the royal car came to a halt. He was nearly beaten to death by police and officers of the royal party; a rib was broken and one arm so badly smashed that eventually it had to be amputated.

At the trial of the conspirators—most of whom were caught by the Austrians—Princip stood out both as the strongest personality and the clearest mind among them.

"I am a South Slav nationalist," he explained in court, concisely summarizing the objectives of the conspiracy. "My aim is the union of all Yugoslavs, under whatever political regime, and their liberation from Austria."

"By what means did you think to accomplish that?" the judge asked.

"By terrorism," was the unhesitating answer.

Because of his youth Princip escaped the death sentence, as did all but six of the conspirators. He was given twenty years, with the medieval provisos that he be obliged to fast one day every month and that he be placed in solitary confinement for one day each year on the anniversary of his crime. He died of tuberculosis and bad treatment in the prison of Theresienstadt on April 28, 1918, a few months too soon to see the outcome of the world war that his act had precipitated.

Looking back from the vantage point of the present we see clearly today that the outbreak of World War I ushered in a twentieth-century 'Time of Troubles'—in the expressive term of the British historian Arnold Toynbee—from which our civilization has by no means yet emerged. Directly or indirectly all the convulsions of the last half century stem back to 1914 and Sarajevo: the two World Wars, the Bolshevik revolution, the rise and fall of Hitler, the continuing turmoil in the Far and Near East, the power-struggle between the Communist world and our own. More than 23,000,000 deaths can be traced to one or the other of these upheavals; all of us who survive have been scarred, at least emotionally, by them. This much is plain.

But why and how did the romantic crime of a nineteen-year-old fanatic lead to such dramatic and far-reaching consequences?

The superficial answer, of course, is that the Austrians believed Princip and his fellow conspirators were simply the agents of an upstart, expansionist Serbian power which in the long-run constituted a real revolutionary and para-military threat to the empire. We know today that many of the specific accusations that served as basis for the brutal Austro-Hungarian ultimatum to Serbia after the murders in Sarajevo were unfounded, though enforced familiarity with conspiracy and subversion on a scale undreamed of by earlier generations suggests to us that there was, after all, some fire behind all that smoke.

The really significant factor explaining not only the crime of Sarajevo but its cataclysmic effects lies deeper, however, than any secret-service skulduggery in the Balkans, deeper even than the rivalry between Russian and Austrian imperialism, than the competition for commercial and maritime supremacy between England and Germany, than French irredentism or the general European armaments race. Francis Ferdinand and Gavrilo Princip typify not merely opposing national interests but two conflicting social orders, two ages of history, two incompatible patterns of human destiny. In a sense they were both victims—and so are all of us—of the same revolutionary process: the decline and fall of the dynastic system in Europe and of the social structures it supported. In necessarily broad strokes it is the story of this twentieth-century *Goetterdammerung* that the present book attempts to relate.

CHAPTER 2

Flashbacks to a Sunset World

O N the last Sunday of June 1914, a young Viennese man of letters sat reading under the chestnut trees at Baden, on the edge of the Wiener Wald, that green embossment of hilly forest which stamps the Danubian plain a few miles south of the capital. From time to time he put aside his book and looked about him in delight, only faintly tinged with irony. To the eye of a connoisseur, the little watering place had the charm of some tasteful bauble from an unfashionable period, offered at a bargain; its authentic Biedermayer villas and the neat, shady park where Beethoven loved to walk, were perfect in their kind. The sky was an even-tempered blue; the air was warm but light and elegant, correct for the season. The wives and daughters of Vienna's insouciant bourgeoisie chattered as they strolled along the flower-bordered paths in the artful innocence of starched, frilly white; well-shined carriages rolled along the gravel drives, the polished brass of their fixtures blinking in the sun like heliographs. In the outdoor music kiosk of the casino the orchestra paid uninspired but respectful tribute to the less exacting masters of a high tradition.

Suddenly, the music stopped in the middle of a bar, jarring every Viennese ear within range. The man of letters, Stefan Zweig, then in his early thirties, looked up from his book. The musicians, as he later described the scene in his memoirs, were packing their instruments and beginning to walk out of the pavilion. Excited promenaders crowded around the little structure, reading or discussing the official communiqué which had just been tacked up on one of its columns: the announcement of the double murder in Sarajevo. It created a sensation, but as Zweig noted, a short-lived one, marked by only perfunctory sorrow. The disappearance of the grumpy *ungemutlich* heir to the Habsburg crown left no irreparable sense of bereavement among his prospective subjects. The circumstances of his death were, of course, shocking, but royal assassinations were not a rarity in pre-war Europe.

"They are shooting us like sparrows from the roofs," Francis Ferdinand himself had remarked a couple of years earlier on hearing of the King of Portugal's violent end.

Elsewhere throughout the Continent the sensation was even milder. News traveled at the time no faster than messages in Morse code could be tapped out on a telegraph key, and Sunday extras were frowned on by the relatively sedate journalism of the era. All over Europe the same brilliant sun that had beaten down in Sarajevo on the Duchess of Hohenberg's parasol, shone on carefree throngs as it had already shone for many days, and would continue to shine, in what surviving Europeans later recalled with nostalgia as the most magical of all summers; on decorously covered bathers lolling beside the café-au-lait waters of the Danube; or upon the Dalmatian beaches; on Parisians promenading in the Bois; on Londoners strolling in Hyde Park; on straw hats in leafy beer gardens; on white sails skimming across the Baltic. To most of these millions the day remained in every way cloudless to the end.

Where the tidings from Sarajevo were known they produced some concern—the Balkan powder barrel was already an established journalistic cliché—but rarely any forebodings of doom. In Munich an unsuccessful student of architecture who had recently moved from Vienna in an inconclusive attempt to escape the loathed promiscuity of proletarian slum life, did experience a kind of somber tingling in his morbidly sensitive nerves when he heard the news, but was characteristically muddled as to its meaning.

"I was filled with muffled dread at this vengeance of an inscrutable destiny," Adolf Hitler relates in his book *Mein Kampf.* "The greatest friend of the Slavs had fallen under the bullets of Slav fanatics."

The other ultimate beneficiary of those same bullets, Vladimir Ilich Ulyanov, then forty-four and already better known in Russian exile circles under his pen name of Lenin, was more lucid in his reactions, but apparently no more clairvoyant. As the leader of the extremist faction of Russian Marxists who called themselves Bolsheviks Lenin was a professional revolutionary, and since the Czar's police did not think highly of this profession, he spent most of his adult life exercising it from bases outside Russia. At the time he was temporarily installed in a remote village of Austrian Galicia (today part of Poland) at the foot of the Tatra Mountains, conveniently near the Russian border, and he learned about Sarajevo on returning from a Sunday walk with some Russian emigré friends. It was basic Marxist doctrine that war between the capitalist powers was inevitable, bringing revolution in its wake, but Lenin was chronically suspicious of the revolutionary romanticism bubbling under the dry crust of Marxist dialectic in the minds of his comrades, and he warned against basing any false hopes on the Archduke's assassination.

"War between Austria and Russia would be very useful to the cause of the revolution in Western Europe," Lenin had written a year earlier to one of the most incorrigible of the revolutionary romantics, the Russian writer, Maxim Gorky. "But it is hard to believe that Francis Joseph and Nicholas will give us this pleasure."

The crime at Sarajevo had not invalidated this pronouncement, he maintained with his usual dogmatism.

"There is nothing to cause anxiety," wrote General Zurlinden, the respected military commentator of the Paris *Figaro,* no less dogmatically.

"I cannot imagine the old gentleman in Schoenbrunn [the Emperor Francis Joseph] will go to war, and certainly not if it is a war over Archduke Francis Ferdinand," Wilhelm II of Germany is said to have declared to intimates.

"It can either be a *débarras* or an *embarras* [an embarrassment or a disembarrassment]," was the diplomatically judicious comment of the Kaiser's Chancellor, Prince von Bulow on Francis Ferdinand's tragic end.

The most superbly uncomplicated—as well as genuinely human—reaction, was that of Britain's King George V.

"Terrible shock for the dear old Emperor," is the laconic notation in his diary.

Francis Joseph himself learned the news sitting at his desk in his summer villa at Bad Ischl, the fashionable watering-place of Vienna society. His seventy-seven-year-old aide-de-camp, Count Edouard Paar, had been called to the telephone—the Emperor refused to have any such newfangled contraptions in his office—and in accordance with standing instructions, had taken down the message from Sarajevo in writing. Breathing heavily, too overcome with emotion to speak, the elderly courtier returned and with trembling hand laid the hastily scrawled note in front of the imperial master he had served and loved for half a century. For a few moments Francis Joseph, to whom fate had already dealt so many cruel blows during his eighty-four years of life, sat woodenly, with his eyes closed, as if stunned by this latest one. When he finally spoke, however, it was not grief for the nephew he had always detested that thickened his voice, but awe at the Divine retribution which at last had punished the dynastic sin of Francis Ferdinand's morganatic marriage, and erased a blot from the Habsburg geneological table.

"Horrible," he murmured, more to himself than to Paar. "The Almighty does not allow Himself to be challenged with impunity. A higher power has restored the order which I unfortunately was unable to uphold."

No words could bring home more sharply the mental gap between our own age of political insomniacs and the generation of sleepwalkers that stumbled unawares over the ledge of doom during that halcyon summer of 1914.

Looking back during the tormented twenties on the pre-war Europe, of which he was one of the most brilliant survivors, Sir Winston Churchill in a few characteristically broad, vivid strokes painted a masterly if slightly nostalgic word portrait of this vanished world, so close to us in time, so distant in mood and temper.

"Nations and Empires, crowned with princes and potentates, rose majestically on every side, lapped in the accumulated treasures of the long peace," he wrote in *The World Crisis*. "All were fitted and fastened, it seemed securely, into an immense cantilever. The two mighty European systems faced each other glittering and clanking in their panoply, but with a tranquil gaze. A polite, discrete, pacific, and on the whole sincere diplomacy spread its web of connections over both. A sentence in a dispatch, an observation by an ambassador, a cryptic phrase in parliament seemed sufficient to adjust from day to day the balance of the prodigious structure. . . . The old world, in its sunset, was fair to see."

Due allowance must be made, of course, for the magic of the Churchillian prose. The sunset view was not so fair from every angle or to all observers, as Sir Winston remembered, nor—as we shall soon discover— was the old-world diplomacy quite so sincere. In stressing the importance of pre-war Europe's dynastic institutions, however, the British historian did not exaggerate. Princes and potentates were in fact dominant—if not always quite majestic—features of the political and social landscape in what was then the heartland of the civilized world. In the first decade of the twentieth century, the monarchic-aristocratic order of society, based on a king by divine right and a ruling class largely recruited from the aristocracy which we carelessly tend to think of as having passed away with the eighteenth century, not only continued to coexist with nineteenth century bourgeois-nationalist democracy—itself beginning to feel the pressure of the nascent racial or collectist movements—but in several parts of the world still overshadowed its supposed successor. It was not Marie Antoinette on the eve of the French Revolution, but Nicholas II on the eve of the Russian one, who, brushing aside the warnings of a friendly diplomat, said, "Do you mean that I am to regain the confidence of my people, Ambassador, or that they are to regain my confidence?"

The New World—taking the crypto-dictatorships of Latin America at their face value—was predominantly democratic and republican. So were France, Portugal (after 1910), Switzerland, Andorra and San Marino. Britain, Holland, Belgium, Luxembourg, and the Scandinavian states were then, as now, constitutional, democratic monarchies—though considerably less democratic in the social sense, than they are today.

Even England's easygoing Edward VII never forgot the royal blood that set him apart from ordinary mortals. While still Prince of Wales (as Virginia Cowles relates the anecdote in *Edward VII and His Circle*) he gave precedence at a ball over the Crown Prince of Germany to a visiting potentate from the South Seas: Kalakua, King of the Cannibal Islands. "Either the brute is a king," Edward explained to the indignant Germans, "or he is an ordinary black nigger, and if he is not a King, why is he here?"

Elsewhere across the whole Eurasian land mass, kings or emperors not only reigned but ruled. From the Vosges mountains to Vladivostok, from the Arctic Ocean to the Arabian Gulf—with the exception of the turbulent peasant-principalities of the Balkans—they ruled, like their ancestors, by divine right, their absolutism tempered only slightly, if at all, by nominal constitutions and feeble, easily manipulated parliaments. So far from having withered away, the autocratic principle on the eve of the great conflict was enjoying, in parts of Europe, a kind of ideological Indian summer, thanks to the ingenious sophistries of various contemporary apologists of neo-despotism.

"Take my word for it Nicky," Kaiser Wilhelm II of Germany wrote to his imperial cousin Nicholas II of Russia to warn him against the danger of an alliance with regicide and republican France, "the curse of God lies heavy on that nation. Heaven had imposed a sacred duty . . . on us Christian kings and emperors—to uphold the doctrine of the divine right of kings."

Yet industrialized Germany was socially and culturally the most enlightened of the great powers at the time and Wilhelm himself an exceptionally progressive representative of the imperial dynasties that constituted the pillars of the traditional European order. There were four of them: the Hohenzollerns in Germany, which then owned Alsace-Lorraine and part of Poland; the Habsburgs in Austria-Hungary, a vast mosaic of subject races and nations which stretched from Switzerland to beyond the Carpathians and from the Bavarian Alps to the Adriatic, including the territory of present-day Czechoslovakia and about half that of Yugoslavia; the Romanovs in Russia, including Finland and most of Poland; and the Osmanlis (Ottomans) in the Turkish Empire which in addition to modern Turkey, comprised Syria, Palestine, Arabia, Mesopotamia and, up to 1912, Libya and substantial parts of Thrace and Macedonia. The empires ruled by these families controlled the greater part of the Continent's military and economic power. Between them they had some 400,000,000 subjects, belonging to hundreds of races and including proud, once sovereign peoples like the Czechs, the Poles, and the Finns.

Clustering around the great imperial powers in frequently shifting patterns of alliance were the minor dynasties of southern and southeastern Europe: Spain, Italy, Serbia, Albania, Montenegro, Rumania, Bulgaria, and Greece. Italy was allied with Austria-Hungary and Germany in the Triple Alliance, while other treaties linked Rumania and Turkey closely to this bloc of central powers; Albania—after 1913—and Bulgaria, originally oriented toward Russia, were more loosely attached. Serbia and Montenegro were clients of Russia, the ally of France; Greece felt the contrary tug of German and of British influence, as did Spain. Within their own realms, the monarchs held sway over vassal throngs of princelings, dukes, tribal chiefs, barons, and lesser nobility. (In Germany the imperial hierarchy included no less than twenty-two ruling dynasties, among them the royal houses of Bavaria and Saxony.) At least in the more civilized states, the nobles had long since yielded up their feudal powers to the central authority, but in most of the monarchies their social prestige—along with the de facto privilege it confers—remained enormous.

The rising new aristocracy of industry, typified by bourgeois dynasties like the Krupps, and the quasi-hereditary bureaucratic caste which earlier had challenged the old nobility, by the turn of the nineteenth century had come to terms with it. Rivalry had largely given way to partnership and partnership was producing an increasing intermingling. Both classes gained materially in the exchange; each seems to have been spiritually bankrupted by the contact. The aristocrats started on the moral decline into cafe society. The *parvenu* power-elites, only moderately attracted by the aristocratic cult of honor, enthusiastically adopted the blue-blooded vices, and aped the haughtiness of the high-born; the generous idealism that had animated their fathers in the revolutionary year 1848 and their great-grandfathers at the time of the French Revolution in 1789 became for many an increasingly dim, discreditable memory. The snobbery of wealth compounded, instead of countervailing, that of birth; the insolence of the successful climber reinforced the arrogance of the titled ancestor-worshiper. At a time when dangerous new pressures were building up from below, the European ruling classes, both supporting and supported by an outdated dynastic system, not only clung to the Victorian credo that social inequalities are somehow part of the divine plan, but following the example of their monarchs, drew on the dialectical resources of contemporary pseudo-science, or perverted the intent of unwary thinkers like Nietzsche, to bolster an already inflated sense of institutional self-esteem. The practical implications of these attitudes were sometimes quite monstrous. When the S.S. *Titanic,* the pride of early twentieth century marine technology, rammed an iceberg and quickly sank on its maiden trip across the Atlantic, most of the first-class passengers, including men as well as women and children, got away in half-empty lifeboats, but 53 children of third-class passengers—not to mention their parents—went down with the ship.

"I only realized that the situation was serious when I saw a working-class passenger on the first-class deck," one of the survivors recounted later.

Our fathers' generation not only recognized class privileges that we consider ludicrous or inhuman, but had a much sharper eye than ours for social frontiers. Pre-war European society was stratified like the passenger list of an ocean liner: first-class, second-class, third-class, and steerage. "To become an officer in the Prussian army," remarks Kuerenberg, the biographer of Wilhelm II, himself a former member of this elite corps, "it was necessary . . . to furnish proof of good origin, and here the fact of having a father who was a shop-keeper was quite sufficient to ensure disqualification. An ambitious man in Germany could become a Commercial Councillor or even a Privy Councillor . . . he might even secure the ennobling 'von' but to become a reserve lieutenant was not so easy." The caste system was pushed to its ultime refinements in Austria-Hungary, where the ruling classes were rigorously divided into the first and the second society, the former consisting only of the old nobility, the latter including the administrative, financial, and intellectual elites, and the newer aristocracy. The Austrian obsession with social status was reflected in the proliferation of honorific titles or appellations that survives to this day. Sigmund Freud's son recalls that while doing his service in the pre-war Austro-Hungarian Army, which allowed him to keep private quarters in Vienna, he once notified the chambermaid at his lodging house that he was expecting a female visitor for tea.

"*Ja wohl, Herr Einjahrfreivilliger* [Yes, indeed, Mr. One-Year-Volunteer]," she replied, "I'll put clean sheets on the bed."

The social stability associated with such a keen sense of hierarchy had, of course, some real virtues to counterbalance its injustices. The security—or at least sense of security—enjoyed in pre-war Europe by most of its population, save for the poorest classes and for certain chronically unfortunate minorities like the Jews in Russia, or the Armenians in Turkey, can hardly be imagined in our anxiety-ridden generation.

The old world, as Churchill saw it in its sunset glory, had undeniable charms, along with some less attractive features. The need for colorful ceremonial to uphold the prestige of a way of life that every year looked more and more anachronistic to more and more men generated a bright social glitter. The two decades before 1914 were the heyday of conspicuous consumption, the age of jade and lobster. The long peace, with its accumulated Churchillian treasures, and a generally expanding economy, had furnished a solid underpinning for both civic display and for private self-indulgence; monuments and waistlines alike took on the bulge of opulence. The liberating influence of *art nouveau*—gradually merging into *modern style* as its lotus tendrils writhed up from the Paris *métro*—was partly responsible for the former; the latter owed something to Paul Poiret, the daring Paris couturier who freed the female body from corsets, and to Edward VII, who introduced a note of easeful elegance, suited to his favorite sports, into masculine attire.

(Edward indulged in various outdoor activities, such as racing, shooting, and romping with the wood nymphs—recruited for him by his faithful valet —in the bushes at Marienbad, where he took the waters every summer. He probably enjoyed himself most, however, at Maxim's famous restaurant in Paris; to his cousin, King Leopold of Belgium and other wealthy or blue-blooded habitués of the establishment, he was noted as a connoisseur both of the cuisine and of the high-priced *cocottes* who at certain levels of contemporary society personified the feminine ideal. To one of these reigning queens of the demimonde, La Belle Otero, Edward once sent a billet-doux of truly regal brevity: his calling card with the dial of a watch scrawled on it, the hands at five o'clock. She accepted the rendezvous and was rewarded to her disgust with a valuable duck-shoot near the Channel Coast.)

The quickening pace of scientific and technological discovery, especially around the turn of the century, contributed to the prevailing euphoria. The revolutionary concepts worked out by the young German mathematician, Albert Einstein, in his General Theory of Relativity (published in 1905) might have no practical significance, but the handful of advanced thinkers able to appreciate their theoretical implications recognized them at once as milestones in the history of civilization. More popular and less esoteric ones in various fields of endeavor were the contemporary achievements of Freud, Marconi, the inventor of wireless telegraphy, Louis Blériot, who successfully attempted an audacious nonstop flight across the English Channel in one of the flying machines recently invented by the Wright Brothers, and Paul Ehrlich, the German chemist, whose discovery of salvarsan—the first effective specific against syphilis—in 1910 came too late, however, to save some of the age's most noted boulevardiers from their chief occupational hazard (Archduke Otto of Austria whose youthful high jinks once included leaping stark naked, except for his sword belt, out of a private dining room at Sacher's cafe in the path of a visiting English peeress, paid the wages of sin in later life by having to wear a leather nose at public ceremonies).

The intellectual and artistic life of the period was equally tonic, at least to bold young minds. The gilded youth of London, Paris, Berlin, and Vienna might generally be content to scandalize the elderly by sipping cocktails as it one-stepped through life to the ping of tennis balls and the gentle tinkling of bicycle bells, but earnest, intelligent—and wealthy—young aristocrats like the early friends of Lady Diana Duff Cooper enjoyed rarer pleasures. They thrilled to the audacities of social iconoclasts like Shaw and H. G. Wells; they cheered the standards of literary and aesthetic innovation or revolt hoisted by Rilke, Rimbaud, the French post-impressionists, Diaghilev, Richard Strauss, Schonberg; they nearly swooned at the thought of Isadora Duncan shedding her neo-Grecian tunic and dancing in prayerful ecstasy on the Acropolis.

"There was a general new look in everything in those last years before the first war," Lady Diana wrote in her memoirs. "We felt it and revelled in it."

The revel was not always joyous, however, even for the privileged. Little by little the optimism inherited from the buoyant nineties began to lose its bounce. As the omens multiplied—as social or political tensions grew sharper, as the war clouds rolled up from the Balkans, as the unsinkable *Titanic* went down in the Northern twilight with all her lights blazing and the band playing *Nearer, My God, to Thee*—a note of doubt and pessimism increasingly crept into the cultural concert. For some, up to the very end the time remained one of those June moments of history, in which to be young is very heaven; for others, of every age, it had never been anything but sheer hell.

Like most transitional periods, it was a paradoxical age, in which millions enjoyed unprecedented well-being and other millions lived in more than usually abject misery. Good taste flourished, and so did the pompous broad-buttocked vulgarity admired by drummers and monarchs. There was a morning tang in the air, and a midnight staleness. The social order was firmly knit, but subject to the torque of mortal stresses. Revolutionaries with murder in their hearts lurked among the geranium beds; counterterrorists, in the guise of policemen, stalked them from behind the potted palms. Out of such contradictions the old world's winding sheet was finally woven. They were apparent nearly everywhere in European society; but probably were most glaring, as well as most colorful, in Vienna.

We all know what peace is, but it is difficult for any of us now living even to imagine the long peace our fathers knew, the sleekness and the fat of it. At the time of Sarajevo there had not been a major war in Europe proper since the Franco-Prussian one in 1870, forty-three years earlier. Within the Habsburg Empire, which had not won a battle since 1848 or even fought one since 1866 (when its armies were brutally but quickly overwhelmed by the rising Prussian militarism) there were fifty-year-old subjects of Francis Joseph who had lived their whole lives without ever being belligerents or learning to call any nation the enemy. Such experiences mark a man, above all in Vienna; the enjoyment of peace has always been a special Viennese talent. In 1683 the city rendered a notable service to Christendom by withstanding a Turkish siege, which if it had been successful, would have opened all central Europe to infidel invasion. Vienna recalls the victory with modest pride, but in the collective memory of its citizens the really noteworthy event occurred after the Turks had withdrawn, when a quick-witted Polish mercenary picked up on the battlefield a sack of dark, aromatic beans, previously unknown in the West. A bronze plaque on the coffeehouse that the Pole founded still commemorates the occasion; from the exotic pleasure to which he introduced his adopted fellow countrymen, the Viennese have elaborated over the centuries an art of living and virtually a whole way of life. The coffeehouse culture that reached its apogee in Vienna before 1914 could flourish only in a peaceful world; to the Viennese, as to most other Europeans at the time, peace itself was something to be savored among habitués in an atmosphere of mild and unhurried sociability, sugared to taste, and with plenty of *schlag* floating on it.

Peace, in the Habsburg Empire was *gemutlich*—that untranslatable and typically Viennese compound of comfort, charm, and sympathy—but it was also gay and even dashing. The aura of romance which in the public imagination still haloes the vanished institutions of the Dual Monarchy, is a reflection not so much of their real or supposed splendor, as of the European and domestic tranquillity which they helped maintain for nearly five decades. The handsome young hussars who waltz their way through so many Viennese operettas are absurd because war had come to seem an absurdity, and this very absurdity made them figures of glamour as well as fun to their audience. In retrospect we tend to see the carefree social life of pre-war Europe as a kind of death waltz on the brink of doom, but to those who took part in it, it was not that at all. People did not throw themselves into a rout of pleasures to forget their worries; they simply joined in the dance to express their sense of well-being and to manifest their solidarity. In a society of the content—the only kind the social conscience of the age recognized—pleasure had come to seem almost a civic discipline.

Nowhere, of course, was this discipline more conscientiously observed than in Vienna. Scholars have estimated that one out of every three babies born in the pre-war Habsburg capital was illegitimate. Various factors contributed to this statistical exploit—the general social and economic backwardness of the Empire, Austrian *schlamperei,* and above all the red tape surrounding marriage and divorce, which made these formalities seem just too much trouble to many of the Emperor's subjects. It would be an error to conclude from such evidence that Vienna was a city of unbridled license, but it was unquestionably easygoing.

On the whole the Viennese, despite their legendary sophistication, stressed the simpler pleasures: eating, drinking, flirting, and dancing. The dance, especially the waltz, was a general passion. Impoverished nobles skimped all year on their country estates to give one of the formal balls, with dancing until dawn, around which the social season in Vienna revolved. At more modest levels of society, the public dance halls were nearly always crowded. One, claiming to be the largest in Europe, maintained a fully equipped emergency maternity room for the convenience of its female patrons. Viennese past the age of romance, if there were any, could console themselves with such innocent pleasures as swaying above the trees of the Prater in one of the red gondolas of the Big Wheel. This giant steel toy was erected in 1898 to commemmorate the fiftieth year of Francis Joseph's reign, an eminently Viennese tribute to a much-loved monarch, and has been turning tirelessly ever since, for the pride and pleasure of those citizens who are not too filled with beer or whipped cream to enjoy the view of their beloved city.

The aristocracy and wealthy bourgeoisie of Vienna, like their peers in other European capitals of that day had no morbid inhibitions about letting the less-favored see that they were having a good time. As James Laver remarks in his delectable *Edwardian Promenade:*

"The Edwardian age was probably the last period in history when the fortunate thought they could give pleasure to others by displaying their good fortune before them."

Extravagant entertainment was one of the forms of display whereby the privileged classes simultaneously kept up the morale of the lower orders and maintained their own station. Describing a ball at the palace of a great Austrian aristocrat, Lord Hamilton, a pre-war British ambassador to the Habsburg court reported the scene as follows:

"It was Prince S——'s custom on these occasions to have three hundred young peasants sent up from his country estates and to have them thrust into the family livery. These bucolic youths, looking very sheepish in their unfamiliar plush breeches and stockings, with their unkempt heads powdered, and with swords at their sides, stood motionless on every step of the staircase."

(A less feudal, but probably no less expensive "Venetian Dinner" given by a British millionaire at the Savoy Hotel in London was served in a large, specially constructed gondola, moored in the flooded courtyard of the hotel, while smaller craft and live swans floated around it. At about the same time the Paris couturier, Paul Poiret, stirred local society writers to a high pitch of ecstasy by one of the balls he gave in his private hotel on the Fauborg St. Honoré. It was transformed for the occasion to an Arabian Nights palace guarded by half-naked blackamoors and enlivened by pink ibises, monkeys, and parrots in the trees, from which hung luminous fruit.)

Dress, of course, was an essential form of display. Being seen in the right clothes at the right time in the right place was one of the obsessions of the age. A male guest at a quiet British weekend party was expected to don, or change into, the approved costumes for breakfast and church, for lounging about in the morning, for eating lunch, for lounging about in the afternoon, for taking tea (a velvet jacket) and for dinner (white tie and tails). Female guests put on filmy tea gowns for the afternoon ritual; for dinner they wore formal dresses with trains and carried ostrich feather fans. For motoring, an increasingly popular sport but one that in 1914 still had considerable snob appeal, both sexes wore full-length sealskin coats, veils or mufflers, and goggles. In Vienna clothes were still more varied and splendid especially the uniforms worn by officers. The annual May Corso of fashionable equipages along the Ringstrasse and in the Pater outshone even such masterpiece group-exhibitionism as Britain's Ascot or the Grand Prix in Paris. Monarchs were naturally expected to set a brilliant example to their subjects in matters of dress and decorations and they usually did; Germany's Wilhelm II had the gaudiest wardrobe, and England's Edward VII was unrivaled in the casual range, but the all-round champion of the sartorial *mot juste* was the veteran Francis Joseph.

A few years before the war the Swedes modified the cut of their uniforms at about the time King Gustavus Adolphus visited Vienna for the golden jubilee of Francis Joseph's reign. "Great heavens," the King of Sweden said as he stepped from the train and saw his host walking toward him, impeccably got up as a Swedish general, "the new uniform already? Why, I don't have one myself yet."

Travel was another fashionable form of display. Crowned heads visited back and forth as frequently as lesser mortals. The German Kaiser rarely failed to take his yacht to the Cowes Regatta, the climax of the social season in Britain, and occasionally won it. Going abroad held magic charm, providing it was at the right season. July was for Deauville, Biarritz, and Le Touquet; in August came the German baths season at Baden-Baden, Marienbad, Wiesbaden, and other fashionable resorts. In winter, after the close of the hunting and country house season, the fashionable migrated to the French Riviera, especially to Monte Carlo with its famed gambling tables. (Just before the war a small adventurous *avant-garde* defected to St. Moritz, where it soon became chic to be seen sliding down the slopes on skis, wearing knee breeches and with a balaclava helmet on one's head.)

Passports were not yet required in most European countries, and the leading currencies could be exchanged everywhere; no customs inspector's eyes turned hard if he heard the chink of gold sovereigns, francs or marks as a traveler's luggage was shifted. This glorious freedom of movement has inspired some writers to draw an overidyllic picture of pre-1914 Europe as a continent practically without internal frontiers. In reality much depended on who you were and what you were traveling for; there were few restrictions for wealthy and titled pleasure seekers, but some 400,000 of Francis Joseph's poorer subjects were annually forced by economic pressures to slip by stealth through the primitive iron curtain set up to halt emigration from his realms, while the long Russian borders were policed almost as closely then as now.

Despite such necessary qualifications, the cosmopolitanism of pre-war Europe often seems amazing by present-day standards. As might be expected, Vienna, the polyglot capital of a multi-racial empire, outshone the rest of the Continent in this respect, too. Stefan Zweig relates how the great Belgian poet Emile Verhaeren shed tears when the German Count Zeppelin's dirigible balloon crashed on its maiden flight after having circled the Cathedral of Strasbourg, and how the Viennese shouted with joy when the Frenchman, Blériot, flew the Channel. In the leading Vienna cafes anyone with the price of a cup of coffee and enough time on his hands could read every day not only the whole Austro-Hungarian press but all the important German and Swiss papers, the *London Times,* the Paris *Le Temps* and *Journal des Débats* and miscellaneous Italian, Russian, and American papers. The young Viennese intellectual with a penchant for the liberal arts could find there the foremost literary and art reviews of the whole world such as the *Mercure de France, Studio,* and the *Burlington Magazine.* He knew all about the latest *avant-garde* play produced in Paris and the newest trends in painting or sculpture everywhere; he could—and did—sit for hours with his friends arguing about European poets who had not yet been published in their own countries.

Admiration for the achievement of foreign writers or artists was enhanced by the reverence among Europeans at the time—above all in Vienna —for art and literature generally. The universal sneer had not yet been perfected; debunking had not come into fashion. To have crossed Gustav Mahler in the street, to have recognized Richard Strauss or Arthur Schnitzler or Hugo von Hofmannsthal sitting in a cafe, were events to be recounted to one's friends like personal triumphs. If one had had the incredible good luck to meet a leading actor or actress of the Burgtheater, mere words could not suffice to communicate the intensity of the experience; one might be quite speechless with hero-worship. The theater was the great Viennese passion and actors were demigods, outside and above the rigid caste system of the Habsburg Empire. When the great tragedienne, Charlotte Wolters, died, Zweig's old cook wept, though she had never seen her, nor set foot inside the Burgtheater.

Before we shed tears ourselves for having been born too late, or in the wrong place, to prove the pleasures of so refined a civilization, it might be well to note the dour comment of the greatest of all modern Viennese thinkers at the apogee of the city's cultural flowering.

"Vienna," Sigmund Freud wrote, a few years before the war to his German friend Wilhelm Fliess, "after all is Vienna, that is to say disgusting in the highest degree."

Freud detested the moral squalor of an age and a society whose sexuality was simultaneously overheated and hypocritical; he was appalled by the submerged vestiges of primitive savagery that his new technique of psychoanalysis was constantly uncovering in the minds of supposedly civilized twentieth-century adults. The roots of Freud's loathing for the city that was his home during seventy-eight of his eighty-three years were more personal, however, as Manes Sperber, himself a Viennese and a psychiatrist, has pointed out in a brilliant essay. By the last years before the war Freud was already famous throughout the medical world and beginning to be honored by intellectuals generally, but in Vienna intellectuals, with rare exceptions, were not considered *hoffahig* (literally, not worthy of being received at court, and by extension, not recognized in the highest social circles). For that matter, not all aristocrats possessed that precious grace; Countess Karoli, the wife of the Austro-Hungarian ambassador in Berlin, was greatly commiserated with in diplomatic circles because, having only twelve of the required sixteen quarters of nobility, she was not *hoffahig*. In England at the time, as the future Socialist, Lady Warwick, explained to the popular novelist Elinor Glyn, "Doctors and solicitors might be invited to garden parties, though never of course to lunch or dinner." Vienna society was stricter, particularly in the case of Jewish doctors. The social and racial arrogance of the European ruling classes, which contributed so largely to the revolutionary upheavals of the following generation—above all to the anticolonialist revolution after World War II—flourished in its most anachronistic, if not in its most extreme form in the cultured, cosmopolitan capital of the Habsburgs before 1914. Moreover, the Viennese anti-Semitism that inflicted many bitter humiliations on Freud and provoked his undying resentment was not confined to the upper strata of Austrian society: it poisoned the whole atmosphere of the capital, in fact of the entire Empire. As a small child before his parents moved to Vienna, Freud once saw his father forced off the sidewalk by an anti-Semitic bully in the family's native Galician town.

"Vienna, where Freud lived from his fourth to his 82nd year . . . was the most anti-Semitic of all the great cities of the world," says Sperber. (Czarist Russia was the most anti-Semitic country, however.) "The American nation owes it to itself to confess its horror when it hears of massacres as terrible as those of Kishinev," said President Theodore Roosevelt after a particularly atrocious pogrom in southern Russia. Hitler, who lived in Vienna from 1907 to 1913, did not have to look far to discover the elements of racial doctrine that he later elaborated into the most monstrous of twentieth-century ideologies. They were ready at hand, as William A. Jenks has demonstrated in the contemporary speeches and writings of Karl Lueger, the immensely popular Christian Socialist Mayor of Vienna, and in those of the Pan-German demagogue Georg von Schonerer. One particularly rabid follower of Lueger, Ernst Schneider, even foreshadowed the

Nazi extermination camps by publicly recommending that all Jews be placed aboard a large ship which would then be scuttled on the high seas.

Vienna's anti-Semitism—along with the conflicting nationalist passions that erupted in incessant student brawls at the university—was no doubt intensified by the social misery of which Hitler got such a bitter taste during his six years in the Habsburg capital. At the time the young would-be architect from Linz was walking the streets of Vienna trying to sell his uninspired water colors, followed—in his own self-pitying but accurate phrase—by his "faithful companion, hunger," there was a grave housing shortage in the city, brought on by rapid industrialization. Some 45 per cent of the Viennese population in 1900 lived in flats of one or two small rooms; one Viennese in twenty had no room of his own at all, but lived as a *bettgeher*, sleeping, for a few pennies, in someone else's bed while its regular occupant was at work, or spending the nights in one of the ghastly "warming rooms" (flophouses) maintained by private charity. The most miserable slept on the grass of the Prater in summer and lived all winter, as Hitler was able to observe, in the damp tepid stench of the sewage canals. Hitler himself was doubtless a *bettgeher* for a time, and Jenks believes that he probably slept on occasion in the Prater or in a "warming room." In later life, the Nazi Fuehrer still shuddered to recall those "pitiful dens" and those "sinister pictures of dirt and repugnant filth, and worse still."

Though housing conditions were worse in Vienna than in most European cities, they were bad nearly everywhere. Sunset to thousands of homeless men, women, and children in London meant the closing of the parks and the beginning of the all-night shuffle from doorway to doorway, from one temporary shelter to another, until the Green Park, the first to open, admitted them at 4:15 A.M. to its lawns and benches. They would still be huddled there, ragged, haggard, and sleeping fitfully, when the well-dressed inhabitants of the West End would turn out for their fashionable morning constitutional. The pitiful spectacle did not unduly distress the rudimentary social conscience of the day, no more than did the grim sociological data that writers like Shaw and Wells were beginning to publicize—the fact, for example, that one out of every three adult workers in contemporary London died on public charity, or that in the poorest areas of rural England, one infant out of four never reached the age of twelve months. The welfare state—except possibly in Bismarck's Prussia—was still two generations and two wars in the future. Few, if any, public controls mitigated the ruthless functioning of the free-enterprise capitalism inherited from the nineteenth century, with its brutal alternations of insufficiently shared prosperity and all-too-widespread depression. Workers' wages, even in good times, were shockingly low—thirty shillings a week, about $7.50, was considered good pay for a married working man in prosperous England. The living standards of farm laborers and poor tenant farmers were even lower, almost everywhere in Europe, owing in part to the competition of cereal grains and meat from the New World.

Rural conditions were specially bad in Russia and in the Austro-Hungarian Empire, where there was a chronic farm problem. In Germany the working day for a farm laborer in 1910 was as long—18 hours—as it had been in 1820, but in the Habsburg lands, hundreds of thousands of peasants could not even find work, except at harvest time. The feudal backwardness reflected in the high rate of illiteracy—63 per cent in Austrian Galicia—was rendered nightmarish (as in Russia) by the social dislocations of a society in the frenzied early stages of industrialization. The result in Austria-Hungary was a steady flow of uprooted and demoralized peasants from the countryside into an already badly overcrowded capital. It was not surprising that the young Hitler, on the occasions when he found manual work, overheard his comrades "reject everything: the nation—an invention of the capitalist classes; the fatherland—the bourgeoisie's instrument for the exploitation of the working classes; the law—a means for oppressing the proletariat; morality—a principle for turning men into sheep."

On the whole it seems remarkable that the working class population of pre-war Vienna was not more revolutionary. The annual May Day parade of workers with red carnations in their buttonholes pouring in from the industrial suburbs and marching along the Nobelallee with their women and children gave some nervous bourgeois the jitters, but the Social Democratic notables who led the procession—Victor Adler, Otto Bauer, Karl Renner—were sober, civilized Viennese intellectuals who liked to be addressed as "Comrade Herr Doktor." Leon Trotsky, an exile in Vienna for several years before the war and a member of the Social Democratic Party himself, listened with scarcely veiled contempt to their academic discussions in the smoky back rooms of the Café Central. In his memoirs he later derided these innocuous mandarins for not perceiving "that history had already poised its gigantic soldier's boot over the ant-heap in which they were rushing about with such self-abandon."

Trotsky was prescient, as he often was, but oversimplified the situation, as he not infrequently did. History's boot was poised, but it did not stamp down in quite the way he and other doctrinaire Marxists had expected. As we shall see more clearly in a later chapter, it was not the forces of social revolution, mainly inspired since the mid-nineteenth century by the writings of Karl Marx and his disciples, but those of nationalist irredentism—within the Habsburg Empire and elsewhere—that doomed the traditional European order handed down from the eighteenth and nineteenth centuries. And even the death sentence pronounced on this order by the nationalist fanatics might not have been irrevocable had it not been for the invisible but fatal processes of decay at work inside the dynastic structures of the four great European autocracies. Before taking up the story of their downfall, let us pause for a moment longer to study a single revelatory incident that was at once a significant milestone on Europe's road to war and an illustration, among other things, of certain fatal weaknesses in the old world diplomacy that Churchill admired.

CHAPTER 3

Dynasts and Diplomats

IN the last week of July 1905, the long white and gold yacht *Hohenzollern,* flying the imperial pennant with its sable cross and the subsequently famous motto, *Gott Mit Uns,* steamed into the Bay of Bjorkoe, off the Finnish coast, and dropped anchor in the clear waters of the Baltic, a cable-length from another luxurious pleasure craft that already lay there. Kaiser Wilhelm II of Germany, with the Kaiserin, and several guests, had arrived to pay a neighborly call on his cousin Nicky— Nicholas II, Czar of all the Russias—who awaited him, with the Czarina, their daughter and the year-old Czarevitch abroad the Romanov yacht *Stella Polaris.* The seemingly casual encounter of two vacationing monarchs and their families was actually the culmination of intense and ultra-secret diplomatic preparations. Last-minute arrangements had been settled by an exchange of wireless messages, in the private cipher of the two Emperors after their yachts were on the high seas.

"Not a soul has the slightest idea," read the text of a final top-priority eyes-only signal from the *Hohenzollern.* "All my guests think we're bound for Gothland . . . have important news for you. My guests' faces will be worth seeing when they suddenly behold your yacht. Tableau! What sort of dress for our meeting? Willy."

This almost giggly communication expressed the Kaiser's inmost personality; the style here was unmistakably the man. A born ham with a compulsive urge for the mock-heroic gesture, Wilhelm ranted and postured like some men drink. His whole life was a series of charades that he acted out with self-applauding zest before a captive audience of European diplomats and crowned heads unable to take their eyes off the grotesque performance for a moment lest fate punish the mountebank by accepting one

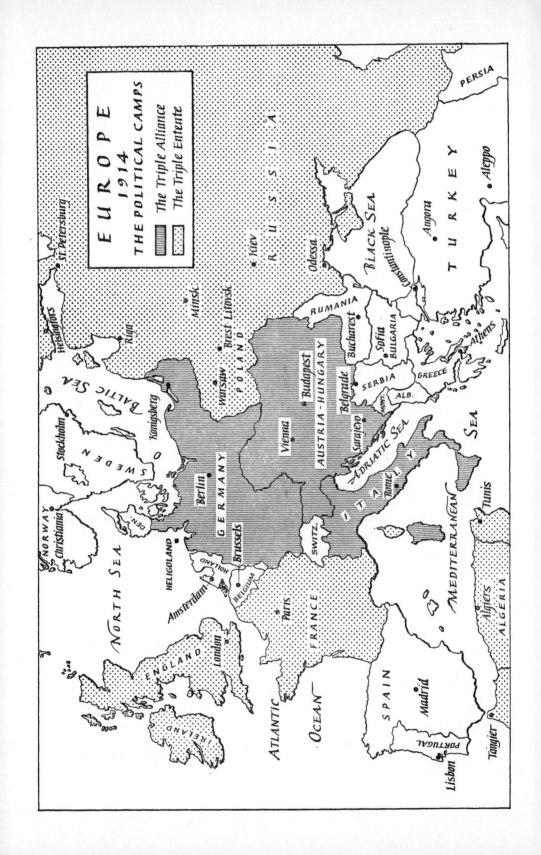

of his impersonations at its face value, thus turning farce into real tragedy. This, of course, is what finally happened in 1914; the Bjorkoe affair was to be a kind of warning.

In stressing the secrecy of his rendezvous with the Czar, Wilhelm had exaggerated only a little. His long-suffering Chancellor, Prince Bernhard von Bulow, knew about it, but no other German official at the policy-making level had been informed. On the Russian side no minister had been taken into the Czar's confidence. Yet the diplomatic implications of the encounter were sensational. Though international tensions were not yet acute in Europe, the two sovereigns belonged to opposing European coalitions. Germany already headed the Triple Alliance, which linked her national ambitions and disquietudes with those of Italy and Austria-Hungary, Russia's traditional rival in the Balkans. Russia was the military ally of a France still mourning over lost Alsace-Lorraine and haunted by dreams of revenge for 1870. In the circumstances any personal contact between the two Emperors other than routine exchanges of civilities when they happened to meet at royal weddings, funerals, and similar occasions was calculated to plunge all the foreign offices of the Continent into orgies of speculation.

Wilhelm, however, had not slipped off to Bjorkoe just to enjoy a family outing with his Russian cousins away from prying journalists and monocled gossipmongers. He had come to make history. He was going to outdo his old mentor Bismarck, who, after forging German unity and seating Wilhelm's grandfather on the Imperial throne, had gained the admiration of all Europe's professionals by his adroit diplomacy.

Bismarck had once taken out reinsurance against the dangers of encirclement and the fundamental insecurity of the European security system by signing a secret nonaggression pact with Russia. The dream of European, or world hegemony based on reconciliation between Slav and Teuton has recurrently tempted some of the strongest as well as the weakest minds in Germany up to the present day; the undulations of Russian Foreign policy, from Alexander I to Nikita Khrushchev, show that it has some appeal to Slavic ones as well. Moreover, in the nineteenth century diplomatic tradition inherited from the princely courts of an earlier day, making a deal with a potential enemy behind the backs of one's friends or allies had an almost irresistible attraction; diplomacy and the *comedia dell' arte* had emerged from Renaissance Italy at about the same time and the two art forms had retained certain basic similarities as they evolved. The young Kaiser, however, shocked by the cynicism of Bismarck's foreign policy, had allowed the Russian treaty to lapse when he dropped the ageing pilot of Germany's imperial destiny after a row over domestic questions in 1890. Now Wilhelm at forty-three was back on the same easterly tack the Iron

Chancellor had tried, maneuvering with the same deviousness, but not, unfortunately, with the same prudence or dexterity.

The Kaiser had already made a tentative and inconclusive move in this direction in the course of an earlier meeting with the Czar aboard the *Hohenzollern*.

"I wish you would assume, from now on, the title of Admiral of the Pacific," he had said to Nicholas on that occasion. "I shall call myself Admiral of the Atlantic." Steaming away from the meeting the Kaiser had ordered the *Hohenzollern* to make the signal, "The Admiral of the Atlantic salutes the Admiral of the Pacific."

Annoyance with his British cousin, Edward VII, had helped Wilhelm's diplomatic evolution. The year before, Edward, already a virtual ally of France in the Entente Cordiale, had been the Kaiser's guest at the Kiel review and had displayed a lack of enthusiasm bordering on rudeness at the spectacle of Germany's nascent naval might. Since then the British press had been filled with insolent warnings to Germany not to challenge Britain's supremacy on the seas. To punish England for thus spurning the knightly hand of German friendship, and to neutralize French hostility, Wilhelm had finally come up with his super-Bismarckian brainwave. Egged on by his gray eminence Baron Holstein, a diplomatic spider who sat day and night in his obscure lair in the Wilhelmstrasse (the German Foreign Office) covering Europe with his endless webs of intrigue, the Kaiser had written the Czar around the end of 1904 suggesting an alliance between their two empires as the best way to safeguard European peace. France, as Russia's ally, would virtually be obliged to join in, Wilhelm had pointed out to his cousin; the proposed Berlin-St. Petersburg axis would thus become in effect a new continental coalition against Britain, Russia's hereditary rival in Asia.

The immediate reaction had been disappointing to Wilhelm. The Czar had shown the letter to his ministers; they had consulted the French allies. The project was quietly pigeonholed while a discrete snicker ran around the chancelleries of Europe. By July, however, the Kaiser felt that the changing European situation justified another try. The Russo-Japanese War, which had broken out in February 1904, was lost. The virtual annihilation of the main Russian fleet in the Straits of Tsushima on May 27, 1905, had deprived the Czar of his last hope. Revolutionary unrest was mounting in Russia. Nicky would be looking for friends.

Wilhelm accordingly proposed the joint yachting excursion in the Baltic, and when Nicholas accepted, ordered Bulow to dust off the draft treaty worked up six months earlier and send it to him (Holstein, its real author, for some reason, was not in on the secret this time). The document was wirelessed to the *Hohenzollern* and Wilhelm copied it in his own hand, incidentally altering the text at a critical point, without informing his Chancellor. Just before the meeting—on July 24—the Kaiser retired to his cabin and placed himself in God's hands.

"And at the end," Wilhelm later reported to Bulow, "I also uttered the prayer of the Old Dessauer [Leopold Prince of Anhalt-Dessau] at Kesseldorf, that if He did not wish to help me He should not help the other side either. Then I felt wonderfully strengthened . . . and decided within me 'You will put it through, no matter what the cost'."

Thus fortified in spirit, the Kaiser went abroad the *Stella Polaris,* wearing a German admiral's uniform, his famous spiked mustaches bristling martially, a manic glitter in his dark eyes. He was warmly embraced by Nicholas, dressed like a British yachtsman and looking, with his gentle blue eyes and neatly trimmed chestnut beard, astonishingly like his distant cousin the Prince of Wales, the future George V. The talks got off to a brilliant start. Overcome by emotion, the Czar's court chamberlain, old Count Fredericks, tearfully exclaimed, "At a moment when we are abandoned by the whole world, ay, despised, and not even a dog will take a bone from us, your Majesty has come as a true friend to comfort us and lift us up again."

The first greetings had hardly been exchanged before Nicholas spontaneously brought up the name of Edward VII, whom he described as "the greatest mischiefmaker and the most dangerous intriguer in the whole world."

The Czarina was a granddaughter of Queen Victoria—who was also Wilhelm's grandmother—and Nicholas himself was the nephew of Edward's consort, Queen Alexandra, but family ties had become strained during the current war by Britain's manifest sympathy with its Japanese allies, especially since the previous October. At that time the Russian naval forces in the Baltic, running at night through the English Channel en route to their distant Pacific doom, had inadvertently shot up a British fishing fleet (and some of their own ships) in the fog off the Dogger Bank. The British Government and public had not been amused by the tragi-comic incident, and a major crisis in relations with Russia had narrowly been averted.

Wilhelm naturally sympathized with the Czar's feelings about Edward, and slyly added that the latter had "a passion for concluding a little agreement."

"Well," Nicholas shot back, "I can only say that he shall not get one from me, and never in my life against Germany or you, my word of honor on it."

Nicholas then went on to complain about the way his French allies had let him down over the Dogger Bank affair and in closing the coast of Indochina to the Russian fleet, at England's behest. Wilhelm rubbed salt into this wound, too, with what he thought was extreme cleverness.

The day passed deliciously, and that evening the Kaiser was host at a gay little dinner party aboard the *Hohenzollern* for the Czar and his family. Nicholas seemed cheerful and relaxed; the famous charm that captivated everyone who had not had occasion to do business with him was radiating warmly. Wilhelm, himself, was a little tense, his mind seething with Machiavellian plans for the morrow. The next morning, after another consultation in his cabin with God, the Kaiser again went aboard the *Stella Polaris,* where, at the end of an excellent lunch, the two blue-blooded amateurs, each as gullible in his own fashion as he was undependable, got down to the serious business of outwitting each other and double-crossing their respective allies. Somehow the theme of British perfidy and French unreliability came up again. Wilhelm hinted that Edward was cooking up another of those "little agreements" of his with France, behind Russia's back.

"That is too bad," the Czar answered, "what shall I do in this disagreeable situation?"

"How would it be if we were to make a little agreement, too?" Wilhelm suggested.

That reminded Nicholas that Wilhelm had sent him a draft along these lines a few months before, but unfortunately he had forgotten its details and had not thought to bring the text along with him on the yacht. The Kaiser quickly reassured his cousin.

"I possess a copy," he said, "which, by an extraordinary chance, I happen to have in my pocket."

The incident would seem unbelievable if Wilhelm himself had not recorded it in his subsequent report to Bulow. The scene that followed was even more fantastic. Here are the essentials of it related in the Kaiser's own inimitable prose:

"The Czar caught me by the hand and drew me out of the saloon into what used to be his father's cabin, then he shut all the doors himself. 'Show it to me, please'—and his dreamy eyes lit up. I drew the envelope from my pocket, unfolded the paper on Alexander's own writing table, right in front of the Empress-Mother's photograph . . . and laid it before the Czar. He read it once, twice, thrice. I sent up a fervent prayer to the good God that He would be with us in this moment, and guide the young monarch aright.

"There was a dead calm; only the gentlest murmur from the sea, and the sun shone bright and clear into the pleasant cabin, while right before my eyes lay the *Hohenzollern* in her dazzling whiteness, and the Imperial Standard fluttering high in the morning breeze. I was just reading there on its sable cross, the words *Gott Mit Uns,* when I heard the Czar's voice beside me say: 'That is quite excellent. I quite agree!' . . . My heart beat so hard that I could hear it; but I pulled myself together and said, quite casually, as it were: 'Should you like to sign it? It would be a very nice souvenir of our interview!'

"He ran over the pages again. Then he said 'Yes, I will.' I flung back the cover of the ink well, handed him the pen, and he wrote with a firm hand, 'Nicolas' and gave the pen to me. As I rose he clasped me in his arms, deeply moved, and said, 'I thank God and I thank you' . . . tears of joy stood in my eyes—to be sure drops of perspiration were trickling down my brow and my back—and I thought, Frederick Wilhelm III, Queen Louisa, Grandpapa and Nicholas I must surely be near in that moment."

To avoid disappointing this celestial audience, Wilhelm hastily reminded the Czar that documents of such import should be countersigned. One of the Kaiser's guests, a minor diplomat named von Tschirschky took care of this formality for the German side by writing his signature below that of his imperial master. For want of anyone more qualified the Czar sent for the doddering old man who was his Minister of the Navy, Admiral Birilow, and waved the folded document before his face.

"Do you trust me, Alexis Alexeivitch?" he asked. "In that case, sign here. Here, under my signature."

The admiral was so overwhelmed with the mysterious honor bestowed on him that he kissed the Kaiser's hand, exclaiming, "God bless you, Sire; you are Russia's guardian angel."

The treaty of Bjorkoe, considered by Wilhelm as a landmark of modern history, provided for a defensive alliance between the two empires which was to come into effect as soon as peace had been concluded between Russia and Japan. The Kaiser had written in a stipulation restricting its scope, originally world-wide, to Europe, where each signatory was pledged to come to the aid of the other if it was attacked by a third party. Article Four laid down that after the treaty had come into force the Czar should invite France to join the pact.

In a letter to the Czar immediately after his return from the Bjorkoe meeting—which he characterized as "a cornerstone of European politics" and a "new leaf in the history of the world"—Wilhelm outlined the role he envisaged for France in the new European order:

"Marianne [France] must remember that she is wedded to you and that she is obliged to lie in bed with you and eventually to give you a hug or a kiss now and then to me, but not to sneak into the bedroom of the ever-intriguing *touche-à-tout* on the Island [Edward]."

Despite the proviso for French adherence, the agreement was a flagrant betrayal of the alliance signed with France fifteen years earlier to support her against Germany. Theoretically under the Bjorkoe treaty Russia could find herself at war with France if the latter was considered to have attacked Germany. Yet France and Russia were already bound by a secret military convention, whose existence and sinister import both came to light in 1914, whereby each partner was pledged to mobilize immediately and automatically if the other did. Somehow the Czar had failed to grasp this implication of the document his wily cousin had handed him to sign, though, as always with Nicholas II, it was hard to tell how much of his shiftiness was due to weakness of mind or character and how much to a kind of passive, feminine guile. In any case, the whole Bjorkoe affair horrified his ministers when he was finally obliged to let them in on the secret. "Monstrous!" We shall be dishonored in the eyes of the French," was the immediate reaction of the professionals in St. Petersburg.

The French themselves speedily realized that some sort of skulduggery was going on when their intelligence agents in Russia learned from a French chef employed by the imperial kitchens that on July 20 orders had been handed down to rush the gala table service, only used in entertaining royalty, to the Czar's yacht. A few days after Nicholas' return from Bjorkoe a French spy overheard old Admiral Birilow mutter, "I've signed something, but the devil only knows what," and flashed the news to Paris, where it provoked extreme agitation. Finally, the Russian ambassador in Paris was instructed cautiously to sound out the French attitude toward the idea of a Franco-Russo-German defense pact, and the reaction being as expected, the Czar was wheedled by his ministers into writing the Kaiser to insist on an amendment that rendered the Bjorkoe agreement inoperative.

Wilhelm had not fared much better in Berlin. Even Holstein castigated Bjorkoe as "operetta politics" and Bulow flew into a rage because the Kaiser, after altering the original text of the draft treaty—the limitation of its scope to Europe—had signed it without consulting his Chancellor. Tears, tantrums and hysterics became daily occurrences at the imperial court. Bulow handed in his resignation; Wilhelm, refusing to accept it, whined and sniveled like a jilted schoolgirl.

"To be treated like this by my best and most intimate of friends," the deflated would-be Bismarck wailed in a reproachful letter to his disgruntled Chancellor. "It has dealt me such a terrible blow that I feel quite broken and cannot but fear I may have a serious nervous attack. Telegraph 'All Right,' as soon as you get this, and then I shall know you are not going. For the day after I receive your resignation, the Emperor will no longer exist! Think of my poor wife and children."

When the Czar's embarrassed letters weaseling out of the Bjorkoe agreement reached the Kaiser, his overwrought nerves were subjected to a further strain. After ranting to his entourage about the "schoolboy ideologue in St. Petersburg," he took up his pen for a last solemn appeal to his defaulting partner.

"We have joined our hands together religiously," he wired Nicholas. "We have given our signatures before God, who has heard the promise we swore. I consider, therefore, that the treaty is still in force. If you desire some alterations of detail, propose them to me. But what is signed is signed. God is our witness."

Nicholas did not reply. He never forgave Wilhelm for having duped him. Consciousness of the shabby role he himself had played, whether from weakness or from duplicity, probably added to his bitterness. The affectionate relations which had existed between the two cousins for ten years were at an end, and the Anglo-Russian accord of 1907, completing the encirclement of Germany and the definitive crystallization of Europe into two hostile power-blocs, was in sight. Wilhelm had indeed succeeded in making history at Bjorkoe, though not in the way he intended.

"To such a man was entrusted so great a part of the destinies of the world!" comments the Italian historian Luigi Albertini. The remark applies with equal force to Nicholas. The two emperors, the most powerful rulers of contemporary Europe, undoubtedly bear a heavy share of responsibility for the catastrophe that eventually shattered both their empires and so much else besides. It would be alike misleading and unfair, however, to exaggerate the personal guilt of either Wilhelm II or Nicholas II, as rival propagandists did after the war. Each in his muddle-headed and disastrous fashion was trying to safeguard peace.

It was the decaying European dynastic system itself, and the whole philosophy and machinery of foreign relations linked to it, that made war inevitable, thereby dooming the social order based on the system. The monarchies of pre-1914 Europe were rushing to their final extinction for the same reason that the dinosaurs of the Carboniferous Age had waddled to theirs. They had simply ceased to be adapted to their environment. Technological and sociological progress had rendered war too dangerous to be used as a means for achieving national objectives, but the rulers of nations had not yet realized it—half a century later, we are just beginning to grasp the idea—and their political imagination had not evolved techniques or concepts of diplomacy capable of settling major international problems without resort to war (neither has ours).

"The political ideas which governed diplomatic intercourse such as balance of power, spheres of interest, national prestige and sovereignty," remarks the German historian Meissner, "provide a poor guidance through the fogs of mistrust. The lights had gone out over Europe long before the conflict arose."

The failure of Churchill's "princes and potentates"—and their agents—to deal satisfactorily with conflicts of interest between their states was dramatically aggravated by maladjustments that generated explosive internal tensions. These maladjustments, arising from the conflict or discrepancy between traditional institutions and contemporary needs, were more or less acute in the various monarchies and empires. Sometimes they were mainly social and political, sometimes essentially administrative—the sheer over-

loading of the bureaucratic machinery, with resultant paralysis and confusion, was a big factor in the breakdown of the old order—usually all
three at once. Revolution or the threat of revolution helped push the decaying European dynasties into war, and war, or the threat of war, touched
off new revolutions in a deadly chain-reaction that is still continuing in our
day. The ultimate aim of my book is to try to identify some of the most
significant or dramatic stages of this apocalyptic process and to trace their
imbrications. A logical starting place is the abortive revolution of 1905 in
Russia, which, as we have seen, was one of the factors that caused the
Czar to accept the unfortunate meeting with Wilhelm at Bjorkoe.

CHAPTER 4

The Year of the Red Cock

TO the Eastern Orthodox Church, which the Viking merchant-princes of early Russia imported from Byzantium (Constantinople), the Epiphany, January 6, is a specially solemn feast, a graver and more hieratic Christmas. In St. Petersburg, before the Revolution, the day was celebrated with Byzantine splendor, in a typically Byzantine communion of the temporal and the spiritual authority. The main public ceremony, the Blessing of the Waters, commemorating Christ's baptism in the Jordan, was a colorful and moving rite. Beneath the dull ochre walls of the Winter Palace, the Czar's rarely used official residence, a brightly decorated tent and a platform were set up on the frozen Neva, the deep, slow-moving river, wide as an arm of the sea, on whose marshy banks Peter the Great had chosen to build his monstrous and lovely capital. There, on the snowy waste, against the fabulous pink granite embankment that for mile after mile holds the Neva in its bed, under the leaden sky of the northern midwinter, the high priesthood of the Russian Orthodox Church and the Imperial Household assembled, forming a barbaric tapestry of silk brocade and fur and scarlet cloth. A hole was cut in the ice. The Metropolitan (the Orthodox equivalent of Archbishop) blessed a cross. Then, in a gesture of ancient Christian symbolism, with overtones of pagan exorcism, he dropped it into the black and gurgling water. On January 6, 1905 (by the old calendar used in Russia until 1918 and thirteen days behind ours) in the presence of the Czar, the traditional ceremony took place with its usual brilliance, despite the gloomy news from the Far East (Port Arthur had fallen to the Japanese only a short time before). It ended, however, on an unexpected note of drama. Here is the account of an eyewitness with a flair for lively reporting, a young tourist from the

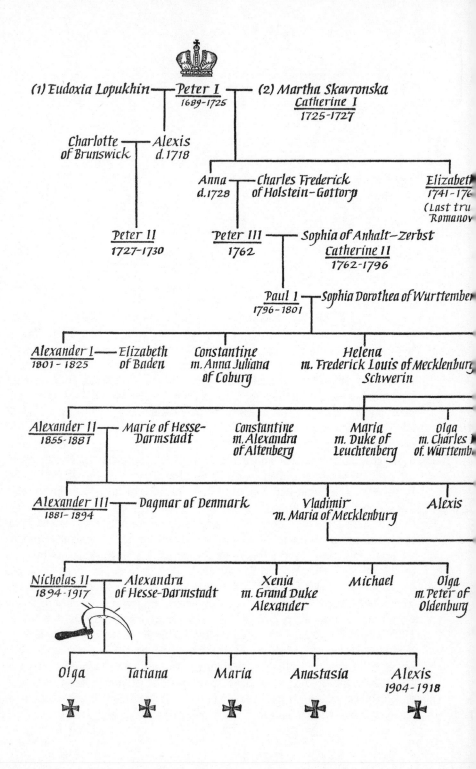

(1) Eudoxia Lopukhin ——— Peter I ——— (2) Martha Skavronska
1689-1725   Catherine I
1725-1727

Charlotte ——— Alexis
of Brunswick   d.1718

Anna ——— Charles Frederick
d.1728   of Holstein-Gottorp

Elizabeth
1741-176
(Last tru
Romanov

Peter II
1727-1730

Peter III ——— Sophia of Anhalt-Zerbst
1762   Catherine II
1762-1796

Paul 1 ——— Sophia Dorothea of Wurttember
1796-1801

Alexander 1 ——— Elizabeth   Constantine   Helena
1801-1825   of Baden   m.Anna Juliana   m.Frederick Louis of Mecklenburg
                                of Coburg   Schwerin

Alexander II ——— Marie of Hesse-   Constantine   Maria   Olga
1855-1881   Darmstadt   m.Alexandra   m.Duke of   m.Charles
                                   of Altenberg   Leuchtenberg   of.Württemb.

Alexander III ——— Dagmar of Denmark   Vladimir   Alexis
1881-1894   m.Maria of Mecklenburg

Nicholas II ——— Alexandra   Xenia   Michael   Olga
1894-1917   of Hesse-Darmstadt m.Grand Duke   m.Peter of
                                  Alexander   Oldenburg

Olga   Tatiana   Maria   Anastasia   Alexis
                                                         1904-1918

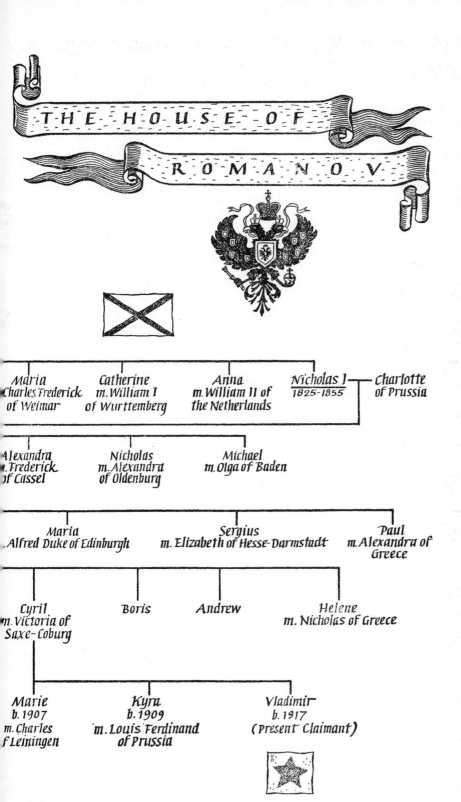

THE HOUSE OF ROMANOV

Maria
Charles Frederick
of Weimar

Catherine
m. William 1
of Wurttemberg

Anna
m. William 11 of
the Netherlands

Nicholas 1 — Charlotte
1825-1855   of Prussia

Alexandra
. Frederick
of Cassel

Nicholas
m. Alexandra
of Oldenburg

Michael
m. Olga of Baden

Maria
. Alfred Duke of Edinburgh

Sergius
m. Elizabeth of Hesse-Darmstadt

Paul
m. Alexandra of
Greece

Cyril
m. Victoria of
Saxe-Coburg

Boris

Andrew

Helene
m. Nicholas of Greece

Marie
b. 1907
m. Charles
f Leiningen

Kyra
b. 1909
m. Louis Ferdinand
of Prussia

Vladimir
b. 1917
(Present Claimant)

West, Dr. Leon Weber-Bauler, the Russian-born son of an emigré woman revolutionary.

"The crowd was kept at a distance; it was glum and silent," Weber-Bauler, who after the war became a well-known figure in Geneva medical and intellectual circles, records in his autobiography. He watched from a bridge. "Bells rang to announce the benediction, and suddenly there was the detonation of a cannon from the esplanade of the fortress of Peter and Paul across the river. The smoke of the discharge rose in a spherical cloud. The regulation salvo was beginning. But, to our amazement, a similar detonation had resounded above the imperial platform. The gun had been loaded with shrapnel and the shell had burst over the imperial party and suite!

"A gunner . . . had loaded the gun with shrapnel instead of with a blank cartridge and had fired on the Czar and his clergy with a piece which had been laid beforehand." The Czar was unhurt. As they removed the dead other officials fled. "The Czar betrayed no fear. 'I'll keep this as a souvenir,' he was reported as saying, as he pocketed a shrapnel bullet which had recoiled from the granite of the quay and had fallen at his feet."

The final anecdote may be apocryphal. If Nicholas II did pick up that pellet, it was a souvenir of something more than centuries' old guerrilla warfare between the Russian autocracy and its oppressed subjects. Though neither the Czar nor the young visitor from Geneva realized it, the shell fired at the imperial platform during the Blessing of the Waters was the opening gun in the desultory, confused but bloody series of uprisings commonly called the Russian Revolution of 1905, a dress rehearsal for the one that brought down the dynasty twelve years later. It was to break out in unmistakable and large-scale violence only three days after the abortive plot against the Czar. To understand its causes and to assess its considerable role in preparing the general European upheaval, let us take a closer look at the curious, tragic personality of the last Romanov emperor, at his family background and at the state of Russia in the eleventh year of his reign.

"In the house of the Romanovs, as in that of the Atrides," notes the Russian writer Merejkovsky, commenting on the 1905 revolution, "a mysterious curse descends from generation to generation. Murder and adultery, blood and mud, 'the fifth act of a tragedy played in a brothel.' Peter I kills his son; Alexander I kills his father; Catherine II kills her husband. And besides these great and famous victims, there are the mean, unknown and unhappy abortions of the autocracy, such as Ivan Antonovitch, suffocated like mice in dark corners, in the cells of the Schlusselburg. The block, the rope, and poison—these are the true emblems of the Russian autocracy."

Nicholas II never murdered anyone—except some thousands of his sub-jects in the line of duty—and his private life, at least to the non-Freudian eye, was free from any unwholesome Aegean taint. He was a dutiful son, a devoted, not to say doting husband, a model father, and a conscientious monarch. Save for a brief early fling with the famous ballerina Ksesinskaya —the height of conventionality for a royal prince in those times—Nicholas was a paragon of Victorian respectability. He had a dull, airless mind, shielded by antimacassars of inherited prejudice from all contact with social or political reality. An autocrat by fanatic conviction, in all his personal attributes he was bourgeois to the marrow. Yet Merejkovsky's in-vocation of the antique curse is appropriate—and prophetic—in commenc-ing the story of Nicholas' reign, for the last Russian emperor, despite his homely, decent, rather stuffy ways, his mild temperament, and his gentle manner, was a true Romanov, heir to some of the most implacably tragic despots that history has known, and in the end, with a kind of macabre dignity that ran in the family, he died a Romanov death in a blood-spattered cellar.

The founder of the dynasty, Michael Romanov, the scion of a noble family that had distinguished itself in the wars against the Poles, acceded painlessly to the vacant, disputed throne at the age of fifteen in 1613, thanks to a general longing for order, and to a surge of patriotic feeling in reaction to foreign invasion after the twenty-nine-year 'Time of Troubles' that followed the death of Ivan the Terrible. Almost immediately, however, Michael had to use ruthless force to crush new peasant or Cossack re-bellions that threatened to plunge the country back into anarchy. So did his colorless successors, Alexis, Fedor II, and Ivan. In the process they reanimated the decaying institution of serfdom, formalized it, made it he-reditary, and gave the gentry increased authority over their peasants. Thus, at the moment when Western Europe was finally emerging, in a social sense, from the Middle Ages, Russia set the clock back to the hours of darkness. It was a regressive pattern that one encounters again and again in the story of the Romanovs—and in that of modern Russia.

Michael Romanov's grandson, Peter the Great (1682–1725), estab-lished or reinforced some other typical Russian patterns. A giant of a man, both literally and figuratively, Peter completed the structure of the cen-tralized, bureaucratic autocracy whose foundations Ivan the Terrible had laid more than a century earlier. He turned Russia into a vast military barracks and transformed the aristocracy into his officer caste. He dragged Russia by the hair out of the Eastern night into the concert of modern Europe. The divorce between technical and political progress that has plagued Russia ever since dates from Peter the Great. With his own hand he shaved off the beards of his chief lieutenants; beards were un-European and un-modern. So was Moscow, the cradle of the Russian monarchy and state; Peter determined to build himself a new capital on the recently conquered Baltic shore, facing west toward the Europe whose technology and culture he admired so intemperately. The marsh at the mouth of the Neva seemed a strategically suitable place, and there, using Italian architects and forced native labor, he built St. Petersburg. Thousands of laborers died of pestilence or accident in the building, not for the last time in Russian history. The city became Peter's monument, figuratively dominated by Etienne Falconet's huge equestrian statue of its founder in the great square of St. Isaak, the "Bronze Horseman," celebrated in one of Pushkin's most famous poems. To the Russian masses, St. Petersburg was from the first an alien capital; the psychological fissure that Peter's ruthless modernizing had opened between the people and the regime grew wider rather than narrower during the reigns of his successors.

More than any other individual in his country's history, Peter created expansionist Russian nationalism and shaped its fundamental strategic doctrines. Russia had already been expanding eastward from the Moscovite nucleus for several centuries. Peter actively encouraged this historic trend, sending explorers as far as the coast of the Bering Sea. To the south and southeast he likewise waged vigorously the already traditional struggle with the Turkish Empire for warm-water ports, and for the liberation of the Christian Slav populations of southeast Europe, who still lay under the heavy Turkish yoke. Implicit in Peter's southern strategy was the dream, that was to haunt the Russian imagination for the next two centuries, of controlling the Dardanelles and hoisting the two-headed Romanov eagle above freed Constantinople, the holy cradle of Russia's civilization. Peter was no dreamer, however, and he concentrated his volcanic energies chiefly in a westerly drive whose objectives were strictly practical. In a long, stubborn war, Peter drove the Swedes out of the Continent, occupied the Eastern Baltic coast and part of Finland, installed an allied, almost puppet, ruler on the throne of Poland, and thus in a few years turned Russia into a major European power.

Throughout his reign Peter had to cope with the usual Cossack and peasant uprisings, which he suppressed without mercy, and with various military or aristocratic conspiracies which he scotched as ruthlessly. His son and presumptive heir, Alexis, was involved in one of these plots. Peter lured the young Czarevitch back to Russia after he had fled abroad, gave him a public pardon, then as the full extent of his treachery became known, had him sentenced to death and executed. Peter himself had gained the throne with the help of a military coup that deposed his half-sister, Sophia, and he inadvertently condemned Russia to more than a century of palace revolutions and contested successions by laying down the principle that the Emperor had the right to choose his successor, as in ancient Rome.

Three of Peter's descendants lost their lives in the incessant *putschs* or conspiracies generated by his fatal dynastic code. One, Peter III, was assassinated by a clique of nobles who installed on the throne his German-born wife, Catherine, known to history as Catherine II or Catherine the Great (1762–1796). Catherine's reign, in many respects a model of eighteenth-century enlightenment—also of eighteenth-century libertinage—was troubled by unusually numerous and grave plots and revolts. She bequeathed new subjects of discontent to her successors by energetically pursuing the expansionist policy of Peter the Great; the first partition of Poland between Russia and the rising Hohenzollern power in Prussia under Frederick the Great was one of its tainted fruits.

Catherine's successor, Paul I (1796–1801), was her son; there was some understandable uncertainty as to who his father was, but he looked upon himself as the rightful heir to the throne and felt that Catherine had usurped it—which she undoubtedly had. Paul hated his mother as a usurper, despised her as an adulteress, probably suspected her of being a murderess, and disapproved of her as an enlightened despot. Paul himself was merely a pathological one. It was in the convulsed attitude of a tyrant at bay that Paul confronted the two great problems of his reign: that of the French Revolution, which broke out in the last years of Catherine's life; and that of his relationship with his eldest son Alexander.

A palace revolution staged in 1801 by a group of aristocratic young liberals, personal and ideological comrades of Alexander, ended Paul's career as a national and family despot. Alexander had naturally stipulated that his father's life be spared, but he does not seem to have stipulated hard enough. There was a scuffle in the Czar's bedroom and one of the conspirators strangled him. A not-wholly innocent Oedipus succeeded a frustrated Hamlet.

With Paul's tragic death, the curse of the Romanovs spent itself, in the sense that from then on accession to the throne, with one partial exception, took place in an orderly and dignified way; son no longer raised hand against father, or father against son. (Paul himself enhanced the legitimacy of the crown by revoking the disastrous code of Peter the Great and substituting a clear law of succession based on primogeniture.) In a deeper sense, however, the curse was merely transposed. The Romanovs became a proper nineteenth-century royal family, like most of the others in Europe, but the old aberrant pattern of doom kept recurring throughout the next five reigns in the relationship between monarch and subjects. As the result of living for nearly two centuries in an atmosphere of Elizabethan or ancient Greek tragedy, the political outlook of the dynasty congealed into a kind of hereditary and officialized paranoia that eventually filtered into the administrative bloodstream of the state itself—so intimately that two revolutions have not yet completely eliminated it.

Alexander I (1801–1825), after beginning his reign in a halo of liberalism and emerging from the Napoleonic Wars as the most idealistic of European sovereigns—the Holy Alliance as originally conceived by Alexander was a "monarchs' League of Nations," in the words of Sir Bernard Pares —turned into the same kind of blind reactionary autocrat that his father had been (no doubt the chastisement of the Furies) and died just in time to escape some revolutionary conspirator's scarf or dagger.

Nicholas I (1825–1855), his younger brother and successor, was both a pettier and a harsher tyrant—he once tried to tell Pushkin how to write verse—and his reign was one of the bleakest periods in modern Russian history. At its outset he had to crush a revolt of the Guard regiments, whose aristocratic officers, in accordance with the tradition dating back to the beginnings of the dynasty, had been plotting against Alexander and wanted to put another brother, Constantine, on the throne despite the latter's formal renunciation of his rights. This so-called Decembrist uprising —it took place on December 26, 1825—was the last palace revolt in Russian history, but it marks a new and no less fatal pattern of disorder, for to a considerable degree it launched the tradition of revolutionary conspiracy in Russia. A number of leaders and sympathizers were liberals or even republicans inspired by the ideals of the French Revolution, and one of its avowed objectives was a Constitution for Russia.

The second Alexander (1855–1881), was a new kind of Romanov. He was devoted to his father and loyal to Nicholas' autocratic principles. Unlike his predecessor, however, he was intelligent. Sir Bernard Pares, the British historian of modern Russia, describes him as an "honest Conservative, forced by the overwhelming logic of facts to put in the forefront of his program the liberation of the serfs." Serfdom was the shame of Russia, the great national canker and the number one social problem of the age. No reform was more urgently needed, or more likely to transform the whole social climate in Russia if drastically carried through. Alexander's reform was drastic, and he carried it through. It not only emancipated the serfs who up to then had been bound to the soil and considered virtually as the chattel of their masters, but it gave them ownership of half the land they had been cultivating in return for payments to the state staggered over a period of forty-nine years.

The emancipation legislation had some injudicious features. Instead of giving each peasant a plot of his own, it turned the land over to the collective ownership of the village communities, thus as Pares remarks, basing the Russian autocracy not on individualist but on collectivist principles. This was to have grave consequences in the future, but in the context of the day it was hardly reactionary, and the reform itself was anything but a timid one.

During the twenty-six years of Alexander's reign, Russia seemed to be rapidly closing the gap that still separated her from the advanced societies of the West. The wave of repression that had swept over Western Europe after the revolutionary disturbances of 1848 had not yet entirely receded, but in Russia, liberalism, after nearly half a century of Arctic night was once more in bud.

Then the curse of the Romanovs struck again. Yielding to its congenital suspicion and the ingrained instinct to repress, the autocracy began to crack down with increasing severity on the Narodniki (literally men of the people) a small body of idealistic intellectuals usually university students, both male and female, who fervently believed in "going to the people," that is, living among the peasants, sharing their harsh conditions of life, helping to raise them up and make them conscious of their human rights. It was a very Russian movement, genuinely noble, a little impractical, potentially important. Many of the Narodniki were merely earnest social reformers; some were harmless Utopian-socialist dreamers; a few were determined revolutionary agitators. Even among the revolutionaries a number disapproved of systematic violence, but there was a hard core of fanatics whom the knouts and torture chambers of the Czar's police, the Arctic prison camp and the Siberian salt mine had helped turn into political psychopaths. The great novelist Ivan Turgenev had coined the name "Nihilists," for them; their models or intellectual masters were the venerable anarchist writer and apostle of terrorism, Mikhail Bakunin, Serge Nechayev, the monstrous prototype of the conscienceless revolutionary in Dostoyevsky's *The Possessed,* and Peter Tkachev, the theoretician of revolution through professionally organized conspiracy, to whom Lenin, among others, owed a great intellectual debt. (Tkachev once recommended that every Russian over the age of twenty-five be put to death as incapable of moving with the times.)

With the help of the imperial police, whose persecution of the milder type of revolutionary agitators had alienated liberal opinion, the influence of the "Nihilists" grew in one wing of the Narodnik movement. The extremists, supported by emigré groups, formed a conspiratorial society, the Will of the People, dedicated to the cult of the bomb. It became the nucleus from which the Socialist-Revolutionary Party, one of the two great revolutionary groups in twentieth-century Russia, eventually sprang up. In the reign of Alexander II, the Will of the People had only a few hundred members, but they were armed, and trained in conspiracy and organized in cells, and that was enough to kill hope. Two attempts to assassinate the Czar failed. The third one, on March 13, 1881, succeeded just after Alexander had signed a decree proclaiming an embryonic Constitution, aimed at reassuring the liberals. A terrorist threw a bomb at the Czar's carriage as he was driving through the streets of St. Petersburg following a military review. He got out to look after some Cossacks of his suite who had been wounded. A second assassin, a young Pole, shouting "It's too early to thank God," threw another bomb. Alexander's legs were shattered, his face mutilated and his belly torn open. "Home to the Palace, to die there," he mumbled. His family, including his grandson Nicholas, the future Nicholas II, then twelve years old and dressed in a sailor suit, assembled in time to see his last moments. The Czar's murder plunged Russia back into the dark night of reaction. It grew steadily darker under the reign of his son Alexander III (1881–1894), whose censor forbade the newspapers even to print the word "Constitution." Almost as tall and as muscular as his remote ancestor, Peter the Great (he wore an impressive beard though), Alexander III resembled the hangmen Czars Nicholas I and Paul I in his political outlook. He abrogated or emasculated many of his father's reforms and took savage, sweeping revenge on the revolutionaries. In 1887 a twenty-year old student-terrorist took part in a plot organized by the Will of the People to kill the Czar on the anniversary of Alexander II's assassination, was arrested and condemned to death. His mother applied for permission to visit him in prison.

"I think it would be advisable to allow her to visit her son," the Czar scribbled on the margin of the letter that the despairing woman had sent him, "so that she might see for herself what kind of person this precious son of hers is."

Explaining his act—or rather his intended act—at his trial, the student said: "Under a system which permits no freedom of expression and crushes every attempt to work for their [the people's] welfare and enlightenment by legal means, the only instrument that remains is terror."

The young man was hanged, with four of his fellow conspirators in the courtyard of the Schlusselberg fortress on the morning of May 20, 1887. His name was Alexander Ulyanov and he had a seventeen-year old brother, Vladimir, who later became a conspirator himself and took the pen name Nikolai Lenin. (Another subsequently famous personage involved in the case of Alexander Ulyanov was Jozef Pilsudski, the future liberator of Poland, who was arrested as an accomplice in the plot against the Czar but got off with a prison term.) It was a brutal psychological shock for the adolescent Lenin to learn that his loved and admired older brother had died like a criminal—and for a crime he had merely planned to commit—with a black hood over his head and his neck broken by a hangman's noose. It had also been a brutal psychological shock for the young Alexander III when the father whom he loved and admired had been carried back into his palace, a blood-soaked, smoke-blackened pulp. The two men reacted in the same way to the same tragic experience. Neither would ever after show mercy to the Enemy (and the Enemy was a dangerously indefinite abstraction called Revolution, or the Autocracy, or even the bourgeosie). Each cherished the martyr's memory but turned his back on the martyr's example. Alexander rejected his father's policy of reform. Lenin repudiated the basically Narodnik revolutionary idealism of his brother, along with the strategy of terrorism, in favor of a more "scientific"—and pitiless—doctrine of revolution ideologically grounded in the economic theories of Karl Marx.

This Russian version of Marxian Social Democracy—which in France engendered the democratic and humanitarian socialism of Jean Jaurès—was oriented toward the industrial workers of the big cities rather than toward the miserable and restive peasantry that was the chief concern of the traditional Russian revolutionaries, the Narodniki, and their successors, the Socialist-Revolutionaries. Russia, right up to the revolution, was primarily an agricultural nation, so the Marxist Social Democrats played only a secondary role in the revolutionary movement there before the war. Industrialization however was progressing by giant leaps in late nineteenth- and early twentieth-century Russia and Lenin's hour would eventually strike.

The reign of Alexander III offers a fascinating case study in the early pathology of diseased social or political orders. Attacked by the revolutionary virus, the regime secretes antibodies of excessive repression that only render it more virulent. The result is Leninism—that is, the revolutionary impulse and doctrine which will be known as Leninism after further human or historic ordeals have enhanced its deadliness. At the same time the ailing system generates counterrevolutionary ideologies that attack its own nerve centers, distorting its vision, disrupting its capacity for co-ordinated action, leaving it incompetent to ward off its enemies. Perhaps the chief agent of this autointoxication in the case of Russia was a pedantic, bigoted, ascetic-looking intellectual named Konstantin Pobedonostsev, whose dry fanaticism somewhat resembled Lenin's. He was the gray eminence—a very black one —of Alexander's whole reign, and drafted most of the manifestoes or decrees promulgated in the name of the Czar. Pobedonostsev's influence was most baneful, however, in his role as tutor to the Czarevitch, Nicholas, and later as his adviser when Nicholas mounted the throne on Alexander's death (from natural causes) in 1894.

Nicholas II was two years older than Lenin. He was born on May 18, 1868. The heir to nearly three centuries of imperial grandeur, tragedy, and crime had few of the Romanov chromosomes in his cells—in view of the indiscretions of Catherine II it is not certain that he had any at all—and very little real Russian blood flowed in his veins. The family had been strongly Germanized since before Catherine's day, and Nicholas' own mother, Maria Fedorovna, was a Danish princess, the sister of England's Queen Alexandra. He had the cosmopolitan bringing-up, the cultural equivalent of grand-hotel cookery, that was standard for European royalty at the time, with the

English element probably predominant, thanks to Victoria. Yet no Czar since Peter the Great had such an essentially Russian soul. Beneath the manners and morals of an English country gentleman, Nicholas possessed in many respects the character that centuries of living under serfdom and tyranny had bred in the Russian muzhik. He was warmhearted, stubborn, brave, sentimental, vague, patient (his birthday was the feast of Job), dreamy, superstitiously pious (or piously superstitious), fatalistic ("Whatever I try, nothing succeeds"), moody, ineffectual, and mistrustful. Nicholas consistently behaved with the meek shiftiness of one of his father's peasants. This was hardly surprising; peasant and Czarevitch had been born under the same tyranny and the latter, during his formative years, lived closer to the tyrant.

Though a stern disciplinarian, Alexander III does not appear to have treated his son harshly, by Victorian standards, but he was so big and so virile, so self-confident and strong-willed and imperious that the frail, small, gentle Nicholas (who was advised to make his public appearances on horseback, whenever possible, in order to offset his unimposing physique) could not help but feel crushed by him. The shock of seeing his grandfather die from a terrorist's bomb no doubt also had a traumatic impact on his emotions. Nicholas was affable in conversation and disliked heated discussion or frank agreement. He almost invariably told others what he thought they wanted to hear and would not tolerate around his person counselors, however obsequious, who told him anything except what he himself wanted to hear.

". . . the minister who had been received with a flattering show of kindness," says Richard Charques in his *Twilight of Imperial Russia,* "learned from an imperial note sent by courrier next morning that he had been dismissed—or worse still, discovered from the morning's newspaper that he had tendered his resignation."

Unfortunately for the monarchy in Russia, and for the peace of Europe, Nicholas was not only an inept autocrat but a systematically deluded one. A number of influences contributed to bemusing the Emperor's mind. The most important one was that of his wife, Alexandra Fedorovna, born Princess Alix of Hesse-Darmstadt, one of the minor German princely houses, and brought up, at least in part, in Kensington Palace by her grandmother Queen Victoria. Alexandra had light chestnut hair, dark blue eyes, firm, classic features that would have made her face beautiful in a regal way if her expression had not been so cold. She held herself with Junoesque grace and walked with the stiff, awkward gait of a cow. Though in a superficial sense Alexandra was the Marie Antoinette of the Russian revolution, she had little in common with the tragic mistress of the Versailles dolls' house. She had earnestness, character, deep religious and social ideals, a stern sense of duty—and all were fatal. Her relationship with Nicholas was as paradoxical as her personality. As we shall see later, there was some un-healthy, almost monstrous element in it; yet there was also a deep, intensely romantic attachment that gave both of them a dignity and a dedication of the heart they never lost. It is a queer unsettling sort of story, half Hans Christian Andersen and half Tennessee Williams.

They met in St. Petersburg, at the wedding of Alexandra's sister, Eliza-beth, to the Grand Duke Sergius, a brother of Alexander III. Alexandra —or Alix—was twelve at the time, Nicholas sixteen, and neither ever for-got the occasion, or the other's image. Nicholas apparently decided then and there that he would marry his shy, awkward English cousin—he thought of her as English—when he grew up. There were serious obstacles to the match when the time came to talk about it. Both Alexander III, the family and national autocrat and Nicholas' mother, whom he adored, strongly disapproved of his choice. Alix, though she had loved Nicholas from the first, disapproved no less strongly of her own heart's choice; she considered Nicholas as a dissipated young waster with no serious goal in life. Both her Victorian bringing up and the kind of idealistic and romantic fiction that nourished her adolescent emotions (even as a grown woman she remained incorrigibly addicted to the vapidly respectable novels of Marie Corelli) condemned such a frivolous union, undedicated by any noble or worthy cause. Moreover, to marry Nicholas she would have to give up the Lu-theran church in which she had grown up, and become converted to the Greek Orthodox faith; priggishness and real conviction combined to make the sacrifice—or the betrayal—seem unthinkable to her. "Religion isn't a pair of gloves to pull on and off," she once smugly told her sister Elizabeth, who had joined the Greek Church after marrying the Romanov Grand Duke.

It was one of love's miracles that the normally weak-willed and fatalistic Nicholas somehow developed the doggedness and the drive that enabled him to triumph over all these difficulties. In 1892—Nicholas was then twenty-four and Alix twenty—he outfaced his parents, left for Germany—disregarding a goodbye-forever letter he had received from Alix—and there persuaded her to reverse her decision. E. M. Almedingen, one of the few writers ever to attempt a sympathetic biography of one of history's least sympathetic victims (*The Empress Alexandra*) offers an explanation for the surrender which is psychologically plausible and which is expressed in the kind of language that Alexandra herself might well have used. "She accepted him in the end," says Miss Almedingen, "because it came to her that she and she alone could make him envisage duty from the only pos-sible point of view; that her passion for him was strong enough to evoke qualities that she considered dormant; that in marrying him she would be able to guide and counsel; and that in their joint happiness they would fulfill their high duty to the utmost. And as she reflected on these points,

she came to see that she would not violate her conscience in any particular
. . . Therein lay God's will for her."

If Nicholas had any qualms about the theological and other considerations that underlay Alix's "Yes," or any apprehensions about the rather
strenuous plans for making him over that she certainly must have hinted to
him, there is no indication of it in his diary. "A heavenly, unforgettable
day," Nicholas wrote with uncomplicated if unoriginal rapture of his be-
trothal to Alix. "In a dream all day long."

In a sense Nicholas never woke up from that dream, nor did Alexandra.
They were married in 1894, shortly after Nicholas mounted the throne.
"With every day that passes I bless the Lord and thank Him from the
depths of my soul for the happiness He bestowed on me," Nicholas wrote
in his diary soon after the wedding. "Never could I believe there could be
such happiness in the world, such a feeling of unity between two mortal
beings," Alexandra added two days later. While they were still engaged she
had started reading her fiancé's diary—so that there could be no "reservations" between them—and occasionally making entries in it in her own
handwriting. The love duet recorded by the Czar's diary—and in the Czarina's letters to him—continued throughout the twenty-three years of their
married life, punctuated from time to time by a nursery chorus as they
gradually acquired four daughters and a son, the semi-invalid Alexis, whose
inherited hemophilia cast the only shadow—albeit a deep one—upon the
imperial couple's domestic bliss.

As a young bachelor Nicholas had been fun-loving and sociable, much
given to dancing, card games, and gambling or roistering with his male
friends. Marriage soon changed him. The passionate communion of souls
with Alexandra over the years turned into an increasingly marmot-like
togetherness of husband and wife and children in a kind of ex-urban snug-
gery: the royal palace at Gatchina, outside the capital, or the larger one at
Tsarskoe Selo, that had been Catherine the Great's Versailles. Alexandra
somehow contrived to make their private quarters in the palace look like
a middle-class English honeymooner's cottage, with bamboo furniture and
beaded gewgaws. Nicholas visited his capital as little as possible; all his
off-duty hours revolved around the family dining room—to which official
guests were rarely invited and where official business was taboo—the nursery
and his wife's boudoir. His evenings were usually spent reading—particularly from English novels—to Alexandra, who hated St. Petersburg society.
She considered it vapid, snobbish, and immoral, which it probably was.
Formal entertaining was reduced to a strict minimum during the whole
reign of Nicholas II, and Alexandra cared just as little for small informal
dinners or luncheon parties. Though she constantly preached the stern code
of autocratic duty to her easygoing husband, she appeared to resent everything, including the accepted social duties of the state, that distracted him

even momentarily from his family. Thus, Alexandra, though she may have deepened and improved Nicholas' moral character, encouraged the tendency to isolate himself from his subjects that was one of his deadly failings as a ruler.

Paradoxically, however, Alexandra's greatest contribution to the fall of the Romanov dynasty stemmed less from her efforts to remodel her husband's character, than from her equally strenuous efforts to refashion her own. In trying to adapt herself to her husband's country and culture she went native with a naive violence that would have seemed ludicrous if it had not proved so fatal. In exchanging her sober Lutheran piety for the Eastern splendors of the Orthodox Church she simultaneously embraced all the mystic excesses, the superstition and the religious quackery to which the Slav soul was prey. In submerging the English liberalism which had once scandalized her husband's family, she not only accepted the doctrine of autocracy but espoused it with a fanatical ardor that seemed a bit medieval, even by Russian standards. In Trotsky's words "she adopted with a kind of cold fury all the traditions and nuances of Russian medievalism, the most meager and crude of all medievalisms, in that very period when the people were making mighty efforts to free themselves from it." In so doing Alexandra re-enforced in her husband's mind the powerful and delusive influence already exercised on it by his father's old counselor, Pobedonostsev.

Nicholas' tutor—he had also been the tutor of Alexander III—was not merely a fanatical reactionary, but a philosopher of reaction. Born in 1827, he spent his life reacting against the wrong revolution—the French one of 1789. His enemies were rationalism, progress, liberalism, personal liberties, constitutions, parliamentary institutions and, above all, popular sovereignty, "the erroneous principle that . . . all power comes from the people." He had failed to notice, or at least to understand, the increasing emphasis on scientific socialism rather than human rights in the Russian revolutionary movement, the steady rise of the Nihilists and the Leninists-to-be, with their cold pessimism, so like his own, and their evident bent toward dictatorship, only a little less openly expressed than his.

It was Pobedonostsev who drafted Nicholas' very first policy statement just after his accession, a sternly worded rebuke in reply to a message of congratulation from a *zemstvo* (one of the provincial assemblies established by the reforms of Alexander II) that had ventured to include a veiled criticism of police oppression and a timid plea for greater participation of the *zemstvos* in public affairs. "Senseless dreams," retorted Pobedonostsev, over the signature of Nicholas, whose statement added that the Czar would "firmly and unflinchingly" uphold the principle of autocracy.

Pobedonostsev's doctrine of autocracy, which the young Nicholas had uncritically made his own, was grounded in religious mysticism. Its essence, as one of Pobedonostsev's disciples explained to the French ambassador, Maurice Paleologue, was that.

"The Czar is the anointed of the Lord, sent by God to be the supreme guardian of the Church and the all-powerful ruler of the empire. . . . As he receives his power from God, it is to God alone that he must account for it. . . . Constitutional liberalism is a heresy as well as a stupid chimera."

In twentieth-century Russia this neo-Byzantine dogma could not fail to push the liberals into a potentially fatal collusion with the radicals of the extreme left. As early as January 1904, a group of representative *zemstvo* liberals founded a nation-wide underground Union of Liberation that marks an ominous milestone in the history of the monarchy. Even the Western-educated supporters of the autocracy—technicians, administrators, businessmen—who might have welcomed rationalizations of absolutism based on less anachronistic principles were alienated or discouraged.

Nicholas II, with Alexandra's encouragement, pushed his old tutor's ideas to suicidal extremes by the literalness with which he conceived his rights and his duties as an autocrat. Pobedonostsev had once complained that Romanov court etiquette prevented him from ever quizzing his pupil, but he need not have worried; Nicholas' subsequent behavior showed that he had done his homework all too faithfully. As Czar, Nicholas not only based state policy on the royal whim, but would hardly trust anyone but himself to carry it out. Delegating authority, he felt, undermined the autocratic principle. He was jealous of officials who were too successful in carrying out his own orders. He tried to run his sprawling twentieth-century empire, with its top-heavy bureaucracy, its chaotically expanding industry and its complex foreign relations, the way Peter the Great had run seventeenth-century Russia. Nicholas, refusing the help of a private secretary, regularly insisted on himself sealing the envelopes into which he sent out official documents; such work-habits had a good deal to do with the chronic bureaucratic anarchy or paralysis that was an important factor in the ultimate collapse of the Romanov dynasty.

Other facets of the political *mystique* that Pobedonostsev instilled into the mind and policies of Nicholas II were hardly less deadly in their ultimate effects. One was the Great-Russian racism implicit in his version of Slavophil nationalism. He and Nicholas both looked on the dominant native stock of European Russia as the master race of the empire, and regarded its other races, even when they were of pure Slavic origin, as inferior, especially when they did not belong to the Orthodox faith. The racism was not openly admitted, but the bigotry was quite official; there were attempts at forced conversion of Catholics in Poland, of Protestants in Finland, of the schismatic sect known as "Old Believers" in Siberia, of Moslems in Central Asia. Jews were at the bottom of the ladder and anti-Semitism was a formal State policy, though Jews could escape official persecution by joining the Orthodox Church. Nicholas II tightened Catherine the Great's edict aimed at confining the Jews to a kind of ghetto zone along the western borders and tolerated the pogroms which fanatics or hooligans periodically instigated against them. These attitudes made it impossible for the dynasty to employ the strategy of playing one minority group against another which greatly helped the Habsburgs and the Osmanlis to hold their crazy-quilt empires together.

At the same time the Czar and his mentor dreamed, somewhat incongruously, of a "Third Rome" (Byzantium had been the second one): a vast zone of Russian hegemony stretching from the Balkans to the China Sea. As a starter, Nicholas talked quite seriously of annexing Manchuria, Mongolia, and Tibet, vassalizing China and driving the British out of India. These expansionist fantasies were encouraged by a succession of picturesque Far Eastern adventurers and by the Czar's cousin, Wilhelm II, who naturally preferred that Russian ambitions should be directed eastward rather than westward.

"The great task of the future for Russia is to cultivate the Asian continent and defend Europe from the inroads of the Great Yellow race," Wilhelm wrote to Nicholas in 1895.

Another time the Kaiser sent the Czar a painting, based on a sketch of his own, showing Buddha presiding over an holocaust in the Far East, while Germany and Russia stood guard as sentinels of the True Faith. "I designed this drawing in Christmas week, under the glitter of the Christmas trees," Wilhelm said in an explanatory note.

The Far Eastern chimera eventually led to the Russo-Japanese War of 1904, precipitated by Russian encroachments in Korea. The idea that "a short, victorious war" as one of the Czar's ministers felicitiously put it, would help avert revolution at home, also contributed to Russia's bellicose attitude. The unbroken, humiliating succession of Russian defeats on land and sea, however, and particularly the spectacle of blunder, confusion, and corruption that produced them, was a nearly mortal blow to the dynasty's prestige. Strikes, riots, and miscellaneous disorders began erupting all over the empire.

"Bloody Sunday," January 9 according to the Orthodox calendar, is considered by most historians as marking the beginning of the 1905 revolution. Weber-Bauler, the impressionable young tourist, who, three days earlier, had witnessed the spectacular attempt to assassinate the Czar during the Blessing of the Waters, also had a close-up glimpse of this vaster, more tragic drama.

"Turning into the Nevsky Prospekt (the monumental boulevard leading to the Winter Palace) I saw advancing along the highway a slow-moving human flood," he relates. "It was a mute and terrible procession, black and gray and brown. The men wore peaked caps; the women's heads were covered with dark kerchiefs. These "pale, haggard faces" were iron-founders, workers from a rubber factory, men out of the Kronstadt work-shops . . . thousands and more thousands of "the true urban proletarians who had suffered for generations from undernourishment, alcoholic excess and syphilis . . .

"Before them went a priest, an Orthodox pope, in black surplice. He was walking between an old white-bearded man and a very beautiful woman of a definitely Jewish type." The pope, a short man in a brown beard "was young and fragile," the report goes on, holding "a great icon of the Savior.

"In full view of the Winter Palace, that palace whose front was the color of clotted blood, the priest, his followers and the foremost ranks of the crowd knelt in the snow. The procession slowly came to a standstill . . .

"Suddenly, moving at the double, a company of infantry swung into the square. They lined up in front of the kneeling crowd. There was an order 'Present; fire.' and the crackle of rifle shots followed by a terrible confusion. The foremost ranks fell; others rose to their feet and fled. The beautiful Jewess was one of the first victims." Bauler escaped through one of the small side-streets, "dragged along by the crowd." His final sight was of "Cossacks charging, their whips falling on the crowd and their horses rearing."

Other eyewitnesses remember various details differently. All agree on the essentials: that a gigantic crowd of workers (some 200,000 moving in five separate columns) led by an Orthodox priest converged on the Winter Palace, along the five great avenues radiating from it; that the crowd was disciplined and pacific in intent—many demonstrators carried pictures of the Emperor and sang the Imperial anthem, *God Save the Czar*—and that the troops, after a perfunctory order to disperse, fired into the mob at close range, leaving at least 500 dead and several thousand wounded lying in the snow.

The background of the massacre, which raised a blood-strained barrier between the Russian masses and the dynasty, was a typical Romanov blend of murder, muddle, and Machiavelli. The priest who led the march, George Gapon, was a former prison chaplain who had made a name for himself as labor organizer. He was the head of a shadowy organization called the Assembly of Russian Factory and Mill Workers, which had been subsidized by the Okhrana, the regime's secret political police in the hope that it would split the working-class movement. Gapon had collaborated in an earlier, more ambitious experiment in "police socialism" that had got out of hand. The same fate quickly overtook the Okhrana's new venture. After organizing a successful strike at the great Putilov steel works, Gapon allowed himself to be talked, by his followers, into heading a mass demonstration to petition the Czar. The petition included a number of flagrantly political—and by Romanov standards, subversive—demands, such as civil liberties and a constituent assembly; its very size was a threat to public order in the wartime capital.

Some historians believe that Gapon, a complex, intensely Russian personality who combined a streak of hysterical idealism with the Judas-bent of a born police spy, was swept away, or pushed further than he had intended to go, by secret revolutionary agents who had penetrated his stooge union. Several years later, however, a high official of the Okhrana, then stationed in Paris, boasted to the future French ambassador, Paleologue, that he had helped Gapon draft his fatal petition. If he was telling the truth, it was neither the first nor the last time that the Okhrana deliberately provoked revolutionary disorder so as to have an excuse for teaching the people a lesson by crushing it. Whether or not "Bloody Sunday" was the work of Okhrana *agents provocateurs,* it could have been averted if the decisions of an inter-ministerial conference the day before had not been sabotaged either by design or by bureaucratic confusion. The Czar, with his family, had prudently moved out of the Winter Palace for Tsarskoe Selo, sixteen miles from the capital, and the workers' march to lay the petition before him was pointless. The ministerial conference issued instructions that this fact be widely publicized, but they were not carried out and the demonstrators, unaware of the Czar's absence, started on schedule. Somebody also failed to pass on the ministerial order to break up the demonstration while the marchers were forming into groups and columns in the suburbs. The Romanov curse was still working.

(As for Gapon, he survived the massacre, escaped from the country and joined an emigré section of the Socialist Revolutionary Party, helped run guns to the 1905 insurrectionists, renewed contact with his old friends at the Okhrana, was condemned to death by his revolutionary comrades, and was finally strangled in an isolated chalet in Finland.)

"Bloody Sunday" helped to shape the revolutionary conscience of a generation, not only in Russia, but throughout the civilized world. In the United States the usually gentle Mark Twain was impelled to write his savage *Czar's Soliloquy* calling for revolution and assassination of the Czar, and attacking those moralists who condemned the use of revolutionary violence against tyrants. Similar incitements and arguments from other intellectuals in the following months or years found only too ready an audience.

A short time after the massacre at the Winter Palace, and at least partly in retaliation for it, there occurred another tragic incident which likewise had far-reaching repercussions on the relationship between the dynasty and its subjects. A Socialist-Revolutionary student threw a powerful bomb at the Czar's uncle, Grand Duke Sergius, the military governor of the Moscow area, as his carriage was entering the gates of the Kremlin, and blew him into bloody gobbets. Sergius, noted for his harshness to Jews and intellectuals had not been a popular figure; gruesome souvenirs, picked up at a considerable distance from the explosion were being sold the next day in the Moscow Thieves' Market for one rouble the fragment, according to public rumor.

Nicholas got the news at the Peterhof Palace, outside St. Petersburg, as he was about to sit down to a family dinner with a royal visitor, young Prince Frederick-Leopold of Prussia. The Czarina did not appear; her elder sister, Elizabeth, it will be recalled, was the widow of the murdered Grand Duke. The Czar, however, insisted on going ahead with the meal; as Frederick-Leopold reported in a letter to the German Chancellor von Bulow, he even seemed to be in a gay humor; so did Nicholas' other guest, his brother-in-law, Grand Duke Alexander. The assassination was not mentioned.

"After dinner," Bulow relates in his memoirs, the "brothers amused themselves by trying to push each other off the long, narrow sofa on which they were sitting."

Prince Frederick-Leopold's amazement suggests that he was not a student of Freud or even of Dostoyevsky. Nicholas may not have been specially attached to his dour uncle, but his horse-play with his brother-in-law a few hours after Sergius' ghastly end was anything but a symptom of indifference. The assassin's bomb had struck too close to the throne for that, and it also reactivated some painful and terrifying memories of childhood. (The reaction of the Grand Duchess Elizabeth, like the Czarina an ardent convert to the Orthodox faith, was equally Dostoyevskian; she spent much of the night in the cell of her husband's murderer, a slender youth named Kalaiev, vainly beseeching him to ask God—and the Czar—for forgiveness.)

Nicholas had no knowledge of the equivocal role played by his own Okhrana in the assassination of Grand Duke Sergius (it had an informer in the terrorist group which plotted the outrage) as well as in the "Bloody Sunday" affair; the facts would not come to light for several years. The Moscow crime simply strengthened his inherited tendency to rely on the knout, the scaffold and the firing squad to uphold the autocracy. "Terror has to be met with terror," he wrote his mother in a letter that was to survive for the Bolsheviks to publish after the war.

Both sides acted in keeping with the same grim philosophy during the revolutionary struggles of 1905–1906, though not yet with the systematic fanaticism they were to display in 1917–1920. Some 1500 government officials lost their lives, many of them by assassination, during the strikes, riots, mutinies—including the famous seizure of the battlecruiser *Potemkin* by its crew—and insurrections that swept the country, rising to a climax in

November 1905. There are no reliable statistics on the number of revolutionists killed in action or shot out of hand during the same period.

The most characteristic disorders were the peasant uprisings that broke out in unco-ordinated violence all over Russia. The wrath of the *muzhiks* —80 per cent of whom were still illiterate—had been smoldering for years; the land reform of Alexander II was not working satisfactorily—the reimbursements were too high and the fields allotted often too poor—repeated crop failures had led to famine and atrocious suffering, farm prices were steadily falling while taxes stayed high. The peasants were not interested in constitutions and civil liberties; they wanted land, tax relief, revenge on the local officials who had chronically humiliated or mistreated them. Egged on by Socialist-Revolutionary agitators, who shrewdly played down political themes in their propaganda, they took up their shotguns or pitchforks and went berserk. Whole provinces were plunged into anarchy; across the Russian countryside there was an orgy of murder, pillage, banditry, and arson—above all arson. "The Red Cock: The Red Cock!" was the favorite battle cry of the marauding bands, and from the heart of Siberia to the western borders, the sinister fowl spread his wings of flaming allegory over rural police stations or tax bureaus, over the barns and stables of wealthy landowners, over the white-columned country mansions of the nobility. In many areas the gentry were systematically looted; sometimes they were threatened or roughed-up; only rarely were they massacred. These twentieth-century *jacqueries* were a form of class warfare, but class hatreds in Russia had not yet reached the ultimate pitch of inhumanity.

In the cities the revolutionary movement was generally less furious, but no less grave. The different socialist groups temporarily put aside their doctrinal quarrels, and in St. Petersburg even the moderate constitutionalists joined them for a while in an anti-regime co-ordinating committee—Soviet —whose designation was to become a revolutionary symbol. Elsewhere the Socialist-Revolutionaries, with their deep peasant roots, were the most important enemies of the autocracy, but in the capital the Marxist Social-Democrats, including Lenin's *Bolsheviks,* played a star role, for the first time in Russian history. Though he theoretically disapproved of it, Lenin himself slipped back from exile to help steer the St. Petersburg Soviet into the course of all-out revolution. Lenin's direct contribution to the dramatic events of 1905 was less substantial, however, than that of a younger Marxist intellectual, Leon Trotsky, whose name for the first time now became known to millions of Russian workers. Trotsky, born Lev Davydovich Bronstein, the son of a well-to-do Jewish farmer, shared many of Lenin's viewpoints, but he refused to take sides in the quarrel that had developed between the Bolshevik and the Menshevik (Minority) factions within what was still theoretically a united Social-Democratic party, and he was not particularly close to Lenin at the time. Only twenty-six years old, Trotsky with his thick glasses and his long unruly mop of hair, looked almost a caricaturist's model of the revolutionary bookworm, but he soon proved that he could act as well as theorize and orate. As vice-chairman of the St. Petersburg Soviet—the chairman was an obscure Menshevik lawyer—he rapidly became the outstanding leader of the 1905 revolutionary movement in Russia. Trotsky was ably seconded by a picturesque but gifted member of the emigré underground named Alexander Helfand, alias Parvus, who between plots to set up the dictatorship of the proletariat, had found time to become a rising publisher and financier in Germany. Trotsky, assisted by Parvus, took command of the nation-wide general strike that had broken out more or less spontaneously after the signing of the humiliating peace treaty with Japan in September, and at one time came fairly close to toppling the Czar off his throne with it.

As the revolutionary threat grew increasingly serious, repression became steadily more savage. The moment came—in mid-October—when Nicholas saw that he would either have to name a military dictator and grant him unlimited authority to restore order by naked force, or make concessions to the constitutionalists. Dictatorship was the lesser evil in his eyes, but the only acceptable dictator, the Czar's Grand Duke Nicholas Nicholaievitch, refused the job and even, according to some accounts, threatened to blow out his brains on the spot if he were pressed to take it. Nothing was left except—as Nicholas explained to his mother—"to cross oneself and give what everyone was asking for." The Czar crossed himself and gave, but he was a notorious Indian giver. He issued an Imperial manifesto largely drawn up by Count S. G. Witte, a sensible Conservative, that transformed Russia into what might be considered the larval stage of a constitutional monarchy, with civil liberties, free elections, and a representative assembly possessing rudimentary legislative authority; Witte himself was appointed as the first Western-style Prime Minister in Russian history. At the same time, however, Nicholas named General D. F. Trepov, the harsh-fisted military governor of St. Petersburg, as the commandant of his palace guard, and made him his de facto Chief of Staff. While Witte maneuvered, with some success, to split the revolutionary front and win back the moderates, Nicholas, with Trepov's help, launched a series of punitive expeditions across the land; a particularly ferocious one, commanded by General Orlov, did what the Czar considered "splendid work" in the Baltic province.

Parallel to the official repression, Nicholas, under the influence of Pobedonostsev and another old friend of his father's, Prince Vladimir Meshcherski, a paleo-fascist, whose incendiary propaganda sheet, *Grashdanin* (*The Citizen*) was the only newspaper he regularly read, encouraged the formation of monarchist-nationalist vigilante groups. These gangs, later known as the "Black Hundred" bands (after one of the medieval guilds), specialized in protecting the throne by beating, robbing, and killing Jews. Nicholas strongly approved. Jews were "nine-tenths of the trouble," he explained to his mother, and this infuriated the people, leading to pogroms. "It's amazing how they [pogroms] took place simultaneously in all towns in Russia and Siberia," he wrote, with more than his usual naïveté.

Some of the ideological roots of German National Socialism were planted in Russia during the year 1905, and Russian Right-Wing Radicals like Meshcherski count among the intellectual ancestors of the Nazi theoreticians Goebbels and Rosenberg.

On occasion the Czar, under the influence of Alexandra's synthetic mysticism, listened to even weirder counselors, among them a French healer and spiritualist from Lyon, Dr. Encausse, known in St. Petersburg occultist circles as Papus. In response to an SOS from some of his highly placed Russian friends, Papus dropped his "practice" in France and rushed back to St. Petersburg, arriving early in October. An interview with the Czar and the Czarina was soon arranged and at their request the necromancer organized a spiritualistic seance at Tsarskoe Selo. The fantastic scene was recalled years later for Paleologue by one of the well-informed and indiscreet ladies of the Imperial Court that he made a point of cultivating.

"By an intense concentration of will and a prodigious expenditure of fluid dynamism, the 'Spiritual Master' succeeded in calling up the spirit of the most pious Czar Alexander III," the ambassador relates in his memoirs. "In spite of the fear which clutched at his heart, Nicholas II bluntly asked his father whether he should or should not resist the current of liberalism which was threatening to overwhelm Russia. The spirit replied: 'At any cost you must crush the revolution now beginning; but it will spring up again one day and its violence will be proportionate to the severity with which it is put down today. But what does it matter! Be brave, my son! Do not give up the struggle.' "

Nicholas did his best to carry out the somewhat chilling instructions from his father's spirit, transmitted—if the anecdote is authentic—through the mouth of Papus. The St. Petersburg Soviet, abandoned by the Moderates, was outlawed and its chiefs, including Trotsky and Parvus, arrested (Lenin escaped via Finland). Among the smaller fry taken was a young Socialist-Revolutionary combat leader named Alexander Kerensky. When ganized a spiritualistic seance at Tsarskoe Selo. The fantastic scene was drowned in blood (more than 1000 workers were killed), though the Socialist-Revolutionaries won themselves new glory by blowing up the local headquarters of the Okhrana. Ruthless clean-up actions of various types followed in all parts of the empire, among them a purge of government offices in which 7000 bureaucrats lost their jobs.

Repression continued to alternate with concession for several years. Liberal ministers were appointed, then disowned; reform policies enacted, then scuttled or suspended. The national assembly (*duma*) was elected, twice dissolved, elected again. At first glance the moderate liberals seem to emerge from the struggle of 1905 as victors, since they achieved their key objective, a constitution, but their victory was a pyrrhic one. They had compromised themselves in the eyes of the Right by their initial collusion with the revolutionary parties and irremediably discredited themselves in the eyes of the workers by their ultimate desertion from the revolutionary cause.

The rudimentary constitution granted by Nicholas II was too imperfect to furnish a new basis for the monarchy, but it was substantial enough to weaken the psychological underpinnings of the autocracy. And by shedding so much blood to postpone according it, the Czar had brought about a fatal, if subtle, transformation in the public image of the reigning autocrat; to the Russian masses it seemed henceforth that the Emperor looked down on them not with the confident gaze of stern majesty, but with the fixed glare of the tyrant at bay.

In final analysis, only the extremists of the right and the left—though the latter fell for a while into public disfavor—benefited from the abortive revolution; they were not merely hardened by the ordeal, in the sense of being fanaticized, but tempered for further combat. Their subterranean duel, at home and abroad, helped to generate the climate of conspiracy in which the seeds of general war finally sprouted.

The year of the red cock was also the year of the dragon's teeth, not only for the Russian monarchy but for Europe and world peace. Its first, but not its most deadly, fruits were to become apparent almost immediately.

CHAPTER 5

The Fossile Monarchy

THE revolutionary crisis of 1905 in Russia seriously joggled the delicate European balance of power. The German Kaiser's abortive meeting with the Czar at Bjorkoe illustrated some of its repercussions on the chessboard of classic diplomacy. Its impact on the domestic equilibrium in the other autocratic empires of Europe was perhaps even more significant.

For more than a century Russia had been the bastion of reaction and the symbol of autocracy. Other monarchs admired the Czars for their uncompromising dedication to the cause of their own absolutism, and envied them the docile, subject masses that seemed to go on accepting it without question, generation after generation. Now these supposedly immutable masses were stirring, and the intransigent autocrat had been forced into compromise. Revolution had broken out in Russia; it could happen anywhere.

In Constantinople—toward which Russian nationalist eyes would soon be turning, now that Japan's proved military strength closed the door on further expansion in East Asia—Sultan Abdul Hamid II, barricaded in his fortress-seraglio, sniffed the winds of political change, like some intelligent, fretful little rodent, quivering in its golden lair, and found them more than ever a bewildering mixture of threat and promise. Along with the delicious reek of dynastic corruption wafted from across the Black Sea came the contagiously antiseptic odor of constitutional reform. Even in stable, prosperous, authority-loving Germany, with its tame Marxists and its ever-dependable Prussian officer-caste, Wilhelm II, as the year wore on, became increasingly uneasy over the ideological implications of the turmoil in Russia. The letters of advice with which he bombarded his unfortunate cousin,

Nicky, throughout the upheaval gradually lost their Wagnerian bombast and took on a tone of sober warning or reproach.

It was in Austria-Hungary, however, that the Russian disorders had both the most explosive and the most paradoxical effect. Starting in September 1905, the Social-Democrats, supported by many spokesmen of the Slav minorities, launched a campaign of agitation for universal suffrage and general electoral reform (the existing system was scandalously weighted in favor of the landowning aristocracy). Strikes, demonstrations, and riots broke out in several parts of the Empire. They rose to a crescendo when news of the Czar's October manifesto, promising the Russian people constitutional government and free elections, reached Vienna at the end of the month. On November 2 there was a large-scale, though not very bloody, clash between demonstrating workers and police along the Ringstrasse of the capital. The very next day Francis Joseph let his subjects know that he had graciously decided to grant them full voting rights, at least in the Austrian half of his realms.

As later events proved, it was one of the most disastrous decisions the aged Emperor ever took, but he seemed to have little choice. The Socialists pointedly underscored the strength of their position later in the month by organizing a peaceful victory parade in which some 250,000 Austrian workers, wearing red armbands and marching in disciplined ranks, filed past the parliament building on the Ring. Pressure from below, however, was probably not the dominant element in forcing the Emperor's hand. The veteran of more unsuccessful rearguard actions against history than any crowned head since King Canute, Francis Joseph had repeatedly demonstrated in the course of a reign stretching from the days of Metternich to the age of Woodrow Wilson that he was not the kind of ruler to panic at a few street demonstrations; he had his own reasons this time for yielding so rapidly to the public clamor, and they were typically Habsburg ones. A venerable, and in some respects, benevolent, despot, thinly disguised as a constitutional monarch, Francis Joseph, as we shall see, was deliberately exploiting the hunger for electoral reform, touched off among the most advanced of his subjects by the apparent liberal victory in Russia, in order to blackmail a peculiarly backward group—the Hungarians—who were threatening to give him trouble for reactionary reasons. His political strategy suggested the naive Machiavellism that one might expect from some harassed overlord of the Middle Ages, emancipating his burghers to humble his barons, and the analogy is not wholly accidental; politically speaking Austria-Hungary was in many ways a fossile remnant of Medieval Europe, embedded in twentieth-century history.

The Habsburg lands had developed into an empire without ever becoming a nation. Stretching from Lake Constance on the Swiss-German border to the Transylvanian Alps, and from Lemberg (today Lvov) in Poland, to

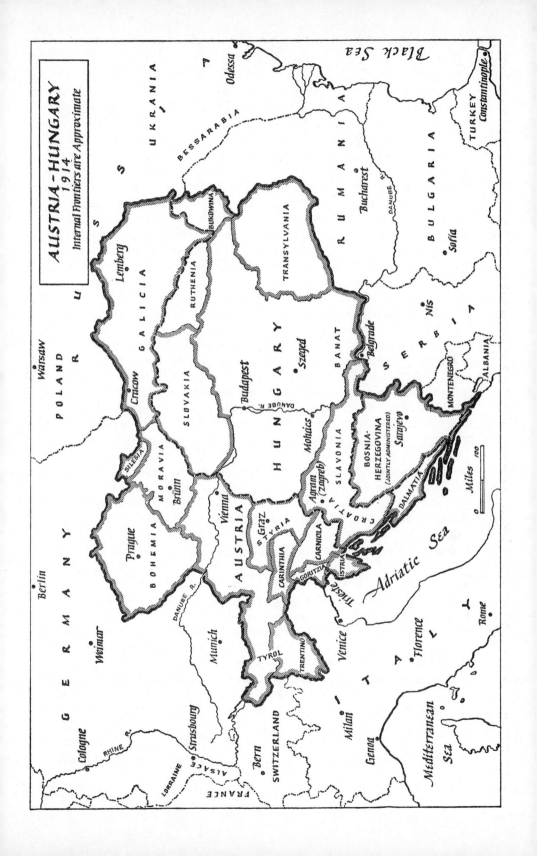

AUSTRIA-HUNGARY
1914
Internal Frontiers are Approximate

Black Sea

Odessa

UKRANIA

BESSARABIA

RUMANIA

Bucharest

DANUBE

BULGARIA

Sofia

TURKEY

Constantinople

Warsaw

Lemberg

GALICIA

Cracow

POLAND

RUTHENIA

BUKOWINA

TRANSYLVANIA

SLOVAKIA

Budapest

Szeged

BANAT

Belgrade

Niš

SERBIA

Berlin

Weimar

GERMANY

Cologne

Prague

BOHEMIA

MORAVIA

Brünn

SILESIA

DANUBE R.

Vienna

AUSTRIA

HUNGARY

DANUBE R.

Mohács

Agram
(Zagreb)

SLAVONIA

CROATIA

BOSNIA-
HERZEGOVINA
(JOINTLY ADMINISTERED)

Sarajevo

MONTENEGRO

ALBANIA

Miles
100
0

Munich

Graz

S.

STYRIA

CARINTHIA

CARNIOLA

GORITZIA

ISTRIA

Trieste

DALMATIA

Adriatic Sea

Bern

SWITZERLAND

TYROL

TRENTINO

Venice

Milan

Genoa

Florence

Rome

ITALY

Mediterranean Sea

Strasbourg

ALSACE

LORRAINE

RHINE R.

FRANCE

Raguss (Dubrovnik) and Trieste on the Adriatic, Austria-Hungary was the second largest state in Europe from the viewpoint of area, with 240,456 square miles and the third largest in population, with something over 50,-000,000 subjects, speaking a dozen different languages and dialects.

"Eight nations, seventeen countries, twenty parliamentary groups, twenty-seven parties," sighed one Austro-Hungarian statesman cited by the French historian, Pierre Renouvin.

The dominant elements in this political goulash were the Germans and the Hungarian Magyars (the descendants of early invaders from the Asian steppes) a little less than 10,000,000 of each, who considered all their other fellow subjects of the Habsburg crown as "minorities." This appellation was understandably contested by the 30,000,000 Czechs, Slovaks, Poles, Ruthenians, Rumanians, Serbs, Croats, Slovenes, and lesser racial groups who constituted the bulk of the population. If one counted the Czecho-Slovaks as a single people they were actually the majority group.

The juridical framework which held together the whole intricate mosaic was a masterpiece of legalistic whimsy that defied the laws of political gravity. The Austrian half, the original family estates of the Habsburgs plus some later acquisitions, did not even have a proper name—it might be argued that between 1867 and 1918 there was no such country as Austria —but was officially designed as "the kingdoms and provinces represented in the Reichsrath (parliament)." They included present-day Austria, Bohemia (the Czech part of Czechoslovakia), Polish Galicia, the Rumanian Bukovina, some of the Slovene areas of present Yugoslavia, most of the Dalmatian coast and the Italian-speaking Trentino. Hungary ruled all the other subject territories and peoples, including Slovakia, Transylvania, and Croatia. There were four parliaments—the two main ones in Vienna and Budapest, and satellite diets in Prague and Agram (Zagreb), the capital of Croatia which had a special statute under the Hungarian Crown, but no common one for the whole empire, which of course was not officially an empire, though it was ruled by an Emperor. (Bosnia-Herzegovina, administered by the Joint Finance Ministry, also had its diet.)

Here we come to the quasi-metaphysical concepts and symbols of dualism, which have provided almost as much subject for controversy to modern jurists as those of the Holy Trinity did to medieval theologians. Roughly, very roughly, speaking, the Dual Monarchy, as established by the so-called *Ausgleich* (settlement) of 1867, consisted of two sovereign states, each possessing semiautonomous dependent territories, linked—but not in identical fashion—to the person of a common ruler. In Austria he held the title of His Apostolic Majesty the King—Emperor of Austria-Hungary, (The title of Holy Roman Emperor formerly used by the Habsburgs had been abandoned in 1806.) There were joint Austro-Hungarian Ministries for War, Foreign Affairs, and Finance. They were termed *Koniglich-und-Kaiserlich* or K-u-K (Royal and Imperial) departments. The other branches were called simply *Koniglich-Kaiserlich* (Royal-Imperial) in Austria, and *Koniglich* in Hungary. The Army was K-u-K. The railroads changed as they crossed boundaries. The railroad carriage that carried a traveler from Vienna to Budapest was K-K up to the Hungarian border and merely K from there on. If requisitioned by the Army, however, it would be K-u-K all the way. The whole relationship was really quite simple if you thought of it in mathematical terms; an Austrian, as the Viennese novelist Robert Musil explained with his unique irony, possessed a citizenship equivalent to that of an Austrian plus a Hungarian, minus that same Hungarian.

The most illogical human institutions are not always the least durable, as demonstrated by the monarchy in Britain, and if the difficulty of defining the Dual Monarchy had been its greatest weakness it might still be flourishing under the royal, royal-imperial and royal-and-imperial sway of the Habsburgs. Unfortunately, the paradoxes of its protocol were only the reflection of basic anachronisms in its structure. It was certain of these structural defects that had obliged Francis Joseph to discipline his Hungarian subjects by enacting an electoral reform which fundamentally was as distasteful to him as it was to them. The Hungarians, prodded by the fanatics of Magyar nationalism—who had apparently forgotten that they were supposed to belong to a "majority" people—were demanding the abolition of German as the language of command in the Royal-and-Imperial Army and were threatening to convert its Hungarian units into a purely national, or single "K" army. This would have transformed the Dual Monarchy, for all practical purposes, from a juridical puzzle into a farce, and the old Emperor, a soldier above all else, was determined not to let it happen. "The Army is not a joking matter," he told his Hungarian ministers.

In the political climate that the Russian uprisings had created throughout Europe, there was only one weapon left to Francis Joseph to ward off the danger of a de facto Hungarian secession. He could frighten the semifeudal Magyar landowners, whose oligarchy in Hungary was based on iniquitous election laws, with the menace of free, direct, and universal suffrage. To impose electoral reform on the Hungarian magnates at once might be risky however; it was essential to Francis Joseph's strategy to keep the threat of it hanging over their heads. It was at this point that his Royal-Imperial Social-Democrats unwittingly came to the aid of their Emperor; by yielding to their demand for an electoral new deal in the Austrian half of his empire, he could give the stubborn Magyars an object lesson in the fate that awaited them if they continued to defy him. This policy seems too devious to have originated in the sensible, unimaginative mind of Francis Joseph; but the Habsburg throne was surrounded wtih subtle, frequently oversubtle, political advisers. By taking their advice in the incipient constitutional crisis of 1905, the Emperor achieved his prime objective—safeguarding the unity of the Imperial Army—but in so doing opened a Pandora's box of national-ist agitation which aggravated disunity in the empire as a whole.

To understand how this came about it is necessary to recapitulate briefly the story of the Habsburg dynasty and that of Francis Joseph's own reign; together they constitute a momentous and fascinating chapter in the chronicle of modern Europe. Such as it is, our world today owes more to both than we generally realize.

The Emperor crypt of the Capuchin chapel in the heart of Old Vienna is the family mausoleum of the Habsburgs. The dust of twelve emperors and fifteen empresses lies there in the golden gloom, watched over by four crowned skulls whose sightless eye sockets are turned toward the red and white tomb of Frederick III (d. 1493), the first member of the dynasty to use the title. To the modern eye there seems as much pride as humility in the baroque symbolism; there was a time when the Habsburg realms were second only to the universal monarchy for which the crowned skulls stand.

It was Frederick who adopted and carved over a gate of the Hofburg the boastful motto AEIOU, an interchangeable Latin-German anagram (*Austriae est imperare orbi universo* or *Alles Erdreich ist Oesterreich unterthan*) signifying that it is Austria's destiny to rule the world. In modest, pacific, republican present-day Austria, the words have a pathetic ring, but then, they never really applied to Austria. The Habsburgs were something else.

"In other countries dynasties are episodes in the history of peoples," comments A. J. P. Taylor, "In the Habsburg Empire peoples are a complication in the history of a dynasty . . . No other family has endured so long or left so deep a mark upon Europe."

The first Habsburg king was born in 1218, exactly 700 years before the last one, the Emperor Charles, abandoned his throne. Rudolph of Habsburg was a feudal lord whose possessions amounted to a few hundred acres of wooded rolling country on the Swiss plateau, in Alsace, and southern Germany. He descended from an already ancient family whose name derived from a castle built in the eleventh century: the "Habichtsburg" or castle of the hawk. The walls of the ruined keep, six feet thick, still stand and can be visited near Zurich, in Switzerland. From his ancestors—one of them was Count of Zurich—Rudolph had inherited the protectorate over the "Waldstatte," the original Swiss cantons whose struggle against their Habsburg overlords was later dramatized in the legend of Wilhelm Tell.

It was not his riches or military strength, but rather the lack of them, that caused Rudolph to be elected "King of the Romans" as the rulers of Germany were then called. This was an optimistic appellation; it is true that the Holy Roman Empire had become the Holy Germanic Roman Empire since a German king, Otto the Great, had knelt before the Pope in

Rome to be crowned with Charlemagne's Golden Crown and hailed like him, Caesar and Augustus, but it had become a hollow title. Medieval Europe had curdled into hundreds of small warring States, whose lords would tolerate no king but one of their own choosing, and the monarchy had become elective. When Rudolph was finally chosen, the crown had gone begging for over twenty years; no one cared to rule the hornets' nest of nearly four hundred feudal baronies which in French chronicles of the day is referred to as *"Les Allemagnes"* and where no writ prevailed but that of the *"Faustrecht"* (Law of the mailed fist).

Rudolph turned out to be more than the German princes had bargained for. Defeating the King of Bohemia, he acquired the Ostmark (roughly Austria and northern Yugoslavia) and thus became the richest landowner in the empire; its wary prince-electors took prudent note and returned the imperial crown to Habsburg hands only intermittently for the next two hundred years. In the fifteenth century however, a Habsburg Emperor, Frederick III, finally made it practically hereditary by the simple device of having his son elected heir-presumptive during his lifetime; successive Habsburgs adopted the practice as a family tradition. The same Frederick, a colorless but ambitious ruler, founded another Habsburg tradition, that of expansion by matrimony. *"Bella gerant alii, tu, felix Austria, nube"* ("Let others wage war, but you, happy Austria, marry") became the unofficial Habsburg motto.

Frederick's son, Maximilian, (1459-1519) who married the Netherlands and a nice strip of eastern France, perfected the policy. He betrothed his heir to a bride whose intellect was cloudy but whose dowry was brilliant; Joan the Crazy, daughter to their Most Catholic Majesties, Ferdinand and Isabella of Spain (and, thanks to Christopher Columbus, of certain lands beyond the ocean sea). The Spanish connection also brought to the Habsburgs the pompous, stiff etiquette of Isabella's court (which was still being observed at that of Francis Joseph), the narrow foreheads and drooping mouths immortalized in the canvasses of Velasquez, the strain of melancholy or even occasional madness that kept cropping up in the family, and the blight of Castillian bigotry; these were the days when the smoke of the Spanish Inquisition's *autos-da-fe* darkened the Mediterranean sky.

With Maximilian the Habsburgs began to bulge out of their purely German frame and become a European dynasty, but Maximilian himself, depicted in a portrait by Albrecht Durer as a sharp-nosed splendid, *grand seigneur,* was above all a Viennese. He was born in the city, and there he lies buried. Brilliant and flighty, he was described by his Florentine contemporary, Niccolo Machiavelli as "the greatest spendthrift of our time, or any other." Naturally, Vienna loved him.

Maximilian's grandson, Charles V (d. 1558), was more cosmopolitan. Born and brought up in the Netherlands, he inherited from his Austrian-

French father the Low Countries, the Franche Comté (the Burgundy-Jura area of modern France) and all the traditional Habsburg possessions. From his Spanish mother he acquired, at the age of eighteen, the crown of Spain and the greatest colonial empire in the world, including the known parts of Central and South America and sizable tracts of what was to become the United States of America. The sun, his courtiers boasted somewhat loosely, never set on his realms. AEIOU became merely a pithy summary of the Habsburg imperial mission.

The universalist vocation implicit in the family slogan developed, with the post-medieval Habsburgs into more than a passion for collecting real estate; it was at once their glory, and their undoing. Though the Habsburgs could hardly be called a family of intellectuals, their story is intertwined with the history of ideas since the sixteenth century, to a degree unmatched in that of any other European dynasty. In each century, right up to the twentieth, as Professor Taylor points out, they identified themselves with some great ideological movement and became the foremost champions of some supranational cause of doctrine. The causes were generally lost ones, and the ideas unpopular, but they were not always so retrograde as they seemed to those who held opposing views. The peculiar tragedy of the Habsburgs is that they were usually as far ahead of their age in some respects as they were behind it in others. They were historic failures, in the sense that they consistently missed achieving their major goals, but they count among the most imposing, or even glorious, failures in history.

"Glorious failure" is certainly the appropriate epitaph for Charles V, the greatest monarch of the Renaissance. For thirty years this essentially peaceloving, introverted, deeply religious man rode at the head of his armies, back and forth across the face of Europe, from the Netherlands to Sicily, from Spain to the Danube, pursuing the grand medieval dream of Christian and European unity. The pursuit was a hopeless one. Charles did succeed in saving much of Europe from Turkish invasion, an achievement that today is sometimes underrated, but the spread of Lutheranism had irremediably split the Western church, and the rise of the nation-state inexorably doomed the Continent to political compartmentation. Charles' victory over his French colleague, Francis I, at the Battle of Pavia was in one respect a triumph of the supranational over the national ideal, but it was the last meaningful one Europe was to see for nearly four centuries. Though neither Francis nor England's Henry VIII could equal Charles' spread, their dynasties were more firmly rooted in the soil of their homelands. The mere extent of Charles' scattered empire made it ungovernable in an age of rudimentary communications. Eventually he had to admit his limitations. Sick and exhausted from his labors, he retired at the age of fifty-six to a small country house in Spain, and renounced the Imperial crown with the Habsburg family holdings in Central Europe, in favor of his brother Ferdinand; at the same time he handed over the Spanish crown to his son Philip, thus splitting into two allied but separate parts the greatest concentration of power in Europe since Charlemagne.

The story of the Spanish Habsburgs is a long decline from grandeur, ending in 1700 when the branch became extinct.

The Austrian line, at first considered as poor relations by their magnificent Spanish cousins, was to go on playing a splendid, if increasingly tragic, role for much longer. It continued to champion the cause of Europe against the Turks for more than a century, after crusading had gone out of fashion (though the need for it was greater than ever); the last Moslem assault was thrown back under the walls of Vienna in 1683. The wars against the Turks earned the Habsburgs numerous rewards in addition to the crusader's halo and the legendary sack of coffee the foe had abandoned on the battlefield. In return for their protection against the infidel, the Bohemians and the Hungarians offered their vacant thrones (in 1526) to Ferdinand I, not to become part of the Holy Germanic Roman Empire over which he ruled, but in personal unions that were supposed to respect their separate national sovereignties. In the seventeenth century the Emperor Leopold I declared the ancient crowns of St. Stephen (Hungary) and St. Wenceslas (Bohemia-Moravia, that is roughly modern Czechoslovakia) as hereditary possessions of the Habsburg family, along with the Holy Roman one made for Otto the Great in 962 and the almost equally famous Iron Crown of Lombardy. At the same time he began the process of whittling away Hungarian and Czech liberties, thus planting the seeds of two particularly virulent nineteenth- and twentieth-century nationalisms. Their future growth proved all the more tangled and prickly because in swallowing up the ancient Kingdom of Hungary, the Habsburgs, like a big fish devouring a slightly smaller one with the remains of an undigested minnow still sticking in its throat, had recognized the claim of their new Magyar vassals to the lands of the no-less ancient Kingdom of Croatia, absorbed by Hungary in the twelfth century after it had two centuries of national independence behind it. As Gordon Shepherd remarks in his *Austrian Odyssey,* the "South Slav Problem" which was to be one of the crucial issues of the twentieth century, had its root in the Dark Ages.

During the sixteenth and seventeenth centuries the Habsburgs likewise continued to identify themselves with the secular aims of the Counter Reformation; it was largely thanks to them that the insurgent forces of Protestantism were contained in northern and northeastern Europe. From the viewpoint of the Empire, however, this defensive victory of the Catholic cause was a disastrous one that aggravated the disunity of the Germanic world. After the shambles of the Thirty Years' War (1618–1648) in which Catholic and Protestant rulers fought each other to a bloody stalemate and reduced much of Central Europe to a ravaged waste, the Imperial crown

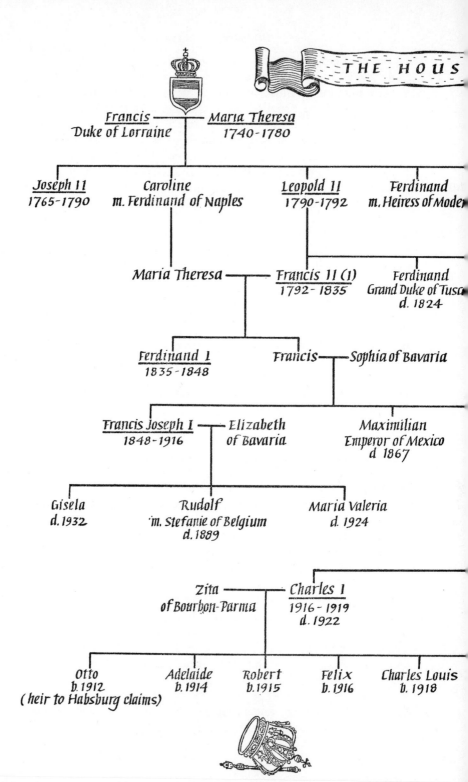

THE HOUS

Francis
Duke of Lorraine — Maria Theresa
1740-1780

Joseph II
1765-1790

Caroline
m. Ferdinand of Naples

Leopold II
1790-1792

Ferdinand
m. Heiress of Moder

Maria Theresa — Francis II (1)
1792-1835

Ferdinand
Grand Duke of Tusca
d. 1824

Ferdinand I
1835-1848

Francis — Sophia of Bavaria

Francis Joseph I
1848-1916 — Elizabeth
of Bavaria

Maximilian
Emperor of Mexico
d. 1867

Gisela
d. 1932

Rudolf
m. Stefanie of Belgium
d. 1889

Maria Valeria
d. 1924

Zita
of Bourbon-Parma — Charles I
1916-1919
d. 1922

Otto
b. 1912
(heir to Habsburg claims)

Adelaide
b. 1914

Robert
b. 1915

Felix
b. 1916

Charles Louis
b. 1918

HABSBURG - LORRAINE

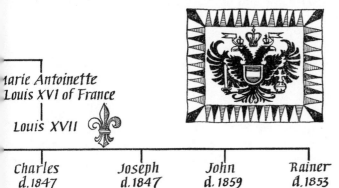

Marie Antoinette
m. Louis XVI of France

Louis XVII

| Charles | Joseph | John | Rainer |
| d.1847 | d.1847 | d.1859 | d.1853 |

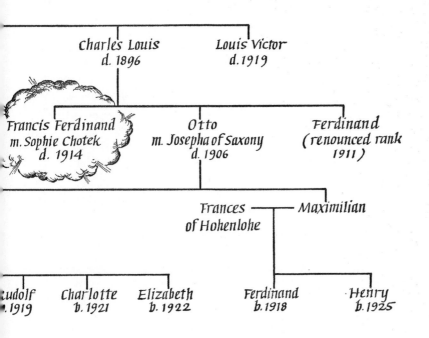

Charles Louis
d. 1896

Louis Victor
d.1919

Francis Ferdinand
m. Sophie Chotek
d. 1914

Otto
m. Josepha of Saxony
d. 1906

Ferdinand
(renounced rank
1911)

Frances ——— Maximilian
of Hohenlohe

| Rudolf | Charlotte | Elizabeth | Ferdinand | Henry |
| d.1919 | b. 1921 | b. 1922 | b.1918 | b. 1925 |

became an empty symbol. The Habsburg dominions at the beginning of the eighteenth century still stretched from Calais to the Russian plain and from north Germany to northern Italy, but the empire was a fragile shell of its former grandeur and the Habsburgs were increasingly being thrown back upon their family holdings. From the religious viewpoint their attempt to uphold orthodoxy by the sword had been equally inconclusive, even in their own fiefs. The Austrian baroque style of architecture which the Jesuits, the indefectible allies of the dynasty, were largely responsible for introducing into the Habsburg lands is an apt symbol of this dubious victory. The worldly triviality, bordering on frivolousness, which so often underlies the baroque striving for magnificence and fervor, came to mark not only the facades of the empire's churches but all too often the attitudes of their congregations; Leopold I was even obliged to promulgate an edict forbidding flirting and gossiping in places of worship.

The original Habsburg branch died out with the death of Charles VI, but his daughter, Maria Theresa, the only reigning Empress in the history of the family, launched a sturdy offshoot by marrying the Duke of Lorraine and bearing sixteen little Habsburg-Lorraines, among them the unlucky Marie Antoinette. The so-called Pragmatic Sanction,[1] a special law which her father bullied or wheedled his vassals into accepting to legalize her accession (only males had hitherto been eligible to mount the Imperial throne) served at the same time to complete the merger of the formerly independent countries or territories, held by the Habsburgs under various feudal conveyances, into a centralized empire. A dauntless woman who upheld her contested right to the throne in two major wars, and a conscientious ruler despite her family distractions, Maria Theresa possessed both the Viennese talent of enjoying herself and the Viennese gift of simplicity.

[1] It is possible to lead a satisfactory twentieth-century life without knowing why the Pragmatic Sanction was pragmatic, or exactly what it sanctioned, but to readers in whose minds the words tend to reverberate with a Thurberesque obsessiveness, the following explanation may save some sleep:

The term, taken from Roman law (*Pragmatica Sanctio*), was familiar to European jurisprudence long before the time of Maria Theresa. Essentially it served to give a cloak of legal respectability to arbitrary decisions of the supreme power intervening on behalf of the state or crown in disputes between private parties or subsidiary authorities. The Pragmatic Sanction of the Emperor Charles VI decreed in effect that it was in the interests of the Empire to alter the Habsburg family rules of succession so as to make sure that his daughter, Maria Theresa, would succeed him. Normally, the eldest daughter of the late Emperor Joseph I should have been crowned after Charles' death (there were no near male heirs). The Sanction stipulated that henceforth the Habsburg dominions would pass undivided to the children, first male, then female, of the last reigning Emperor, starting with the issue—Maria Theresa—of Charles himself. By this high-handed procedure Charles not only deprived his niece of her birthright to the profit of his own daughter but imposed an arbitrary change in Habsburg family law as the supreme writ of the Empire, thereby overriding a number of traditional and contractual arrangements between the Imperial crown and the vassal nations that acknowledged its authority, not to mention several international treaties. The result was to embroil the House of Austria in a long series of wars.

To announce to her subjects the birth of one of her numerous grandchildren, she once stood up in her loge at the Vienna Opera and shouted, "Leopold has a son!"

Her successor, Joseph II (1765–1790), was a new kind of Habsburg. The others had exploited ideas; he generated them—and most un-Habsburg ones at that. In the seventeenth century Vienna had been the supreme bastion of the Counter Reformation; in the eighteenth, Joseph converted it into one of the most advanced outposts of the Enlightenment. He was the most benevolent and the least despotic of the benevolent despots (Frederick the Great, Catherine the Great, and himself). He liked to think of himself as the "Emperor of the People," and in donating to the city of Vienna the Prater, the lovely and frivolous park that has been the delight of its citizens ever since, he dedicated it "To my fellow-men from their true servant."

Joseph undertook a sweeping program of reforms, abolishing serfdom and the legal use of torture, antagonizing the feudal nobility by his egalitarian fiscal doctrines. It was probably due to Joseph's timely eradication of economic and social abuses inherited from the Middle Ages that Austrian society stood up as well as it did against the storm winds of the French Revolution—if his brother-in-law Louis XVI had been as alert there might never have been one—but he could not eliminate the basic anachronism of the Habsburg system without undermining the very foundations of the dynasty. In Taylor's words, "The Habsburg lands were a collection of entailed estates, not a State; and the Habsburgs were landlords, not rulers." Their empire, the British historian points out, "rested on tradition, on dynastic rights and on international treaties"; they could not be anything but the implacable foe of the French Revolution and of the upstart Corsican adventurer, Napoleon. Joseph's son, Francis I, it is true, gave his daughter Marie Louise, to the usurper but this was only a temporary gesture of appeasement. Francis managed to be on the losing side of most of Napoelon's great battles and had to yield up the German territories on which his title was based. He accordingly laid aside the crown of Otto the Great—the emblem itself was thriftily stored away and can be seen today in the museum of the Hofburg—and changed his own designation from "Francis II, Holy Germanic Roman Emperor," to "Francis I, Emperor of Austria."

After the downfall of Napoleon, the Habsburgs recovered many of their lands but did not attempt to revive the Holy Roman Empire. Their immovable Chancellor, Prince Klemens von Metternich, a prim-faced, iron-willed zealot of reaction, took charge of the Habsburg destinies and in their name propagated the ideology of the traditionalist counterrevolution. It was mainly due to Metternich's influence that the Holy Alliance of Christian monarchs, proposed by Czar Alexander I at the Congress of Vienna in 1814, emerged as a repressive league for the maintenance of the dynastic and territorial status quo in Europe. Nationalism, one of the dynamic ideas generated and spread by the French Revolution, was his particular *bête noire*.

Metternich's phobia was an understandable one. Austria, that is the remains of the Habsburg empire, was not a nation in the sense that France, England, Prussia, Spain, and even Alexander's Russia were nations. It was a supranational community, artificially bound together by the authority of a dynasty that derived its mandate from a mixture of habit and medieval land-jurisprudence. Patriotism itself was a suspect virtue in Habsburg Austria. When one of his subjects was recommended to him as an outstanding patriot, Francis I testily inquired, "But is he a patriot for me?" In the twentieth century this outlook enabled two Habsburgs—one of them being the Archduke Francis Ferdinand—to figure as at least timid pioneers of a new pattern of European federalism, but in the nineteenth century it doomed the dynasty not only to oppose the rising Slav, Magyar, and Italian nationalisms with bayonets, but to throw up a fragile barricade against the movement for German unification, which a rival feudal family, the Hohenzollerns of Prussia, exploited to achieve imperial grandeur. The brunt of this double mission fell mainly on Francis Joseph I, the nephew of Francis I's feeble-minded son, Ferdinand. In his remote courtesy, unwavering sense of duty, quiet authority, old-fashioned simplicity, and narrow-minded singleness of purpose he was the ideal captain for a sinking ship. The reign of Nicholas II in Russia demonstrates with Elizabethan starkness some of the mechanisms of historical nemesis; the less garish drama of Francis Joseph's life illustrates the dignity as well as the inevitability of the tragic principle in human history.

To the world of our fathers, Emperor Francis Joseph I of Austria-Hungary was a symbol of human and institutional permanence. Middle-aged men who had known him since childhood as a grizzled old gentleman with bushy sideburns that drooped like jowls felt reassured every time they saw the changeless, familiar face in their newspaper. After Britain's Queen Victoria, he was the supreme personification of nineteenth-century values and tradition; he was born eleven years later than she was, but survived her by fifteen. In all he reigned sixty-eight years. Woodrow Wilson was President of the United States when Francis Joseph died, in 1916 at the age of eighty-six. Andrew Jackson was President the year he was born, 1830. Metternich, Talleyrand, and Wellington were all active in public life; Goethe and Lafayette were yet alive; Francis Joseph's grandfather, Emperor Francis I, who had been defeated at Austerlitz and Wagram by Napoleon, was still reigning.

The year 1830 saw the first significant break in the legitimist restoration which Metternich had helped impose on Europe. A few weeks before

Francis Joseph's birth (on August 18, at the castle of Laxenburg, outside Vienna) his Bourbon cousin, the diehard Charles V, had been chased off the French throne by a bourgeois revolution, but along the banks of the Danube, the dikes of Metternichean reaction held as firmly as ever. No breath of independent thought was allowed to trouble the provincial stillness that had settled upon the Habsburg lands since 1815. Metternich, it was true, did permit one cafe in the capital to keep a few foreign journals on its reading racks, but that was purely for the convenience of the police, so that they might more easily identify suspect intellectuals (contemporary dictatorships, in Central Europe and elsewhere, follow the same practice on occasion). The police were efficient; so was the bureaucracy, reorganized by Francis I. They were the twin pillars of the dynasty, and the guardians of the post-Napoleonic social order. The bourgeoisie of the Empire dozed in a snug, tepid Biedermayer world of *Sachertorte, Caffee mit Schlag,* and Schubert's *Trout Quintet,* while Napoleon's son, the young Duke of Reichstadt, *L'Aiglon* of fanatical Bonapartists, was systematically coddled to death in the boudoirs of Schoenbrunn Palace.

There was no coddling, however, for Francis Joseph. He had a Spartan bringing up, together with his younger brother, Maximilian (the same Maximilian who was destined to die stupidly and tragically before a firing squad in Mexico), in the drafty, smelly old Hofburg, under the vigilant eye of their mother, the Archduchess Sophia, a tough, ambitious Wittelsbach, without any of the romantic traits for which the Bavarian dynasty was later noted. (His father, Archduke Frederick, died early.) Metternich, who as president of the council of regency, became the virtual dictator of the Empire after the epileptic, intermittently insane Ferdinand I, Francis Joseph's uncle, mounted the throne in 1835, personally groomed the young Archduke to be the next Emperor. At seventeen his curriculum, in the words of one Austrian historian, included, besides the usual classical studies, "newspaper reading, Polish, and one hour a week with Prince Metternich."

Francis Joseph was not yet eighteen when he was sent off to Italy to get a taste of army life. He showed considerable aptitude for it, and when the test eventually came bore himself well under fire. It was prophetic that the first time he heard bullets whistle around his head or saw men die in combat was in action against nationalist revolutionaries. He was serving in northern Italy where local patriots, encouraged by a liberal Pope (Pius IX) and helped by the armies of the Piedmontese dynasty, the House of Savoy, had revolted and driven the Imperial forces out of Venice and Milan.

This was the fateful year, 1848; invisible but dynamic new pressures had been building up under the crust of Metternichian conformism, and the February revolution in France which overthrew the stuffy, bourgeois monarchy of Louis Philippe had touched off a series of political eruptions across Europe. In March the Hungarians and the Czechs rose up, demanding self-government and parliaments of their own. Then insurrection broke out in Vienna itself, led by liberal students and supported by most of the population. Metternich escaped from the capital hidden in a laundry cart and went into exile. Revolution died down momentarily in Austria when the puppet Emperor, Ferdinand, granted his subjects freedom of the press and promised a constitution, but in May it flared up more violently than ever. A Committee of Public Safety took power in Vienna and the Court fled to Innsbruck; Francis Joseph, recalled from the Army, rejoined it there. Toward the end of the summer the Imperial Family returned to Vienna, but a new and bloodier uprising obliged them to take flight again almost immediately, this time to the old fortress town of Olmutz, in Moravia.

This humiliating forced retreat in the face of revolution was the final, traumatic touch in the political education of the hapless young Archduke whom nothing had prepared to understand the great historic movements of his day and who was doomed to oppose them all, piling defeat upon defeat, both in his public and in his private life. Momentarily, however, the escape to Olmutz marked a turning point in the fortunes of the dynasty.

The Archduchess Sophia, Francis Joseph's mother, became one of the chief instigators of the monarchist counterrevolution that steadily gathered momentum during the last few months of 1848. "I could have borne the loss of one of my children more easily than I can the ignominy of submitting to a mess of students," she declared at one critical moment during the struggle. She organized an ultraroyalist cabal with two of Metternich's most incorrigible disciples, Prince Alfred Windisch-Graetz, the imperial commander in Prague who had "restored order" there by bombarding the city in violation of the Emperor's promise, and his brother-in-law Prince Friedrich Schwarzenberg, an energetic, stubborn reactionary, whose lack of scruple matched his aristocratic contempt for democracy. With her help, they succeeded in persuading the feeble, good-natured Ferdinand to abdicate in favor of his nephew; the youth was not hampered by any promises to the revolutionaries that might hamper the task of repression, and the "Ultra" clique reasoned, correctly on the whole, that he would be amenable to Schwarzenberg's vigorous guidance.

Planned in secrecy and performed in privacy, the coronation, which took place in the gloomy old castle of Olmutz, was not much of a ceremony; the atmosphere was less that of a dynastic festival than that of a high-level hanging. Francis Joseph, blond and slender and handsome in the romantic taste of the day, looked pathetically boyish with the muscles in his narrow, stern Habsburg forehead corded to achieve a manly frown, and his pouting Habsburg lips drawn into a wan, prim line. Surrounded by whispering relatives, with Schwarzenberg acting as unofficial master of ceremonies, he knelt in front of the silly, kindly old uncle who had been so easily persuaded to abdicate. Ferdinand stroked the nervous boy's cheek. "Bear yourself bravely," he said with the insight of inspired idiocy. "It's all right."

It was a long time, however, before things were all right, even in Schwarzenberg's sense. Revolution had not yet been stamped out in Italy; in Hungary it had still to reach its climax. Ferdinand, before his abdication, had granted the Hungarians national sovereignty and a liberal constitution. Francis Joseph, after his coronation refused to recognize his predecessor's grant, whereupon the Hungarian Diet, galvanized by the Magyar Patrick Henry, Lajos Kossuth, in Budapest, refused to recognize him as King of Hungary. Windisch-Graetz, with the grudgingly accepted aid of the Croats who had caught the fashionable nationalist fever from their Magyar overlords and risen against them, occupied Budapest, but the Hungarian patriot forces rallied and inflicted a series of sharp defeats upon him; this encouraged the Diet to depose the Habsburgs and proclaim total independence.

Ever since their tribal ancestors rode out of Asia to settle in the flat, rich Danubian plain, bringing with them an inextinguishable breath of nomad freedom and an unappeasable nomad lust for domination, the Magyars have been a problem to themselves as well as to their less turbulent neighbors. To a greater degree perhaps than any other people in Europe their relationship to history has been that of a chronic invalid to his malady, an endless alternation of political elation and depression, an infernal cycle of martyrdom and imperialism. In 1956 a dim, fragmentary successor to the Habsburgs, the Soviet prison warden, Kadar, had to call for Russian help to master an ungovernable paroxysm of national feeling that had seized his compatriots. In 1848 Francis Joseph, invoking the Holy Alliance, had to call for Russian military help to reconquer his subjects, possessed by a similar passion for national freedom, and Nicholas I, like Nikita Khrushchev always ready to aid a brother or vassal tyrant in distress, sent an army to his succour.

(With this historic precedent in mind, it is not surprising that Austro-Hungarian reactionaries were so disturbed by the 1905 revolution in Russia, the ultimate stronghold of reaction.)

Thanks to the Czar, the Hungarian revolution was quenched by August 1848; Habsburg rule had already been restored in Venice and Lombardy. A new and more bitter frost of repression cut short the precocious "springtime of the peoples." Kossuth escaped to America and successfully transplanted his political idealism in the generous soil of the New World, but many other Magyar patriots paid with their lives for their love of freedom, as they had done before and have done since, and doubtless will do again. To suggestions that it would be both magnanimous and expedient to treat the Hungarian rebels mercifully, Schwarzenberg replied with aristocratic casualness, "Yes, yes, a very good idea, but we must have a bit of hanging first." In Habsburg Italy the imperial police again set up its whipping posts, and its stolid Teuton or Croatian gendarmes, planted on either side of the stage—to discourage subversive enthusiasm in the audience—once more infuriated Italian opera and theater lovers. The King of Sardinia, Charles Albert, the father of Italy's future ruler, Victor Emmanuel II, was forced to abdicate, and the whole marvelous adventure of the Italian *Risorgimento* set back for a decade—but only for a decade.

With Schwarzenberg's prompting, Francis Joseph drew what he imagined was the deep lesson of his narrow escape from revolution: the torrents of history can be dammed if one is strong and determined enough. He thought he had the strength, and he expressed his antirevolutionary determination on New Year's Day 1852, by proclaiming a new charter for the Empire based on unlimited, centralized absolutism, that, with a stroke of the pen, wiped out everything his people—and peoples—had gained in two revolutions. The Emperor, by this virtual coup d'état, not only assumed for himself the whole weight and power of government, but abolished all the rights that had existed from time immemorial between the monarch and his vassal kingdoms or territories. Metternich himself had never dared to go so far.

Like the suicidal policies of Nicholas II in Russia, Francis Joseph's youthful and naive experiment in autocracy illustrates what is perhaps the deadliest weapon in the arsenal of revolutionary movements: their ability to goad their adversaries into self-slaughtering madness. Ironically, Francis Joseph was probably saved from destruction by the very enormity of his error. He had so radically misread the whole politico-diplomatic situation in Europe that the saber of reaction was wrenched out of his hands before he had time to chop off his own head with it.

"Keep an eye on the Piedmont; it is a hotbed of unwholesome tendencies," the Emperor once wrote to his brother Maximilian then serving as Viceroy in Lombardy. To repress these tendencies before they got out of hand again, Francis Joseph in 1859 sent an ultimatum to the government of young Victor Emmanuel II demanding, in terms which foreshadow the fateful note to Serbia after Sarajevo, that Sardinia and Piedmont disarm— no doubt as a prelude to purging them of their unwholesome nationalism. The ultimatum was exactly what was desired by Victor Emmanuel's Prime Minister, Count Camillo di Cavour, a sophisticated nationalist who had read Machiavelli as well as Rousseau. He had a defensive alliance, valid in case of Austrian aggression, with France's new Emperor, Napoleon III, a nephew of the great Corsican, who possessed both the looks and the mentality of a Mississippi riverboat gambler, and he had been waiting eagerly to be aggressed. The eventual clash of the Austro-Hungarian and Franco-Italian armies, first at Magenta, then at Solferino, was a low-grade, somewhat inconclusive, but extremely bloody retake of Bonaparte's Italian epic—

which badly frightened both the opposing Emperors. (Each had taken the field at the head of his armies.) Peace was patched up, Lombardy was freed from the Austrian yoke (Victor Emmanuel was crowned King of Italy two years later), and Francis Joseph returned to Vienna to lick his wounds and offer his subjects a liberal-seeming, if not wholly sincere, constitution.

The twenty-nine-year-old Emperor not only abandoned his experiment in personal despotism but for a while even sought to exploit in his own behalf the subversive dynamism of the nationalist idea. In 1863 he tried to take the head of the movement for German reunification by convoking a diet of all the German princes at Frankfurt. The idea of a Habsburg Emperor proposing an emasculated, denatured nineteenth-century version of the vanished Holy Roman Empire of his ancestors and offering himself as the leader of a nationalist new Germany bubbling with the ferment of Marx's ideas, not to mention those of Treitschke, was patently ludicrous. It was also rashly provocative; the Hohenzollern dynasty of Prussia had long since staked its claim to play the same unifying role in Germany that the House of Savoy was playing in Italy, and the Prussian Chancellor, Prince Otto von Bismarck, was determined to settle the question of Germanic hegemony by blood and iron. In 1866 he lured Francis Joseph into much the same kind of trap that Cavour had laid for him, and declared war. Italy, seeing a chance for booty, followed suit. Most of the German princes, including Bavaria and a strong Saxon contingent, fought on the Austrian side, but the brutally efficient Prussian military machine under the command of Field Marshal Helmuth von Moltke shattered the Imperial forces near Sadowa, in northern Bohemia.

Defeat cost Francis Joseph Venice and its rich hinterland. ("Is this what they made me abdicate for?" exclaimed the old Emperor, Ferdinand, living under medical supervision in Prague, when he heard the news. "I could have lost those provinces myself.") A far graver humiliation was to see the Habsburg dynasty, which, for so many centuries had worn the crown of the Holy Germanic Roman Empire, expelled from the Germanic community and German unity virtually achieved under the aegis of the victorious Hohenzollerns.

The blow to the Emperor's prestige would have shaken an empire more solid than that of Francis Joseph; Sadowa upset the internal political balance within his composite realm no less than that of Europe as a whole. The only alternative to revolution—and the only hope for effective support in an eventual war of revenge against Prussia—was to come to terms with the Hungarians, the strongest and most militant of the national minorities. The result was the Compromise of 1867—establishing the Dual Monarchy —a compromise that in reality was an unconditional surrender to Magyar imperialism. This fatal accord granted Hungary a constitution that was extremely liberal in the privileges it gave the Magyars within the Empire, and infamously reactionary in the power it allotted them to establish a racial dictatorship over the Rumanians, Slovaks, Ruthenians, Serbs, and Croats living inside their historic frontiers. The Serbs and Croats who had supported the throne in 1848 felt that the dynasty had betrayed them, and said so. In fact, the *Ausgleich* scrapped the traditional Habsburg policy of maintaining the various nationalities of the Empire in a balanced state of well-tempered discontent, and substituted the principle of minority rule.

Francis Joseph had originally intended to promulgate a fairly liberal and federalistic constitution, within the Austrian half of the Empire, but the Hungarians, fearing the contagion, forced him into adopting a centralized form of government that confirmed the hegemony of the German ethnic group, while theoretically recognizing the equal rights of all nationalities. The inevitable effect of this was to alienate the Czechs, and to some degree the other Slav elements in Austria.

In the circumstances, democratic constitutional procedures were a dangerous luxury. Francis Joseph remained convinced—with some justification —that they could not work anywhere in his Empire, and he put his faith in the famous Article 14 he had caused to be written into the Austrian constitution, which permitted the Emperor to resort "exceptionally" provisionally but almost at will, to government by emergency decree without consulting parliament. The word *ausnahmsweise* (exceptionally) became the key to effective government and the catchword of all satirical doggerels. Austria, the wags said, was neither an autocracy nor a democracy, but a state of emergency. By 1867 Francis Joseph's political outlook had evolved considerably from the reactionary oversimplifications of Schwarzenberg's day and his character had developed under misfortune, but the pattern of failure that dogged his whole long reign had been irrevocably established. This was true in his private, no less than in his public life.

The narrative of Francis Joseph's marriage and family disasters is a hard one to tell for several reasons. In the first place it is like rummaging in an attic trunk and coming upon some old albums and love letters of one's great-grandparents' day that reveal a forgotten tragedy. One is startled, almost embarrassed, to discover that the vanished beings whose grotesquely artificial likenesses stare at us from a faded daguerreotype once suffered such authentically contemporary torments; that a crinoline could cover such unconventional sorrows; that such a delicate and infinitely painful tenderness could lurk behind a pair of bushy sideburns. Then too, the floods of celluloid or pulpy romance inspired by the life and death of Elizabeth of Austria, not to mention those inspired by her unhappy son, the Archduke Rudolph, have inevitably tended to blur in our minds the features of the one genuinely romantic figure in the whole sad story; Francis Joseph himself.

He was twenty-three when he encountered Elizabeth, then sixteen, a

Wittelsbach, like his mother, and the youngest daughter of the King of Bavaria. The young Emperor's amorous well-being had been looked after by a succession of hygienic baronesses but none of them had made the least impression on his emotions. He fell in love with Elizabeth almost on sight. The Archduchess Sophia had planned for her son to marry the eldest of the Wittelsbach princesses, but after they came for a visit to Bad Ischl, the fashionable watering place in the Salzkammergut, in 1853 and Francis Joseph met Elizabeth, there was no question of any other bride for him. They made a glamorous couple, the perfect materialization of millions of naive young dreams of happiness, including no doubt their own. Elizabeth was a beautiful creature, a fine-featured, long-limbed dark-haired girl with a straight slender figure that was half a century ahead of fashionable taste. Francis Joseph's virile good looks were more conventional, but he wore his brilliant officer's uniform with dash; he was a skilled horseman and an accomplished dancer; he had charm and gaiety and easy good manners.

A gifted, spirited undisciplined child of nature, used to roaming alone on horseback across the Bavarian countryside, Elizabeth was a bad risk as a Habsburg empress; without training for the exacting job of being a royal personage, intoxicated with bad literature, and given to writing gushing verse in her diary, she could not adapt herself to the prisonlike Hofburg with its implacable etiquette. There were a few years of relative happiness with her prince-charming husband, but life at the Court of the Habsburgs was no fairy tale and Elizabeth was not emotionally equipped to cope with reality, either as Empress or as wife and mother. Francis Joseph, for all his love, could not help her. He was full of attention, and eager to grant her every wish—he even went to the length of installing an English bathroom in the Hofburg for her—but his duties did not leave him enough time for her, and he lacked imagination. He does not seem to have learned anything really useful from the hygienic baronesses, and like most romantics, was probably something of a bore at home. His quality as a lover, like his greatness as a monarch, only revealed itself in adversity.

Elizabeth was barely twenty-five when she escaped abroad for the first time—a trip to Madeira on pretext of her health. From then on she cultivated poor health with neurotic intensity, fleeing from one fashionable watering place or health resort to another, taking up each new diet-fad—she once adopted a curative regime of sand. A kind of royal Madame Bovary in her intellectual and artistic pretensions, she was infatuated with sea travel, Homeric poetry, psychiatry, and above all, herself. Her neo-Greek palace in Corfu, the Achileon, was a monument to escapism and bad taste —not to mention extravagance. Elizabeth was an early-day parlor-pink whose liberalism expressed itself mainly in the prodigality with which she squandered the revenues allotted her by her husband and her subjects on horses, houses, yachts, doctors, and the gambling tables at Monte Carlo.

By the time he was forty, Francis Joseph had to admit to himself that the only role left for him to play in Elizabeth's life was that of an indulgent father toward a willful and capricious daughter. He played it with unflagging devotion to the last. While Elizabeth pursued her endless travels in search of health, youth, and aesthetic experience, Francis Joseph sat uncomplaining at his desk twelve or fourteen hours a day, snipping the unused blank paper off incoming letters to use as scratchpads (perhaps he was trying to compensate for her extravagance), lunching off a tray of boiled beef, or goulash or sausages washed down with a glass of pilsner. She left the housekeeping and the social aspects of Court life entirely to him and he handled them with the same efficiency he displayed in the execution of his more official duties. He never forgot a birthday in the family—including those in most of Europe's royal families—and he would notice a tarnished button on a coachman's uniform, or a plate set down too brusquely by one of the white-wigged footmen at a state banquet. From afar he kept a discreet eye on Elizabeth's safety and welfare, respecting her mania for incognito in the prosaic, impersonal telegrams: HOW ARE YOU? WEATHER IS FINE HERE (from) COUNT HOHENEMBS to COUNTESS HOHENEMBS. His letters to Elizabeth, however, especially those in Hungarian, which seems to have been their language of intimacy, were tender and wistful, without ever sounding mawkish.

"Let me also tell you," he wrote in 1892, "since I cannot show it (and you would be bored if I showed it forever) how boundlessly I love you."

Six years later—the Emperor was then sixty-eight and his wife sixty-one—the old wound was still unhealed. "There is no end to my need of you," he wrote. "My thoughts are near you, and with pain do I think of our everlasting separation; especially do your vacant, dismantled rooms sadden me."

Elizabeth loved the riding and hunting in Hungary; the untamed element in the Magyar soul appealed to the strong literary element in hers. Moreover, the Archduchess Sophia hated the Hungarians, and the Empress detested her mother-in-law. Those were reasons enough to manifest sympathy for Magyar political aspirations, and in so doing, Elizabeth doubtless exercised a pro-Magyar influence on the Emperor, especially in 1867, at the time of the disastrous Compromise. Her main contribution to the broader tragedy of our times, however, was a negative one, less ugly and direct than that of the Czarina, Nicholas II's wife, but perhaps no less deadly. By depriving her husband of the warmth which, because of the exalted loneliness of his official life, he needed even more than other men to develop into a complete human being, Elizabeth's essential immaturity condemned him increasingly to submerge his private personality into his public one, to change from a man into a mask of office. As old age grew upon him, Francis Joseph acquired the stiffness, and the imperturbability of the Imperial symbol in a Byzantine mosaic; it was with eyes of gilded marble that he gazed down, unseeing and untouched, on the gathering disorder of his Empire.

The meager nourishment for the life of the heart that the old Emperor derived from his relationship with his wife was further impoverished by a tragic series of losses starting well before the time when longevity begins to exact its normal ransom. Their first-born, a daughter, died while the Imperial couple were on a state visit to Hungary in the early years of their married life. In 1867 Francis Joseph lost the favorite comrade of his boyhood, his younger brother Maximilian, who had inexplicably allowed himself to be lured into one of the more hare-brained political speculations of the riverboat gambler in Paris, the tragi-comic "Mexican Empire" sponsored by Napoleon III and paid for, as usual, with other men's blood. Then in 1889 the heir to the throne, Francis Joseph's son, Rudolph, was found dead in the hunting lodge of Mayerling, beside the corpse of his seventeen-year-old mistress, Baroness Marie Vetsera. All sorts of hypotheses have been put forward to account for this obscure and scandalous tragedy; the most likely explanation is that it was in fact a double suicide, but that on Rudolph's side the motivation was not purely sentimental. He was an intellectual with a bold, free mind, a liberal, if not an out-and-out revolutionary, and like his mother, he could not bear life in the Hofburg. Whatever the real story of his death, the shock of it was all the worse for the old Emperor because it followed shortly after a stormy father-and-son scene, provoked by Rudolph's desire to divorce his wife, the Belgian Princess Stephanie, in order to marry his mistress.

The crowning bereavement for Francis Joseph, of course, was the death of Elizabeth, stabbed, for purely symbolic reasons, by an Italian anarchist as she was about to step aboard a paddle-wheel excursion steamer on the Lake of Geneva in 1898. The Emperor sobbed when he heard the news. "The world will never know how much we loved each other," he is reported to have said. On another occasion, in a rare fit of self-pity, he gloomily remarked, "I am a *pechvogel*" (a bird of misfortune). It was hardly an exaggeration.

Naturally, Francis Joseph's existence was not unrelieved tragedy from adolescence to senility; there were some consolations. In the last quarter-century of his life one of the most important was a plump, comely retired actress named Katharina von Schratt. It was Elizabeth herself who introduced Katharina to the Emperor, and eventually installed her as the companion of his old age, one of those wise, wintry accommodations with life that are something of a Viennese specialty; it was one of the few kind things Elizabeth ever did for her husband. Katharina had a cheerful uncomplicated nature that thrived on *mehlspeisen* and operetta; Elizabeth preferred raw carrots and Heine. The two women were good friends however and had one trait in common: their extravagance. Though Katharina came high, at least she gave good value; she appears to have had a genuine affection for her venerable admirer, and showered him with tangible mementos of it. They included a music box that warbled like a nightingale when wound up—the delight of the Emperor's grandchildren on their frequent visits to his study—and a little mirror framed with the words *Portrait de la Personne que j'aime* (Portrait of the one I love) which always stood on his desk.

The garden of Katharina's little Biedermayer villa near the Maximilian Platz conveniently opened on the Imperial park of Schoenbrunn, and Francis Joseph walked over almost daily to have breakfast with her, particularly after Elizabeth's death. By the time he arrived the mistress of the house would be out of curlers, dressed and smiling—though Francis Joseph invariably got up at five—and the coffeepot would be steaming next to a bouquet of fresh flowers on the breakfast table. While the Emperor drank his coffee from a cup of fine old porcelain and munched on his *kipferl,* Katharina put him in a good humor for the day with Viennese gossip and small, domestic talk. She was a daughter of the sun; if she had also been the daughter of a king and Francis Joseph had met her thirty years earlier, the course of European history might have been different.

Apart from his visits to Katharina Schratt, Francis Joseph had only one relaxation—hunting. In the corridors of the nondescript yellow two-story villa at Bad Ischl where he spent his summers are 2200 mounted and tagged trophies of big game killed by the Emperor—the last one dated 1911, when he was eighty-one. He was a real hunter though, not a mere butcher of game like his nephew Archduke Francis Ferdinand or the German Kaiser. Nearly every day at Ischl the old gentleman—he was one in every sense of the term—would rise before dawn, put on his well-worn Tyrolean *lederhosen* (it was rumored that he had his valet wear them for several years to break them in for him), his knee socks, his boots, and an old felt hat, and creep downstairs to avoid waking his daughters and grandchildren. He would clamber around the surrounding mountains with a gamekeeper as his only companion until eleven o'clock, then settle down at his desk for the rest of the day. Work was his most reliable antidote for the sorrows and frustrations of his life.

Francis Joseph had the knack of splendor but no taste for the artificial glitter of Court life. A state banquet at the Hofburg during his reign was an awesome ordeal for the guests. The magnificence of the uniforms and furnishings, the perfectly trained lackeys, the historic plate and crystal, the famous wines, the great blazing chandeliers (according to Eugene Bagger, one of the Emperor's biographers, their periodic crashing was the regretted but accepted cause of frequent casualties), made even the haughtiest royal visitors feel like parvenus. Since Francis Joseph did not believe in wasting time over his food, and detested small talk, he had trained the palace staff to serve and clear away a twelve-course dinner in less than an hour. A new course was served the moment the Emperor finished his plate, and guests at the bottom of the table were likely to have theirs whisked away before they had taken a mouthful. On army maneuvers the imperial table etiquette was simpler but even more Spartan. Once when Kaiser Wilhelm II, who had been invited to attend an important Austro-Hungarian field exercise, asked the Imperial Chief of Staff if he might have some champagne with his meals, Francis Joseph indignantly forbade it. "Not a drop," he growled, "let him drink beer."

In Austria the Emperor was the effective head of the government as well as the chief of state and commander-in-chief of the army; Francis Joseph's rule has been described as one of latent absolutism," and he was shrewd enough to preserve the element of latency whenever possible. He had some gift for administration, and unlike Nicholas II was not unwilling or afraid to delegate authority. The ramshackle political structure of the Empire, however, made it difficult to establish orderly channels of administration or efficient mechanism of co-ordination and control. As the Emperor aged, he inevitably lost touch with the increasingly complex problems of government, and real power slipped out of his hands into those of irresponsible bureaucrats governing in his name; the once admirable Austro-Hungarian military and civilian bureaucracy fell into a feudal anarchy of warring cliques or services, largely free from either democratic or autocratic controls. The consequences, as we shall see in a later chapter, were particularly grave in the fields of foreign and defense policy, but they were also disastrously felt in the domestic sphere.

Francis Joseph was too much of a Habsburg to identify himself exclusively with either the German or the Magyar ruling classes in his Empire; the master race to him was his own family. Autocracy seemed to him a sound principle, but he did not have a religious feeling about it, as Nicholas II did; what counted was maintaining the position of the dynasty. In all dynastic matters, small or great, the Emperor's policy was strict conformity to tradition. He humorlessly insisted that the guards on duty at the Imperial Palace present arms every time a carriage bearing a baby Archduke with a nursemaid entered or left the grounds. He tried to forbid Francis Ferdinand's morganatic marriage as he had forbidden Rudolph's divorce, and when the marriage eventually did take place, he permitted his courtiers to snub and humiliate the wife of the heir to the throne, even after he had reluctantly conferred the title of Duchess of Hohenberg on her. For a Habsburg to marry a commoner was a sin against the dynasty in the old Emperor's eyes, and the wages of sin had to be paid. In such matters he was a fanatic and a tyrant.

On the broader issues of national policy, including the crucial question of the "minorities," Francis Joseph could on occasion show himself extremely flexible. He was not too stubborn to make concessions to the developing national conscience of the peoples over whom he ruled; what he lacked was a political concept for reconciling their conflicting aspirations which the dynasty could champion, as it had once championed the concept of Christian unity in Europe. In this respect the rift between the Emperor and his heir—which was also a rift in the Court, in the administration, and in the Army—caused by Francis Ferdinand's marriage was doubly unfortunate for the Empire.

The case that some present-day Habsburg apologists make for Francis Ferdinand as an enlightened spirit who, if he had not been struck down by Balkan fanatics, might have transformed the Empire into the prototype of a supranational European community, does not seem wholly convincing; his character was probably too autocratic and his temper too reactionary to play such a role. He had an alert mind, however, and he unquestionably recognized the need for some radical solution to the nationalities problem. The little brain trust he gathered about him in his shadow cabinet at the Belvedere Palace included several bold and original thinkers. Under their influence the Archduke had once championed the cause of "Trialism"— the idea of converting the Dual Monarchy into a union of three national states, one of which would be created, largely at the expense of Hungary, by a partial liberation of the South Slavs. Later Francis Ferdinand came to the conclusion that this formula was inadequate as well as impractical, and, according to his admirers, was groping his way toward the concept of a democratic, multinational federation of equals, a true United States of Austria-Hungary, which if it could have been realized, would have saved the Habsburgs—not to mention Europe.

How far the Archduke really got in his intellectual gropings is immaterial. He was doubtless headed in the right general direction, but the old Emperor was not prepared to accept his errant and arrogant nephew, a mere whippersnapper in his forties, as a guide. Apart from personal considerations, Francis Joseph did not believe in experimenting with political novelties like federalism. It never occurred to him that in the ancient supranational tradition of his family he possessed, albeit in raw and imperfect form, an ultramodern antidote to the toxins of modern nationalism. He put his faith in the tried and tested—and unfailingly calamitous—nostrums of cautious expediency; a dram of repressive firmness, an ounce of gracious concession, a pinch of genteel trickery. It was in this spirit that the aged autocrat, confronted as we have seen earlier with the threat of Magyar separatism and harassed by left-wing agitation for electoral reform, hit on the idea of playing Austrian Socialists against Hungarian reactionaries and thereby inadvertently set in motion forces which were destined to plunge the last years of his reign into growing turmoil.

A few years before the war, an American journalist living in Vienna, Wolf von Schierbrand, attended a session of the Austrian Reichsrat (parliament) which, though it was by no means exceptional, left an indelible impression on his mind. In his entertaining and useful book, *Austria-Hungary: Polyglot Empire,* he gives the following description of the preposterous scene:

". . . the bulk of the 500 delegates or thereabouts whom I saw on entering the press gallery looked and behaved like a band of madmen. It was a question about the rights and privileges of one of the eight officially recognized 'national tongues,' I think it was Ruthenian, that had brought them all to such a fearful pitch . . . This is what burst upon my astonished view: About a score of men, all decently clad, were seated or standing each at his little desk. Some made infernal noise, violently opening and shutting the lids of these desks. Others emitted a blaring sound from little toy trumpets; others strummed jews-harps; still others beat snare drums. And at their head, like a bandmaster, stood a gray-bearded man of about 65, evidently the leader of this wilful faction, directing the whole pandemonium in volume and tempo . . .

"I was told that not only this Ruthenian fraction, but every other in the Reichsrat as well, in its fraction and committee rooms had stowed in a locked and safe place a complete assortment of such instruments of torture —whistles and sleigh bells, mouth harmonicas, cow bells and trombones . . ." (Other authorities include hunting-horns.)

Nationalist agitation and interracial friction were not new phenomena in the Habsburg Empire. All during the nineteenth century the ferment of nationalism had been working more and more intensely in ever-wider layers of the population. The Crown itself, practicing the classic imperial strategy of divide and rule, had more than once encouraged the trend by granting special concessions to ethnic groups, like the Czechs or the Magyars, who were strong enough to make serious trouble, or who, like the Poles in Galicia, were willing to act as Imperial Janizaries. Maintaining a constant, controlled strain between the different "minorities" was an ancient Habsburg tradition. After 1907, however, the situation got completely out of hand; Austria-Hungary was never quite the "prison of peoples" that hostile propagandists called it, but in the last years before the war it turned bit by bit into a madhouse of nationalities.

Though there were deeper reasons for this development, the universal suffrage law decided on by Francis Joseph in 1905 and finally put into effect in 1907 was a major factor. (It is by no means the only instance in history of a despotism undoing itself with reform.) In Hungary the threat of honest elections heightened the tension between the dominant Magyars and the subject races. In Austria the sudden enfranchisement of the illiterate peasant masses opened up a new Golconda to demagogic exploitation. The chronic tumult in parliament was one of its fruits.

All things considered, there was surprisingly little separatist sentiment in the Dual Monarchy. The chief exceptions, perhaps, were to be found in the Germanic "majority," itself; the followers of Georg von Schonerer and similar demagogues wanted the break-up of the Empire and an Austrian *Anschluss* with Hohenzollern Germany. Most of the "minorities" preferred putting up with the slovenly paternalism of Habsburg rule to being absorbed in either the German or the Russian empires. For a long time there seemed to be no other feasible alternatives. Between 1905 and 1914, however, there occurred several new developments in Europe, which, among other effects, had a revolutionary impact on the nationalities problem in Austria-Hungary (and which in turn were influenced by it). The time has come to turn to the southeast, picking up the winding Balkan road that finally led to Sarajevo.

CHAPTER 6

Sick Man's Legacy

THE worm-eaten Ottoman dynasty was the first of the great autocracies still standing in twentieth-century Europe to go down before the winds of change, and the resultant crash was more fateful than most contemporary observers realized. Today, in the wake of all the tempests and upheavals the world has witnessed since, we can better gauge the importance of the event. Though the monarchy was not formally abolished in Turkey until after the Great War, the overthrow of the absolutist regime there dates back to 1908. On July 23 of that year Sultan Abdul Hamid II, in a desperate, eventually futile attempt to save his throne, yielded to an ultimatum from a junta of military revolutionaries—the so-called Young Turks—and proclaimed a constitution. The reform brought about a real transfer of power that for all practical purposes put an end to seven centuries of Oriental, semitheocratic despotism in an empire, once the largest West of the Great Wall, which still stretched astride three continents from the Danube to the Indian Ocean, and from the Caucasus to the shores of Tripoli.

Modern Turkey understandably solemnizes the anniversary of July 23, 1908, as a great national holiday; for somewhat different reasons the date should be underscored in the calendar of our own historic outlook. Reading over the accounts of Western eyewitnesses who were present at the time in Constantinople (Istanbul), the ancient capital of the Byzantine emperors taken over by their Ottoman conquerors and successors, one has the feeling of reliving one of those moments of lucid pathos that often usher in an age of revolutionary turmoil, when for a brief span history seems to break free from the gravitational pull of destiny, and events retain only the inertia of innocence. Such a moment, for instance, was the famous Night of the

Fourth of August (1789) at the outset of the French Revolution, when the delegates of the nobility sitting in the Constituent Assembly spontaneously renounced their hereditary privileges. It was a similar eruption of hope, reason, fraternity, and reform, lasting for several days, that occurred in Istanbul in July 1908.

As soon as the newspapers carrying the Imperial proclamation appeared on the streets—in the early morning of July 24—lighthearted throngs, as if wakening from a nightmare of centuries, began to gather on the Galatea Bridge across the Golden Horn, and in the heart of Stambul, the city's original Byzantine nucleus. "Men and women in a common wave of enthusiasm, moved on radiating something extraordinary, laughing, weeping," a witness reported. "The motley rabble, the lowest pariahs, were going about in a sublime emotion, with tears running down their unwashed faces, the shop-keepers joining the procession without any concern for their goods."

In those days Istanbul, a disheveled but gleaming cluster of cities and suburbs scattered between Europe and Asia along the hilly shores of the Bosporus and the inland Sea of Marmora, was still the seat of government to a vast empire. Then as now, it was a fascinating jumble of East and West, of seediness and magnificence, but no doubt it was both more Oriental and more opulent than it is today. Along with the slender needles of its minarets and the domes of its mosques, there was more of the slatternly grace of the old Turkish quarters, spared by fire and progress, with their tall, narrow houses jutting over cobblestone streets, and their windows grilled with blue or green wooden lattice work. The street scene, even on normal days, was a vivid and exotic human tapestry, as it could hardly fail to be in the capital of an empire almost wholly made up of "minorities" at every stage of cultural development, ranging from the fierce Druse tribesmen of the Lebanon mountains or the desert Bedouins in their ragged, flowing robes, through the swarthy Anatolian peasant in his billowing trousers—the only authentic Turk of them all—to be slightly caricatural Paris or London elegance of the cosmopolitan aristocracy. Rarely could all these contrasts have been gaudier than they were on this day of cloudless revolution. The crowds were particularly thick around the Sublime Porte, the huge tasteless marble block that then housed the key ministries of the government (it has since been largely destroyed by fire) and in the square of Aya Sophia, the temple of the Holy Wisdom, the foremost basilica of Eastern Christendom—and to Christian subjects of the Empire the symbol of a never-healed historic traumatism—erected in the sixth century on the foundations of Constantine's original church, converted since 1453 into a Moslem mosque. From every convenient vantage point young officer-agitators with the white and red cockade of liberty pinned to the tunics of their Prussian-style uniforms harangued the people in the name of the revolutionary society calling itself the Committee of Union and Progress which had risen up against the Imperial authority a few weeks earlier in Macedonia and progressively won over the military forces sent to crush the revolt. Intoxicated with their own generous enthusiasms, the military revolutionaries promised freedom, brotherhood, and equality "under the same blue sky" for all the Sultan's subjects in a reborn Ottoman national commonwealth.

There was no fighting, nor any disorder, except of the joyful sort, and in the general euphoria even the self-deposed tyrant, miraculously transformed into an enlightened Western-style constitutional monarch, temporarily recovered the popularity forfeited in the course of a thirty-two-year reign marked by an unbroken succession of humiliating national defeats, by countless foreign and domestic treacheries, and by dreadful excesses of bloodsoaked repression. Abdul Hamid's career is an interesting example of political nature seemingly trying to imitate journalistic art; long known to newspaper readers of the West as The Red Sultan, Abdul the Damned, or the Ogre of Yildiz, Abdul Hamid, in so far as he was a monster at all, was a monster of apprehensiveness rather than of cruelty, but from the viewpoint of his unfortunate subjects he might as well have been Bluebeard or Caligula. His pathological dread of assassination had led him more than once in blind panic to shoot down inmates of his palace with the little pearl-handled automatic that never left his person (he always handled it expertly even when he was too frightened to think straight)—and he had just as delusively, if more coolly, ordered the appalling massacre of Armenians—some 86,000 of them by the most conservative count—suspected of mass disloyalty. Despite these and many other horrors that lay between the Sultan and his people, a crowd of sixty thousand of them on July 26 stormed the gates of Yildiz Kiosk, the strange fortress-palace-menagerie on a hill above the city, looking out across the narrowing of the waters toward the shores of Asia—not to lynch the aged ex-despot, but to acclaim him. When Abdul Hamid appeared on the balcony, looking shrunken and owl-like in his gold-encrusted state uniform, with his great beaked nose, his dark, fevered eyes, his cheeks carefully rouged as usual and his beard dyed the traditional red, the crowd greeted him with hysterical devotion; men sobbed and wept as the Sultan—who notoriously had never kept a promise in his life—swore to uphold the constitution which the army had forced him at gunpoint to accept three days earlier.

It must have been a curious spectacle, but no less extraordinary and colorful scenes were taking place at the time everywhere throughout the capital, in fact throughout much of the sprawling Euro-Afro-Asian Empire whose jumble of antagonistic races, religions, and cultures made Austria-Hungary by comparison look almost homogeneous (just as the archaic, corrupt Ottoman administrative institutions made those of the Dual Monarchy seem modern, dynamic, and even rational). "Murder ceased," noted a contemporary European observer, "there was no thieving . . . Pacifists, idealists, and some others had flocked from all over Europe to see the vulture turn into a dove of peace." Age-old intercommunal hatreds that Abdul Hamid and his predecessors for centuries back had nurtured with deft, devoted hands, convinced that universal spite and suspicion were the surest cornerstones of empire, seemed to evaporate like miasmas of the night. Some of the examples cited by contemporary witnesses appear even more remarkable in retrospect than they did at the time. Jews and Arabs publicly embraced; Christian Armenians, an ancient, once-independent people of Asia Minor, exchanged the kiss of forgiveness with Moslem Kurds who a few years earlier had been incited to slaughter them; Phanariot Greeks, descendants of Constantinople's original Byzantine population, fraternally clasped the descendants of their Turkish conquerors—not to mention their hardly-less-hated Bulgar or Macedonian fellow Christians from the unliberated Balkans. Turkish officers in uniform attended a Requiem Mass for the victims of the Armenian massacres.

All had been subjects, that is virtually slaves, of the Ottoman autocracy, and it was in the name of all that the young officers of the Committee of Union and Progress, nominally Turkish Moslems for the most part, actually free-thinkers steeped in the ideas of the French Revolution—preserved, like flies in amber, in the traditions of the European Masonic lodges of Salonika and the capital—had risen up against their common secular master, the Sultan, who was at the same time the Caliph of Islam, the successor of the Prophet Mohammed, and as such the Shadow of God on Earth to 300,-000,000 orthodox Moslems throughout the world. The real paradox was much deeper, graver, and more complex than that, however.

For centuries the Ottoman despotism had been an inflamed tumor in the sensitive underbelly of Europe. The processes of retraction and internal decay had gradually transformed it during the nineteenth century into a kind of localized malignancy—painful, debilitating, but not immediately fatal. In applying to it the rough surgery of military revolution, the Young Turks of 1908 achieved a temporary relief—expressed in the naive popular rejoicings during the July days in Constantinople—but provoked a deadly metastasis that helped to bring about the vast and multiple revolutionary disorders the world has since experienced. Before attempting to analyze this process it will be useful to trace some of the main channels of Ottoman history and to consider more closely the personal role of Abdul Hamid, one of destiny's most sinister, but curious and pitiable instruments.

By certain reckonings, the House of Osman, which ruled the Ottoman Empire (Ottoman is a corruption of Osman) from its foundation in 1288 to its end in 1922, is the longest-lived dynasty known to history. The claim involves some semantic complications, but the 634-year lifespan of the empire itself is impressive by any count. For centuries it was the world's largest power—in its heyday it held substantial remnants of the ancient empires of Egypt, Assyria, Babylon, Persia, Macedonia, Rome, and Byzantium—and in a military sense it was for long periods the most formidable one. It was also one of the oddest, though not most attractive, human polities ever to exercise wide-spread and lasting dominion.

Like the Habsburgs, the Osmanlis never put down firm national roots. Osman I (1258–1325), who founded the dynasty, belonged to a Turkish-speaking tribe of people that had recently migrated from Central Asia to settle in Anatolia (the Asiatic core of modern Turkey), up against the Byzantine frontier, as vassals of the neighboring Seljuks, the more civilized descendants of earlier Turkish invaders, who then ruled in Bagdad. The hulking but sclerotic empire of Christian Byzantium was both a permanent menace and a permanent temptation to the weaker, though more warlike, Moslem societies on its southern flank. Need and greed combined to develop in the Anatolian marches bands of Moslem *ghazis*—fighters for the Faith—who were at the same time part brigands and part mercenary border guards. Osman inherited one of these crude fighting machines from his father. No doubt it was composed to a considerable measure of his own kinsmen but it also included many recruits from the more settled Islamic lands. As Osman and his successors extended their conquests, they attracted or pressed into service new recruits—often hasty and purely nominal converts to Islam—from the subject populations, thereby intensifying both the cosmopolitan, or colonialist, and the secular character of their armies; the Ottoman Empire that came into being increasingly took the shape of a supranational power system ostensibly dedicated to the propagation of Islam, but essentially concerned with the aggrandizement of its own chiefs and cadres.

From a brotherhood of free warriors, the Ottoman hierarchy turned into a slave society that anticipated by centuries certain aspects of contemporary totalitarianism. It recruited its members by simply taking them from their parents—usually Christian—in early childhood and subjecting them to a conditioning process of almost Pavlovian ruthlessness which simultaneously castrated them of their humanity and trained them for specific functions in the state. Those with military aptitudes were sent to the corps of Janizaries, the shock troops of the Ottoman armies, and for several centuries probably the most dreaded fighting force in the world. The intellectuals were trained for the civil service, the court, and the government.

Such a system works, as we know from examples much closer to us, but it also has drawbacks that contemporary admirers of totalitarian efficiency would do well to study. By the early nineteenth century the admirable Janizaries had become a permanent menace to the throne that employed them and a reformist sultan—Abdul Hamid's grandfather, Mahmud—after vain attempts to impose discipline, ordered the whole corps put to death —its strength at that time was about 25,000 men. As for the civil service, whose efficiency for long was unmatched by any in the West, by the early twentieth century it had become a byword for corruption, laziness, and disloyalty. The rise of Ottoman power was, of course, swifter and more spectacular than its decline. Orkhan (1326–1359), the son of the dynasty's founder, exploited factional strife in the Byzantine Empire to gain himself a solid bridgehead on the European shore of the Dardanelles. In 1389 the destruction of Serbian power on the famous field of Kossovo opened most of southeastern Europe to the Ottoman invaders. In 1453 the Sultan Mohammed II, the Conqueror (1451–1481), stormed Constantinople, then defeating Venice, the great naval power of the Eastern Mediterranean, overran Albania and Bosnia; he also seized the Crimea and the adjacent Black Sea coasts. With the occupation of Constantinople and the extinction of the Paleologus dynasty, the Ottoman Empire became the political heir of Byzantium and took over many of its administrative institutions, along with the refinements and the vices of Byzantine civilization. (The so-called Turkish bath, for example, was actually the Byzantine version of a Roman institution.) The high-water mark of Ottoman expansion was reached in the sixteenth century under Suleiman the Magnificent (1520–1566) and his successors, when much of Central Europe, practically all of Greece and the Greek Islands, vast tracts in southern Russia, and North Africa, as far west as Algiers, fell under the Ottoman sway.

Today the traveler in Greece and the Balkan countries easily identifies the cities and the villages which remained until the threshold of the twentieth century under Ottoman rule by the lingering atmosphere of Oriental squalor and lethargy, "like dirt ringing an old bath-tub," that still marks them. It was the long night of Turkish colonialism, one of the deep traumatisms of European history, that bred the nightmare-politics of the Balkan peninsula; the flashes at Sarajevo were among the fatal discharges of tensions of hatred built up over the centuries between oppressors and victims, between the various rival clans of native traitors and avengers. The Ottoman yoke does not always seem to have lain harshly on the Christian peoples of Europe— some welcomed it in preference to Venetian corruption or indigenous anarchy—but it was nearly always stultifying to them. This was particularly true during the last two or three centuries of the empire when the gradual decay of Ottoman dynasty chained its subject peoples to a political corpse.

Starting in the seventeenth century, the Habsburg and Romanov empires, with their stronger technological and political bases, began to push back the Ottoman frontiers. Then, following the French Revolution, came the Nationalist awakening in Europe. Greece was the first to revolt against Ottoman rule, followed by the resurgent kingdom of Serbia. Throughout the rest of the nineteenth century the Balkans were in constant revolutionary ferment. Even the Christian Armenians of Asiatic Turkey began to stir. France and England, in the hot flush of colonial expansion, took over respectively Algeria and Egypt, though the latter remained nominally for a time under Ottoman suzerainty. By the middle of the century ambitious politicians in Moscow and Vienna were sure that the fairest fruit of all —control of the straits—was ripe for the plucking.

This fabulous waterway that divides Europe from Asia has been an objective of warfare back to the period when history is indistinguishable from legend. Jason passed through the straits on his way to the Caucasus in search of the fleeces—in the plural—which the Caucasians suspended in mountain torrents to trap the flakes of gold the streams deposited on them. It was not a face which launched a thousand ships, and burned the topless towers of Ilion, but the desire of the Achaean trader-pirates to penetrate into the Black Sea, barred to them as long as Troy remained in the basin of the Sea of Marmora. The Sea of Marmora, indeed, is a natural prison for shipping, which could not have been better designed for the purpose of permitting a nation holding both its European and Asiatic banks to control absolute passage through this strategic bottleneck. Almost landlocked, it is entered through two narrow straits. From the Aegean, the entrance is through the Dardanelles—the swimmable Hellespont of the ancients—running along the peninsula of Gallipoli on the European side, where archaeologists have located the capital of the Trojan kingdom. From the Black Sea, the entrance is through the somewhat shorter Bosporus, so narrow it can be closed by chains, and not enough of an obstacle to prevent European Istanbul and Asiatic Scutari from being parts of the same city. Running these two gauntlets by ruse or surprise is virtually impossible.

The international importance of the straits was intensified when modern Russia came into being. "From the moment that Russia achieved something of political unity," the British historian Marriott wrote, "from the moment she realized her economic potentialities, the question of access to the Black Sea, of free navigation on its waters, and free egress from them into the Mediterranean became not merely important, but paramount."

Free passage of the straits became vital to Russia, whose great waterways of the Dniester, the Don, the Bug, and the Kuban empty into the Black Sea, when the Ukraine was converted from grazing country into one of the world's richest granaries. Practically all of the grain exported from this region went through the straits, and enough other exports as well, so that on the eve of World War I 60 per cent of Russia's outgoing seaborne trade passed this way, which meant 45 per cent of all the exports of the Russian Empire. But if control of the straits was vital for Russia, it was vital also to those who wished to hold her in check. The Marquis de Caulaincourt suggested to Napoleon that in view of Russia's predominance of interests there, she might be permitted to hold the Dardanelles. "Constantinople!" Napoleon cried. "Never! That means the empire of the world!"

Napoleon was doubtless exaggerating, but to nineteenth-century diplomacy it seemed clear that for any one of the great European powers to get control of the Straits would upset the always precarious European balance; only the most elaborate system of compensations and safeguards for the others could avert war in such a case. The danger of Austro-Russian rivalry for possession of the straits leading to a major conflict was considered especially grave. The easiest way to avoid trouble was evidently, therefore, to leave the "Sick Man of Europe"—as the British statesman Gladstone had once termed the Ottoman Empire—in possession of the vital passage. This implied an unspoken gentlemen's agreement among the great powers—after the Russo-Turkish War of 1877 it was formalized in some measure by the Treaty of Berlin—to confine their plundering of the invalid's estate to such peripheral tidbits as Bosnia or Egypt, and to refrain from asserting any too-exclusive claims of predominant influence over the remainder.

There were two weak spots in this otherwise sensible understanding. One is that it put extreme demands on the self-restraint of the great powers, who from time to time could not resist the temptation of seeking through intrigue or violence to enhance their interests in the Ottoman Empire at the expense of their rivals. The Ottoman rulers, especially Abdul Hamid, aggravated the tensions thus generated by systematically playing off one Western nation against another. An even greater threat to the status quo along the straits, upon which the tranquillity of Europe depended, was the dry rot eating away the basic structures of the Empire.

Like the Byzantine emperors before them, but to an even more extreme degree, the Ottoman dynasty ruled over a political conglomerate of semidetached protectorates and unassimilated ethnic minorities. From Byzantium, long the victim of Western European colonialist penetration, the Ottomans had inherited the so-called millet system of quasi-autonomous foreign colonies, originally planted by contemporary European powers like Venice, Genoa, Amalfi, Pisa, Ancona, and Narbonne, each with its own churches, schools, and courts administered by governors from the home countries. The Turks continued this system of special regimes for minority communities and extended it to large new units like the Greeks in Turkey proper. Suleiman the Magnificent even signed a treaty with Francis I of France according similar privileges to the latter's subjects. Besides creating precedents for various European powers later to appoint themselves the protectors of racial groups inside the Ottoman frontiers, as the Russians were fond of doing on behalf of the Bulgars and other Balkan Slavs, the millet system doubtless played a major role in preventing the different peoples of the empire from eventually knitting together into a single nation.

On the other hand, the tolerance which the Ottoman sultans manifested toward Christian and other minorities in their empire did not go quite deep enough for it to evolve into a multi-racial commonwealth. The reef on which brotherhood constantly splintered was the dynasty's traditional policy of exploiting Islam for political ends by combining the sultanate and the caliphate in one office. Claiming the Moslem title of the Shadow of God on Earth while acting as the secular head of an empire in which the Christian "minorities" outnumbered the Moslem "majority" was not merely an anomaly but a congenital blunder. It not only antagonized the Christians but it delivered the Sultans more or less completely—depending on how seriously they took their roles as Caliph—into the hands of the *ulemas,* the traditionalist and professionally fanatical Moslem priesthood.

Perhaps the most striking symbol of Ottoman decadence—and the actual root of much of it—was the sultanate's harem system. In the morning of the empire the unveiled Turkish women were the free and respected companions of their warrior-husbands. With the accumulation of wealth based on conquest, they gradually changed from partners into luxuries, and finally into luxury-objects. The superabundance of female slaves that were one of the prized spoils of war led to a kind of erotic inflation; the Sultans, and their principal warlords acquired increasingly imposing retinues of concubines, and the harem came into being. At first it was no doubt both a useful and—from the owner's viewpoint—an agreeable institution; it provided distraction for the Sultans while adding splendor to their reigns and serving as an inspiration to their captains. Bit by bit, however, the conspicuous-consumption principle, and the absolute-dominion principle got out of control, as they are apt to do in all societies, and the harem turned into a social cancer that eventually devoured both the ruler and the realm. Byzantium, of course, made its contribution to the social hypertrophy of the harem, many of whose more elaborate rituals can be traced back to the *Gynasceum* of the Byzantine emperors. Some of the most exotic harem functionaries—that is the Master of the Girls, the Keeper of the Parrots, and the Chief Nightingale Keeper—were copied from Byzantine originals, and reflect the Byzantine talent for making even luxury as complicated as possible.

From about the fourteenth century onward, the Osmanlis no longer legally married their queens—who thus ceased to be queens—and depended alike for their pleasure and for their posterity upon their slaves, thereby completing their own enslavement. Suleiman, it is true, did go through a ceremony of marriage with one of his slaves, the Christian Khurrem, more widely known as Roxellana, but the exception aggravated as well as confirmed the rule. Roxellana's domination of her master launched the 150-year "Reign of Women" in Turkish history.

In a more institutional sense, for a good many centuries the harem continued to rule the Empire. For the Sultans, it became the main setting of their lives. It forged a chain about them in infancy, which most of them were never able to break. The job of fighting had been turned over to mercenaries, the job of thinking and governing to foreign-born vizier-slaves, while the spoiled and frightened Sultans took refuge from all their problems among the women whose constant, self-interested adulation prevented them from developing the will, decisiveness, or firmness which are necessarily stifled in an atmosphere of chronic indulgence. It was not the master's virile lusts, but the women's covert ambitions which dominated the seraglio.

The fact that the harem was a whole slave society led to disastrous results. Its considerable population—under Abdul Medjid, the Red Sultan's father, there were 900 women in the harem, served by innumerable domestics (300 cooks alone), black and white eunuchs, mutes, guards, pages, etc.—being utterly dependent upon the favor of a despot, waged continual war among one another for first place in that favor, using the arts of sycophancy, flattery, bribery, subordination, spying, denunciation, wheedling, and pandering to all the weaknesses and vices of the Sultan, which were sedulously cultivated to provide opportunities to curry favor by satisfying them. It was in this atmosphere that the future Sultans spent the formative years of their lives.

While the women strove to exploit the influence which, even though slaves, their charms gave them over the Sultan, their custodians, the eunuchs, used them as instruments to sway the ruler. Their ability to do so was facilitated by the fact that for centuries they were authorized at will to apply the whip to the carefully tended bodies designed to beguile the Sultan. Often the Kislar Agha, the chief black eunuch, "Guardian of the Gates of Felicity"—usually a mountain of a man, for the same outrage which turned whites into drawn, emaciated skeletons made the blacks monsters of obesity—was the most important man in the kingdom, though he was usually a coarse, ignorant Negro slave. This indirect influence which the eunuchs exercised over the Sultans continued the direst domination which they acquired during their boyhood, when the eunuchs were entrusted with the education of the royal princes—with such education as they were permitted to have. It varied at different periods, but there was no epoch in which it was considered seemly for the princes to receive any genuine schooling, and the eunuchs who taught them up to the age of eleven had every incentive to maintain their royal charges in an ignorance even more dense than their own. By Abdul Hamid's time, the princes' school in the harem did make some pretense of teaching its pupils—they were told romanticized and inaccurate stories about their glorious forebears, acquired a smattering of French and a touch of musical appreciation, and for the rest read the Koran. A few of the most gifted were allowed to consult the ancient poets, in Persian and Arabic. But the subjects an apprentice-ruler might seem most to need—history and politics—were definitely forbidden. There *was* a good school in the harem, with a four-teen-year course and a curriculum running all the way from cultural sub-jects to hairdressing, but it was for the royal pages, not for the royal princes. Its students were Georgians, Circassians, Armenians, Persians, Austrians, Hungarians, Russians, Greeks, Italians, Bosnians, Bohemians, Germans and Swiss, for they were all slaves, but never Turks.

The harem not only failed to produce rulers of quality; it barely suc-ceeded in producing heirs in sufficient quantity to maintain the succession. A ruler who counts his women by the hundred should not be plagued, as some European sovereigns are, with the fear of having no issue. But ex-cessive sexual indulgence, which tended to render the Sultans sterile or impotent, made their progeny less numerous than it might otherwise have been—Abdul Medjid, despite a renowned collection of erotic drugs and gadgets, was impotent at thirty-five—and their offspring, once in this world, had a better than even chance of being very quickly ushered out of it again.

In the intense rivalry which reigned among the women of the harem, there were two chief objectives. Though the Sultan as a rule had no wife, he usually named four favorites as Kadins, or concubines. The ranking concubine, or First Kadin, was often a power in the kingdom. But the status of concubine was uncertain—divorce was a mere formality, and the Bosporus was handy—and therefore the real prize was to become Sultane Valide—the mother of the Sultan. She became head of the harem, and the fact of having borne a Sultan secured her position for life. If, therefore, it was the goal of every ambitious woman in the harem to bear the Sultan a son and bring him to the throne, so it was the object of every other woman in the harem to prevent either the birth or the accession of any son but her own.

The perils of a potential Sultan thus began before birth, and the first care of an expectant mother was to keep her pregnancy secret as long as possible, no easy feat in the public life of the harem, shared with several hundred other jealous women. Once a child was brought into the world, the second problem was to preserve it from "accidents"—also difficult, as is evidenced, for instance, by the fact that of the thirty or so children sired by Abdul Medjid half died in babyhood.

The princes had to escape not only the jealousy of the women of the harem, but also that of their half-brothers, as a result of a rule of succes-sion which passed the Sultanate not from father to son but, as long as the supply held out, from brother to brother in the order of age. This caused every Sultan to regard with distrust the half-brothers ready to step into his shoes, many of them often not at all scrupulous about the means for emptying these shoes. Bayazit, who became Sultan in 1389, solved the problem by putting his younger brothers to death. The simple logic of this method appealed to his successors, who followed it for several centuries.

Those heirs to the Ottoman Empire who survived remained in their youth prisoners of the harem, cut off completely from the outer world, and denied even an elementary education. For centuries, the typical successor to the throne was an ignorant old man, worn out by sexual excess, accustomed only to the society of slaves and eunuchs, and imbued by the latter with the fear, hatred, and suspicion of all the world which their own fate had developed in them. For generations the harem system had revealed itself an almost infallible hatchery of mis-rule; in nineteenth century Europe it could scarcely fail to prove itself as well a predestined recipe for revolution. Western technological progress, and even Western political ideas, were beginning to transform Turkish society at many levels, but within the Sultan's harem the only reform in centuries had been the introduction by Abdul Hamid's father of the four-poster bed.

It was in one of these beds that Abdul Hamid, himself, was born, on September 18, 1842. He started life inauspiciously, even by harem standards. His mother was a consumptive Circassian slave, who was more hated in the harem than any woman presumptuous enough to bear the Sultan a male heir had necessarily to be. She was never well after Abdul Hamid's birth, and gave her son a thoroughly unhealthy start, physically and mentally, by keeping him shut up with her in her sickroom until she died; he was seven at the time. He was unpopular with his brothers and sisters—they accused him of being a tattletale—and his father denied him the affection that he lavished upon Abdul Hamid's older brother, Murad. Small and frail and furtive, with his huge nose and heavy-lidded eyes, the future Red Sultan was an unprepossessing child, and he was bitterly aware of it.

Abdul Hamid received the usual harem education—or lack of it; history and politics were still taboo. What he learned he picked up as a result of his own natural curiosity. His teachers reported with disapproval that he showed an interest in everything concerning the Empire, always considered an unsuitable study for the princes who would one day be called upon to reign over it. His passion for figures, not noticeable in many previous Sultans, was also discouraged by his tutors, but he managed to instruct himself in them by poring over the account books of the eunuch who acted as harem treasurer, and to such good effect that as he grew older he began to speculate on the Galata Bourse and accumulated a private fortune of some $350,000 before he acceded to the throne. He acquired a knowledge of French by sitting in, at the age of sixteen, on the lessons that were being given to a married sister.

What the harem did teach the future Sultan was wiliness and fear, the two subjects it knew best. He learned the art of intrigue from its women, and fear from the eunuchs. He had the good luck when his mother died to be entrusted as a foster child to one of his father's Kadins, named Peresto, a woman of unusual intelligence for a harem beauty, to whom he probably owed much of the mental agility he later displayed. He also struck up a strangely close and lasting friendship with his uncle's mother, the Valide Sultane (dowager), Pertevale, the first lady of the harem, and a past mistress of all its ruses.

Thanks to the kindness of these two women, Abdul grew up with one part of his warped and shriveled personality almost straight and whole. He was perhaps incapable of love, but he liked women, and when he eventually inherited the imperial harem he was a gentle, considerate master to its inmates; his mild lusts were a healthy contrast, as far as they went, to the erotic excesses and aberrations of his ancestors. As a young man, Abdul Hamid even managed for a while to escape from the cloying embrace of the harem through an outside liaison with a European woman— an innocuously sentimental affair with a little Belgian *modiste*.

From earliest childhood on, Abdul Hamid lived in fear as in a private cloud that he carried with him—the protean, all-pervading anxiety of the neurotic, cowering before the teeming phantoms of the imagination, occasionally evaporating in the face of real danger. He was morbidly afraid of disease (his consumptive mother), electricity (after he became Sultan he reluctantly allowed the architects to install electric lighting in his palace, but not a telephone), and above all, crowds. The harem eunuchs, hated by the common people for their graft and arrogance, had the dread of the crowd in their own bones; they gave to little Abdul Hamid's nightmares the specific shape of the lurking assassin. After he mounted the throne, this childhood bogie, rendered plausible by the palace tumults and treacheries which throughout Ottoman history had often done away with his predecessors, grew to monstrous dimension. Feeling insecure in the old waterfront palace in the city, Abdul Hamid chose Yildiz Park, a commanding position high above the Bosporus, and built himself a new one, Yildiz Kiosk, in the scattered style of a nomad encampment, that formed a strongly walled fortress. The parakeets, peacocks, monkeys, and other furred or feathered creatures that also made it an exotic menagerie were conceived as a kind of supplementary alarm system, to warn of approaching enemies. To foil possible conspirators, Abdul Hamid kept shifting beds—he had plenty to choose from—and at times of special stress the most important responsibility of the duty-concubine who shared with him the bed he had chosen for the night was to make sure that no one, or no thing, was hiding beneath it. The kitchens where the Sultan's meals were cooked had barred windows, and the food arrived on his table in sealed containers; even so, the chief chamberlain had to taste each dish before the Sultan did.

The very cows in the model farm at Yildiz were kept under guard, to make sure that no one tampered with the ruler's milk. When he was obliged to appear in public, the Sultan always had one of his little sons ride beside him in the Imperial carriage, as a psychological deterrent to assassination. To give himself the illusion of freedom in his self-imposed prison, Abdul Hamid had several fully staffed cafes set up in the grounds of Yildiz for his exclusive use, and he would often stroll into one or the other of them, take a solitary seat at one of the tables, clap his hands for the waiter, and on leaving would even fling down a coin to pay for his coffee—which, however, could only be prepared for him by the *Cafedfi Bachi,* the Royal Coffeemaker. His other relaxations, apart from the usual harem sports, were riding in the Yildiz Park, rowing on its artificial lake, carving elaborate wood scrollwork, playing the piano—Offenbach was his favorite composer—and reading the adventures of Sherlock Holmes.

Abdul Hamid's phobias and his pathological cowardice were personal afflictions, but they had a historic component—not to mention historic consequences. Like such European colleagues as Nicholas II and Wilhelm II—who underneath his bluster was almost as great a coward—Abdul Hamid was chronically unnerved by fear of the future itself. He was a natural-born reactionary who, in an age of swift and universal change, not only identified himself with the old order but tried to set the political clock back to an earlier time that he himself had never known. (Perhaps the hundred clocks whose ticking, audible in every room, startled Western visitors to the Sultan's pavilion at Yildiz were one symptom of his obsession.) Unlike the other two regressive autocrats, however, Abdul Hamid was neither a weakling nor a myth-addict. His nerves were ragged, but his will was steely, and his appreciation of immediate political events, within the limits of his education, was generally clearheaded. The harem, scandalized by two modernizing, reformist Sultans—Abdul Medjid, with some Western prodding, had once tumbled out of bed long enough to sign a decree granting all his subjects equal rights under the law—had taught Abdul Hamid as a child to equate social progress with dynastic and national humiliation. He was determined to restore the autocratic prerogative to its ancient splendor, but he was intelligent enough to realize that progress can only be fought with progress; he gave a prudent welcome to technological modernism wherever it could help him to crush liberal reform. He kept in his office a map of the Ottoman Empire as its frontiers stood in Suleiman's day to remind himself of its lost grandeur, but he was realistically aware that its weak remnants could only be saved from colonial subjection or dismemberment by craft and dissimulation, and by playing one powerful enemy against another.

Abdul Hamid demonstrated his tactical gifts in maneuvering his way to supreme power. In 1876, a palace revolution instigated by a secret society called the Young Ottomans—the political ancestors of the Young Turks—deposed the reigning Sultan, Abdul Hamid's uncle Abdul Aziz, in the name of constitutionalism and progress.[1] The thirty-four-year-old prince's older brother, Murad, was next in line of succession, but he was a hopeless drunkard—Abdul Hamid was rumored to have discreetly encouraged his vice. After three months he was declared insane, and deposed. Abdul Hamid, who had somehow convinced the revolutionaries that he was a liberal at heart, succeeded to the throne with their support. Murad was locked up in his own harem—the uncle had conveniently committed suicide —but otherwise treated with every kindness; the new Sultan saw to it that his brother's cellar never ran dry.

A few months after his accession Abdul Hamid, on December 23, 1876, proclaimed the constitution for which the Young Ottomans and their sympathizers had been clamoring. The move was beautifully timed; an international conference—which the Ottoman Empire had not been invited to attend, but to which it was the involuntary host—was then sitting in Constantinople. It had been called by Queen Victoria's subtle Prime Minister, Benjamin Disraeli, following some specially frightful Turkish massacres in Bulgaria, with the double objective of protecting the Christian minorities and of dissuading the Russians from seizing the Dardanelles in a fit of righteous indignation. The delegates of the European Concert, meeting in the Russian embassy, were within a few commas of completing a joint ultimatum to the Sublime Port demanding autonomy for the Christians of Bulgaria and Bosnia when an artillery salvo announced the proclamation of a constitution—the first one in Ottoman history. That salvo blew up the conference; the constitution gave the Sultan's subjects all the guaranties they could ask for—on paper—and after such a gesture there could be no further question of international sanctions.

Two weeks after the European diplomats had packed their bags and gone home, Abdul Hamid put his constitution into effect in a somewhat disconcerting way. Invoking an apparently innocuous amendment which he had drafted himself, he banished the document's chief author, his liberal grand vizier (premier), Midhat Pasha, whose help had enabled him to mount the throne. Without Midhat, the constitution soon became a dead letter. This Asiatic duplicity revolted the conscience of nineteenth-century Europe—especially in Vienna and St. Petersburg. Despite the rivalry in the Balkans between Russia and Austria-Hungary, Czar Alexander II wrung a personal promise from his cousin, Francis Joseph, to keep hands off if Russia undertook to chastize the treacherous Turk, and in April 1877 the chastisement got under way.

[1] In addition to his other failings, Abdul Aziz had been addicted to such unprogressive amusements as releasing cratefuls of hens and roosters in his harem and trying to catch them amid the shrieks or giggles of his wives.

Less than a year after the war had started, the Russians were camped at San Stefano, seven miles from Constantinople, where, on March 3, 1878, Turkey was forced to sign a peace treaty which practically pushed her out of Europe: Rumania, Serbia, Montenegro, and Bosnia-Herzegovina were to become completely independent, and a Greater Bulgaria under Russian domination was to be created, taking in, among other territories, most of Macedonia.

The terms were supposed to be secret, but Abdul Hamid carefully allowed to leak toward London and Vienna such details as he thought might seem most alarming to those capitals. (No doubt his childhood training as a tattletale helped.) Austria suddenly began to have second thoughts about the gentleman's agreement that had been arrived at between her Emperor and the Czar, and started to mobilize her forces to check the Russians. When Queen Victoria was informed that the Russians were on the shores of the Sea of Marmora, she said: "Then they must get out!" The Russo-British crisis of 1878 introduced a new word—jingoism—into the English language when the British public began singing, *We don't want to fight, but by jingo if we do, we've got the men, we've got the ships, we've got the money too"*—and then, in a rousing *tutti: "The Russians shall* not *have Constantinople."*

The men and the ships, propelled by the money, anchored within firing range of the Russians, stayed there for six months, and Russia in fact did not get Constantinople—nor even the territory stipulated in the Treaty of San Stefano, which did not go that far. Pressure by the other European powers obliged her to submit the terms of the Treaty of San Stefano to the Congress of Berlin, which met under the chairmanship of Bismarck in June and July, 1878. It was preceded by a deal between England and Turkey in which Britain received Cyprus. As payment for Cyprus, which he called "the key to eastern Asia," Disraeli got back for Turkey two-thirds of what she had ceded in the Treaty of San Stefano. Serbia, Montenegro and Rumania remained independent, but Bosnia-Herzegovina, though handed over to Austrian administration, was theoretically under Austrian trusteeship in behalf of Turkey; Bulgaria was to be a principality under nominal Ottoman suzerainty.

More important than what the Congress of Berlin did to Turkey was what Turkey at the Congress of Berlin did to Europe. Agreement at Berlin to leave the Ottoman Empire in control of the straits averted a European war, but thanks to Abdul Hamid's adroit diplomatic well-poisoning, the underlying Austro-Russian rivalry was permanently envenomed. The temporary award of Bosnia-Herzegovina to the Dual Monarchy had an even more inflammatory effect on Austro-Serbian relations. Once again the old world diplomacy displayed its genius for creating the irreparable while postponing the inevitable. In one respect Abdul

Hamid overplayed his hand. The smoldering animosity between Russia and Austria-Hungary growing out of the Russo-Turkish war and the settlement of Berlin burned away the foundations of the *Drei Kaiserbund,* the dynastic entente of the three emperors—Russia, Austria-Hungary, Germany —a slightly anemic descendant of Metternich's Holy Alliance, which Bismarck had cemented in 1873. In so doing, the Sultan dealt a new blow to the solidarity of monarchs and to the divine right of autocrats, in which he himself was a fanatical believer. No doubt he was unaware of this—just as his fellow autocrats in Europe were unaware that the wasting sickness of the Osmanli dynasty might be contagious.

Yet the interaction of domestic political regression—which in Abdul Hamid's reign was the gravest symptom of dynastic decay—and of an Ottoman foreign policy aimed at fomenting discord between the great powers, should have been clear to all. As soon as the war with Russia was over, and while the European crisis that it produced was simmering, Abdul Hamid returned to his lifework of resurrecting Ottoman absolutism.

"I made a mistake in wanting to imitate my father," he declared in dissolving the short-lived parliament. "From now on I shall follow in the footsteps of my grandfather, Sultan Mahmud, who understood that only by force can one move the people with whose guardianship Allah has entrusted me."

Like Nicholas II and other belated champions of neoabsolutism, Abdul Hamid was not content to lay down basic policy; he interfered in the smallest details of its execution. For all practical purposes he was his own foreign minister and his own minister of the interior. The result was that though he rose every morning between four and five, and worked until late in the night, he rarely managed to catch up with his paperwork. He also felt that it was beneath the Sultan's dignity to confer with his ministers or palace officials; either he contented himself with giving his orders while the subordinate listened in silence and then departed to execute them, or he listened while the subordinate gave his report, and then commented upon it with a brief word, a nod, or simply a frown; it was the subordinate's duty to translate these symptoms of the imperial will into a formal decree—an administrative technique which not infrequently inverted the roles of bureaucrat and autocrat.

By nature Abdul Hamid was a gentle creature who shrank from violence and had no penchant for inflicting wanton cruelty on his subjects. It was usually fear that goaded him into acts of inhumanity—he once forced himself to listen from behind a lattice while some wretches who had tried to assassinate him were questioned under torture—but he could also be ruthless in punishing or avenging any slights upon the imperial dignity. As a fundamentalist of harem tradition, he is said to have ordered the execution of a slave girl who had been one of his pets from her childhood because she committed the offense of flirting with his son. Abdul Hamid lacked the temperament to be a political fanatic, but he was something perhaps more dangerous—a political pedant. He was a prig of despotism.

Hoping to cut off liberalism at the roots, the Sultan forbade the teaching of literature and history in his realms. The foremost Ottoman liberal, he exiled Midhat Pasha, was lured back with promises of high office, then dispatched as governor to the remote province of Syria, and finally banished to Arabia where on Abdul Hamid's orders, he was murdered. Though it is doubtful that Abdul Hamid had any deep religious convictions, after the Turkish war he delivered himself into the hands of the retrograde Moslem clergy, and began to put increasing stress on the hitherto largely ritual function of Caliph. Throughout the Moslem world the late nineteenth century witnessed a reaction against Western influence, which was in part an Islamic Reformation, in part a retreat back into the ancient night of Oriental superstition and fanaticism. Influenced by a retinue of zealots and adventurers from the backward Arabian provinces, the Sultan gave powerful encouragement to the emerging doctrine of Pan-Islamism, the dream of a united Islamic community of 300,000,000 souls, from Java to Morocco, from Zanzibar to the steppes of Turkistan, under the leadership of the Caliph—who, by a fortunate coincidence, also happened to be the temporal head of the Ottoman Empire.

There is at least a faint analogy between Abdul Hamid's attempt to revivify the wasting Osmanli dynasty with the supranational dynamism of Pan-Islam, and that of the seventeenth-century Habsburgs to identify theirs with the Catholic counter-Reformation. The former, in any case, was even less successful than the latter. The Sword of Islam soon proved a double-edged weapon in both domestic and foreign affairs. When xenophonic nationalist disorders occurred in Egypt, the Concert of Europe[2] summoned Abdul Hamid, as the country's nominal suzerain to put them down. As Caliph of Islam, however, he could not afford to punish Moslem rebels against Christian colonialism. He refused. Britain thereupon occupied Egypt (1881). In retaliation, Abdul Hamid, up to then something of an Anglophile, turned away from England toward Germany. He accepted a German military mission to reorganize the Ottoman armies and gave German firms railroad concessions which eventually culminated in the German-financed project for a line to the Persian Gulf—the famous Berlin-to-Bagdad

[2] Technically, this popular term of the Old World diplomacy, stemming from the Congress of Vienna in 1814, merely signified the major powers of Europe acting in agreement, or Concert. Though the European powers then were agreed about as rarely as the members of the United Nations today feel united, there was something of the same white word-magic in "Concert of Europe" that there is in "United Nations." It implied the existence of an actual, if mystic, European community, and however shadowy this may have been, it was an ominous symptom when the terminology fell into disuse toward the end of the nineteenth century.

railway. In 1889 Kaiser Wilhelm II arrived in Constantinople for a state visit to cement the new friendship. Abdul Hamid turned on the personal charm for which he was noted among Western diplomats, and Wilhelm responded sympathetically to the personality of his brother-neurotic. The Kaiser's trip gave a powerful impetus to Germany's *Drang nach Osten* (eastward thrust, in the sense of pressing for expanding economic and political influence in the Balkans and Asia Minor), which played some part in poisoning Anglo-German relations, and thus setting the stage for a European war. The nascent Anglo-German tensions—they did not become acute until after 1906—were sharpened after the discovery of oil in Mesopotamia —by German "archaeologists"—and by a second visit that Wilhelm paid to Turkey in 1898. Traveling through Palestine and Syria, the Kaiser laid a wreath on Saladin's tomb, and in Damascus, where he appeared in public dressed as a Bedouin sheik, he commemorated the friendship between Haroun al-Raschid and Charlemagne and pledged Germany's armed might to help his friend, the Caliph Abdul Hamid, defend the cause of Islam. (Queen Victoria, who as Empress of India ruled over nearly 100,000,000 Moslems, was definitely not amused by her grandson's antics.)

At home Abdul Hamid's exploitations of religion as an adjunct of despotism indirectly led to the most hideous episode of his reign—the Armenian massacres. To punish the Armenians for the nationalist agitation that had developed among some of the Armenian communities in the wild, mountainous region near the Caucasian border, the Sultan in 1891 authorized the use of Kurdish tribesmen as auxiliary police to put down the unrest. The Kurds, most of whom were Moslem, were a neighboring mountain race that had lived on bad terms with the Armenians for centuries. To send them into the Armenian areas to track down suspected nationalist revolutionaries was a sure recipe for religious and race war, and that is what broke out. The killing—which was one-sided since the Armenians were mostly unarmed—got under way in earnest in 1894, when the Kurds penned some 2000 men, women, and children in the Christian cathedral at the Urfa, ancient Edessa, and burned them alive. As a protest against Europe's failure to put a stop to such atrocities (the Sultan's friendship with the Kaiser helped to neutralize any European intervention), Armenian terrorists in 1896 seized the Ottoman Bank, in the heart of Constantinople. This aroused the conscience of Europe—the bank was mainly European-owned —but before any effective pressures could be brought to bear on Abdul Hamid, he ordered a retaliatory massacre of Armenians living in the capital, in Smyrna, and in other large cities, who up to then had escaped persecution. The order for the massacre was secret, but the execution was virtually official, and very tidy. Moslem mobs, usually organized and led by police officers, roamed through the streets armed with heavy clubs, and whenever they spotted an Armenian—or someone who looked and dressed as if he might be an Armenian—they bludgeoned him, as one pole-axes steers in a slaughterhouse. The killing lasted four days and then stopped with impressive discipline, on another secret order from the Sultan. Some 7000 Armenians perished in the capital alone. The total number of Armenians exterminated throughout the empire between 1891 and 1900 is still controversial—some estimates run to more than 300,000—but considering that the Sultan's agents had neither gas chambers nor nuclear weapons at their disposal, they undoubtedly perpetrated one of the most efficient attempts at genocide between the days of Genghis Khan and those of Hitler. Of course, Abdul Hamid, in ordering—or tolerating—the Armenian massacres, was not motivated solely by religious fanticism. He disapproved of nationalism, and he believed, not without some foundation, that Armenian terrorists were plotting to assassinate him.[3]

No sooner were the embers of Armenian nationalism quenched in blood than another Christian uprising took place—this time (1896) on the island of Crete. To everyone's surprise, the Sultan's German-renovated army defeated a Greek force sent to aid the Cretan rebels. Although the island was put under a sort of European trusteeship and eventually joined with Greece, the prestige of victory temporarily shored Abdul Hamid's wobbly throne. He was not unduly worried when in the early years of the new century bands of Bulgarian or Macedonian *comitadjis*—the traditional brigand-revolutionaries of the Balkan Peninsula—went on the offensive in Macedonia, with secret support from the Serbian, Greek, Montenegrin, and Bulgarian governments.

The approach of old age had not weakened the Sultan's will to rule (he was fifty-eight in 1900), and he had lost none of his ruse, but without realizing it, he was more and more falling victim to the administrative hardening of the arteries that often marks the terminal phase of extreme despotisms. The upward flow of information and ideas, without which even an autocratic ruler cannot long survive, was being choked off by venal, biased, and benighted officials or courtiers who controlled the channels of access to the monarch's private cabinet. For the most part they were not the comparatively educated, though usually corrupt, ministers in the Sublime Porte who were nominally responsible for administering the empire under the Sultan, but the palace clique of eunuchs, adventurers, and fakirs. The most important figure in this group, and thereby one of the most powerful men in the Empire, was the Sultan's secretary, a quick-witted and unscrupulous Arab named Izzet Pasha. Because this camarilla alone had the Sul-

[3] A minority of Western observers has tried, not very convincingly, to exculpate Abdul Hamid in the Armenian massacres. One of his most enthusiastic contemporary apologists was the American minister, Judge Terrel of Texas, who after dining with the Sultan at Yildiz as the trouble was starting in Turkish Armenia, confided to one of his British colleagues that Abdul Hamid was "the best man that ever breathed, and only his agents were vile."

tan's ear, its members were able to impose their policies upon him, simply by suppressing all contrary views, and gradually he became their puppet while imagining he was their master. The one chink in the curtain of censorship that Abdul Hamid's entourage threw around him proved more harmful than helpful. His suspicious nature and his morbid fear of assassination led him to employ what, even by Ottoman standards, was a prodigious number of spies (20,000, according to one count). He insisted on personally reading their daily reports, which became more voluminous as opposition to his despotism mounted throughout the Empire. In the end he was swamped by a flood of paper; he was so busy poring over reports filled with the gossip of stoolpigeons and the minutiae of routine police surveillances—he would trust no one to summarize them for him—that he failed to discern the most dangerous pattern of revolutionary conspiracy that was developing—not among the minorities and the agents of foreign powers, but among his own Turks, and particularly in the Turkish officer-caste upon whom the protection of the dynasty ultimately depended.

The Young Turks were not originally an organization but a current of opinion—with numerous undercurrents. Ideological descendants of the Young Ottomans of Abdul Hamid's early reign, they were both politically and socially a good deal more radical than their predecessors. While not extreme revolutionaries in terms of their objectives—most of them accepted the idea of a constitutional monarchy under the Osmanli dynasty—their philosophy of revolutionary violence made them kindred spirits to those political "activists" of the extreme right and the extreme left who between them have contributed so much to shaping the contorted physiognomy of our age. The deepest roots of the movement were indicated by the reactions of the Young Turks to the Russian revolution of 1905, which had so disturbed the Sultan. Like their liberal counterparts in the Dual Monarchy, in Germany and elsewhere, they were encouraged by the apparent defeat of the autocratic principle in Russia. They seem, however, to have responded even more enthusiastically to the victory of emergent Japanese nationalism over Russian imperialism which had touched off the revolution.

One of the significant undercurrents in the Young Turk movement was embodied by a secret revolutionary organization in the army that called itself Vatan (Fatherland). Its members believed passionately in constitutionalism, in representative government, in education, in modernizing Ottoman social and cultural life, and above all, in nationalism. Exactly what the word meant to the young conspirators is not clear—like "patriotism" in the Habsburg Empire, "nationalism" in the Ottoman one was of necessity an ambiguous concept—but one of its chief ingredients was a bristly resentment of European encroachments or domination. Vatan was not anti-Western in the sense that some of Abdul Hamid's Pan-Islamic sheiks were, since it was hospitable to Western ideas as well as Western technology; in fact many of its members had an almost extravagant admiration for everything Western. They preferred, however, to do their own Westernizing. They criticized the Sultan for allowing foreigners to enjoy extra-territorial privileges on Ottoman soil, for accepting an international commission to supervise Ottoman finances on behalf of the Empire's European debtors, for having let Crete slip under a virtual international mandate despite the glorious victory of the Ottoman Army. They were eager to have a modern army, but resented the arrogant Prussian instructors who were helping them to achieve it.

The essential—though not yet completely explicit—philosophy of Vatan was perhaps best exemplified by the volcanic but rigidly self-disciplined personality of one of its most dynamic younger leaders: a handsome, fastidiously dressed cavalry officer with steely blue eyes and a predatory mouth named Mustapha Riaz, better known, because of his cocksure efficiency, by the nickname, Kemal ("Perfection"). Mustapha Kemal, whom history now remembers under still another name, Ataturk, joined Vatan when he was attending the army staff college in Constantinople. On his graduation in 1904 he was arrested for sedition, but after two months' detention managed to talk the Sultan's inquisitors into releasing him—no easy feat. Posted to the garrison in Damascus with the rank of captain, he set to work organizing Vatan cells throughout Syria, then in 1907 had himself transferred to Salonika, at that time the main center of revolutionary unrest in the Empire. There he switched from Vatan to a more powerful and important conspiratorial group—the Committee of Union and Progress.

It was this committee that represented the dominant trend in the Young Turk movement. Virtually all of the younger officers of the Third Army Corps in Macedonia belonged to it, and its outstanding leader was a brilliant staff major named Enver Bey, a drawling, cosmopolite dandy in manner and appearance (despite his humble birth), at heart a twentieth-century condottiere. The Committee was not exclusively military, however—it was in close touch with a group of emigré intellectuals in Paris—and its aims, while similar to those of Vatan, were more articulately suffused with eighteenth-century rationalism and eighteenth-century political idealism, along with nineteenth-century nationalism. Many of its members belonged to Masonic lodges affiliated with the politically militant Grand Orient "obedience" of France and Italy, and there seems to be no doubt that this form of Freemasonry played a big part in framing its ideology. Whether European Freemasonry likewise gave direct support to its revolutionary activities is a more controversial matter. Possibly some European politicians or government officials who were also prominent members of Grand Orient Masonic lodges were not averse to undermining the Sultan's authority over his subjects. It seems likely, in any case, that the Italian consul in Salonika who furnished extra-territorial protection to the Masonic lodge, Macedonia Risorta, to which several prominent CUP leaders belonged, had at least a finger in the conspiracy.

In keeping with its Masonic background, the Committee fraternally accepted members of every race and creed; its leaders included Greeks, Armenians, Jews, and Turks, and it had clandestine contacts with some of the rebellious minorities in Macedonia. It explicitly professed the doctrine of "Ottomanism"—loyalty to the cause of a multi-national empire, with every ethnic group enjoying equal civic and political rights under a constitutional ruler. Though they were known abroad as Young Turks, the members of the CUP did not think of themselves as Turkish nationalists. In fact, apart from the peasants of Anatolia, few of the Sultan's subjects called themselves Turks at that time. "The word 'Turk' to an Ottoman was an insult," remarks a modern Turkish writer, Irfan Orga. The "Ottomanism" of the CUP was hardly less prickly than the vaguer nationalism of Mustapha Kemal's former Vatan comrades. It was finally a series of external threats or humiliations that detonated the so-called Young Turk revolution of 1908. The most determinant of them was a meeting between the Russian Czar and his uncle, Britain's Edward VII, off the Baltic coast, another of those royal yachting parties, but from the diplomatic viewpoint a much more professional affair than the Kaiser's ill-fated expedition to Bjorkoe three years before—which concluded in a Russo-British pact of friendship. This agreement ended—or at least limited—the traditional rivalry of British and Russian imperialism in Asia and the Near East upon which the survival of Ottoman independence largely depended; it thereby marked the ultimate failure of Abdul Hamid's divide-and-rule diplomacy. The Salonika revolutionaries decided the time had come to save the fatherland —whatever that might be.

At the beginning of July 1908, Enver Bey took command of a detachment of 150 Ottoman troops in eastern Macedonia near the present Greek-Yugoslav border and proclaimed the revolution. One of his fellow conspirators stationed in another part of Macedonia looted the battalion treasure and fled with his troops to the hills, joining forces with the Christian rebels he had been sent to suppress. A few days later the revolutionaries murdered the loyalist general commanding the Ottoman garrison in Monstir (today a town of southern Yugoslavia) and set up their headquarters. A battalion of supposedly loyal troops rushed in from Anatolia, went over to the insurrection almost as soon as they landed in Salonika. Before the Sultan, caught off guard by a real conspiracy after a lifetime of hunting down more or less imaginary ones, fully realized what was happening, the whole Third Army Corps was in revolt and threatening to march on the capital. When the Committee of Union and Progress sent its formal ultimatum on July 23, Abdul Hamid found himself with no trustworthy forces available. Since there was no immediate hope of licking the revolution, he decided to join it—in his fashion.

The Young Turks did not take over the government themselves. They were content to demand the removal of Abdul Hamid's sycophants and their replacement by politicians or officials sympathetic to the cause of reform. They allowed the Sultan to keep Yildiz Kiosk, including its harem, but they closed its private theater, cut down the number of his aides-de-camp from 290 to 30, and left him only 75 out of 300 musicians for his private orchestra. They also fired the Sultan's spies.

Abdul Hamid, on his side, made a seemingly conscientious effort to play the role of constitutional monarch. On December 17, 1908, he attended the first session of the newly elected parliament, sitting impassively in the royal box while one of his secretaries read his inaugural address, full of pious hopes and sound liberal sentiments.

The honeymoon between the crypto-nationalist freethinkers from Salonika and the retired autocrat, who remained Caliph of Islam, lasted for only a few months, however. The old conspirator still had some tricks to teach the young ones. In the early spring of 1909 the Moslem Brotherhood, a recently created secret counterrevolutionary society—for whose activities Abdul Hamid accepted no responsibility—instigated a mutiny of private soldiers and non-coms against their Young Turk officers in the main barracks of the capital. Mobs of religious fanatics, led by Moslem theological students—and in some cases by unemployed former spies of the Sultan—joined the rioting troops. For a few days the counterrevolution took over Istanbul; the Committee of Union and Progress had to go underground again, and a return to autocracy seemed close at hand, though Abdul prudently refrained from committing himself.

On April 23, however, a Young Turk force from Salonika, with Enver Bey commanding one of its leading columns, and Mustapha Kemal serving on the staff, fought its way back into the city. Two days later Abdul Hamid was deposed, and his colorless brother, Mohammed V, installed on the throne. When a delegation from the Committee of Union and Progress arrived at Yildiz to break the news, the ex-Sultan, looking frailer and more shrunken than ever with a military dress-greatcoat thrown over his shoulders, at first bore himself with kingly dignity.

"In accordance with a *fetva* (a decree of the highest Moslem religious authority), the Nation has deposed you," General Essad, the leader of the delegation, told him. "The National Assembly assumes responsibility for your personal security and that of your family. You have nothing to fear."

"This is *Kismet* [fate]," Abdul Hamid answered impassively. A few moments later, however, he started hysterically begging for his life; when the delegation returned later in the day bringing an order for his banishment —to Salonika, of all places—he fainted away. On being revived, he was informed that he would have to leave at once with his family and suite. He was warned that the Nation was rationing him to three wives, four concubines, four eunuchs, and fourteen servants. Other tyrants have fared worse.

The Young Turk revolution was destined to have a second and more consequential flowering in the 1920s; the first one withered on the tree. Autocracy was deposed for good with Abdul Hamid, but in its place the Young Turks set up a de facto oligarchy which exercised power through the political party that they controlled—the Party of Freedom and Progress, sprung from the secret society of the same name. Opposition and criticism were theoretically tolerated, but practically discouraged—by means that were often reminiscent of the Red Sultan's. The survivors of Abdul Hamid's fabulous spy corps soon found steady employment; the prisons that had been emptied after the July revolution rapidly filled up again, and not merely with the supporters of the March counterrevolution. Progress was encouraged, after a fashion, but hardly with a vigor sufficient to justify the dictatorship exercised in its name. Perhaps the most durable reform of the new regime was to round up the famous pariah dogs that infested the streets of Istanbul—the verminous symbols of Moslem charity—and to banish them to a small island in the Sea of Marmora, where they speedily came to a grisly but progressive end.

From the first there had been an implicit contradiction between the democratic "Ottomanism" which the Young Turks professed and the nascent Turkish nationalism which was their deepest motivation. The revolutionary brotherhood-in-arms between Turkish conspirators and Macedonian *comitadjis* did not long survive the triumph of the revolution. Confronted with continued unrest among the subject peoples of the Empire—there were simultaneous uprisings in Moslem Arabia and in partly Christian Albania —and harassed by the incessant intrigues of the great powers, the new regime gradually reverted to the oppressive nationalities policy of the old one; in time it even resurrected Abdul Hamid's Pan-Islamic doctrines, and had its own Armenian massacres. Arrogant, chauvinistic, and often brutal, the Young Turk oligarchy conducted foreign policy in the same barracks-room style with which it handled domestic affairs. It thereby achieved the remarkable feat of leaguing all the Balkan powers against the Ottoman Empire and laid the stage for the disastrous Balkan war of 1912. This in itself was no small contribution to the general European conflict which broke out two years later. Ironically, however, it was not the Young Turks' betrayal of their early ideals that contributed the most directly to the World War; it was rather the fleeting threat that they might live up to them. The great powers hoped to keep the Sick Man alive, but none of them wanted to see him get well. By creating the illusion that recovery was imminent, the Young Turk revolution of July 1908 spurred two of the larger European predators, Austria and Russia, to plunder the invalid while he was still helpless. Inevitably, their claws tangled.

CHAPTER 7

Rehearsal for Doom

O NE of the first by-products of the Young Turk revolution
—and ultimately one of the most fateful—was the Austro-
Russian conference which took place on September 5–6, 1908, at the
Castle of Buchlau in Moravia (today part of Czechoslovakia). Officially,
it was only a diplomatic house party given by the owner of the castle,
Count Leopold von Berchtold, at that time the Austro-Hungarian minister
in St. Petersburg, who was destined to reappear on the international stage a
few years later in more dramatic circumstances.

From the viewpoint of contemporary journalists who covered the affair,
it must have made a baffling and rather unsatisfactory story. The first tip
on it had come from the Ballplatz (the Austro-Hungarian Foreign Office)
itself, which had discreetly passed on word to reporters that the Austrian
Foreign Minister, Baron Alois Aehrenthal, and his Russian colleague,
Count Alexander Izvolsky—then taking the waters at Karlsbad—would be
fellow guests at Buchlau. Such official helpfulness was sufficiently rare in
Vienna, where the tradition of Metternichian diplomacy was still strong, to
give the press the idea that something momentous must be in the wind. Yet
when the correspondents were finally admitted into the castle, after spending
the greater part of two days waiting outside its gates, with only an occasional tantalizing glimpse of the two foreign ministers strolling under the
ancient trees of its park, it was to be handed a communiqué that contained
little but pious platitudes. The somewhat mushy kernel of the statement
appeared to be in a paragraph which voiced the hope that the new regime
in Turkey might prove to be an element of peace in Europe and declared
that the two foreign ministers were agreed on the need of adopting toward
it a "benevolent and expectant attitude."

The unspoken question in the journalist's minds—Why issue a communiqué if that is all that the two governments had to say?—was answered within a few days, but the Buchlau meeting remains in certain respects one of the residual enigmas of the prewar period, even though the margin of controversy as to what actually happened is small. Like the fiasco at Bjorkoe in 1905, Buchlau was both a milestone on the road to war and a symptom of the institutional decay that was eating away the foundations of the old order in Europe. (It was also one more striking illustration of the sinister imbrication between the international tensions of the period and the internal political strains of its crumbling autocracies.) Unlike that earlier meeting between Nicholas II and Wilhelm II, the Buchlau conference was not "operetta diplomacy" conducted by a couple of royal amateurs. The European crisis that stemmed from it was the inadvertent handiwork of two trained, experienced professional diplomats utilizing the traditional techniques of their calling, and operating within the ideological frame of reference accepted by most of their colleagues—including those of the Western European democracies—at the time.

Izvolsky, a big, moon-faced man with marbly, blue eyes and ponderous mustaches, looked somewhat like a confidence man trying to pass himself off as a guileless country squire. In reality he was a well-read, at least moderately intelligent specialist in international affairs (though perhaps handicapped by the small scope for initiative and responsibility which the Czar left his ministers), and basically no more dishonest than an Old World diplomat—especially a Czarist one—was expected to be. His chief failings were extreme conservatism, mental indolence, and an almost mystic self-satisfaction. The idea of organizing a quiet little meeting with the Austrians was largely his own—or so he thought. The Czar, after some hesitation, had approved his suggestion for an informal tour of Europe to sound out the signatories of the Treaty of Berlin about a revision of its Article 25, which since 1878 had closed the Black Sea exit to the Russian fleet.

In Russian minds, easing the stringencies of the treaty was, of course, merely an opening gambit in a series of moves aimed ultimately at realizing the age-old Russian dream of reaching Constantinople and gaining control of the straits. The Russian defeat in the war with Japan had reactivated the dream, and the Revolution of 1905 had bred the need—of which Izvolsky as stanch supporter of the monarchy was keenly aware—for some success abroad to bolster the Czar's prestige at home. The Young Turk revolution, in Izvolsky's view, gave his plans a particular urgency. For the moment, the Young Turks had too many domestic problems on their hands to resist concerted foreign pressures; if their reforms succeeded, however, the Ottoman Empire might pull itself together at last, and the golden moment would be lost. Aehrenthal, Izvolsky correctly reasoned, would be receptive to this argument. He knew that Vienna, too, was eager to revise the Treaty of Berlin so that Austria-Hungary could formally annex Bosnia and Herzegovina—this treaty was the instrument which had sanctioned Austro-Hungarian occupation of the provinces in 1878—before a renovated and reformed Ottoman Empire could demand their return. A clause in the Ottoman constitution provided that seats in the new parliament should be reserved for the two provinces, and the Young Turks were even talking about eventually holding elections there. Conditions—in Izvolsky's analysis—thus seemed propitious for one of those "little agreements" between Russia and Austria-Hungary—naturally behind the backs of their respective allies—despite their traditional rivalry in the Balkans. Even before the triumph of the Young Turk movement, Izvolsky had written to Aehrenthal hinting at the possibility of such a deal, and had not been rebuffed.[1]

Unfortunately for Izvolsky—and for the future of Europe—he does not seem to have grasped the full subtlety and complexity of Aehrenthal's Balkan policy, though Aehrenthal, who had earlier served as Austro-Hungarian minister in St. Petersburg, was well known to him. The Austrian foreign minister, a stiff, nearsighted man, whose bullet head topped with irascible gray fuzz gave him the look of a provincial notary, had one of the most brilliant—and in certain respects one of the most unscrupulous—diplomatic minds of his day. He was as vain as Izvolsky, and believed as fanatically in the historic mission of the Dual Monarchy as he did in his own—which proves that he, too, was a mystic. His brain, like some swollen gland, secreted ideas in an uncontrollable stream. His numerous enemies accused him of having a Talmudic mentality—he was the grandson of a Jewish grain merchant—but it could be more accurately described simply as an extreme example of late Viennese baroque. This type of convolute intelligence, widespread, though in a less genial form, among Francis Joseph's subjects, is characterized by the ability to turn ideas upside down and inside out; it can recognize duplicity as the supreme expression of good faith, or war as being merely a noisy form of peace.

The Balkan policy that Aehrenthal had developed since he took over the Ballplatz in 1906 was his masterpiece—a majestic labyrinth of thought,

---

[1] The key passage of Izvolsky's letter, from Albertini's book, is a superb example of Old World diplomatic prose:

"We continue to be of the opinion that the question of changing the state of things laid down in Article 25 of the Treaty of Berlin, i.e. the annexation of Bosnia-Herzegovina and the Sanjak of Novibazar is eminently a European concern and not of a nature to be settled by a separate understanding between Russia and Austria-Hungary. On the other hand, we are ready to recognize that the same reservation applies to the question of Constantinople, its adjacent territory and the Straits. However, in view of the extreme importance to our two countries of seeing the above-mentioned questions settled in accordance with their mutual interests, the Imperial Government would be prepared to enter into the discussion of them in a friendly spirit of reciprocity."

endlessly negating its own negations, which only the pictorial genius of a Saul Steinberg could render fully comprehensible to a present-day reader. Contrary to what Izvolsky supposed, pushing down through the Balkans to Salonika was no longer an objective of Austro-Hungarian diplomacy, as it had been under some earlier foreign ministers. In Aehrenthal's opinion, the hankering for acquiring Balkan real estate was a weakness of vulgar minds. The Balkans were largely peopled with Slavs, and the Austro-Hungarian Empire could not afford to burden itself with any more Slavic minorities. If Aehrenthal wanted to revise the Treaty of Berlin and to formally annex Bosnia-Herzegovina, it was not to use these provinces for further expansion at the expense of Turkey; it was to contain Serbian expansion at the expense of Austria-Hungary.

Here a broad look at the over-all political situation in the Balkan Peninsula in Aehrenthal's day may be helpful. The complex geography and the tormented history of the region need not be gone into deeply at this point; what is important to stress is that the whole area in the early twentieth century was heaving in a turbulent anticolonialist revolution somewhat akin to the one that is going on today throughout the Middle East and parts of Africa. The first phase of this revolution, the phase of violent de-colonization had almost been completed by the end of the nineteenth century. The Ottoman Empire—for it was against this Moslem and Asiatic imperialism that the Christian colonies of the Balkans were revolting—had been forced to recognize the independence of Greece, Serbia, and Montenegro. Bosnia and Bulgaria were still nominally part of the Ottoman Empire but the former was actually under Austro-Hungarian rule and the latter was for all practical purposes already a free nation. The Albanians, the Macedonians —a Slav people akin to the Bulgars—and hundreds of thousands of other Christians remained under the Ottoman yoke but their liberation was clearly only a question of time.

In 1908 the second phase of the Balkan revolution was already well under way; that of nationalist expansionism, of blind groping for the limits of nationhood, of extravagant irredentisms. As in Africa and the Middle East today, the juvenile greeds or idealisms of the newly liberated nations in the Balkans repeatedly clashed not only with interests of the established, imperialist powers, like Austria-Hungary and Italy—not to mention the hereditary enemy, Turkey—but with those of their anticolonialist brothers. Serbia, Bulgaria, and Greece all had conflicting territorial claims, either on yet-to-be-liberated Ottoman holdings, or on each other. The inherent instability of the area was aggravated by the overlapping or contradictory appeals of supranational movements roughly analogous to such contemporary trends as Pan-Arabism, Pan-Islam, and Pan-Africanism.

One of the most dynamic of these Balkan supranationalisms—or supernationalisms—was the Pan-Serb movement, whose goal was the union of all the Serb (or Serbo-Croat) populations of southeastern Europe. A few bold thinkers already had an even more ambitious dream: the creation of a Yugoslav commonwealth embracing all the South Slavs. Naturally, the main impetus for this project, in its varying degrees of ambition and extremism, came from the kingdom of Serbia itself, which could reasonably hope to provide the leadership for a larger South Slav Confederation. As an example of free national life, the very existence of an independent Serbia on the borders of the Austro-Hungarian Empire had an unsettling influence on the millions of South Slavs who lived under the mild but alien Habsburg yoke. But Serbia was not content merely to exist and be an example. Influential elements in the little mountain kingdom began actively propagandizing their racial brothers in the neighboring empire, and encouraging subversive conspiracies against the Emperor's authority. This Pan-Serb (or Yugoslav) agitation increased sharply after 1904 when a group of ultra-nationalist (i.e. Pan-Serb) army officers murdered the relatively pro-Austrian King Alexander Obrenovitch and his queen, Draga, and installed Peter Karageorgevitch, a more aggressively patriotic monarch, on the throne. Undeveloped Serbia with its population of 4,000,000 Balkan hillbillies, supported, it is true, by the distant might of a sympathetic Russia, began to seem a real threat to the integrity of the Austro-Hungarian Empire with its population of 50,000,000.

For a while the authorities in Vienna tried to force the new regime in Serbia into clamping down on Pan-Serb agitation by applying economic sanctions against the kingdom. This was the "Pig War" of 1906, so-called because the heaviest Austrian sanction was an embargo on Serbian pork—a major item in Serbia's foreign trade—which up to that time had crossed the frontiers of the Dual Monarchy freely, and usually under its own power, in the form of immense herds of live Serbian pigs, squealing and jostling under the goads of their drivers as they plodded almost shoulder-deep in the dust or mire of the Empire's backroads, en route to the Royal, Royal Imperial, or Royal-and-Imperial sausage factories of his Apostolic Majesty. Though Austria-Hungary was virtually the sole market for Serbian livestock and other farm produce, economic logic had not assured victory in the "Pig War," and Aehrenthal, shortly after he took over the foreign ministry, had shown good sense by calling for a re-examination of the Dual Monarchy's relations with its peppery little neighbor to the south.

"Our policy of making Serbia economically and politically dependent and treating her as a negligible quantity has foundered," the new foreign minister declared at a cabinet meeting in Vienna on October 27, 1907. "Only a third party would profit by a conflict between Serbia and the Monarchy. Politically we must urgently beg for such a conduct of Croatian, Dalmatian and Bosnian affairs as would place the center of gravity for the Serbo-Croat peoples within the Monarchy."

While not entirely clear, Aehrenthal's remarks indicated that at the time he was not anti-Serbian in the ordinary sense of the word. (Of course, Aehrenthal was never anything in the ordinary sense of the word.) His views seemed close to those of certain thinkers in Archduke Francis Ferdinand's "Belvedere Group" who favored a reconciliation with Belgrade in order to placate the South Slav elements within the Dual Monarchy, and even dreamed of luring Serbia into a freely accepted federal union presided over by the Habsburg dynasty.

Since the Serbians were known to covet Bosnia-Herzegovina themselves, and therefore passionately opposed annexation of the provinces by Austria-Hungary, it might be supposed that any Austrian statesman who favored improving relations with Serbia—the policy that Aehrenthal seemed to advocate—would necessarily favor delaying annexation until some friendly understanding on the Bosnian problem could be worked out with Belgrade. Aehrenthal's logic was of a more sophisticated variety, however. According to one of his loyal subordinates at the Ballplatz, he maintained that the annexation of Bosnia-Herzegovina was actually the "precondition of any further step towards a satisfactory solution of the Monarchy's Southern Slav question," while an Austrian withdrawal from there would be a form of "political hara-kiri."

Ultimately, Francis Joseph's foreign minister, who liked to think of himself as a Danubian Bismarck, or as a twentieth-century Metternich, worked around to the curious view that the best way to cement the loyalty of the Emperor's Serbo-Croat subjects was to woo Bulgaria, a country for which they had no affection, rather than Serbia, with which they had, at the very least, strong sentimental ties.

"They had to make up their minds to tear the evil up by the roots and put an end to all Pan-Serb dreams for the future," Aehrenthal wrote in secret memorandum outlining the salient features of his Balkan policy. Explaining that a conflict between Bulgaria and Serbia was inevitable—a shrewd prophecy—he continued:

"If in this struggle we favor the Bulgarian cause and the creation of a Big Bulgaria at the expense of Serbia, we shall have completed the necessary preparation for laying hands on what remains of Serbia as soon as a propitious star is in the ascendant in Europe.

"He looked to an independent Albania (under his aegis, of course) a friendly Montenegro and "a Big Bulgaria bound to us by ties of gratitude."

It is hard to translate this Old World diplomatic gobbledygook into contemporary language without oversimplifying Aehrenthal's reasoning and thereby doing him an injustice. The policy he proposed was not a stupid one, but it was fatally devious—and deviously fatal. It was also almost the reverse of the course he had urged earlier. The Empire, he argued in effect, was permanently threatened by Pan-Serb agitation fomented from across the frontiers by Serbia, and inspired by Serbian expansionist ambitions, which could be satisfied only at the expense of Austria-Hungary. To make the Empire's frontiers safe, the evil—and independent Serbia—must therefore be torn up by the roots. The best way to do this was encourage Bulgarian ambitions to expand at Serbia's expense. War would break out between the two Balkan rivals, Serbia and Bulgaria, and the latter, discreetly backed by Austria-Hungary, would win, annexing a lot of formerly Serbian territory. Serbia would be ruined by the defeat, and Austria-Hungary would quietly annex what was left of her at the first favorable moment —i.e. when the great powers were too busy elsewhere to interfere. (The Habsburgs would thus acquire a million or more new South Slav subjects, despite Aehrenthal's earlier warning against this very mistake.) Then the Dual Monarchy would have only safe frontiers to the south: an enlarged but grateful Bulgaria, a friendly independent Albania (which Aehrenthal proposed to liberate from Turkish rule and set up as a sovereign state) and a friendly or at least harmless little Montenegro. No enemy would be left to foment unrest—at least from the outside—among the Empire's South Slavs.

These were a few of the ideas leaping in Aehrenthal's restless mind, like apes of thought swinging from branch to branch in some equatorial jungle, as he prepared himself—with his usual meticulous care—for the talks at Buchlau. In certain respects they were painfully different from what Izvolsky—who like other Czarist diplomats looked on both Bulgaria and Serbia as Russian protégés—imagined them to be. The house party at Count von Berchtold's castle turned out to be a thoroughly pleasant affair—as long as it lasted. The guests included Count Paul Esterhazy, Aehrenthal's inseparable Hungarian *chef de cabinet* (Aehrenthal was married to a Magyar Countess and habitually surrounded himself with Hungarian die-hards), and one of the young secretaries of the Russian legation in Vienna. The atmosphere was an agreeable blend of the social and of the official. Thoroughly relaxed, puffing on a good cigar, while liqueurs were being handed around after dinner, Izvolsky did not find it difficult to touch on the subject close to his heart, and he was gratified to hear his Austrian hosts assure him—at least he thought he heard them—that for their part, they had no objection to the idea of reopening the straits to the Russian fleet. As he expected, the Austrians in return raised the question of Bosnia and Herzegovina, and asked with unusual directness how Russia would feel if Austria-Hungary simply annexed the two provinces.

Izvolsky, who has been described as "unwilling to say anything which might appear to be displeasing to his interlocutors," replied a little vaguely that he could not see any objections, "but, of course, a satisfactory procedure would have to be found."

In addition to the general conversation at mealtimes, the two foreign ministers spent six hours talking together, first as they strolled around the park, then in Berchtold's crowded little study. Except for the innocuous press communiqué, nothing was put in writing; there was no formal record of the talks. This was not only secret diplomacy; it was gentlemen's diplomacy in its most gentlemanly form. Izvolsky, as he drove away from Buchlau for a holiday in the Bavarian Alps, was even more pleased with himself than usual. It seems strange that he was so unwary; Aehrenthal was noted among his colleagues all over Europe for his outstanding skill at slipping important elements into casual conversation—the fine print of verbal exchange—in such a way that they passed unnoticed.

A month later, on October 5, just after Izvolsky, fresh from his rest in Bavaria, had reached Paris, the time bomb set at Buchlau went off. News agency dispatches from Vienna announced that the Austrian annexation of Bosnia-Herzegovina was a *fait accompli*. The dispatches added that Bulgaria—which under the Treaty of Berlin still owed nominal allegiance to the Ottoman Sultan—had at the same time proclaimed its formal independence, with Austrian approval, but without consulting its Slavic big brother, Russia. This was another blow to Russian prestige in the Balkans.

In the tense Europe of 1908 the "Balkan Powder Barrel" was already a well-worn cliché; any unilateral action in that region was bound to usher in an atmosphere of crisis. There was an explosion of fury in Serbia, where the dream of South Slav unity had received a cruel blow. Belgrade announced the mobilization of 120,000 men. Russian opinion reacted nearly as violently. Sympathy for the oppressed Slav brethren flooded Moscovite hearts. In every European capital there was talk of possible war.

Izvolsky was in hot water. The Austrians proclaimed loudly that, through his voice, Russia had agreed to their move. Count Berchtold even went so far as to put up a tablet in the study of his castle to commemorate the "conversations, of such major importance to Austria, when Izvolsky gave his consent to the annexation of Bosnia-Herzegovina." It was difficult, under the circumstances, for Izvolsky to protest. His explanations to St. Petersburg fell on unsympathetic ears—he had informed the Czar, but none of the ministers, of the deal he was preparing. His only hope was to press for the compensation which he thought had been promised him at Buchlau. He called loudly for a conference of the signatories of the Berlin Treaty to take up the Bosnian question, such a meeting would have the double advantage, in his eyes, of bringing Austria to heel, and of opening the way for a revision of the straits statute.

But in London, where Izvolsky had rushed from Paris, the idea of letting the Russian fleet into the Mediterranean, athwart Britain's main line of communications with India, was no more popular than it had ever been; polite evasiveness was all that the unfortunate diplomat got. In Paris his only satisfaction was hearing Premier Clemenceau, at a brilliant diplomatic reception, greet the startled Austrian ambassador with a loud, *"Eh bien, avez-vous bientôt fini de mettre le feu aux quatre coins de l'Europe?"* ("Well! How soon are you going to be finished setting fire to the four corners of Europe?")

Feeling cheated and desperate, Izvolsky hastened to Berlin. The Kaiser was furious at his Austrian ally's coup, and reviled "that Jew, Aehrenthal" for his independent action. "Why," he fumed, "I am the last one to be informed in Europe." Wilhelm had no desire to be involved with the perpetual witch's cauldron of Austro-Russian rivalry in the Balkans. He was acutely embarrassed by the memory of his flamboyant visits to Turkey, and of the no less flamboyant speeches he had delivered in the course of them. And now his Austrian ally was snatching two provinces from his Turkish friends.

Izvolsky's spirits rose when an invitation bidding him to lunch with the Kaiser arrived, but they were at an all-time low when, the afternoon still young, he emerged from the Imperial Palace; he had not been able to allude to his problems even once. His host had sternly confined the conversation to trivialities. Izvolsky rushed to see the Kaiser's Chancellor. "I am in a terrible mess," he confided, but Bulow was unmoved. He could do nothing for Izvolsky, except advise him to keep the ebullient Serbs on a tight rein.

From St. Petersburg, to which the hapless Izvolsky eventually had to return, he continued to bombard the European powers with note after note. By December, the situation had become so tense that an Austrian invasion of Serbia seemed imminent. Nicholas wrote Wilhelm to beg him to restrain his ally.

"You must realize the difficult position in which I would be put if Austria declared war on Serbia," the Czar pointed out. "To maintain peace I would have to choose between my own conscience and the unleashed passions of my people."

To Francis Joseph, Nicholas wrote complaining of Aehrenthal's duplicity.

The Austrian Emperor was unimpressed. He could not see what the Russians were fussing about; they had consented to the annexation, hadn't they? It was only to put a stop to the Serbian agitation against the Dual Monarchy that the step had been taken. Expansion in the East was of no interest to Austria. "Those people are unprofitable," he had once said, referring to the Southern Slavs. Aehrenthal had given him his solemn word that there was no danger of warlike complications. Otherwise he would never have signed the decree of annexation. He replied coldly to the Czar's letter:

"When your foreign minister gave us assurances, [that Russia had no objections to the proposed annexation] my ministers could not suppose that he was giving them in his own name, rather than in that of the imperial government, without being authorized to do so by you."

By January 1909, the general staffs of Austria and Russia were preparing to mobilize. England, France, and Italy offered to mediate. They called on Germany to join in this measure of appeasement. But Bulow had other ideas.

The German Chancellor, then sixty, had recently lost the Kaiser's confidence and he knew that his days in power were numbered. (He was to resign in July 1909, after having held the chancellorship since 1900.) No doubt he welcomed the chance to make one last brilliant appearance on the stage of history, the more so because the role in which he saw himself cast was one for which he had been preparing all his life. Amiable, witty, urbane, handsome in a silver-haired, somewhat un-Prussian way, and endowed with a definitely un-Prussian nimbleness of mind, Bulow had been a disciple of Bismarck. He admired above all the Iron Chancellor's amoral dedication to the power goals of the Prussian state, and prided himself on following this high example in his own policies. He was, in fact, unscrupulous enough in a shallow, diplomatic way, but he lacked the fierce personal integrity that went with Bismarck's lack of public scruple, and he had neither his hero's nerve, nor his farsightedness. Most of his career had been spent in diplomacy. He had risen, mainly by merit, from secretary of legation to head of the Imperial foreign office, before becoming chancellor. Like Izvolsky and Aehrenthal he stood at the top of his profession in Europe. In fact he was a much better diplomat than either of them: more adroit, clearer-headed, lacking only the Bismarckian gift of realizing what a dangerous thing victory can be.

"I trusted my skill and strength to set the points so that the Austrian express should not collide with the Russian one," he had boasted to the Kaiser.

The situation was ideal for a display of brinkmanship—if one did not worry too much about the future. Russia, weakened by revolutionary troubles, insufficiently recovered from the Far Eastern fiasco, was quite unprepared for war. Her French and British allies had demonstrated that they did not consider her dispute with Austria over Serbia as warranting more than diplomatic support.

As soon as Turkey, pressed by Germany, and bribed by Austria, finally recognized the annexation, Aehrenthal in a series of notes to the European powers demanded not only that Serbia recognize the rape of the sister provinces, but also give a written promise of future good behavior: No protesting, no more attacks on the Dual Monarchy; good-neighborly relations were to reign from now on. A particularly stiff warning was sent to Russia.

Next, it was Germany's turn to play. On March 21, 1909, the German Ambassador in St. Petersburg, Count Friedrich von Pourtales, presented himself at the foreign office. He was in receipt of drastic instructions from Berlin. They had to be assured, he said, that Russia accepted the Austro-Hungarian note, and gave her formal and unreserved agreement to the abrogation of Article 25 [of the Treaty of Berlin]. His Excellency would stress to Mr. Izvolsky that a definite answer was in order: "yes or no."

A hastily summoned council of ministers decided that there was no other course but to swallow what was virtually a German ultimatum. Russia was forced to recognize the Bosnian *fait accompli* and to drop Serbia like a hot brick. (A week later, Belgrade accepted the humiliating Austrian demands.)

"It is a bitter pill," Izvolsky admitted to the British Ambassador, Sir Arthur Nicolson, "but the whole Austro-German plan had been carefully prepared, and the favourable moment chosen. Three or four years later, Russia would have sufficiently recovered her forces to reply in other tones."

Bulow was delighted with the results of his saber-rattling. Under the threat of war he had forced Europe to condone Austria's act of diplomatic brigandry in the Balkans, and had demonstrated to Russia the unreliability of her allies. "The continental power of Germany," he crowed, "has burst the meshes of encirclement."

Because none of their vital interests were threatened, France and England had averted their eyes while a European treaty to which they were signatories was being violated. With smugness that recalls certain Western reactions to what happened at Munich twenty-nine years later, the *London Times* dismissed the crisis with these words: "The danger of war has thus, we may confidently hope, been averted."

Yes, war had been averted. But both the way in which the crisis had arisen and the way in which it was resolved should have made thoughtful Europeans shudder—and did in fact make some shudder—at the outlook for a peace dependent on monarchs and ministers who conducted the affairs of twentieth-century world powers in the spirit and style of eighteenth-century rulers-by-divine-right wrangling over the dismemberment of a grand duchy or preparing to shed their subjects' blood to avenge an affront to an ambassador's honor. As to the practical consequences of the international crisis launched by that pleasant houseparty in that charming little Moravian castle, it is hard to overestimate them.

One consequence, and not the least one, was the transfer of an embittered Izvolsky from the Foreign Ministry in St. Petersburg to the Russian Embassy in Paris. There for the next few critical years he labored with vindictive zeal to tighten the noose of the Franco-Anglo-Russian alliance around the throats of Germany and Austria, while his aides bribed the venal French press of the day on a huge scale, thereby helping to inflame the chronic French chauvinism. In both these tasks, he worked closely with

like-minded French officers or officials in the General Staff, in the Foreign
Ministry and in the police, and with strident spokesmen of French nationalism like Théophile Delcassé, still smarting over the rejection of his tough
foreign policy in the 1905 Moroccan crisis with Germany, and Raymond
Poincaré, the dour Lorraine politician who was soon to become premier,
then president of the republic. While Izvolsky was thus employed in Paris,
his successor in St. Petersburg, Serge Sazonov—a loyal former subordinate
who still tended to look to his old chief for guidance—mobilized against
Austria-Hungary the powerful apparatus of Russian overt and covert
political warfare in the Balkans. "I have the impression," Sazonov wrote
in 1910 to his minister in Belgrade, N. H. de Hartwig, "that Austria-Hungary, despite the German brotherhood in arms, is on her last legs . . .
Serbia's promised land lies within the orbit of present-day Austria-Hungary
. . . Under these circumstances it is a matter of vital importance for Serbia
to put herself by hard and patient work in the position of readiness necessary
to face the inevitable outbreak of future war."

In Serbia itself, the repercussions of the Bosnian crisis were, as might
have been expected, dramatic—how dramatic we shall see in a later chapter. They were hardly less so in terms of the Dual Monarchy's internal
strains and fissures.

"When the Turk gets up from the Sick Man's bed, Austria will take
his place," Albert Sorel, the French historian, had once predicted. The bed
remained occupied, despite the Young Turk revolution, but in 1908 Austria
moved at least into the same ward—and unfortunately there was no international quarantine for such contagious cases.

It was in Germany, however, that Izvolsky's disingenuous bumbling, and
Aehrenthal's self-defeating finesse, had the direst consequences. Forgetting
Bismarck's advice about not tying the trim Prussian craft to the rotting
Habsburg hulk, Bulow, with the Kaiser's approval and participation, had
underwritten in advance Austria's patently suicidal Balkan policy. Militarily, the whole character of the alliance between the two central empires
was transformed. The decision taken by the German General Staff to
support Austria if she invaded Serbia, and Russia intervened, inevitably
tended to crystallize German strategy in a fatal pattern. For Russia had an
ally, France, who, though not bound in all circumstances, might join her
in declaring war on the Dual Monarchy. In that case, where would Germany launch her first counterblows? This was the question raised by the
Austro-Hungarian Chief of Staff, General Franz Conrad von Hotzendorf,
in an exchange of letters with his German opposite number, General Helmuth von Moltke, that he had initiated in January 1909. Moltke's reply
had been brutally explicit: His plan was "to hurl the main body of the
German forces first against France."

Thus, as one courageous German editor put it, the defensive alliance created by Bismarck had turned into an offensive alliance by which "Germany with all her Pomeranian Grenadiers and all the rest of her panoply of war —her entire army—pledged herself to shed her blood for Austrian Balkan policy." Worse still, the decision to strike the first blow at France eliminated all hope of localizing an eventual conflict in southeastern Europe; any Balkan war involving Austria and Russia would automatically become a European war. And since a blow against a great, modern military power like France could only hope to succeed if it were delivered with stunning speed, Moltke's strategy—based on the famous Schlieffen Plan[2]—implied the minimum delay in mobilizing and concentrating his forces, and in launching them headlong across the French frontiers. Once set in motion, the German war machine could not be halted momentarily without compromising the Plan. This time factor virtually doomed in advance any diplomatic moves to avert war, after the crisis had reached a certain pitch. In our age, the time lag between "mobilization" and total war has for all practical purposes shortened to the countdown for firing a ballistic missile, but in pre-1914 Europe armies massed ponderously at the railheads and moved to battle by forced marches, the boots of their infantry and the caissons of their horse-drawn artillery echoing hour after hour through winding cobblestone streets of sleepy border villages. There was a logistic interval between diplomatic crisis and military clash which left some opening, however slight, to last-minute peace-makers; the German General Staff, groping toward what twenty years later became the concept of blitzkrieg, had ominously narrowed the gap. To grasp fully the chilling implications of this situation, we must now take a closer look at the personality of Wilhelm II, the Supreme War Lord, who, at least in theory, controlled the hair-trigger German military machine; at the same time let us note certain ominous new trends in the overenergized society that had produced both him and it.

---

[2] The Schlieffen Plan, named after its author, Count Alfred von Schlieffen, then chief of the German General Staff, was first drafted in 1899 and progressively elaborated over the next six years. It called essentially for a vast German offensive into northern France through Belgium—whose neutrality would thus have to be violated—so as to achieve the partial envelopment of the main French armies and their destruction in a decisive battle.

CHAPTER 8

The Unlucky Brinkmanship of Wilhelm II

O N the grand piano in many a plush-upholstered, velvet-hung German drawing room before the war there stood a court photograph of Kaiser Wilhelm II, framed in silver and autographed in his flamboyant, slightly hysterical scrawl. The portrait depicts the All-Highest in the uniform of a Grand Admiral of the German Navy, holding an outsize telescope under the left arm. Wilhelm is frowning sternly, chin stuck out, mustache martially twirled, his right hand resting on the gold braid of the belt, the other one grasping the hilt of the dress sword. Rows of medals cover the chest; coils of fourragères entwine the shoulders. Every inch an Emperor, here stands the man whose motto was "Full Steam Ahead."

But a photograph, however official, never completely conceals reality. The jauntily cocked hat hides the Kaiser's graying hair; it cannot wholly distract attention from the dispirited middle-aged sag of his jowls, tautened though they be by the virile thrust of the chin. The theatrical pose with the telescope shows that it is a prop, meant to camouflage the awkward twist of the left arm; to the instructed eye the tawdry print turns into a psychological X-ray plate that reveals a far deeper and more pitiable scar. Behind the posturing and the ranting which for years have made Wilhelm the *enfant terrible* of Europe, one catches a sudden glimpse of the crippled child he once had been, compulsively trying to attract notice from his mother, who stubbornly turns her face away in shame and cold distress. It is the expression of the eyes, however, that is the most striking feature of the Kaiser's favorite portrait. Something in the subject's fixed, almost hypnotic gaze gives the lie to everything it is supposed to say. Under the mask of arrogant self-satisfaction there lurks a sickly doubt; breaking through the look of manly resolution one senses a dawning panic. The admiral stands on the bridge in his bravest uniform; the engines throb in proud obedience to his orders; but the rudder of his ship is jammed on a collision course, and he is just beginning to realize it.

Whether or not the Kaiser really did suspect the truth—and there is evidence more explicit than the portrait's to indicate that he did—the nautical analogy is a fairly close one. Imperial Germany in the last years of peace actually was like a vessel headed full steam ahead for disaster, and no longer responsive to the helmsman's hand, or—if one prefers the terrestrial simile of a British historian—like a runaway locomotive. It is known approximately when the partial breakdown in the empire's control system took place—the decisive accident seems to have occurred shortly after the Bosnian crisis of 1908–1909—and in a general way what went wrong. The apparent success for Germany's mailed-fist diplomacy that marked the end of the crisis was itself a factor of some importance.

Wilhelm himself unquestionably bears part of the blame. His militaristic belligerence, his boasting and his verbal intemperance over the years had built up a public image of him which had hardened almost beyond revision. In certain respects it was a disastrously misleading image. Wilhelm was something of a bully, but he was far from being the furious war lord that the average newspaper reader in France, England, and Russia imagined him to be. Yet the mistake—even if it was sometimes encouraged by chauvinist propagandists in these countries—was natural. Ever since he had mounted the throne at the age of twenty-nine his martial impersonations had scandalized the royal courts of Europe, and given its foreign offices the jitters.

As a young Emperor, Wilhelm had once presented the German Embassy in Paris with an oil portrait of himself, dressed in the black cuirasse of a Garde du Corps and brandishing a field marshal's baton, that was so incendiary it had caused an eminent French general to remark, "This portrait is a declaration of war."

Replying to the manifesto drawn up by the Hague Peace Conference of 1898, the Kaiser had said:

"Can we picture a supreme war lord disbanding his illustrious historic regiments . . . and thus delivering his cities over as a prey to anarchists and democrats?"

"I trust in God and in my unsheathed sword," he had later exclaimed in more informal comment on the same conference, "and I ********* on all resolutions of international conferences."

In 1905, a few days after President Emile Loubet of France, defying chauvinist opinion, had voiced his readiness to receive the Kaiser in Paris, Wilhelm had reciprocated this hospitable intent by delivering a speech to his army which concluded:

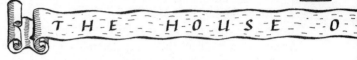

Frederick II the Great
1740–1786

Augustus William

Frederick William II
1786–1797

Frederick William III
1797–1840

Frederick William IV m. Elizabeth of Bavaria   William I ── Augusta of Weima
1840–1861   1861–1888

                Frederick III ── Victoria of England
                1888   (daughter of Queen Victoria)

William II ── Augusta   Charlotte m. Bernard   Henry m. Irene
1888–1918   of Schleswig-   of   of
             Holstein   Meiningen   Hesse

Frederick William ── Cecilia   Eitel Friederich m. Sophie   Adalbert m. Adelaide   Augustus
                     of   of   of Saxe-
                     Mecklenburg   Oldenburg   Meiningen

        William m. Dorothea   Louis Ferdinand m. Kyra   Huber
        b. 1906   de   b. 1907   Grand Duchess   b. 190
                   Salviati   of Russia

...lotte m. *Nicholas I of Russia*   Charles   Alexandrine   Louise   Albert

Louise m. *Grand Duke of Baden*

...ria m. *Adolf*   Waldemar   Sophia m. *Constantine*   Margaret m. *Frederick Charles*
    of   d. 1879   *of*   *of Hesse*
  Schaumburg-   *Greece*
    Lippe

...xandra   Oscar   Joachim m. *Marie*   Victoria Louise m. *Ernest Augustus*
...chleswig-   *of Anhalt*   *of Cumberland*
...olstein   d. 1920

...rederick   Alexandrine   Cecilia
  b. 1911   b. 1915   b. 1917

"The Order of the Day is: Keep your powder dry; keep your sword sharp; and keep your fist on the hilt."

Above all there had been the memorable—all-too-memorable—speech to his marines, departing in 1900 to help put down the so-called Boxer Rebellion in China, and to avenge the fanatics' massacre of Western diplomats, including the German Minister:

"Give no quarter. Take no prisoners . . . Even as a thousand years ago when the Huns under King Attila made such a name for themselves as still resounds in terror . . . so may the name of German resound through Chinese history for a thousand years . . . may you so conduct yourselves that no Chinaman will ever again so much as dare to look crooked at a German."

It was perhaps a bit unsporting for Allied propagandists in two wars to pin the Hun label on Germany because the Kaiser had gone on an unusually disgraceful verbal binge in the course of a colonial expedition where Germany was allied with all the Occidental powers—including the United States —in defense of Western interests and civilization, but the anecdote is a good example of the effect often produced by Wilhelm's speeches on a scandalized—if sometimes hypocritically scandalized—world.[1]

It was Germany's misfortune to have such a ruler at a time when the very appearance on the world stage of a new and vigorous latecomer was bound to arouse the resentment of the established powers. It was Wilhelm's misfortune to have every one of his boasts or threats underscored by possession of the most heavily equipped, best disciplined army in the world, by a navy second only to England's, by an aggressive commercial policy that threatened vested trade interests in all the markets of the world, and by an exuberant birthrate. Finally, it was the world's misfortune that Wilhelm's reign and Germany's bid for bloodless hegemony in Europe should have coincided with a kind of lopsided revolution in German society that swept away old restraints, while it sharpened ancient hungers; that reenforced anachronistic political or social institutions while creating unrecognized and therefore irresponsible new forms of power. As indicated earlier, the critical years in this revolution were those between 1908 and 1914, but to understand fully what happened during this period, it is necessary to retrace the story of the Hohenzollern dynasty and of the Pomeranian bog which in less than three centuries they turned into a world power: Prussia.

The Hohenzollern dynasty rose to fame and far-flung dominion at the head of a state which it fashioned from nothing. The kingdom of Prussia

[1] Among other extreme examples of Wilhelm's reckless use of language, he is cited as having once said to his American dentist:
"Don't worry about hurting me; I never feel pain."

was their creation; the history of the dynasty and the history of Prussia are one.

Before the sixteenth century, the word Prussia designated lands in north-west Poland, beyond the borders of the Empire, which had been conquered from a heathen Baltic people—the Borussians—in the early thirteenth century, and colonized ever since by a Germanic order of crusading knights. The Hohenzollerns were a family of feudal counts whose original keep in Swabia lay not far from that of the Habsburgs. In the fifteenth century they climbed several rungs in the feudal ladder by becoming Margraves of Brandenburg, in north Germany. Their conversion to the Reformed faith brought them as a reward the colonial territories which eventually gave their name to the Hohenzollern kingdom: In 1525 a Hohenzollern secularized (we would say liberated) the lands of the Teutonic Order of Knights and annexed them to his domains as the hereditary duchy of Prussia. By the seventeenth century the Hohenzollerns were the biggest landowners in the Empire after the Habsburgs, though their estates were largely disconnected stretches of sandy waste, marshes, and somber pine forests. Situated east of the Elbe, for the most part, these were frontier lands, sparsely populated by the remnants of the Slavic tribes from whom they had been conquered, utterly remote from the civilization of Germany's free cities and princely courts. Such was the unpromising raw material from which sprang the Hohenzollern dream.

Using as their agents the *junkers*—the baronial landowners of eastern Germany, stiff-necked but efficient autocrats of the turnip patch—four ambitious Hohenzollerns between the middle of the seventeenth century and the French Revolution created the new Prussian power. Frederick William, the Great Elector (1620–1688), merged the two Hohenzollern possessions, Brandenburg and Prussia, into a single administrative unit, though they did not yet have a common frontier. His successor, Frederick I, was a bit frivolous, by Hohenzollern standards, but he nonetheless talked the Emperor into recognizing Prussia as a kingdom. Frederick William I, the "Sergeant King," forged the Prussian Army as a precision tool of conquest. His son, Frederick the Great (1740–1786), put the tool to work; by ruthlessness and generalship he defeated the combined armies of most of Europe, knit his scattered realms into a strong, coherent nation and provided it with an industrial base by wresting the Silesian coal basin from the Habsburg Empress Maria Theresa.

Militarism was a Hohenzollern attribute from the beginning, for power alone could hold together a state, built from the top down, which had no historic basis, no riches of its own and hardly a population (the Hohenzollerns were obliged to colonize their lands by encouraging immigration). "All my subjects are born to be soldiers," the Sergeant King had said in decreeing compulsory military service for Prussia. It was a natural attitude for the ruler of a state which had created its subjects instead of having been created by them.

The barracks room and the parade ground put their stamp of harsh efficiency not only on the Prussian Army and civil service but on the Prussian tradition of education, and thereby on the Prussian character. As an adolescent, the Hohenzollern prince who was to become Frederick the Great had been an undisciplined dilettante with artistic leanings; his father licked him into shape with a long term of imprisonment, and by beheading one of the youthful companions of his escapades before his eyes. Frederick retained enough of his early enthusiasm for the life of the mind to convert it into a valuable public relations asset in an age of enlightenment—the friendship with Voltaire and the concerts at Sans Souci, that creampuff imitation of the Trianon, strongly appealed to the imagination of his contemporaries— but in adult life he never forgot that for a Hohenzollern ruler there could be only one aim, one preoccupation, one recreation—the making of Prussia.

The story of Frederick's education reveals not only the brutality but the artificiality of the Prussian tradition. Both to its rulers and to the elites who served them, Prussia was an obsessive ambition rather than an ideal; its service was a compulsion rather than a dedication. Frederick the Great was himself a typical victim of this Moloch tradition. "I will sustain my power or let everything perish, so that even the name of Prussia shall be buried with me," he exclaimed at a particularly critical moment in his career. The words have a sinister twentieth-century ring, and their note of almost hysterical commitment to a mission beyond one's strength has in fact been a recurrent theme in twentieth-century German history.

Frederick died three years before the French Revolution broke out. His immediate successors, by first appeasing Napoleon and then surrendering to him, helped to deliver Germany into the Corsican adventurer's crafty grip. It was Napoleon who was the original, if inadvertent, artisan of German unity—he suppressed no less than 300 petty German sovereignties—and the French armies of occupation which were the begetters of German nationalism.

"Vivat Teutonia," was the rallying cry which in 1813 led the German people in the war of liberation against Napoleon. After the Congress of Vienna, however, the ideas of German unity and constitutional reform which this slogan had implied were no longer fashionable. Prussia became a member in good standing of the Holy Alliance and for a brief period the Hohenzollerns resumed their place as deferential seconds to the imperial Habsburg dynasty. When in 1848 the German liberals, ignoring their various sovereigns, called a constitutional assembly in Frankfurt and offered the Prussian King the crown of a reorganized and united Germany, he refused it. What was a crown conferred by a gaggle of excited professors who purported to represent the popular will? "Mud and wood," scoffed the

King of Prussia. The Parliament of Frankfurt was dissolved, short-lived revolts in various German states—Prussia among them—were snuffed out, and the old order was restored.

Not for long, however. Strong material as well as idealistic forces supported the trend toward German unification. Economic ties and a remarkable railway network, fostered by a customs union gradually spreading all over Germany, but excluding Austria, were setting a new pattern. Prussia, as the largest, most populated, and most industrialized of the German states, was in the lead of the movement; soon it was ready to seize political leadership as well.

German unity was finally achieved by a Hohenzollern, the grandfather of Kaiser Wilhelm II, and it was done in true Prussian style: from above, without reference to the popular will, in the fire of three wars, and for the greater glory of Prussia.

Wilhelm I was a man of sixty-four when he succeeded to the crown of Prussia. He was a Hohenzollern of the austere, thrifty, and soldierly type who believed that Prussia belonged at the head of Germany, that only power could put her there, and that all power was rooted in a good army. Four years of ruthless dictatorship were needed to ram the necessary military reforms down the Prussian parliament's throat. The dictator was the Iron Chancellor, Prince Otto von Bismarck, who was called in for the purpose in 1862 and who for the next twenty-eight years dominated Prussia, Germany, his king, and European politics. The aims of this great hulk of a man, blunt to the point of rudeness, Prussian to the marrow, were cynically explicit. "The great problems of our times will not be resolved by speeches and majority decisions," he scoffingly told the Prussian Landtag, "but by iron and blood." It took Bismarck six years and three wars to reach his goal.

After the Austrian rout at Sadowa had shattered the Habsburg bid for German hegemony, a North German confederation, excluding Austria, was formed under the leadership of a Prussia, enormously swollen by the arbitrary annexation of various German and Danish duchies and kingdoms. Twenty-one German states adhered to this confederation, but it was still necessary to bring to heel the four South German states—Hesse-Darmstadt, Baden, Wurttemberg, and Bavaria—who did not consider Prussian leadership as an unmixed blessing.

Bismarck was convinced—and later made no bones about saying so—that the rift between the northern and southern German states could best be healed by "a national war against the neighbor people, our age-old aggressor (France)." With the help of a doctored press report—the famous "Dispatch from Ems," an early classic in the manipulation of mass media—he maneuvered the French Emperor, Napoleon III, into declaring war on Prussia. All the German states rallied to Prussia's defense in a national

crusade, and three months later the victorious German armies were be-
sieging Paris, where the republic had been proclaimed. German might,
German unity, and Prussian hegemony all received a memorable consecration at Versailles on January 18, 1871; the German Empire, including all the
German states and the freshly annexed French provinces of Alsace and
Lorraine, was solemnly proclaimed in Louis XIV's Hall of Mirrors, and
the King of Prussia became Kaiser (Emperor) Wilhelm I.

In assuming the Imperial crown on a hereditary basis the Hohenzollerns
retained the royal crown of Prussia; they never supplanted the reigning
dynasties of the lesser German states who, as we shall see later, remained
significant elements in the fabric of German society.

The new German Reich, as fashioned by its architect, Bismarck, was a
confederation, and its constitution sought to strike a balance between the
sovereignty of the four kingdoms, five grand duchies, thirteen duchies or
principalities and the three free cities which composed it, and the popular
representation of a united Germany. The states were represented in the
Federal Council (Bundesrath) which initiated laws and could alter the constitution by a two-thirds majority. In the Bundesrath, however, Prussia, as
the most populous of the states, held 17 out of the 43 seats, so that in effect
this body was gradually reduced to a distinguished debating society. The
states had kept their own constitutions, parliaments, electoral laws, local
taxes, and administered their educational and religious affairs, but they
had relinquished to the federal government, headed by the King of Prussia
who was also the Emperor of the Reich, diplomacy, the Army, and the
Navy. Communications, external commerce and customs were also in the
hands of the Imperial government.

In the Reichstag sat the representatives of the people, elected by universal suffrage (not universal enough, however, to include anyone on the
dole, and dependent on electoral laws which were rigged to favor the conservative and agricultural vote). The Reichstag had only limited control
over the Imperial government; it could do little except refuse to authorize
expenditures other than those permanently authorized by the Constitution.

The Kaiser had supreme executive power. He was Commander-in-Chief
of the Imperial Army and Navy. He governed through a chancellor, named
and dismissed by him, responsible to him alone. The state secretaries under
the chancellor were glorified office boys. It was the chancellor's task to act
as buffer between the Kaiser and the Reichstag: he usually got his way with
the latter by playing off the three conservative parties against one another.
The opposition was represented by the Social-Democrats, and by the representatives of various small national groups such as the Danes, the Poles,
and the population of Alsace-Lorraine. The great German parties represented interests rather than ideas, their attitude on the whole was one of
respect for authority. In any case, whenever they proved troublesome, the

chancellor could, and did, dissolve the Reichstag, as in 1906 when the Catholics and the Socialists objected to his colonial administration and refused to vote credits.

The Prussian constitution, and the Empire's, remarked Wilhelm's biographer, Emil Ludwig, "were a tissue of contradictions." Responsibility moved from King to Chancellor-Premier, and then "back on the King, until in the inextricable meshes it disappeared once and for all. Actually no one in Prussia or in Germany was responsible in the democratic sense which today prevails in all European countries. In very truth, the Emperor King was absolute," said Ludwig, the only limit on his authority the right of the Houses to deny supplies.

Undoubtedly the German constitutional labyrinth, by the opportunities it offered for evading democratic controls, exposed its rulers in the nineteenth and twentieth centuries to the anachronistic temptations of eighteenth-century autocracy. Neither the authoritarian traditions of the Hohenzollern family nor the kind of bringing-up to which he was subjected, had prepared Wilhelm II to resist these temptations. His failure to do so was to have tragic consequences both for Germany and for Wilhelm himself.

The future Wilhelm II—christened Friedrich Wilhelm Viktor Albert—was born at Potsdam, the Prussian Versailles, in 1859. His father was Prince Friedrich of Prussia, eldest son of the Crown Prince. Little Fritz, as he was known in the family, got off to a dolorous and unpromising start in life. His mother, Princess Victoria, the eighteen-year-old daughter of the reigning British Victoria, was ashamed of her sickly first-born, and resented the German doctors who could not cure his paralyzed left arm, as she resented generally the deplorably un-English ways of her husband's family. The marriage had not been exactly a misalliance—Friedrich, after all, had "prospects"—but Queen Victoria's daughter could hardly be dazzled by the possibility that her husband might one day inherit the crown of Prussia, one of those upstart little Continental powers, even if the most important one in Germany.

Wilhelm was two years old when his grandfather, the Crown Prince, succeeded to the throne of Prussia as Wilhelm I. He was twelve when the same grandfather stood in his defeated enemy's palace at Versailles and assumed the Imperial crown. He therefore saw the drama of German unification acted out before his eyes—with all its sordid aspects deleted—like some Arthurian epic brought to date. Its hero, of course, was the Prussian warrior-king, the victor of Sadowa and Sedan, Wilhelm I. The shining figure of the tall, upright, awesomely remote old Emperor-grandfather was the one bright beacon in a joyless childhood. Wilhelm resented his parents, especially his mother, who reserved her pallid affection for her other, healthier children; her rejection of him undoubtedly helped to mold the ambivalent feelings toward England that he later manifested. The child-hood traumatisms of hereditary rulers inevitably have a political frame of reference—not to mention political consequences; Wilhelm's martial swag-gering after he became Kaiser was at least in part an attempt to act out on the stage of twentieth-century Europe the fantasies of martial derring-do, based on an idealized version of his grandfather's exploits, that had peo-pled the picture-book universe of his unhappy boyhood.

The bitter struggle to overcome his physical handicap and to dominate his unhealthy nerves, to become the stoic, stiff-backed Prussian youth that his ancestors—especially his grandfather—expected him to be, further helped to warp Wilhelm's character. He learned to grit his teeth, as a Prus-sian boy should, during the painful electric treatments that failed to im-prove his arm, and to goose-step with the little junkers during cadet-drill in a Guards regiment, but the relative success of his efforts encouraged the tendency to arrogance and bombast he later manifested so unfortunately. (And as usually happens in such cases, under the tough, braggart shell there continued to lurk a weak, timorous, childishly dependent creature.) A victim, as he thought, of his mother's "English" and his father's "liberal" ideas, he was sent to study with common mortals at the lyceum (high school) in Kassel. Conceit being no substitute for work, he was graduated tenth in a class of seventeen, with the sober comment "satisfactory." Al-though his intellectual gifts were much above average, his tutors and their charge heaved a simultaneous sigh of relief, when, after two years at the University in Bonn where he studied constitutional law and political econ-omy, he devoted himself to the life of a Guards officer.

It was in the mess room, with his Prussian fellow officers, that young Hohenzollern felt happiest—in the mess room or on the parade ground rid-ing at the head of his regiment. One of his proudest memories was standing, at the age of eighteen, in front of the old Emperor in the newly conferred mantle of the Most Noble Company of the Black Eagle, swearing to "main-tain the honour of the Royal House, and to guard the Royal privileges."

He made it abundantly clear that he was determined to keep his oath. Emil Ludwig relates that, while still a prince, Wilhelm was in the habit of giving birthday presents of his own bust, and that he sent to England a photograph of himself under which he wrote *I bide my time.* This did not make him welcome at home, where the family atmosphere was increasingly soured by his father's impatience with the insipid duties of a perennial Crown Prince, so that he was no more amused than his mother was with Wilhelm's increasing pushiness.

At the age of twenty-three Wilhelm married Princess Augusta Victoria of Schleswig-Holstein. A handsome girl of simple and pious upbringing, she became the self-effacing, admiring wife which a Prussian pater-familias required. She gave Wilhelm six sons who were brought up in the stern

Hohenzollern tradition—Friedrich Wilhelm, who as Crown Prince was to play a significant role in German public life, Eitel Friedrich, Adalbert, Augustus Wilhelm, Oscar, and Joachim. There was also one daughter, Victoria Louise, whose penwipers, bookmarkers, and embroidered slippers graced the Kaiser's gift table on every January 27 when the Court celebrated his birthday. This was usually the date when the Berlin season began and the purple pennant flew from the ugly, square gray *Schloss*—the royal palace in the capital—to indicate that the All Highest was in residence. Home, to the Royal Family, was first the Marble Palace, then the rococo New Palace in Potsdam, pleasantly surrounded by gardens. But there were frequent and cumbersome moves to outlying country estates and hunting lodges where Wilhelm could indulge in his passion for vigorous hiking—wife, children, governesses, and courtiers puffing in the rear, willy-nilly—cook-outs and organized massacres of stags, boar, and wildbirds. His favorite spot was the hunting lodge at Rominten, in East Prussia, a huge log cabin with gingerbread adornments and neo-Gothic interior decoration. After he became Emperor he designed an official hunting costume, prescribed for all his guests at Rominten: green coat and britches, high tan boots, a tan leather belt with a hunting knife hanging from it, a jaunty felt hat adorned with pheasant feathers or the beard of a *gemsbock*. Although he jibed at his uncle Edward VII as a "silly old peacock," Wilhelm was something of a dandy himself. His wardrobe, tended by twelve full-time valets, contained more than two hundred military uniforms. Like his latter-day imitator, the Nazi Field Marshal Hermann Goering, the Kaiser had an almost compulsive belief in the importance of fitting his costume to the occasion; when he attended a performance of *The Flying Dutchman* at the Berlin Opera he put on his grand admiral's uniform; in Palestine—except when dressed as a Bedouin—he wore a white cloak adorned with a Crusader's cross; he was once dissuaded with great difficulty from dressing as a Roman general to inaugurate a museum of antiquities.

Wilhelm, when he was in the bosom of his family—and both as Crown Prince and as Kaiser he was away a great deal—led the stodgy bourgeois existence followed in most royal courts of the day. His wife, who divided her time between her children and good works, was mentioned in his speeches as "the shining jewel at my side! The embodiment of all the virtues proper to a German princess." These virtues were summarized in the words *"Kinder, Kirche, Kuche,"* and they were unquestionably dull. Irreverent Berlin wags sometimes referred to Wilhelm's jewel as *die Kirchengustl*—the Church Gussie. Evenings in the family circle had a heavy Teutonic quality; the Kaiserin sewing, the Kaiser reading dispatches and clippings, often aloud, the suppressed yawns of the ladies-in-waiting and of the courtiers. In true Prussian fashion, Papa's most often repeated remark to Mama was, "You don't understand these things." Naturally, he was glad to escape whenever he could. It is perhaps too bad that Wilhelm's strict Lutheran principles—and the Kaiserin's sharp eye—kept him from relieving the tedium of married life as his British Uncle Bertie did; his reign might have been less hectic.

As a young man he preferred the congenial atmosphere of the Guards Club, which also kept him away a great deal from the sterner necessities of training for his future job under the guidance of Bismarck. It seemed as if the training were due to go on forever. The old Emperor lived on and on, until it began to appear that he would outlive his son, Wilhelm's father. In the spring of 1887 the hapless Crown Prince developed cancer of the throat. When he came back posthaste from San Remo in Italy, where he was trying to keep alive, to be present at the old Emperor's death, he was already completely speechless. At the funeral he rode in a closed carriage, while Wilhelm, who had been flexing his muscles with increasing impatience, strode at the head of all the princes through the mourning multitude.

He did not have long to wait, and when his father died on June 15, 1888, three months later, he was ready. The day before he had garrisoned the palace with his men, and as soon as the king was dead, sentries challenged everyone who entered or left; Wilhelm had long suspected his mother of transferring vital papers for safekeeping to England. He ordered an autopsy of his father's body, so as to humiliate his mother, who had denied until the last days that her husband's illness was cancer.

The Wilhelmine era opens with two characteristic proclamations. The one to the Army contains these words: "You will soon swear fealty and submission to me, and I promise ever to bear in mind that from the world above the eyes of my forefathers look down upon me, and that I shall have one day to stand accountable to them for the glory and honour of the Army." The other proclamation, issued a day later and addressed to the German people, strikes the same note. "Summoned to the throne of my fathers, it is with eyes raised to the King of Kings that I assume the sceptre . . ." The cast of Wilhelm's rhetoric is set. It is one in which the word God recurs regularly. For Wilhelm, who compared his grandfather to Charlemagne, had no doubts about the sanctity of his own crown. That there was a shrill, parvenu note in his constant reiterations of the Divine Right of Kings was only natural. His was an upstart dynasty. Six centuries of absolutism flowed in the Austrian Emperor's veins; God's approval of the Habsburgs was so obvious that it did not have to be incessantly invoked. But the German Kaiser evidently felt more comfortable when he could bring his Celestial Ally into the picture. As in a Renaissance painting, God is usually hovering in the upper third of the background, in the same cloud as the revered ancestors, while Wilhelm, sword in hand, is slaying dragons in the forefront. Later, the Kaiser became so convinced of his direct communication with the Almighty that he would read the office on Sunday morning, and sometimes even preach a sermon, to his long-suffering guests aboard the *Hohenzollern.*

Wilhelm had the theory that most of humanity's progress was the work of ten great geniuses specially chosen by God for the purpose: Hammurabi, Moses, Abraham, Homer, Charlemagne, Luther, Shakespeare, Goethe, Kant and Kaiser Wilhelm I. There is little doubt that he considered himself as belonging to the same select company.

"Inasmuch as I regard myself as an instrument of Heaven," the Kaiser once declared in a speech at Koenigsberg, "I go my way without regard to the events or opinions of the day."

Though Wilhelm was probably in some respects a genuinely religious man, it did not always seem clear from his utterances just who was the senior partner in his unique relationship with God. As his official biographer, Joachim von Kuerenberg, points out, the Kaiser was always careful to write both *"Sein"* (His), with reference to the Deity, and *"Mein"* (My), in alluding to himself, with capital letters. "This morning the All-Highest paid his respects to the Highest," the Court Circular is alleged to have reported one Sunday.

Wilhelm not only professed the anachronistic doctrine of the Divine Right of Kings—in defiance of the German and Prussian Constitutions—but gave it a neoabsolutist twist that sometimes resembled the royal totalitarianism of Louis XIV.

"Regis voluntas, suprema lex" (The King's will is the highest law), he wrote in the golden-book of Munich's city hall, during a visit to Bavaria in 1891.

"If it should ever come to pass that the City of Berlin revolts against its monarch," the Kaiser once warned his sullen subjects, "the Guards will avenge with their bayonets the disobedience of a people to its King."

Naturally, Wilhelm had a poor view both of parliamentary institutions and of parliamentarians, whom he referred to as "those owls, those muttonheads." Curiously, the most effective resistance to Hohenzollern absolutism, both in and out of parliament, came not from the Socialists, but the right; From the very *junkers* who formed the Prussian governing class, and above all from the reigning dynasties and the nobility of the minor German states. The princely courts were picturesque survivals of the past which undoubtedly slowed down the development of German democracy, but at the same time they stood out as beacons of sanity and of traditional German culture in the gathering Wagnerian murk of Wilhelmine Germany.

"Let Bavaria protest against the reproach that she ought to look on it as a favor to be allowed to belong to the Reich," the Prince Regent Luitpold of Bavaria warned the Kaiser in 1900. ". . . we wish to be regarded, not as minors, but as brothers of full age."

The conflicts between Wilhelm and his brother-dynasts in Germany were not invariably over lofty principles—loyal subjects of Grand Duke Adolf Friedrich of Mecklenberg-Strelitz never forgave the All-Highest for having given their young ruler a playful but Imperial smack on the behind in the officers' mess of the Guard Uhlans—but they helped to remind him that the Divine Grace in the name of which he claimed supreme power was not a Hohenzollern monopoly.

Like his cousin Nicholas II of Russia, and his friend Abdul Hamid II of Turkey, Wilhelm II was a firm believer in personal rule. So was Bismarck, but the Kaiser and his Iron Chancellor did not have the same person in mind. A clash was inevitable between the old Prussian dictator and the imperious young autocrat in whose name he exercised the dictatorship. It finally came in March 1890—over the issue of the Kaiser's right to bypass the chancellor in dealing with his ministers—and after a tense, ten-day crisis Bismarck was persuaded to resign.

"The duty of watch-keeping officer in the ship of State has now devolved upon me," Wilhelm proclaimed in a triumphant speech. "The course remains as it was! Full steam ahead!"

In the mouth of a responsible, dedicated ruler such lordly words might inspire reluctant respect. But Wilhelm was an amateur, with an amateur's dislike of hard work and real responsibility. His neurotic traits, the love-hate complex which he transferred from his mother to England, his perpetual discordant whistling in the dark, have been recorded and analyzed by all his earlier biographers. More recently published evidence confirms the verdict. The memoirs, published in 1959, of the Kaiser's naval *chef de cabinet,* Admiral Georg Alexander von Muller, a member of what was known as the court camarilla, point up Wilhelm's pathological unrest, his lack of discipline and self-control, his incapacity for doing a systematic job of work. *Did the Kaiser Govern?* is the book's suggestive title. Muller, who lived in his intimacy for nearly fifteen years, describes the Kaiser as a lonely man, with no true friends, but one who could not bear to be without a constant swarm of courtiers, sycophants, and cronies.

Wilhelm reigned in a hothouse atmosphere carefully tended by his entourage who managed him like a hysterical prima donna, coddling and deceiving him in turn. The tone was set by the Kaiser's bosom friend, Count Philipp zu Eulenburg, alias Phili, an occasional diplomat, drawing-room poet, singer of ballads, fluent in the fashionable Wagnerian jargon. He was twelve years older than Wilhelm, and it is something of a surprise to come on a photograph of him that reveals a bearded, shifty-eyed, elderly beau, for he was renowned for his distinguished languor and perverse charm. (A charm that did not work on Bismarck, who said he had "eyes that would spoil the best breakfast.")

"The Prince's affection for me was an ardent one . . . my musical performances drove him into almost feverish raptures," Eulenburg records in his memoirs, speaking of his early relations with Wilhelm.

The effeminate, gushing sentimentality so glaringly evident in the relationship between Wilhelm, Eulenburg, and at times Bulow, was the fashionable tone in society friendships, when the new century was ushering in *art nouveau*. The wave of bad taste which all over Europe was twisting furniture like plasticine, bloating stone monstrously, filtering daylight through colored glass and electric light through silk and beads, put out blossoms of a particularly lurid mauve in Germany. Foreign diplomats whispered that Berlin was as full of scandals as Tiberius's Rome. Friedrich Alfred Krupp's death in Capri in 1902 was whispered to be suicide. "He did so like handsome young waiters," people tittered. The King of Wurttemberg's boon companion was a mechanic, and had not poor, mad King Ludwig of Bavaria, before drowning himself and his psychiatrist, given his coachman the prerogatives of a chancellor? And wasn't the Berlin chief of police a bit that way himself . . . ? As for the Kaiser, it all depends upon whether you look at him with a clinical or with a moralizing eye; even his harshest critics admit that these heliotrope-scented friendships of his were as blameless as they were peculiar.

High personages managed for years to dodge the notorious article 175 in the penal code, which dealt with what for a time became known as the "German vice," but after 1906 a series of politically inspired press campaigns ushered in a wave of puritanism. Poor Eulenburg, no worse than most, but more exposed, was embroiled by his enemies into a number of law suits. Finally in 1908 he was tried for homosexuality. A hypochondriac all his life, he was carried on a stretcher into court, where his relations with a Bavarian fisherman, twenty years earlier, were exposed as an example of his perversions. As a result Phili, whom many accused of influencing the Kaiser toward pacifism, was dropped by Willy—suddenly and completely.

Eulenburg owed his disgrace to the machinations of another member of the Kaiser's entourage, Baron Friedrich von Holstein, the mysterious gray eminence of the Wilhelmstrasse, who from Bismarck's dismissal until 1906 ran Germany's foreign policy. Ranking as a privy councilor, but with no formal responsibilities, Holstein, a tall, bearded man in an undertaker's frock coat, sat entrenched in an obscure office which contained, it was believed, card files on everyone who was anybody in Berlin. Lurking in voluntary obscurity, he was at the center of a web of intrigue by which he controlled Germany's relation with the exterior world. Ambassadors and ministers who came to Berlin saw Holstein first, as a matter of course. His telegrams and letters were acted on, and many official reports were marked "private for Baron Holstein"; important papers were often unavailable because the Baron had locked them up. Holstein shunned all social contacts (eating oysters and playing the stock exchange were among his rare pleasures), disdained official recognition, and consented to see the Kaiser only once, because he dreaded responsibility as a mole dreads daylight. He liked to elaborate policy with his rare cronies in a discreet but luxurious wine cellar, and had pronounced paranoid tendencies; he never went out unarmed, and, after office hours, practiced revolver shooting in an obscure gallery. Eulenburg, for many years his friend, provided a link between him and the Kaiser, but Holstein came to hate him for not being subservient enough, and was convinced that Eulenburg was responsible for his dismissal in 1906.

Eulenburg represents the classic type of court parasite that surreptitiously drains power from its host; Holstein was a primitive example of a new twentieth-century phenomenon: the anonymous servant of state who, without formal authority, wields tremendous power, because he alone possesses the specialized knowledge upon which power-decisions in the modern world must be based. In Metternich's day premiers and even monarchs could easily function as their own foreign ministers, and foreign ministers carried their planning staffs, their research departments, and their area experts under their own powdered wigs. By the end of Bismarck's tenure, however, the age of the specialist was beginning to dawn; rulers—whether by Divine Right or by the People's will—might proclaim decisions, but more and more it was getting to be the experts who actually made them. The problem of establishing controls over the specialists, which is an acute one for present-day democracies, was no less acute for early twentieth-century autocracies, but it was as yet unrecognized; the nominal masters and the masterful servants had not learned to live with each other. The executive "Indian" stalked undetected, and therefore untamed, through the rapidly growing thickets of bureaucracy. The monarchs and the ministers of the Old World looked like nincompoops, not only because they often were, but because they felt obliged to claim an encyclopedic competence that they could no longer be reasonably expected to possess.

The role of the Kaiser in the Moroccan crisis of 1905 throws some light on the true relationship between the nominal autocrat and the diplomatic specialists whom he thought of as the humble executors of his august policies. Germany had been a party to the international covenant which set up the statute of Morocco. When in exchange for a free hand in Egypt, the French obtained British support for a policy of French supremacy in Morocco, the Germans had a legitimate cue for another sensational performance by the Kaiser, although this time he was not a willing actor. On March 31, 1905, reluctantly carrying out the suggestion of his advisers, he interrupted a Mediterranean cruise long enough to land at Tangier, mount an Arab steed and proclaim Germany's support of an independent Morocco whose Sultan was to safeguard German interests there. This slap at France was planned by Bulow and Holstein with a double motive: the world must be shown that Germany could not be ignored when it came to dividing colonial spoils, but more important still, France must be scared out of relying on the Entente Cordiale. France's ally, Russia, was hopelessly tied up in the Far Eastern war; the moment was favorable for vindicating German honor and raising German prestige.

The Kaiser needed some convincing. He had no desire to antagonize France, and the whole enterprise seemed hazardous—he was not a man who disregarded his personal safety easily. On the fateful day, the sea was rough, and he stepped into the bobbing motor launch with the greatest misgivings. Arriving on shore wet and queazy, he found that he was expected to ride into Tangier on a mount whose fiery appearance was disquieting—Wilhelm's lame arm made him shy of strange horses. His nervousness was increased by the presence in the crowd of ruffianly looking individuals whom his secret service described as Spanish anarchists. Amid the welcoming din of rifle fire from whirling Arab horsemen, Wilhelm delivered his speech, not to the Sultan, but to the Sultan's uncle. Then he returned to his ship as fast as possible.

The worldwide sensation did little to mollify him, nor did a letter of commendation from Bulow:

"I shook with fear. When the news reached me that your Majesty had come away alive out of Tangier, I broke down and sat weeping at my desk while I uttered a thanksgiving to Heaven," the chancellor wrote. When his master objected, a bit plaintively, that he still could not see the point of the whole thing, Bulow replied that it was necessary for his (Bulow's) policy. He had thrown down a gauntlet to challenge the French. He wanted to see, he wrote, "whether they would mobilize."

Perhaps the most striking illustration of the complete internal power-situation in Wilhelmine Germany was in the relations between the Supreme War Lord and his Army. The eighteenth-century Hohenzollerns had been virtually their own chiefs of staff, at times their own drill sergeants. Wilhelm had been brought up in this tradition of personal command, considerably distorted by his boyhood fantasies about his grandfather's role in the wars of German unification. As a young man he had a fairly thorough grounding in tactics, command, and administration up to the regimental level. As Kaiser he was prepared to carry out his constitutional duties as Commander-in-Chief in the most literal sense.

"I don't need a general staff," he explained to one of his generals (though some historians suspect the anecdote is apocryphal). "I can handle everything myself, with my aides-de-camp."

Naturally, the Imperial General Staff, a professional aristocracy within an aristocracy, did not share the Kaiser's optimism. His mania for designing new uniforms and insignia was a constant minor source of irritation to the Army, and his meddling at maneuvers was such a nuisance that on one occasion the General Staff pretexted measles at headquarters to keep him away. The little anecdote has symbolic significance. The harder the Kaiser tried to play the anachronistic role of soldier-king, the more determined the General Staff became to deny the Commander-in-Chief any share in the decision-making process, when vital issues were at stake.

Wilhelm's attempts to govern in accordance with the doctrines of eighteenth-century autocracy were subtly distorted—and at times nullified—by the emergence during his reign of other new patterns of power. One was the influence of monopoly capitalism, a by-product of Germany's prodigious industrial growth after unification. Before 1870 Germany had been primarily an agricultural region; by 1914 it had become an industrial power on a level with Great Britain or the United States. Here is a contemporary description of the great Krupp works at Essen, the spearhead of German economic might:

". . . a great city within a city, with its own streets, its own police force, fire department and traffic laws. There are 150 kilometres of rail, 60 different factory buildings, 8500 machine tools, seven electrical stations, 140 km. of underground cables and 46 overhead. More than 41,000 workers are employed there."

The sole owner of this vast concern—the most important supplier of artillery and other weapons to the German Army—was Friedrich Alfred Krupp, the head of a dynasty whose role in shaping the nation's destiny sometimes seemed second only to that of the Hohenzollerns. At the Essen works and in his other enterprises Krupp employed a total of 78,334 men and women. The great German industrial barons displayed in some respects more social sense than those contemporary "malefactors of great wealth" in the United States whom Teddy Roosevelt had castigated; at least they had accepted without too much grumbling Bismarck's paternalistic version of the welfare state, which had made the Prussian worker the most privileged—from a material viewpoint—in Europe. On the other hand, the concentration of economic power—untrammeled by anti-trust legislation or restraints on lobbying—in the hands of a few families or closely related interest-groups had reached an extreme pitch in prewar Germany. Exposés of this hypertrophic German—and European—capitalism by contemporary Marxist and other muckrakers, including Lenin, have supplied anticapitalist propaganda with ammunition to this day (and many of the attacks would be unanswerable if the capitalism that is being attacked were the same one which now prevails in the great Western democracies). The "internationale of cannon-makers" which figured prominently in pacifist and Marxist folklore between the two wars dates back in good part to

Wilhelmine Germany, and beneath the legends there is a stratum of hard fact.

In 1913, for example, the left-wing Social-Democrat deputy Karl Lieb-knecht threw the German Reichstag into an uproar with a heavily documented exposé of the more sordid factors underlying the mounting international tension in Europe. He painted a lurid picture of ". . . the greatest armaments factory in the world bribing war-office employees; of most confidential state documents straying by mysterious means into the safe of an assistant director of the Krupp works; of a great illustrated paper in Leipzig collaborating with representatives of the General Staff and of the munitions makers to bring out a special supplement in support of a pending bill for new military appropriations; of the director of a weapons factory . . . feeding the most violent diatribes against France to the Pan-German newspaper *Die Post,* and then with stupefying Machiavellism, after having aroused French opinion with provocations in the German press, using these same bellicose articles in the French press to push Germany toward war."

Liebknecht's jeremiad was perhaps too sweeping, but it calls attention to another important, and at the time largely unrecognized, factor in shaping the basic decisions of national policy that the Kaiser assumed were the effects of His august will: the role of patriotic pressure groups (they were not called pressure groups in those days, of course, but we can easily identify them in the light of our own subsequent experience with this characteristic phenomenon of twentieth-century public life). There were several powerful, interlocking organizations working toward the same broad ends. The most important ones were the Pan-German League, the Colonial Society, and, above all, the Navy League—backed of course by the maritime and armaments lobbies—which both exploited and were exploited by the Secretary of the Navy Admiral Alfred von Tirpitz. This fateful personage, a tall, thick-set, overbearing Prussian with a flowing two-pronged beard, became the dominant figure in the German government for some years after 1897. He had little difficulty in convincing the Kaiser that a great navy was essential to a great power, and with the All-Highest's blessing launched the patriotic societies on an intensive propaganda campaign to make the nation conscious of the need for one. In time, as A. J. P. Taylor remarks, "the demagogic organizations of imperialism took the government prisoner." The Navy League's slogan, "Our Future lies on the water," resulted in the top-heavy Navy bill of 1900 which set the nation's helm straight for war. Thanks to Tirpitz and his friends, the Kaiser, before he fully realized it, found himself saddled with a policy that could hardly fail to turn England—the only uncommitted great power in Europe—into a mortal enemy, thus completing Germany's encirclement.

There is a disquieting parallel between Anglo-German relations in the years 1900–1914 and U.S.-Soviet relations after World War II. The Kaiser —and most of his subjects—did not want war with England, not even a cold war. Germany merely wanted equality with England. But, as the liberal German historian, Ludwig Dehio, points out, equality, particularly on the seas, implied "the expulsion of England from her position of supremacy." And the British considered supremacy on the water and control of the sea lanes as vital to the survival of their empire. "Seen in this light," continues Dehio, "the incidents which led to World War I were merely the shell around a hard core of diametrically opposed vital interests, like the aureole of light around the moon on a damp night."

Once the Big Navy program of 1900 had been adopted, the incidents became increasingly frequent and serious. They were aggravated by the German political and commercial penetration of the Ottoman Empire, by Germany's openly displayed sympathy for the Boers in the South African war, by Wilhelm's weakness for private theatrics in public places, by his lifelong detestation of Edward VII—Uncle Bertie had once dubbed him "the most brilliant failure in history"—and by his ambivalent feelings toward England generally. Though he frequently railed against British arrogance, the Kaiser was inordinately proud of his honorary rank as a British admiral, and on one occasion he startled the British Undersecretary for Foreign Affairs, Sir Charles Hardinge, by declaring in the course of an acrimonious discussion about relative sea power, "I am a British admiral, and I understand these questions better than a civilian like you."

Wilhelm's attitudes toward England resembled those of certain anti-British Americans, and it was significant that he usually got along better with Americans, despite their deplorable breeziness and familiarity, and their misguided ideas about democracy, than he did with British aristocrats. After the brush with President Theodore Roosevelt over some German muscle-flexing off the Venezuelan coast in 1903, the Kaiser developed a warm admiration for the wielder of the Big Stick, about whom he later said, "Of all the men I've known he showed the strongest moral courage." Wilhelm even enjoyed showing visiting American millionaires around the royal palace and bragging about his ancestors, while they talked about their millions. The Kaiser was much impressed by great wealth, and as a young prince had dreamed of establishing some colossal charitable endowment.

"Sometimes," he wrote his friend, Poultney Bigelow, the son of an American diplomat with whom he had played Indians in childhood, "I wish one of your millionaires would have the splendid idea on his deathbed of willing his fortune to me." Neither Wilhelm's cordial feelings toward American dollars and their owners, nor respect for the U. S. Navy's big stick kept him from continuing to cast a slightly colonialist eye in the direction of the New World. (On the eve of World War I he toyed for a while with a weird scheme for appeasing European tensions by creating a United States of Europe—though not organized on quite the same basis as Jean Monnet's later version—allied with Great Britain against the United States of America.)

Conclusion of the Franco-British entente, in April 1904, marked an ominous new stage in the crystallization of European antagonisms. So did the Moroccan crisis of 1905, brought to a head by the Kaiser's visit to Tangier, in which England supported her new ally against Germany; the abortive encounter between the Kaiser and the Czar at Bjorkoe; the Anglo-Russian entente signed in 1907, followed by the Reval talks in 1908; and the Bosnian crisis of 1908–1909, whose ending, though a seeming triumph for German diplomacy had made Germany appear as an overbearing bully in the eyes of Europe. Even before the Bosnian crisis had died down, a new one that was destined to have a particularly grave impact both on Anglo-German relations and on the future of the Hohenzollern dynasty broke out.

On the morning of October 28, 1908, the German Ambassador in London, Count Paul von Wolff-Metternich, laid down his *Daily Telegraph* with shaking hands and said to one of his staff, "Now we might as well shut up shop." At the same moment, thousands of *Telegraph* readers were choking on their kippers, and many an indignant sputter disturbed the ritual silence of the British breakfast table.

In a long interview accorded to a British visitor "for the purpose of giving utmost publicity to the Anglophile views held by himself and his House," the Kaiser had appealed to the British people in such auspicious terms as these: "You English are like mad bulls; you see red everywhere! What on earth has come over you, that you should heap on us such suspicion? What can I do more? I have always stood forth as the friend of England . . ."

Recalling the Boer conflict, during which he admitted that German opinion was hostile to England, the Kaiser had conjured up a pathetic picture of his grandmother, Queen Victoria, confiding in him her anxiety about the unsatisfactory progress of the war. Wilhelm, like an affectionate grandson, had drawn up a plan of campaign for crushing the Boers and had submitted it to his own general staff before sending it to Windsor Castle.

"And let me remark on an extraordinary coincidence," the Kaiser had said to his interviewer. "My plan almost exactly corresponded with that which Lord Roberts ultimately adopted . . . And now I ask you, was this not the behavior of a man who wishes England well? Let England give a fair answer."

Even worse than the explosion of fury touched off in England by the unfortunate interview was the wave of criticism in the German press over the Kaiser's bumbling attempt at personal diplomacy. For the first time, the most submissive public opinion in Europe revolted. One irreverent German cartoonist even went so far as to portray the Old Emperor, Wilhelm I, trying to intercede with the Almighty on behalf of his grandson on the grounds that it was due to the Divine Grace, after all, that he sat on the throne (an allusion to one of the Kaiser's famous speeches). "Now you want to put the blame on me," God replies.

Actually, there was no one on whom the blame could fairly be put because in Wilhelmine Germany no one was really responsible for anything that happened; the dichotomy between parliamentary democracy and absolutism—the Kaiser, if we can believe the French historian Maurice Muret, sometimes boasted that he had never read the German constitution —had completely falsified the decision-making process at the highest levels; the Prussian efficiency of the German administrative machine merely served to bureaucratize irresponsibility. The *Daily Telegraph* incident was a neat illustration. Wilhelm had concocted the "interview" himself, with the help of a British Army officer who had once entertained him in Scotland, but had sent the text to Bulow for comment before publication. Bulow, who was on vacation at the time, had not bothered to read it carefully—or perhaps had been quite satisfied to see the Kaiser inadvertently sabotaging his own hopes of a reconciliation with England—and had forwarded it to the Wilhelmstrasse with a noncommittal note. At the Foreign Office it had been passed from desk to desk like a hot biscuit plate; loyal Prussian bureaucrats could hardly be expected to censor the All-Highest's imperial prose. In the end the draft had returned to the Kaiser without objections, and he had dispatched it to England, naively convinced that he was ushering in a new era of good will in Anglo-German relations, and thereby promoting the cause of peace.

When Wilhelm discovered his mistake, he hastily departed on a hunting trip, leaving Bulow to face the storm. The Chancellor, however, proved to be lacking in the Niebelungen spirit. When the outcry, both in the Reichstag and in the Bundesrath—where there was even talk among the princely houses of forcing the Kaiser to abdicate—reached a dangerous pitch, he implicitly laid the blame at his master's door by declaring that the Emperor would henceforth "observe more closely even in his private conversations, that reticence which is indispensable to consistent policy and to the authority of the throne."

Wilhelm never forgave Bulow for what he considered his disloyalty—he got rid of the Chancellor in 1909—and the whole incident left a deep scar on his neurotic soul. The strains of the political crisis were aggravated by Wilhelm's distress over the recent Eulenburg scandal and by a tragic incident of his hunting trip: the head of the Emperor's military staff, Count Hulsen-Haeseler, a fifty-six-year-old wag greatly loved for his high spirits, had dropped dead a few moments after he had enlivened a hunt supper by cavorting around the table dressed in a ballerina's *tutu*.

On returning to Potsdam in mid-November 1908, the Kaiser took to his bed with what he called a nervous prostration and informed his family that he was going to abdicate in favor of his son, Crown Prince Friedrich Wilhelm. Eventually the Kaiserin and the Crown Prince himself talked Wilhelm out of his proposed dynastic hara-kiri, but he never completely recovered from the stormy trials of 1908; his self-confidence was irremediably shaken.

"Here started the process of the Kaiser's psychological abdication, although it was frequently interrupted by violent, irrational, temperamental outbursts, and by exaggerated aggressiveness to still the gnawing doubts," writes Admiral Muller, who was in almost daily contact with his master. The Crown Prince in his memoirs likewise refers to his father's growing irresolution and unwillingness to take decisions.

After Bulow's departure, the zigzag course of German foreign policy, the reflection of its contradictory impulses, was more erratic than ever, the absence of a firm guiding hand more noticeable. The new Chancellor, Theobald von Bethmann-Holliveg, a plodding bureaucrat, lacked the personality to counterbalance the influence of the new State-Secretary (foreign minister), the brutal, heavy-handed Alfred von Kiderlen-Waechter. The ultramilitarists, headed by the infernal Tirpitz, grew stronger than ever. Their influence on the Kaiser was reinforced by the support of the Crown Prince—until the Emperor grew jealous of his oldest son and sent him into virtual banishment after 1912. The heir to the Imperial throne, nicknamed the *windhund*—greyhound—because of his lean, aristocratic good looks, was a steadier and more responsible person than his father, but his political outlook was close to that of the most irresponsible Pan-Germanists and Big Navy fanatics. He had published writings stressing the moral wholesomeness of war and had denounced the ideal of universal peace as an "un-German monstrosity."

The Kaiser himself fell more and more under the spell of the militarist and Pan-Germanist clique (due in part to his friendship with the English racist, Houston Stewart Chamberlain, whose ideas later inspired Hitler), and German foreign policy became increasingly aggressive at every level and in every field: commercial competition, colonial rivalry—Germany, a latecomer in the European race for colonies, was dissatisfied with her modest territorial prizes in Africa, China, and the Pacific—the struggle for spheres of influence, and above all, the armaments race.

The last few years of peace in Europe progressively degenerated into a kind of cold war—they called it the "dry war" in those days—between the two rival power blocs: the Triple Alliance (Germany, Austria, Italy) and the Triple Entente (England, France, Russia). International crisis followed crisis, each one bringing Europe closer to the brink of a shooting war. The Agadir incident of 1911, when Germany for the second time challenged French colonial ambitions in Morocco, the election as President of the French Republic in 1912 of the Irredentist leader, Raymond Poincaré, the stepping-up of the German naval program, the lengthening of compulsory military service in France to three years, the reckless Austrian and Russian intrigues superimposed upon the two Balkan wars of 1912 and 1913—these were some of the fatal milestones along the road to Armageddon. The changes in the climate of European opinion that accompanied the deterioration of the diplomatic situation were no less ominous. In the early years of the new century Europeans had pinned their faith—as we do now—on the deterrent power of huge armaments programs. Gradually this faith gave way to the fear—and finally to the conviction—that the arms race in Europe made an eventual military clash between the two blocs inevitable. Instead of devoting all their energy and imagination to trying to avert war, the rulers and captains of Europe by 1914 seemed to be mainly concerned with trying to make sure that when war did come it would be at the right moment and over the right issue from the viewpoint of their respective strategic imperatives.

The ruling clique in Germany was perhaps more outspoken in expressing its cynicism than the other European elites, but it is not sure that it was basically more cynical. "Barbarism lit by neon" was the merciless verdict on Wilhelmine Germany—a generation before Hitler's Reich—handed down by the Viennese satirist, Karl Kraus, and it was a marvelously apt one. But if the neon was brighter in Germany than anywhere else in Europe, and the barbarians perhaps a bit noisier, regression to barbarism was a general European trend. We shall see this perhaps more clearly if we pause for a brief last look at the more shadowy corners of Europe, beyond the neon's reach, where the fuse for the final explosion was already being laid.

CHAPTER 9

The Gravediggers of Autocracy

A S might be expected, the pattern of outward growth and inner rot that characterized European civilization in the last years before the Great War manifested itself most paradoxically in Russia, the most backward of all the European powers. The period from 1907 to 1914 was one of the most prosperous in Russian history. In certain respects it was also one of the most brilliant. Science and technology made rapid, if uneven, progress. Industry surged ahead, laying the foundations for the spectacular economic expansion achieved after the 1905 revolution; agricultural output climbed at a prodigious rate. The army was modernized, education reformed, the administration rationalized. After the stern repression of the 1905 uprisings the Czarist despotism itself became somewhat less harsh; the parliament established by the new constitution had little real authority, but its very existence modified the climate of Russian public life and gave the country at least a superficial resemblance to a twentieth-century commonwealth. The impression that Russia was catching up with the century culturally and politically as well as materially was not wholly illusory; it was merely misleading. The progressive influences that were at work in Russian society were real enough, but they were not the decisive ones.

Two men exemplified the rival tendencies that were competing for the soul of Czarist Russia. Each in his own way was a catalyst, as well as a symbol of essential historic processes.

Peter Stolypin, who was the Prime Minister from November 1906 to his assassination in September 1911, was the chief artisan of the monarchy's recovery after the crisis of 1905. A big, burly, black-bearded man with frank and virile features, Stolypin was not exactly an enlightened conservative, but he was an honest and thoughtful one. His goal was not so much to reform the autocracy as to renovate it. As a provincial governor during the 1905 revolution he had put down insurrection in his area with a ruthless hand, and he had been Minister of the Interior during the period of repression. Yet he welcomed the constitution of October 1905—perhaps because it offered increased scope for the talents of loyal, but independent-minded servants of the Czar like himself—and during his five years' premiership would not allow it to be sabotaged or evaded. Not a parliamentarian by temperament or conviction, he was nonetheless both liked and respected in the Duma—even by its liberal members—because of his good faith and of his basic decency in human relations. Stolypin was only moderately intelligent, and the best that can be said for his political outlook is that it was based on contemporary rather than on anachronistic concepts of capitalism, but he had something that Russia in those days needed far more than deep or original ideas: character. It was Stolypin who, in the teeth of criticism both from the left and from the reactionaries, gave Russian peasants the right to withdraw from the village communes and to own their own land—the most fundamental social reform since the emancipation of the serfs. By 1914 nearly 9,000,000 peasant families were tilling their own fields in Russia, and the embers of revolution were fast dying out in the countryside.

If anyone could have saved the Russian monarchy after 1905 it was Stolypin. His antithesis in Russian history—and in a sense his victorious rival—was not Lenin, or any of the revolutionary leaders, but Rasputin, whose emergence as a public figure almost coincided in time with Stolypin's, though his final triumph came long after the latter's death. Just as Stolypin was simultaneously a symbol of residual vitality in the wasting autocracy and the main instrument of its potential recovery, Rasputin was both an ominous symptom of its decay and the ultimate agent of its collapse. One was the scientific healer, the other the irresponsible quack. Stolypin stood for the kind of rational political conservatism that seeks to preserve traditional values by modifying existing institutions to meet changed conditions. Rasputin expressed the inverted radicalism that in its panic flight from contemporary reality tramples down tradition and replaces it with synthetic legend. It is hard to believe that such an implausibly lurid figure as Rasputin could have played a significant role in the history of even a backward country like Czarist Russia—but he did.

To the politically sophisticated eye of the 1960s there is something vaguely unsatisfactory about the surviving photographs of Gregory Efimovich Rasputin. They usually depict a sturdy man of medium height wearing a peasant blouse or caftan, baggy trousers and heavy boots. He has a coarse, fleshy nose, long, brown, not-very-well-combed hair, parted in the middle, and a wiry, unkempt beard, so dark as to be almost black. He is staring hypnotically into the camera, with enormous, deep-set Ancient Mariner eyes. (Contemporary memoirs describe them as being of a piercing steely blue, with pupils that contracted to pinpoints when their owner was concentrating.) The general impression is of a genuine rascal who is inexplicably going out of his way to look like one.

The same odd effect is produced by the portrayal of Rasputin's character in most accounts of the Romanov dynasty's twilight period. His contribution to the ultimate collapse of the Czarist regime is variously evaluated by different authorities—the majority view is that it was substantial—but there is agreement so complete as to be almost suspect on his vices and short-comings. Rasputin, it appears, was a charlatan, a grafter, a simonist, a drunkard, a blasphemer, and a debauchee. He was as lecherous as a baboon and he stank like a rancid billy goat. He once pulled out a tuft of his father's beard in a public brawl, and he had a scar on his own scalp that Trotsky uncharitably links with suspected horse stealing. He was probably a secret sympathizer with one of the more disreputable heresies of Eastern Christendom, and it is not unlikely that he was even scheming to usurp the Imperial throne. He washed as seldom as possible—at least in the early stages of his public career—and he dipped his hands in the soup—preferably fish soup.

While both the adversaries of the Russian monarchy and its apologists had reasons of their own for painting Rasputin darker than life—and sometimes larger than life—the evidence that he actually was an unprepossessing scoundrel is almost overwhelming. The trouble with the conventional picture of Rasputin is not so much that it makes the subject look too much of a villain—though perhaps in some ways it does—but that it leaves a misleading impression about the nature of his villainy. Rasputin's boorishness, like his debauchery, unquestionably came naturally to him, but like the peasant smock and the matted hair, they were also props that he used deliberately to build up his public image.

At the outset Rasputin was a kind of Russian equivalent to a backwoods revivalist, but one who specialized less in evangelism than in soothsaying and healing. (His gifts as a healer, though doubtless mainly dependent on mental suggestion, were not completely bogus.) The calling was an ancient one, overlaid with a rich patina of tradition. An almost indispensable requirement for practicing it was an adequate term of preparation as a *strannik,* a variety of pious hobo. The wanderer, after acquiring sufficient sanctity in his travels, might eventually gain recognition as a *starets:* a holy man and lay religious teacher of the type made fashionable in modern times by Dostoyevsky.

The atmosphere of neomedieval religiosity—with faint undertones of Satanism—that naturally surrounded what might be termed Rasputin's paratheological career has tended to obscure his other one. For Rasputin was not just a lay preacher who dabbled in politics: he was a politician. Like his spiritual vocation, his political one was unorthodox and unofficial, but despite the exotic trimmings it conformed to a pattern that we have no difficulty in recognizing. Essentially, Rasputin was a political boss—at least he became one—and his business was power; its acquisition and manipulation. Mysticism was part of his stock in trade, but the mystique that he exploited the most significantly was a political and comparatively modern one. He was the embodiment of the unspoiled muzhik—glorified by Tolstoy and the early Populists—the Russian offshoot of Rousseau's noble savage, and the ideological cousin of all those unwashed masses in whose name homespun demagogues from every land have labored to build up the widespread twentieth-century confusion between folksiness and democracy. In a sense, Rasputin personified, among other things, the Czarist version of the Common Man, and he had to look and act the part; he dipped his fingers in the soup and scratched his behind in public for the same reason that Nikita Khrushchev takes off his shoes.

It may be useful at this point to summarize briefly the main stages in Rasputin's career from peasant lout to self-anointed holy man, and from professional mystic to political boss. The future starets was born in 1872 in the Siberian village of Pokrovskoe, near Tobolsk, just beyond the Urals. His father, Efim, was a farmer and a horse dealer. The family, like many peasant families in Russia, had no surname; eventually Gregory adopted the legal name Novyk. "Rasputin" was a nickname given him as a young man by his neighbors. It means "the dissolute," and there is every reason to suppose that it was well earned. From earliest adolescence Rasputin manifested exceptionally strong sexual urges and powers. ("Gregory can take care of them all," his wife, a sturdy Siberian peasant, commented when she heard about the swarms of society women who were pursuing him in St. Petersburg.) At the same time he was deeply—and apparently sincerely—religious, with a bent for the contemplative life. The traditional solution to his problem in Russia was to flee the temptations of the flesh by entering a monastery. In young Rasputin's case, however, there was a major contraindication. "Rasputin," once testified a Czarist police official who knew him well, "was aware of certain unhealthy and perverse tendencies which had manifested themselves in him from earliest youth. He realized that he was not made for the closely confined life of a monastery and that if he entered one he would soon be banished from it."

Instead of a monk, Rasputin became a *strannik*. He twice made the traditional pilgrimage to the Holy Land, and he wandered all over Russia, praying at its most noted shrines. No doubt he often drifted into less sanctified establishments as well, but in yielding to the more banal temptations of the flesh he could reassure himself with the thought that he was saving his soul from even graver jeopardy. His soul proved to be so often in need of rescue that for his own spiritual comfort—and for the eventual salvation of others—he was led to work out his famous dogma of redemption through repentance. Stated in its crudest terms—which Rasputin was usually careful to avoid doing—the doctrine postulated that to be saved it was first necessary to sin; at least it was essential to be humble in heart, and nothing was more truly humble than a repentant sinner. Therefore, brothers—and sisters—let us humble ourselves by sinning. The influence of the *Klysti,* an illegal and heretical sect of erotic flagellants that flourished underground in Rasputin's part of Siberia, seems apparent in his teaching, but he managed to camouflage it sufficiently to avoid prosecution or anathema; he preached mainly by example. His basic message could hardly fail to have a wide appeal—especially in Czarist Russia. Its popularity was an important factor in his rise to power.

In 1903 Rasputin, then thirty-one, arrived in St. Petersburg and set himself up as a reformed drunkard and rake. He had already acquired a wife and three children, but he had left them behind in Siberia and he was gaunt and ascetic-looking from his wanderings. His phenomenal filth, his verminous rags and his burning eyes attested the sincerity of his repentance. He was accepted as a kind of hanger-on in a fashionable theological academy, and soon found himself some influential sponsors. They included Hermogen, the Bishop of Saratov, and a monk named Illiodor, who was regarded as a pious mystic in certain drawing rooms of the capital. Thanks to such connections, Rasputin eventually came to the attention of the Grand Duchess Militsa, a noted collector of seers, mediums, and similar para-ecclesiastical bric-a-brac. His reputation as a healer was firmly established when he successfully treated a hunting dog belonging to the Grand Duke Nicholas after the animal had been given up for lost by the veterinary science of the day. He had equally good luck with the two-footed patients—especially the female ones—who submitted themselves to his ministrations, and he was also credited with some accurate forecasts of future events; among them was the prediction that the Czarina, who up to then had borne only girls, would give birth to an heir in 1904 (she did).

Introducing Rasputin to the Czar and the Czarina was probably the idea of the Grand Duchess Militsa, though it seems to have been her brother-in-law the Grand Duke Nicholas who made the actual arrangements. It was the first of numerous attempts by various schemers to build up Rasputin's influence in order to extend their own. The Imperial couple's ingrown family life constituted a kind of magic palisade that sheltered them from the normal intrigues of an autocratic Court, but their tragic obsession with the little Czarevitch's health—along with their ignorance and superstition—rendered them abnormally vulnerable to quackery, especially to quackery in pious dress.

Rasputin made the most of his opportunities. His first visit to the Imperial Palace at Tsarskoe Selo took place in November 1905. He was invited to return after a trip back to his Siberian village, and soon he was virtually commuting between Siberia and the capital. The Czarina was convinced that he had the power to stop her son's bleeding attacks, and thus to preserve his life whenever it was threatened. Any trace of doubt that may have lingered in her mind vanished in 1912 when the Czarevitch, who was near death from uncontrollable internal hemorrhages, rallied after the starets sent a telegram promising that the boy would get well. On other occasions he relieved painful or alarming symptoms merely by talking to the Czarevitch on the telephone. Many of these symptoms were no doubt aggravated by emotional stress—perhaps the child's unconscious response to his parents' anxiety—and Rasputin, like other noted charlatans, had extraordinary tranquilizing powers. He supplemented them on occasion with secret Tibetan remedies borrowed from a fellow quack, and for a time he took lessons from a professional hypnotist. The Czarina, of course, was unaware of these earthly expedients: to her mind Rasputin's success in treating the Czarevitch was miraculous; only saints could perform miracles; obviously, therefore, the starets was a saint. The Czar was inclined to agree with her.

Rasputin, however, was more than a saint: as we have noted, he was also a symbol.

". . . In the eyes of the sovereigns," observes the conservative jurist and historian Basil Maklakov, "Rasputin was the authentic representative of the 'real' people, as distinguished from High Society—the 'bridge-players,' as the Czarina termed them. In the second place, he was the prophet, the holy man whom God had sent to them for their welfare. By following his advice the Czar would thus have on his side both God and the People. What could counterbalance such an influence?"

The idea that Rasputin typified the real people, or as we would say, the common man, in Russia, was no doubt literary and oversimplified, but it was not completely delusive. The starets did not typify the urban factory worker—an increasingly important element in Russian society owing to the country's rapid industrialization—but he was an authentic muzhik, even if at times he overdid the effort to look and smell the part, and this had enormous political significance. Numerically, the peasants were still the most important class in Russia—they remained so right up to the revolution—and from the viewpoint of the Czarist state they were the most radically alienated. The muzhiks' attitude toward the Russian elites was almost that of a colonial people toward the master race: in their eyes the nobles, as Rasputin put it, were not real Russians. They regarded with bottomless distrust not merely the monarchy's tax collectors and its gendarmes, but the liberal or revolutionary intelligentzia of the cities, and the often high-minded country squires.

Rasputin correctly diagnosed this fundamental cleavage in Russian society—in one sense, his own public career was a symptom of it—and he repeatedly called it to the Czar's attention. The dynasty, he advised, should identify itself less with the noble, more with the muzhik. Reversing the slogan of the early Narodniks, it should seek to bring the people to the throne. Most of Rasputin's advice lay essentially in the field of public relations, but it was no less shrewd for that—if TV had existed in 1912 and a captive audience in the most remote villages had been able actually to see the starets bestowing his verminous blessings upon Mama and Papa, as he called the Czar and the Czarina, the destiny of the Romanovs might have been different. (Sometimes Rasputin's recommendations were more substantive: As we shall see later, he tried to warn the Czar against going to war in July 1914, and he boasted that he had saved peace in 1909 and in 1912. This was an exaggeration, but it seems established that over a period of several years Rasputin consistently advocated a cautious and pacific foreign policy—the best counsel Nicholas received from any quarter on the most important issue of the time. Rasputin also appears to have taken a curiously enlightened stand in condemning anti-Semitism, one of the major political and moral evils of Czarist Russia.)

Rasputin unquestionably had great natural gifts, perhaps even moral ones, greatly debased. And no doubt he honestly believed that he was serving the best interests of the dynasty. It was the occasional flashes of real wisdom and sincerity that made his charlatanism so destructive. There was some kind of affinity between the Dostoyevskian chaos of his personality and the regimented anarchy of the Czarist state that made him a prodigious catalyst of corruption. The Czar and the Czarina were the foremost, though by no means the most innocent, victims of this mortal chemistry. Nicholas, like many weak men, had a guilty, only half-acknowledged lust for power; he wanted to be told that it was both a pious duty and a politic course to satisfy it. His need for reassurance was all the greater after the revolution of 1905, when he had accepted to become, in name at least, a constitutional monarch and to yield some fragment of his authority to an elected parliament, however feeble.

Rasputin, whose own lust for power was the most unbridled of his passions, told the Czar exactly what he wanted to hear. Speaking as a man of God, he declared that the autocracy—just as Pobedonostev had taught—was a Divinely ordained institution for whose maintenance Nicholas would be held accountable before the Supreme Judge. Speaking as a man of the people, he affirmed that the muzhiks revered their autocrat and were unconditionally devoted to the autocracy, while they had nothing but loathing or contempt for the revolutionaries and reformers of every stripe. Consequently it was expedient as well as lawful for the Czar to disregard the constitution and put the clock back to the untrammeled absolutism of his father's day. This doctrine of despotic populism, or progress through reaction—the political analogue of Rasputin's private dogma of salvation through sin—had a tonic effect on Nicholas' morale, but it was the most dangerous intellectual drug that could have been prescribed for him. He was not the kind of ruler who misuses power; he simply did not know how to use it at all, and the more he tried to grasp in his own hands, the more slipped through his fingers.

Rasputin's influence upon Alexandra, the Czarina, was not merely unfortunate; it was definitely pathological—both in political and in psychiatric terms.

"I kiss your hands and I lean my head on your beloved shoulders," she wrote to the starets in 1909. "Oh, how light, how light I do feel then. I only wish one thing: to fall asleep, to fall asleep forever, on your shoulders and in your arms. . . ."

This is somewhat empurpled prose, even for an inveterate reader of Marie Corelli, and it is not surprising that aristocratic eyebrows were raised in St. Petersburg when the Czarina's letters were filched from Rasputin and, through an oversight on the part of the Czar's censors, found their way into print. Most sober historians, however, believe that the relationship between Queen Victoria's granddaughter and the son of the Siberian horse dealer was clinical, rather than carnal, and there are abundant precedents for it in the annals of psychiatry. No doubt Alexandra herself was blissfully unaware of the strong erotic element in her feelings toward Rasputin; it was precisely because she was a granddaughter of Victoria that she could, in all innocence, write such letters to him.

To understand fully Rasputin's role in Alexandra's life, however, it is necessary to take into account both the complexity of one of her character and the peculiarities of her unique social position. Underneath her Victorian dedication to family and duty, she was morbidly ambitious; like many other ambitious women, especially in that day, she had to satisfy her power-addict's cravings vicariously, through her husband and children. She was the kind of woman who completely dominates her husband at home while incessantly prodding him to "assert himself" outside of it. Where a suburban housewife might insist that her husband walk straight into the boss's office and demand a raise, Alexandra kept nagging at hers to act the part of the absolute autocrat that he was supposed to be. So long as she confined herself to general principles there was no problem, and as the mother of a future autocrat she could properly stress the need for handing down intact to "Baby"—the Czarevitch, Alexis—the heritage of absolutism that Nicholas himself had received from his ancestors. But Alexandra could not indulge in the detailed, day-to-day meddling in her husband's affairs that is food and drink, and the breath of life itself to a domineering woman without violating the very creed she invoked to justify her interference. By definition, there can be only one autocrat in an autocracy, and it is *lèse-majesté* even to offer him unsolicited advice. This is where Rasputin came in; in his dual capacity as the emissary of God and as the Voice of the People he could without disrespect volunteer suggestions to the Czar. And Alexandra, without seeming to intrude on her husband's prerogatives, could effectively influence his actions as a ruler by instigating, communicating, and on occasion interpreting the starets' policy recommendations.

". . . listen to me, which means Our Friend [Rasputin]," Alexandra puts it in one of her letters to the Czar. ". . . only believe more in Our Friend," she urges in another. "Be the boss," she writes in still another. "Obey your firm little wife and Our Friend." Finally there is this revelatory gem of conjugal prose: "Ah! my Boy, my Boy, how I wish we were together . . . think more of Gr. [Rasputin] . . . Oh! Let me guide you more."

The letters from which these quotations are taken were written during the war when the weird triangular relationship had assumed its final form. At the beginning both the starets and the Czarina were less blatant in their efforts to influence the dreamy and wavering Nicholas, but the pattern was established almost from the first. Rasputin knew what was expected of him; he gave the Czarina the pretexts she needed for meddling in state affairs at the same time that he exploited his influence over her to further his own ends. The emotional bond between Alexandra and Rasputin was far more complex than it appeared. In certain respects he exercised an almost hypnotic control over her, but at the same time he served as the indispensable instrument of her own will to dominate; naturally she loved him for that, as well as for other reasons, just as in a different way she sincerely loved the emotionally immature husband whose weakness enabled her to rule an empire. In matters of the heart Alexandra looked up to Rasputin with a child's awe and devotion, just as Nicholas looked up to her, but politically speaking they were partners in the power game, and the Czar himself was almost as much their accomplice as their victim. None of the three was wholly innocent or totally cynical.

A lesser, but nonetheless indispensable, cog in the power machine that Alexandra and Rasputin gradually built up was a protégé of the Czarina's named Anna Vyrubova, a dowdy, whey-faced lump of a woman with heavy dull braids of blond hair coiled around her head, and eyes like badly rinsed glassware. Anna was the daughter of a senior court official and had been briefly, unhappily married before she settled down to a poor relation's existence at Tsarskoe Selo, living in a little house assigned to her near the palace grounds. She is another almost archetypal figure: the household parasite burrowed into the intimate core of a conjugal relationship and slowly rotting it with a flaccid, excremental taint. She was Alexandra's closest companion outside the family circle and this unappetizing feminine friendship was in its way as great a triumph of self-ignorance over instinct as the Czarina's infatuation for Rasputin. Anna was herself infatuated with starets, even more submissively than Alexandra was—though equally shielded from the more goatish implications of her passion—and besides helping Alexandra celebrate the cult of Our Friend, she joined with reptilian avidity in the common task of shearing Nicholas of the few poor shreds of his manhood. (This, of course, did not prevent her from "adoring" the Czar—to the point of causing Alexandra an occasional jealous twinge.)

On the practical level Anna's chief function was to act as a liaison agent between the Czarina and Rasputin; the starets could not appear at the palace every day, but Anna could and did; thanks to her a continuous two-way communication was established. When a face-to-face conference was necessary out of normal visiting hours Alexandra could meet Rasputin at Anna's house. She was useful in other ways. There were a certain number of down-to-earth requests or suggestions—particularly those relating to the starets' personal finances—that Rasputin could not make without stepping out of his other-worldly role. Anna made them for him. There is reason to believe that she likewise prompted Rasputin at times to tell the Czarina what—for purposes of husband management—the latter wanted to hear him say. Anna Vyrubova was generally regarded by those who knew her as an abnormally stupid woman, but she must have had a good deal of sly cunning, and it included a knack for appearing even more moronic than she was which at moments may have taken in the starets himself. While loyally serving her two friends, Anna by no means neglected her own interests; even protégés of Rasputin had to pay their personal court to her if they wanted to be called to the favorable attention of the Czarina, and, through her, to that of the Czar.

Not content with influencing state policy at the highest level, Rasputin and the Czarina eventually created a huge political organization, to implement their will. Like all such machines from the precinct or courthouse level up, this unofficial "Empress's Party" operated on a basis of patronage and favors. Rasputin obtained jobs and honors for his henchmen, government contracts or inside information for his financial backers. His clique ultimately included ministers—in fact two prime ministers—bishops, high officials, and generals. It also included a couple of shady bankers, a provincial Jewish jeweler who thanks to the starets became a confidential moneylender to the St. Petersburg aristocracy and the proprietor of a prosperous gambling club, a titled, homosexual influence-peddler, and a former Okhrana operative turned professional blackmailer. General Vladimir Sukhomlinov, the corrupt, uxorious War Minister, and his pretty, somewhat scandalous young wife were among the charter members of the camarilla. Count Sergius Witts, the Prime Minister at the time of the 1905 uprising was one of the shrewd political minds behind it. A senior police official named Stephen Beletsky, who for a while was one of the key figures in the band, put Rasputin on the secret payroll of the Okhrana for a salary of 3000 rubles a month—about $800—and with the Czarina's authorization assigned an Okhrana general to supervise the starets' personal bodyguard.

Rasputin took his duties as a political boss seriously. When a major appointment or a fat contract for one of the machine's supporters was at stake he would concentrate on the tactical problem with the aid of several bottles of Madeira—his favorite drink—take a steam bath and then write himself a memo and put it under his pillow (before he learned to write he had used a notched stick as an *aide-memoire*). In the morning he would pick up the memo, declare, "My will has prevailed," and telephone Anna Vyrubova to inform the Czarina, who would then give the necessary instructions to the Czar.

For relaxation from the cares of office the starets caroused with his friends and henchmen at gypsy cabarets, and climbed, tumbled or fell into bed with an heroic number and an amazing range of feminine companions. Contrary to legend, few of them were authentic aristocrats, but the list of Rasputin's conquests, if the word can be used, included jeweled and sabled beauties from the fringes of high society, de luxe adventuresses and the wives of respectable businessmen or officials trying in their fashion to promote the interests of their spouses. Once on his birthday Rasputin organized an all-night orgy at his flat on Gorokhavaia Street in St. Petersburg that came to a near-dramatic end the next morning when the husbands of the two most indefatigable bacchantes burst into the apartment with drawn swords (the Okhrana agents detailed to guard the starets held them off long enough for him to escape with his guests down a back stairway).

On another occasion Rasputin created something of a stir in a public bath in Siberia when he brought with him a bevy of female acolytes from St. Petersburg whom he ordered to scrub him down—a salutary spiritual discipline for them, as he explained later to an inquisitive journalist. While Rasputin preferred what he called society women because, as he said, they smelled better, he did not believe in losing the common touch. Police reports note an unending disheveled stream of "yelling, cursing and spitting" prostitutes, peasant wenches, servant girls, and other women of the people emerging from the little bedroom next to the dining room in Rasputin's flat.

Neither the Czarina nor even the prudish Anna Vyrubova—though the latter often witnessed the beginning of some queer evening entertainments at Rasputin's—could be brought to believe, or at least to admit, that the starets ever behaved like anything but a saint. "Read the Apostles; they kissed everybody as a form of greeting," declared Alexandra in refuting the scandalous tales about her favorite. When the Czarevitch's nurse accused Rasputin of having seduced her the Czarina dismissed it as an hysterical delusion. Rasputin's early backers, the monk, Illiodor, and the pious if slightly gullible Hermogen were less obdurate in the face of the evidence. Following upon the lurid and documented revelations of a nun named Xenia, Hermogen called in Rasputin and extorted a confession from him. "You are smashing our sacred vessels," the sturdy bishop roared, whacking Rasputin over the head with his episcopal cross. As penance he made the starets swear on a particularly holy icon that he would never touch a woman again. The next day Rasputin, hysterically crying, "Save me, save me" (a night's reflection, presumably, had brought him to realize the implications of his vow), sought to enlist the help of Illiodor, but when the two of them returned to Hermogen's study, the bishop turned his back on the petitioner, saying, "Never, and nowhere."

Neither Rasputin's sexual extravagances nor his political influence reached their apogee until after the start of the war. The fantastic and fatal epoch in Russian history that might be termed the reign of Rasputin will be chronicled in due course; it was only foreshadowed at the time of Stolypin's death. Rasputin's rise to power had been so gradual as to be scarcely perceptible, and though he was already a national scandal in 1911 he was hardly yet a national calamity. Had Stolypin lived, he might never have become one. The virile and healthy minded Prime Minister was untouched by the morbid fascination which the starets exercised upon many otherwise sensible Russians of both sexes. He had bluntly rejected a suggestion from the Czar that Rasputin be called in as a healer for Stolypin's daughter, who had been injured by the explosion of a bomb thrown at her father in 1906, and later on when Rasputin sought an interview and tried to hypnotize him, his mind was made up. Early in 1911, on the strength of police reports about Rasputin's malversations and misbehavior, Stolypin ordered him out of the capital. The Czar was unhappy and the Czarina raged, but the order stood and Rasputin went into exile. Stolypin's action, of course, turned Alexandra into one of his mortal enemies.

By a queer coincidence, Rasputin, accompanied by Anna Vyrubova, turned up in Kiev when Stolypin and the Czar arrived for an official ceremony in November 1911. As the Prime Minister drove the streets of the town behind the Imperial carriage, Rasputin, it is said, suddenly called out "Death is after him! Death is driving behind him."

The next night, Stolypin was shot down by a terrorist in the local opera house, under the eyes of the Czar and of his two eldest daughters. It was to prove one of the most fateful political crimes in modern history—in part because it removed the only serious stumbling block in Rasputin's path— but it provides a somewhat double-edged argument to historians who believed in the unqualified primacy of the individual leader as the ultimate molder of history. It is true that the history of Russia, and therefore of the world, might have been very different if Stolypin had lived longer. Statistically, however, the odds were heavily against his survival. The dark forces that were sweeping Czarist Russia to its doom were too strong for one man to stem, and long before his assassination Stolypin had missed whatever chance he might have had to do so. His efforts to reform the monarchy had overlooked the area of most deadly abuse. Stolypin's failure is part of the story of the downfall of the Old World as a whole. The processes of social decay that at least indirectly were responsible for his death were simultaneously eating away the underpinnings of civilization—and with it the chances for continued peace—throughout much of Europe.

CHAPTER 10

Murder, Muddle, and Machiavelli

DOCUMENTARY evidence on certain aspects of the "dry war"—uncomfortably reminiscent of our own "cold war" —that preceded the outbreak of military hostilities in 1914 is tantalizingly fragmentary. Some of it is still buried in secret archives; much has doubtless been deliberately destroyed; a good deal in all probability was never written down. Scrap by scrap, however, information has been accumulating over the last quarter-century, and in the light of what our generation has witnessed, we can now both see more clearly than our fathers did, and evaluate more realistically, what might be termed the conspiratorial background of World War I. Some of the particular incidents that figure in it may at times have been oversensationalized, or exaggerated for propaganda purpose, but the rising curve of espionage and subversion, of secret violence and of public deception, in Europe between 1900 and 1914 is a phenomenon that deserves the most serious attention. As we know from examples closer to the present, when policemen imitate the methods of the underworld, while revolutionaries adopt the outlook of policemen, that is a symptom of a disordered or a decaying civilization. Before 1914, this symptom—which was also a significant factor in the ultimate breakdown of the monarchic order in Europe—manifested itself in a specially malignant form within Russia and Austria-Hungary, and above all, in the efforts of the two rival empires to exploit the revolutionary movements inside each other's borders. The secret-service duel between the Romanov and the Habsburg dynasties played a prominent part in creating the morbid climate of opinion in which the seeds of European war germinated; in the far-from-negligible degree to which it involved both duelists in the endemic conspiracies of the Balkan states, it contributed directly to the *casus belli*.

A spy scandal that came to light in Austria shortly before the war provides us with an instructive case history, as a starting point. On May 29, 1913, the Viennese press revealed that Colonel Alfred Redl, then serving as Chief of Staff of the 8th Army Corps in Prague, had committed suicide five days earlier. He had been caught, the authorities reluctantly admitted, selling secret military information to a foreign power—which, of course, turned out to be Russia. In addition to its obvious gravity from the military viewpoint—Redl had been in the Russian pay for at least seven years—the case had exceptional journalistic appeal. The unfortunate victim, the enemy agents who corrupted him, and the counterintelligence officers who discovered his treason, had all behaved in accordance with the strictest traditions of espionage fiction; the case was authenticated in the public mind by numberless examples from the real world of pulp and screen. Every detail was perfect: from the little slip that ultimately brings down even the Napoleons of crime—in Redl's case a penknife which he had dropped in a hansom cab—to the classic nocturnal visit from a stony-faced delegation of brother officers, the revolver wordlessly laid down, and the long vigil outside the traitor's bedroom, waiting for the penitential shot. (This ritual suicide for the sake of military honor led to a politically important break between the Austro-Hungarian Chief of Staff, Conrad von Hoetzendorf, who had authorized it, and his former patron, the Archduke Francis Ferdinand. The heir to the throne had his faults, but as a believing Catholic in an age of mingled fetishism and cynicism, he was profoundly shocked to see a Catholic monarchy making itself the accomplice to a self-murder, and as one of the few practical-minded men to hold high office in the Habsburg Empire, he was no less scandalized by the discovery that Redl had been allowed to blow his brains out before revealing everything that he knew about Russian espionage operations.)

Underneath its pseudoromantic trimmings, the Redl case was not only inexpressibly sordid, but definitely ominous, both in its political and in its moral implications. Unless there are depths-within-depths to the affair that have not yet been discovered, one has no choice but to view Redl as a figure of such towering shoddiness as to be almost archetypal. He certainly was not a typical Austrian or Viennese of his generation, but at the root of his felony there seems to have lain a bottomless pit of the triviality which was perhaps the most characteristic failing of Habsburg society in its last days. One cannot even say that Redl was a kind of moral cretin; he merely seems to have been an extreme case of moral *schlamperei*. As far as we know, he had no subversive, or other convictions; no overpowering passion or inexorable necessity led him to betray, not only his country—an ideal that was hazy to many of Francis Joseph's subjects—but his uniform and his personal oath to the Emperor. He was a practicing homosexual, and the Russian agent who had recruited, or debauched him, was a Moscovite nobleman with numerous contacts in the fashionable male demi-monde of the day, but the bond of perversion between them seems to have been no more significant than a common interest in tennis or stamp collecting might have been; it merely brought them together. There may have been some hint of blackmail, but it is not likely that before the first act of treason it was a compelling factor; the Austro-Hungarian army was fairly broad-minded about its officers' private failings, as long as they were somehow connected with sex. Redl's vice, however, cost him a good deal of money. He had a kind of male concubine, a handsome but flighty and spendthrift lieutenant, whom he passed off as his nephew and on whose behalf he was constantly running into debt; Redl, himself, liked to drive a flashy automobile and generally to cut more of a figure than he could afford to do.[1] The wages of treason were comfortable, but on a petty-bourgeois scale in keeping with the whole climate of the affair. Redl got a regular salary from the Russians, but it does not seem to have amounted to more than a few hundred dollars a month—no doubt there were occasional bonuses—and it was handled with the contemptuous sloppiness of a dishonest public-works contractor bribing a municipal inspector. Redl's clandestine pay was sent him in a bulky envelope mailed at fixed dates to a postal-box address in Vienna from the same village near the Russian border. (This unimaginative practice naturally was a factor in his eventual detection.)

There is some controversy about the exact importance of the secrets that Redl betrayed but by even the most conservative estimates it was great. They included at least one document on the highest strategic level—the so-called Plan Three for a lightning Austro-Hungarian attack against Serbia—detailed tactical information of major significance such as the pertinent data on the great Austrian fortress of Przemysl in Galicia, and last but not necessarily least, everything that the Russians wanted to know about Austrian espionage and counterespionage activities. For Redl, from 1900 to a short time before his arrest, had been chief of the Austro-Hungarian counterespionage and military secret service; among other services rendered his clandestine masters, he had revealed to them the identity of a high-level Russian traitor, also a staff colonel, who had started selling information of strategic value to the Austrian military attaché in Warsaw (the Russian had been discreetly encouraged by his superiors to commit the same "honor suicide" that was later imposed on Redl).

Not all these facts were divulged to the public at the time, but what was generally known or approximately surmised was enough to impair seriously public confidence in the Imperial government, if not in the dynasty itself. At the same time the "activist," or militarist clique in the Austro-Hungarian army and government reacted to the discovery of Russian spying upon

[1] When police raided Redl's flat in Prague, among strange discoveries they found a large and expensive collection of life-size female dolls.

Austria almost as if it had been an outright act of aggression, calling for violent retaliation. To the "Activists" the Redl case underscored the need for eliminating the Serbian menace without delay, so as to be able to mobilize Austria's full strength against Russia when the inevitable showdown came. This reaction was not wholly logical, but it was understandable—especially when we recall the impact of major spy scandals on foreign policy in other countries, including the United States and Soviet Russia. Spying has been an ineradicable aspect of the power struggle between nations ever since they have existed; kept within reasonable limits, it disturbs international relations no more seriously than prostitution or crime, within certain bounds, disturbs the basic order of society. But just as crime or prostitution when they get out of hand become intolerable social plagues, so espionage when it is conducted on a spectacular scale, or with a blatant disregard of the conventional hypocrisies of international life, is likely to be considered, with some justification, as a form of aggression. The Russian operations based upon Redl's treason constituted such a case.

Perhaps the Russian secret service had some cloudy notion of the grave responsibilities it was incurring in recruiting as one of its agents the head of the Austrian secret service. Colonel Batiouchine, the operating head of the relevant military branch in Russia, through sheer slackness or recklessness occasionally exposed his Austrian colleague to unnecessary and terrible risks, but he went to even more terrible lengths to protect him. If we can trust apparently sober contemporary sources, Batiouchine systematically supplied Redl with the identities of important Russian spies on the soil of the Dual Monarchy so that he could build up his reputation for reliability and efficiency by arresting them. This deliberate sacrifice of one's own agents is not without precedent in the history of espionage, but in the Redl affair it was carried out by the Russians on an unprecedented scale, with unprecedented ruthlessness and cynicism. Within the small but important segment of the Czarist state represented by Colonel Batiouchine's military espionage service, it is probably not excessive to say that one of the essential dikes of civilization had crumbled and that kind of localized regression had taken place to the value-systems of barbarous times. What is graver than that the break was not limited to one area. It was widespread throughout what might be called the police sector in Czarist Russia, and in those organisms of Czarist diplomacy which by function, preoccupation or tradition, shared the police outlook. This bureaucratized barbarism deserves closer study, but it may help to give us better perspective if we first examine the parallel regression from earlier ideals and restraints that set in after 1905 among the revolutionary adversaries of the Czarist state, particularly among those who were destined eventually to succeed it: the Bolsheviks.

The name "Bolshevik" dates back to a congress of the Russian Social

Democratic party (composed of revolutionary Marxists) held in London in 1903. The faction headed by Lenin—who after a term of prison and banishment to Siberia had escaped to Western Europe in 1900—won a majority (in Russian, *bolshinstvo*) on every major issue under discussion. Underlying the purely technical ones were the basic problems of whether the party should be run along normal parliamentary lines or whether it should be a disciplined combat group under the leadership of "professional revolutionaries" like Lenin himself; whether it really believed that violent revolution was the ineluctable road to socialism, or whether, like most Western Socialists, it merely paid lip service to the formula; above all, whether or not it accepted Lenin's doctrine that once the revolution had triumphed, a dictatorship of the proletariat must be established to build a socialist society. To earnest Russian Marxists these were grave and fundamental options; the bitterness generated by the division of opinion over them was aggravated by the fact that while Lenin won over a majority of the delegates who had been able to reach London, his main opponents, the Mensheviks (minority) undoubtedly represented a majority of the party as a whole. A third body in Russian Marxism, an organization of Jewish Social Democrats called the *Bund,* stood close to the Menshevik position.

After the 1905 revolution the split between Bolsheviks and Mensheviks steadily widened, as Lenin's doctrine of revolution became increasingly rigid and implacable. In his own mind Lenin was merely applying, or at most developing to their logical conclusion, the classic dogmas of Marxism; in reality he was laying the foundations of a new philosophy which was destined much later to become known—after it had already been half-superseded in its turn by an even grimmer *mystique* of power—as Leninism. To understand it, one must study, among other things, the personality of its creator, though Lenin, himself, would no doubt have indignantly denied this.

Lenin was one of the great human paradoxes of all times, not only because he was so full of contradictions, but because these contradictions of character fused into such astonishing consistency of action and thought. There was a paradoxical element even in his physical appearance. There was undoubtedly something of the intellectual revolutionary in the looks of this stocky little Slav, with his domelike head, nearly bald from early manhood, his snub nose and high Tartar cheekbones, his slightly disquieting hazel eyes, and his small reddish-brown beard and mustache, but there was more of the neighborhood confectioner. Lenin's cheap, sometimes shabby, but always neat and proper clothing contributed to the bourgeois effect: during his period of exile—from his thirtieth to his forty-seventh year—he was more often seen in a bowler hat than in the workman's blouse and cap.

Whether in Munich, Geneva, London, Paris, or Zurich, Lenin's life was as bourgeois as his appearance. Weekdays he studied in some library or

wrote; on Sunday he and his wife, Nadejda Konstantinovna Krupskaya, bi-
cycled in the suburbs or strapped on rucksacks and went for long walks in
the country. Occasionally Lenin indulged in a game of chess with some
friend at a neighborhood cafe, but he sedulously avoided such bohemian
meeting places as the famous Café de la Rotonde in Montparnasse, the
Left Bank artist's quarter in Paris, where many of the Russian emigrés gathered night after night, to smoke, to drink, to argue endlessly about politics
and art.

There was only one anomaly in the studious middle-class correctness of
Lenin's personal life, but it was a highly significant one: his strange rela-
tionship with a French-born woman revolutionary who called herself Inessa
Armand. (There is a certain obscurity about her background; some sources
give her maiden name as Elizabeth Pecheux d'Herbenville, others as Ines
Stephane.) Inessa, who had been brought up in Russia by an aunt serving
as governess in a wealthy Russian family, was five years younger than
Lenin. She was a statuesque, handsome blonde with slightly bovine features
(Lenin's wife, Krupskaya, was frankly homely and dressed with a lack of
glamour notable even in emigré Marxists circles). Inessa had drifted away
from her husband, a well-to-do Russian landowner with intellectual leanings, after bearing him five children, and had joined the Bolsheviks during,
or possibly before, the 1905 revolution. She had been imprisoned and de-
ported to Siberia and had escaped to the West in 1909. It is not certain
when she first met Lenin, but from 1910 until the end of his exile she kept
popping up in his life. (She returned to Russia with him on the famous
sealed train, and died of cholera in the Caucasus during the Civil War.)
She was a constant visitor to his lodgings and frequently accompanied
Krupskaya and him on their Sunday hikes.

Krupskaya treated Inessa almost like a younger sister, and after her death
spoke of her with a curious mixture of reticence and affection. Nina Gour-
finkel, who has written a popular but solidly documented biographical
sketch of Lenin, based in part on interviews with one-time members of his
entourage in exile, suggests that Inessa was the great love of his life. There
was certainly a romantic—and intensely Russian—element in their friendship; Inessa, besides helping Lenin at times with his professional correspondence, lightened his rare off-duty hours by playing Chopin and
Beethoven on the piano to him—his favorites were Kreutzer and the Moon-
light sonatas—and they had a common literary enthusiasm. This was a once-
famous Russian novel called *What to DO*—significantly the title chosen by
Lenin for one of his early tracts—about a woman revolutionary who in an
emancipated and idealistic way shares her life with two men, but who is so
prolixly honest with both of them in analyzing her problems that she cannot
have had much time left for any other sharing. According to Mme. Gour-
finkel, Lenin read this revolutionary pot-boiler, steeped in Narodnik sen-

timentality, no less than five times; Inessa was inspired by it to write a pamphlet in favor of free love.

Here the complexity of Lenin's character reveals itself with extraordinary clarity. Replying to a letter from Inessa about her proposed pamphlet, Lenin lectured her in the same doctrinaire, pedantic tone with which he habitually reproved deviants from the party line, as fixed by him:

"You write: 'Even an ephemeral passion or a liaison are purer and more poetic than kisses without love between vulgar and trivial married couples'. Is this opposition really logical? . . . Why passion, rather than love? . . . Why ephemeral? . . . Wouldn't it be better in this popular tract to hold in contrast to the kind of dirty and vulgar marriage without love practiced by the bourgeoisie, the peasantry and the intelligentzia, the ideal of civil, proletarian marriage with love?"

This is the familiar Lenin, the revolutionary prig, the dry fanatic, the calculating propagandist, the intellectual who prided himself above all else on being down to earth. But underneath one clearly sees the repressed idealist, despising mere "passion" as against "love," aspiring after the eternal rather than the ephemeral. One also sees the naive cultist with his sacramental belief in the rites of civil anti-marriage, with his radiant myth of the love-worthy and love-able proletarian, the inverted twentieth-century version of Rousseau's noble savage. Lastly, one sees the blight of the corrosive, and corroding, contempt for human weakness—inspired, perhaps, by the memory of how supposedly liberal and humanitarian-minded friends had turned their backs on the Lenin family when his brother had been arrested—that sometimes betrayed Lenin into betraying his own humanity.

Leninism—that is the total body of Lenin's thought and practice, not the mummified corpse of Leninist theory propagated after his death—transposes all these conflicts of Lenin's personality to the political plane. They were both aggravated and put into practical harness by the early Bolshevik cult of the revolutionary will and by their vocation for the heroic life. These nearsighted, stoop-shouldered, incorrigibly urban intellectuals were no less incorrigible—though one suspects, usually synthetic—men of action than such chest-beating bourgeois contemporaries as Teddy Roosevelt, Winston Churchill, or Cecil Rhodes. Thanks, however, to their Marxist intellectual formation, they were not mere believers in action for the sake of action, but something even more dangerous: dervishes of the effective act. They had an almost idolatrous admiration for professionalism.

In Czarist Russia conspiracy was the precondition for effective revolutionary action—or so the Bolsheviks believed—and being a professional revolutionary therefore implied being a technician of conspiracy. Lenin deliberately, almost ecstatically, steeped himself in the professionalism of his calling. His letters and many of his newspaper articles are peppered with technical, do-it-yourself advice on the preparation and use of invisible inks, bomb-making in the home, how to be a success in street fighting, and related subjects. During the 1905 revolution Lenin came close to bridging the psychological gap that had hitherto separated the Marxist revolutionaries in Russia from the cultists of terror like the Social Revolutionaries and the Anarchists. In fact he even shocked some of the more high-minded terrorists by organizing bank holdups and other systematic acts of brigandage— termed expropriations or "exes"–to raise funds for the party.

A congress of Russian Social Democrats—including both Bolsheviks and Mensheviks—held in Stockholm early in 1907 banned further "expropriations" but unwisely authorized Lenin to create a "Military Technical Bureau" for defensive action against the attacks of the extreme-Right Black Hundreds gangs. Under this cover Lenin and several of his trusted lieutenants who had remained in Russia proceeded to organize the expropriation raids on a bigger and bolder scale, utilizing squads of so-called *boyeviki*– who were officially supposed to be free-lance desperadoes over whom the party had no control. To support this fiction Lenin kept the proceeds from the "expropriations" to build up his factional machine, instead of turning them over to the central party treasury. The *boyeviki,* though they also perpetrated some daring robberies in Moscow and even in the capital, were particularly active in the Caucasus where their operations were directed by a sullen pock-marked Georgian, a former theological student named Josef Vissarionovich Dzhugashvili, who also used the conspiratorial pseudonym Koba, and the pen name Stalin. On occasion Stalin took part in the raids— he also took part in the party congress at Stockholm which had outlawed them—but his field commander was usually a tough, cheerful, cross-eyed incredibly daring young fellow Georgian named Ter Petrossian, alias Kamo, the Jesse James of the Russian revolutionary movement.

Kamo raised an outlaw band of several hundred mountaineers, trained them, and indoctrinated them, more or less, with Marxist principles; some of these highwaymen-comrades were perhaps a bit hazy on dialectical materialism but they could—and did—pass the stiffest examinations in laying ambushes, and in diversionary bomb-tossing. At their head Kamo carried out a brilliant series of train and bank robberies, attacks on police posts and guerrilla skirmishes in the hills. He was several times captured and questioned under torture. Twice he was sentenced to the gallows, and he was once forced to dig his own grave. During one period of detention he avoided execution by pretending to be insane and successfully kept up the simulation for four years, finally escaping from his prison-asylum in the Caucasus and making his way to France.

Off duty, Kamo was a gentle, warmhearted fellow with a kind of schoolboy hero-worship for Lenin. Lenin and Krupskaya were touched by his devotion and he was a special favorite with Krupskaya's mother; when

Lenin was hiding in Finland after the collapse of the 1905 revolution, Kamo would sit for hours in the old lady's kitchen munching almonds and boasting to her about the sparrows he had tamed while he was in prison; then he would strap on a rucksack weighted with revolvers and bombs and head back for St. Petersburg on some hazardous underground mission. Krupskaya relates how Kamo during this Finnish period of Lenin's once threw a scare into the emigré group by walking up to them in a restaurant, flamboyantly dressed in the Caucasian national costume and carrying under his arm a big round parcel that everyone supposed must contain a bomb. It turned out to be a melon that his aunt had sent him from the Caucasus and which he had smuggled across the border to present to Lenin.

Kamo's most famous exploit was the Tiflis stagecoach robbery carried out under Stalin's personal supervision in June 1907. The stagecoach, containing the equivalent of more than $100,000 in Russian banknotes, was rolling through the streets of the city, headed for the bank, with a military guard and an escort of armed Cossacks. Kamo's men dropped a large bomb on the convoy from the roof of a house, then attacked it with revolvers and grenades. They made off with the money, and Kamo got away with part of it to Berlin.

Difficulties inevitably arose in changing the loot—the Russian authorities had naturally circulated the serial numbers of the stolen banknotes, which were all in 500-ruble denomination. Maxim Litvinov, who later became the Soviet Commissar for Foreign Affairs, was arrested trying to pass some of them in Paris. One of Lenin's associates—who, as we shall soon see, had been the brains behind most of the "expropriations"—hatched a complicated scheme for doctoring the serial numbers of the notes that Kamo was holding. Either as part of this operation, or in an attempt to add forgery to robbery was a means of raising funds, some watermarked paper was purchased by Bolshevik agents in Germany. Thanks to one of the numerous Okhrana spies in the party, the Prussian police were tipped off about the plot, and Kamo was arrested with the Tiflis banknotes in his possession. It was while awaiting extradition that Kamo, on the advice of his German lawyer, decided to feign madness.

The police investigation in Berlin revealed that the Bolsheviks had cynically and ruthlessly exploited their unsuspecting Prussian comrades; the watermarked paper for the proposed venture in forgery had been shipped without the knowledge of the German Social Democrats to the address of their Berlin newspaper *Vorwaerts*. There were also indications of a somewhat nebulous plan on Kamo's part to "expropriate" the Mendelsohn Bank in Berlin.

The resultant scandal was tremendous. To most Western Social Democrats—and even to some Bolsheviks—the *boyeviki* had ceased to be revolutionaries and had turned into plain criminals. Lenin came under heavy criticism, but he remained unperturbed and scornful. Under Menshevik pressure a party investigating committee was set up to look into the Tiflis affair and the Berlin scandals but Lenin by clever maneuvering managed to have them hushed up. Stalin was suspended from the party, but eventually reinstated. At the time no evidence directly linked Lenin with the activities of the Caucasian *boyeviki,* but it was later revealed that most of the spectacular expropriations, including the Tiflis raid, had been explicitly authorized by a self-appointed secret committee—an underground within the Bolshevik underground—one of whose members was Lenin himself.

The other two members of this clandestine planning board, afterward nicknamed the *Troika,* were Alexander Bogdanov, a scientist and Marxist theoretician, and Leonid Krassin, one of the most extraordinary personalities of the Russian revolution. A high-paid engineer working for a big German firm, Krassin was also a conspiratorial genius. Neither the Okhrana nor most of his Bolshevik comrades suspected his true role in the party, which at one period was more important than Lenin's. For many years Krassin was the real head of the underground Bolshevik organization in Russia; his most essential activity was smuggling in arms for the revolution —especially in 1904 and 1905—but he was also the planning brains behind the *boyeviki* gangs. It was Krassin's fertile mind that concocted the scheme for changing the serial numbers of the Tiflis banknotes, and he who had ordered the mysterious watermarked paper in Berlin.

Eventually, Lenin came to the conclusion that the *boyeviki* were getting out of hand and ordered them to be disbanded. Apparently he also felt that Krassin was allowing conspiracy to become an obsession with him, and in 1909 the two men quarreled; Krassin dropped his revolutionary activity, and when he rejoined the Bolshevik ranks after 1917 it was to serve the revolution as its ambassador—as far as is known an impeccably respectable one—in Paris and London.

Despite his break with Krassin and his suppression of the *boyeviki,* Lenin never completely repudiated bankrobbery as a legitimate adjunct to revolution. In 1912 he sent Kamo—who had escaped from prison in 1911— on a clandestine arms-buying mission through the Balkans and then ordered him back to Russia for a desperate and ill-fated "expropriation."[2]

2 Kamo, after completing his Balkan assignment, made his way back to the Caucasus and reassembled a group of his old *boyeviki* to engage in fund-raising activities for the party. They attempted an attack on a bank in the dashing old-time style, but it failed and Kamo was once more captured. Imprisoned in the fortress of Metekh with four death sentences now hanging over him, he was saved from the scaffold by the public prosecutor who so admired Kamo's lion-hearted courage that he purposefully dragged out the legal proceedings until a general amnesty celebrating the tricentenary of the Romanov dynasty in 1913 commuted his sentence to twenty years of forced labor. He was released by the 1917 revolution and played a heroic part in the civil war. He finally was killed during the early 1920s in a traffic accident—in Tiflis.

He also continued to make use of various shady or unsavory characters, including several who he almost certainly knew were double agents.

"A central Committee, to be effective," he once said (according to David Shub), "must be made up of gifted writers, able organizers and a few intelligent scoundrels."

The formula unquestionably fitted the Bolshevik central committee, whose quota of intelligent scoundrels at different times included from one to as many as five informers of the Okhrana.

Lenin's cynicism, his ruthlessness, and his dictatorial management of party affairs were repeatedly denounced by both Western and Russian Social Democrats as contrary to true Socialist ideals. "No party could exist under the regime of this Social Democratic Czar, who regards himself as a super-Marxist, but who is in reality nothing but an adventurer of the highest order," thundered Charles Rappaport, a Socialist of Franco-Russian background who later became a well-known Communist journalist. Even Trotsky, an early admirer of Lenin who held himself aloof from the Menshevik-Bolshevik quarrel, could no longer swallow some of Lenin's methods. "The entire edifice of Leninism at present rests and lies on falsification, and carries within itself the poisonous seeds of its own disintegration," he wrote to a Menshevik leader.

Curiously, there was little contemporary criticism among European Socialists of what today seems one of the more questionable episodes in Lenin's revolutionary career: his move from Paris to Austrian Galicia in 1912. Both in Cracow, where he first settled—with Krupskaya and Inessa Armand—and later in Poronin, in the mountains he was conveniently near the Russian border. Whether for conferring with overt representatives of the Bolshevik center in Russia—it was legally tolerated after 1907—or for smuggling in clandestine propaganda and instructions to underground groups, Galicia was a much better base of operations than Paris or Geneva. It was also, however, one of the most sensitive frontiers in Europe—especially after the Redl case. The police and military authorities of the Dual Monarchy kept a particularly vigilant eye on all comings and goings across the Russian border; while not as pathologically suspicious as their Russian counterparts, these guardians of an empire where the Metternich tradition was still honored were notable neither for their liberalism nor for their naïveté.

Naturally, Lenin needed to have the authorization of the Austro-Hungarian authorities before settling down in Galicia with his wife and helpers. It was obtained for him by one of his more mysterious friends, a Polish Social Democrat—by nationality an Austrian subject—named Jacob Fuerstenbuerg, also known at various times as Ganetsky and Hanecki, who was later to play a role in connection with an even more questionable phase of Lenin's career. Undoubtedly the Austrians reasoned—quite cor-

rectly—that allowing the emigré Bolsheviks to set up an operational base—
for that was what it amounted to—on the Russian border would help the objectives of their cold war with Russia. Austrian appreciation of Galicia's
strategic potentialities had already been indicated by the support given
another group of exiled revolutionaries from Russia—Jozef Pilsudski's
Polish nationalists—who, with the help of certain friends in the Austro-
Hungarian General Staff, were receiving training for guerrilla warfare at
secret camps in Galicia. The Austrians were also in touch with an Ukrainian
nationalist underground. However useful the Bolsheviks might be considered, however, it seems highly unlikely—on the basis of everything that
we know about the Austrian bureaucratic mind—that they would have
been allowed to operate across the Russian border without some discreet
Austrian supervision of their activities; if nothing else the Austrians would
need to make sure that no "expropriations" were being organized too pro-
vocatively close to the border; they would probably want to take precau-
tions, too, against the Russian secret service slipping some agents into the
stream of legal or clandestine visitors to Lenin's headquarters.

If it is possible, of course, that arrangements were made by the Austrian
authorities to supervise Lenin's revolutionary activities without his knowing it—possible but somewhat improbable. Of course, depicting Lenin as an
"agent" of the Emperor Francis Joseph is even more absurd than the attempts that were made later to depict him as an agent of Wilhelm II. Lenin
was never the agent of anyone, or of anything, but his own implacable
dream of revolution. There is a strong suspicion, however, that in the service of his dream he deliberately allowed himself to be exploited for a while
as a weapon in the Austrian secret-service duel with Russia. To that degree he bears some modest share of responsibility—along with the autocrats
and the gun merchants—for World War I.

There was one daily newspaper in Russia that had a single subscriber:
the Czar. It was published by the Ministry of the Interior, and it consisted
exclusively of information about the activities of the secret police and of
the penal administration for political prisoners. The sheet probably contained everything of importance known to the Minister of the Interior himself, but like every other newspaper in Czarist Russia it was heavily
censored; some of the police news was not considered fit to print, even in
a classified publication for the Emperor's eyes alone.

The censoring was done, of course, by the policemen themselves, that is
by the officials—not necessarily at the top level—of the Okhrana, the political
secret police. Nominally reporting to the Ministry of the Interior, but actually a law unto itself, the Okhrana was only one of several Russian secret
services; leaving aside the unofficial and the purely military ones for the
time being, the general police, which was also under the Minister of the

Interior, had some specialized undercover departments, and the Police of the Imperial Court, responsible for the protection of the Czar and his family, had an important secret branch which employed numerous spies and stool pigeons. To further complicate things, the Okhrana itself was highly decentralized; it had branches in several of the larger Russian cities and in foreign capitals, each with its own network of secret informants.

In one form or another the Okhrana had existed since the days of Peter the Great, but its most spectacular proliferation took place after the assassination of Alexander II in 1881. From 1905 on its growth was quite monstrous, by 1914 it was believed to employ regularly some 20,000 officers and agents. Its regular budget was around $2,000,000 a year, some of it earmarked for press and propaganda use, but it could also draw when necessary on a $5,000,000 secret state fund under the Czar's personal control. These sums look modest by present-day standards, but they were enormous in the society where the salary of a secret agent was often as low as $15 a month.

Like other political police services in Europe at the time—for example the French Sureté Générale—the Okhrana tried to plant or recruit undercover informants in the various revolutionary organizations. Its uniqueness lay in the scale of its operations, and in its encouragement to these informants to play an active role within the groups they had penetrated, even when it meant breaking the law. After the revolution a former chief of the Okhrana, General Guerassimov, who headed the organization from 1906 to 1909, revealed that he never had fewer than 120 secret agents in the left-wing revolutionary organizations. Most of these agents, he added maliciously, were still active in the Soviet state. One of the Okhrana's most remarkable undercover men was a florid, flashily dressed one-time St. Petersburg metalworker and labor organizer named Roman Malinovsky, who first spied upon the Mensheviks, and then with police approval joined the Bolsheviks, where he soon became a special protégé of Lenin's. His career in the party was spectacular; he was one of the "intelligent scoundrels" on the Bolshevik central committee, and he rose to be the chief Bolshevik spokesman in the Imperial Duma—the Okhrana is said to have facilitated his election as a deputy by arresting his leading rivals. Lenin named him as the St. Petersburg manager and nominal publisher of the Bolshevik organ Pravda, and Malinovsky faithfully submitted copy for it both to Lenin and to his chiefs in the Okhrana.

Thanks to Malinovsky, the Okhrana obtained invaluable information about the revolutionary plans and activities of the Bolsheviks, but though it occasionally arrested undercover Bolshevik organizers, it made no use of its inside knowledge to cripple the party. On the contrary, it encouraged its growth, not only to build up its own agent, Malinovsky, but apparently because it considered the Bolsheviks, with some justification, as a disruptive element in the ranks of the Russian Marxists. According to some sources, the Okhrana at Malinovsky's suggestion enabled Lenin to win a majority at a special party congress in Prague in 1912 by arresting three of his leading opponents. The symbiosis between the Okhrana and its Bolshevik enemies, not only through Malinovsky, but through a host of lesser though no less active double agents, was close enough to leave a lasting mark on the operational attitudes of both organizations: the Bolshevik spy-phobia which later attained such monstrous proportions in the Stalin era was certainly in part the heritage of the Okhrana.

The Okhrana's relations with the out-and-out terrorist groups were no less equivocal than its relations with the Social Democrats. For many years the head of the Social Revolutionary assassination squads, a bearded, appropriately villainous-looking individual named Evno Azew, was the Okhrana's star undercover agent. Unquestionably he was strategically placed: the most formidable terrorist organization in Russia could not plan a murder without the Okhrana receiving warning in advance. There was, of course, one slight drawback to the arrangement: if Azew were not allowed a reasonable quota of assassinations his professional reputation might suffer, and eventually the terrorists would replace him with a more efficient and reliable killer. On the other hand there was a feeling in some police circles that Azew had been allowed perhaps a little too much scope when in 1904 he helped plan the murder of his own employer, Minister of the Interior V. K. Plehve; the feeling grew sharper the following year when Azew's associates blew up the Czar's uncle, Grand Duke Serge in Moscow. Strictly speaking, Azew was not to blame for this outrage; he had reported it in good time for perpetrating it, but the Okhrana, apparently fearing to expose a useful agent by being too explicit, had passed on to the local authorities a warning, so vague as to be worthless.

When Azew later reported a plot to assassinate the Czar himself, General Guerassimov decided that to avoid any further slips he would personally take over the management of his talented but redoubtable agent. Thanks to this high-level supervision the plot was eventually foiled without damage either to the Czar or to Azew. Eventually Azew was exposed, but he was never brought to justice. When the scandal became serious the Okhrana helped him to escape abroad, where he remained in genteel retirement until his death in 1918.

Employing terrorists as double agents is inescapably a tricky business; this was particularly true in Russia where the national temperament lends itself to complex and subtly shaded relationships intermediate between absolute loyalty and total treason. There were probably Okhrana agents in the revolutionary organizations—Azew may actually have been such a case—who did not know themselves which side they were ultimately betraying, or betraying the most. Uncertainties on this score were compounded by divergencies among different factions in the Okhrana—never exactly a band of brothers—over whom the empire could best spare if someone had to be sacrificed to preserve an agent-terrorist's "cover." Regulations promulgated in 1907 instructed *agents provocateurs* to refrain from participating in terrorist activities whenever possible; in no case were they to participate without first obtaining authorization from their immediate supervisors. These rules tended to eliminate some of the incidental abuses that had developed, but did not solve the basic moral and practical problems of a police force trying to protect the state by conspiring with its enemies.

The evils of the system were dramatically underscored by the assassination of Prime Minister Peter Stolypin in 1911, who was shot down under the eyes of the Czar during a gala performance in the opera house of Kiev. The Kiev branch office of the Okhrana had received warning of a plot to assassinate Stolypin from one of its former agents, a man named Dimitri Bogrov, who had remained in touch with revolutionary circles. The Okhrana held off arresting the terrorists identified by Bogrov in the hopes of learning through him the complete details of their plan, but it passed on the warning to the Ministry of the Interior, which ordered drastic re-enforcement of the security arrangements for the protection of the Czar and of the high government officials scheduled to arrive in Kiev. Police threw an impenetrable cordon around the opera house and packed it with detectives, while passes and invitation cards were subjected to expert scrutiny. It seemed inconceivable that a terrorist could slip into the building—until Bogrov, who had been admitted in order to brief the chief of the local Okhrana on the last-minute arrangements of his confederates, pulled out a pistol as soon as he caught sight of the Prime Minister, and shot him dead.

On occasion the Okhrana organized escapes and prison breaks to build the "cover" of its agents, and though it clung to the fiction that these were merely passive informants, many of them were *agents provocateurs* in the most literal sense. Though the investigating committee set up under the Kerensky regime could not find documentary proof that the Okhrana had deliberately instigated street demonstrations and rebellions, there is a wealth of informed testimony that it did so, notably in the great Moscow uprising of 1905 and in similar bloody disorders in Kronstadt and Viborg.

During the 1905 revolution the Okhrana got into the habit of working closely with the counterterrorists of the Extreme Right. Its chiefs sometimes disapproved of the "unauthorized" assassinations of liberal politicians carried out by the Rightist Black Hundred gangs, but they generally co-operated in organizing the anti-Semitic pogroms that were the main *raison d'être* of the extremist bands. The most glaring instance of this co-operation —and perhaps the most striking symptom of the moral regression provoked by the 1905 revolution—occurred in Kiev in 1911. Local "patriotic"—i.e.

extremist—organizations accused a Jew named Mendel Beiliss of having murdered a little Christian boy to obtain his blood for ritual purposes. (There is an ancient and tenacious folk legend in parts of Eastern Europe that human—and gentile—blood is used in the preparation of *matzoth*.)

Finding that the evidence presented by the local patriots was a trifle flimsy, the Kiev authorities appealed to St. Petersburg for help. The Imperial Minister of Justice, M. Shcheslovitov, took a keen personal interest in the case. He not only made it clear to the prosecutor that a conviction was expected, but arranged that the Okhrana send a team of agents to Kiev to help "collect" better evidence, and also, apparently, to rig the jury. In a memorandum to the Czar, Shcheslovitov affirmed that the examining magistrate in Kiev had information from an unimpeachable source establishing the guilt of Beiliss. The Okhrana drew on its secret funds to bring an obscure religious fanatic from distant Tashkent to testify as an expert witness at the trial. The expert, an Orthodox pope named Pranaitis, a self-appointed authority on Hebraic tradition, solemnly maintained in court that ritual murder was not only enjoined by various esoteric Jewish texts, but was sanctioned by the Old Testament itself. Despite—or because of—the demential nonsense to which it had to listen, and the heavy pressures to which it was subjected, the jury finally acquitted the defendant.

At the session of the investigating committee in 1917 when Shcheslovitov confessed his role in the affair, one of the jurists on it asked the former Minister of Justice a loaded but pertinent question: "Didn't you realize that the indictment [of Beiliss] was at the same time an indictment of the religious convictions of millions of our fellow citizens? Didn't you consider in general that this indictment was a disgrace to Russia, because in the twentieth century it served as a basis for a trial worthy of the Middle Ages?"

"No," replied Shcheslovitov.

Yet this deluded and dishonest guardian of the law was not himself a backwoods fanatic. He was an eminent jurist, an intelligent and cultivated man. He had once been a civilized one. Before 1905 he had even been a liberal, and more than once had courageously opposed the Czarist establishment, according to B. Maklakov, who edited the proceedings of the 1917 committee and wrote a judicious commentary upon them.

"Frightened by the prevalent disorder and the threat of revolution, he [Shcheslovitov] turned into a Rightist," explains Maklakov, who knew him personally. "Shcheslovitov resolved to break the traditions of our judicial system and to subject it to political control. He terrorized the magistrature, he became the great corrupter of justice."

Russia has always been a police state and no doubt the Czarist police force, secret and public, served as a reservoir of barbarous attitudes and traditions handed down with little softening from the times of Ivan the Terrible. It was not, however, the primitives—the moral fossiles imbedded in the darker strata of the Czarist administration—who opened the flood-gates of barbarism in twentieth-century Russia; as in the other disintegrating autocracies, it was the decadents, the self-made barbarians—like Shche-slovitov. We have seen the same phenomenon occur many times since—and not only in dynastic states.[3]

The infiltration of the police and the secret-service outlook into the higher policy-making levels of the Czarist state was no less evident in for-eign than in domestic affairs. The Okhrana was particularly active in Paris, a major center of emigré revolutionary activities. It operated much as the GPU and the MVD were later to do. The chief agent was usually attached to the Russian Embassy with the rank of counselor; he rendered no ac-counts to the ambassador but was authorized to correspond with his chiefs through the diplomatic pouch. Co-operation between the Okhrana unit in Paris and the French Sureté was always close in the prewar years. The Sureté helped one Okhrana official set up a special Franco-Russian or-ganization, disguised as a private-detective agency, to spy on the emigrés. The Okhrana likewise organized, without protest from the French authori-ties, a French branch of the Russian "patriotic" organizations called the League for the Salvation of the Fatherland, which co-operated with French right-wing extremists like the Royalist Camelots du Roi.

To neutralize the chronic protest of French Socialists and Liberals against its operations on French soil, the Okhrana bribed French newspapers and journalists of the right who were willing to follow a pro-Russian line. According to an exposé of the Okhrana written in 1919 by one of its former senior officials, V. K. Agafonov, it financed a journalists' club in Paris and paid regular subsidies to several important French newspapers, including

[3] A closely related phenomenon that might be termed "the transmigration of nightmares" is illustrated by the case history of the so-called *Protocols of Zion,* an anti-Semitic forgery which, like the Beiliss case, sprang from the collaboration between the Okhrana and right-wing fanatics in Czarist Russia. The *Protocols*— a kind of blueprint for a secret Jewish plot to dominate the world—were concocted in 1905 by a Russian writer named Sergius Nilus, who was on the payroll of the Okhrana. Although Nilus claimed to have obtained his manuscript from a reliable person who had stolen it in the course of an ultrasecret Masonic meeting somewhere in France (needless to say, the Masons were depicted as tools of the mysterious plotters) it was later demonstrated that he had merely adapted for purposes of anti-Semitic propaganda an obscure pamphlet against Napoleon III, published in Geneva in 1864. Nilus' forgery was republished in 1911, with Okhrana help, and again in 1917 when it was utilized by certain White authorities for anti-Bolshevik propaganda. It was brought to Germany by refugees from the Baltic provinces, fleeing the Bolshevik revolution and the civil war in Russia. The first German publication of the *Protocols* was in 1919; in the following years the forgery became a major source of National Socialist anti-Semitic propaganda and contributed to poisoning the minds of millions of Germans. The person chiefly responsible for this exploitation of Nilus' fake was the Nazi theorist Alfred Rosenberg, a refugee from Russian Esthonia (though of Ger-man descent, Rosenberg was born in Reval) who was one of the main ideological transmission belts linking the neobarbarians of Czarist Russia with those of Hitler's Germany.

the *Echo de Paris,* the *Gallois,* and the *Figaro.* The last-named organ, according to Agafonov, for a while received 24,000 rubles—about $10,000—monthly from the Okhrana.

When Izvolsky took over the Russian Embassy in Paris he promoted an arrangement with the French government for influencing French opinion that was more official, but hardly less conspiratorial, than the crude undercover operations of the Okhrana: the Russians would open a special credit, drawn upon the Czar's secret funds, for the French government, which would then undertake to buy up the consciences—and the pens—of its own journalists in behalf of joint objectives. A letter sent by the Russian Prime Minister in October 1912 to his French opposite number—at that time Poincaré—pointed out one of the advantages of the proposed system: It would help keep within bounds "certain appetites and certain rivalries" in the French press which the Russians had learned from bitter experience were apt to be stirred up when they approached foreign journalists directly.

There was another advantage that the Russian communication did not spell out but which Poincaré may have been able to read between the lines. Izvolsky looked upon the dry, little Lorrainer, with his implacable irredentism as the heaven-sent instrument of Russian foreign policy in France— "If Poincaré were defeated it would be a catastrophe for us," he warned St. Petersburg before the French presidential elections of 1913—and one of the secret objectives of the press campaign that Russia was proposing to finance was to combat the "pacifist"—we would say today "appeasement"— and therefore anti-Poincaré, elements in French public life. "Do not forget," Izvolsky once wrote his nominal chief in St. Petersburg, "that Poincaré has to struggle with very influential elements in his own party which are generally hostile to Russia and openly preach that France must not be dragged into any war arising out of Balkan affairs." To the degree that the Russian propaganda-credit was likely to aid Poincaré in his "struggles," and thereby to help his political career, it came perilously near to being a personal bribe to him, as well as to the French journalists who were actually to pocket the funds.

Despite this slightly sordid implication, Poincaré, who was normally more fastidious, received a secret emissary of the Russian treasury and worked out with him and Izvolsky an agreement in principle for handling a Russian slush fund of 300,000 gold francs (about $60,000). An official of the French Ministry of the Interior was appointed to deal with the Russians in the matter, but it was some time before both parties could agree on details. The Russian officials thought their French colleagues were too generous with the Czar's funds in proposing to pay some $600 monthly for three months to the editors of several relatively obscure dailies with which certain male or female protégés of various French politicians had particularly close connections. When the first Balkan war broke out in October 1912, however, Izvolsky, fearing that a general European crisis was imminent, relented and urged that $20,000 be released to the French without too close scrutiny as to how it was spent.

The following year St. Petersburg at first disapproved a French request to unfreeze another $20,000 to neutralize an expected left-wing campaign against the newly established three-year military service, and also to bolster "the generally difficult situation of the French cabinet." Izvolsky, however, intervened again to break the deadlock by proposing the subsidies be made conditional not only upon supporting the purely French objectives already named, but also upon furthering "our interests, for example in Balkan questions."

Izvolsky, of course, worked closely—perhaps connived would be the better word—with like-minded French diplomats and with the French general staff, as well as with several politicians who shared Poincaré's intransigent nationalism. They included Alexandre Millerand, who was President of the French Republic immediately before Poincaré, then Minister of War, and Théophile Delcassé, who was Minister of the Marine from 1911 to 1913, then French Ambassador to St. Petersburg until shortly before the outbreak of the war.

"If, God forbid, a crisis should occur," Izvolsky wrote in 1912, "the decision will be taken by the three strong personalities who head the cabinet: Poincaré, Millerand and Delcassé. It is our good fortune that we shall have to deal precisely with these three."

To make sure that the trio of nationalist leaders in France retained its decisive position, the Russian Ambassador had no inhibitions about using his influence—including the influence he had acquired, thanks to the generosity of the Czar or of the Okhrana, over important press organs like Le Matin—to undermine their less nationalist or more moderate domestic rivals. (As is normal in such intrigues, the intrigants were not always completely frank with each other: Poincaré was not quite as much in Izvolsky's pocket as the Russian Ambassador liked to imagine, and Izvolsky sometimes neglected to inform his French allies about Russian activities in the Balkans that vitally concerned every member of the alliance.)

After the Revolution the Soviets published an aptly termed Black Book of Izvolsky's official correspondence which was largely intended as an exposé of the secret diplomacy that had brought the Old World to its downfall. The indictment, it must be admitted, is a damning one, but the illustration is perhaps too extreme; Izvolsky was not conducting mere secret diplomacy in Paris, but a kind of diplomatic conspiracy. What made it sinister was not so much its aims as its methods. Neither he nor Poincaré was deliberately plotting a European war, but the fact that their relations constituted a kind of permanent plot, meticulously concealed from public opinion and bypassing constitutional controls in both nations, had a great deal to do with making war inevitable.

The conspiratorial toxins generated by the dying Russian autocracy contaminated Russia's relations with her allies—and sometimes the allies, too —just as they corrupted the revolutionary opposition at home. Aside from its moral implications, all this plotting and counterplotting contributed to the administrative breakdown of the Czarist state and to the fragmentation of authority. The Czar could not control the Okhrana; the Okhrana could not control its own agents—though it controlled some that Lenin thought were his. The Minister in St. Petersburg officially responsible for conducting Russia's foreign relations was dominated and manipulated by his nominal subordinate, the Ambassador to France, but the Paris Embassy could not be, even unofficially, the co-ordinating center for the Russian diplomatic service.

Czarist diplomacy with its supporting networks of spies and secret police and undercover propagandists was probably more unscrupulous than most others in prewar Europe, but its cardinal sin was the irresponsibility which almost of necessity permeates any system that functions to a considerable degree through invisible chains of command—especially multiple ones. Conspiracy involves never letting the right hand know what the left hand is doing. On occasion this averts unpleasantness, but at other times it can be dangerous—for instance, if the left hand happens to light a match at the moment that the right one is manipulating slabs of cordite. Russian diplomatic and paradiplomatic operations in the Balkans between 1909 and 1914 furnish the classic example.

The foundations for a new Russian policy in southeastern Europe were laid by Izvolsky, himself, before he quit St. Petersburg, and it seems probable that he conceived it as a kind of diplomatic revenge for the humiliations that Austria and Germany had inflicted on Russia after the Bosnian crisis of 1908-1909. The Czar and the Russian new Foreign Minister, Sazonov, do not seem to have understood it in so aggressive a spirit, but the Russian minister in Belgrade, N. H. de Hartwig, almost certainly did; he was an ardent Pan-Slavist and had been specially picked for his critical post by Izvolsky. The avowed aim of the policy was to encourage better relations between Serbia and Bulgaria, and thereby to promote stability in the Balkans; the real aim—at least in Hartwig's mind—was somewhat less idyllic. It was expressed in a secret annex to a defensive treaty signed in March 1912 between the two chief Balkan rivals. This annex provided for carving up Turkish Macedonia between Bulgaria and Serbia; one of its clauses stipulated that the Czar's arbitration would be accepted for any contested territories—a foresighted arrangement, in view of Balkan history.

When Poincaré learned the full text of the treaty—completed by a military convention—during a state visit to St. Petersburg in August 1912, some five months after it had been signed, he blew up.

"This convention in no way corresponds to the account of it that was given me," he protested to Sazonov. "To tell you the truth, it is a convention for war. Moreover the treaty contains the germ not only of a war against Turkey, but of a war against Austria."

Sazonov tried to reassure him by declaring that Russia had the right to veto any aggressions projected by the Balkan allies, and would not hesitate to do so. Despite this assurance, Serbia and Bulgaria, their appetites whetted by Turkey's impending defeat in the Tripolitanian war (started by Italy's invasion of Tripolitania in 1911), broadened their alliance into a coalition with Greece and Montenegro, and opened hostilities in October 1912—without, of course, a Russian veto, and without any significant manifestations of Poincaré's displeasure.

In one sense the French President had been unusually prophetic, but in another he had overestimated the danger. The Balkan war produced a violent European crisis that gave the Kaiser a chance to do some more saber-rattling, and it left the whole diplomatic situation in Europe in a more precarious state than ever, but the only other war that came out of it directly was a second one in the Balkans. The first one ended with the defeat of Turkey and its virtual eviction from Europe, but the victorious allies, as might have been expected, almost immediately fell to squabbling over the loot. Bulgaria attacked Serbia and Greece; Rumania, which had been left out of the first conflict, attacked Bulgaria, and the Turks naturally joined in, hoping to recoup their losses. When it was all over, Turkey had lost a good deal of mountainous real estate; Bulgaria, Montenegro, Rumania and especially Greece had gained some; Serbia had acquired more than 1,000,000 new subjects but her dream of getting a window on the Adriatic had been blocked, at Austrian insistence, by the creation of an independent Albania. The map of the Balkans had changed, but not the political climate; everyone continued to hate everyone else, perhaps a little more bitterly than before.

The gravest repercussions of the Balkan conflicts were indirect. Germany, fearing a new Balkan attack on the Ottoman Empire that might lead to its final dismemberment, drew closer to Austria—whose Balkan policy had earlier inspired serious misgivings—and with the agreement of the Young Turks, dispatched a German general, Liman von Sanders, to reorganize the Ottoman Army. This move infuriated and frightened the Russians: if German military power with the connivance of a puppet Turkish government established itself astride the Dardanelles, it would be a threat not only to Russia's ambitions but even to her security. An imperial crown council held in St. Petersburg on February 21, 1914 came to the gloomy conclusion that only a general European war would enable Russia to realize her "historic aims"—i.e. seizure of Constantinople and control of the straits. The same council estimated, however, that Russia would not be adequately prepared to face a major conflict for at least two or three years. This estimate, while it did not basically modify Russia's Balkan policy, injected a note of prudent realism into it that was apparent even in Belgrade. Unfortunately, this was true only of official Russian policy—the right-hand one. The left-hand policy remained as reckless as ever—particularly in Belgrade.

For several years Hartwig, the Russian Minister, had worked with both hands to build up the Balkan coalition against Turkey and to encourage Serbian ambitions for uniting the South Slavs, under Serb leadership, at the expense of Austria-Hungary. With the right hand he pursued these objectives through his normal diplomatic contacts with King Peter, Crown Prince Alexander, and the Serbian government. With the left hand—especially through his military attaché, Colonel (later General) Victor Artamanov—he gave financial, paramilitary and other kinds of support to ostensibly private but actually semiofficial organizations of what were euphemistically termed Serbian nationalists (in Austrian, Turkish, and Bulgarian eyes, they were Great-Serbian imperialists).

The most fateful of these Russian-supported irredentist, or expansionist, groups in Serbia was a secret society that called itself Union or Death but which was popularly known as the Black Hand, because of its conspiratorial mentality and organization. According to its statutes, the Black Hand aimed at achieving the union of "all the Serbs," including, of course, those of Turkish or Bulgarian Macedonia, and those living in Bosnia and elsewhere in the Dual Monarchy. At home it operated as an extremist pressure group dedicated to the task of committing Serbian official circles and Serbian public opinion to Serbia's proposed mission as "the Piedmont of the South Slavs"—i.e. playing the same role in South Slav unification that the kingdom of Savoy had played in Italian unification. Beyond Serbia's borders the Black Hand sought to promote its objectives by subversive action with emphasis on terrorism rather than what it somewhat contemptuously termed "intellectual propaganda." With such a program, the Black Hand had to organize itself and to operate along conspiratorial lines, though the Balkan love of conspiracy for its own sake no doubt was responsible for some of its more melodramatic trimmings. Members were known to each other only by number; they swore extravagant oaths of secrecy and blind obedience, and observed colorful rites borrowed from the Freemasons, the nineteenth-century Italian Carbonari, and similar sources.

Despite all these operetta flourishes, Union or Death was a serious organization of serious-minded and influential men. Its members were fanatics, but political fanaticism in the Balkans was neither abnormal nor discreditable. The army was strongly represented in the society, and its head was none other than Colonel Dragutin Dimitrijevic, the chief of the military intelligence department of the Serbian Army. For several years, in fact, the Black Hand was an unofficial auxiliary of the Serbian Army—and to a lesser degree of the Serbian foreign office. Dimitrijevic, known in conspiratorial circles as Apis, seems to have got into the habit of switching hats—the military one and the Black Hand one—so casually that neither his colleagues on the executive committee of Union or Death, nor his superiors in the army, ever knew exactly what he was doing. By playing one connection against the other, he was able to exploit the considerable assets of both without being subject to the control of either—a situation that was wholly to his taste.

Apis—the pseudonym suits him better, as well as being shorter—was a heavy-shouldered, bull-necked, bullet-headed man with the luxuriant black handlebar mustaches of the typical Serbian Army officer in his day. From his photographs he does not look particularly intelligent, and probably he was not, but he was a prodigious worker and had a forceful personality. He was brave, and he could be brutal, but essentially he was a staff-officer type, a military bureaucrat. He excelled in desk warfare even more than in the mountain variety; he was a master of administrative guerrilla, as well as of the other kind. He does not appear to have possessed much imagination and his patriotic fanaticism, or idealism, seems to have been of a rather formal and pedestrian strain.

"I die innocent and in the belief that my death is necessary to Serbia for higher reasons," Apis declared after a Serbian court condemned him to death on an obscure and confused indictment of treason in 1917. There are grounds for believing that Apis had some specific—and to him, adequate—reasons in mind for concurring in his own execution, but his use of the administrative cliché at such a solemn moment seems revelatory. In the world of routine fanaticism that was Apis'—as in the world of bureaucratized conspiracy that was peculiar to the Okhrana—"higher reasons" was as definite a justification as was ever needed for murder, judicial or otherwise. (Twenty years later, it will still be valid for the successors of the Okhrana, but in keeping with the spirit of a more progressive age, their victims will no longer have the right to die innocent.)

Apis had few interests outside his job—or rather his jobs—but what little private life he had was normal and decent. His nephew remembered him as affectionate and relaxed in the family circle. Nothing, apparently, in Apis' character or background fitted him to play a role as one of history's star villains; it was the context that made the man.

The Russian Embassy was an important element in the context. Before and during the first Balkan war—in which the Black Hand played a conspicuous role, organizing guerrilla bands behind the enemy lines—the Russians gave financial and political support to the organization, as did Crown

Prince Alexander. For a long time, not only the Russian military attaché but the Ambassador, Hartwig, were in intimate contact with Apis. There is no suggestion that he personally pocketed any Russian funds, but the Russians looked upon him as their particular friend, if not quite their agent, and quite naturally tried to build him up in influence. Their success—with the help of the Black Hand's guerrilla achievements in Macedonia—was altogether too brilliant. The Balkan wars dangerously inflated the prestige, the egos, and the recklessness of the Serbian officer caste. This was particularly the case with those who belonged to the Black Hand—starting with Apis.

Apis became, in fact, such a powerful figure in Serbian political life that he fell out both with the Crown Prince—according to one version Alexander never forgave Apis for not yielding to him the secret chairmanship of the Black Hand's executive committee—and with the Prime Minister, Nicholas Pasic. Apis had participated in the assassination plot against the last Obrenovitch king and his devotion to the Karageorgevitch dynasty which he had helped set upon the throne was probably lukewarm (though the attempts which have been made by the Tito regime to portray him as a republican, or even crypto-Marxist revolutionary are not convincing). He is said to have been on the point of launching a military coup against the government when war broke out. For all these reasons, and because the bloody anarchy unleashed by the Balkan wars had somewhat put him off the role of apprentice-sorcerer, Hartwig from early 1914 on was unusually attentive to the counsels of prudence that were now coming from St. Petersburg, and in keeping with them adopted a more aloof attitude toward Apis.

Artamonov, the military attaché, continued, however, to see his Serbian colleague and friend nearly every day. It was natural enough: they were conducting a joint secret-service operation across the nearby Austrian border, with the help of a chain of Serbian customs inspectors and frontier guards who had been recruited as secret operatives of Apis. Artamonov's contribution to the operation had been to furnish some $1600—an impressive sum by contemporary Balkan standards—toward financing the clandestine network that Apis was setting up on Austro-Hungarian soil, particularly in Bosnia. His agents collected military intelligence, but they also engaged in subversive propaganda activities—among other things they distributed copies of the Black Hand's monthly organ, appropriately entitled *Piedmont*—and it would be surprising indeed, in view of the Black Hand's statutes, if they did not also try to encourage local terrorist groups. According to former collaborators of Apis, Artamonov was fully informed about the subversive as well as the intelligence aspects of the project; whether he reported both of them to St. Petersburg and to Hartwig is not definitely established. In any case, if any Russian official eyebrows were raised over these pyrotechnics at the bunghole of the Balkan powder barrel, Artamonov could reply that he was just a simple soldier doing his duty by helping to collect military information in regard to a potential enemy of his country. No doubt Apis turned over to him from time to time reports of some value from the viewpoint of military intelligence, and Artamonov could justifiably—and perhaps did—send his chiefs maps of Austria peppered with crossed Russian and Serbian flags symbolizing the steadily expanding Serbian intelligence network that he was helping to subsidize.

From here on we are on haunted grounds. Some of the original controversies about the origins of the crime at Sarajevo have died down as more information became available to historians but there is still enough obscurity about certain important details to sustain quite divergent interpretation. The viewpoint that the assassination was essentially a local plot that spontaneously generated in the minds of young Princip and his fellow conspirators, to which some irresponsible nationalist elements in Belgrade gave rather offhand assistance, cannot be formally disproved. Neither can the contrary hypothesis that the murder of the heir to the Habsburg throne was systematically planned at a high government level in Belgrade, or even in St. Petersburg. The most convincing version, at least to a journalist who has had occasion to investigate—or to cover the investigations—of later political assassinations in Europe, lies between the two extremes, and is based in the main on the conclusions reached by the Italian historian, Luigi Albertini, after exhaustive documentary research and interviews of surviving key witnesses.

According to this version, it was in fact Apis who organized the assassinations of Francis Ferdinand and Sophie Hohenberg in Sarajevo. He admitted this himself in a long confession which he handed to the judge during his trial at Salonika (the base of the Serb Army during the war). The fact that the alleged text of the confession, published with the authorization of the Yugoslav government in 1953, contains some passages that look suspiciously like Titoist propaganda, does not prove that no parts of it were authentic. Moreover there is the testimony of several persons to whom Apis talked about the affair.

"Now it is clear to me, and it must be clear to you, too," Apis told one of the officers riding with him in a truck to the place where the firing squad was waiting for him, "that I am to be killed today by Serbian rifles solely because I organized the Sarajevo outrage."

There is a mass of circumstantial evidence to support this direct testimony. On the other hand there is much evidence, too, to indicate, if not to prove, that he acted without the consent of any higher Serbian authority, and probably without realizing that this act would start a European war— whether it would have made any difference to him if he had realized, is more doubtful.

What then was his motive? The most plausible one is that Apis considered Francis Ferdinand a dangerous enemy—precisely because he was a relatively enlightened one—to the Black Hand's goal of a South Slav Union. When the heir to the Habsburg throne succeeded his aged uncle he might impose reforms that would end the discontent of the Dual Monarchy's Serbo-Croat subjects, in Bosnia and elsewhere, and they would no longer wish to secede and unite with Serbia. Hence it was important that Francis Ferdinand should die before the old Emperor, and the visit to Sarajevo offered almost unique opportunities for arranging his assassination.

Pan-Serb, or embryonic Yugoslav, nationalism had deep roots in newly annexed Bosnia-Herzegovina, and by 1914 it was beginning to put them down in Magyar-ruled Croatia. In free Serbia, public opinion undoubtedly sympathized with the oppressed race brothers in the Habsburg Empire. It should not be overlooked, moreover, that after the Austrian annexation of Bosnia—in itself a deadly affront to Serb national sentiment everywhere—Aehrenthal's policy had seemed to many patriotic Serbians a threat to their national independence as well as a humiliating slap at their national pride. Not all Serbs, or Serbo-Croats, however, whether inside or outside the Dual Monarchy, were as intransigent as the Princips or the Apises in determination to realize their aspirations, to defend their honor, or to safeguard their independence. It is possible that a majority of Serbo-Croats, both in the kingdom of Serbia and in Austria-Hungary, would have been satisfied—for some time at least—by the type of reform or accommodation that Francis Ferdinand was credited with seeking (whether he could actually have succeeded in bringing them about seems more doubtful). Thus, if the version of Apis' motivations that has just been given is the right one—as seems probable—Sarajevo conforms to a pattern of nationalist political crime that has since become all too familiar to us. It was —on this reading—the type of outrage which the fanatical minority in a national movement perpetrates in order to block compromise solutions and to commit the more moderate majority to its extremist program.

Above all, Sarajevo was in its conception and instigation, a typical secret-service crime whose real purpose and meaning was withheld even from the agents who carried it out; Princip and his fellow schoolboy-conspirators were hardly less victimized than their victims. For Apis—operating through one of his trusted lieutenants (a senior Black Hand member named Major Voja Tankosic)—did not merely come to the aid of the Princip group, or arm them or stiffen them; he manipulated them. The boys, whether one looks on them as heroes or delinquents, were bona-fide romantics, inspired, or deluded, by a belated vision of the nineteenth-century national ideal. Apis, though he doubtless shared their ideal, did not share it with them; to him they were not subjects, in the philosophical sense, but objects, mere pawns in the never-ending chess game of conspiracy. Probably their adolescent idealism was less useful to him than the ingenuousness that went with it; they would be too naive to realize exactly how they were being used, and he could hope that their patent amateurishness would disguise the professional planning back of their deed.

It was particularly from his own government that Apis needed to conceal his role in organizing the murder—perhaps that is the deepest reason why he chose to rely upon amateurs rather than to utilize the professional killers that he unquestionably had available in Bosnia. Sarajevo was the result of a secret-service plot, but it was not plotted by a responsible secret service; Apis was not wearing his military hat when he sent the Princip group on its fatal mission. It is not even certain that he was wearing the Black Hand hat; according to some accounts, when the Black Hand executive committee learned what he had dispatched the young Bosnians to do, it ordered him, by a majority vote, to call them back (if such an order was actually given, Apis disregarded it).

The Serbian government, that is Apis' enemy, Prime Minister Pasic, learned of the assassination plot through a secret informer planted inside the Black Hand, and actually took official steps to block its execution. Instructions were wired to the Serbian Minister in Vienna to warn the Austrian government. The warning could not expose the role of the Black Hand or give any details that would enable the Austrians to arrest the killers before they could strike—otherwise Pasic and the Serbian Minister would have been signing their own death warrants. Accidentally or not, the Serbian Minister sabotaged Belgrade's instructions, by the vague and bumbling way in which he delivered the warning. The Austrian government official to whom he delivered it—the Joint Finance Minister, responsible for administration in Bosnia—did not appreciate its full gravity, though he passed it on, after a fashion. Austrian red tape and *schlamperei* did the rest; the administrative anarchy of the disintegrating Habsburg power fatally coincided with the disorganized backwardness of the nascent Yugoslav power.

The deepest unresolved mystery of Sarajevo is the degree of direct Russian guilt in the assassination. Did Hartwig, the Russian minister, or Artamanov, his military attaché, know in advance what Apis was plotting? Albertini demonstrates convincingly that it is most unlikely Hartwig was informed of the murder plot. Artamanov is another story—a very queer and confused story. There is some testimony that he not only knew Apis was organizing the assassination, but that he asked St. Petersburg for approval —and got it. After the war, and the Russian Revolution, Albertini—whose dogged quest for the truth about the origins of the conflict is as fascinating as a good detective story—found Artamanov, then a retired general, living in Yugoslavia, and asked him point-blank if his was the hand behind the hands that launched the war. It must have been an extraordinary interview.

Artamanov admitted his close co-operation with Apis, but denied that he had been consulted about the assassination. He declared that he had been away from Belgrade on leave in Switzerland and Italy for some time before the crime was perpetrated, and to back this up, showed the Italian sleuth-historian his diary for the months of June and July, 1914. It contained no mention of the tragedy at Sarajevo. For the fateful date of July 24, there was merely the laconic note, "Austrian ultimatum to Serbia," followed, Albertini says, by the usual statement of Artamanov's daily expenses: "coffee—2 lire."

Albertini came away from the interview unconvinced. The general impressed him as being not overly intelligent and without much character. He remained puzzled by Artamanov's continued absence from Belgrade after the crime and during the early days of the European crisis it engendered; indeed this was a strangely prolonged vacation.

There may be one man still alive who knows the whole story; the Russian assistant military attaché, Captain Alexander Werchovski, who replaced Artamanov during his absence. A friend of Werchovski, a Polish nobleman named Louis de Trydar-Burzynski, stated in his memoirs, published in Italy in 1926, that "the assassination [at Sarajevo] was perpetrated with the support of the Russian military attaché at Belgrade, Captain Werchovski . . ." Werchovski, he continued, "was later War Minister in the Kerensky government; he was a young man whom I had known very well for years, and he told me quite frankly the truth about the origins, preparations and execution of the plot." Unfortunately, Werchovski, if he is living today, is not likely to tell any more about the case; when last heard of, he held a high command in the Red Army—a curious detail in itself.

Albertini's final conclusion is that Artamanov was informed of the plot and did nothing to obstruct it. Contrary to some sources, the Italian historian does not believe Artamanov gave assurances to Apis that Serbia could count on Russian military aid in case the crime led to war with Austria. Whether Artamanov—or Werchovski—reported the assassination plan to anyone in St. Petersburg is still a wide-open question. He—or they—might have informed the Russian Minister for War, General Sukhomlinov, who for reasons of his own, did not pass it on to the Czar. Perhaps the recipient of the information—if there was one—was some unofficial but powerful behind-stage personality in Russia: one of the more bellicose Grand Dukes, or even one of the still more bellicose Grand Duchesses. Perhaps it was simply lost somewhere in the Russian bureaucratic labyrinth. Anything is possible. It is even conceivable that Artamanov decided to keep the whole thing a little secret between his friend Apis and himself. The moral and administrative decay of Romanov Russia had reached the point by mid-1914 when it was conceivable not only for the left hand to act in affairs of the gravest importance without the right hand knowing what it was doing, but for one of the fingers of the left hand, twitching independently of the rest, to pull the trigger that detonated a world war.

Like the treason of Redl, the intrigues of Izvolsky, and the conspiratorial Witches' Sabbath of the Okhrana, the murderers at Sarajevo demonstrate that overlaying the local power vacuum in southeastern Europe caused by the breakup or decrepitude of the Habsburg and Ottoman Empires, there was a vacuum of responsibility affecting a much wider area. Responsible government was beginning to collapse under the strains of the modern age, just as civilization was beginning to crumble, in all the autocracies—and in some of their more-or-less democratic allies. (In the Balkans responsible government had never existed, at least not for centuries.) The breakdown, it is true, was limited; the regression to barbarism was noticeable only in certain contexts, the relapse into anarchy was confined to certain sectors. Philosophers continued to philosophize, and the plumbing, where it already existed, worked as well as ever. The trains ran—often on time—mail was delivered and taxes collected: drunkards were jailed and prostitutes had their cards stamped. Only the higher policy-coordinating centers of the state were affected. How grievously, was demonstrated, not only by Sarajevo, but as we shall now see, by the failure of the Old World diplomacy to prevent the crisis inevitably engendered by it from ending in the general European war that virtually nobody in Europe wanted.

CHAPTER 11

The Failure of Diplomacy

IF there was one thing that the Habsburgs did superbly, it was to bury their dead. Other dynasties exploited coronations, marriages, or jubilees to refurbish the splendor of their public image and to rededicate the loyalty of their subjects; the Habsburgs, with their essentially baroque *weltanschauung,* usually tended to put the stress on funerals. Even in normal times the death of a Habsburg Emperor, of his heir, or indeed, of any member of his immediate family, was the occasion for grandiose, slightly macabre, awesomely anachronistic, mortuary pageantry. The tragedy at Sarajevo, one might have thought, offered the monarchy an opportunity to celebrate its own grandeur on an almost Pharaonic scale—and in a highly significant political context. Though the Archduke Francis Ferdinand had never been popular, his death on the field of honor from the bullets of revolutionary assassins—a death rendered more poignant by that of his wife at his side—had stirred the somewhat lethargic patriotism of loyal Austrians and shocked the consciences of many among the minority groups of the Empire who believed in freedom, or self-determination, or South Slavdom, but not yet in murder. (Throughout most of the Old World, except in Russia and in the Balkans, people were still backward in this respect.) The impact of the outrage on what might be termed the dynastic conscience—the vestigial solidarity of Divine Right rulers—in the other European monarchies was naturally no less great. Since 1848, both the family ties between the reigning dynasties of the Continent, and the elements of a common ideology that they shared, had steadily lost importance as political factors, but in 1914 they were not yet negligible ones. A new Metternich might have effectively exploited these classic themes of early nineteenth-century diplomacy to win sympathy for Austria's understandable desire to punish Serbia for her suspected complicity in the crime, and to cushion hostile reactions to any retaliation that might be decided. A state funeral for the martyred Archduke would have facilitated such a neo-Metternichian policy by bringing together in Vienna at a solemn, cere-monial moment most of the crowned heads of Europe. At the very least, it would have muted for a while the international tensions that Sarajevo had begun to generate, and it would have favored British or other efforts to discover some face-saving formula for averting the incipient world crisis. Unfortunately, the Empire, though it still had plenty of diplomats who clung to Metternich's doctrines, had none that possessed his tactical skills; in fact, it was no longer capable of producing even a good funeral director. The same contradictions and decrepitudes that had helped send Francis Ferdinand to his death, dispatched him to his grave in a botched and sordid foretaste of the unceremonious trip to the potter's field of history which awaited, not only the entire Habsburg dynasty, but virtually all that sur-vived of the old monarchic order in Europe—together with the civilization built upon it.

The mortal remains of Francis Ferdinand and the Duchess of Hohen-berg arrived in Vienna at 10 P.M. on July 2. They were met by the new heir apparent, the Archduke Charles, a nephew of the murdered Archduke, and by the officers of the Vienna garrison, who escorted them through the night to the little Hofburg chapel. There, the coffins, of different make and size, were placed side by side, but not on the same level. That of the Archduke was adorned with the symbols of his rank: the crown of an Im-perial Prince, a general's cap and saber, an Archduke's hat. That of the Duchess bore only a fan and a pair of white gloves—a reminder of the time when she had been a lady in waiting.

The next morning the public was admitted to view the bodies, but promptly at 12 the gates were closed and the coffins remained locked in the chapel until the start, at 4 P.M., of the brief requiem service. The Em-peror attended but no foreign heads of state or their representatives were present, although the wreaths they sent made up for the absence of floral tributes from the Emperor and the Court. Foreign royalties had been kept away on the official pretext that the aged Emperor's health permitted only a very brief ceremony. Wilhelm, who had nevertheless wanted to come "as a friend," was discouraged by hints that a band of anarchist assassins were plotting against his life. (Officially, it was announced that the Kaiser's ab-sence was due to lumbago.) A wreath of white roses, inscribed *Sophie, Max, Ernst,* lay at the foot of the catafalque, but the dead couple's three children were not present at the ceremony. No bells tolled, no candle bearers followed the procession as it left the Hofburg at dusk to wind its way to the West Station. Francis Ferdinand had left a will expressly stating that he wished his body, and that of his wife, to be laid to rest side by side at their castle on the Danube, at Artstetten. He knew his family—Sophie Chotek would never be allowed to lie beside him in the Capuchin crypt where 137 members of the August House, including the suicide, Crown Prince Rudolph, were awaiting his company.

Vienna was agog at this shoddy performance. Everyone knew who the culprit was: Prince Montenuovo, the Imperial Chamberlain. (It was less generally known that the old Emperor had personally approved Montenuovo's arrangements.) The Chamberlain's disapproval of Sophie Chotek bordered on hatred, perhaps because he was a morganatic offshoot of the House of Habsburg himself—he was a descendant of Napoleon's second wife, Marie Louise, who after leaving her turbulent spouse to his fate at Elba had married again. Among other things, the funeral was Montenuovo's revenge on the "Belvedere crowd" for their jibes at the Court's antiquated Spanish ceremonial, of which he was the high priest.

But he had overreached himself. As the cortege proceeded through the darkening capital, over a hundred members of the Austrian and Hungarian aristocracy who had not been invited to the services, wearing gala uniform, forced their way on foot into the procession.

If any of the small suite who accompanied the bodies by train to their final destination had the least premonition of the horror soon to be unleashed on the world by the Sarajevo outrage, the trip to Artstetten must have seemed to them nightmarish beyond belief. At two in the morning, when the train reached the little station of Pochlarn on the Danube, where the coffins were to be ferried across the river, an apocalyptic thunderstorm drove everyone into the dingy, minute waiting room. Lightning and thunder on a *Gotterdammerung* scale made the night hideous, and those who felt their necks bristling with the primeval fear inflicted by the warnings of Heaven could not resort to drink, or even levity, for they had to share their shelter with the two august corpses. When, in the gray light of dawn, the hearse was finally loaded on to the barge, a delayed thunderclap made the horses rear and plunge, and a gruesome catastrophe was barely avoided.

For more than a week after Sarajevo, Austrian policy teetered on the brink of decision. Vienna seethed with excitement. Anti-Serbian sentiment, kindled by a majority of the press, ran strong, and several demonstrations took place in front of the Serbian Embassy, where the flag at half-mast seemed to the crowd an infuriating piece of hypocrisy. Francis Joseph, who returned to his summer villa at Ischl a few days after the funeral, remained, however, unmoved by the tumult in his capital.

"Surely the Emperor thinks that today's crime may have political consequences?" his aide-de-camp, Count Paar, was asked on the day of the assassination.

"Not at all," replied this worthy. "Why should it? . . . This is just another of those tragic occurrences which have been so frequent in the Emperor's life. I don't think he considers it in any other light."

It is quite likely that Francis Joseph, who, although he had been seriously ill only recently, still had all his wits about him, did not discuss higher policy with his aide-de-camp, who was as old as he was, but whose favorite pastime was napping. Visitors whom he received in the first days of July report that although he was quite unaffected by the demise of his nephew, he shared the general feeling in Vienna that "things could not go on in this way." He confided to the German Ambassador that he saw a very black future. From all that we know of his character, Francis Joseph can have had but one desire, that of finishing his days in peace. He had never been lucky in battle, and he was a tired old man. But revolution, and the disintegration of the Empire, seemed the inevitable outcome if Serbia were once more to remain unpunished. "If the Monarchy is doomed to perish, let it at least go down decorously," he said to his Chief of Staff, General Franz Conrad von Hotzendorff, an assiduous visitor, intent on wresting an order of immediate military measures against Serbia from his master. The Emperor, supported by his two Prime Ministers, the Austrian and the Hungarian, was for temporizing at least until Serbia's guilt had been officially established. (The conscientious Ballplatz official who was sent to investigate Serbian complicity in the crime reported on July 13 in the words that he was to rue all his life, "There is nothing to indicate, or even to give rise to the suspicion, that the Serbian Government knew about the plot, its preparation, or the procurement of arms.")

General Conrad, however, was straining on the leash. Events had presented him with a unique opportunity—the last one, he was convinced—to destroy Serbia and to restore the prestige of the Monarchy. Twice his plans had been frustrated. "In the years 1908–1909 it would have been a game with open cards," he said. "In 1912–1913 the chances were in our favour. Now it is a sheer gamble (*ein va-banque Spiel*)." But the gamble had to be taken, Conrad insisted. Time was working against the Monarchy.

Conrad, a simple military man with a straightforward manner, was the foremost Austrian warmonger; he was also one of the most forceful personalities in the Empire. His chief accomplice, Foreign Minister Leopold, Count Berchtold (Poldi, to his friends), was by temperament the least bellicose of men. A wealthy aristocrat, the owner of a racing stable, who likewise appreciated the slenderness of a feminine ankle, a man about town with great charm of manner, a bit of a fop, a bit of a snob, he was often snapped by contemporary photographers in a rakishly tilted silk hat, looking the perfect boulevardier. "Poldi's" vacuity of mind and flabbiness of character were to prove even deadlier to the world than the deviousness of his predecessor, Aehrenthal. He was a living, if somewhat extreme, caricature of the professional inadequacies of the European diplomat in his time, and his appointment as Austro-Hungarian Foreign Minister (in 1912) was evidence, no less striking in its way than Redl's treason, that the Habsburg Empire was indeed on its last legs.

Conrad had been a great nuisance to Berchtold for years, badgering him with secret memoranda on the theme of *"Serbia delenda est."* But after the two Balkan wars, in which Austria had cut a sorry figure, and the Foreign Minister had come in for much criticism, he had swung over to Conrad's views, much to the delight of the select society of lesser counts (the war counts, as they were known) which peopled the offices of the Ballplatz and liked to imitate Poldi's mania of drinking iced coffee (brought up specially from Demel's Café) at all hours of the day. Berchtold's quite unmilitary spine had been further stiffened by reports that the German ally, who had proved tiresome and evasive during the Balkan wars, was veering toward an attitude of much firmer support. Shortly after the assassination, the German Ambassador in Vienna, Herr von Tschirschky, had bluntly said to a high Austrian official, "If you take this lying down, you are not worth . . . on!" Moreover, a German publicist known to be a spokesman of the Wilhelmstrasse had sought out Count Berchtold's *chef de cabinet* and spoken to him at great length observing that in Berlin, the Foreign Ministry, plus the army and navy, found the "idea of a preventive war against Russia" less distasteful than they had a year earlier. He had assured him that if Kaiser Wilhelm was spoken to in the right way, he would not hesitate to support Austria and "this time go to the length of war."

Francis Joseph, too, needed to be spoken to in the right way. But he was much less easily swayed than the Kaiser. Conrad, who once again tried to persuade him that war with Serbia was unavoidable, was received by him on July 5 and found him in a very skeptical frame of mind.

"Quite so," said the old man testily, "but how can we wage war if they all jump on us, especially Russia?"

"But do we not have German re-insurance?" countered the Chief of Staff.

The Emperor looked doubtful. "Are you sure of Germany?" he growled.

To get an unequivocal answer to that question, Count Alexander Hoyos, Berchtold's *chef de cabinet,* had left for Berlin, bearing a memorandum on the Balkan situation and an autographed letter to the Kaiser from the Emperor.

The German capital on that Sunday, July 5, was a sleepy, empty town. Everyone was vacationing. (If Sarajevo had occurred a month earlier during the height of the social season in the leading European capitals, responsible consultation between governments, both allied and adverse, would have been facilitated, and the chances for saving peace would have been better. The work habits of high-level European officialdom, still strongly influenced by the aristocratic tradition of leisure, lagged far behind what the French historian Daniel Halevy has termed the acceleration of history—resulting from the technological and social progress of the last two centuries—and were not geared to the increasing proletarization of events.) The Foreign Minister was away on his honeymoon, Tirpitz was drinking the waters in Switzerland, the Chief of Staff was taking the cure at Karlsbad, the Chancellor was in the country, but due back on the same day.

The Kaiser was in his summer residence in Potsdam. He had been attending the naval regatta at Kiel on the day of the Sarajevo outrage. The news of his friend and hunting companion's horrible death had interrupted the regatta and brought Wilhelm back to the capital.

On learning that a special messenger had arrived from Vienna, bearing important documents, the Kaiser bade the Austrian Ambassador bring the papers to him in Potsdam and stay for lunch.

The resultant talks at the Hohenzollern New Palace were in the classic tradition of informal diplomacy: easy, elegant, and ultimately fatal. The Kaiser, who was preparing to leave the next morning for his annual summer cruise in northern waters, received the Austrian Ambassador, Count Marish Szogyeni, with friendly courtesy but with somewhat more prudence than he usually displayed. Reading over the communications from Vienna in a businesslike way, he was careful to voice reservations about a passage in the personal letter from his Imperial cousin which mentioned "eliminating Serbia as a factor of political power in the Balkans." This, the Kaiser sagely remarked, involved "possible serious European complications." He could therefore give no definite answer before consulting with his Chancellor (Bethmann-Holliveg). Szogyeni was an amiable, good-natured man of the world, and also an experienced diplomat who knew his Wilhelm. If he felt any disappointment over the Kaiser's attitude, he was careful to conceal it.

Lunch—at which the Kaiserin and a few guests were present—was a pleasant affair. We are told that the conversation was general and that the Kaiser was affable. In view of that luncheon's subsequent importance to the world, one cannot help feeling a certain morbid curiosity about some of the details connected with it that appear to have become lost in the haze of years. What, for example, was the menu? It seems a fair inference that the soup course was clear turtle—everything in the situation cries for clear turtle—and no doubt there was plenty of well-chilled hock, the day being warm. Whatever was eaten, or drunk, or said, seems to have acted disastrously on the Kaiser's centers of diplomatic inhibition.

In fair weather the Kaiser was accustomed to entertain his guests—and even to transact much of his official business—in the garden; it is there that he led the Austrian Ambassador for coffee and cigars. While the Kaiserin and a valet hovered in the background—the other guests somehow evaporated—the two men installed themselves on one of Wilhelm's favorite benches and resumed their portentous conversation. Lunch, however, had subtly changed the Kaiser's outlook: he was now more sanguine and less constitutionally minded. Without waiting for his Chancellor, whose views he was sure would coincide with his own, he assured the Ambassador—according to the latter's official dispatch—that "even if matters went to the length of war between Austria-Hungary and Russia, we could remain assured that Germany, in her customary loyalty as an ally, would stand at our side." Although none of the Austrian written communications specified what measures against Serbia were contemplated, the Kaiser added, in the words of the Ambassador's report:

"He quite understood that His Imperial and Royal Apostolic Majesty with his well known love of peace, would find it hard to march into Serbia, but if we have really recognized the necessity of military measures against Serbia, he [the Kaiser] would deplore our not taking advantage of the present moment, which is so favorable to us."

Later in the day, when the shadows were lengthening in the park, the Kaiser strolled under the trees with Bethmann-Holliveg who had been summoned from his country estate and acquainted him with what he had said to the Austrian Ambassador. If the Chancellor had any objections, he did not air them. Likewise, there were no objections from the Minister of War who was summoned later, nor from the acting chiefs of the General Staff and of the Navy Ministry whom Wilhelm saw next morning before leaving for Kiel.

"I do not believe in any serious warlike developments," he said to the Navy man. "The Czar will not place himself on the side of regicides. Besides, neither Russia nor France is prepared for war." Anxious, then, "not to create any uneasiness," he said that he would "on the Chancellor's advice," leave.

Having thus dispatched current affairs, Wilhelm embarked on a cruise which was to keep him away from his capital for nearly three weeks, feeling apparently no uneasiness himself at having pledged the lives of some ten million of his subjects, who were still blissfully unaware of what was going on, to support an Austrian punitive expedition, the nature of which he did not inquire about, and the consequences of which he tried to put out of his mind. The Wilhelmstrasse and the German Staff heaved a sigh of relief.

When Count Hoyos returned to Vienna with Wilhelm's blank check, the Emperor Francis Joseph sighed, "Now we can no longer turn back. It will be a terrible war."

Few European leaders, or observers, were so prescient.

The bitterness against Serbia was reported by Sir Maurice Bunsen, the

British Ambassador to Vienna, at about the same time that Hoyos was returning from his deadly mission. Bunsen had been chatting with the Russian Ambassador. "Mr. Schebeko doubts if the animosity penetrates deep down among the Austrian people . . ." The country would not "be rushed into war, for an isolated combat with Serbia would be impossible and Russia would be compelled to take up arms in defence of Serbia."

Sir Arthur Nicolson, Permanent Undersecretary of State at the Foreign Office, annotated the dispatch as follows:

"I have my doubts as to whether Austria will take any action of a serious character and I expect the storm will blow over. Mr. Schebeko is a shrewd man and I attach weight to any opinion he expresses."

Bunsen may have been a particularly woolly minded diplomat, but Nicolson certainly was not. The whole system and technique of diplomatic reporting, with its loose generalities, its fuzzy abstractions, its technical and sociological naïvetés, was—and to a large degree still is—archaic in terms of the requirements for twentieth-century policy planning. To make matters worse, because of the long peace, hardly any of the European statesmen or diplomats who gambled away the lives of a generation had personal experience of combat. The aged Francis Joseph remembered the horrors of the bloodsoaked field of Solferino, but most of his younger contemporaries, in every European nation, and at every administrative level, were as blind to the human and moral implications of modern war as they were ignorant of its technical imperatives.

(A number of able European diplomats, of course, operated competently, if not effectively, within the antiquated conventions of their craft, but it is hard to think of any professional who in the 1914 crisis matched the lucidity and insight earlier displayed by that roving amateur observer from the New World, Colonel Edward M. House.)

As for the nameless millions who were as yet unaware of their approaching rendezvous with death, little was heard from them in those early days of July. To the general public in Europe, the ripples of the Sarajevo outrage seemed to have faded out. Even many persons with access to inside information held this cheery view.

"The London season of 1914 had been a disappointing one for me," writes Margot Asquith, wife of the British Prime Minister, in her *Autobiography*, "and not an amusing one for Elizabeth [her daughter], and I was anxious that she should have a little fun. I sent her alone on the 25th of July to stay with Mrs. George Keppel, who had taken a house in Holland."

Even Sir George Buchanan, the British Ambassador to Russia, wrote in his memoirs:

"As several weeks had elapsed since Sarajevo, it was hoped Austria had
given up her punitive expedition. I had been granted leave of absence and
had taken tickets for our journey to England."

London at the time was sweltering in a heat wave, and perspiring newspaper readers were more likely to turn to accounts of the Henley regatta
on the sports page, than to the political section, which day in day out
featured the glum development of England's chief headache: the Irish
Question. In Paris the newspapers were providing their readers with
the best possible entertainment: *a crime passionnel* with political implications, in the best style of the period. The heroine was the wife of former
Finance Minister Joseph Caillaux, one of the leading French "appeasers."
She had found it necessary to call on Gaston Calmette, the editor of the
ultrapatriotic *Figaro,* and shoot him dead to prevent him from publishing
the letters which her husband had written to his mistress—a gesture of conjugal *delicatesse* which won her a prompt acquittal from the gallant French
jury.

The French government itself was blissfully unaware of the detonator of
doom, which was being readied with genteel leisureliness but with diabolical
thoroughness, between sips of *eiscaffee* in the Ballplatz. On July 15, President Poincaré of France, accompanied by Prime Minister René Viviani,
sailed on the five-day sea voyage to St. Petersburg for their long-planned
ceremonial visit. By that date the Austrian ultimatum to Serbia was nearing
final-draft form, and quite a few persons already knew what that form was
going to be. This was demonstrated by the selling wave that hit the Vienna
Bourse after July 12, and even more by the spectacular bearish operations
conducted on the Paris Bourse between July 12 and July 15 by a famous
Viennese speculator. Apparently the foreign offices of Europe did not read
the financial pages of their newspapers. They also appear to have neglected more traditional channels of information. It is quite inconceivable
that some young French, British, or Russian embassy attaché in Vienna was
not at the time on intimate terms with the wife of some Austro-Hungarian
minister, department head, or *chef de cabinet*—or at least that he was not
sharing with a high level Austrian official the intimacies of some opera
singer—and it seems equally inconceivable that none of these ladies knew
what was going on, or was too security-minded to drop a hint of it.

When the detonator finally went off, on July 23, the statesmen and the
diplomats were only slightly less surprised than the novelist Elinor Glyn,
then at the height of her slightly scandalous success, who commented with
asperity on the bad manners of the Austrian Ambassador in rushing
away from a weekend house party in a château near Paris at which they
were fellow guests. Anthony Glyn relates in his entertaining biography of
his famous sister that when Fielder, Elinor's chauffeur, suggested the dis-

appearance of the Ambassador was possibly a sign of impending war, "everyone searched hurriedly in the newspapers to see what he could mean and with whom the war could be."

A brief flashback to what had been happening behind the scenes in Vienna and in Belgrade, while the rest of Europe settled into its normal midsummer torpor, may be helpful at this point. From the moment the Kaiser had given his unconditional backing, the government of Austria-Hungary had virtually made up its mind to take some kind of military action against Serbia. The Emperor's ministers and chief military advisers were not unanimous, however, as to its form. General Conrad wanted all-out war, with as little advance warning to the enemy as possible. Count Koloman Tisza, the influential Hungarian premier, a bushy-bearded, high-living, but exceptionally clear-thinking Magyar aristocrat, feared that this course would bring Russia in. Berchtold's view, which ultimately prevailed, was a kind of sleazy compromise between two antithetical policies. As he told the German Ambassador on July 14, he proposed to send the Serbian government a note "so phrased that its acceptance will be practically impossible." At the same time, the door would be left very slightly ajar to some solution short of full-scale war if the Serbian government showed last-minute evidence of reasonableness. In provoking Serbia, every effort would be made to minimize the provocation to Russia and France. For this reason the Austrian ultimatum to Belgrade would be held up until the French President had started home from his Russian visit; there would be no chance for a warlike brotherhood "being sworn at St. Petersburg over the champagne under the influence of Mssrs. Poincaré, Izvolsky and the Grand Dukes."

A tragic accident in Belgrade may have heightened the dangers that were inherent from the first in Berchtold's recklessly calculated risk. On July 10, Baron Vladimir von Giesl, the Austrian Minister in Belgrade who had been recalled to Vienna for consultation returned to his post. At 9 o'clock that evening he received an unexpected call from his Russian opposite number, the redoubtable Nicolas Henrikovitch de Hartwig. The Russian Minister said that he had come to express his condolences "for the atrocious outrage" (Sarajevo), but there were undoubtedly other things that he wanted to say. What they were we shall never know. At 9:20 P.M., just as Giesl was launching into a soothing—and quite false—interpretation of Austria's attitude toward Serbia, Hartwig suddenly slumped to the floor, unconscious. He was dead when a doctor examined him a few minutes later (he was overweight, and had suffered from angina pectoris for some years). An unpleasant scene ensued after the arrival of Hartwig's daughter, Ludmilla. She brusquely repulsed the sympathy expressed by the Giesls, and poked about the room, sniffing at an eau de cologne bottle, and rummaging in some large Japanese vases. Her father had smoked only his own Russian cigarettes, but Ludmilla had wrapped up the two butts and put them in her bag. Had her father had anything to eat or drink? she asked with unveiled suspicion. In the tense atmosphere of the time, public rumor immediately made a poisoner of the unfortunate Giesl, who was even accused of having brought back from Vienna an electric chair which instantly killed anyone sitting in it.

Hartwig had inside knowledge of the Serbian Black Hand and its methods (the Austrians were strangely uninformed on the subject, though the alert French Minister in Belgrade had already been able to ferret out for his government the Black Hand's role in the Sarajevo assassinations). As was noted in a previous chapter, he is believed to have broken off his originally close relationship with the fanatical brotherhood's head, Colonel Apis, and in general, to have started putting the brakes on extreme Serbian nationalism, which he had earlier encouraged. His influence on the Serbian government was enormous; if his personal outlook on the Balkan problem had really changed as much as many historians think, his death at that crucial moment was undoubtedly a catastrophe for Europe. Giesl himself believed so. He later wrote that if Hartwig had lived beyond the "critical 25th of July," the war would not have occurred.

Perhaps that is an exaggeration, however. Vienna's final instructions to Giesl left little room for maneuver on either side. They stated that the Austrian Minister should call at the Yellow House (the Serbian Foreign Ministry) at 6 P.M. on July 23—the date and the hour had been fixed to make sure that Poincaré and Viviani would be safely aboard ship, headed for the open sea—and deliver the Dual Monarchy's note to the Serbian government whether or not Prime Minister Pasic was on hand. Moreover, Giesl was instructed, the answer must be one of unconditional acceptance within the stipulated time limit of 48 hours; no additional delay was to be granted under any pretext.

The Austrian ultimatum to Serbia, which the British Foreign Minister, Lord Grey, called the most formidable document ever addressed by one state to another, had been minutely and interminably hatched in the Vienna Foreign Office. It was finally adopted in a Joint Council of Ministers on July 19. Count Berchtold's main concern had been candidly described by the German Ambassador in a dispatch to Berlin:

"Were the Serbs to accept all the demands, this will be a solution not at all to his [Count Berchtold's] liking and he is turning over in his mind what demands could be made that would render acceptance by Serbia absolutely impossible."

Berchtold's soul-searching had already resulted in a list of conditions, the acceptance of which would have implied a revision of the Serbian constitution. Points 5 and 6 in particular, which called for the participation of the Austrian police in the investigation of the crime on Serb territory, were so clearly unacceptable to a sovereign power that at the Ballplatz they were referred to, with a satisfied smirk, as *"die zwei punkterl"* ("the two little points"). Other clauses would have committed the Serbian government to disavow "the unhealthy propaganda" directed from Serbian territory at subjects of the Dual Monarchy, and under the supervision of Austrian officials to disband the societies engaged in such propaganda. The kingdom of Serbia in 1914 resembled in certain respects those make-believe nations to which the proliferation of nominal sovereignties since World War II has accustomed us. Its inability to exercise real sovereignty over some of its own officials—e.g. Apis—was patent. But whatever the Serbian state lacked in administrative cohesion, the Serbian people, irrepressibly fumbling its way toward true nationhood, made up in bristly patriotism. The Austrian note was one that no self-respecting brigand chief could have accepted in its entirety. It is not certain, however, that Berchtold in approving the final terms of the ultimatum had unconditionally joined the war-at-any-cost camp in Vienna. He may have had some unparalleled feat of acrobatic brinkmanship in mind. Albertini even suggests that by a display of purely verbal toughness he thought, in some convolute Viennese fashion, to cut the ground from under the real Austrian warmongers, who were being egged on—in the Kaiser's absence—by the German General Staff and the Wilhelmstrasse. (The Kaiser, himself, cruising in the Norwegian fjords, did not fully realize what was going on between Berlin and Vienna, but he was unperturbed by the Austrian ultimatum when the text reached him aboard the *Hohenzollern*, following an after-dinner card game, in the night of July 24. "A spirited note, what?" he remarked to his naval aide, Admiral von Muller, strolling on the sunny deck next morning.)

As the Serbian Premier was out in the provinces electioneering on July 23, the Finance Minister received the ultimatum from Baron Giesl's hand, observing, with some dismay, that as it was election time, most of the ministers were out of town and that a Cabinet meeting was impossible in such a short time limit. Giesl brusquely replied that this was the age of railways, telegraphs, and telephone, and that if Serbian acceptance was not forthcoming by 6 o'clock on Saturday, July 25, he would leave Belgrade with his whole staff.

Forty-eight hours later, a few minutes before the 6 P.M. deadline, a tall old man with a bristly beard walked up to the Austrian Embassy. It was Pasic, the Serbian Premier, carrying an envelope under his arm with his government's reply to the Austrian note. It was a messy document, for the cabinet, in continual session, had kept amending it until the last hour, and under the ministrations of an exhausted and nervous secretary the only available typewriter had jammed so that several copies had to be made by hand. It was not customary for the Prime Minister of even a small kingdom to deliver messages, however vital, himself, and on foot. But when, half an hour earlier, Pasic had asked, "Now, who will deliver this?" one look at the distress on the faces of his colleagues convinced him that this was a job he must do himself. Now he handed the envelope to the stiffly waiting Austrian and said in broken German:

"Part of your demands we have accepted . . . for the rest we place our hopes on your loyalty and chivalry as an Austrian general."

Giesl was, in fact, a former army officer, and he seems to have been a man of heart, but his instructions left him no scope for chivalry. Conditional or partial acceptance was to be considered as a rejection. He already knew what to expect before reading the Serbian reply. Encouraging news from St. Petersburg earlier in the day had made the Serbian leaders feel that in rejecting dishonor they were not necessarily accepting death for their little nation, and during the afternoon a train had left Belgrade with the state archives and treasury. When Pasic arrived at the Austrian legation, Giesl received him in his traveling clothes. The legation cipher books were a smoldering heap of ashes, and the luggage was ready to be loaded into the waiting automobiles. Within an hour of the Serbian premier's departure, Giesl, accompanied by his wife and his staff, was across the border, informing the Ballplatz by telephone that he had just broken off diplomatic relations with Serbia.

A few minutes before seven on that same Saturday evening, the War Ministry in Vienna telephoned the news to Bad Ischl, where the Emperor was staying. Baron Margutti, one of the Imperial aides-de-camp, took it down. Francis Joseph listened with a wooden face while he read it off, then muttered, *"Also doch"* (literally, "So, after all"), one of those prosaically indefinite bits of familiar German that because they mean so little can signify so much. Reaching for his pince-nez with trembling hands, the old man sat down at his desk to study the text of the message. As he was making unconscious gestures with his hand, as if to push back a nightmare, the Emperor struck a glass bowl. "The jarring sound, as if something had finally broken, I will never forget," relates Margutti. But Francis Joseph had not yet given up all hope. "Well," he sighed, collecting himself, "the breaking off of diplomatic relations still does not mean war." Later in the evening, Berchtold persuaded him to sign an order of limited mobilization. (Serbia had already started to mobilize.)

Publication of the Austrian ultimatum, followed by the news of the rupture with Serbia and that of the two mobilizations, launched a shock wave of alarm throughout Europe, but did not lead to immediate panic. Some Europeans, grasping at straws like the aged Francis Joseph, tried to convince themselves that rupture—or even mobilization—did not necessarily mean war. Others felt that war was now inevitable, but expected it to be one of those localized Balkan conflicts—a brushfire war, as we would say today.

Localized war was, in fact, the official catchword in Berlin and Vienna. The sooner it came, the better, according to the experts.

The bolder Austria became, and the more strongly she was supported, "the more likely Russia is to keep quiet," said Herr Gottlieb von Jagow, the German Secretary of State (Foreign Minister).

On this theory, Bethmann-Holliveg—a political lightweight a bare notch above Berchtold's level—Jagow, and the German General Staff kept trying to prod Austria into hostilities before anyone could intervene. The intervention which they probably feared the most was that of their master, the Kaiser, and they took care that the information of the developing international crisis which reached him on board the *Hohenzollern* was as little, and as late, as possible. (One more illustration of how fictitious the Kaiser's claim to supreme responsibility had become.) No direct German interests were involved in the dispute between Austria and Serbia. Berlin officialdom was trying to push Germany's Austrian allies into war for their own good, and to strengthen the alliance. The Habsburg Empire was visibly crumbling, the Wilhelmstrasse argued; only military victory over the forces of South Slav irredentism could save it. To achieve this result the risk of a general European conflict had to be accepted.

In retrospect, the policy of the irresponsible German official camarilla seems criminal, and it was—but criminal negligence or recklessness, rather than criminal premeditation. The limited-war clique reasoned that it would actually reduce the danger of European complications if Austria-Hungary confronted the world with a military *fait accompli* in Serbia. Russia would protest and France would growl, but with Germany making it plain to them that she was standing by her ally, they would back down again as they had done in 1909. If worse came to worst, England would remain neutral, while Italy, in accordance with her obligations under the Triple Alliance, and even neutral Rumania, would join the Central Powers.

Events soon demonstrated that all the premises underlying the German limited-war policy were false. Austria could not forestall intervention by a bold *fait accompli* because she lacked the forces in readiness. General Conrad maintained that he would not be able to start hostilities before August 12, and wanted a formal declaration of war against Serbia to be held up until then (Berchtold and the Germans had naively dreamed of an Austrian blitz attack before mobilization was complete). Russia, through the mouth of her Foreign Minister, Sazonov, made a statement in St. Petersburg that sounded ominous by its very restraint:

"Russia cannot allow Austria to crush Serbia and become the predominant power in the Balkans."

French opinion began to sound increasingly resolute, Rumanian opinion more neutral, Italian opinion more aloof. Worst of all, England, from July 24 on began to show increasing concern over the situation—a concern which the German Ambassador, Prince Lichnowsky, one of the few European diplomats to cut a good figure during the 1914 crisis, faithfully and speedily transmitted to Berlin.

The Kaiser, himself, began to show agitation. Sudden—and fully justified—suspicion of the Wilhelmstrasse caused him to cut short his cruise. A meandering report from the Chancellor full of understatements and omissions and concluding with the news that "the diplomatic situation is not quite clear" put him in a thundering bad temper on his return to the capital, July 27.

This was probably the decisive day of the crisis. The text of the Serbian reply to Austria's ultimatum reached the Wilhelmstrasse—which had not bothered to ask for it sooner—about midafternoon, along with the first foreign reactions to it. The document caused dismay, as it had done in Vienna, where the Ballplatz official who had himself drafted the Austrian note termed it "the most brilliant example of diplomatic astuteness" in his experience. In reasonable and moderate terms the Serbians had accepted most of the Austrian demands, formulated some reservations on others and rejected only point six, which called for the participation of Austrian police in the investigations on Serbian territory. So much reasonableness might make too great an impression on the Kaiser; he must not see the Serbian note any sooner than could be helped. The Wilhelmstrasse accordingly dawdled so long about getting the document—already two days old—to Potsdam that Wilhelm did not read it until the next morning—a fateful delay.

Another key development of the day took place in London. The British government had been slow to appreciate the gravity of the crisis. The Foreign Secretary, Sir Edward Grey—tall, taciturn, tight-lipped, a passionate trout fisherman addicted to rural solitude—had taken a long time to perceive the terrible implications for England of the war clouds piling up over Europe. The carefully understated reports of his ambassadors on the Continent had not stirred him out of his native phlegm. He attached little importance to the hypocritical cluckings of the Germans about the need for keeping the Russians in check. As for the French, whose pleas for more precise commitments had been a recurrent nuisance for nearly ten years —their hysterical proddings were an affliction to be borne with equanimity like the weather.

The threat suddenly called up by the rupture between Vienna and Belgrade was something else. The British traditionally dislike tackling problems before they have become urgent, but the urgency of the Balkan situation could no longer be doubted. Action was called for if peace was to be saved, and Grey, more than any European statesmen then in power, really was attached to peace. It was not easy to act with a divided Cabinet and Parliament, with an uninformed public opinion, and with both allies and potential adversaries chronically addicted to misunderstanding Britain's attitude. In the circumstances Grey took what he felt was the most vigorous possible action. He called in the German Ambassador, Prince Karl Lichnowsky, spoke to him frankly about his worries, and made a formal plea that Germany use its good offices in Vienna to facilitate acceptance of the Serbian reply at least as a basis for further negotiation. The whole conversation, backed by the announcement in the British press the same day that leave had been canceled in the British Navy—the personal initiative of the First Sea Lord, Winston Churchill—constituted the most explicit warning yet given not to count on British neutrality. Prince Lichnowsky, like the alert and conscientious diplomat that he was, immediately grasped its import and relayed it to Berlin with the sense of urgency that the situation called for.

Lichnowsky's dispatch reached the Wilhelmstrasse at about the same moment as a message from Vienna informing the German government that Austria would declare war on Serbia the next day, or at the latest on July 29. Thereupon Bethmann-Holliveg committed either an incredible blunder, or—as Albertini and some other historians believe—an act of almost equally incredible duplicity. Acting upon instructions from the Kaiser, he forwarded to Vienna Sir Edward Grey's suggestion about German good offices, but on his own initiative he omitted a key passage in the message he had received from the German Embassy in London which stressed the seriousness of the British warning, and he failed to indicate any official German endorsement of the suggestion; he merely asked for the Austrian views about it. He even allowed his colleague, Jagow, to call in the Austrian Ambassador, and in effect to advise him that the Austrians should pay no attention to any British suggestions that Berlin might feel obliged, for the sake of the record, to forward. (The Ambassador, of course, immediately transmitted the advice to Vienna.)

The gravity of the German Chancellor's maneuver in sabotaging the British mediation proposal was underscored the next day when the Kaiser received simultaneously the report on his Ambassador's conversation with the British Foreign Secretary and the text of Serbia's reply to the Austrian ultimatum. Wilhelm often behaved irresponsibly, but he was neither a fool nor a lunatic. Far better than Bethmann-Holliveg or the Wilhelmstrasse, he grasped immediately the threat to the Austro-German daydream of a localized Balkan war implied by the awakening British concern over the situation. Unaware that for the past three days his Chancellor and Foreign Office had been doing their best to prod their Austrian ally into declaring war on Serbia without delay, Wilhelm set a new course for German policy in his comments on the Serbian note:

"A brilliant achievement for a time-limit of only 48 hours! It is more than one could have expected!" A moral coup for Vienna, he thought, but now "all reason for war is gone and Giesl ought to have quietly stayed on in Belgrade! After that I should never have ordered mobilization."

This was a complete change from the swashbuckling marginal notes, calling for the wiping out of the Serb bandits, with which Wilhelm had decorated the dispatches received on board the *Hohenzollern*. Bulow, who knew him well, writes of him: "Wilhelm II did not want war. He feared it. His bellicose marginal notes prove nothing . . ."

It was too late to change course, however. The diplomatic incendiaries in the Wilhelmstrasse had made too good use of the Kaiser's absence, and their Viennese accomplice, Berchtold, had been playing the same game on his aged master. The day before—July 27—he had purposely gone out of town to avoid seeing the Russian Ambassador, who had conciliatory proposals to make.

"Count Berchtold," noted the German Ambassador, speaking as of a promising pupil, "is in excellent disposition and very proud of the great number of telegrams of congratulation received from every part of Germany."

On the same fatal July 27, Berchtold had obtained Francis Joseph's signature to a declaration of war against Serbia. To overcome the eighty-four-year-old Emperor's lingering doubts, he had sent a telegram to Bad Ischl reporting a completely fictitious Serbian attack upon an Austro-Hungarian border detachment (though whether the Austrian premier deliberately faked the incident to deceive his master has never been established). Thus, on the morning of July 28, when Berchtold received the British Ambassador— at about the same moment the Kaiser in Potsdam was coming to the conclusion that war between Austria-Hungary and Serbia was both unnecessary and dangerous—it was to tell him that it was now unfortunately too late for any attempts at mediation, since His Royal and Imperial Apostolic Majesty had already signed the declaration of war. It was telegraphed to Belgrade shortly before 1 P.M. the same day—the first time in history that war was declared by wire. (After the Austrian Ambassador had left Belgrade, Berchtold was at a loss for a while as to how to serve the declaration of war. Berlin had refused to let the German legation transmit it on the ground that "it might awaken the impression in the public unfamiliar with diplomatic usage that we had hounded Austria-Hungary into war.")

Vienna, the capital of frivolity and *gemutlichkeit,* foamed with patriotic hysteria when the official proclamation of the state of war, signed by the Emperor, appeared on the walls of the city. The whole town, an American observer noted, suddenly "went frantic with joy. Total strangers embraced each other . . . The nightmare of humiliation, of disdain gulped down like a nauseous drug for ages, was off their breasts."

And yet, at the moment the declaration of war was laid in front of the Emperor for signature, the Austrian Army was not mobilized, and no military operations were contemplated for another two weeks. It is quite possible that Berchtold still believed some last-minute miracle would keep war from actually breaking out. But what neither Berchtold nor the Wilhelmstrasse realized is that by formally proclaiming war, even in such a remote and unimportant corner of Europe, they were relinquishing control everywhere to the military, whose heavy hand would soon wreak havoc with their diplomatic chess game.

Although saber-rattling had for ten years been a major diplomatic technique, the statesmen of 1914 were for the most part quite ignorant of what a mobilization involved. The Austrians, at war, but unable to move a single battalion against the enemy, were the first to find out. The Russians were the next to be swept to the point of no return by the rigidity of their army's mobilization plans.

Like his fellow autocrats Wilhelm II and Francis Joseph, Nicholas II of Russia dreaded war. "Everything possible must be done to save peace," he told a member of his entourage just after he had received an alarming telegram from the Kaiser. "I will not become responsible for a monstrous slaughter." Unfortunately, though he was theoretically the most absolute of all the European despots, the Czar had no more real control over events than the others had. The reactionary, militarist, and fanatically Pan-Slav clique that Nicholas relied upon to save the autocracy included many influential officers or officials who were bent on pushing him into a ruinous war.

"I foresee," he wired Cousin Willy in a futile appeal to him to restrain his Austrian ally, "that very soon I shall be overwhelmed by the pressure brought upon me and be forced to take extreme measures which will lead to war."

The pressure did in fact build up with terrifying speed. After the Austrian declaration of war on July 28, sheer muddle played an increasingly significant role in generating it. Too much was happening too fast in too many places. Consultation between allies, and co-ordination within national governments, became more and more unsatisfactory as the stacks of urgent telegrams grew steadily higher and higher on the desks of Europe's statesmen. Old World bureaucracy was simply snowed under by the blizzard of information that descended upon it. The keenest and most orderly minds could no longer digest and assimilate the raw data that were being fed into them, and in every capital decision tended to lag behind event, so that each new move on anyone's part was likely to be a false move, adding to the general confusion. Nowhere were the fatal effects of this process more clearly illustrated than in St. Petersburg where the bureaucracy was disorganized at the best of times, and where the cloudiest judgments and the weakest characters were generally to be found in high places.

Even before the sheer velocity of events became intolerable, the Russian Foreign Minister, Sazonov, a slight, shallow, conscientious man with a close-trimmed beard and a sharp foxlike face that made him look cleverer and more tricky than he was, had committed a momentous blunder. After the Austrian ultimatum to Serbia he obtained the agreement of the Cabinet and the approval of the Czar to the principle of a partial mobilization of Russian forces—involving a little over 1,000,000 men—along the Austrian border. This move, Sazonov argued, might scare the Austrians out of attacking Serbia, but would not threaten Germany, and in any case a soothing note to Berlin would accompany public announcement of the call-up.

Orders to put the limited mobilization in effect throughout four southern districts were supposed to go out on July 29, the day after the Austro-Hungarian declaration of war against Serbia. The Russian General Staff, however, had developed second thoughts about partial mobilization. There was a serious risk, its chief told Sazonov, that such limited measures would throw out of kilter the cumbersome machinery of military administration and thus compromise eventual full-scale mobilization if the latter should become necessary. At this point, Sazonov, as a man of peace, should have withdrawn his original proposal and insisted on canceling any form of mobilization; the Czar would almost certainly have backed him. Instead, he suddenly veered around to the military viewpoint and joined the generals in urging the Czar to decree general mobilization at once. Nicholas at first consented, then at 9:30 on the evening of July 29, just as the official telegrams transmitting the order of mobilization to all the military headquarters of the Empire were about to be sent, he dispatched an officer to the central telegraph bureau to stop them and to substitute the original order of partial mobilization.

Summarizing the historic, if somewhat incoherent, events of the day, Nicholas wrote in his diary for July 29:

"During the day we played tennis. The weather was magnificent. But the day was singularly unpeaceful. I was constantly being called to the telephone . . . Apart from that I was in urgent telephonic communication with Wilhelm. In the evening I read, and received Tatishev [a Russian General attached to the Kaiser's personal staff as a kind of special military attaché] whom I am sending tomorrow to Berlin."

Two days before, the Russian Minister of War, General Sukhomlinov, had recorded his impressions of an audience with the Czar in the following terms:

"To judge by the calmness, or more exactly the equanimity, with which the Czar listened to my report of current business, one might have come to the conclusion that there was nothing that might affect in any way the peaceful life of Russia. I was amazed at His Majesty's impassiveness and the slightness of his interest in what I had to say."

There is no doubt that poor Nicholas had neither the character nor the intellect to cope with the terrible responsibilities that confronted him, but his aloofness and his preoccupation with the trivia of daily life during that critical last week of July 1914 preserved him from the hysteria to which most of his ministers and generals had succumbed. During the last days of peace "Nicky" and "Willy" were blamelessly employed exchanging telegrams or telephone calls that had little bearing, for good or ill, on the actions of their respective governments. And Nicholas at least, did make one last futile attempt to assert himself. Late on the night of July 29, after issuing his dramatic order to cancel general mobilization, the Czar again wired the Kaiser giving warning of the rising pressures that were about to overwhelm him and suggesting that the Austro-Serbian dispute be submitted to the Hague Conference. The telegram was signed, "Your loving Nicky."

The proposal for arbitration by the Hague Tribunal had no chance of acceptance—"Rubbish," Willy scrawled on the margin of the dispatch—but at that particular moment in the European crisis any move that offered a hope of postponing the eventual showdown was important. The Czar's telegram came on the heels of a message from London which had rocked, not only the Kaiser, but even Bethmann-Holliveg and the Wilhelmstrasse. "So long as the conflict remains confined to Austria and Russia we can stand aside," Grey had told the German Ambassador. "But if Germany and France should be involved, then the British government would be forced to make up its mind quickly." If the Czar had stuck to his refusal not to let Russian mobilization go beyond the limited call-up in the south, peace might have been saved (although the Russian Generals had already begun surreptitiously to exceed the terms of the Imperial ukase). But between 3 and 4 P.M. on July 30, just as Bethmann-Holliveg in Berlin was drafting new instructions to his Ambassador in Vienna advising him that Germany "must decline to be drawn wantonly into a world conflagration without having any regard paid to our counsels," Nicholas' vacillant will suddenly buckled.

It was Sazonov who effected this fatal result. Accompanied by a staff officer, he came to the Peterhof Palace, some 17 miles out of the capital, to try to convince the Czar that general mobilization could no longer be delayed. For more than an hour, in deferential but urgent tones, he marshaled his arguments in favor of mobilization. He had two particularly strong ones: a somewhat vague report that Germany, too, had begun to mobilize, and the arrogant tone of the Kaiser's latest telegram declaring that he could not mediate in Vienna if Russia went ahead with the partial mobilization against Austria.

Nicholas, however, appeared adamant. Sitting behind his bronze-trimmed mahogany desk, littered with maps, in his office on the ground floor of the palace, overlooking the Gulf of Finland, he hardly seemed to hear what his Foreign Minister was saying. His bearded face, though pale and lined with fatigue, remained expressionless, and his dreamy eyes stayed fixed on the remote blue sea-horizon.

"Think of the responsibility you are asking me to take if I follow your advice!" he finally exclaimed. "Think what it means to send thousands and thousands of men to their death."

Unluckily, Sazonov's companion, General Tatishev, chose that moment to speak up.

"Yes, it is a terrible decision to take," he said.

"I am the one who decides," Nicholas snapped.

From then on he seemed more attentive to Sazonov's arguments. He was particularly impressed by the Foreign Minister's view—an erroneous one we now know—that Germany was bent on war and would go ahead whether Russia mobilized or not. At last, after what seemed a terrible inner struggle, the Czar gave in.

"All right, Serge Dimitrievitch," he said, "telephone the Chief of the General Staff that I give the order for general mobilization."

Sazonov was inside the telephone cabin on the ground floor of the Peterhof as soon as etiquette permitted. "And now, General," he said, after passing on the glad news, "disconnect your telephone."

The advice proved unnecessary. The Czar hastened to wire his cousin Willy, pledging that his troops would commit no provocative actions, and urging continued negotiations in the interest of the "universal peace dear to our hearts," but he issued no further counterorders. On the morning of July 31—"a grey day, in keeping with my mood," as Nicholas wrote in his diary—the red mobilization posters went up on the walls of public buildings throughout the Russian Empire.

Russia's mobilization triggered the irreversible chain reaction that vaporized the last hopes of the apprentice-sorcerers in the chanceries for achieving their diplomatic objectives by mere saber-rattling or through limited or "localized" war. The statesmen kept assuring themselves—and each other—that mobilization did not mean war, but the soldiers in every country knew they were wrong. Mobilization implied countermobilization, and when practiced on a Continental scale, in a Europe long since divided into two tensely hostile camps, the reciprocal but never exactly equal, insecurities thereby generated would suffice in themselves to make an armed clash inevitable. Moreover it was the season for battle. All over Europe the cereal harvest was virtually finished—armies in those days were almost as dependent upon bread as upon bullets—and the silos or elevators were filled with a bumper crop. The military conscience, which quailed at the thought of tender green shoots being trampled down by booted feet—whatever might happen to the owners of the feet, or to the cities from which they had marched—at last was tranquil. From the Urals to the Atlantic, the fields of stubble lay naked and tawny under the blazing sun, inviting the deployment of armies. War was possible; therefore it must be necessary.

The first big power after Russia to order full mobilization was Austria-Hungary. The decree was signed on July 31, only a few hours after the posters started going up in Russia. The decision to mobilize had been taken the day before, despite a series of frantic appeals from Bethmann-Holliveg in Berlin to heed a new British proposal, already endorsed by Russia, for calling off the war against Serbia once the Austro-Hungarian armies had occupied Belgrade (which was virtually on the frontier). Any lingering doubts Berchtold may have had about the wisdom of the decision to mobilize were dispelled when the Chief of Staff, General Conrad, rushed into the Ballplatz early on the morning of July 31 brandishing a telegram he had received during the night from his German colleague, Moltke, urging Austria to reject the British proposal and to mobilize at once against Russia.

"How odd," mused the dapper little count. "Who runs the government in Berlin—Bethmann or Moltke?"

It was a naive question. In Russia, in Germany, and in Austria the generals were now in the saddle. Their business was war, and war under the best conditions. All that was left for the diplomats was to put a good face on the brutal dictates of the military plans.

The Kaiser himself had for all practical purposes tossed in his hand. The solemn warning from Grey on July 29 that had thrown the Wilhelmstrasse into panic, merely plunged Wilhelm II into rage and despair when he read it on the thirtieth. On the margin of the dispatch, opposite the paragraph voicing Grey's fear that if war broke out it would be "the greatest catastrophe the world has ever seen," the Kaiser scrawled, *"That means they are going to attack us."* Both Wilhelm and his Chancellor had based their truculent support, or incitement, of Austria on the childish assumption—stemming from the former's mythological concept of the solidarity of monarchs, and fed by a recent, unguarded luncheon-table remark made by Britain's George V to the Kaiser's brother, Prince Henry of Prussia—that in case of a Continental war England would stand aside. Wilhelm's fury broke out in the long footnote he penned at the bottom of his Ambassador's report:

"England shows her hand at the moment when she thinks we are cornered, and in a manner of speaking, done for. The low-down shopkeeping knaves have been trying to take us in with banquets and speeches. The grossest deception is the King's message to me by Henry . . . England alone bears the responsibility for peace or war, not we now."

Later in the day, Wilhelm dejectedly exclaimed to one of his intimates, "My work is at an end."

Bethmann-Holliveg, who like Wilhelm, had unwittingly helped to light the fatal conflagration by his earlier blunders, made an even more pathetic confession of failure in a statement to the Prussian Council of Ministers on July 30. "All governments, including Russia's, and the great majority of their peoples are peacefully inclined," the Chancellor said, "but the direction has been lost, and the stone has started rolling."

As Bethmann was speaking, the low bovine rumble of human herds surging back and forth in the Unter den Linden as they chanted *Deutschland uber Alles,* counterpointed his words. His remark was a surprisingly profound one to issue from such a shallow mind, but in one sense at least, it was not quite accurate. The men of peace had, in fact, lost control, but the men of war assumed it. Mob-hysteria itself was no longer a significant factor in the situation; it was merely a symptom of the lucid death-wish embodied in the war plans of the opposed general staffs.

The inflexibility of Germany's contingency plans for a major diplomatic crisis—reflecting a primitive version of the massive-retaliation doctrine—would have sufficed to kill the last chance for peace, if one had remained after Russia's mobilization. General Helmuth von Moltke, the mediocre nephew of the great Moltke, was actually a diffident neurotic, but his thought-processes were as typically Prussian as his bull-necked, pot-bellied body. Even if he had possessed the cool nerve necessary for brinkmanship, his staff planners had left him no room for maneuver on the brink. Germany, it now became clear, had no mobilization plan—only a plan for war, and one that virtually assured immediate generalization of the conflict because it called for an attack on France through Belgium, whose neutrality Germany was pledged by solemn treaties to respect, thereby installing the German Army on the coast of the English Channel. Accordingly, when confirmation of the Russian mobilization reached Berlin just before noon of July 31, Moltke after declaring a state of national emergency—the last stage before general mobilization and martial law—instructed the Wilhelmstrasse to set in motion the diplomatic machinery that would enable Germany, whose standing armies in the West were already poised, to strike without incurring the odium of unprovoked aggression. Two German ultimatums were dispatched in the afternoon of July 31: one to Russia, enjoining her to halt all military measures against Austria-Hungary and against Germany within twelve hours, the other to France, demanding that she remain neutral in case of a Russo-German war. (The ultimatum to Belgium, demanding right of passage for the German armies, had already been sent to the German Minister in Brussels, though it was not to be delivered until August 2.) Like the earlier Austrian note to Belgrade, they were formulated and timed in such a way that refusal would be certain, thus giving Germany a pretext for declaring war. So the juggernaut which was to devastate the face of Europe began to roll.

On August 1, at 7 P.M. Count Friedrich von Pourtales, the German Ambassador to Russia, red in the face and laboring under the nervous strain of a sleepless week, entered the office of Sazonov, whose amiable features were unusually taut. Rather brusquely the Germans asked whether the Russian government was disposed to give a satisfactory answer to the ultimatum presented by Germany the day before and timed to run out at noon. Receiving an evasive answer, he repeated his question, in a staccato voice. Once again Sazonov replied that the Russians could not demobilize, but that they were, as before, prepared to continue negotiations for a peaceful settlement. Both men were on their feet. The Count fumbled in his pocket and drew out the German declaration of war, which he read, breathing hard as he reached the final sentence:

"His Majesty the Emperor, my august sovereign, accepts the challenge in the name of the Empire and considers himself at war with Russia."

Then, losing all control of himself, he ran to the window which looked out over the Winter Palace reddened by the evening sun, and turning his back on Sazonov, burst into tears. Sazonov wordlessly patted his shoulder, whereupon Pourtales burst out, "Never did I think that I would have to leave St. Petersburg under such conditions." The two diplomats, who were also old friends, embraced each other, in the Russian style, for the last time.

The Czar was less emotional about his rupture with Cousin Willy. Late that night, after drinking a glass of tea and chatting with the Czarina, who was already in bed, he decided to take a bath. He had just lowered himself into the tub when a footman knocked on the door to inform him that there was an urgent personal telegram from his Majesty, the German Kaiser.

"I read the telegram, I reread it, I repeated it out loud to myself, but still I did not understand," Nicholas subsequently related to the French Ambassador. "What, Wilhelm pretends that it is still in my power to avoid war? He implores me not to let my troops cross the border . . . Have I gone mad? Has not the Court Minister, my old Fredericks, brought me less than six hours ago the declaration of war handed to Sazonov by the German

Ambassador? I returned to the Czarina's room and read her Wilhelm's telegram. She wanted to read it herself to believe it, and said, 'You will not reply to it, will you?' 'No indeed.' . . . On leaving the Czarina's room I felt that all was finished for ever between Wilhelm and myself. I slept soundly."

There were few other public figures in Europe who slept soundly that night. Probably Francis Joseph did, because he was old and tired, and accustomed to disaster, and because he had done his duty as he saw it. Perhaps Gavrilo Princip, the assassin of the Archduke, slept in his cell, if he was not still in too much pain from the injuries inflicted on him by the crowd and by the police at the time of his arrest. His work was done. So was that of the mysterious chief he had never seen, Colonel Apis; of Apis' friend, the Russian military attaché, Colonel Artamanov—back on duty after a refreshing two-months' leave—of Izvolsky; of Izvolsky's fellow-plotter, Théophile Delcassé, the former French Minister of Foreign Affairs.

"I thought I saw the work of the little spider into whose web Germany was throwing herself," Abel Ferry, the French Undersecretary of State for Foreign Affairs, jotted down in his secret notebook after an interview with Delcassé on the eve of the German ultimatum. "Germany could no longer live in the world he [Delcassé] had made for her . . . and for the first time I understood that no one since Bismarck had had such an influence on European events as this little man who never saw French ambassadors, disregarded parliament, and lived only in his work. He was no longer minister, but the net was up and Germany was bumbling into it like a fat fly."

Most of the other crowned heads and statesmen and diplomats of Europe, who had worked for war without realizing it, stumbled through the last hours of peace in a kind of waking nightmare. In the night of July 31 the French government decided to reject the German ultimatum, which had been delivered at 7 P.M., and to order general mobilization. While the ministers, with President Poincaré in the chair, were still deliberating around the big horseshoe table, covered with green baize, in the council chamber of the Elysée Palace, the news reached them that Jean Jaurès, the bushy-bearded leader of the French Socialists, mortal foe of the Franco-Russian alliance, and the last hope of European pacifists, had been shot dead by a nationalist fanatic. There were gasps of horror around the council table, followed by deathly silence. If the Socialist ideal had taken as deep root in the minds of European workingmen as Jaurès and his friends liked to believe, his martyr's death might have saved peace at the last minute. For a little while almost anything seemed possible. According to Abel Ferry, the Paris Prefect of Police threw the Council of Ministers into panic by calling up the Elysée to warn them that revolution would break out in the capital within three hours.

It was a false alarm, however. Some workers did turn out into the streets, but the anti-war demonstrations were literally swallowed up by the vaster, more Dionysian frenzy of the patriotic mobs screaming and chanting on the boulevards. Scattered shouts of *A bas la guerre* turned into the many-throated roar of the *Marseillaise,* and finally into the strident mass-cry, *À Berlin.* Next day, August 1, when the little yellow mobilization posters with the crossed tricolor flags went up on walls throughout France—almost at the same moment that general mobilization was proclaimed in Germany —the workers and the peasants of France greased their boots and filled their packs with their usual shrug. Cheering crowds, chiefly made up of women waving flags and throwing flowers, rushed to the stations to see them off, and as the long trains pulled out for the East, the reservists jammed themselves into the open windows, like clusters of gesticulating ants, and waved and sang.

Similar scenes were taking place at the time nearly everywhere in Europe, except in the traditionally neutral countries, and in Italy, which despite its long-standing alliance with Germany and Austria had decided to turn neutral.

In the Prussian capital the approach of war was greeted with a collective fervor not matched anywhere else. "The general feeling among the Germans is that their years of preparation would now bear fruit," wrote the American Ambassador, James W. Gerard.

Neither Bethmann-Holliveg nor the Kaiser shared the martial elation of their compatriots.

"How did it all happen?" Bethmann's predecessor, Prince von Bulow, asked the Chancellor a few days after the outbreak of war.

"Ah, if only one knew," Bethmann replied, throwing up his arms in despair.

"I have never seen a more tragic, more ravaged face than that of our Emperor during those days," recorded Admiral von Tirpitz.

On August 1, the day of the French mobilization, to the accompaniment of a distant, ever swelling roar of acclamation from his subjects, Wilhelm II sat down in the Star Room of the Berlin *Schloss* at a desk made from the wood of Lord Nelson's flagship *Victory* to sign the order that would start his armies rolling toward the Grand Duchy of Luxembourg and Belgium—whose neutrality was still guaranteed by the solemn international treaty which Bethmann-Holliveg, in a famous conversation a few days later, dismissed as a "scrap of paper." When he got up, the Kaiser, suddenly clairvoyant, as the doomed sometimes become, looked into the faces of his naval and military chiefs, standing respectfully around the desk. "Gentlemen," he said in a low, harsh voice. "You will live to regret this."

Two days later, Lord Grey, standing with bowed shoulders at the window of his room in the Foreign Office, while dusk brought relief to the sweltering, exhausted city of London, had a similar chilling vision of night falling on a whole continent, on a whole social order and way of life.

"The lamps are going out all over Europe," he said. "We shall not see them lit again in our time."

In reality, the lamps had started going out long before Grey or Wilhelm, or any contemporary, was aware of it. And the darkening of the Old World was to prove both more total and more cataclysmic than the most fearful, or the most lucid, imagined.

CHAPTER 12

The Failure of Arms

B Y present-day standards, the First World War was a parochial and technologically rather low-grade struggle. Only
the westerly jut of the Eurasian land mass was seriously involved, and
topographically speaking, it was scarcely pitted. Yet because of what it did
to Europe in the human sense—and because of what Europe then meant to
the world—the 1914 war remains the greatest trauma in Western history
since the Wars of Religion. The fears expressed shortly after its outbreak
by U. S. President Woodrow Wilson that it would "set civilization back by
two or three centuries," may have been excessive, but they have not proved
wholly groundless. World War I killed fewer victims than World War II,
destroyed fewer buildings, and uprooted millions instead of tens of millions,
but in many ways it left even deeper scars both on the mind and on the map
of Europe. The Old World never recovered from the shock.

In part, the war's devastating impact was due to the vast, revolutionary
upheavals that came in its wake. The dynastic empires of Central and
Eastern Europe, whose moral and political decay had engendered the conflict, were—as we shall soon see—its foremost victims, and their downfall
could not fail to be momentous. This cause, however, was also an effect.
The war was a cataclysm in its own right. However strange it may sound
to the veterans of Omaha Beach, of Monte Cassino, and of Stalingrad—or
to the survivors of Hiroshima—the trench warfare of 1914–1918 was perhaps the cruelest large-scale ordeal that the flesh and spirit of man have
endured since the beginning of the Ice Age.

The opening battles in France and on the eastern front—the greatest
shock of armies the world had seen up to then—already gave some hint of
the nightmare to come. They were heroic but murderous engagements. In

East Prussia, where the Kaiser's armies were outnumbered three to one, German gunners laying their pieces wheel to wheel in the gaps between the marsh-ringed lakes and patchy, dark pine forests fired over open sights into the massed Cossack squadrons—and still the Russian hordes came on. Among the wooded, flinty hills of German Lorraine, where the French Army rashly took the offensive, infantry in baggy red trousers—sometimes led by young officers fresh from St. Cyr in white gloves and waving plumes— fixed bayonets on their unwieldy Lebel rifles and charged into the teeth of concealed machine-gun batteries. To the north and west, in the tangled thickets of the Argonne, on the chalky, tilted plains of the Champagne, il- lumined with their ripening, lemon-colored vineyards, the French took their revenge, raking the *feldgrau* columns marching down from Belgium along the poplar-shaded roads with round after round of shrapnel from their fast, vicious little 75-mm fieldpieces.

Moltke, who took supreme command of the German armies, stood on the defensive in East Prussia, warded off the French in Lorraine, and in accordance with a slightly modified version of the Schlieffen Plan, flung the bulk of his forces headlong through Belgium and Picardy around the French left flank, in a vast enveloping movement. His objective was the classic one of squeezing and crushing the main body of the enemy—six French armies, together with the small but professional expeditionary force the British had rushed across the Channel—deployed between Paris and the German border. He very nearly achieved it. A bare month after the out- break of war, German Uhlans, patrolling in advance of Moltke's leading column north of the capital, checked their horses and gazed in awe at the Eiffel Tower etched against the slatey blue sky of the Ile-de-France.

Moltke had hoped to knock France out of the war within six weeks and then throw the whole combined weight of the German and Austrian armies against Russia. His own errors of judgment and failure of nerve—he had weakened his striking force in the west to bolster the hard-pressed eastern front—helped to cheat him of the victory that was in his grasp. Stolid as an ox—and hardly more imaginative—the French commander-in-chief, Gen- eral Joseph Joffre, retreated as best he could under the sledgehammer blows of the enemy, then sensing a slackening, lowered his head and butted back. The three-day French counterattack (September 6–9) on the Marne and along the Nancy-Verdun front, brilliantly improvised by Joffre's subordinate commanders, shivered the German offensive. A week earlier General Paul von Hindenburg, a wooden-faced, mineral-nerved Prussian called out of retirement to cope with the crisis on the eastern front, had similarly thrown back the Russians in the so-called Battle of Tannenberg. The Austrian invasion of Serbia, after initial successes ended in a humiliating fiasco. (Later in the war Serbia was entirely overrun by the Central Powers, the remains of its army, following an epic retreat to the coast, had to be evacuated by the Allies.)

By the time that winter closed down, with its pall of mud and fog in the west, its white shroud of blizzard in the east, the opposing armies were deadlocked from Switzerland to the North Sea, from the Baltic to the Carpathians. The fearful vigil had begun.

Diplomacy—abetted more recklessly than ever by propaganda and conspiracy—vainly strove to tip the balance. New allies, enticed by secret treaties and secret subsidies, joined one camp or the other; new fronts were opened; peripheral stalemates prolonged the main one. Little Montenegro was in with Serbia almost from the start. Japan joined the Western Powers in August—but contented herself with scooping up the German possessions on the China coast and in the Pacific. Turkey threw in with the Central Powers in November. Italy declared war on her former allies of the Triple Alliance in May 1915. Bulgaria lined up with Germany, Austria and Turkey in October of the same year; Rumania came in—on the side of the Entente —in 1916.

The decisive intervention was that of the United States, which declared war against Germany on April 6, 1917—mainly the consequence of Germany's desperate attempt to break the tightening stranglehold of the Entente's naval blockade by unrestricted submarine warfare. With America in, a whole swarm of new belligerents—mostly Platonic—rallied to the Allied cause. Honduras—July 1918—was the last. By that time the planetary coalition against the four Central Powers already totaled 27 nations, counting in Greece, Portugal, Brazil, China, San Marino, and such nominal partners as Liberia, Siam, and Bolivia.

The sixteen active belligerents suffered total casualties—in military personnel alone—of 37,494,186, substantially more than half of the forces mobilized. More than 8,500,000 were killed or died from wounds or disease. In the French, British, German, Russian, Austro-Hungarian, Turkish, and Italian armies at least one man out of every ten mobilized died or was killed; the ratio of fatal casualties was, of course, very much higher than that among front-line units, particularly in the Russian and Austro-Hungarian armies. France and other advanced industrial countries with a low birthrate were demographically and psychologically debilitated for a generation by the hectacomb of vigorous young males, while the more backward nations suffered cruelly from the decimation of their educated elites.

During World War II—except possibly in the Soviet and Japanese armies —a unit's morale was presumed to be dangerously shaken when it lost 10 per cent or more of its effectives in an attack. In World War I, battalions —and even regiments—after weeks under fire might lose three-fourths of theirs in the first hours of an offensive, and still be expected to keep on fighting. Because aerial bombardment was still in its infancy, service troops, like the civilian population, were less exposed in World War I than they were to be in World War II, but front-line service in a good combat division was more dangerous, as well as more harrowing. On the British sector of the Western Front between January 1915 and September 1918 it was generally reckoned that a private soldier in such a unit had only about five months of trench service in front of him, and that the wound which eventually put him out of action would be fatal in at least one case out of four. Life expectancy was higher on the German side, except during the great offensives, but it was considerably lower in the elite Russian and Austro-Hungarian units.

The momentary ascendancy of the defensive over the offensive—mainly due to the killing power of the machine gun, the mortar and the quick-firing fieldpiece—had obliged the belligerents to dig in, and the longer the stalemate lasted, the more elaborate their defensive systems became. Along most of the front there stretched on each side two or three successive lines of deep trenches, connected by lateral passages, and strengthened with sandbagged parapets. Tangled thickets of barbed wire bristled in front of them; their walls were honeycombed with dugout shelters. The shell-cratered no man's land between the enemy lines was rarely more than 500 yards wide; most of the time it was between 100 and 200 yards, and in a few places barely the width of a normal city street, from curb to curb. Each command was loath to yield to the enemy so much as a foot of ground won at a terrible cost or fortified at great labor; on the contrary, bloody minor skirmishes were constantly fought to gain a few yards, or to occupy some insignificant feature, at the enemy's expense. In between such futile engagements the two armies—observing the military proprieties and imagining they were keeping up front-line morale—harassed the opposing trenches throughout the long days and nights with desultory fire. Thus developed the most horrible absurdity—and the most absurd horror—in the history of warfare: a pointless battle of mutual attrition, involving millions of combatants and lasting, with occasional lulls but no break for some 1400 days.

The trenches, recalls the British poet Robert Graves, were "like air-raid shelters hastily dug in a muddy field, fenced by a tangle of rusty barbed wire, surrounded by enormous craters; subject not only to an incessant air-raid of varying intensity but to constant surprise attacks by professional killers, and without any protection against flooding in times of heavy rain."

Life in these warrens of death, which men shared with their body-vermin and with hordes of fat, gray rats, attained, as Graves remarks, "the absolute zero of discomfort," and it was as sordid as it was miserable: "we fed like pigs, we stank like pigs."

"Cold, dirt, discomfort are the ever-present conditions, and the soldier's life comes to mean for him simply a test of the most misery that the human organism can support," reported the young American poet, Alan Seeger, who was soon (1916) to be killed in action. "It is ignoble, this style of warfare. We are not in fact leading the life of men at all, but that of animals living in holes in the ground and only showing our heads outside to fight and to feed."

Seeger, the author of the once-famous bit of verse, *I Have a Rendezvous with Death,* volunteered in the French Foreign Legion in 1914. Thousands of other young Americans who came over to France after 1917 with General Pershing's American Expeditionary Force faced their share of hardships and dangers, but few of them arrived in time to experience the full desolation of trench life as their French and British comrades knew it for more than three years during the stalemate phase of the conflict.

Poison gas, widely used by both sides after the Germans tried it out near Ypres in 1915, was one of the nightmarish features of trench warfare. Another was the difficulty in disposing of the dead when they fell in no man's land. Rotting bodies, or scraps of human flesh, lay in the shell craters between the fences or in the wire entanglements for weeks or months, particularly after a heavy engagement, poisoning the air with their stench. "Do you want to find your sweetheart?" ran the chorus of a popular British army song. "I know where he is: Hanging on the front-line wire!" Undoubtedly the harshest ordeal of trench warfare was the slowly building stress of anxiety in the minds and nervous systems of men who had to stand still under heavy fire for days or weeks at a time. Certain particularly active sectors of the Western Front received an average of one ton of steel and high explosive per square yard. During the Battle of Verdun, probably the most murderous in history, the French alone fired more than 12,000,000 shells of all calibers between February 21 and June 16, 1916. Thirteen years after the end of the war when as a young correspondent in France I had occasion to visit the former battlefields there were still sizable areas, particularly around Verdun and near Rheims, where the ground was cratered like a lunar landscape, and truncated hilltops with all their topsoil blasted off, standing stark and naked as if the splintered skeleton of the earth were showing through its wounds. Yet, I knew, parts of this man-made wasteland had for a while been as thickly populated as many a city street. The imagination went numb trying to picture how it must have felt to live through one of the synthetic cataclysms that produced such devastation. Sweating out a major bombardment in a front-line shelter was an apocalyptic experience; even the routine fire-fights which blazed up along a sector of the front from time to time could be a severe strain after one had lived through a certain number of them.

"We came at an unhealthy moment," writes Douglas Read, a British journalist, reminiscing after the war about a conducted visit to the front he once made as a cadet. "I shared a trench bay with a private of the Worcestershires, an old soldier, steady, grizzled, resigned. Wrapped in a blanket I lay on the fire-step while heavy shelling rocked the trench, splashed dirt in my face, grazed my nose with a tiny fragment of metal.

"The old soldier told me not to be afraid. I was not, very much . . . If you are young, in good health and have not been much bombarded, steadiness under fire is not difficult; but I admire those men, like my old soldier-companion, who know what a bombardment is and does and still remain masters of themselves.

"In the next bay was a machine-gunner. He was at the end of his nerves and shivered as if with ague."

". . . we became jittery after six months," says Robert Graves, "morose and unreliable after a year, a dead loss after eighteen months. In World War II the deterioration would have been early diagnosed as 'combat fatigue' and the sufferer rushed to a base hospital for treatment. In World War I nothing like this happened . . . Before being diagnosed as a 'shell-shock' case [the soldier] had to be either paralyzed or maniacal."

The endless strain and the physical misery of trench life often caused the infantrymen of World War I to look forward to clambering over their parapets and rushing across no man's land through the deadly hiss of machine-gun bullets and the tight curtain of flying metal from the enemy's artillery barrage. It seemed worth running the infernal gauntlet and grappling hand to hand with death in the enemy lines if there was a chance that the attack would achieve the decisive breakthrough that meant final release, if not from war, at least from the nightmare of war in the trenches. Again and again the hope seemed on the point of being realized for one side or the other—at Verdun, on the Gallipoli Peninsula, in Austrian Galicia, in the Champagne, along the Isonzo, the Somme and the Yser—and each time up to the spring of 1918, the offensive petered out in mud and blood. The epitome of all these futile massacres was probably the four-months' British campaign in Flanders during the summer and autumn of 1917, sometimes known as "Passchendaele," after its terminal battle near the village of that name, which cost the attacking side some 400,000 casualties and achieved no results of even momentary importance. The British attack literally bogged down, almost from the first; the artillery preparation, considered necessary for ripping up the enemy's wire and for smashing his forward machine-gun positions, had also destroyed the drainage system of the Yser flats, and thereby converted the battlefield into a marsh. On the rare occasions when an attacking army punched a real hole in the enemy's front—as the Russians twice succeeded in doing to that of the Austrians—the difficulty of moving the immense quantities of artillery and ammunition needed across the mire and shell craters of the original battlefield soon slowed down the momentum of the offensive, giving the defense time to plug the gap with new trench systems.

The frustration, the horror, and the despair generated by war on such a scale and under such conditions gradually spread from the battlefields, darkening the whole mind of the twentieth-century West, somewhat as the Thirty Years' War darkened that of the Baroque Age. War was not yet total—Coventry, Hamburg, Lidice, Buchenwald, and Hiroshima were still in the future—but the need for mobilizing every energy at home, for cowing underground resistance by the civilian population in occupied territory, for stimulating or combating treason and subversion, gave it a ruthlessness Europe had not known for nearly three centuries. Such officialized atrocities as the cynical German violation of Belgian neutrality, the execution of civilian hostages by the Germans in Belgium and occupied France, the systematic attacks by German submarines on unarmed passenger ships far from the battle zone, and the maintenance of the Allied blockade after the starving German and Austrian people had laid down their arms, were ominous symptoms of an accelerating retreat from civilization.

In the beginning, when it had been generally assumed that the war would be over in a few weeks, patriotic enthusiasm had been widespread everywhere in the belligerent countries. All that was best and worst in the Old World shared in the orgy of mass emotion.

"I am not ashamed to acknowledge today," Adolf Hitler wrote, "that I was carried away by the enthusiasm of the moment [the outbreak of war] and that I sank down upon my knees and thanked Heaven out of the fullness of my heart for the favor of having been permitted to live in such a time."

The same berserker frenzy seized Charles Péguy, the most luminous of modern French poets, and flung him to his death on the battlefield of the Marne. Here is how one of the survivors of the infantry platoon that the warrior-poet led relates the scene:

"Bent over double to offer a smaller target, stumbling among the beetroot stalks and the lumps of earth, we rush to the attack.

"'Hit the dirt,' Péguy shouts, 'and fire at will.' But he remains standing . . . directing our fire . . . 'Down,' we shout, but the glorious madman, insane with courage, is still on his feet . . . 'Shoot, God-damn it, shoot,' we hear the lieutenant yelling . . . At the same instant, a deadly bullet shatters the noble forehead. . . ."

Alan Seeger was hardly less ecstatic over his first taste of war.

"I go into action with the lightest of light hearts," he wrote his mother from the front, early in October 1914 . . . I think you can count on seeing me at Fairlea next summer, for I shall certainly return after the war to see you all and recuperate. I am happy and full of excitement over the wonderful days ahead."

Even so civilized and sensitive a spirit as Edith Wharton, the American novelist then living in France, at first found the great holocaust a purifying experience.

"Looked back on from these sterner months," she wrote, "those early days in Paris . . . the sudden flaming up of national life, the abeyance of every small and mean preoccupation, cleared the moral air as the streets had been cleared, and made the spectator feel as though he were reading a great poem on war rather than facing its realities."

As the war dragged on and the casualty lists grew ever longer and privations increased, the mood changed. In 1915 a Russian author named Gregory Alexinsky, reporting for a French publisher on his country's role in the conflict, coined a new word to describe a certain trend that was beginning to develop in St. Petersburg and Moscow. The term, which shocked contemporary grammarians but quickly found its way into the journalistic vernacular in several tongues, was "defeatism." As an organized and systematic movement, defeatism was at first largely confined to Russia and Austria-Hungary, but in all the belligerent countries the concept of the war as a meaningful and purposeful struggle for the achievement of heroic goals gradually gave way to the view that it was a kind of impersonal natural catastrophe, or as the German poet Rainer Maria Rilke put it, a "dreary muddle of trumped-up human doom." The British common soldier remained a hero to the end—as did the French and the German one—but he grimly thought of himself as a mere ingredient for the "sausage machine" at the front, so-called, Graves explains, because "it was fed with live men, churned out corpses, and remained firmly screwed in place."

Resentment of the "slackers" and "profiteers" behind the lines increasingly embittered the outlook of the front-line soldier; his faith both in the civilian leadership that had been unable to avert the catastrophe of general war, and in the military leadership which seemed incapable of winning it, turned into doubt, then into cynical revolt or despair. The myth of the bungling or heartless "brass hat," ruthlessly throwing away the lives of his men, was born. It was to reach full flower after the war in books and plays like Robert Graves' *Goodbye to All That,* Ernest Hemingway's *A Farewell to Arms,* Erich Maria Remarque's *All Quiet on the Western Front,* Laurence Stallings and Maxwell Anderson's *What Price Glory?* and Louis-Ferdinand Céline's *Journey to the End of the Night,* perhaps the absolute zero in literary nihilism.

Unlike many myths, that of the brass hat as a cheerful mass murderer had a solid foundation in fact. Some generals were more incompetent or more inhuman than others—the Germans were the least inefficient and usually the least wasteful of their men's lives—but the whole military caste in pre-1914 Europe, like its diplomatic and ruling castes, was neither technically nor emotionally equipped to face the challenge of modern war. It always takes men a long time to adjust to new conditions, and nothing like World War I had ever been seen, or even imagined before. (By the out-break of World War II military leadership in most countries had caught up with the times, or at worst was only one war behind, instead of two or three, as in 1914.) The consistent failure of the staff-officer mind in World War I to absorb either the tactical or the psychological lessons of trench warfare is attested by crowds of reliable contemporary witnesses, at every level.

"Most of them [the brass-hats] seemed capable of limitless folly," Graves comments. ". . . One I knew ordered gas to be discharged from our trenches 'at all costs' though the wind was blowing in our faces . . . None ever tried a short spell of trench life himself to discover in what con-ditions his troops lived . . ."

Conditions were no better in the French Army.

"In the army the ravages caused by the failure of the April 16 offensive were frightful," reported Abel Ferry, the young French minister who had abandoned his office in the Quai d'Orsay for the trenches. He was referring to General Nivelle's disastrous Champagne offensive of 1917. "Spontane-ously, whole regiments and divisions revolted," he continues. "The inci-dental causes of this state of mind were numerous: Excessive drinking, sometimes poor food, bad behind-the-lines quarters, inadequate rest and finally the failure of the offensive. Alas, this is the price of our military policy of the last three years—2,000,000 casualties. The life of the French soldier has been protected neither against his chiefs, who have managed it abusively, nor against his allies, who have asked too much. He knows it, and he is revolting . . . We are headed towards peace by revolution. . . . All the nations, belligerent or not, are approaching the stage of revolution, with the peoples threatening to make peace against their governments."

Ferry, who was killed by a German shell in 1918, turned out to be al-most right as far as France was concerned. Several mutinous divisions from the Champagne front, singing the Socialist anthem, *L'Internationale,* started to march on the capital and were only turned back in the nick of time. To restore discipline in the demoralized French Army drumhead courts-martial handed down 253 death sentences—sometimes virtually at random—though it is claimed that only 25 of them were actually carried out. Elsewhere in Europe the tide of revolutionary defeatism steadily mounted, as Ferry had predicted.

The loss of faith in leadership, including military leadership, on the part of the European masses was one of the most significant results of World War I. Its full effects were not to become apparent for another generation—the debased form of pacifism which paralyzed French and British resistance to the aggressive expansionism of Nazi Germany in 1938, and partially paralyzed it in 1939, was an emotional hangover from the 1914–1918 war —but even its immediate fruits were momentous. Naturally, it was the most anachronistic leadership-systems—i.e. the Divine Right autocratic dynasties and their supporting aristocracies—which were the most vulnerable to the blasts of doubt and revolt blowing from the battlefields. A few reigning monarchs—in particular young King Alexander I of Serbia, and Albert I, King of the Belgians—saved the prestige of their dynasties by the way in which they shared the hardships of their subjects, but the Habsburgs, the Hohenzollerns, and the Romanovs, along with other handicaps, lacked the common touch.

From the outbreak of war the autocrats had been obliged to surrender most of their power to the generals who nominally functioned as their advisers. The transfer of real authority was most nearly total in Austria-Hungary. "I can't do anything for you," the aged Francis Joseph is supposed —apocryphally—to have told a petitioner. "Don't you know a sergeant with influence?"

The Kaiser took the field in his capacity as Supreme War Lord shortly after the opening of hostilities, but this consisted merely of moving to GHQ at Charleville, a safe distance behind the front, where he shared the hardships of his troops by cutting his lunches down to four courses and drinking beer instead of champagne. He almost never showed himself in the trenches, but perhaps this was just as well from the viewpoint of morale; with his completely whitened hair, deeply lined face and conspicuous lame arm, Wilhelm, after August 1914, bore little resemblance to the martial figure that had so long ruled victoriously over the imagination of his subjects. He made no serious attempt to guide the strategy of the war, and for the most part contented himself with listening meekly to the briefings of his generals. After 1916 the Kaiser was a mere figurehead; the real dictator, not only in military but in civilian affairs, was General—eventually Field Marshal—Erich Ludendorff, the politically illiterate apostle of rule by the sword, who as First Quarter Master General of the armies completely dominated his nominal superior, the new Commander-in-Chief, General von Hindenburg.

The official camera portraits of Ludendorff at the peak of his extraordinary career are prime fossil specimens of European history. Brutal and blubbery, he looks almost literally bloated with self-awe. The features are unmistakably plebeian—Ludendorff was one of the few Prussian staff officers of lower middle-class origin—but without any redeeming touch of homely humanity. In the cold, hooded eyes, the gross pompous jowls, the overfed old woman's chin and the mouth like a cuttlefish's, we can recognize a kind of transitional form between the men of blood and iron who created the German Empire and the "flabby monsters" (in the words of Georges Bernanos) who finally destroyed it. Ludendorff, who was forty-nine at the outbreak of war counts among the foremost wreckers of European civilization in his generation. Before he collapsed into his

Wotan-worshiping senility, during the 1930s, he was to play a substantial role in pushing the Hohenzollern dynasty to its doom, in launching the Nazi nightmare on the world, and in assuring the ultimate triumph of Bolshevism in Russia. It was the war, of course, that gave him his chance—he planned the brilliant German attack on the fortress of Liege and was Hindenburg's Chief of Staff at Tannenberg—but his meteoric rise to a position of almost unbounded if irresponsible power is a devastating commentary on Wilhelmine society, on the limitations of the German military caste and on the deficiencies of the Hohenzollern family.

The Kaiser's sons, and several of the minor German princes, held active wartime commands, but this turned out to be a liability rather than an asset to their dynasties. The martial career of the Crown Prince was particularly disastrous, though it had begun with a hopeful little piece of make-believe. At the outset of the war the Hohenzollern heir had been put in nominal command of the German Fifth Army, on the Lorraine front. Its initial successes earned him the award by the Kaiser of the Iron Cross, First and Second Class. "I rejoice with you in Wilhelm's first victory," Wilhelm Sr. wired the Kaiserin. "How splendidly God stood by his side." Some eighteen months later the Celestial Ally defected. The Crown Prince was theoretically in command of the German armies attempting to take Verdun and although he had criticized with unusual shrewdness the plans for the offensive drawn up by his Chief of Staff he had been obliged to countersign them, and was thus left saddled with supreme responsibility for the costliest failure of German arms.

"Weeks and months of slow, hard-fought offensive battles, claiming heavy sacrifices," the Crown Prince wrote after the war, "had followed the February assault, which was boldly executed, with every confidence in its success; then came the halting of the offensive, the result of the progressive dissociation of our forces; and now . . . two unexpected set-backs had wrested away a large part of this battlefield soaked with our blood. For the first time I realized what it was like to lose a battle. Self doubt, self-reproach, bitter feelings, unfair judgments of others, struggled in my heart and weighed heavily on my mind . . . it was a long time before I regained my composure and recovered my faith."

The German Army and the German people never wholly recovered theirs—and it was not only faith in ultimate victory that was lost, but faith in the social system and in the dynasty that had led them into massacres like Verdun.

As for the Russian people and Army—which by 1917 had already lost nearly 9,000,000 men, killed, wounded, or taken prisoner—the real problem is not to explain why they finally revolted or why the revolution took such a catastrophic turn, but why it was so long in coming.

CHAPTER 13

The Suicide of the Russian Monarchy

M OST of the belligerent nations had staggered off to war in a fog of patriotic inebriation; Czarist Russia dedicated itself to Armageddon with ritual solemnity. The ceremony, which took place in the afternoon of August 2, was both grandiose and moving, perhaps the most poignant moment in modern Russian history. For once the official actors were worthy of their tragic theme. So was the setting: the imperial heart of St. Petersburg, then at the zenith of its splendor but already marked with the fey, twilight beauty of the self-doomed. "The city . . ." writes George F. Kennan, one of the latest in a long series of Western visitors to fall under its watery spell, "is one of the strangest, loveliest, most terrible, and most dramatic of the world's great urban centres . . . The heaven is vast, the skyline remote and extended. . . . Under such a sky, fingers of fate seem to reach in from a great distance, like the beams of the sun, to find and shape the lives and affairs of individuals; events have a tendency to move with dramatic precision to denouements which no one devised but which everyone recognizes after the fact as inevitable and somehow faintly familiar."

The denouements still lie ahead; the scene enacted that August afternoon of 1914 in and around the ponderous Winter Palace serves as a kind of dramatic antithesis in the unfolding of the grim, foreordered plot. It has been reported by a Western eyewitness who was well qualified to appreciate both its color and its pathos.

To the French Ambassador, Maurice Paleologue, the stage setting was majestic. "In the immense St. Georges Gallery which overlooks the Neva embankment, 5000 or 6000 persons are assembled. The whole Court is in gala costume; all the officers of the garrison are in field uniform." An altar

stood in the center "and the miraculous icon of the Virgin of Kazan, removed for a few hours from the national sanctuary on the Nevski Prospect,
has been transported there . . . In religious silence, the Imperial cortege
traverses the gallery and takes position on the left of the altar."

The holy office began, and with it "the moving and ample chants of the
Orthodox liturgy. Nicholas II prays with an ardent concentration that
gives his pale features a strikingly mystic expression. The Empress Alexandra Feodorovna stands close beside him, holding herself stiffly, her head
high, her lips livid, her gaze fixed and her eyes glassy; from time to time
she shuts her eye-lids and then her ashen visage reminds one of a death-
mask."

After this, the chaplain read a manifesto from the Czar. ". . . Then
the Emperor approaches the altar and raises his right hand toward the
Bible which is presented to him. . . . In slow, short tones, stressing each
word, he proclaims, 'Officers of my Guard here present, I salute in you the
whole army, and I bless it. Solemnly I swear that I shall not conclude peace
so long as a single enemy remains on the soil of the fatherland.'"

This was word for word the oath that Czar Alexander I swore in 1812,
when Napoleon invaded Russia. After pronouncing it before the brilliantly
and frantically cheering throng of courtiers in the St. Georges Gallery, the
Czar stepped out on the balcony overlooking the great square of the Winter
Palace, where on that other Sunday—the Bloody Sunday of 1905—his soldiers had mowed down the ranks of unarmed demonstrators. This time,
too, the crowd filled the square—the third largest in Europe—waving flags,
banners, icons and portraits of the Czar, but this time sovereign and subjects shared the same solemn exaltation. As the Czar repeated his ancestor's historic oath, the crowd dropped to its knees and sang the Imperial
anthem, *God Save the Czar,* followed by the lovely hymn, *Lord, Save the
People and Bless Thine Inheritance,* invoking the divine protection in time
of war.

"In this minute," comments Paleologue, "for these thousands of men who
are prostrate there, the Czar is truly the autocrat consecrated by God, the
military, political and religious chief of his people, the absolute sovereign
of bodies and souls."

The almost incredible demonstration of patriotic fervor and dynastic
loyalism witnessed by Paleologue and other Western observers in St. Petersburg was not an isolated phenomenon. It was typical of the mood in
which the whole Russian people went to war. (One of its minor manifestations was changing the name of the capital to Petrograd—a pure Slavic
word with no German taint.) Not only was there a deep surge of national
feeling, uniting all classes and all but a few extremist opinion groups, but
there was an unmistakable reconciliation between the Romanov dynasty
and the Russian masses. For a while it seemed almost as if the memory of

1905 had been magically erased from the Russian mind, and that the doom pronounced upon the autocracy by its own victory over the revolutionists had been rescinded. History appeared to be offering Nicholas II the rarest of its benefactions: a second chance.

It was all the more remarkable because ever since the murder of Stolypin in 1911, the Czar's regime had been sinking deeper and deeper into the mire of reaction, and popular discontent had accordingly been rising. The prosperity of the middle classes, due to Russia's industrial boom, and the emergence of a class of peasant landowners, thanks to Stolypin's agrarian legislation, had somewhat cushioned the violence of the opposition forces, but the temper of the factory workers was turning revolutionary again as the chastening remembrance of the repression after 1905 gradually faded. In the last years before the war the curve of strikes and social disorder had been steadily mounting; another year of peace might have brought new upheavals.

Sarajevo completely transformed the social and political climate. To the chauvinists in the bourgeoisie—not to mention those entrenched in the army or the administration—the war was a chance to wipe out the national humiliation suffered in the Russo-Japanese conflict and to achieve Russia's millennial goal—control of the Dardanelles. To the Orthodox traditionalists and the Pan-Slav idealists it was a crusade to liberate the Slavic brothers in the Balkans. To the liberals it was a just war at the side of enlightened allies—France and England—whose example would inspire deep reforms in Russia after the common victory. To many of the left-wing revolutionaries —except, of course, the Bolsheviks—it was an ideologically progressive war that would sweep away German militarism as a potential ally of Russian autocracy, and win new privileges for the armed workers and peasants.

Both in the autocracy and in the nation as a whole, war brought to light treasures of loyalty, of heroism, and of social co-operation that had lain hidden for years under the corruption and barbarism of the decaying despotism. Nicholas himself was transformed in many ways. Alexandra took a course in nursing and threw herself into an orgy of war-work. Unfortunately, if war galvanized all the latent strength in Czarist Russia, it also exacerbated the weaknesses of the regime. Raw idealism had never been wholly wanting in Russia—even when overlaid by bureaucratic cynicism; it was lucid dedication that was in short supply. Both the Russian Czar and the Russian liberals were eventually undone as much by their virtues as by their vices. Neither conservatives nor reformers in Russia were intellectually equipped to face the ordeal of modern war.

"Let Papa Nicholas not plan war," Gregory Rasputin—for once the guardian angel instead of the evil genius of the monarchy—had telegraphed from Siberia to the Czarina's confidante, Anna Vyrubova when he learned of the crisis, "for with war will come the end of Russia and yourselves and you will lose to the last man."

It was only gradually that the fatal weaknesses of Czarist Russia came to light under the strains of the conflict. At first it seemed that the Russian Army had put to good use the lessons of its defeat by Japan ten years earlier. It was still short on heavy artillery and machine guns—as all the other belligerents were—but its infantry masses were adequately trained and they were led into battle by tough, professionally competent, almost extravagantly courageous officers. What surprised foreign military observers the most was the good relations that seemed to exist in the early days of the war between the muzhiks who comprised the bulk of the Russian forces and the young scions of the overprivileged Czarist aristocracy who commanded them. In the line regiments at least—the staffs were less admirable—the officers had ceased to be playboys in uniform that they had sometimes been in the past. Despite the anachronistic discipline and etiquette of the Russian Army, the officers understood their men and were respected by them.

Both the virtues and the faults of the Russian military caste in 1914 were exemplified in the army's Commander-in-Chief, Grand Duke Nicholas, the Czar's uncle. The Grand Duke, a tall, broad-shouldered man with a frank, energetic expression, probably was not the "really great soldier and strategist" that his adversary, Ludendorff, credited him with being, but he was a professional who had mastered the fundamentals of his trade. He had a gift for leadership, a soldierly sense of duty, and great moral, as well as physical, courage. He was undoubtedly somewhat old-fashioned in his tactical conceptions, he considered that supply and logistics were something you turned over to the quartermaster general and forgot about, and he was almost illiterate in politics, economics, and administration. Above all, like many Russians of his generation, he was a fervent idealist who constantly tended to confuse aspiration and reality. Paleologue, who in accordance with instructions from Paris called on the Russian Commander-in-Chief a few days after the outbreak of war to plead for an immediate offensive on the eastern front, was almost disconcerted by the quasi-mystical enthusiasm with which the Grand Duke responded.

He told the startled diplomat that God and Joan of Arc were with them. "Victory will be ours. Is it not providential that war broke out for such a noble cause? . . ." He would order an offensive and strike with everything he had. "I may not even wait for all my corps to be assembled. As soon as I feel strong enough I shall attack."

Neither the Grand Duke nor the Czar ever rejected or evaded an appeal from Russia's allies to sacrifice Russian lives in order to relieve the pressure from the German armies in the West, and the diversionary offensives ordered from on high were usually executed with vigor—if not always with great skill—by the Russian corps commanders, sometimes under suicidal conditions. A particularly gruesome example was the Russian drive of 1916 in the Baltic sector around Lake Naroch, east of Vilna. Despite adverse weather conditions, it was ordered by the Czar, Paleologue explains, "to satisfy the public conscience," which had been quickened by the heroic French defense of Verdun. After a sketchy artillery preparation, the Russian infantry attacked, and disregarding unusually heavy losses, reached all its initial objectives. A sudden thaw transformed the battlefield into a morass; the Russian field guns bogged down, depriving the infantry of artillery support, and the field kitchens could not be moved forward with the advancing troops. Soaked to the skin, without food, almost without ammunition, the Russian infantry doggedly struggled ahead under heavy fire through the knee-deep mire; the wounded frequently smothered in it where they fell. Then an icy wind started blowing from the Arctic, and a hard freeze set in. The wounded men who managed to escape drowning in the mud and slush were caught in the ice and froze to death before they could be evacuated; the rare survivors suffered horribly from frost-bite. Virtually all the ground originally gained by the Russians had been yielded up again by the end of April when the fighting slacked off. From the allied viewpoint the five weeks' Russian offensive proved moderately useful; it drew several German divisions away from the Verdun front. The cost to the Russian Army was 250,000 dead, missing and wounded. The public conscience in Russia could rest easy.

In the history of coalition warfare few nations have displayed the loyalty toward their allies that Russia consistently manifested between August 1914 and October 1917. And few have in turn been so mercilessly exploited by their allies. The Russians, poor in heavy weapons, rich in manpower, had to use human flesh where the other main belligerents, especially the Germans, relied on steel and high explosives. Russia lacked the railroads and the industrial base needed to sustain prolonged, large-scale offensive operations. The Russian forces, unit for unit, were generally a match for their Austro-Hungarian enemies, but they were substantially below the German standard in organization, training and staffwork, as well as in equipment. Yet the Western members of the Entente, especially the French, were constantly prodding the Russians to take the offensive—whether they were in shape to do so or not—and to attack their toughest enemy, along the most difficult sectors of their front. The exorbitant demands of the West on the Russian Army were a major factor—perhaps the major factor—in creating the conditions that finally produced the revolution. They would not, of course, have proved so fatal if the Czarist military mind with its curious mixture of chivalry, cavalryman's dash, and humility had not been peculiarly vulnerable to such pressures. Russia in 1914 was an underdeveloped country, and there is a definite trace of colonial awe, almost of a hunger for immolation

—Trotsky sneeringly termed it the comprador mentality—in the attitude of many Russians toward their more "advanced" Western allies; it was to express itself most disastrously under the Kerensky regime.

"We owed this sacrifice to France," the Foreign Minister, Sazonov, said to Paleologue after the battle of Tannenberg—the result of the Grand Duke's pledge to take the offensive without delay in East Prussia—which cost Russia 110,000 men.

In addition to being afflicted with Quixotic commanders and short-sighted—or simply desperate—allies, the Russian Army suffered from several handicaps that exposed it to abnormally heavy losses. Its weaknesses in staff work and in equipment have already been mentioned. Their effects were monstrously aggravated by other factors. One was German espionage. The charges made after the February Revolution that Germany had agents in the Imperial entourage and in the administration at the ministerial level have never been fully confirmed but there is no doubt that a vast and ef-ficient spy network, based chiefly on German commercial penetration, had been built up in Russia before the outbreak of war. The military informa-tion it supplied was often of great importance; it may have been a decisive element in the Russian defeat at Tannenberg.

An even graver Russian weakness was the red tape, inefficiency and cor-ruption prevailing in certain vital sectors of the Czarist bureaucracy which deprived the front of the munitions that Russian industry was potentially capable of delivering. It was bad enough to be short of heavy artillery and machine guns; all too often corps commanders found themselves obliged to oppose an enemy attack—or even to take the offensive—without shells for their light fieldpieces or cartridges for the rifles of their infantry. At times there were not enough rifles to go around; the Russian units had been known to go into battle when two men out of three were armed with noth-ing better than a bayonet tied to a stick. The Minister of War, General Vladimir Sukhomlinov, a member of the Rasputin clique, was fired in the summer of 1915 for allowing such conditions to develop—later he was even condemned to prison—and thereafter the munitions situation improved somewhat, but it was too late. The Russian Army had suffered nearly 4,000,000 casualties in the first year of the war. (Russia's total casualties for the war were more than 9,000,000—76.3 per cent of the men mobilized.)

"You know, sir, we have no weapon except the soldier's breast," a Rus-sian infantryman told the British historian, Pares, when he visited the front in 1915. "This is not war, sir," another said. "It is slaughter."

Hindenburg, not exactly a sensitive observer, was horrified by the carnage on the eastern front. ". . . Sometimes in our battles with the Russians," he writes in his memoirs, "we had to remove the mounds of enemy corpses from before our trenches in order to get a clear field of fire against fresh assaulting waves."

Defeat in battle often creates a vicious circle, or spiral, of conditions that the defeated army finds it increasingly difficult to break. This is what happened to the Russians in World War I. The heavy losses in the first ten months of fighting almost wiped out the admirable generation of young professional officers that had been its major asset—and one of the regime's bulwarks against revolution. Both the technical and the moral quality of combat leadership steadily declined, and so did its political reliability. Avoidable losses mounted, and the morale of the ranks declined with their confidence in their officers and with their hopes of victory. Similarly, the great German offensives in the spring and summer of 1915 which pushed the Russians out of Poland, most of the Baltic provinces and part of the Ukraine, deprived them of their best railways, thus accentuating their logistic weaknesses.

In trying to counteract or minimize the difficulties at the front, the Russian High Command inadvertently contributed to the demoralization and disorganization of the rest of the country. It uprooted the civilian population—mostly Jewish—throughout a vast zone behind the lines, tying up precious transportations and dumping several million demoralized refugees upon the overburdened towns of the interior with as little regard for the social and economic problems as for the human misery thereby created. With equal recklessness the army alienated the peasant masses by continually squeezing them to make good the wastage of effectives and of livestock for transport. Its ill-considered exactions fell particularly heavily upon those muzhiks who had become small private landowners thanks to Stolypin's reforms. With their sons mobilized and their horses requisitioned, they could no longer work their fields; a great many of them had to sell out. Thus the army unwittingly sabotaged the agrarian program that might have averted the Bolshevik Revolution—Trotsky, at least, thought it might have done so—just as it was beginning to take effect.

The fatal error of Czarist leadership between 1914 and 1917 was letting the war occur at all; one way or another, most of the subsequent ones stemmed from that initial blunder. Naturally, as the disasters and the stresses accumulated, the aberrations of leadership became more frequent and more glaring. Probably no regime in history was ever so thoroughly overkilled as the Russian despotism. The last days of the Romanov dynasty recall one of those obsessive suicides where the victim swallows poison, slashes his wrists, and climbs over the parapet of a high bridge before blowing his brains out. The most unmistakable symptoms of the dynastic death wish were manifested at the very pinnacle of the autocracy. The weird political and psychological drama in which the Czar, the Czarina and the so-called starets or Man of God, Gregory Rasputin, were the principal actors, has already been mentioned; the time has come to relate its climax.

Though the power of the starets had been growing since Stolypin's death in 1911, the true reign of Rasputin dates from 1915. Two events which occurred in September of that year simultaneously assured his ascendancy and paved the way for the ultimate downfall of the regime. The first one was the rupture of the tacit political truce which had existed since the beginning of the war between the Czar and the democratic or reformist parties in the Duma. Early in September the leaders of these parties pooled their forces to create the so-called Progressive Bloc—the strongest coherent group in the Duma—on the basis of a common program calling for some mildly liberal reforms and for an intensified war effort. From the constitutional viewpoint there was nothing revolutionary in the program but it asked the Czar to appoint a new council of ministers in which the country could have confidence. If Nicholas had accepted, it would have made the monarchy more popular but at the same time it would have implicitly repudiated the doctrine of absolutism which he felt himself committed to uphold. Understandably he hesitated. Alexandra, whose personal itch to rule was reinforced by her fanatical dedication to the *mystique* of autocracy, had no doubts what the Czar's response would be; when a majority of his ministers recommended acceptance of the Progressive Bloc's program, Alexandra denounced them to her husband as "fiends worse than the Duma." Rasputin, whose absolutist convictions were probably sincere, naturally supported her. Under pressure from them Nicholas eventually rejected the plea for a "Ministry of Confidence" and prorogued the session of the Duma, thereby opening a latent constitutional crisis that was to remain unresolved until March 1917.

The other irremediable blunder of September 1915 was the Czar's decision to relieve the respected, dependable Grand Duke Nicholas at GHQ and to assume personal command of his armies in the field. The Czar had long been covertly jealous of his uncle's popularity, and Alexandra, egged on by Rasputin, had insidiously exploited the sentiment. She had a double score to settle with the Grand Duke; "overshadowing" the Czar, and disrespect for the starets (when Rasputin had suggested visiting GHQ to hang a votive icon the Grand Duke, now thoroughly disillusioned about his former protégé, had sent the terse telegraphic reply: "Come and I'll hang you").

From the narrow military viewpoint the change in command was not important; the Chief of Staff, General Mikhail Alexeyev, handled things quite competently in the Czar's name, and Nicholas for once showed good sense by refraining from any interference in the conduct of operations. The fiction that the Czar was actively commanding—which Alexeyev went to elaborate lengths to maintain—was no help to the prestige of dynasty, however, since the war was going from bad to worse. The circumstances of the shake-up at Supreme Headquarters had infuriated or disheartened the enlightened elements in Russian public life, thus aggravating the conflict with parliament. Above all, the Czar's mythical command kept him away from the capital much of the time and in his absence Alexandra established what was almost a de facto regency, with Rasputin as her clandestine Chancellor. "Think, my wifey, will you not come to the assistance of your hubby now that he is absent?" Nicholas imprudently suggested in one of his first letters home from the *Stavka* at Moghilev on the Dnieper.

Alexandra had been offering assistance rather freely for some time— "don't laugh at silly old wifey, but she has 'trousers' on," as she put it in one of her letters—but now she cast aside all discretion. Not content merely to bombard her husband with advice and to influence appointments she began intervening directly in the governance of the country. In one of her letters to Nicholas she even boasted naively that she was the first Empress to receive ministers regularly since Catherine the Great—who usurped her husband's throne and took his murderer into her bed. Alexandra's mauve boudoir in Catherine's old palace at Tsarskoe Selo became the secret command post of the empire.

Rasputin was equally active. Despite his initial opposition to the war he displayed an unexpected interest in military affairs that is reflected in Alexandra's letters to her husband:

October 10, 1915: "He (Rasputin) says you must give the order that only waggons with flour, butter and sugar should be allowed to pass: there are to be no other trains for three days. He saw the whole thing in the night in a vision."

November 8: "He dictated to me the other day I saw Him walking about, praying and crossing himself, about Rumania and Greece and our troops passing through."

November 15: Rasputin has another strategic vision and on the strength of it orders an offensive near Riga, "prompted," the Czarina says, "by what he saw in the night." (Next June we hear that he categorically forbids a scheduled attack in the same sector.)

December 15: Alexandra transmits some new instructions from Our Friend, reporting that there was an additional one which unfortunately "He cannot remember." Nonetheless, she concludes, "He says we must always do what He says."

Much to the Czar's discomfort—not to mention that of the General Staff —Rasputin frequently insisted on being told in advance the exact date on which an offensive was scheduled to be launched. The usual pretext was that he needed the information to pray for victory. Sometimes, however, his curiosity was inspired by more worldly considerations, as illustrates the following excerpt from the testimony of one of his high-level henchmen—

A. N. Hvostov, a former Minister of the Interior—before the provisional government's investigating committee:

"Rasputin went to Tsarskoe Selo and Rubinstein [a shady banker who was also suspected of being a German spy] asked him to find out if an offensive was going to take place; he explained to his friends that he needed to know because he was thinking of buying some forest lands in the province of Minsk [at the time occupied by the Germans] and if we are going to launch an offensive in that area their value would go up, so it would be a good investment. I learned that Rasputin discharged his mission, and on his return he related what he had said at Tsarskoe Selo."

Rasputin was always handsomely rewarded for the information or other services that he supplied to his profiteering friends, some of whom were almost certainly German agents. Though not quite as shiftless in financial matters as he has sometimes been portrayed, the starets was not primarily interested in making money for himself. As his power grew the scale and recklessness of his traffic in influence increased proportionally, but the bulk of it consisted in collecting payment in kind from female petitioners seeking exemption from military service for their men-folk or such perquisites for themselves as the pay-toilet concession in some provincial railroad station. It was not uncommon for Rasputin to pick up a prostitute and in lieu of payment rendered to give her a penciled note of introduction to one of the ministers.

From the end of 1915 on there is a rising note of madness accompanying Rasputin's extravagances. The desire to flaunt his power by inflicting grotesque humiliations not only upon his adversaries but upon his accomplices is evident. At times Rasputin seemed almost to be courting disaster for himself; he once created a national scandal in a Moscow night club by drunkenly boasting of his intimacy with the Czarina in such terms as to create the impression that she slept with him. Whether Rasputin's more lurid transgressions were inspired by megalomania, despair, guilty conscience, or some extraordinary Russian blend of all three, is a matter of speculation. He was generally protected from the consequences of his recklessness by a succession of highly placed rascals, who looked upon him as a valuable supplier of patronage and graft, and naturally did not want him to come to grief. Most of these parasites were connected in one way or another with the Okhrana, whose resources were mobilized to keep the starets out of trouble. The last of Rasputin's self-appointed managers was a colorful but sinister rogue named I. F. Manasevich, a former Okhrana operative who had once been sent to Rome to try to organize a Russian spy network in the Vatican, and who had later handled the Okhrana's slush fund in Paris for a time.

Manasevich-Manuilov had a curious weakness: he liked to be frank about himself when at all possible. "I am a vicious man," he once told a noted anti-Czarist journalist. "I love money; I love life." With his pomaded hair, flashing, dark Levantine eyes, sparkling rings and overtailored clothes he certainly looked the part he had chosen to play. Born a Jew and converted first to Lutheranism and then to the Orthodox faith, he had started his career as the henchman of an ultraright-wing fanatic and had personally helped to launch several bloody pogroms. Eventually he proved too gamey even for the Okhrana and he was fired from the service. Thereafter he made his living as a journalist—it was he who had got the scoop on Rasputin's bathhouse escapades—as a low-level fixer and above all as a blackmailer. He had prospered in these occupations, but the nostalgia from his police days never left him and the dream of his life, was to create a new super-secret service in Russia and to be appointed its head. In tenacious pursuit of this goal he joined Anna Vyrubova's clique and attached himself to Rasputin as a kind of confidential secretary. Manasevich-Manuilov saw to it that the starets had his daily quota of Madeira and wenches, but managed to surround his revels with an unwanted curtain of discretion. Even the Okhrana could no longer keep score on Rasputin's fornications and shady business deals; his new confidential secretary had taken the precaution of requisitioning for his private use a powerful army car that was too fast for the Okhrana's motorized agents to keep up with. In the political sphere, however, Manasevich-Manuilov encouraged Rasputin's maddest fantasies and helped to shape them into a coherent form that made them all the more dangerous; from time to time he seems to have been in direct contact with the Czarina as well. Under his influence both she and Rasputin lost what little touch with political reality they still possessed and embarked on a wild power spree.

All the ministers or high officials who had ever dared to criticize or resist the starets were marked down for removal. One of the first to go was General A. A. Polivanov, the able energetic war minister who had succeeded Sukhomlinov, perhaps the most indispensable man in Russia from the viewpoint of the war effort. When Nicholas showed some reluctance to deprive the army of the efficient administrator who for the first time since the beginning of the war had succeeded in getting an almost adequate flow of munitions moving to the front, Alexandra kept nagging at him in her letters until he gave in. "Get rid of Polivanov," she wrote on January 9, 1916. "Remember about Polivanov," she reminded him a few weeks later. "Lovey, don't dawddle."

Sazonov, the honest, loyal Foreign Minister who enjoyed the confidence of Russia's allies soon followed Polivanov into the discard. Early in 1916, Alexandra persuaded the Czar to appoint as Prime Minister, Boris Sturmer, an obscure political hack with some rather dubious associations; now she caused him to be named Foreign Minister as well. Sturmer was the discovery of Manasevich-Manuilov, who arranged to get himself named to the new Prime Minister's personal staff so as to help keep an eye on him. To make sure that there was no misunderstanding, Rasputin peremptorily summoned Sturmer to a nocturnal conference at a friend's house and gave him his orders. "Never allow yourself to interfere with any of Mama's [Alexandra's] plans," he roared at the Czar's first minister. "Watch your step— if I drop you, you are finished."

Both the most grotesque and the most disastrous ministerial appointment was that of Alexander Protopopov as Minister of the Interior in charge of the nation's police forces, among other things. Protopopov was a member of the Duma, but it is an understatement to say that he did not enjoy the respect of his colleagues. He was a fob, a fool, a dilettante, a dabbler in the occult and an advanced syphilitic with nervous symptoms rapidly developing toward the strait-jacket phase. To top all these disabilities, he had allowed himself to get involved in some indiscreet and very nearly treasonable "peace talks" with a German agent in Stockholm. To certain members of the Rasputin clique this was no doubt a recommendation; whether or not the camarilla was intriguing behind the Czar's back to get Russia out of the war through a separate peace, as some historians charge, it was unquestionably surrounded by a strong aura of defeatism. Protopopov's other assets in the eyes of his backers were his probably sincere devotion to the starets, his eagerness to please his friends, and a gift for not asking awkward questions. As the liberal politician and historian Paul N. Milyukov described him to Sir Bernard Pares, Protopopov was "the typical noble in debt who is always prepared to do everything that is wanted." Needless to say, he made an excellent impression on the Czarina. "Gregory begs you earnestly to name Protopopov," she wrote her husband in September 1916. When the usually docile Nicholas balked slightly—"Our Friend's opinions of people are sometimes very strange"—Alexandra hounded him until he gave in.

The appointment of Protopopov brought to a head the long-gathering conflict between the autocracy and the Duma. There were a series of violent speeches by both Liberals and Conservatives denouncing Sturmer, Protopopov, and the whole Rasputin clique.

"Impertinent brutes," Alexandra wrote her husband, referring to the Duma as a body. "It is war with them and we must be firm." When Nicholas showed signs of wavering she returned to the charge, "All my trust is in Our Friend, who thinks only of you, Baby and Russia, and guided by him we shall get through this heavy time. It will be a hard fight but a Man of God is near to guard you safely through the reefs and little Sunny [the Empress herself] is standing as a rock behind you, firm and unwavering. . . ." Despite this imposing support Nicholas chose to compromise. He dropped Sturmer, replacing him with one of the few surviving anti-Rasputin members of the cabinet, the Minister of Transport, A. F. Trepov. Alexandra saved Protopopov in the nick of time by a lightning visit to her husband at Headquarters. She realized that there could be no co-operation with the Duma, or with any of the politically enlightened forces in Russia, if the Czar retained his Minister of the Interior, who despite his personal insignificance was fast becoming in the eyes of the Opposition the symbol of everything that they hated in the government, but that did not worry her. On the contrary she was eager for a showdown with Parliament; her ultimate goal, shaped for her by Rasputin and Manasevich-Manuilov was to dissolve the Duma, to scrap the Constitution of 1905 and to establish a neoabsolutist regime with some demagogic features. Alexandra does not seem to have taken her husband fully into her confidence, but her general intention is clear from the tone of the letters to him during the month of December 1916:

"Now comes your reign of will and power. . . . The good is coming, the turn has begun. . . . We must give a strong country to Baby and dare not be weak for his sake . . . draw the reins in tightly which you let loose. . . . Russia loves to feel the whip. . . . How I wish I could pour my will into your veins. . . . I suffer over you as over a tender, soft-hearted child. . . . Be the Emperor, be Peter the Great, Ivan the Terrible, the Emperor Paul—crush them all under you—Now don't you laugh, naughty one. . . . Send Lvov [Prince George Lvov, one of the liberal leaders in the Duma] to Siberia. . . . Milyukov, Guchkov and Polivanov also to Siberia."

One letter is signed, "Russia's mother, blessed by Our Friend." One of Nicholas' replies expresses "Tender thanks for the severe written scolding. . . . Your poor little weak-willed hubby."

To contemporary Western observers, looking at the Russian scene with a liberal bias and through glasses tinted by wartime propaganda, the policies pursued by the Czarina and her coterie seemed deliberate sabotage of the Russian war effort. Today we are virtually certain that Alexandra was not a German agent, or even pro-German in the sense of secretly hoping for a German victory, and it seems more likely than not that Rasputin himself was faithful in his fashion to the national cause. Both of them, however, equated the cause of Russia with that of the autocratic dynasty, and though they realized that military defeat would probably be fatal to the regime, they had good reasons to fear that victory would be no less so. The politicians in Russia who were the most reliable partners for the prosecution of the war were often the least reliable as bulwarks of the throne; many of them in fact were insidiously exploiting the war to undermine the monarchy, or at any rate the autocracy. Shipping them off to Siberia as the Czarina had proposed was probably not feasible, but it was not mere spite or megalomania that had caused her to make the suggestion. To intransigent believers in the autocracy the situation looked desperate whichever way one turned—perhaps that was one reason for Rasputin's increasingly mad behavior—and the temptation to seek desperate remedies was understandable. The trouble with all the remedies envisaged by Alexandra or Rasputin or Protopopov was that they were ultimately self-sabotaging in terms of the autocracy itself.

It is by no means unlikely that Alexandra was planning to top off her projected coup d'état against the constitution by having Rasputin officially named Prime Minister. Rasputin himself, according to Manasevich-Manuilov, had an even more revolutionary aim: to depose the Czar and to enthrone Alexandra as regent, after the example of Catherine the Great. It has not been definitely established that any such scheme existed, other than in the starets' drunken babble—if it did, Manasevich-Manuilov was probably its real author—but it was suspected, and even rumored at the time, and that in itself was another damaging blow to the moral authority of the monarchy. The final one, paradoxically, was the murder of Rasputin on December 29, 1916.

All sorts of Russians, from wronged husbands to disinterested patriots, had sound reasons for wanting to kill the starets. The little group of conspirators who finally succeeded in ending his unofficial reign (there had already been several halfhearted plots to do so) was composed of ultra-right-wing monarchists. Their political ideal was essentially the same one professed by their victim: to make Russia safe for autocracy. It was because Rasputin was ruining the cause of autocratic monarchy—as well as that of the nation itself—that he had to die.

The actual executioner was Prince Felix Yusupov, an orchidaceous young man about court who had married one of the Czar's nieces. He carried out his gruesome mission with aristocratic amateurishness, and Rasputin's end in consequence was as grotesquely messy as his whole career had been. Yusupov lured the starets to his home for a midnight drinking bout, served him Madeira spiked with potassium cyanide. While waiting for the poison to take effect Yusupov played the guitar for the man he was murdering. His co-conspirators upstairs steadied their nerves by playing *Yankee Doodle* over and over again on the phonograph. When it was clear that the cyanide had failed, Yusupov used a revolver. Rasputin fell on his back, seemingly dead. Later, however, he revived and was only finished off —by one of the shaken young prince's accomplices—after a ghastly scuffle. The blood-spattered corpse was weighted and dropped through a hole in the ice into an arm of the Neva.

The macabre crime produced results far different from what its authors had intended. They had, after a fashion, avenged the honor of the monarchy by slaying its chief corrupter, but in so doing they had inevitably underscored in the public mind the scandal of its corruption. The damage to the prestige of the regime was irreparable. The wound to the morale and the cohesion of its natural supporters was unhealable. The assassination of the starets simultaneously revealed and aggravated a split at the highest levels of the Czarist power-elites. All the progressive elements in the nation had long since been driven into opposition; now it was made clear that the lucid conservatives and the honest reactionaries were no less alienated. "The bullet which killed him [Rasputin] reached the very heart of the ruling dynasty," wrote the revolutionary poet Alexander Blok, whose verdict Trotsky endorses. The bullet proved to be all the deadlier because in a sense it had missed its real target. In killing Rasputin it had only strengthened Rasputinism and made it more vicious. The Czarina clung more stubbornly than ever to her suicidal plan for a sort of neoabsolutist coup against the constitution of 1905. The Czar remained tied to her apron strings. The court camarilla kept on intriguing and profiteering. The incredible Proto-popov incredibly remained at his post as Minister of the Interior. Thanks to him the late starets even continued to guide the destinies of the monarchy from the other world, for Protopopov in moments of crisis consulted Ras-putin's spirit through a professional medium. The dynasty was clearly de-termined to keep its rendezvous with death. It did not have long to wait.

CHAPTER 14

The Lost Revolution

SOME disorders occurred today," Sir George Buchanan, the British Ambassador in Petrograd reported to his government on March 9, 1917, "but nothing serious." A more perceptive observer would no doubt have realized that in the bitter third winter of the war any disorders in the Czarist capital were potentially serious, but Sir George's prosaic dispatch, unwittingly announcing the onset of the most momentous political upheaval in Western history since the French Revolution—actually, it had started the day before—was not quite so fatuous as it sounds. Riots and strikes were not novelties in wartime Petrograd; at the end of October 1916 they had broken out on such a dramatic scale that two entire regiments of the local garrison, called in to restore order, had caught the insurrectionary fever and fired on the police instead of on the mob. Even that bloody clash—150 of the mutineers were subsequently executed by firing squads—had not touched off a general uprising, and the British Ambassador had no grounds for supposing that the initially milder disturbances that began on March 8 would do so. The leaders of the revolutionary parties themselves showed hardly any more flair. Both the regime and its enemies, as Trotsky remarks, had long been preparing for the revolution, but both were caught unawares when it exploded in their faces. Undoubtedly the Bolshevik historian is right in saying the real leadership of the March movement came from below; he is far less convincing when he tries to demonstrate that its leaders were mainly professional, if obscure, revolutionaries. The professionals—whether liberals or Marxists—may have proposed, but it was the amateurs who seem to have disposed. The March Revolution was schizophrenic from the beginning, not only in its ideals but in its very texture. Its basic relationship to the historic context was warped: in a sense the

Russian monarchy collapsed before it could be overthrown, and smothered the revolution under its own ruins.

The particular tragedy of the Democratic Socialists like Alexander Kerensky, of the liberal monarchists like Paul Milyukov, of the more-or-less enlightened conservatives like Alexander Guchkov, who for several weeks or months had been actively plotting an anti-autocratic coup of some kind— Kerensky in February had publicly called for the elimination of the Czar "by terrorist means if necessary," and the Chief of Staff General Alexeyev had a plan for arresting the Czarina and forcing a change of government on Nicholas at gun-point—is that before they could act they were thrust into honorary leadership of a ready-made revolution which they had had no hand in organizing. Trotsky and other Bolshevik historians have held the leaders of the bourgeoisie opposition up to scorn as typifying the poltroonery and futility of a doomed class in a time of social upheaval, but in the light of what we have witnessed during the last half century these hapless men deserve some indulgence. They were no more ineffectual, after all, than the leaders, whatever their social origins, of the anti-Nazi opposition in Hitler's Germany. And how daring, lucid, and resolute were the present rulers of Soviet Russia during the Caligulesque twilight of Stalin's reign? For that matter, what mysterious influence dulled Trotsky's own conspiratorial reflexes when the *epigoni* started trimming the old lion's claws? The real lesson of history is that while despotism almost never succeeds in totally stamping out all active opposition, it invariably mutilates its opponents in some way, and the closer they stand to the seat of despotic power, the graver the mutilation. Naturally when slaves try to strike off their chains, their movements are less uninhibited than those of men who were born free, or who early escaped to the free life of outlaws.

That much having been said, for the sake of justice and out of common humanity, it must be admitted that the oppositional role of the Russian elites—whether officers, aristocrats, or bourgeois intellectuals—on the eve of the March uprising was as pathetic as it was afterward. Their conspiratorial agitation was an important factor in paralyzing the reactions of the old regime when the insurrection occurred, but they were themselves the ultimate victims of the chaos thereby induced. Their predicament can be compared to that of a timid and inexperienced bridegroom whose inept fumblings arouse the passions of his adolescent bride just enough to push her into the arms of the first tramp who knocks at the door, leaving the poor cuckold with the responsibility for trying to raise the congenital little rebel that she later brings forth. The tramp—if the essential factor must be personalized—in the March Revolution, and particularly in the breakdown that followed it, was the demoralized soldier or ex-soldier, absent from the front through desertion, convalescence, or administrative hazard, and consciously or unconsciously prepared to tear society to shreds rather than to risk going or returning there.

"The soldiers will return like wild beasts," Rasputin had accurately warned the Czar in urging him to halt the useless slaughter of General Brusilov's offensive on the Galician front, which between June and mid-September 1916 had brought in 375,000 prisoners but had cost the Russians 550,000 men without achieving any really decisive result.

It was the soldiers, whether mutineers from units of the Petrograd garrison or deserters and stragglers back from the front, who supplied the leaven of revolutionary violence to the doughy mass of proletarian discontent in Petrograd and the other industrial centers. Wages had naturally risen since the beginning of the war, but the cost of living had risen three times as fast. The nation's food production was theoretically adequate to feed the whole population, but there were often local and temporary shortages of staples. Housewives spent hours standing in lines in front of stores (Rasputin had once shrewdly suggested ordering the bakeries to sell pre-sliced bread, so as to shorten time that the women spent waiting in queues and thereby to diminish the opportunities for collective grumbling and rumor-mongering). The scarcity of coal and firewood was an additional hardship, especially in the capital where the biting cold of the Russian winter is preceded by bleak weeks of damp and mud. Sharpening the pinch of these bodily tribulations were the normal irritants or depressants of casualty lists, the spectacle of flagrant profiteering, the Rasputin scandal, Protopopov's harsh and stupidly vexatious measures against organized labor.

". . . the industrial proletariat of the capital is on the verge of despair," a police report noted with unusual lucidity in November 1916. ". . . the smallest outbreak due to any pretext will lead to uncontrollable riots."

The pretexts that finally did touch off the uprising were obscure and diverse. One was a labor dispute in the great Putilov steel works that had culminated in the lock-out of some 30,000 workers. Another was a shortage of bread, due mainly to unusually heavy snowfalls during the first week of March which had hampered communications and deprived many bakeries in Petrograd of fuel (there seems to have been no lack of flour). A third, more formal pretext was the observation of International Woman's Day, a new institution of vaguely socialistic origin, set for March 8. Some of the revolutionary movements in the capital had planned to exploit the occasion by instigating anti-war demonstrations. A little-known Bolshevik agitator in the Vyborg industrial quarter named V. N. Kayurov—the important Bolshevik leaders were mostly in exile or prison—was particularly active in organizing parades of female textile workers to march through the streets chanting subversive slogans like "Down with the war" and "Give Us Bread." In haranguing his feminine audiences Kayurov seems to have stressed the warning to avoid any provocative action that might give the police an excuse for firing on the demonstrators; for the same reason most of the leftist leaders were initially opposed to any city-wide strike. As the rumor of projected demonstrations spread through the factories of the Vyborg quarter, however, more and more workers, men as well as women, decided to walk out. Once in the streets—from early in the morning on March 8—they forgot the prudent advice given them by Kayurov and other experienced agitators, and started looting the bread shops. At its beginnings the Russian Revolution was a series of scattered bread riots in the capital.

The authorities were naturally nervous about the impending demonstrations—police spies had given early warning of them—but they were not seriously alarmed. The Czar, brushing aside a not-very-insistent plea by Protopopov to remain in the capital, left for Moghilev early on March 8. ("I shall take up dominoes again in my spare time," he wrote the Czarina on his arrival there.) Responsibility for maintaining order in Petrograd rested on Protopopov (of all people); on the commander of the military district, General Khabalov, a harsh but bumbling officer; on the City Prefect, Balk, a creature of Rasputin's; and ultimately on the Premier, the decrepit Prince Nicholas Golitsyn who had been appointed a few weeks earlier (the old prince had not wanted the premiership but according to Trotsky he finally accepted it to round out his career "with one more pleasant memory"). The Petrograd garrison consisted of some 160,000 men, plus 3500 heavily armed police and some cadet training units, the so-called Yunkers. To minimize the risk of serious bloodshed the official defense plan worked out a month earlier called for relying initially on the police alone to control any disorders that might break out in the capital. If they proved unable to control the situation, two mounted regiments of the dreaded Don Cossacks would be sent in to scatter the crowds. The infantry had to be held as a last reserve for desperate circumstances. Khabalov's decision to avoid exposing his shaky garrison troops to the contagion of the mob, lest it produce another mutiny like the October one was understandable but he showed bad judgment in sticking to the plan too rigidly and too long. In particular he committed a fatal error by not pitting his Cossacks against the rioters before the tumult became uncontrollable, and by failing to issue them their usual cruelly effective whips when he finally did send them into action.

By the end of the second day, March 9, it was already plain that a popular rising was gathering in Petrograd. In a sense it was true, as the British Ambassador had cabled, that nothing serious had happened: no major public buildings had been stormed, no troops had mutinied; police casualties for the two days amounted to twenty-eight men slightly wounded, mostly from pieces of ice, rocks, or cobblestones hurled by the demonstrators. The crowds, however, had been growing steadily in size and aggressiveness; the red flags of 1905 were beginning to reappear; cries of "Down with the

Autocracy," or "Down with the German Woman," were ringing more and more frequently in the snow-carpeted streets; students and white-collar workers were beginning to join in the demonstrations or scuffles with the police, which were no longer confined to the industrial suburbs. Surprised by the revolutionary temper of the masses, the top leadership of the left-wing organizations—Social Revolutionaries, Bolsheviks, Mensheviks, and a small but at that time extremely militant Marxist group called the Mezhra-yonka—started issuing incendiary manifestoes, set up co-ordinating committees and proclaimed a three-day general strike. A number of the responsible leftist leaders were promptly arrested, but the main effect of this, as Trotsky remarks, was to give a free hand to their more combative lieutenants, like Kayurov, at the district or factory level. (The local Bolshevik cadres played a part in organizing the Petrograd insurrection, in so far as it was organized, but there is no evidence that they played the leading part.)

Saturday, March 10, was a significant turning point in the disorders. It marked the stage when riot merges into revolt. The transmutation—if it is checked before it has gone too far—does not always have grave political implications, and at first it may not even produce an increment of noise or violence: sometimes there is a deceptive lull. Most newspapermen who have covered the more unsettled regions of our planet during the last half-century have witnessed the phenomenon at least once in their careers. It is an unforgettable experience but never an easy one to report. The air thickens to a mustard haze that is heavier and more smarting than the physical smoke of battle; contours grow ragged and objects seem to bulge; the firing and the bursting of grenades, the shattering of glass, the thuds and crashes, the screams of horses and throaty cries of men are muffled by the elemental surf pounding in the inner ear. As the power of the state totters, so does the mental authority which in a civilized society polices through-ways of causality and guards the intersections of our categories: the rational world of our normal vision splinters into a mosaic of vivid discontinuities. The battle scene becomes a succession of tableaux unrelated to each other in time and space, or perversely related as in the old newsreels. An agitator in a fur hat harangues the crowd with jerky, puppet movements of his arms; suddenly it scatters; here and there a figure crumples on the sidewalk, apparently struck down by his mortal rhetoric. The crowd reassembles—or perhaps it is another crowd: shapeless female bundles covered with shawls, men in long overcoats and baggy trousers, marching in an uneven column, that seems wracked by spasmodic tremors of discipline or enthusiasm, behind a wide red banderole. A file of soldiers with short-visored caps and gray overcoats, holding long rifles with needlelike bayonets, lines up to block the street: an officer with shoulder boards on his greatcoat and a contorted face threatens the camera. At his order the soldiers drop to one knee aiming at the oncoming marchers, but whether they fire or not we never learn: there is a flickering of quicksilver and next we see a knot of soldiers and civilians, closely intermingled, gesticulating around a bonfire; the caps or shoulders of some of the figures are dusted with fresh snow; apparently dusk has fallen.

Such are the celluloid or cardboard images of the March Revolution that have been preserved for us; their very incoherence, however accidental, probably furnishes a closer approximation to psychological reality than the spoken word can give. The mental universe of a revolutionary mob, as the nineteenth-century French sociologist, Gustave Le Bon, has pointed out, is a prelogical one, and the mob itself is not so much a social chaos as an archaic society, swept by intense collective hates and fears, responding almost magically to charismatic leadership, displaying an antlike capacity for spontaneous organization and endowed with an instinctual sense of strategy like that possessed by pack-hunting animals. These characteristics are not manifested by a normal political crowd, however indignant or agitated; they sometimes develop with eerie suddenness in the course of large-scale and prolonged civil disorders when the prestige of authority wears off in clashes and skirmishes with the rioters. In the Russian Revolution it was during the third day of rioting, when some 240,000 demonstrators were in the streets, that this awesome precipitation occurred.

Trotsky, though not an eyewitness—he was living in New York at the time—has written a superb and probably accurate account of how it happened:

"By noon [March 10] tens of thousands of people pour to the Kazan Cathedral and the surrounding streets; a series of armed encounters with the police occurs. Orators address the crowds around the Alexander III monument [this means they had succeeded in reaching the administrative heart of the capital]. The mounted police open fire. A speaker falls wounded. Shots from the crowd kill a police inspector, wound the chief of police and several other policemen. Bottles, petards and hand-grenades are thrown at the gendarmes. The war had taught this art. The soldiers show indifference, at times hostility, to the police. It spreads excitedly through the crowd that when the police opened fire by the Alexander III monument, the Cossacks let go a volley at the horse 'Pharaos' (such was the nickname of the police) and the latter had to gallop off."

The rumor about the Cossacks may have been merely an illustration of how such a mob intoxicates itself with myths of hope or dread, but Trotsky thinks it was correct. In any case he cites an authentic incident that occurred later the same day, as related by Kayurov, the Bolshevik agitator, who was one of the few mob leaders to write down his recollections. When the group of rioters that Kayurov was egging on were scattered by police

262 THE FALL OF THE DYNASTIES

whips within sight of a detachment of Cossacks, he and several of his followers took their caps in hand and humbly approached the Cossacks. "Brothers—Cossacks—help the workers in a struggle for their peaceable demands," Kayurov pleaded. "You see how the Pharaos treat us hungry workers. Help us." The response is given by Trotsky in Kayurov's own words: "The Cossacks glanced at each other in some special way, and we were hardly out of the way before they rushed into the fight."

It was a spectacular victory of the insurrection. The Cossacks—these "age-old subduers and punishers" as Trotsky calls them—were the last hope of the regime. They had already betrayed symptoms of disaffection the previous day, charging the crowds as ordered, but tacitly acquiescing when the demonstrators dived to safety under the bellies of their horses (this was when the lack of whips proved disastrous). No doubt Trotsky is justified in praising the shrewdness of Kayurov's revolutionary tactics, and in arguing that the Cossacks were sick of war and repression like everyone else, but Kayurov's anecdote illustrates above all the tremendous power of contagion and absorption that every mob possesses regardless of the ideological pretexts that brought it into being. This almost magical power of winning over the enemy was demonstrated again and again during the Petrograd rising, and the insurgents systematically exploited it, cheering the very troops charging to attack them.

Every time the soldiers were exposed to direct contact with the mob they returned to their billets carrying with them, like an invisible mold upon their uniforms, the ferments of fraternization. "I order that the disorders shall be stopped tomorrow," Nicholas had wired from Moghilev on March 10. The command was not really absurd; it was merely fatal. In trying to execute it General Khabalov almost succeeded in driving the insurrection off the streets; it then exploded in the barracks. On Sunday afternoon March 11, a few hours after the Czarina had wired her husband, "All is calm in the city," and about the time that the Bolshevik leader Kayurov was dejectedly proclaiming that "the insurrection is dissolving," a company of the Pavlovsky regiment of the Imperial Guards mutinied in protest when they learned that a training unit in their regiment had fired into the crowd of workers. That night there were tumultuous meetings in barracks throughout the city. Self-appointed agitators, most of them without any previous revolutionary background—those first "forever nameless" voices of the revolution in the army whose role Trotsky stresses—harangued their comrades, consciously or unconsciously reiterating the slogans of fraternization that the mob had all day been dinning in their ears.

This phenomenon—the "molecular work" of the revolution as Trotsky terms it—was the decisive process of the March uprising, and as always when we come to the basic chemistry of history, it remains a mystery. There is only scanty evidence as to the substance and pattern of the discussions in these impromptu barrack-room parliaments of revolt that were to have such far-reaching influence upon the destiny of the world, but through the fog of tobacco smoke and the reek of unwashed bodies we get tantalizing glimpses of an eternal debate in the central core of the human personality itself. The garrison troops in Petrograd had been exposed to many competing propagandas—among which the atavistic herd appeal of the mob itself was by no means the least potent—but they do not appear to have been swept away by any of them. They contended with each other's thoughts, and with their own, neither like animals, nor like automatons nor like intellectuals, but simply like men in a human predicament. Two psychological factors seem to have been decisive in the end.

The first was the sense of human brotherhood: the refusal to be an executioner. Most of the soldiers in the Petrograd garrison, even in the Guards' regiments, were civilians recently put into uniform. Whatever they thought of the Czar, or of the monarchy, or of the army—and they certainly felt little enthusiasm for any of them—they were indignant and aghast at the prospect of being ordered out into the streets again to shoot down other civilians, most of them unarmed and friendly, many of them women or children. It was an authentic feeling in every sense, very natural, very clear, and it was intertwined with an equally clear realization that there were only a few hours in which to decide. The Pharaos were good executioners but there were not enough of them: when morning came and riots resumed the army would have to take over their work. This meant shooting: not firing in the air; shooting to kill.

Here the other factor came into play: the antithetical idealism of private salvation, the prospective deserter's intuition of his moral duty to dissociate himself from collective disaster. It would be dangerous to refuse obedience, but it might prove no less dangerous to obey. The firing squad was waiting for deserters and mutineers; but the mob had more savage ways of punishing its enemies—as the luckless Pharaos were discovering. It might be beastly to turn against one's officers; but some of them were beginning to get a beast-look in their eyes. Underlying the immediate choice of terrors was the more general issue of perilous conformity or of heroic defection posed by the war itself. Sooner or later whether or not the garrison troops did their duty, sheer necessity would cause them to be sent to the front.

Thus angel and demon wrestled in the souls of the Czar's soldiers, and as often happens, walked away from the struggle arm-in-arm. Love, hate, brotherhood, egoism, courage, and cowardice jointly prevailed over social habit. At 7 A.M. on March 12, after a whole night of fevered discussion, the Volinsk regiment of the guards, led by a sergeant named Kirpichnikov and by an officer-candidate named Astakhov—neither of these key figures in the revolution ever appears again on the stage of history—marched out of its barracks under arms with its band playing the *Marseillaise;* what happened to the unit's officers is obscure. The mutineers, seeking safety in numbers, proceeded to the nearby quarters of the Preobrazhensky and Litovsky regiments and called out their comrades. From that moment on the revolution became irreversible. The Imperial Army in Petrograd disintegrated. Regiment after regiment either rose against its officers—sometimes killing them—or melted away through individual desertions. The Cossacks, and some other elements of the garrison, held themselves aloof, reluctant to join the rebellion, but unwilling to fire on their comrades.

The soldiers who had mutinied or deserted joined the civilian insurgents in storming the precinct police stations where the Pharaos had barricaded themselves—often defended with machine guns—and then began attacking other public buildings. In the early afternoon of March 12, a mob spearheaded by its military elements, successfully attacked the Arsenal; from then on virtually every revolutionary who wanted a rifle had one. Later the same afternoon the revolutionaries sacked the headquarters of the Okhrana, set the central court buildings on fire, and finally captured the seemingly impregnable island fortress of St. Peter and St. Paul, the Czarist Bastille. Various jails were raided and the prisoners released. By the end of the day General Khabalov's command had dwindled for all practical purposes to about 2000 loyal troops, concentrated around the Winter Palace and the Admiralty.

Here is the street scene in the heart of the Czarist capital at this dramatic moment as reported by an objective and thoughtful eyewitness, a Dutch professor named L. H. Grandijs, writing in the French weekly *L'Illustration:*

"It is four in the afternoon when I reach the Nevsky Prospekt [the wide monumental avenue starting from the Admiralty square near the river] . . . I hear firing all around. Just as I am starting up the steps that lead to the bridge, the crowd that had been on it scatters. We just have time to duck our heads before there is a salvo. The crowd is astonishingly calm. As soon as the fusillade is over people rush out to look. . . .

"Stretcher-bearers pass by, carrying a corpse and a wounded man. A Red Cross auto is loudly cheered by everyone . . . A sister of charity leans out of the ambulance and frantically waves her red handkerchief . . . The crowd is composed of workers, of students belonging to the petty bourgeoisie and of a certain number of toughs who come from God knows where. . . . In the distance orators are haranguing the people from the statues on the Anitschkov bridge. . . .

"Soldiers appear in the Liteiny Prospekt [another wide avenue that bisects the Nevsky]. They look tired, anxious, but resolute; all have rifles in their hands. They are followed by young workers and students armed with revolvers, officer's sabers, bayonets, military rifles and shotguns. Nobody is in command but all the same there is a kind of order stemming from unity of purpose and depth of conviction. . . . There is a noise of steel against wood; some hooligans are trying to force open the door of a tobacco shop. But arms are thrust out and the older workers cry out, 'Brothers, don't do that. Move along brothers. . . .'

"All the cafés are closed since this morning, so I enter a lower-class tea house in Kazanskaia street. It is full of soldiers, workers and small shop-keepers, all discussing the events of the day—with amazing calm . . . For the time being there is no hatred of the Czar and there seems general willingness to continue fighting the war . . . The common people are concerned with the problems of daily life, not with principles or political systems. . . . They want bread. They accuse the present minister of criminal negligence . . . the remedy as they see it is a change of cabinets, not of regimes . . . Others will make the revolution. The soldiers who are drifting around the city in little groups, and who are growing increasingly aware of their power, form the hard core of the movement that is developing. . . ."

By the time the Dutch professor got back to his hotel, late in the night of March 12–13, armored cars manned by insurgents were dashing through the streets, incessantly blazing away with their machine guns—mostly at random, it seemed to him. Scattered firing could be heard all over the city, there was a ruddy glow in the sky from burning buildings, and the situation appeared to be wholly chaotic.

In reality an embryonic revolutionary authority was already beginning to take shape, and even to impose a recognizable, if loose, pattern on events. Its geographical focal point was the vast neo-classic Tauride Palace, built by Catherine's lover Potemkin, in the northeast corner of the capital, conveniently situated between the barracks of the insurgent regiments on one side and the Vyborg workers, just across the frozen Neva, on the other. The incongruous structure with its cupola and marble columns had housed the Imperial Duma, before becoming the general headquarters of the revolution. The Duma itself, or at least its principal members, had joined the rebellion on March 11, by defying an Imperial decree of prorogation. Instead of disbanding, the deputies had on the following day set up a so-called Emergency Committee, chaired by the Duma's President, the portly, Conservative M. V. Rodzianko, and consisting of the chief Progressive Bloc leaders—Milyukov, Lvov, Guchkov, Basil Shulgin, et al—plus a left-wing maverick, the former Revolutionary Socialist Alexander Kerensky. We are so used to thinking of him as the Kerensky of the Russian Revolution, that we tend to forget he was really its Danton. A lean, tense, jerky man with short-cut hair and the sharp peak of a high-minded cormorant, Kerensky, despite his subsequent reputation, had exceptional energy and courage, and he was the greatest soap-box orator in Russia (certainly with Trotsky in America). The situation was made to order for him (and he, alas, for it).

The revolutionary crowd instinctively drifted to the Duma, the nearest thing to an opposition forum in Czarist Russia, seeking news, inspiration, and instructions. Kerensky was prodigal with all three. He alone of the Duma Committee was in his element receiving the impromptu delegations of battle-stained, disheveled soldiers, of red-eyed, grim-featured workers and of hysterical students who milled around the lobbies of the Tauride Palace, shouting, sweating, gesticulating, brandishing weapons, and spitting on the floor. Between inspirational harangues he would dart into the crowd to rescue with his own hands some elderly, terrified general, countess, or ex-minister whom the revolution had dragged in, like a cat with a crippled bird in its mouth. (Protopopov, found hiding at his tailor's, was narrowly saved from lynching by Kerensky's intervention.) Everyone was quaffing down great draughts of raw history, the most intoxicating kind.

At the same time and in the same place that the Duma Committee began functioning—as the supreme executive of the revolution—the Russian genius for purposive chaos was illustrated by the establishment of a rival authority: a resurrection of the 1905 workers' soviet. A handful of socialist intellectuals, meeting in one of the caucus rooms of the Tauride Palace, set themselves up as its organizing nucleus, and so called on the revolutionary organizations to name their delegates. In response to this appeal about 50 rather summarily chosen workers and some 20 soldiers showed up at the Tauride Palace on the evening of March 12. While the Duma Emergency Committee was sitting in one wing of the building the workers' and the soldiers' "delegates" met in another and set up a Central Executive Committee of all the soviets—few of which were yet elected. This body, whose name was soon shortened to Ex Com, started out with some 20 members but gradually swelled by co-option to nearly 100. Its chairman was the Menshevik leader, Nicholas Chkeidze, and its political coloration was more Menshevik (orthodox Social Democrat) than anything else, but it also included Revolutionary Socialists, Bolsheviks—among them such subsequently well-known figures as V. M. Molotov, and A. G. Shlyapnikov— and a sprinkling of miscellaneous radicals or progressives. One of these was Kerensky, who thus had a foot in both camps.

The Ex Com theoretically represented the proletarian revolution; but it was pink, not red. It was dedicated to socialism as St. Augustine in his younger days was dedicated to chastity: ardently, but not yet. In accordance with orthodox Marxist doctrine it took the view that the bourgeois would have to complete their revolution before the workers could take over; hence it was generally content to leave the formal responsibilities of power to the Duma Committee—or to its successor the Provisional Government—but from the first it systematically competed with the bourgeois authority by issuing direct orders to the workers and even to the revolutionary soldiers. Russian democracy was born a two-headed monster; its chances of survival were almost non-existent from the start.

On March 12, 1917, however, the adversaries of the regime, though by no means unaware of the long-term difficulties that lay ahead of them, had their hands full with those of the moment. The Imperial government still held a redoubt in the administrative heart of the capital; outlying garrisons that theoretically were loyal to the autocracy ringed the city; the Czarina was safe in Tsarskoe Selo (by March 12 she was so busy looking after her children who had all come down with measles that she had little time for suppressing the revolution, but the revolutionists were not aware of this); the Czar was at Headquarters nominally in command of all his armies. It was hard for anyone to realize after only five days of intermittent street turmoil in Petrograd that the iron despotism of the Romanovs was tottering, that its foundations had, in fact, already collapsed. In the context of the seemingly undecided revolutionary struggle, the bicephalous executive at the Tauride Palace had its uses. The Duma Committee reassured fence-sitters in the army or the civil service and it represented something to opinion throughout the nation; the Ex Com of the soviets had more influence over the insurgent workers and mutinous soldiers of the capital. By co-operating, after a fashion, the two bodies on March 13 succeeded in consolidating their victory and in restoring a semblance of order in Petrograd. The government had collapsed, General Khabalov had abandoned the Admiralty, and only a small group of officers barricaded in the Hotel Astoria were still holding out against the forces of the revolution.

The last hope of the regime vanished on March 14 when a task force which on the Czar's orders had set out by rail from Moghilev three days earlier stalled on the outskirts of Petrograd, demonstrating that the rising had ceased to be a local affair. The commander of the force, General Nicholas I. Ivanov, a bluff, sensible old soldier, long in disgrace for suspected disrespect of Rasputin, had been promised four regiments from the front for stamping out the revolt in Petrograd. He entrained from Headquarters with his staff and an incomplete *bataillon* of elite troops but the trip, which normally took 24 hours, proved both slower and more tumultuous than he had expected. Informed at one of the main junctions on his route that on the previous day—March 11—a trainload of soldiers from Petrograd had mutinied in the station and seized their officer's weapons, General Ivanov decided to police all trains arriving from the capital whenever he had the opportunity. One soon arose. A train pulled in, packed with soldiers, some of them brandishing weapons, others proudly showing off new civilian clothes, obviously looted from some provincial store. Suddenly, the General, inspecting one of the wagons, found himself face to face with a soldier wearing an officer's sword strapped around his waist and holding one in each hand. "On your knees," he roared, putting his hand on the man's shoulder and shoving downward. The same technique had enabled Ivanov to check a riot between soldiers and sailors many years earlier, but the times had evidently changed. The mutineer sank to his knees as ordered; at the same time he also sank his teeth in the General's hand. Ivanov could have had the man shot, but as he later explained to a commission of inquiry, to do so would have been to "pour fuel on the flame."

While the officer-biter was being locked up in the baggage compartment, another train arrived from the direction of Petrograd and Ivanov was intrigued to see a group of soldiers who had clambered off it tossing their caps in the air. "As I came up to them," he testified, "I heard them shouting: 'Freedom,' 'Now everyone is equal,' 'No more superiors, no more authority.' I saw several officers, surrounded by common soldiers. 'Gentlemen,' I said, 'what has got into you?' Seeing them look shame-faced I gave the same order: 'On your knees.' Immediately they all dropped to their knees."

Having locked up several ringleaders and recovered some stolen arms, General Ivanov resumed his voyage, but the nearer he got to the capital, the more unsettled conditions became. Somewhere along the way the chaos swallowed up the four front-line regiments that he had been promised in Moghilev. On arrival at Tsarskoe Selo, General Ivanov found the little town abandoned by its garrison and learned that the Czar's ministers had been arrested in Petrograd. To try to fight his way into the capital with his understrength *bataillon* would, he concluded, merely lead to useless bloodshed, and so he notified Headquarters. After a rather unsatisfactory consultation with the Czarina, whom he found bewildered by the ingratitude of her husband's subjects, Ivanov, who like many high-ranking professional soldiers, seemed dutiful but hardly zealous in defending the regime, entrained again with his troops on an aimless ramble among the outer suburbs. For some reason he had not considered it necessary to reinforce the Imperial Family's guard at the Alexander Palace. The next day the Imperial Escort Regiment, which was responsible for their safety, deserted to the revolution. (The Duma, however, sent delegates to assure their protection.)

On March 15, one week after the start of the Petrograd rising—which despite the occasional violence of the clashes had cost only some 1500 lives—the Duma's Emergency Committee transformed itself into a Provisional Government. Prince Lvov was named Premier, Milyukov, Foreign Minister, and Kerensky, Minister of Justice. The new government called on civil and military authorities throughout the nation to honor its decrees. One of the earliest to respond was the Czar's first cousin, Grand

Duke Cyril, who at the head of his Marine Guards marched to the Tauride Palace and pledged his allegiance.

As if in retaliation, the Red Ex Com on the same day broadcasts its subsequently famous "Order Number 1" to the armed forces of the nation, proclaiming that in all political matters they were under the authority of the Petrograd Soviet—or of the local soldiers' committees that were beginning to spring up—and instructing the troops to obey only such orders of the Duma as were not in conflict with those of the Soviet. The order also abolished saluting and laid down the principle that weapons should be in the keeping of the soldiers' committees instead of in that of the officers. Thus chaos was institutionalized.

The Provisional Government and the Ex Com were agreed that Nicholas must abdicate, but whereas the Ex Com—and the whole Soviet—were determined to abolish the monarchy at once, most of the new ministers originally wanted to save it in some modified form under a different monarch. To this end Milyukov drew up for the Czar's signature an act of abdication in favor of the 12-year old Czarevitch, with the boy's uncle, Grand Duke Michael, named as Regent. Without waiting for the approval of all colleagues—or even for the Provisional Government, to be officially proclaimed —a two-man delegation consisting of the new War Minister, Guchkov, and the Conservative Deputy, Basil Shulgin, set out from Petrograd early on March 15 to get the Czar's signature on this document.

Nothing in Russia or in world history proves that the attempt to save the monarchy was foredoomed, but in the context of the moment it was clearly a delicate operation. It could only have succeeded if the Russian monarchists had all been agreed on what to do, and if they had displayed a rare combination of toughness and political adroitness in doing it. Also they needed some co-operation from the Romanovs—starting with Nicholas. In the event, none of these conditions was realized.

Nicholas met the supreme crisis of his life with the same mixture of dignity, fortitude, and apathy that he had exhibited in all the lesser ones. He had started out with his suite from Moghilev for Tsarskoe Selo a short time after General Ivanov's departure, and his special train had finally been blocked in the railroad yards of Pskov, an ancient town a little more than halfway to the capital. It was there, in his office-sleeping-car, that he received the two emissaries from Petrograd on the evening of March 15. He greeted them with his usual grave, imperturbable courtesy, and sat down with them around a little table while an aide took notes on the conversation. Guchkov tried to explain as tactfully as possible the reasons that made an abdication imperative. He might have saved his breath. Nicholas had already received concerted telegrams from most of the army leaders including his uncle, Grand Duke Nicholas, commanding on the Caucasus front, urging his abdication, and he had even sent off a reply indicating his assent.

On the insistence of his entourage this telegram had been held up—or at least an attempt had been made to hold it up—but the incident merely reflected his normal tendency to vacillate in the face of any decision. When Guchkov concluded by offering to retire while the Czar reflected in private before giving his answer, Nicholas brushed aside the suggestion. "I have already reflected," he said, "and I have decided to abdicate."

The two deputies were shocked by the Czar's apparent indifference to his fate and could not believe that he fully grasped the implications of his decision.

"It was all too simple, too normal," Guchkov reported later. "The Emperor did not appear to realize the tragic nature of the scene."

It was only when Nicholas alluded to the future of the little Czarevitch that his voice betrayed some emotion, and it was only in regard to this question that he made any difficulties. He would not agree to the child being named Czar since this would imply that his parents could no longer be near him, day and night, to watch over his fragile health. The attitude was understandable enough in a loving father, but it was nonetheless a flagrant betrayal of the dynasty credo that was bound to accentuate confusion among the supporters of the monarchy. Guchkov and Shulgin realized that any change in the Milyukov formula was tactically dangerous, but they eventually yielded to Nicholas' gentle obstinacy. "In agreement with the Imperial Duma we have thought it good to abdicate from the throne of the Russian State and to lay down the supreme power," read the final text of the abdication act as amended by Nicholas. "Not wishing to part with our dear son we hand over our inheritance to our brother, the Grand Duke Michael Alexandrovich, and give him our blessing to mount the throne of the Russian State."

By the time Guchkov and Shulgin got back to Petrograd—on the morning of March 16—the outcome of their mission was known in the capital. The Soviet was adamant against any attempt to preserve the monarchy and opinion in the Provisional Government was hardening against the idea. A conference was already under way at the Grand Duke's palace to decide whether he should accept the throne. All the ministers were present, as was the President of the Duma, Rodzianko. Guchkov and Shulgin, after shaking off a delegation of indignant workers, drove straight from the station to join them. Kerensky led the faction urging Michael to refuse the throne; Milyukov and Guchkov pleaded for at least conditional acceptance. The latter proposed specifically that the Grand Duke should reign until the election of a constituent assembly which would freely decide on a permanent regime for the country. The formula, at least in theory, had real merit; it would have rallied the officers, the big industrialists and most of the nobility to the support of the Provisional Government and possibly would have given it greater prestige in the eyes of the muzhiks. Most of the liberals, who had earlier favored some such solution, now were opposed to it however; they feared an open break, perhaps an armed clash, with the Soviets. The argument raged for hours, confused and emotional, at moments almost hysterical—few of the participants had enjoyed a whole night's sleep for a week—while the Grand Duke, a tall, frail, youthful-looking man known in quieter times mainly for his love of horses, sat in an armchair listening attentively, occasionally putting in a question, seldom offering a comment. Finally, he asked to be excused and retired to a little study adjoining his drawing room for some solitary reflection. It was soon interrupted by Rodzianko and Prince Lvov, both proponents of abdication, who followed the Grand Duke into his study. The brief, three-way exchange, that followed was decisive for the fate of the dynasty, at least in a formal sense. After a few minutes the Grand Duke, looking sad but composed, returned to the drawing room and announced his decision. He would accept the throne if it should some day be offered to him by a constituent assembly, but in the meantime he would abdicate. The instrument of this curious and, as it were, provisional abdication, which nonetheless prejudged the future of the monarchy, was soon drafted and signed. Thus came to an end the 300-year reign of the Romanovs. Unlike the wooden ceremony in the railway carriage at Pskov, the previous evening, it was at least marked by some flashes of human drama. "Monseigneur, you are the noblest of men," Kerensky exclaimed when the Grand Duke announced his intention to abdicate. "I cannot follow you along the path you have chosen," Guchkov warned his colleagues, his poise breaking. "You are pushing the country to its ruin."

Non-Communist Russian historians have been arguing ever since about whether that "Fatal Third of March"—March 16 by the new calendar—as Basil Maklakov terms it, signed the death warrant of Russia's new-born democracy. Both the monarchists and the anti-monarchists have some cogent arguments. Perhaps the truth lies not so much between them as beyond them. The course of the Russian revolution after March 1917 was influenced at least as much by forces bearing upon it from outside Russia as by those seeking to guide it from within; essentially it was tributary to the deeper, vaster, increasingly violent crisis of civilization unleashed by the war itself.

CHAPTER 15

The Age of the Witch Doctor

O N March 23, 1917, exactly one week after the conference in Petrograd that had led Grand Duke Michael to re-nounce the throne of Russia, there took place near Vienna a much more intimate—and secret—meeting which had no direct connection with the Russian situation but which potentially was of crucial importance to its development. The setting was a living room in the old Habsburg castle of Laxenburg, a few miles south of the Austrian capital, at the unusual hour of six on a dark and snowy morning. Initially only four persons were present: the Emperor Karl—Francis Joseph had died four months earlier—a slender man of twenty-nine with a trim mustache, whose handsome features habitually wore a look of slightly timid earnestness; his wife, the Empress Zita, four years younger, dark-eyed and beautiful in a strong-minded way; and her brothers the Princes Sixtus and Xavier of Bourbon-Parma, who looked like what in normal times they were: two elegant young Parisian men about town. Zita had not seen her brothers, for whom she had considerable affection, since 1914; her country of adoption and theirs were at war with each other. The Bourbon-Parmas were a charac-teristically cosmopolitan European family of royal descent; Zita, nominally an Italian princess had naturally acquired Austro-Hungarian nationality (if it could be called that), while Sixtus and Xavier lived in France and con-sidered themselves French. Debarred by the law of the Third Republic—because of the Bourbon taint—from serving in the French Army, they had enlisted as stretcher-bearers in the forces of their cousin, Albert, King of the Belgians, and eventually risen to the rank of second lieutenant. The some-what conspiratorial-seeming encounter over the ersatz coffee in the medie-val chill of Laxenburg castle was a family reunion; in the circumstances of the day it would have been rather moving even if it had been nothing but that. Of course it also had a broader significance. This was Old World diplomacy once more—and doubtless for the last time—at its Old Worldliest, though perhaps not at its worst.

The new Habsburg Emperor was neither a philosopher-king nor a man of iron; he was a decent, fairly sensible, intensely civilized young Central European who retained the supranational outlook of his ancestors but had shed much of the anachronistic feudalism that had still colored it in the reign of his great uncle, Francis Joseph. Like his deceased uncle Francis Ferdinand, Karl was fervently dedicated both to the Dynasty and to the Empire; again like Francis Ferdinand he was intelligent enough to see that preserving the former implied liberalizing the latter. Unlike either his uncle or his great uncle, however, Karl was not much of a military man; he hated war and he realized that unless there was an early end to the ghastly and calamitous conflict, which the folly of the Austro-Hungarian government itself had done so much to launch, there would be an end to the Empire. The problem was how to get Austria out of the war. He had often wrestled with it as heir to the throne, while indulging in his favorite recreation of pushing the latest of his frequently recurring offspring around the park of Schoenbrunn in a perambulator. Any Austrian initiative aimed at exploring the possibilities of a compromise peace through the customary diplomatic or paradiplomatic channels would, Karl knew, immediately be scotched at the outset by the Dual Monarchy's implacable German allies. Peace could not be sought honestly and directly; it had to be conspired.

Immediately after his coronation Karl began to hatch his peace plot. It was not, perhaps, strictly honest toward his allies—though he does not appear to have contemplated a separate peace that would have abandoned Germany to her fate—and it was extremely dangerous, politically and even personally. Nonetheless the young Emperor, encouraged and probably spurred on by his wife, who was particularly susceptible to Vatican influence, determined to make the try. He decided to use his brothers-in-law as unofficial agents for approaching the Entente leaders, and got in touch with them through family channels. In due course they were provided with false papers, smuggled into Austria from Switzerland, and secretly brought to Laxenburg. Their mission was by no means a safe or comfortable one, as the two young princes had pointed out to their sister, but they had yielded in the end to her passionate entreaty: "Think of all the poor men who are in the living hell of the trenches, and who are being killed by the hundreds daily, and come."

The whole affair was intensely romantic and amateurish, but it was not irresponsible. Sixtus and Xavier had insisted on clearing their mission with the French government before agreeing to undertake it, and had had several interviews with President Poincaré and Prime Minister Aristide Briand, the latter of whom had definitely encouraged them. Karl had taken his Foreign

Minister, Count Czernin, into his confidence (though not, unfortunately, completely). Czernin, tall, thin, pale, wearing the expression of an undertaker about to view the body, joined the youthful peace plotters at the end of their private conversation and lectured them on some of the pitfalls in their path; the lecture was chilling but useful. At the close of a second conference on the evening of the same day Czernin gave the two princes a note drafted with professional care—and consequently limited to platitudes—setting forth the position of the Austro-Hungarian government as the basis for ulterior official peace negotiations. Karl, without informing Czernin, slipped them a handwritten letter to be shown to Poincaré which was a great deal more explicit. In this letter, written in elegant if not quite faultless French, the young Emperor offered to use all of his personal influence with his German allies to persuade them to accept the "just French claims" to Alsace-Lorraine—a dramatic offer in the context of the time—and proposed as further basis for a general peace the evacuation of all Belgian territory and the restoration of Serbian sovereignty, subject to Serbian undertakings to suppress Pan-Serb agitation on its soil. Karl even evoked the possibility of granting Serbia an outlet on the Adriatic.

The letter created a sensation in Paris. Briand's successor as Premier, Alexandre Ribot, promptly informed the British of the new development. "This is peace," exclaimed Prime Minister David Lloyd George after a talk with Ribot early in April. The prospect was a thrilling one. There was no crystal ball in which the Allied statesmen could read the future; even the most perceptive could hardly be expected to foresee in detail the infernal chain reaction of catastrophes that Karl's peace offer at least stood a chance of interrupting: the Bolshevization of Russia, the Balkanization of Central Europe, the Hitlerization of Germany, the Anschluss and the rape of the Sudetenland, war and revolution all over again and the iron curtain cutting the heart of Europe in two. Yet the end of the nightmare in the trenches was exciting enough in itself, and though the Western leaders could not foretell what was going to happen in Russia they were already seriously worried about what might happen there; a few of them—Briand for one—even had time for an occasional faint twinge of apprehension about what might follow the break-up of the Habsburg Empire. Thus the initial French and English reaction to the Austrian peace feeler was positive, if cautious; it was decided to sound out the Entente's allies, Italy and Rumania (the Russians were too enmeshed in their own revolution to count for much in the international picture) without revealing the full circumstances of the Bourbon Parma mission. Karl on his side demonstrated the sincerity of his offer by attempting to soften up the Germans, particularly on the subject of Alsace-Lorraine. Without admitting his approach to the Entente, Karl stressed Austria's urgent need for peace and warned his allies that the impending American intervention in the war would be fatal to the cause of the Central Powers. Peace without victory was therefore preferable to defeat. Czernin was instructed to hint at the possibility of ceding a slice of Austrian Galicia to Germany if the latter would give up Alsace-Lorraine, or part of it, in an eventual general settlement.

For perhaps a month there seemed a real chance that something might come of all the peace talk. Then the obstacles began to pile up. The Germans were totally unresponsive to Karl's insinuations. "You have been listening to your womenfolk again," Wilhelm sneered after a private talk between the two emperors at Bad Homburg early in April. When Ribot learned of this conversation his previous enthusiasm for negotiations began to flag. The Rumanian, and particularly the Italian attitude, proved even graver snags. These former allies (or clients) of Germany had been enticed into the war on the side of the Entente with secret treaties promising them lavish spoils from the Habsburg Empire. (There were other secret treaties at the expense of Turkey promising the Dardanelles to Russia, Palestine to the Arabs—and the Jew—Syria to the French—and the Arabs.) Karl had been extremely generous with Alsace-Lorraine, which did not belong to him; he was less forthcoming in offering to satisfy Italian and Rumanian greed out of his own inheritance.

Eventually the hope for peace faded away, after reviving intermittently throughout the rest of 1917. There was a brief renewal of optimism when Germany showed some initial interest in peace proposals submitted by Pope Benedict XV, but nothing came of the move. The final result of Karl's well-intentioned attempt to save Europe was, as we shall see in a later chapter, merely to precipitate the destruction of the Habsburg Empire. Some historians put the blame on the lack of resolution that they detect beneath the young Emperor's good intentions. Others denounce Italian rapacity, French pettifogging or German militarism. It is even possible to make a case against President Wilson as one of the chief culprits, by omission; certainly if he had been better informed and more open-minded about the political situation both in Austria-Hungary and in Russia, he could have made the world safer for democracy at less than it finally cost the people of the United States, by putting his moral authority and potential military power in 1917 behind the move for a compromise peace. (Wilson in December 1916 had urged the belligerents to state their war aims as a basis for possible negotiations and Karl's letter was thoroughly in keeping with the spirit of the proposal.)

The fact is that by the spring of 1917 no individual leader and no single nation could be held accountable for sabotaging the chance of peace, because the war-making machinery in every country had for all practical purpose escaped from human control. Though all the belligerent nations—except America, which was just entering the war, and Russia, which was half out of it—had become virtual dictatorships, power was not held in any of them by a true dictator, or even by military oligarchies. In a sense, it was not wielded by men at all, but by the administrative mechanisms which existed or had been specially created to institutionalize the national will to victory, and by the multiple, deeply entrenched, special interests that had crystallized around them. Certain of these mechanisms which played an important role in the breakdown of the 1917 peace talks are also of special significance from the viewpoint of the present book. Though by no means new, they operated on a scale that the world had never seen up to that time, and the revolutionary upheavals that marked the last two years of the war, as well as those which occurred after the Armistice, cannot be fully understood without taking them into account.

Two world wars and a decade of cold war between the West and the Communist-bloc nations have made us all familiar with the miscellaneous manipulations and unpleasantnesses that for purposes of administrative or journalistic convenience are lumped under such headings as "psychological warfare" or "political warfare." (The two terms, at least in official usage, are loosely synonymous, the former being preferred in the United States, the latter in Britain. Like the French equivalent, *action psychologique,* they are catch-all designations covering a variable but wide spectrum of activities ranging from propaganda to the fomenting and support of revolutionary movements and certain aspects of guerrilla warfare.) The words are relatively new, and so of course are some of the techniques, but the basic tactical patterns go back to the dawn of human history. Indeed, they go even farther. The whir of the rattlesnake, the cry of the howler monkey, are forms of psychological warfare. So are the war whoops of the American Indian, the jeers and boasting of the Homeric warrior, the spells and incantations of the primitive witch doctor. Throughout the ages what the French quaintly call "St. George's Cavalry"—i.e. bribing the troops or generals of one's enemy to betray their cause—has been the indispensable auxiliary of nearly every great conqueror; it was the golden charges of this legendary brigade that won the battle of Valmy, the first great military victory of the French Revolution, rather than the valor of its conscript citizen-soldiers. Long before Hitler's propaganda chief, Dr. Joseph Goebbels, Napoleon had made good use of the printed propaganda tract as a weapon of war. It was a native fifth column organized by John Paul Jones that really secured the shores of Tripoli for the U. S. Marines, and the employment of similar political warfare techniques by President James K. Polk helped them reach the halls of Montezuma.

During the first world conflict, however, these black arts of war (and of diplomacy) were practiced so systematically and on such an unprecedented scale that they virtually constituted a new dimension of warfare. For the first time in history, elaborate specialized machinery was set up to furnish unorthodox support to the conventional operations of armies, foreign offices, and police departments. That peculiar modern phenomenon, the psychological (or political) warrior—the militarized version of the advertising man or public relations expert and the bureaucratic cousin of the professional revolutionary—was born.

At the beginning of the war the emphasis, at least in the propaganda field, was defensive rather than offensive, and focused on the home front (in itself a new concept). There were several reasons for this. One was the increased importance of the economic factor in warfare, which made the morale of the farmer and of the industrial worker a matter of high strategic concern. Another, as we have already noted, was the unheard-of strains to which the front-line soldier himself was subjected. And underlying the problem of morale, civilian or military, was the gradually developing impact of the romantic and revolutionary eighteenth-century affirmation of the individual's right to life, liberty and the pursuit of happiness. As Professor Harold A. Lasswell remarks in his classic work, *Propaganda Technique in the World War,* "propaganda is a concession to the willfullness of the age." In the twentieth century—or at least in its first decade—men could no longer simply be ordered to give up their right to private happiness at a ruler's whim; they had to be persuaded. The spread of literacy and the development of rapid mass means of communication facilitated the task of persuasion. Naturally—though at first glance paradoxically—the worst propaganda excesses were committed in the Western democracies, where the common man was, in Lasswell's terminology, the most "willful."

One type of Western morale-building propaganda which proved to be particularly self-defeating and even traumatic in the long view was the abusive appeal to the latent idealism of the masses through slogans such as The War to End War (originally inspired by H. G. Wells) and Make the World Safe for Democracy (derived from President Wilson's message to Congress of April 2, 1917). No doubt the politicians who thus exploited the hopes of their peoples with these high-sounding but demagogic pledges of a better world were the first victims of their own propaganda; the unending wonder, when we look back upon it, is how intelligent and cultivated men—including a trained historian—could ever have deluded themselves into believing that prolonging the sordid massacre in Europe would make it possible to build a better world. The apathy and skepticism of the Western masses a generation later, when confronted with Hitler's naked threat to the survival of their most elementary freedom, can be traced in good measure to the overdoses of war medicine that the new witch doctors had brewed for their fathers between 1914 and 1918.

Even more deadly in its ultimate effects than the propaganda of misdirected idealism was the propaganda of hate. Again the democracies were the worst offenders. In France a kind of forgery mill, supported by secret government funds, ground out fake photographs of German atrocities to back up the no-less cold-bloodedly fabricated news reports of Belgian babies with their hands wantonly hacked off, of women with their breasts cut off by German bayonets or sabers, of factories for making soap out of human corpses. The British were a trifle more subtle, but hardly more scrupulous in exposing the outrages of the savage "Hun" (an epithet originally inspired by the Kaiser's unfortunate address to his marines at the time of the Boxer Rebellion in China). Twenty years later the scars left on the public mind by this wartime atrocity propaganda—which of course was speedily exposed after the fighting ended—were still so inflamed, that American newspaper correspondents in Europe had the greatest difficulty in persuading their editors to print authenticated reports of authentic Nazi atrocities.

As the war advanced the propaganda activity of the chief belligerent powers became increasingly intensive and organized. The British eventually set up a full-fledged Ministry of Information, under a magnate of the popular press, Lord Beaverbrook. Propaganda to Enemy Countries was a semi-autonomous service under Beaverbrook's rival, Lord Northcliffe. Within a few days of America's entry in the war, President Wilson established a Committee of Public Information, under the chairmanship of George Creel, a well-known U.S. journalist, with sole responsibility for propaganda work both at home and abroad, and with censorship functions as well. The French, Germans, and Italians favored a less co-ordinated but no less active form of organization. In all the belligerent countries the propaganda bureaus worked more or less closely with the General Staff, with the military censors, with the secret police and intelligence services and with an extensive volunteer (sometimes covertly subsidized) network of journalists, writers and politicians. The end result was a series of what amounted to immense—and immensely powerful—lobbies with a vested interest in fighting the war to the bitter end; the remorseless pressure of these bellicose lobbies on both the German and the Entente governments seems to have been a substantive factor in blocking the movement for a compromise peace that was launched so promisingly by the Emperor Karl in March 1917.

The political warfare activities of the several belligerents, aimed at demoralizing or splitting up their enemies, were an even greater impediment to peace negotiations. The stalemate in the trenches facilitated the distribution of defeatist propaganda by such crude means as scattering leaflets over the enemy lines from a low-flying airplane; it likewise spurred the search for some diplomatic or political substitute for a decisive military breakthrough. As the deadlock continued each side became increasingly irresponsible and unscrupulous in attempting to foment revolution behind the enemy's front. Every racial or religious minority, every disaffected social category became the target of subversive incitements and appeals. Every group hatred, fear, or greed was played upon; every irredentist ambition was encouraged. Generally, it was only the most extreme minority leaders who would accept to work for, or with, the enemies of their nominal fatherland. Sometimes, however, the heavy-handed repressiveness of the wartime dictatorships—or hatred of the war itself—drove previously responsible and moderate minority leadership into collaborating with the enemy; in such cases it inevitably turned extremist, and in the process sometimes succeeded in committing its new allies to more radical objectives than they had originally contemplated.

The career of Thomas G. Masaryk, the son of a Bohemian coachman who became the founder and first President of the Czechoslovak Republic, was a case in point. Before the war Masaryk's hard-bitten peasant face adorned with the obligatory professorial goatee, was a familiar landmark in both the cultural and the political life of the Habsburg Empire. He was professor of philosophy at the Universities of Prague and Vienna, and the author of distinguished works in several intellectual fields. He was also the outstanding political leader of the Czech national minority and its most effective spokesman in the Austrian parliament. His unadorned but solidly constructed and impressively documented speeches flailed the Emperor's ministers without mercy; he was a sharp critic of the Dual Monarchy's foreign policy and a muckraker of dishonesty or oppression in its treatment of the subject peoples. Masaryk, who had married an American woman, the former Charlotte Garrigue, was a convinced democrat as well as a Czech nationalist, but up to the outbreak of war he had served the Emperor as a chief of his loyal opposition.

When war came and the Czech people was dragooned to fight under the Habsburg flag against its Slav brothers in Serbia and Russia, the loyalty of even the most moderate Czech nationalists was strained to the breaking point. An underground resistance movement took form in Prague and Masaryk was chosen to be its standard bearer abroad. In December 1914, at the age of sixty-five, the respected philosopher-politician escaped into Switzerland and embarked on a new career as a revolutionary conspirator. He was soon joined by a younger and slightly more radical nationalist colleague, Eduard Benes, a thirty-year-old professor of sociology at the University of Prague whose name was later to be identified both with the proudest and with the most tragic occasions in modern Czech history.

Polarized by repression and by the imperatives of the conspiratorial struggle, the Czech nationalist movement became the Czech independence movement—and eventually the Czecho-Slovak independence movement—and steadily hardened against any compromise with the oppressor power. Soon the complete dismemberment of the Austro-Hungarian Empire became the explicit, unwavering aim of the emigré organization headed by

Masaryk and Benes. In 1915 they moved to Paris and with the blessing of the Entente founded a Czech National Committee. Counseled by several distinguished French and British historians and journalists, turned political warriors, the Czech emigrés threw themselves with enthusiasm into the task of subverting the Austro-Hungarian armies. They drafted surrender leaflets to be showered on the regiments of conscripts from Bohemia and from Hungarian-ruled Slovakia, they co-ordinated the work of the underground spy rings or passive resistance networks, they indoctrinated and trained Czech prisoners of war. Their success was spectacular, particularly on the Russian front. By the end of the war they claimed to have induced the desertion of some 400,000 Austro-Hungarian soldiers of Czech, Slovak, or other Slav origin, while in the army of Archduke Frederick alone, more than 12,000 soldiers were hanged for attempted desertion. A number of the Czecho-Slovak deserters or prisoners of war enrolled in the Czech legions that were organized to fight on the side of the Allies both in the West and on the eastern front. The Czech Legion in Russia was particularly important; by the time of the Russian revolution it numbered some 40,000 well-equipped fighting men; it was to play a role in the Russian civil war.

The genius for political warfare displayed by Masaryk and Benes was not exercised solely at the expense of the Central Powers.

"Independence will not be attained by talking about independence," Masaryk explained to his supporters. "We must induce the Allied governments, influential diplomats and politicians, parliamentarians and newspapers to associate themselves with our claim. . . . We must convince political Europe that this Czech state is necessary, that it is advantageous to the allies also."

By the spring of 1917, when the Emperor Karl launched his peace feeler, the Western governments were still not quite convinced that a totally independent Czech state was either necessary or advantageous. As late as January 1918 Lloyd George felt it advisable to specify publicly that the breakup of Austria-Hungary was not one of the British war aims, and President Wilson echoed this caution in his message to Congress of January 8, 1918 (the same one that set forth his famous Fourteen Points).[1] Even at the time that Ribot and Lloyd George were consulting over Karl's letter, however, their diplomatic freedom of maneuver, as far as peace negotiations with Austria were concerned, was seriously hampered by the Allies'

[1] The Fourteen Points provided Allied political warriors with some of their most effective ammunition, but it would be misleading and unjust to consider them primarily in this context. They constitute one of the basic political texts of our century. Moreover, despite their liberalism and their stress on the self-determination of peoples—particularly the Polish people and the peoples of the Austro-Hungarian Empire—they were not inherently incompatible with either the dynastic or the imperial principles. Both the Habsburgs and the Hohenzollerns ultimately attempted to sue for peace on the basis of the Fourteen Points, but foolishly waited until their thrones were already crumbling.

tacit commitments to the Czech National Committee. During the rest of 1917 it steadily dwindled owing to a number of reasons, among which the Czech talent for propaganda and behind-the-scenes diplomacy was by no means the least. Perhaps the final victory of political warfare over diplomatic prudence and flexibility was the so-called Congress of Oppressed Nationalities of Austria-Hungary held in Rome in April 1918. It was attended by delegates of the Czech and Yugoslav national organizations and by representatives of the Polish and Rumanian Transylvanians (Transylvania, most of which was awarded to Rumania after the war, was a border area of mixed population belonging to Hungary). The Congress concluded with the announcement of a "common front" of oppressed peoples, dedicated to the abolition and dismemberment of the Dual Monarchy. Though not an official gathering, the Congress had been organized by the now-powerful anti-Habsburg lobby in the official political warfare services of the Allied governments, and its deliberations were heavily publicized by directive of their domestic propaganda services. (One of the journalists who helped convince public opinion in his country that the Balkanization of the whole Danubian Basin would somehow advance the cause of freedom and civilization, was a talented, splashy young Italian editor named Benito Mussolini, a former firebrand of revolutionary socialism whose conversion to the war to make the world safe for bourgeois democracy had been facilitated by lavish subsidies from the French secret service—an operation which in the light of subsequent history must count among the witch doctors' more dubious triumphs.)

While the Habsburg Empire was to be one of the most tragic victims of the political warfare that accompanied and prolonged the military conflict of 1914–1918, it was not an innocent victim. As we have seen earlier, the Dual Monarchy had launched its own political warfare offensive in the Ukraine and in Russian Poland before the assassination at Sarajevo. When the shooting started a Polish freedom corps (to use the modern terminology) armed by the Austrians was ready to accompany the spearhead of the Austro-German offensive into Russian Galicia. Its commander, Jozef Pilsudski, who was to be the first head of the resurrected Polish state, rivaled the talent for conspiratorial organization of his Czech analogues (and enemies) Masaryk and Benes, but he was utterly unlike them in nearly every other way. A complex, slender catlike man with a small head and sensitive gray-blue eyes, Pilsudski had something about him that suggested the artist and the dreamer, but his dreams were often strangely akin to other men's nightmares. He had been conspiring almost ever since he had started breathing, and even by Russian revolutionary standards was considered a ruthless terrorist. During the Russo-Japanese War he had sought the support of the Japanese government for a Polish insurrection—whether or not he got it is a subject of controversy—and his exploits as a guerrilla leader during the 1905 revolution had rivaled those of Stalin's Caucasian *banditti*. As might have been expected, the efforts of the Austrian and German political warfare service to build him up as a reliable puppet of the Central Powers backfired on them. After the Austro-German declaration of 1916 proclaiming Poland's nominal independence, with virtually all of Russian Poland liberated, Pilsudski's enthusiasm for fighting the armies of the Czar rapidly cooled, and from the viewpoint of the Austrians and Germans, he became an increasingly cantankerous ally. On various pretexts, he entered into contact with the pro-Entente Poles in Russia and in France, and began a kind of underground flirtation with the West. Eventually he proved such a nuisance to the Germans that Ludendorff had him locked up in a fortress.

Pilsudski was not Ludendorff's sole headache in the area of political warfare. The German witch doctors—with the active support of Ludendorff himself—must be credited with what was at once the most brilliant and the most calamitously self-defeating operation in the entire history of political warfare: the encouragement and support of the Bolshevik Revolution.

When the victorious United States Army in 1945 stumbled upon the cache where the secret files of the German Foreign Office had been stored, there were several documents going back to the times of the First World War that our Soviet Allies would have given a great deal to lay their hands on first. One of these items, of outstanding interest to historians was a memorandum dated March 9, 1915, setting forth a comprehensive program for German political warfare against Czarist Russia. The paper included the usual proposals for blowing up bridges and for spreading defeatist propaganda among Russian conscripts; it urged getting in touch with, and giving financial assistance to, most of the socialist opposition and a number of national minority organizations (with the exception of the Zionist Jews, whom the author of the plan considered "incapable of any political action"). More noteworthy was the overriding importance attached to working with the emigré leaders of the Russian Bolsheviks, who at the time were generally considered in the West as a splinter group of doctrinaire extremists. Among eleven specific recommendations for achieving the objectives of the program, number one was "Financial support for the majority group of the Russian Social Democrats [Bolsheviks], which is fighting the Czarist government with all the means at its disposal." The broad philosophical sweep of the memorandum was likewise striking.

"Thus," read one specially lofty passage, "the armies of the Central Powers and the [Russian] revolutionary movement will shatter the colossal political centralization which is the embodiment of the Czarist Empire and which will be a danger to world peace for as long as it is allowed to survive, and will conquer the stronghold of political reaction in Europe."

Such language is unexpected in a state paper of the German Imperial government, not exactly a stronghold of political liberalism or a champion of world peace at the time. The mind that framed it clearly had both scope and originality. Naturally, for the author of the memorandum was Dr. Alexander Helfand, alias Parvus, whom we last heard of as Trotsky's right hand in the Petersburg Soviet of 1905. Parvus had his critics, but no one has ever accused him of lacking either scope or originality. Before explaining how Parvus' prose found its way into the files of the Wilhelm- strasse and before recounting what came of his proposals, it may be well to sketch briefly the unorthodox personality and career of this colorful operator.

Parvus was a Russian Jew, born in 1869. He studied in Germany and very early joined the German Social Democratic party. He belonged to its left wing, headed by Rosa Luxemburg. Though he had contributed to Lenin's paper *Iskra,* Parvus held himself aloof from the Bolshevik-Men- shevik quarrel that divided the Russian emigration. His closest friend among the Russian revolutionaries was that other maverick, Trotsky, whose theory of the permanent revolution Parvus strongly espoused. Trotsky on his side had considerable respect for Parvus both as a revolutionary and as an in- tellectual. In 1904 Trotsky and his wife, on their way back to Russia, stayed with Parvus at the latter's home in Munich, and Parvus at that time wrote a preface to one of Trotsky's monographs. Trotsky describes his friend as having a big, fleshy head like a bulldog. Even at that early date Parvus dressed with an elegance that was frowned upon in earnest revolutionary circles and he had a queer, slightly disreputable foible: he wanted to make a lot of money—for the revolution, of course. He was the owner of a Mu- nich publishing firm that at first did quite well—later it proved a failure—but he had a far more ambitious project in mind: founding a great Marxist daily, to be published in three languages. To do that he would obviously have to be fabulously rich, and since the revolution could not wait, he had to get rich quickly.

In the 1905 revolution, Parvus' preoccupation with finance helped him to draw up an audacious but technically sound scheme for starting a run on the Czarist government's gold reserves that came very near to wrecking the ruble. With Trotsky, Parvus co-edited an enormously successful left- wing daily in St. Petersburg and he probably inspired many of the revo- lutionary tactics applied by the Soviet. In the intervals of his conspiratorial activity Parvus found time to continue his career as a big-time international playboy. The Czar's police when they finally arrested him were baffled to discover a book of fifty theater tickets in his pocket. They assumed it was in preparation for some kind of outrage: in reality it was just for a little party that Parvus was giving. Parvus shared a spell of prison and then of Siberian exile with Trotsky, and like him finally escaped to the West. In the summer of 1907 he joined the Trotskys for a hiking trip in Saxony.

Gradually, Parvus seemed to lose interest in the revolutionary cause, while his interest in getting rich grew steadily keener. He left Germany—with some encouragement from the German police—and launched into various journalistic and financial operations throughout the Balkans. The outbreak of the war found him in Constantinople, about to realize his dreams of fortune, thanks to some contracts on behalf of the German Army. Outraged by the unpatriotic attitude of his former friends in the left wing of the German Social Democratic party—despite his Russian background Parvus by now considered himself a German—he broke with them and became one of the guiding spirits of the party's right wing. He also offered his services to the German Ambassador in Constantinople and was soon deeply immersed in smuggling separatist propaganda into the Ukraine, launching a pro-German newspaper in Bucharest, and similar enterprises. His success in these ventures caused the Wilhelmstrasse to take him seriously when he submitted through embassy channels suggestions for a more ambitious revolutionary offensive against the Russians, and he was invited to Berlin for a conference. The memorandum which has been cited was the first fruit of this meeting.

Others soon followed. The special section of the German foreign office set up under Dr. Diego Bergen (who later served both the Weimar Republic and Hitler as German Ambassador to the Vatican) to co-ordinate political warfare operations against Russia provided Parvus with a German passport and an initial fund of some $250,000 to draw on. (He was soon asking for $5,000,000.) It was decided that he would make his headquarters in Copenhagen under cover of establishing and directing a scholarly institute.

Before going there Parvus visited Switzerland and talked with a number of Russian emigrés, including Lenin. The latter treated him with some suspicion—in part, according to certain sources because he looked on Parvus as a political rival—but did not refuse all co-operation. In fact, Lenin encouraged one of his friends to accept the paid job on the staff of Copenhagen "institute" that Parvus offered him. By an interesting coincidence, the friend turned out to be the well-connected Polish-Austrian Social Democrat, Jacob Fuerstenburg, alias Ganetsky, who before the war had helped obtain permission from the Emperor's police authorities for Lenin to settle in Galicia. Another trusted friend of Lenin's who worked closely with Parvus in Copenhagen was the journalist and noted Marxist theoretician Karl Radek, also a subject of the Emperor Francis Joseph, but like Fuerstenburg a complete internationalist in outlook and a Bolshevik at heart. Both men knew a great deal about Parvus' operations in Russia and kept Lenin regularly informed on their progress. Through other channels Lenin was in touch for a while with a German secret agent in Stockholm named Keskuela, an Esthonian emigré and former Marxist revolutionary, who had organized a left-wing underground network inside Russia altogether distinct from Parvus'. Here we come to the heart of the controversy that has raged for nearly half a century as whether Lenin was himself a German "agent."

The dispute hinges in part upon whether Lenin's associates, Fuerstenburg and Radek, realized that in working with Parvus they were technically working for the Kaiser, and if so whether they acted with Lenin's approval. No historical evidence that has yet been authenticated supplies an irrefutable answer to either question. The evidence found in the Wilhelmstrasse files, however, strengthens the case for believing that the two Austrian collaborators of Parvus knew where the money was coming from and why it was being supplied so lavishly; if they did not know, they must have assumed that the stork brought it. Fuerstenburg and Radek were thus almost certainly German "agents" in one sense, but it is highly unlikely that either was the kind of agent the German government could count upon to obey orders. (Even Parvus and Keskuela, though more deeply committed to the German cause, were by no means its unquestioning tools.) In their hearts they were not striving for the Kaiser's victory, but for Lenin's. After the triumph of the Bolsheviks in Russia, Radek was to become a leading Soviet agent seeking to promote the cause of revolution in postwar Germany, while Fuerstenburg eventually served the Soviet government loyally in a number of responsible posts. It is possible, of course, that neither man ever admitted to Lenin that they were taking German government money and collaborating with the German political warfare apparatus as a means for promoting the revolutionary cause, but if they had not been perfectly frank with him it is hard to believe that he would later have trusted them as much as apparently he did.

Actually, the accumulation of evidence, particularly since World War II, about the relations between the Kaiser's government and the Bolsheviks in the earlier conflict renders the controversy over Lenin's role almost pointless. If he sanctioned the collaboration between some of his prominent supporters and his country's enemy—which seems probable but not yet proved—he did it indirectly so that it gave the Germans no hold over him and thus left him at all times not their agent but a free agent. On the other hand, whether Lenin knew about it or not, the Germans, chiefly through Parvus and Keskuela, were giving substantial assistance to his underground organization at home. They produced revolutionary propaganda and smuggled it in bulk into Russia. They provided arms and munitions. They handed over to the revolutionary underground sizable cash subsidies, including the ruble balances from some large-scale illicit trade operations conceived and directed by Parvus. Social-Revolutionaries, Mensheviks, and various minority organizations benefited from clandestine German assistance, but much of it undoubtedly went to the Bolsheviks. The Germans furthermore propagandized Russian prisoners of war on a vast scale—one of the agents used for this work was Roman Malinovsky, the former colleague of Lenin and of the Okhrana. In return for the German help the Bolshevik underground in Russia, with or without Lenin's knowledge, supplied the Germans with what they considered valuable intelligence reports, (there are explicit references to them in the Wilhelmstrasse files).

The decisive German contribution to the Bolshevik cause was, of course, allowing Lenin after the March Revolution to return to Russia across German territory—he had no other dependable way of reaching his destination. As far as is known, the idea originated with the Bolshevik emigrés in Switzerland, and the approach to the Germans was made unofficially, through a Swiss Socialist leader and the Swiss government. There may have been earlier direct or indirect contacts between individual emigrés and German agents concerning the project, but if so there is no record of them in the Wilhelmstrasse files. The first official German mention of the affair is a telegram from the German minister in Bern, dated March 23, 1917, and apparently inspired by information from the Swiss Foreign Office, reporting the desire of the leading Russian revolutionaries in Switzerland to return to their homeland via Germany.

The political warfare implications of the enterprise seem to have been thoroughly realized on both the Russian and the German sides, from the beginning. Lenin was acutely aware that any appearance of collusion with the Kaiser's government would discredit him in the eyes of the Russian people and expose him on his arrival in Russia to possible prosecution for intelligence with the enemy. He was reluctant to have any direct contact with German representatives in Switzerland, and negotiated the arrangements for the trip through a neutral intermediary, the Swiss Socialist, Fritz Platten. Among the conditions Platten was instructed to insist upon were: extra-territorial status for the railway carriage in which the emigrés would cross German soil; no one except the travelers to be admitted to the carriage at any time without Platten's authorization; tickets to be paid for at the normal tariff; no passport inspection on entering or leaving Germany; bona-fide Russian emigrés to be accepted for the trip regardless of whether they held pro-war or anti-war views. Platten likewise stressed the necessity for avoiding publicity, and particularly for discouraging any optimistic editorial discussion of the trip in the German press that might compromise the emigrés.

The Germans showed themselves understanding and co-operative on all these points. Their realization of the need to protect the reputations of the travelers is brought out in several of the Wilhelmstrasse documents. The military and police authorities raised no pedantic issue of "security"; it was assuring the security of the emigrés that mainly seemed to cause them concern. The final decision to authorize the trip was referred to the highest governmental and military authorities, including Ludendorff and the Kaiser. Judging from a memorandum in the Foreign Office files, Wilhelm took a keen, if somewhat fatuous, interest in the operation. "His Majesty the Kaiser," records the memorandum, "suggested at breakfast today that the Russian Socialists traveling through Germany should be given White Books and other literature, such as copies of the Easter Message and of the Chancellor's speech, so that they may be able to enlighten others in their own country. In the event of the Russians being refused entry into Sweden, the High Command of the Army would be prepared to get them into Russia through German lines."

Lenin's party, conducted by Platten, finally left Zurich on April 9, after a lively scuffle between hostile and friendly demonstrators who had come to the station to see them off. There were thirty-two Russian emigrés in the group: nineteen Bolsheviks including Lenin, Krupskaya, Inessa Armand, and Zinoviev; three left-wing Mensheviks; six members of the Jewish Bund; and four politically unclassified passengers, one of whom was a four-year-old child. Radek joined the train at the German frontier.

"They transported Lenin in a sealed truck like a plague bacillus from Switzerland into Russia," wrote Winston Churchill, but the sealed truck —or train as it is usually styled—was as metaphorical as the bacillus, and its passage across Germany was prosaic. The Russians had a private carriage, kept locked by mutual agreement, that was hitched on to various trains in the course of its journey. The Russians had brought some food with them and the Germans, through Platten, provided more, including milk for the children. At one stop a German officer in civilian clothes—Headquarters instructions had specified that he be an "understanding" type of officer— visited the carriage and talked to Platten. The Swiss assured him that the Russians were gratified with the co-operation shown by the German government. At Frankfurt the special carriage missed its connection and there was a delay of several hours. In Berlin it was shunted about in the yards for a long time. Altogether the trip took two days. The second night was spent in Sassnitz, a little German port on the Baltic, where the Russians were locked up in what the Wilhelmstrasse report described as good accommodations that had been provided for them.

From Sassnitz, the party crossed by boat to Malmo, in Sweden. The Swedish government, at the request of the Germans, had agreed to give them transit to Finland. They stopped over in Stockholm, where Lenin conferred with Ganetsky and other Bolsheviks resident in Sweden, though he sensibly refused to see Parvus who was on hand for the occasion. A Swedish train took the party to the Finnish border, where Platten dropped off: the emigrés crossed by sled on to Russian soil (Finland was still under Russian sovereignty) and then took a train south for Petrograd.

Lenin arrived at the Finland Station in Petrograd on the evening of

April 16. He had half expected to be arrested. Instead there was a huge crowd—a tribute to his reputation as an incorruptible revolutionary leader —a band and a delegation of Bolsheviks, brandishing triumphant banners and carrying an enormous, incongruous bouquet of hot-house flowers with which to welcome the returning exile. There was even the Menshevik leader Chkeidze, the chairman of the Ex Com, to greet him officially in the name of the Petrograd Soviet, and in that of the Revolution. In his carefully prepared address of welcome, Chkeidze stressed the importance of cooperation among the various democratic groups in Russia, and the need for defending the Revolution against its enemies "from within or from without."

Lenin, wearing a round fur cap and carrying his implausible bouquet, took no notice of Chkeidze, according to an eyewitness (the Menshevik writer and memoralist of the Revolution, N. N. Sukhanov). By way of reply, he turned away from the official delegation and spoke directly to the crowd. "Dear Comrades, soldiers, sailors and workers," Lenin began. "I am happy to greet in your persons the victorious Russian revolution, and greet you as the vanguard of the world-wide proletarian army . . . the piratical imperalist war is the beginning of civil war throughout Europe . . . any day now the whole of European capitalism may crash. . . . Long live the world-wide socialist revolution." In a second address on leaving the station, Lenin briefly denounced "the shameful imperialist slaughter."

In the context of the occasion it was a declaration of war against the Provisional Government, and an undisguised appeal to organized defeatism and sedition. The local Bolsheviks who were present—they included Kamenev and Stalin—looked acutely unhappy. The representatives of the other revolutionary parties naturally were furious. Sukhanov even heard a soldier later in the day declare, "We ought to stick our bayonets into a fellow like that." From the German viewpoint everything had gone off perfectly.

LENIN'S ENTRY INTO RUSSIA SUCCESSFUL, a telegram from the German Ambassador in Stockholm reported on April 17. HE IS WORKING EXACTLY AS WE WOULD WISH.

Perhaps if the German political warriors had seen the verbatim text of Lenin's remarks at the Finland Station their admiration at their own cleverness might have been tinctured with some slight uneasiness for the more distant future.

CHAPTER 16

To the Bitter End

IN certain respects the fate of the Russian Imperial Family after the abdication of Nicholas II is unique in the annals of fallen royalty. The ex-Czar and his wife died neither as martyrs to the cause of autocracy, nor as formal scapegoats for its crimes. After a harrowing, vexatious, but not systematically cruel detention, they were slaughtered, together with their children, for somewhat fuzzy reasons of revolutionary expediency, in circumstances of prosaic squalor that recall the gas ovens of Hitler's Germany rather than the tumbrils of eighteenth-century France or the scaffold of seventeenth-century England. Their private ordeal is merely a footnote to the immense collective tragedy of the Russian Revolution. This footnote, however, is of the kind that sheds essential light upon a cloudy text. Retracing the long calvary of Nicholas Romanov and his family, first under the Provisional Government, then under the Bolsheviks, to its grisly end in the house at Ekaterinburg, serves to remind us of the human reality—all too often the piteous human reality—that underlies the mineral glaze of historical generalization. At the same time it lays bare, as no abstract analysis can, some of the basic political or psychological mechanisms that sabotaged Russia's brief experiment in democracy and prepared the way for a new, more efficient, more implacable despotism.

For the first few days after Nicholas gave up the throne nobody seems to have taken very seriously the problem of his future. The readiness with which he had abdicated in favor of his brother—he had resigned as commander-in-chief of the armies at the same time—appeared to guarantee the sincerity of his renunciation. The fact that the Grand Duke Michael had provisionally refused the crown complicated the juridical situation somewhat, but there is no evidence that Nicholas ever had the least intention of trying to recover, either for himself or for his son, the power he had given away. (Alexandra, it is true, was once heard to murmur, "Some day the people will change their minds and call on Alexis, and then everything will be all right.") On the contrary, the former autocrat went out of his path to support the Provisional Government. In his farewell message to the army from Moghilev on March 20, 1917, he implicitly repudiated the doctrine of absolutism and recognized the de facto republic that Russia had become, pending the constituent assembly. "After my renunciation of the Russian throne for myself and for my son," Nicholas wrote, "authority passes to the Provisional Government formed on the initiative of the Duma. May God aid it to lead Russia on the path of glory and of prosperity."

No doubt it was mainly in the hope of committing the army to fight on until complete victory that the ex-Czar penned his message—"Whoever now dreams of peace, whoever desires it . . . betrays . . . the land of his fathers," reads one passage. The final injunction to accept the authority of the Provisional Government is linked with an appeal to "defend our glorious fatherland" and to "obey your chiefs." The influence of the General Staff, haunted by dread of the soldiers' soviets, is discernible in the text, but there is nothing subversive or counterrevolutionary in it from the viewpoint of the new government. While Kerensky's enthusiasm for continuing the war may have been moderate at first, the "Cadet" ministers who held the majority in the cabinet, were as wholehearted in their determination to keep Russia in the war at the side of her allies, as were Nicholas and most of the generals.

When Nicholas left Moghilev on March 21, escorted by three special envoys from Petrograd, it was with the understanding—arrived at somewhat vaguely between the General Staff and the Provisional Government—that he would live in discreet retirement at Tsarskoe Selo until arrangements could be made for the entire Imperial Family to sail for England, via Murmansk. Military honors were accorded Nicholas as he entrained, but at almost the same moment, General L. G. Kornilov, the new commander of the Petrograd district, presented himself to Alexandra at Tsarskoe Selo with the words, "Your Majesty, it is my heavy duty to inform you of the decision of the Provisional Government. You are henceforth to consider yourself under arrest." The real status of the ex-Czar became painfully apparent on his arrival the following day. At the station of the little town several of the courtiers or members of his military household who had accompanied him from Moghilev, scrambled out of the train and disappeared, abandoning their former master to his fate. When Nicholas punctiliously saluted the guard at the gates of the Alexander Palace, his salute was not returned.

The official prisoners, or detainees, were Nicholas, Alexandra, their oldest daughter Olga, a tall well-built girl of twenty-two, Tatiana, twenty, Marie, eighteen, Anastasia, sixteen, and Alexis, thirteen, the former Czarevitch, a high-spirited and rather unruly boy. Nicholas was visibly aged by the strain and despondency of the last few months; his hair and beard were streaked with gray and deep lines were beginning to appear in his face. The change in the appearance of the once majestic and coldly beautiful Alexandra was even more shocking; though not yet forty-five she had turned into an elderly invalid, crippled with sciatica and heart trouble.

Sharing the detention of the former Imperial Family, but free to leave if they wished to, were three former courtiers, Count Paul Benckendorf, Prince Dolgoruki, and Madame E. A. Naryshkina, the last Mistress of the Robes; Dr. E. S. Botkin, their family physician; the governess and assistant governess of the girls; the ex-Czarevitch's Swiss tutor, Pierre Gilliard, his English teacher, Gibbs, and a handful of faithful domestic servants. (Anna Vyrubova had been living in the palace at the time of the revolution—she had caught the measles from the children—but she had been transferred to prison on Kerensky's orders for having helped Alexandra to burn some confidential papers.) Responsibility for custody and protection of the whole group was divided between Colonel Korovitchenko, a Kerensky appointee, who acted as commandant of the palace, and Colonel Kobylinsky, commander of the Tsarskoe Selo garrison troops, a brave and kindhearted officer with monarchist leanings.

The decision to put the former Imperial Family under arrest had been taken on March 20, upon the recommendation of Kerensky as Minister of Justice; originally it was conceived as a temporary measure. Like most acts of the Provisional Government, it was inspired by contradictory motivations. One was a wholly sincere desire to assure the safety of the former sovereigns. Kerensky was determined not "to play the role of a Russian Marat," as he heatedly told a meeting of the Petrograd Soviet which was clamoring for Nicholas' head; a counterproposal to hold the ex-Czar pending eventual trial before an "impartial tribune" seemed the best way to undercut extremist agitation for more summary justice. There is some reason, however, for suspecting that the pressure on the Provisional Government from the left, while real enough, was not yet irresistible, and that there was a weightier, quite different reason for signing the order of arrest that was to prove the death warrant of the Romanovs. "While the mass of workers and peasants were indifferent to the foreign policies of the Czar and his government," Kerensky later testified, "the intellectuals, the bourgeoisie and some of the higher-ranking officer-class thought they detected in the foreign and domestic policies of the Czar, and more particularly in the intrigues of the Czarina, a definite tendency to lead the country to its ruin for the sole purpose of concluding a separate peace and an alliance with Germany."

Whether even those who suspected Alexandra of being a German agent ever believed that Nicholas had connived in the supposed sabotage of the Russian war effort is highly doubtful. The smear campaign against the former rulers served a useful purpose, however, from the viewpoint of the new ones. It helped to make the war look like people's war, and its continuation a revolutionary as well as a patriotic duty. Even a number of monarchists joined in the attacks on the fallen monarch, whom they blamed for the revolution. The Allied governments were likewise quick to see the point. Despite an indignant protest from King George V—perhaps the last, as well as the first gentleman of the Entente powers—a British offer of asylum for the former Imperial Family was quietly withdrawn; the French government, then headed by Clemenceau—a true heir of the Jacobin tradition—was equally unsentimental about the fate of the man who had been his country's most loyal and accommodating ally. The de facto wartime dictatorships of the West did not want to compromise themselves with an ex-autocrat-by-Divine-Right.

A special investigating commission had been set up as early as March 18 in Petrograd to look into possible "illegal acts committed by former ministers and high officials of the Empire in the exercise of their functions." Kerensky informally broadened its terms of reference to include investigation into the conduct of the former Imperial Couple, particularly from the viewpoint of their loyalty toward the nation over which they had ruled. In practice the commission turned into a kind of grand jury charged with determining whether there were grounds for an indictment of high treason against Nicholas and Alexandra. Kerensky himself played the role of special prosecutor on occasion and subjected the couple to numerous interrogations. The commission was still sifting the evidence when the Bolsheviks came to power. Everything that it had turned up indicated the wild improbability of the principal charge, or suspicion, and though its work was to prove a boon to future historians, it made hardly any effort to deplore the ex-Czar's personal responsibility—which was doubtless substantial—in some of the real crimes against humanity committed by officials acting in his name. The Commission did not judge, but in a sense it punished, for its exigencies gave Alexandra and Nicholas a taste of the Kafkaesque malevolence that the repressive machinery of the Czarist regime had often enough manifested toward its victims. To this degree justice of the retributive sort—an eye for an eye, a life for a life, a nightmare for a nightmare—was meted out.

On pretext of avoiding "collusion," Kerensky gave orders that Nicholas and Alexandra should be kept apart except at mealtime when the whole family was to be maintained under close surveillance, and table talk was to be restricted to banalities (this last proviso, it is true, was not much of a hardship in the Romanov family circle). No visitors were to be admitted without written authorization from Kerensky. Walking in the park was limited to certain hours; neither Nicholas nor his children could take a step without being followed around the grounds (Alexandra was usually confined to her wheel chair). This strict regime lasted only for a month. After personally questioning the former rulers some eight or ten times, Kerensky came to the conclusion that any suspicion of treason in their case was absurd. His manner, at first cold and arrogant, thawed under exposure to Nicholas' wistful charm. He restored the relative freedom of movement inside the palace grounds that the detainees had earlier enjoyed, and tried to relieve their anxiety about the future. Negotiations for asylum in England or France were going forward, Kerensky assured Nicholas. The family's detention was only a temporary measure for their own protection. There was absolutely nothing to fear; the Provisional Government, on Kerensky's own recommendation, had even abolished capital punishment.

The platonic nature of these reassurances soon became clear to Nicholas and his entourage. As the attitude of the Provisional Government softened toward the former rulers, that of the soldiers who guarded them became increasingly spiteful and suspicious. Even many of the junior officers were infected with the hostile mood—or thought it expedient to seem to be. One day at the changing of the guard, when Nicholas, according to his custom, offered his hand to the officer who was being relieved, the latter refused to shake hands with him. "Why so, my friend?" the ex-Czar asked, putting his hands on the officer's shoulders and looking him straight in the face. "I am a man of the people," the officer replied, stepping back. "When the people offered you its hand you didn't take it. Now I won't give you mine."

Such incidents reflected, among other things, the growing influence of left-wing propaganda in the army—the work not merely of the Bolsheviks and of other revolutionary extremists, but of the soviets which were ostensibly co-operating with the Provisional Government while stealthily—and in some cases perhaps inadvertently—undermining its authority. Shortly after the revolution a soviet was set up in Tsarskoe Selo, in imitation of the Petrograd one, and in keeping with the doctrine of dual power, it attached a sort of political commissar to the local garrison. Kobylinsky managed to keep this individual, an officer-candidate of revolutionary background, away from the palace but could not prevent him from conducting incessant agitation among the soldiers aimed at whipping up their hatred against the Imperial Family and at arousing suspicion of the Provisional Government. The Romanovs were plotting against the Republic, the commissar-agitator charged; the authorities in Petrograd were criminally lenient toward the conspirators; the soldiers and workers of Tsarskoe Selo must therefore redouble their vigilance, and if necessary, take the law into their own hands.

Naturally all these incitements and insinuations poisoned the mind of the soldiers against the high-level prisoners they were guarding; they came to look on the ex-Czar and his family as dangerous criminals, and treated them accordingly. Discipline gradually broke down and the garrison which at first had seemed wholly reliable from the viewpoint of the Provisional

Government began to show alarming symptoms of disaffection. Of course, other and more general factors were contributing to the demoralization of the forces stationed at Tsarskoe Selo; the phenomenon was virtually nation-wide during the spring and summer of 1917. The noose of circumstance was gradually tightening around the throats of the new rulers in Petrograd as well as round those of the former ones in Tsarskoe Selo. Perhaps at this point we should interrupt the story of the Imperial Family's last days for a brief look at the general situation in Russia during the first few months of the democratic regime.

The most tragic thing about the period immediately after the March Revolution in Russia is that it was a time of hope. A number of policemen and a few officers had been lynched during the Petrograd uprising, or just after it, but in the main the Russian people showed themselves astonishingly free of vindictiveness toward their former oppressors. The nobles not only retained their heads, but in most cases their estates. Arson and pillage were far rarer in the countryside than they had been during the insurrectionary troubles of 1905. Disorder, in the sense of the breakdown of discipline and of methodical administration, was almost universal—it was particularly evident in the army—but at first it was seldom accompanied by violence. The Russian people misused their new-found freedom in nearly every possible way, except by failing to enjoy it, and their enjoyment kept them good-humored in the midst of chaos. Their gravest revolutionary excesses were the excesses of verbalism. After the censorship and snooping of the Czarist regime it was a delight to speak one's mind freely. To this delight the Russians abandoned themselves utterly and irresponsibly. It was the golden age of demagogy, and democratic Russia was the Eldorado of the soap box. In the big cities every factory, every office, every street corner was a forum.

"Crowds form in the streets on any occasion," noted a Western observer in Petrograd at the end of April. "One man stops to chat with another; passers-by gather around to listen in. Soon the first man is delivering an ideological harangue, and hecklers in the audience are answering him back."

Oddly enough, the Bolsheviks, though they were better staffed with experienced and uninhibited agitators than most of the revolutionary parties, were not spectacularly successful in these bloodless street battles of ideas, at least when this target was the masses. The Russian peasant, the Russian worker and the Russian soldier in 1917 were all for pie-in-the-sky and peace on earth but they generally disapproved of civil massacre and organized defeatism as means of attaining them. Lenin's ruthless bid for power, his program of revolutionary dictatorship and his call for immediate peace at any price seemed shocking to idealistic Russian leftists, including some of his own party. In June when he announced before an all-Russian congress of soviets that the Bolsheviks were ready to take over the government at any moment, and that their first act would be to hang fifty or a hundred capitalists, Kerensky indignantly interrupted him. "You Bolsheviks," he shouted from the floor, "what are you? Socialists or police of the old regime?" Not only the congress, but most of Russia applauded the rebuke.

Yet the Bolsheviks, galvanized by Lenin's audacity and driven on by his implacable will, were making steady headway all the time. Much of their effort was devoted, as it had been in Czarist times, to underground organization and agitation, but at certain levels their progress was clearly visible. They did not care greatly about the intellectuals and they were unable to win over the masses—even after they came to power, in the last free (or semi-free) elections ever held in Russia the Bolsheviks still trailed behind the Social-Revolutionaries, the old-fashioned party of agrarian discontent—but they succeeded better than any Russian party in converting to their views what might be termed the revolutionary elites: the soldiers and workers who would be most valuable as the cadres or technicians of a coup d'état.

Lenin's prize recruit was Trotsky, who arrived from America in mid-May and after a few weeks of fellow-traveling formally joined the Bolsheviks in July. A big name in Russian revolutionary circles because of his role in 1905, Trotsky, now thirty-eight, was at the height of his volcanic powers. With his dark eyes flashing behind his spectacles, his wild upstanding shock of hair that always seemed about to shoot out sparks of static electricity, and his heavy authoritative mustaches, Trotsky was Kerensky's only rival—or master—as a mob orator. What was more important from the Bolshevik point of view was that he was a trained, wily conspirator, a brilliant revolutionary organizer, and a genius in respect to the tactics and strategy of revolutionary war. Lenin incarnated the indomitable power drive of the Bolsheviks, the party's operational conscience; Trotsky was to be the technician of victory. It was a formidable partnership—Robespierre plus Napoleon—and any regime threatened by such a combination of deadly talents obviously had cause for concern. Probably no other revolutionary movement in history has had such superbly effective leadership at the highest level as the Bolsheviks possessed in 1917. It was unquestionably one of the reasons for their ultimate triumph—but it was not the only one.

"Would you have mastered the Bolsheviks if you had made a separate peace?" Lord Beaverbrook, the British publisher, asked Kerensky when they were introduced in a London club by Sir Bruce Lockhart, who relates the anecdote in his memoirs, British Agent, "Of course," Kerensky replied (according to Lockhart). "We should be in Moscow now."

Some skepticism is permissible, given the caliber of the opposition that Kerensky faced and the inherent weaknesses of the dual-power system in Russia that he had helped to set up. Moreover Kerensky frittered away

Russia's hopes for a democratic future by failing to come up with sufficiently clear-cut solutions to two of the country's most basic problems. One was the land-hunger of the peasants which left-wing demagogy exploited by agitating for immediate distribution of private estates. The other was the national aspirations of the Empire's subject peoples: Poles, Finns, Ukrainians, Baltic nations, and the smaller ethnic minorities. All these submerged nations began to stir after the March Revolution; a bold federalist program might have held their separatist tendencies within bounds and at the same time have won over their middle classes as allies of Russian democracy against the Bolshevik threat. Instead, as the German historian Georg von Rauch puts it, "The Provisional Government remained as before a slave of the narrow, nationalist and centralist thinking of the overthrown Czarist regime," and the minorities became more and more alienated.

There is no doubt, however, that the Provisional Government in trying to keep Russia in the war killed whatever slender chances of survival it may have had. George Kennan argues rather convincingly that only a general compromise peace might possibly have saved the democratic regime in Russia. President Wilson, who in his speech of April 2, 1917, calling for a declaration of war against the Central Powers had hailed "the wonderful and heartening things that have been happening the last few weeks in Russia," made no move in the direction of peace—quite the contrary—and neither did the other Allied leaders. Instead they put heavy pressure on the new Russian government to fight on to victory. When Milyukov at the beginning of May pledged Russia to do exactly that—the pledge was in the form of a diplomatic note to Russia's allies—he provoked the first political crisis of the new regime. The Finnish Regiment threatened to mutiny and there were riots in the capital. To ease the strain, Milyukov and Guchkov resigned, Prince Lvov brought several moderate socialists into the government and Kerensky took over the War Ministry.

The warning did not suffice. The Allies not only stepped up their pressure on the Provisional Government to stay in the war—"No fight, no loans," as former Secretary of State Elihu Root succinctly put it when he arrived at the head of an American aid mission in June—but began insisting that the battered, disorganized Russian armies once more take the offensive. Kerensky, despite his earlier misgivings (and his later hindsight) responded enthusiastically to this suicidal demand. Wearing a peasant blouse and a military cap he toured the trenches, haranguing the troops. He replaced Alexeyev as commander-in-chief with General A. A. Brusilov, the most brilliant, and reputedly the most socialist of the Russian generals; he somehow persuaded the military soviets to co-operate with the officer corps in restoring discipline. On the home front he instigated a vigorous campaign against defeatism. Even the Ex Com of the Petrograd Soviet joined in with an appeal to the soldiers which informed them that they were no longer "fighting for the Czar, for Protopopov, Rasputin and the rich, but for Russian freedom and the Revolution."

The army's response was almost miraculous. Overnight, it seemed, it became again an effective fighting force. July 1, after a two-day artillery preparation, 31 Russian divisions clambered out of the trenches on the Galician front and rushed at the enemy with their old-time elan. For two days they made good progress. Then the offensive bogged down. When the Russian shock troops were used up and the reserves sufficiently exhausted, the Germans launched a devastating counteroffensive. The Russian front collapsed. This was when the Russian soldier started voting with his feet, as Lenin was later to put it.

On the day that the German counteroffensive started, a left-wing insurrection against the Provisional Government broke out in Petrograd. It was spearheaded by anarchist sailors from the Kronstadt naval base, and covertly supported—possibly instigated—by the Bolsheviks. For a few hours the result was in doubt. Then the government collected a sufficient force of Cossacks and other loyal troops and after three days of fighting in the streets stamped out the rebellion. Lenin went into hiding, eventually escaping to Finland. Trotsky and several other Bolshevik leaders, who had scorned flight, were imprisoned and the Bolshevik headquarters in the palace of the dancer Ksesinskaya—the early flame of Nicholas II—was closed down. The party paper, *Pravda,* was suppressed.

The leftist fiasco in the July days, as the abortive uprising is usually termed, temporarily saved the Provisional Government from the consequences of the debacle at the front, and brought Kerensky to the Premiership—he succeeded Prince Lvov on July 20. The Bolshevik role in the disorders had destroyed any remaining illusions Kerensky may have had about Lenin, Trotsky, and their companions as being "normal" Socialist leaders, just a little more extreme in their views perhaps, than others. The Bolsheviks, Kerensky now realized, were ruthless and incorrigible conspirators. Evidence collected by the Russian military counterespionage service purporting to establish that Lenin was a paid German agent played a big part in this phase of Kerensky's political education. With his acute sense of propaganda he made the dubious information the basis for a violent campaign against the Bolsheviks, accusing them—among other crimes—of having deliberately fomented the July rising on orders from their German employers to support the counteroffensive on the Galician front. The evidence available to Kerensky in 1917, while sometimes close to the truth, was not true evidence; it led him to underestimate his adversaries—if the Bolshevik leaders had been German agents, mere venal adventurers, they would have proved much less dangerous than they turned out to be—and it may help to explain why the governmental smear campaign against the party, after initially arousing a great deal of patriotic indignation, eventually ceased to interest the Russian public.[1]

By mid-August the Bolsheviks, though their leaders were still proscribed or under arrest, had largely recouped their political losses of July; history often forgives those who dare too much too soon. Agitation was spreading again in the factories and in the demoralized army. The Petrograd Soviet which at first had been deeply impressed by the revelations of Bolshevik iniquity, was drawing away from the government again. At the same time, the conservative elements in Russia who had applauded Kerensky's crackdown on the Bolsheviks were unmistakably losing confidence in him as a reliable bulwark against revolution. The ground was beginning to quiver under Kerensky's feet. In trying to stave off disaster, he carried out a series of overly subtle—or perhaps simply wild—moves on the political chess board that eventually precipitated it. One of his luckless pawns was the ex-Czar.

Like many other members of the old regime, the Romanovs were relieved at the outcome of the July days and their confidence in the ability of the Provisional Government to save Russia from disaster was momentarily restored. "It is all such chaos," Nicholas wrote when he heard about the fighting in the capital. "Luckily the troops remained loyal to the government and order is restored." The soldiers of the Tsarskoe Selo garrison were among those who had remained loyal, but their loyalty, like everything else in Russia at that time, was provisional; it soon began to waver again, and the prisoners in the palace could gauge the steady worsening of the political climate by the increasing rudeness of their guards. Simultaneously, the soviets in Tsarskoe Selo and in Petrograd renewed their sniping at the government for "pampering" the former Imperial Family.

The decision to move the ex-Czar and his family away from the vicinity of the capital had been taken even before the July insurrection, and Nicho-

---

[1] The real facts were that the Germans had increased their financial and other assistance to the Bolsheviks after the March Revolution, but that the Bolsheviks continued to pocket it as before and do as they pleased. They needed no outside orders or encouragement to attack the Provisional Government. A telegram from the German Foreign Ministry to GHQ dated December 3, 1917, but referring to the period before the November Revolution puts the matter in sound perspectives: "Russia appeared to be the weakest link in the enemy chain. The task therefore was to loosen it, and when possible, to remove it. This was the purpose of the subversive activity we caused to be carried out in Russia behind the front—in the first place promotion of separatist tendencies and support of the Bolsheviks. It was not until the Bolsheviks had received from us a steady flow of funds through various channels that they were in a position to be able to build up their main organ *Pravda* to conduct energetic propaganda, and appreciably to extend the originally narrow basis of their party. The Bolsheviks have now come to power . . ." The message goes on to recommend continued support on the grounds that it is in the German interest to keep the Bolsheviks in power. There is no claim to exercising any direct control over them; there is the claim that German financial help contributed to their victory.

las had been informed. He was neither surprised nor worried when Kerensky warned him early in August that it was now imperative to execute the decision without further delay. The actual departure on the early morning of August 14 was tumultuous. The soldiers of the palace guard were indignant that the prisoners were being allowed to take along all the luggage they liked and reluctant to see them go at all. The trial of the Romanovs would soon be taking place in Petrograd, the soldiers argued, and they should be held where there was no chance of their escaping; in fact it might be better all round if "things were managed without a trial." It took all of Kerensky's powers of persuasion to get the family and their party safely to the special train that was waiting for them. "Remember that one does not strike a fallen adversary," he sternly reminded the train guards at the station.

Up to almost the last minute, the Romanovs had supposed they were being transferred to their estates in the Crimea; according to some accounts, it was not until the train had pulled out of Tsarskoe Selo that Nicholas learned their real destination was Tobolsk, in western Siberia. The choice of this remote provincial center—it was off the main railroad line to Vladivostok, and the last lap of the trip was by river steamer—reflects the complexity both of the political situation in Russia and of Kerensky's character. The Romanovs would probably have been safer in the south where there was a good deal of monarchist, or at least conservative, sentiment, but the train trip would have required a strong military escort and sending them there might have triggered a major political crisis. Tobolsk was virtually untouched by the revolutionary unrest that prevailed in European Russia; Nicholas and his family would be quite safe there, they would be out of the public eye, and eventually it might be possible to slip them discreetly out of the country to Japan. At the same time Tobolsk was in Siberia —the traditional place of exile for political and other criminals. It had overtones of prison camp and salt mine. Nobody could accuse Kerensky of betraying the revolution because he had sent the Romanovs to Siberia; on the contrary, it demonstrated that he was a loyal son of the Revolution, a true man of the left. The demonstration seemed all the more useful, from Kerensky's viewpoint, because at the moment he was drawing closer to the right. He had agreed to restore the death penalty in the army and had appointed General Kornilov, a stern disciplinarian, commander-in-chief.

Transferring the former Imperial Family to their ambivalent haven-exile was a dexterous maneuver, but dexterity was not what the situation chiefly called for. Kerensky's problem was to win the confidence and respect of the numerous elements both to the right and to the left of the Provisional Government who were ready to follow, or at least accept, his leadership if they could be brought to feel a little more sure that he knew where he was going. The sleight of hand by which he had managed to whisk the Romanovs away to Tobolsk reassured nobody; its very cleverness tended to sharpen the vague mistrust that he had inspired from the first in the minds of many Russians. It is possible that his handling of the affair was in itself a significant factor in the misunderstanding that now arose between Kerensky and General Kornilov; in any case it illustrated the self-defeating, slightly shysterish disingenuity on Kerensky's part that contributed to the fatal break between the two men.

Kerensky, of course, was not solely to blame for what happened. Kornilov's lack of political maturity, his impatience, and probably his ambition were contributory factors. So were the divergent intrigues or pressures of Russia's allies: the British and French military attachés were egging on Kornilov, while the U. S. Embassy encouraged Kerensky to resist his demands. At first the two men agreed, or thought they had agreed, on the need for a firm hand both in the army and on the home front. Then Kornilov began to feel that Kerensky was weaseling out of his agreements, while Kerensky came to look on Kornilov as a potential rival and as a threat to Russian democracy. The noisy support that the right gave to what soon became known as "Kornilovism" naturally added to these fears. Kornilov, who was the son of a Siberian Cossack, was not a monarchist, but he believed that some form of rule more authoritarian than the existing Provisional Government was needed to rescue the nation from chaos, and he was quite frankly preparing a military coup against the Petrograd Soviet and its left-wing supporters. Kerensky gave the pugnacious commander-in-chief the impression that he acquiesced in the scheme, but he may have been misled about its full scope. The whole affair was a fearful and complex imbroglio in which reciprocal lack of confidence led each man to act more and more behind the other's back, thereby generating graver suspicion. Finally, on September 9, with Kornilov's Cossacks moving on Petrograd, Kerensky trapped him into some incriminating admissions and dismissed him from his post.

Kornilov retaliated with a *pronunciamento* against the Provisional Government and ordered his cavalry under General Krymov to occupy the capital. Kerensky appealed to the Petrograd Soviet for help and called the workers to arms. Trotsky, from his prison cell, urged the Bolsheviks to rally round the government, and a kind of informal popular front sprang up. Lenin's followers eagerly accepted the weapons which were thrust in their hands. Apparently the Kornilovists had not expected mass resistance and the risk of civil war unnerved them. General Krymov allowed himself to be captured without a fight, then blew his brains out. Kornilov and his staff tamely submitted to arrest.

That was the end of the *putsch*. It was, of course, also the end of Kerensky's anti-Bolshevik front, which since the July days, had held together the more responsible elements of the left and the more intelligent elements of the right. Trotsky and most of the other imprisoned Bolshevik leaders were released. Kerensky proclaimed the republic, nominated himself president and commander-in-chief of the armed forces and set up a new government which included several leftists—among them the new War Minister, General Verkhovsky, the acting military attaché in Belgrade at the time of Sarajevo. For political support it relied upon the most incorrigibly fuzzy-minded elements of the non-Communist left; Mensheviks, Social-Revolutionaries, and allied splinter groups.

The Kornilov revolt was both a fatal and a fantastic episode in Russian history. The tough little general with the Tartar eyes and the hard mouth behaved, when the chips were down, like a military Kerensky; the former socialist lawyer whose name was to become a by-word for flabby liberalism played the part of a typical condottiere, intrepid and irresponsible. His lightning switch from a center-right coalition against chaos to a center-left alliance with it was not mere sleight of hand; it was the political equivalent of the circus performer's *saut perilleux* a double flip-flop from the high trapeze without a net. These suicidal acrobatics were inspired not by desperation but by overconfidence. Kerensky believed that in crushing the Kornilov *putsch,* which he had earlier encouraged, he had somehow won a major victory over the left as well as over the right. While he may have underrated the sincerity of the Bolsheviks as revolutionaries, he was anything but blind to their duplicity as associates; he counted on his own cleverness and agility to outwit them. Insofar as Kerensky's strategic miscalculations were influenced by an ideological factor, it was the familiar failure of the literary of forensic mind to appreciate how much the power of ideas depends on the efficiency of the social machinery through which they are put into action. Kerensky thought of himself as the savior of democracy and assumed that democratic opinion in Russia was with him; even if he had been right—which is doubtful—it was largely unarmed and even unorganized opinion, the kind that can scarcely win an election, let alone a revolution. Russian liberals were prone to overlook such details, not because liberalism and realism are antithetical, but because the old-fashioned Russian upper-class education which had nourished their special variety of liberalism did not take adequate account of modern social and political reality.

An even deeper factor helps to explain the extraordinary ineptitude of most Russian anti-Bolshevik leadership—both liberal and conservative—particularly the instability of character which was its chief common trait. The Provisional Government had to some extent filled the power-vacuum created by the collapse of autocracy, but it could not inspire the awe needed to fill the vacuum of authority. The sudden eclipse of the formidable father-image that the Czar represented left the Russian people—especially its ruling classes—rudderless, and their disorientation was not only emotional, but in a sense functional. The old Russia had been the most bureaucratic and the most hierarchic society in the modern world; its very titles of nobility were but the hereditary ranks of service. The decision-making process in the Russian state when it worked at all, had worked strictly from the top down, and co-ordination, where it existed, was inseparable from command. It was in the Czar's name that the trains ran on time—when they did. Only a despotic will could effectively replace the institutional will of the fallen despotism, and nobody but Lenin seemed to possess one. His adversaries, cut off from any central source of authority that they respected, unaccustomed to taking the initiative, frightened of responsibility and without the gift or habit of spontaneous co-operation that most Western peoples possess, could not learn in time to pull together, or even to pull themselves together. Sometimes they wavered and dithered, sometimes they rushed prematurely and recklessly into action. On certain occasions they threw their lives away on lost causes, on others they gave up at the first touch of adversity. They quarreled incessantly among themselves over secondary issues. On the rare occasions when they agreed on a common objective they could not concert their efforts to achieve it. Without a Czar on his throne, it seemed, his partisans could not even synchronise their watches.

The collective failure of the Russian elites to meet the challenge of revolution—as illustrated by the Kornilov fiasco, among others—reflects the inadequacies of their training for leadership, but it was also a symptom that Russian society, and not merely the Russian state, was breaking down. This was no less true in Tobolsk, despite the appearance of provincial calm, than it was in Petrograd or on the Western Front.

For a short while life at Tobolsk was easier and pleasanter for the Romanovs than it had been at Tsarskoe Selo. The former residence of the provincial governor, a large two-storied stone building, provided comfortable, if not luxurious, quarters for them. For service and companionship they had a retinue of some 40 persons, including domestic help, who had followed them to Siberia. Food was plentiful. Nicholas missed his long walks in the park at Tsarskoe Selo—for exercise he sawed wood—but the family felt less shut in than before since they were now permitted to go to church in town once a day. The services were open to the public, and the guards who escorted them through the streets did not seem to intimidate the townspeople, who saluted their former rulers with respect whenever they encountered them. The relaxed and unrevolutionary atmosphere of the locality tended to make the soldiers themselves more civil toward their prisoners. The guard was now under the sole command of Colonel Kobylinsky—whose monarchist sympathies had not changed—and it was the only military unit in the immediate vicinity; discipline naturally improved.

The first warning of impending danger, from the viewpoint of the royal exiles, was the arrival in Tobolsk during the month of September of two political commissars sent by Kerensky to keep watch on them. Their mission reflected the growing influence of the left upon the Provisional Government after the Kornilov revolt. Both envoys were Social-Revolutionaries of rather extreme views, and both had served time in Siberia under the autocracy. Though the senior commissar, an idealistic revolutionary of the old type, treated his fallen enemies with marked kindness, the presence of the two inevitably introduced a new chill into the hitherto mild Siberian air. To the Romanovs—and particularly to Alexandra—they were no better than Bolsheviks. Kobylinsky was more discerning, but he blamed the commissars for inadvertently undermining the discipline and loyalty of his garrison through the indoctrination course that they conducted for the soldiers. The change in the attitude of the soldiers from mid-September on was undeniable, but it probably stemmed more from the general loss of confidence in the Kerensky regime—aggravated in this particular case by the government's failure to honor earlier promises of extra pay—than by ideological factors.

In November news of the successful Bolshevik *putsch* in the capital reached western Siberia. It spread gloom and anxiety in many circles, but even in the ex-Czar's entourage it did not have the bombshell effect that one might suppose. The "ten days that shook the world" (the title of John Reed's idealized but vivid firsthand report on the November Revolution in Petrograd) did not at first shake Tobolsk. The reasons for this relative equanimity are interesting.

In the first place, Lenin's followers did not at that time command either the admiration or the hatred and the dread that they later inspired. They were Communists, but so in theory were all other Marxists. They were also Maximalists, meaning that they were in a hurry to achieve their maximum objectives, and therefore prepared to use extreme methods, but there were various other Maximalists in Russia, among whom the anarchists and certain of the left-wing Social-Revolutionaries, sounded wilder, more extreme, than the Bolsheviks. The ruthless and cynical perversion of the Marxist ideal that Bolshevism was destined to become under the dictatorship of Stalin had not as yet had a chance to manifest itself; it was only a virtuality, and the elements in Lenin's own thought or behavior which might have seemed to foreshadow the future nightmare were not taken at quite their face value by his adversaries. In the eyes of Russian reactionaries like the ex-Czar, all revolutionaries, including democratic ones, were just Reds, and they were all equally abhorrent except to the degree that they admitted the necessity of fighting for Mother Russia. Though Nicholas, himself, had often treated Russia as if it were his private family estate, at heart he was a nationalist, and in his fashion a patriot. What seems to have distressed him the most about the developments in Petrograd is that they had finally brought to power men whom he regarded essentially as internationalists and pacifists—which many of the Bolsheviks themselves thought they still were. Nicholas' feelings about the Bolsheviks were in some respects akin to those of a Daughter of the American Revolution about UNESCO; the habit of viewing with alarm eventually dulls the centers of apprehension upon which survival may depend.

In the second place what was known about the circumstances in which the Bolsheviks had taken over control of the state encouraged the widespread belief that events would soon wrest it from their grip. The Communist Dream, as interpreted by the Bolsheviks and their other Maximalist allies, had unquestionably captured the imagination and enthusiasm of many Russian workers, but it had not displayed an irresistible power of attraction in the country at large. In Petrograd itself, with its huge industrial population, the Bolsheviks had only won a bare majority in the last elections for the local soviet. The insurrection against the Provisional Government—even as witnessed through the eyes of such True Believers as John Reed—does not evoke the spectacle of spontaneous mass enthusiasm that characterized the March uprising. As we know now, it was a premeditated coup d'état inspired by Lenin (and ultimately directed by him) but organized mainly by Trotsky, who exploited with consummate skill the tactical possibilities inherent in his newly won office as president of the Petrograd Soviet. Preparations for the coup had been camouflaged as defensive measures against a renewed assault of the "Kornilovists," and a justificatory pretext for launching it was furnished by provoking the government into striking the first blow. During the night of November 6–7, the Bolshevik shock troops, mainly the Red Guard worker-militiamen whom Kerensky had thoughtlessly armed during the Kornilov scare stealthily infiltrated a number of key positions in the city. The sailors from the cruiser *Aurora*—which Kerensky had ordered to the capital in September—along with some mutinous machine-gun units and other troops joined the Bolsheviks. The bulk of the still-dependable army units with which the government might have crushed the revolt as in July had been removed from the vicinity of the capital out of fear of another rightist *putsch*. The loyal forces immediately available in Petrograd were inadequate, and within twenty-four hours the government, under bombardment in the Winter Palace, from the *Aurora,* was forced to capitulate. It was probably the Bolsheviks' good luck that while most of the ministers were arrested Kerensky managed to escape and reach army headquarters at Pskov. His fiery appeals to drive the usurpers out of the capital led to a piecemeal and improvised counter-offensive that was doomed before it started. Many of the Russian generals who still retained some authority over their troops refused all support to the man they considered mainly responsible for the country's misfortunes, while others were paralyzed by the fear of antagonizing the soldiers' soviets. Finally Kerensky persuaded a Cossack commander, General P. N. Krasnov, to move on Petrograd with a sketchily equipped detachment of some 700 men. Whatever chance Krasnov had of regaining control in the capital with this force was lost through delay—mainly the result of a strike called by the railway workers in the queer belief that they were making a useful protest against the Bolshevik coup d'état. After a brief skirmish with a body of Red militia at Tsarskoe Selo, Krasnov's Cossacks began to show signs of disaffection, and Kerensky, who was accompanying them, gave up the fight, escaping in disguise. (He later slipped across the Finnish border with the help of the British agent Bruce Lockhart, and vanished into the wings of history.) A Bolshevik rising in Moscow to support the Petrograd one barely succeeded in the face of uncoordinated resistance.

The political victory, like the military one, went to the Bolsheviks largely by default. A congress of delegates from all the soviets in Russia was just starting to meet in Petrograd when the Bolsheviks rose against the Provisional Government. (Trotsky had deliberately timed his coup to coincide with the opening of the congress.) Even in this body, representing the revolutionary elements of the Russian masses, the Bolsheviks could not command an absolute majority. They obtained a nominal one when their opponents—chiefly the Mensheviks and the less extreme Social Revolutionaries—walked out in protest against the insurrection instead of remaining in the assembly and blocking the Bolshevik attempts to legitimate it. It was thus a rump congress consisting only of Bolshevik delegates and the dissident left wing of the Social Revolutionaries which next day gave the stamp of Soviet approval to the new governmental authority, the Council of People's Commissars, formed and headed by Lenin. The November Revolution which was to prove so fateful in its consequences did not seem enormously impressive—except to its most enthralled adherents—while it was in progress. The Soviet power that it set up scarcely looked formidable to its adversaries. No doubt if the Bolsheviks had conducted themselves like their predecessors it would never have proved so.

As far as Tobolsk was concerned, the fragility of the new authority in Petrograd seemed to be demonstrated by its failure to assert itself locally. In the first few weeks after the *putsch* the Tobolsk region turned neither Red nor White; like much of the Russian countryside remote from the chief industrial centers it remained the same pinkish gray as before. The letters that Alexandra was able to continue sending to Anna Vyrubova and other friends in the capital until well into 1918 reflect a rising sense of personal insecurity and a deepening distress over the plight of Russia, but not the impact of a single overriding and irreversible calamity. The resignation and "meekness" with which her husband continues to bear his trials is mentioned in tones that are half admiring, half exasperated.

Kerensky's two political commissars at Tobolsk presumably became Lenin's—it was not entirely clear—and stayed where they were. More surprisingly Colonel Kobylinsky neither arrested them in the name of the counterrevolutionary authority that was beginning to raise its head in the south, nor was arrested by them as an unrepentant monarchist. No orders arrived either to execute the former Imperial Family or to return them to Petrograd for trial. The Bolsheviks merely suppressed the living allowance they had been receiving from the Provisional Government with the painful result that the Romanov credit soon ran out in the local shops. By the end of the year Alexandra was being kept busy patching and darning her husband's clothes, knitting wool socks to replace her invalid son's last pair. The increasing grimness of life in Tobolsk is reflected by the entry in Nicholas' diary for the last day of 1917 (it was also the last time he wrote in it): "After tea we all parted for the night—without waiting for the New Year. Lord, my God, save Russia. . ."

Uncomfortable—and dangerous—as their situation was, Nicholas and his family did not lose heart. Plans to rescue them were nearing fruition—or so they imagined. The story is fascinating in a way, but like so much Russian history, it reads as if it had been laboriously contrived by some third-rate dramatist with no flair for the emotional authenticity of his scenes, and few scruples about the plausibility of his intrigue; the kind of tragic playwright who can take his nemesis but never, never leave it alone. The man on whom the Romanovs pinned their hopes was a glib and personable young adventurer named Boris Soloviev, an army lieutenant formerly attached to the staff of a rather left-wing general; he also happened to be the posthumous son-in-law (if the term can be used) of Gregory Rasputin. It was only in October 1917 that Soloviev married the starets' daughter Matrona, who was then living in Tobolsk; a few days later, thanks to his family connection with the late Man of God, he established contact with the ex-Czarina and her husband. Soloviev represented himself to them as the accredited agent of a mysterious monarchist underground called the Brotherhood of St. John of Tobolsk and explained that he had been sent to Siberia to organize their rescue. He had, of course, no difficulty in convincing the Romanovs that their salvation was at hand, and he easily persuaded them to have no dealings with any other monarchist groups that might try to come to their aid, lest such contacts jeopardize the plans of the Brotherhood. The Brothers, Soloviev declared, were assembling around Tiumen, the nearest railhead on the Trans-Siberian, and he would establish his own headquarters there, coming to Tobolsk from time to time to keep his sovereigns informed about the progress of the conspiracy for their liberation.

While the Brotherhood was no doubt largely fictitious, it was not a one-man organization. Soloviev had agents in European Russia who demonstrated their existence by collecting substantial funds from monarchist sympathizers. A scout sent independently to western Siberia by a Petrograd group which included Anna Vyrubova came back with the news that Rasputin's son-in-law had assumed sole responsibility for rescuing the Im-

perial Family. On hearing the magic name, Anna urged all her fellow conspirators to avoid any interference with Soloviev's network and to confine
their activity to raising funds for it. In so doing, she inadvertently helped
to doom her exiled friends. The emissary of still another monarchist organization who reached Tiumen was warned off by Soloviev and gave up
the attempt to establish direct contact with the captives in Tobolsk.

Faith in Soloviev's honesty and competence helped sustain the Romanovs
through the bleak Siberian winter, while day by day the physical hardships
of their captivity increased and the attitude of their guards—who now refused to take orders from anyone—became more menacing. Alexandra's
faith was still intact at the end of March 1918 when a detachment of Red
troops from Omsk, at that time under Bolshevik control, paraded through
the streets of Tobolsk. The ex-Czarina was convinced that they were members of Soloviev's Brotherhood in disguise. "There go some good Russians,"
she told her maid as the Bolsheviks marched past.

During the civil war, Soloviev joined the Red Army in Siberia, and was
later arrested, along with his wife, by the Whites. He finally escaped somehow to Berlin, where he turned up in the 1920s. Whether he was a German
agent, a Bolshevik agent, a confidence man, or simply an irresponsible
schemer is still obscure. In any case, like his deceased father-in-law, he was
a curious but deadly instrument of destiny. He made no overt move to get
the Romanovs away from Tobolsk but his presence in Tiumen effectively
blocked all other rescue attempts at a time when they had a real chance
of success.

Things might have been different, possibly, if the Rasputin scandal had
not previously split the ranks of Russian monarchists and discredited the
very idea of the monarchy in the minds of many who had once been its
loyal supporters. "It is precisely because I knew the monarchy as it really
was, that I don't want to have anything more to do with it," General
Alexeyev, who was to be one of the chief organizers of the anti-Bolshevik
counterrevolution once explained to a monarchist friend. Some leaders of
the White movement that began to crystallize in southern Russia (and later
in Siberia) during the winter of 1917–1918 were monarchists, but others
were socialists; the movement as a whole was not dedicated to putting the
Romanovs back on the throne, and saving the lives of the former Imperial
Couple does not seem to have been a high-priority objective in the minds of
its adherents.

It is possible that an attempt was made to rescue the ex-Czar and his
family—or at least part of his family—after Soloviev dropped out of the
picture, but that is another queer story. Before going into it, a brief summary of events on the main theaters of political and diplomatic action during the first few months of the new Soviet power may prove useful.

On the day—November 8, 1917—Lenin took office as chairman of the Provisional Government's revolutionary successor, the Council of People's Commissars, his chance of remaining in power for more than a few weeks seemed slight. The Bolshevik dictatorship had only the flimsiest juridical basis, it possessed no overwhelming military strength, it was hated or despised by most of the nation's officialdom, and it lacked the support of public opinion. In the elections for the Constituent Assembly on November 25—the date had been fixed before the Bolshevik coup d'état—the Bolsheviks polled a little less than a quarter of the national vote. The chief victors were the Social-Revolutionaries who won 370 out of 707 seats, while the Bolsheviks won 175, and the dissident left-wing Social-Revolutionaries, their only political allies, obtained 40. As Leonard Schapiro observes, more than half the country had voted for Socialism, but against Bolshevism. In the face of this result Lenin proceeded to demonstrate the essential difference between the Bolsheviks and nearly all other Socialists: their contempt for democratic principles. When the Constituent Assembly met on January 18, 1918, and a Bolshevik resolution supported by the dissident Social-Revolutionaries, was rejected, Lenin ordered the meeting hall to be occupied by Red Guards and locked out the delegates. That was the end of Russian democracy. "The dissolution of the Constituent Assembly means the complete and open repudiation of the democratic idea in favor of the dictatorship concept," Lenin declared with his customary brutal frankness. From that time all overt opposition to the new despotism would be considered as counterrevolutionary. And to meet the threat of "counterrevolution" the Bolsheviks had already forged the weapon of revolutionary terror in the form of the special security committees that were soon to be known as the Cheka. "Do not believe that I am concerned with formal justice," warned the first head of the Cheka, Felix Dzerzhinsky, the strange Polish fanatic who was to be the Grand Inquisitor of the Bolshevik regime. ". . . I demand the forging of the revolutionary sword that will annihilate all counter-revolutionaries!"[2]

Lenin, of course, was too intelligent to rely on terror alone. While preparing to crush his left-wing rivals by force he had already appropriated one of the key planks in the Social-Revolutionary platform which the Bolsheviks had earlier condemned as demagogic. Instead of nationalizing privately owned land in accordance with orthodox Bolshevik doctrine, Lenin had promulgated a decree simply authorizing the village committees to seize and distribute it among the peasants—which they had already started doing without authorization before the Bolsheviks came in. Above all Lenin counted on the magic in the word "peace." In his first address to the Con-

[2] Quoted by Georg von Rauch in *A History of Soviet Russia* (Praeger 1958) from the Soviet writer N. Zubov. The quote from Lenin in the same paragraph is also taken from von Rauch, citing Trotsky.

gress of Soviets on November 8, he had called on all the belligerent governments to open negotiations for a "just and democratic peace" without annexations or indemnities. A "peace decree" along these lines was solemnly published by the Soviet government and its provisions embodied in a diplomatic note dispatched to all belligerents by Trotsky in his new capacity as People's Commissar for Foreign Affairs. The note specifically proposed negotiations for a general armistice. When Russia's allies disregarded the proposal, the Soviet Government, on December 15, concluded a separate four-week armistice with Germany and Austria-Hungary.

Formal peace negotiations between Russian and Central powers got under way at Brest-Litovsk, a railhead in western Russia then occupied by the Germans, on December 22. They were destined to leave a traumatic imprint upon the personality of the emerging Soviet power at the same time that they helped to transmit the revolutionary virus into the bloodsream of the Kaiser's Empire.

The Russian delegation was headed first by A. Joffe, then by Trotsky himself. Both he and Lenin, despite the realism on which they prided themselves, had no realization of the trap into which they were walking. They took it for granted that the proletariat of the Western world would follow the revolutionary example of their Russian brothers within a matter of months or even weeks; in the meantime they counted on the German workers to exert irresistible pressure upon the Kaiser's generals and diplomats. Perhaps, too, the earlier clandestine contacts between the German government and certain of their comrades had given them a misleading impression of the peace conditions that the Germans were prepared to offer or accept.

For the Bolsheviks, the awakening was terrible. As a starter the Central Powers demanded that Russia cede Poland and the Baltic territories. Recognition of Finnish independence was soon added to the conditions. Then came the crusher: Russia must also recognize the independence of the Ukraine, which had been proclaimed by the anti-Bolshevik and pro-German local government in Kiev on January 1. Some of the Austrian and even German delegates felt that the precarious Soviet regime was being strained to the breaking point, but this did not worry General Ludendorff, the occult dictator of Germany and the real author of the Brest-Litovsk *diktat.* "Paranoia had him [Ludendorff] in its grip," declares John W. Wheeler-Bennett in his masterly *Brest-Litovsk: The Forgotten Peace,* and the diagnosis seems plausible. Ludendorff's ultimate aim was the total dismemberment of Russia and though this objective implied the final liquidation of the Romanov dynasty it had seemingly been approved by the Kaiser. In fact, according to Wheeler-Bennett, a dangerous rivalry had developed among the minor German royal or princely houses over the distribution of the expected Eastern spoils; the Duke of Urach in Wurttemberg, for example, was claiming the crown of Lithuania, Prince Friedrich Karl of Hesse that of Finland, and Wilhelm was planning to reserve for himself the title of Duke of Courland subsequently of Latvia.

Bolshevik demagogy had disintegrated the Russian army as a force-in-being, and the Soviet government was virtually at the mercy of the victorious Germans. In a feeble attempt to exert counterpressure the Bolsheviks intensified revolutionary agitation and propaganda among German or Austro-Hungarian prisoners of war held in Russia—a fateful step from the long-term viewpoint, but one without significant immediate results. Trotsky meanwhile used all the resources of his cunning to drag out the negotiations. Finally on March 3 after the German armies had resumed their advance, and were nearing Petrograd, the Soviet government accepted Ludendorff's terms, signing away more than a quarter of Russia's national territory and some 75 per cent of her coal and steel plants.

The dissident Social Revolutionaries resigned from the government in protest against accepting such conditions, and the Bolsheviks themselves were badly split. Lenin had the greatest difficulty in persuading Trotsky to give up his dreams of resisting the German Army by sabotage and guerrilla warfare. The Whites in the south, encouraged by the demonstration of Bolshevik weakness and enraged by what they considered the Bolshevik betrayal of the national cause openly raised the standard of counterrevolution, with French and British support.

By the spring of 1918 sizable White forces, led first by Alexeyev and Kornilov, then by Generals Krasnov and Anton Denikin, advanced from the northern Caucasus into the Don Basin, while Japanese military intervention in support of the local anti-Bolshevik forces began in the Far Eastern provinces. A combined British-Russian intervention force took shape on the Arctic coast at Murmansk. The Russian civil war, one of the most decisive conflicts in modern history—and also one of the cruelest—was under way. It was to rage back and forth across the former empire of the Czars—and even into some neighboring territories—until 1921, leaving famine and pestilence in its wake.

Opposed within his own party, repudiated by his only allies, under armed attack by his counterrevolutionary enemies, Lenin, who had moved the seat of the government to Moscow in March 1918, realized that in submitting to the peace of Brest-Litovsk, Soviet Russia became for the time being a hostage of Imperial Germany. The Bolshevik power could only survive as long as the German Army was willing to see it survive. A policy of cooperation, almost of partnership, with Germany was therefore a vital necessity from the short-term viewpoint; from the long-term viewpoint discreet preparations for renewing the struggle against the oppressor, possibly with Allied help, and for throwing off the chains of Brest-Litovsk were no less essential.

The German attitude toward the Bolsheviks was even more complicated. Indeed, like the German attitude toward the "liberated" populations of the Soviet Union in World War II, a quarter of a century later, it was compounded of so many contradictory guiles and greeds that it was finally incoherent. In order to release as many troops as possible for transfer to the western front, and to insure a steady flow of grain and other raw materials, it was imperative to avoid any new exactions that might goad the Soviet government into denouncing the Treaty of Brest-Litovsk; in fact it might be necessary to shore up the Soviets with financial and economic assistance (which the Germans did actually provide during the summer of 1918) to make sure that they were not replaced by a more hostile regime. PLEASE USE LARGER SUMS the German Secretary of State (Foreign Minister) wired Count Mirbach, the Kaiser's special Ambassador to the Soviet government, in May 1918, AS IT IS GREATLY IN OUR INTEREST THAT THE BOLSHEVIKS SHOULD SURVIVE. At the same time Ludendorff was determined to keep the Bolsheviks weak, so that they would be easy to liquidate after Germany had won the war in the West, and in the meantime he wanted to squeeze every possible drop of blood out of them. Ludendorff's Soviet policy was a large-scale version of the human-icebox technique by which Papuan cannibals keep their captives alive while progressively slicing off pieces of their flesh. Thus while the large German mission in Moscow—where the government had established itself in March 1918—backed the Soviets against the counterrevolutionary authorities in the south, whom the Allies were supporting, the German forces in Finland and in the Ukraine—and eventually in the Caucasus—helped the local anti-Bolshevik governments to fight the Reds who were loyal to the central government.

Ideological factors naturally aggravated the imbroglio. Most of the White leaders were pro-Allied, but some were ready to accept support from any quarter and a few were actively pro-German. From the German viewpoint these were worth building up as a sort of second team to put in in case the Bolsheviks proved unco-operative or were overthrown. But the pro-German Whites were nearly all monarchists and restoring the Romanov dynasty might seriously hamper the ultimate German plan for dismembering Russia.

"Famine is on the way and is being choked off with terror," the counselor of the German mission wrote at the beginning of June in an informal report that vividly sketched the difficulties of the Bolshevik situation and urged making a deal with their likely successors. "People are quietly shot by the hundred. All this in itself is not so bad, but there can be no doubt that the physical means with which the Bolsheviks are maintaining their power are running out . . . To facilitate the restoration of a Russia which would again be imperialist is not a pleasant perspective, but the development may perhaps be inevitable."

Even Ludendorff agreed that a new approach might be necessary.

"Though we now negotiate only with the Soviet government," he wrote on June 9, ". . . We have to acquire contacts with the right-wing monarchist groups and influence them so that the monarchist movement would be governed by our wishes as soon as it gained influence."

Such was the complex background to the last act in the tragedy of the Romanovs.

Though the swift Tobol River was still frozen and the snow still lay deep under the dark pines, spring was on its way to Tobolsk, bringing with it the magic sense of resurrection that is felt only in the High North at the breaking of winter, when an ominous new development was reported to the ex-Czar and his family. On April 22, 1918, a special representative of the Moscow government had marched into Tobolsk at the head of 150 Red soldiers. The town had been under full Bolshevik control for more than a month; in fact it was occupied by two rival Bolshevik detachments, one from Omsk and one from Ekaterinburg (today Sverdlovsk) in the Urals. In addition, the Imperial Family's special guard had formed its own soviet and chased away the two commissars sent by Kerensky (the soldiers remained, however, on speaking terms with their nominal commander Colonel Kobylinsky). The new commissar, a returned emigré named Vassili Yakovlev, was greeted with suspicion on all sides, but he had an impressive collection of written orders signed by the Bolshevik Central Committee enjoining the local authorities to give him full co-operation in carrying out an important special mission and authorizing him to shoot on the spot anyone who disobeyed him. The mission, he informed Kobylinsky, was to conduct the former Imperial Family to another place, which he declined to name. Yakovlev told the same story to the Tobolsk Soviet and to the soldiers of the special guard. Though he stubbornly refused to reveal where he had been ordered to take the Romanovs he gave the impression that it was to Moscow, where they would stand trial.

To Nicholas and Alexandra, with whom he had a private and confidential interview of April 25, he dropped some rather different hints. On the basis of this talk Nicholas seems to have come to the conclusion that Yakovlev was a German agent disguised as a Bolshevik commissar and that his real mission was to deliver the Romanovs to the Germans for some sinister political purpose. Alexandra was even more explicit in her suspicions. She was convinced that the Germans wanted to get hold of her husband to obtain his signature to the Treaty of Brest-Litovsk. "I mustn't leave him [Nicholas] alone at such a moment," she said to Gilliard, her son's Swiss tutor. "They want to bring him to sign something ignominious by threats against his family. It's my duty to keep that from happening." So strong was Alexandra's feeling of danger, not so much to her husband's life as to his honor, that she decided to leave the next day, April 26, with him and Yakovlev, temporarily abandoning her children—including the invalid Alexis who was in a serious condition from a recent fall—until Yakovlev could return for them. Finally her daughter Marie and six followers were added to the party.

The trip was a dramatic one, marked by several puzzling incidents. Yakovlev seemed desperately anxious to avoid passing through Ekaterinburg, whose Soviet had been demanding the imprisonment of the Romanovs. He first tried to reach European Russia on another and more roundabout line through Omsk, but the special train he had requisitioned was stopped by Red Guards before he could get there and when he wired Moscow for instructions he was ordered to proceed via Ekaterinburg. On arrival in the station of Ekaterinburg, April 30, the whole party was put under arrest. Yakovlev's soldiers were disarmed and locked up, while the Romanovs were kept under strong guard in a house that had formerly belonged to a local merchant. Yakovlev waved his orders in front of the Ekaterinburg Soviet without avail. Finally he left alone for Moscow, threatening to return and punish the saboteurs of his mission. That was the last heard of the strange commissar, except for a wire signed with his name which was sent from Moscow a few days later to the members of his detachment who had remained behind in Tobolsk: ASSEMBLE DETACHMENT AND RETURN. HAVE RESIGNED. CANNOT ANSWER FOR CONSEQUENCES.

No evidence has turned up to support the theory that Yakovlev was actually a German agent, and there is no trace of any serious German attempt to assure the safety of the ex-Czar and his family, much less to rescue them. But it seems likely that the whole confused story of the abortive Yakovlev mission was connected—in some way as yet unrevealed—both with factional rivalries or policy disputes at the highest Bolshevik levels and with German clandestine intrigue in Russia.

For the Romanovs the house in Ekaterinburg was the end of the line. It was a big, white two-story structure, dingy and pretentious, like dirty underwear beneath a starched shirt, built against the slope of a hill so that the ground floor was really a kind of cellar. The house had a second-floor veranda across the whole width, and a mean little yard, enclosed by a wooden palisade, where Nicholas took his exercise every day. Often he carried the ailing Alexis in his arms as he walked. (The children who had remained behind in Tobolsk rejoined their parents in Ekaterinburg on May 23.) Most of the uniforms that Nicholas had brought to Siberia with him were now lost or worn out and to avoid the jeers of his guards he usually wore plain trousers of some sort and a soldier's khaki tunic, without officer's shoulderboards. Whatever he wore, he always managed to look neat and dignified; his frowsy local militia guards were impressed in spite of themselves, though not to the point of following his example.

Nicholas, Alexandra, and their son slept in one bedroom, the girls another. The faithful Dr. Botkin and five servants shared the Romanov's captivity. Family and servants ate together out of a common pot in the merchant's dining room and the guards who lounged about the room helped themselves as they felt like it over the shoulders of the diners. The guards frequently got drunk and baited their prisoners by singing revolutionary or bawdy songs under their window, and sometimes they followed the girls down the corridor when they went to the toilet, teasing them with coarse jokes, but there was no systematic mistreatment of the family. Almost up to the end a priest was allowed in on Sundays to celebrate mass for them. The daily routine of life at Ekaterinburg was simple. The whole family rose about eight, then gathered together for prayers. Dinner was at 3 P.M. After a walk in the yard they had their meager supper at 9 P.M. and retired for the night. Nicholas did a great deal of reading, while Alexandra and her daughters busied themselves with needlework. Sometimes they all sang together.

Witnesses—including both the servants and several of the guards or local Bolshevik authorities who were later interrogated by the Whites—agreed that Nicholas and Alexandra bore themselves up to the end not only with dignity, but with every appearance of serenity. The affectionate tranquillity of their family life remained unbroken by the frustrations and strains of what was virtually a prison existence. The preoccupation with domestic rather than official duties that had been one of their grave failings as monarchs now helped to ennoble what would otherwise have been a sordid experience. Of the manly virtues, the only one that Nicholas possessed to any outstanding degree was fortitude; in Ekaterinburg it was the only one he needed. Alexandra had been a domineering matriarch; with her dreams of power shattered and her husband and children at the mercy of others, maternal solicitude rose above her possessiveness.

The ordeal of the Romanovs must have been all the harder on their nerves because rescue was so near at hand; yet the nearer it approached the more deadly became their peril. The White forces under Denikin were advancing into the politically unsettled area between the Volga and the Urals. At the end of May the Czechoslovak Legion, 40,000 strong, which had started withdrawing through Siberia toward Vladivostok after the peace of Brest-Litovsk, turned upon the Bolsheviks, who had foolishly tried to disarm them, and launched an offensive westward. Almost immediately there was a general anti-Bolshevik rising in Siberia and in eastern Russia. Day by day, the Czechs, reinforced by local White partisans, drew nearer to Ekaterinburg. Lenin knew that the town's capture by the Whites was inevitable and he apparently feared that the rescue of the former Imperial Family—especially that of the little Alexis whom many monarchists continued to look on as the legitimate heir to the throne—would give increased cohesion to the counterrevolutionary movement (actually it might have had just the contrary effect). Moreover, relations between the Bolsheviks and the Germans were beginning to spoil as a result of the increasingly close contact between the Germans and right-wing Russian monarchists. Consequently it no longer mattered so much how the Kaiser might react to the news that his cousin Nicky—and above all the German born Alexandra —had been murdered or executed by the Bolsheviks. Concern over this point may have been the chief reason why they were not killed earlier.

The final development which, somewhat paradoxically decided the fate of the Romanovs was an anti-Bolshevik rising by the Social-Revolutionaries, the ancient foes of the monarchy, now fiercely opposed to the new Leninist despotism and inflamed with patriotic as well as libertarian passion. Organized by the arch-terrorist and master conspirator Boris Savinkov, who had helped plan the murder of Grand Duke Sergius in 1905, financed by French money, supported by certain liberal groups, but inadequately coordinated with other White movements, the insurrection broke out in the new capital, Moscow, on July 6, with the assassination of the German Ambassador, Count Mirbach (provoking a break between the Soviet government and the Germans was one of the insurgents' objectives). It quickly spread to 23 other centers and for a few days threatened the Bolshevik power. Lenin probably saved his regime by the ferocity as well as by the speed of his riposte. He not only stamped out the rebellion wherever it blazed up but in a psychological sense scorched the earth around it by ordering a pitiless mass terror aimed at cowing all the elements in the country who might be tempted to support a counterrevolution from any quarter. As far as the Cheka's arm could reach across the Russian countryside it rounded up *kulaks* (so-called wealthy peasants) along with nobles, priests, former officers, and bourgeois of every category and—on Lenin's personal orders—shot them in more or less random batches, first by the hundreds, then by the thousands. The Romanovs—especially the former Czar—were perhaps the most innocuous subjects of the Bolshevik dictatorship, but they were a prominent symbol of the past and in the public mind their execution would serve to punctuate the terror with a bloody exclamation point. That, apparently was the decisive reason for ordering it.

The actual slaughtering—that is the best word for it—was carried out by a Cheka squad, under the command of an officer named Yurovsky, which on orders from Moscow had replaced the local guards early in July. About midnight on the night of July 16–17 Yurovsky roused Nicholas and his family, ordering them to dress and move down to one of the ground-floor cellar rooms on the pretext that fighting in the streets of Ekaterinburg was imminent. (The Czechs and Whites did as a matter of fact take the city on July 25.) When Nicholas, holding Alexis in his arms, Alexandra, their four daughters, their doctor, and three servants were all assembled in the sinister little room, Yurovsky hastily read out the sentence of death, then without further warning drew his revolver and fired point-blank at Nicholas. That was the signal for the massacre. Alexis and one of the girls were not quite dead when the murder squad had used up its ammunition and had to be finished off with bayonets. The Romanov children's little dog was similarly dispatched for good measure. The bodies were then hastily searched for documents and jewelry. After that they were piled on a truck and taken to a deserted crossroads in a nearby wood where they were splashed with gasoline and set afire. The charred remains were buried in a pit. When it was all over a cipher message was sent to Moscow; INFORM SVERDLOV THAT THE ENTIRE FAMILY SHARED THE FATE OF THE HEAD OF THE FAMILY.

The following night, July 18, five Grand Dukes of the Romanov family and two Grand Duchesses—one of whom was Alexandra's sister, Elizabeth —were put to death under similar conditions not far from Ekaterinburg. Nicholas' brother, Grand Duke Michael—in whose favor he had abdicated —had been kidnaped several days earlier from the hotel in Perm, west of Ekaterinburg, where he was being detained, and presumably was also murdered. The two Romanovs who had avoided internment survived to lead— and to split—the monarchist movement in Russia. They were the late Czar's uncle, Grand Duke Nicholas, the paladin of traditionalist elements, and the more liberal Grand Duke Cyril, a cousin of the deposed ruler.

The Russian people learned of the ex-Czar's execution through a brief official press release from Moscow on July 19 announcing that "sentence of death had been passed on Nicholas Romanov and carried out" by the Ekaterinburg Soviet. It is now admitted, even in the USSR, that in reality it was Lenin himself who ordered the execution, while another member of the central government, Jacob Sverdlov, was responsible for co-ordinating the details with the local authorities in Ekaterinburg. Nothing was ever said officially about the killing of the Czarina and the Romanov children. When the counselor of the German diplomatic mission in Moscow registered a platonic protest at the execution of Nicholas and inquired about the fate of the rest of the family he was given to understand that they were being moved from Ekaterinburg to a safer place. Inspired rumors and news leaks to the same effect were put out, and later similar techniques were used to create the impression that the Romanov Grand Dukes who had been killed in or near Perm had actually escaped and somehow disappeared in the confusion of the civil war.

There is no need to shed tears for any of the Romanovs, and it is hard to glamorize them as martyrs to a lost (and intrinsically abominable) cause, though we can properly respect the memory of Alexandra and Nicholas as belated exemplars of the Victorian tradition. They were two passengers, at least, who kept their manners and did not rush for the lifeboats when their world started going down. The Romanov family was not the only family massacred during the Russian civil war, and as always in such struggles, each side had its atrocities, its martyrs and its butchers. In the murders of Ekaterinburg and Perm it was not the killings themselves that were significant, nor even the identities of the victims—from the viewpoint of the ultimate political outcome in Russia it probably made little difference whether most of the Romanovs lived or died—but their style. They bear the characteristic stamp of twentieth-century totalitarianism—or more exactly of the anti-civilization fostered by the twentieth-century totalitarianism —and this was neither an accident, nor a mere symbol. The personality of governmental systems like that of individuals is the product not only of their environment, but of their reaction to it. The policy murder of Ekaterinburg was one of the normative reactions that helped shape the personality of the Soviet regime for the next two generations. In a sense akin to primitive magic it was also the consecration of the new rulers. It made them authentic successors of the vanished dynasty, lawful heirs to the Romanov tradition of the "block, the rope and poison."

CHAPTER 17

Exit the Hohenzollerns

"WHOEVER sets fire to his neighbor's house cannot complain if the sparks land on his own roof," says a German proverb. Whether any of the military or civilian witch doctors who organized Lenin's return to Russia in the famous sealed train of April 1917 remembered the saying at the time is uncertain; they had numerous occasions to recall it when, a bare year later, His Excellency, the Ambassador of the Union of Soviet Socialist Republics, Comrade Adolf Joffe, arrived in Berlin to take possession of the long-empty Russian Embassy at 7 Unter den Linden. As head of the Soviet delegation which had concluded the peace negotiations with Germany at Brest-Litovsk six weeks earlier, Joffe was a logical choice for the assignment. The first Soviet Ambassador to the Kaiser's Court and government, he was also an admirable one—from the Soviet viewpoint. With his sensitive, Semitic face, his dark professorial beard, his gold pince-nez, his fur-collared overcoat topped with a bowler hat, the emissary of the proletarian revolution had a reassuringly bourgeois look, but appearances could not have been more deceptive. A close friend of Trotsky from the latter's Vienna period, Joffe belonged to the same type of intellectual condottiere that had played such an important part in organizing the October revolution, and like the famous Red commissar, he was a daring professional conspirator who had been playing hide and seek with the gallows for years. Trotsky, in fact, had pulled him out of a prison camp in Siberia to direct the peace delegation.

The new ambassador had arrived with a staff of three hundred. His first official act was to hoist the hammer and sickle over the embassy; he refused to present his credentials personally to the Kaiser, and on the list of the guests invited to his first dinner party were the names of two left-wing German socialists serving prison terms for sedition and treason: Karl Liebknecht and Rosa Luxemburg. The Soviet Embassy soon became a head-quarters for the Independent Socialists and other revolutionaries who later formed Germany's first Communist Party. The group's clandestine "Letters of Spartacus" had spread anti-war propaganda ever since 1916. The circulation of these tracts now increased considerably, and no less than seven independent Socialist newspapers were supported by the vast funds which Joffe dispensed for propaganda purposes. Curiously undiplomatic-looking attachés of the embassy constantly traveled back and forth between Moscow and Berlin fully protected by diplomatic immunity; diplomatic usage did not, however, prevent members of Joffe's staff from appearing at German left-wing meetings where they harangued increasingly feverish audiences in increasingly fiery terms.

The amount of curiously shaped baggage traveling as "diplomatic pouch" from Moscow to Berlin worried the German government, which knew that both subversive pamphlets and arms were being distributed to the left-wing extremists by 7 Unter den Linden. Joffe scarcely bothered to hide his role as agitator; he himself later wrote, "It is necessary to emphasize most categorically that in the preparation of the German revolution, the Russian Embassy worked all the time in close contact with the German Socialists."

Ludendorff and Hoffmann had voiced misgivings from the first over introducing the Bolshevik Trojan horse into the German capital. Eventually even the Wilhelmstrasse, and the Imperial Chancellery, along with the moderate Socialists, came around to the view that it was a mistake to let the Bolsheviks have a diplomatic mission in Germany before a general peace was signed. Hampered by diplomatic usage from collecting the evidence that would have justified a rupture, the German authorities finally hit on an ingenious but desperate expedient: the police planted a package of faked and flagrantly subversive propaganda tracts in the Russian "pouch" and arranged to have it dropped in the railway station so that it burst open.

Joffe and his whole staff were expelled on November 7, 1918. By then their work had been done. The departing Soviet Ambassador, in his own "sealed train," must have remembered with a satisfied smile a dinner party he had given a few days ago. Karl Liebknecht and Rosa Luxemburg, recently released from jail, had been present, and toasts were drunk to a naval mutiny which had broken out at Kiel. ("Even at that early date," remarks the British historian John Wheeler-Bennett, "the Bolshevik diplomats had established a reputation for the excellent quality of their champagne.") Karl Liebknecht had not believed that the time was ripe yet for the final revolution. "On the contrary," Joffe had said, "within a week the Red flag will be flying over the Berliner Schloss."

Joffe's subversive activities were, of course, only one element in Germany's breakdown. His gifts as a technician of conspiracy contributed significantly to the German revolution, but the impact of Russian Bolshevism in Central—and even in Western—Europe after 1917 cannot be explained solely in terms of subversive propaganda or manipulations, however massive, however adroit. To a continent wracked by the most suicidal and the most senseless of modern wars, the fierce light of revolution blazing in the Eastern sky seemed the dawn-glow of a new hope for martyred humanity. Lenin's unwavering opposition to the war, underscored by the Soviet government's appeal for an immediate peace without annexations or reparations, had given him immense prestige in the eyes of Western intellectuals, including some—Rosa Luxemburg among them—who recognized and condemned the anti-democratic tendencies inherent in the Bolshevik dictatorship. The political dynamism of the Bolshevik ideal could be measured by the quality of Lenin's earliest sympathizers or adherents abroad; in many cases the most committed ones belonged to the elite of the European labor or socialist movements, and a few years later were to become the intransigent adversaries of post-Leninist Communism. The prisoners of war who started streaming back into Germany from Russia after the treaty of Brest-Litovsk also helped to spread the virus of revolutionary defeatism; some of them had been systematically indoctrinated with Bolshevik propaganda, but many more had been brainwashed by the ordeal of captivity itself, or had been spontaneously won over by the delivery of revolution.

The most dangerous carriers, their influence both on the civilian population and on the exhausted troops fighting off the final Allied onslaughts in the West was disastrous. Under the spell of such slogans as "Peace and Bread," whole units gave themselves up to the Allies without resistance in August 1918 and retreating troops jeeringly called reservists coming up to relieve them "strikebreakers."

War weariness, subversion, and treason, however, did not of themselves bring about the German collapse in November 1918. Only when Germany had been militarily defeated in the field, only when the High Command publicly proclaimed defeat by suing for an armistice, did the exhausted population, so worn out by four years of privation and a diet of nauseous *ersatz* foods that workers fainted in the factories, lose faith both in victory and authority. And only then did the ingrained habits of obedience give way beneath the incitements of revolutionary propaganda.

In March 1918, with Russia knocked out of the war and with American troops still mostly at the training camps, the German High Command had unleashed the "Kaiser's Battle" which was to be the final and fatal offensive against the Allies on the Western Front. The pompous name given this attack—or rather series of attacks—turned out, however, to be an injudicious compliment to the All Highest. None of the sledgehammer blows delivered against the Allies proved decisive. By July the tide began to turn, and General Ludendorff, faced with the growing buildup of fresh American troops on one hand—General Pershing already had 19 infantry divisions at the front in early August—and with the dwindling of German reserves on the other, privately conceded that all hope of victory in the field was gone. But he would do nothing to prepare peace, and he refused to inform the government. "The Wilhelmstrasse is frightened enough now; if they knew the true military situation it would be a catastrophe," he said. Obstinately the High Command, whose dictatorship over the government and even over the Kaiser, was complete, continued to maintain that "there is no ground for doubting our victory."

By September all the gains of the great spring offensive had been lost, and the outer bastions of the Central Powers were crumbling everywhere. Austria was beginning to buckle, and, on September 26, Bulgaria dropped out of the war.

Suddenly, Ludendorff's nerves gave way. The Great General Headquarters of the German Army was in the little Belgian watering resort of Spa, famous for its mineral springs. In the late afternoon of September 28, the faint buzz of conversation, heel-clicking and spur-jangling which had replaced the peacetime clinking of teacups under the potted palms in the hall of the Hotel Britannique was suddenly hushed as General Ludendorff, escorted by his aides, his face gray above the "pour le Mérite" cross at his throat, made his way to Marshal Hindenburg's office. Gaspingly he told the Marshal, who looked more than ever like a wood carving of a St. Bernard dog, that an armistice must be concluded immediately, and that a new German government capable of obtaining favorable terms on the basis of President Wilson's Fourteen Points must be formed at once.

Next day, the Chief of the General Staff and his Quartermaster General, bent on a painful mission, showed up at the Kaiser's villa, a large, turreted, gabled, balconied and ivy overgrown structure in the neo-Norman style still seen on Long Island estates today. It lay in more than 100 acres of beautifully kept grounds on a hill outside Spa and had been requisitioned from a Belgian senator and textile magnate. Much of the furnishing came from the Belgian royal palace of Laeken. A concrete bomb shelter that could be entered from the cellar, with an emergency exit through an underground tunnel ending in a clump of trees had been built for the All Highest. Wilhelm felt much happier in these holiday surroundings at Spa than at Berlin, where, it was said, "the pavement burnt the soles of his feet." He clung to the fiction of the Supreme War Lord, at the head of his armies. Pictures appeared from time to time in the newspapers, showing him visiting the trenches, wrapped in a field gray coat, and wearing the famous spiked helmet so dear to Allied cartoonists. Most of them were taken not far from the villa, where a trench had been dug and decorated with sand bags for the purpose.[1] In a moment of pathetic self-recognition he once confided to a visitor at headquarters: "The General Staff tells me nothing and asks me nothing. If anyone in Germany thinks I lead the army, they are quite mistaken. I drink tea, chop wood and take walks, and from time to time I hear that this and that has been done, according to the wishes of those gentlemen."

According to all accounts, the Kaiser received the news that the German armies were defeated and that an armistice must be promptly obtained with unusual dignity. The decision to proclaim a parliamentary regime and to form a new government was taken easily, since the General Staff said it was needed, although the Kaiser countered Ludendorff's frantic pleas for haste with some asperity. "You could have told me all this a fortnight ago," he said. "I can't work miracles."

"Wilhelm II had never opposed the High Command's wishes, nor did he demur when it chose to transfer the responsibility of defeat to others, to burden the Reichstag parties with the odium of making the catastrophe palatable to their own people and to conclude a disappointing peace with the enemy," writes the Swiss historian, J. R. von Salis. On the contrary, when the new chancellor, Prince Max von Baden, shocked by the icy wind of panic which blew straight from Spa, objected that so much haste seemed unpolitic, and suggested that the military situation might not be all that bad, the Kaiser told him sharply ". . . you have not been brought here to make difficulties for the Supreme Command."

Prince Max, a cousin of the Kaiser's, a grandson of Czar Nicholas I and next in succession to the throne of the Grand Duchy of Baden, was an urbane man with well-tempered liberal ideas. On October 4 his government, which was for the first time in German history composed of responsible ministers and included such Socialist leaders as Philip Scheidemann and Gustav Bauer,[2] appealed to President Wilson for an armistice on the basis of the Fourteen Points—via the Swiss government—thus informing the German people and the world at large that Germany had lost the war.

It is likely that neither Ludendorff nor Hindenburg had seriously read Wilson's speeches. An armistice was needed to save the German Army from destruction. Peace would be a matter of negotiation, they thought.

---

[1] Shortly before his abdication it was felt that the Kaiser might regain a measure of popularity if he went for a visit to a really exposed part of the front. He consented without enthusiasm and returned with harrowing accounts of the ordeal; several bombs had dropped not far from the imperial train.

    "Cowards die many times before their deaths;

    "The valiant never taste of death but once,"

he quoted to his entourage in lofty, if slightly strained tones. Actually he had not been beyond the rear depots.

[2] When the Kaiser received his first Socialist Ministers he is reported to have said "I have nothing whatever against Social Democracy except its name. The name, you know, must be changed."

But now the ground upon which they stood crumbled. By their démarche they had utterly destroyed the morale of the German people. The soldiers in the trenches who had suffered terrible losses ever since the *Kaiserschlacht* had been launched could see no reason to procrastinate. What stood in the way of peace? On October 14, a note of President Wilson gave them the answer, by drawing attention to one of his conditions: "The destruction of every arbitrary power anywhere that can separately, secretly and of its single choice disturb the peace of the world."

That this meant the German monarchy first became clear to big business; the Kaiser's abdication would buy a better peace, it was felt. Wilhelm's abdication was soon the subject of conversations and arguments everywhere, in government offices, drawing rooms, political meetings, streetcars. Everywhere but in the press, where every mention of it was censured. At the rallies of the extreme left, cries of "Down with the Kaiser" became as loud as the cries for peace.

In the hope of saving the Hohenzollern dynasty Prince Max proposed that the Kaiser should give up the throne at once, not in favor of the Crown Prince—who among other liabilities was saddled with formal responsibility for the disastrous Verdun offensive—but in favor of the Crown Prince's twelve-year-old son, Prince Wilhelm. The Kaiser would have none of it. To escape the pressure building up against him in Berlin, he returned to Spa, where he still had the support of the High Command. Prince Max sent him one emissary after another to plead that he abdicate. "How can you, a Prussian official, reconcile such a mission with the oath of loyalty you have taken to your king?" the irate Kaiser asked one of them, a Prussian minister, on November 1. But it was later than the Kaiser realized.

On October 28 a naval mutiny broke out in Wilhelmshaven. On November 1 it spread to the High Seas Fleet in Kiel. By November 4 full-fledged revolution had broken out in all of northern Germany.

The city of Kiel lies at the end of a picturesque Baltic fjord and overlooks one of the best natural deep water harbors in Europe. In pre-war days tourists admired the gold and white splendor of the *Hohenzollern,* riding at anchor, always ready to receive the Kaiser and his suite. He spent much time in Kiel, where he liked to play host to the great and the rich, surrounded by the symbol of Germany's world power, his shiny toy, the German Navy.

The picture on November 4, 1918, was a little different. The navy was there, practically unscathed. It had been tucked away ever since the battle of Jutland, in June 1916. For more than two years the crews had swabbed decks, polished brass, and saluted irritable officers. But now the Red flag flew from the masts of the grim, battle-gray warships, thousands of mutinous sailors were parading through the streets of the city, singing the *Marseillaise,* and the flags they were carrying were blood colored, too. Few officers were in evidence, and those who were, were disarmed and had red cockades pinned on their uniforms. A number of U-boats loyal to the Kaiser fled the harbor; the crews of the others formed the first soviet of the German revolution, which in the next few days was to engulf all the coastal cities of northern Germany.

The mutiny had been sparked a week earlier, on October 28 when the German high seas fleet was ordered into the North Sea to relieve the pressure on the German armies retreating along the Belgian coast. Immediately a rumor spread from ship to ship—the crews had long since evolved a secret signaling system—that the fleet was to be sacrificed in a last spectacular action against the British Grand Fleet rather than accept surrender. As a number of rabid Pan-Germans were left who advocated such a course, the danger seemed real and urgent. On several cruisers the fires were doused, on others the men refused to weigh anchors. The fleet stayed in the harbor, but the mutineers were arrested and jailed. Attempts to enforce discipline merely fanned the revolt. The sailors became the heroes of the day; the appearance of a small detachment of bluejackets was enough to trigger the uprising in one north German city after another.

On November 7 the railway lines to Berlin were cut to protect the capital, but the infection had already reached south Germany and shaken the foundations of the federal state for on that day revolution broke out in Munich. It was led by a fifty-one-year-old Bavarian, Kurt Eisner, a former journalist who had carried on a persistent campaign against the war since its beginning and had gathered around him a small but faithful group of workers and intellectuals. His convictions had forced him to break with the majority socialists, and had finally earned him a sentence for treason. He was released from jail in time to organize the mass meeting that triggered the Munich revolution. It was called on the Munich Fair Grounds, the Theresienwiese, where once a year was celebrated the huge, beery *Oktoberfest* (October Festival). In a mounting frenzy, twelve successive speakers called for the abdication of the Kaiser. As the excitement grew, the soldiers in the crowds formed ranks behind Eisner and marched to the nearest barracks, where the garrison was easily persuaded to join the parade. As it marched through town, it acquired more soldiers, and a brass band. The railroad stations, post offices, and government buildings were occupied by revolutionary commandos, and toward evening a soldiers' and workers' soviet, with Eisner as president of the small group, established its headquarters in a brewery and proclaimed Bavaria a socialist republic.

When the revolution erupted the Bavarian King, Ludwig, the sedate, burgher-like descendant of the magnificent Ludwig I—Lola Montez's admirer—and of the mad Ludwig II, was walking with his daughters in the English Garden, a long narrow park which extended its well-kept lawns, artificial lakes, cascades, gazebos, and kiosks to the north of the Royal

Residence, on the opposite side of town from the Theresienwiese. He was accosted by one of his subjects who respectfully but urgently advised him to go back to his palace. There he learned from his ministers that a republic had been proclaimed. He and his family packed some hand baggage and left the city by automobile, unaccompanied and unmolested. They took up abode in Berchtesgaden, and on November 13 Ludwig formally abdicated, releasing all Bavarian officials and soldiers from their oath of allegiance. Thus the Wittelsbach dynasty became the first to capitulate to the new order in Germany. As Kurt Eisner said: "The Wittelsbach ruled over Bavaria for seven hundred years. I got rid of them in seven hours with seven men."

In the first two weeks of November all the other German thrones collapsed. The last to give up was the ruler of a wooded patch of Thuringia, the Prince of Schwarzburg-Rudolstadt. "The red flag floated over the palaces, while royal mottoes vanished from the courts, the newspapers and the commercial world," says Ralph Haswell Lutz in his scholarly study, *The German Revolution.*

Though the princely houses of Germany had been the traditional bulwarks of regional particularism, their fall generated a strong centrifugal movement away from the Empire. *"Weg vom Reich, Los von Preussen"* ("Away from the Reich, Break with Prussia") was one of the slogans of the Bavarian revolution, while the representatives of the Polish and Danish districts, not to mention those of Alsace-Lorraine, had already proclaimed their separatism in a public session of the Reichstag. Germany thus appeared to be simultaneously threatened with communism and with the breakup of its national unity. To avert both dangers it was essential that the central government itself take the leadership of the revolutionary movement and guide it into safe, national channels. Realization of this seems to have occurred simultaneously to Prince Max von Baden, and to the more conservative Social Democratic leaders, in particular to Friedrich Ebert.

"If I go to Spa and obtain the abdication of the Kaiser, can I count on your support in the fight against social revolution?" the Chancellor asked.

"I don't want social revolution," replied Ebert, a former saddlemaker and a man much respected for his integrity. "I hate it like sin."

Both the Chancellor and Ebert, who knew the German's attachment to monarchic institutions, were doing their best to save the dynasty by sacrificing its figurehead. But the Kaiser was not co-operative. In despair, Prince Max, who had been ill with influenza for nearly two weeks (the terrible pandemic of so-called Spanish influenza was then raging throughout Europe) sent in his resignation. It was refused, and the plea for abdication simply ignored. Appeals to Marshal Hindenburg were equally unsuccessful; the old soldier could not even contemplate any action against the sovereign to whom he had sworn unconditional fidelity.

On November 8 the war, as far as Germany was concerned, was virtu-ally over. On that day in a clearing of the Forest of Compiègne, in a con-verted wagon-restaurant attached to Marshal Foch's special train, the stony-faced German armistice commission, headed by Secretary of State Matthias Erzberger, having answered "Yes" to Marshal Foch's curt query, "Do you request an armistice?" listened to the terms that were to be im-posed on them. As article after article was read, first in French, then in German, they grew paler and stonier, and the young German interpreter-officer wept openly, for, as Foch had wanted it, the armistice was designed "to put Germany at the mercy of the victors." On the evening of November 8, however, the Kaiser still had not grasped the implications of the drama at Compiègne. Earlier in the day he had ordered a plan to be drawn up for the restoration of order in the country by the army. He had never varied in his belief that the army, whose military oath included uncon-ditional obedience to the Kaiser's commands, stood as a shield between revolution and the dynasty, and the Supreme Command had, so far, not seen fit to disillusion him. As Wilhelm saw it, it was the army's duty to obey him and his duty to take the head of the operation: he had said so to Prince Max, who had kept him on the phone for nearly half an hour with a heart-to-heart appeal "as a parent and a German prince" to consent to immediate abdication. Once again, in the face of the Kaiser's refusal, the Chancellor had begged to be allowed to resign. But Wilhelm would not let him off the hook. "You asked for the armistice," he said sarcastically, using the familiar thou. "You stay and see it through!"

It was the last night of Imperial Germany, and its last Kaiser went to bed without being told by his staff that his plan was a pipe dream, and that nothing now could stop the revolution scheduled to break out the next morning in Berlin.

The Kaiser's order for a plan of operations against the revolutionary home front had been addressed to the new Quartermaster General, Gen-eral Wilhelm Groener. (Ludendorff had finally toppled off his pedestal, a prey to nervous prostration and to the Berlin government's cries for his scalp.) A south German, the son of a noncommissioned officer, Groener was a man of cool judgment and an immensely able administrator. A close rival of Ludendorff, he had been passed over only because his family did not belong to the military caste. When he received the Kaiser's instructions he decided that the time for illusions was past. In a heart-to-heart talk, he put the facts to his chief, Hindenburg, whose position at Headquarters has often been described as that of a much respected zero.

Far from being *Kaisertreu* (unconditionally devoted to the Emperor), he told the old marshal, the army was the spearhead of the revolution. Soldiers' and Workers' Councils had taken control of railway centers and supply depots. The bridges across the Rhine were in their hands. The

Kaiser's plan was unworkable. Hindenburg wept. The Emperor's seventy-seven-year-old Adjutant General von Plessen wept. He had been Adjutant General to Emperor Wilhelm I, and his motto was "The Kaiser must hear only good news." But no one went to see Wilhelm in his hill-top sanctuary. Prince Max von Baden telephoned again and informed Headquarters that if the news of the abdication was not on the front pages of the newspapers at breakfast time, the workers, in accordance with instructions from the Socialist leaders, would take to the streets after the mid-morning coffee break.

The night's crop of warnings and abdication pleas from Berlin were brought to the Kaiser with his breakfast. They did not, however, keep him from his *Spaziergang,* that particular addiction of elderly German gentlemen, which consists of strolling, cane in hand, along well-kept paths, pausing on an occasional bench, conversing earnestly all along. Wilhelm did warn the sentries at the gates that he would remain in the immediate surroundings, and left orders to send for him if Marshal Hindenburg should call. It was a foggy morning, and the trees dripped drearily from nearly leafless branches, but the cold seemed to invigorate the Kaiser, who held forth at length, to the staff officer accompanying him, on the perils of Bolshevism. He could not believe, he said as they walked past the frost-blackened flower beds, that the Allies would fail to recognize the danger of exposing Germany to such a plague. The revolutionary movements, though worrisome, could still be scotched. "We'll surmount these difficulties by a rapid military action," he prattled.

But the moment of truth was approaching. A guard came running to announce the Marshal's arrival.

In the closely curtained garden room, where a fire was burning in the grate, half a dozen men in *feldgrau* uniforms stood around, biting their lips, shifting uneasily from one foot to the other. As Hindenburg, fighting to control his emotions, started to speak, the Kaiser held his numb hands to the fire.

With tears in his eyes, the massive gray-headed old soldier begged his War Lord's leave to resign. He could not, as a Prussian officer . . . Choking, he motioned to Groener to finish the sentence. It fell to the "good Swabian" as he was known a little pityingly at Headquarters, to tell the German Emperor that his day was over. The situation, as he saw it, was hopeless: the army was beaten and Germany was in the hands of the revolutionaries. It was quite impossible to fight a rear-guard action against the enemy and a civil war at the same time. The army was unreliable. The Emperor's plan was totally unfeasible. The urgent need was to ask for an armistice, immediate and unconditional.

Groener, though he did not share the semi-mystical attitude of Prussian officers toward the All Highest, avoided pronouncing the word "abdication." He supposed that the Kaiser would spare them all the final ordeal and himself draw the inescapable conclusion.

But the heavy silence that followed was broken by one of the officers present, who had listened to Groener's exposé with impatience, and had been mutely begging the Kaiser for leave to speak. Count Friedrich von Schulenburg, described in most memoirs as a "Prussian officer of the old school and a gentleman," was the Crown Prince's chief of staff (and the father of another Prussian officer and gentleman who was to die on the gallows for plotting against Hitler in July 1944). He denied heatedly that the army was unreliable. "Give them time to sleep and to get rid of their lice," he said. "In eight or ten days they will be all right, and anxious to fight the rabble of Jews and war profiteers who have betrayed them."

General von Plessen chimed in enthusiastically, and a general discussion developed. Wilhelm, after listening to both sides of the argument, retreated to a new position: he would at least, he said, lead the army home in good order after the armistice had been concluded.

Groener heaved a sigh: the Kaiser had still not understood. He prepared to deliver the coup de grace:

"The army will return home in good order under the command of its chiefs, but not under the orders of Your Majesty. The army is no longer behind Your Majesty."

Stung to the quick, the Kaiser turned on Groener. "Excellency, I shall require that statement from you in black and white," he snapped.

Wilhelm then looked questioningly at Hindenburg. The Marshal mumbled soothing words, but he too had to admit that the loyalty of the troops to their War Lord could no longer be guaranteed. An impasse had been reached.

In the embarrassed hush the constant ringing of the telephone in an adjoining office, the querulous voice of the official replying to Berlin's queries, suddenly became unbearable. The Kaiser adjourned the meeting; the French windows were thrown open. Wilhelm waved aside an officer who whispered that the Chancellor was on the phone once again and wished to speak to his Majesty, and everyone drifted into the garden.

Groener, who had been challenged by his Emperor to prove the validity of his assertions, returned to the Hotel Britannique, where a meeting of army commanders hastily summoned from the front was in progress. Orders to proceed to Headquarters immediately had reached them in their front line positions in the night. Most of them had motored through the small hours and had arrived at dawn, frozen to the bone, yawning and hungry. In the confusion nobody had arranged to serve them breakfast, and they could only guess at the reason for the summons by the long faces and distraught looks of the headquarters personnel, who brushed off their questions in nervous haste. Shortly before ten, the Marshal had finally appeared, red-eyed and ash-gray, and had drawn for them such a grisly picture of the general situation at home and on the front that when he ceased speaking there fell a "silence as of a tomb," interrupted only by the discreet sniffles of the Kaiser's Adjutant General, who had drifted into the meeting by accident. After the briefing by Hindenburg, a staff officer had been ordered to interrogate each of the thirty-nine army commanders separately and privately.

He was to ask two questions. The first was: "Would it be possible for the Kaiser to regain control of Germany by force of arms, at the head of his troops?" By the end of the morning only one unequivocal "yes," to twenty-three "noes" and fifteen ambiguous answers, had been registered. To the second question, "Would the troops march against the Bolshevists in Germany?" the replies had been eight "yeses," nineteen "noes," and twelve uncertain.

It was a little before one when Groener, accompanied by the officer who had examined the army commanders, once more made his way to the villa. The Kaiser was still in the park, standing in the center of a motionless group of officers, talking in high-pitched tones and gesticulating with his right hand. The Crown Prince was there too. He had arrived around noon, and had winced at his father's appearance.

". . . His face was livid and haggard, his features drawn . . . I felt sorry for him," he later wrote in his memoirs.

During the informal and feverish discussions in the garden, the officers of the Kaiser's military house, Schulenburg, the Crown Prince, all had offered advice to the hapless man whose fate was being decided. He was now grasping at a new straw that had been held out to him: he would sacrifice himself to avert civil war (he had reigned long enough to know what an ungrateful job it was, let others try to do better, etc.) and would abdicate as German Emperor. But not as King of Prussia. Never as King of Prussia. And as King he would remain at the head of his Prussian troops.

The men whose distracted coming and going churned up the neat gravel on the walk were too intimately involved in the situation to realize that their words had already been robbed of meaning by the swift rush of history. Telegrams from Berlin indicated that revolution had broken out punctually on schedule, and that some of the Emperor's most trusted regiments had hoisted the Red flag. The telephone kept ringing in the villa. "What about the abdication?" the Chancellor's office in Berlin wanted to know. "The decision is being taken," the Kaiser's office in Spa replied.

As soon as Groener appeared, the Kaiser asked for a report, and at a nod from the prim Swabian—whom only the uniform kept from looking like a rural high-school principal—the officer accompanying him read off the results of the poll of army commanders. In tones which were felt to be unnecessarily loud he summed up the consensus: "The Army is true to your Majesty, but tired and indifferent. It wants only one thing: rest and peace. Nor will it now march against the country, not even with Your Majesty."

There was another one of those silences. Once again von Schulenburg jumped into the breach with a tirade about the officers' oath to the flag and to their Supreme War Lord.

Then Groener, the only one present whose vocabulary was adapted to the times, pronounced the verdict which put an end to an era. "The oath to the flag? The Supreme War Lord? These are now but words."

There seemed little to say after that, and indeed little was said. A messenger came running from the house with further news from Berlin: the situation was getting out of hand, one regiment after the other was deserting to the "Bolsheviks."

Wilhelm stood silent for a few minutes, and then finally took his last decision as Kaiser: He would abdicate as Emperor, but not as King of Prussia. The armistice terms must be accepted. Hindenburg was to take over supreme command of the army.

He then dismissed his generals and went in to lunch. A committee sat down to work out the wording of the abdication act—a waste of time, as it turned out shortly, for the decision was no longer Wilhelm's.

Lunch in the friendly dining room of the villa, at a table laden with freshly cut flowers from the garden, was recorded as a nightmarish memory by the Crown Prince. The Kaiser sat brooding, nervously biting his upper lip; no one cared to break the silence; the food remained on the plates. But it was soon over, and Wilhelm, his son, von Schulenburg, and a few of the intimate staff had just drifted dejectedly into the living room for coffee, when a door was thrown open and a stricken voice called from an adjoining office, "Would Your Majesty be so good as to come here a moment?" Admiral Hintze, the Foreign Office representative at Spa, still held the telephone receiver in a trembling hand. It was two o'clock and he had just called Berlin to transmit the text of the abdication act. The Chancellor's spokesman in Berlin had rudely interrupted him right at the start to ask, "Is it abdication at last?" As Hintze read the passage relating to the Kaiser's abdication as Emperor but not as King of Prussia, the voice in Berlin had gasped, "This is insane!" and before Hintze had reached the end of the declaration he was interrupted again. "Special editions have just gone on sale in the streets," the voice now said with a new urgency. "I have one here. Let me read you what it says."

Prince Max's spokesman had been on the telephone all morning trying to get a decisive statement from Spa. He had therefore not been informed that at 11:30 A.M. the Chancellor, believing the abdication to be imminent and faced with an increasingly threatening situation in the streets, had issued a communiqué to the Wolf Agency announcing the Kaiser's decision to renounce the throne for himself and for his son. At 12:30, with all the troops of the Berlin garrison mutinous, including the famed Emperor Alexander Regiment, the Kaiser's special pride, Prince Max had transmitted his powers to Ebert.

If the special edition with the screaming headlines announcing the abdication came as a surprise to the Chancellor's spokesman—now the ex-Chancellor's spokesman—in Berlin, the text of the Wolf telegram, as read to him over the phone, literally stunned the unfortunate Hintze in Spa. He called out to his Kaiser, who stood dumfounded as the situation was explained to him.

It was the affront to the Emperor which struck Wilhelm and his luncheon guests, and loosened their tongues. "Unheard of . . . Decision taken out of my hands . . . Treachery . . ." There was a babel of such confused, jittery exclamations, then a burst of activity: telegram blanks covered feverishly, orders for arms to be brought to the villa, orders to inform Hindenburg and Groener at once. Wilhelm's apparent resolution to stand his ground made it easier for the Crown Prince to take his leave. He, too, was urgently required at his battle post. The armistice terms had been received at Spa, but no one had studied them yet, and fighting was still in progress all along the lines.

"I did not guess," says the Crown Prince, "as I shook his hand that I would only see him [the Kaiser] again a year later, in Holland."

Back at Headquarters, Hindenburg, Groener, and their advisers went into conference to decide what to do with their discarded monarch and War Lord. Groener had already made plain his views ten days earlier in an informal talk with Hindenburg and Plessen. He thought that the Kaiser should go to the front and get himself killed. The other two generals had been horrified, and Wilhelm himself had disapproved of the suggestion—it was never submitted to him as a formal proposal—on lofty humanitarian and religious grounds.

"Some say the Emperor should have gone to some regiment at the front, hurled himself with it upon the enemy and sought death in one last attack," the ex-Kaiser notes in his memoirs. "That would not only have rendered impossible the armistice . . . but would also have meant the useless sacrifice of the lives of many soldiers."

Wilhelm also records his feeling that a *Heldentod* ("hero's death") at the front would have been a violation of Christian principles incompatible with his honorary position as first bishop of the Evangelical Church in Germany. Presumably their ex-master's views were known to the conferees at the Hotel Britannique, and in any case by the afternoon of November 9 Groener's idea—which might conceivably have saved the monarchy if carried out in time—was no longer practical. It was equally impossible for Wilhelm to return home for a last stand against the revolution. The roads back to Germany were blocked by the Reds. Spa itself was no longer safe; soldiers' councils had begun to form; the men's faces were turning sullen and officers—to the sardonic joy of the Belgian civilians—were no longer saluted when they appeared on the streets of the little town. It was not even certain that the regiment assigned to guard the Emperor's person would remain loyal. Hindenburg, recalling the massacre of the Czar and his family at Ekaterinburg, insisted that Wilhelm must leave at once, while it was still possible, to seek refuge on neutral soil. Groener and the rest finally agreed.

At 4 P.M. they returned to the villa to inform the Kaiser of their decision. "My God, you again, already!" he exclaimed when he saw them. Then, turning to Groener in a burst of spite, he said, "You have a War Lord no longer." Wilhelm clearly was not in a co-operative mood. "The declarations of his Majesty took quite a while," one of the officers present noted with restraint. Eventually Wilhelm authorized "preparatory measures" for a flight to Holland to be taken.

With or without his consent, such measures had already been decided. Witnesses of the period recall that earlier on the same day a Dutch general spent several hours in the town, and that some sort of military exercise was put on for his benefit; its senselessness on that particular day struck local observers as quite out of the ordinary. Holland had been picked in preference to Switzerland as a sanctuary for the ex-Kaiser, not only because its border was a mere 40 miles from Spa, but also because it was a monarchy.

After so many years of posturing to hide his inner uncertainty, it was not easy for Wilhelm to decide on a becoming exit. The idea of selling his life dearly, surrounded by his faithful followers in the besieged villa, appealed to him long enough to order arms to be brought to the residence. But at the end of the day, with darkness falling rapidly, he was persuaded to return to his special train, which served him as traveling headquarters, and which was always ready for him.

He had still not admitted the idea of flight, and when he reached the train he found a message from the Kaiserin, who was in Potsdam and reported that she was in good spirits, and wished him well. "My wife stays," he exclaimed, "and they want me to leave for Holland . . . It would look like fear!" Two naval officers who met him on his way to the dining car found him determined to remain. They had begged him to be released from the service. "No," he said. "No. You must stay. I am staying." And banging on the table with his fist, "I am staying, not leaving."

It was after ten at night, when Wilhelm finally gave his consent to departure. "But only tomorrow," he insisted. Hindenburg was getting into bed when General von Plessen came to inform him that his master had finally decided to leave for Holland in the morning. Utterly worn out by the emotional strain of the day, the old Marshal nevertheless decided to hasten to the train. Plessen advised against it. The Kaiser should not be disturbed again tonight. There would be time tomorrow.

While merciful oblivion came to the aged Commander-in-Chief, his Quartermaster General settled down to a night's work. The dynastic question had been solved with relative ease. Groener may not have agreed with the German socialist who said, "Wilhelm's greatest service to his country in thirty-one years of reign was to leave it," but it was a relief to be able to turn one's attention to serious problems.

The most urgent one was to bring the German army home in good order, and to save Germany from a Bolshevist revolution. The Allied armistice terms had been transmitted to Spa from Rhetondes on that day. They called for the evacuation by the German army of Belgium and Alsace-Lorraine within fifteen days, for the occupation by the Allies of the left bank of the Rhine, and for the delivery into the victor's hands of practically all the nation's armaments. It was necessary for Germany to have a strong government to cope with such demands. The key to the situation lay in Berlin. Groener picked up the telephone which connected headquarters directly with the Chancellor's office "Do all that is in your power for the Reich," Prince Max had said to Ebert that afternoon just before leaving for Baden where he had his own little revolution to cope with. "I have given it two sons," Ebert had replied sadly. But he had few illusions about his further services to the country. Defeat coupled with civil war were staring him in the face, and there was no one he could depend on. He sat dejectedly, listening to the brawling of the crowd beneath the Chancellery windows.

The telephone rang and he reached nervously for the receiver. His relief at hearing Groener's voice was great; the two men knew and respected each other. Groener came to the point with military abruptness. Was Ebert willing to restore order? "Yes," replied Ebert fervently. Rapidly the two men reached an agreement. Groener would maintain discipline in the army and bring it home in good order; Ebert would co-operate with the Officers' Corps in the suppression of Bolshevism and it would see to it that no disturbances interfered with the transport system. Hindenburg, it was decided, would remain at the head of the army.

This telephone conversation determined the future of the German Republic. The revolutionary government would have the army's support and thus be strong enough to bear the responsibility of the armistice. Ebert may not have realized that he was delivering the new regime into the hands of the army. But Groener, the strategist, had every reason to go to bed satisfied. The important business of the day had at last been attended to.

Wilhelm, meanwhile, had been quietly attending to some business of his own. At 4:30 A.M. on Sunday, November 10, his train slid out of the Spa station into the foggy night. Among the numerous persons who failed to receive notice of the Kaiser's pre-dawn departure was the newly appointed chief of his civilian cabinet, Clemens von Delbruck, who had rushed away from Berlin the previous evening to die at his master's side; Delbruck had managed to get through the revolutionary barricades, but when he alighted at Spa shortly after daybreak with a grim, dedicated expression, it was to discover that he was several hours late for his rendezvous with death.

There was no slip-up, however, in the arrangement for the Kaiser's escape. His chauffeur had driven out of town during the night in a car stripped of all insignia with instructions to wait beside the railway track a few miles from the Dutch frontier. Ten other cars joined him en route. They were lined up at the designated spot, their headlights dimmed by the thick fog, when the Imperial train halted in the middle of the countryside. It was still dark. Muffled to the eyes in a greatcoat, Wilhelm walked from his railway carriage to the lead automobile in the caravan and climbed in. His suite occupied the others.

The cortege reached the border post at Eyden at 7:30 A.M. It was several hours before any Dutch officials of sufficient rank to deal with such an exalted situation showed up. When they finally appeared, they treated the Imperial refugees with every courtesy, but there were a few formalities they had to insist upon observing. Some of the officers in the Kaiser's party were turned back as belligerents, and Wilhelm himself had to deposit his sword with the Dutch customs for safekeeping. A little later he reached the castle of Amerongen, in Holland, where he was to spend the first months of his comfortable exile.

"And now, my dear Count," he said to his host, stretching out his legs in front of the fire, "I would like a cup of really hot, strong, English tea."

Two days later the Crown Prince, who had promised his corps commanders, with a firm clasp of the hand, that he would remain with the army, also reached Holland. There have been both more tragic and more disgraceful exits from the stage of history, but few more inglorious ones.

In a purely formal sense, the 250-year reign of the Hohenzollern dynasty did not come to an end until November 28, 1918, when Wilhelm, safe in exile, signed an official act of abdication both as Prussian King and as German Emperor. (The Crown Prince renounced his rights to the two thrones on December 1.) As we have seen, however, responsibility for the fate of some 60,000,000 war-exhausted Germans—and for accepting the hard armistice conditions of their victorious enemies—had already shifted to the new men in Berlin. It was they who had to pick up the pieces.

Friedrich Ebert and his colleagues were no revolutionary firebrands. Since 1914 they had dutifully voted all the credits required for the greater glory of German arms and earned their nickname of *"good sozis"* (good socialists). When at the request of Prince Max von Baden Friedrich Ebert assumed the chancellorship, his frock coat was correctly buttoned over his paunch and a blamelessly starched collar supported his comfortable jowls. His ideas were no more subversive than those of the Grand Duke from whom he took over. Like Prince Max he would have favored a liberal, parliamentary monarchy along British lines. He had hoped for a regency and an eventual restoration in the person of Wilhelm's youngest son, Prince August Wilhelm (a poor choice, as it later turned out, when "Auwi" showed up in the ranks of the Nazis). In fact, the form of Germany's government was decided without Ebert. As he was lunching with his colleague Scheidemann in the Reichstag restaurant on the afternoon of November 9, a workers' delegation broke into the building clamoring for a speech. Scheidemann got up from his clear-soup, and as he walked toward the balcony, his excited escort informed him that Liebknecht was going to proclaim a Soviet Republic from the steps of the Imperial Palace. With great presence of mind, the elderly, professorial Scheidemann ended his short address to the seething crowd below with these words: "The old and the rotten, the monarchy, has collapsed. Long live the new. Long live the German Republic." Thus German democracy was born as an improvisation to head off a proletarian revolution.

Ebert was furious at his colleague's high-handed announcement, but he could see for himself how timely it had been. Gray-faced, ragged masses from the suburbs were pouring into Unter den Linden, brandishing Red flags, sweeping along with them crippled veterans, released jailbirds, bearded and dazed prisoners of war, in the great fraternal delirium of the *Internationale*. Prince von Bulow, a bitter old man, stood behind a window at the Adlon Hotel and saw his world go down. "I have seldom witnessed anything so nauseating," he wrote, "as . . . the spectacle of half grown louts, tricked out with the red armlets of Social Democracy, who in bands of several at a time, came creeping up behind any officer wearing the Iron Cross or the order *Pour le merite,* to pin down his elbows at his side and tear off his epaulettes."

To an excitable observer the first dawn of the democratic German republic—November 10—might well have seemed likely to be its last one. The thick black headlines announcing the Kaiser's flight were only one of many shocks that came to dazed inhabitants of the capital along with their *ersatz* coffee and their morning newspaper. The papers themselves had in many cases taken on a new look during the night: the royalist *Lokal Anzeiger,* for example, had turned into *Die Rote Fahne* (The Red Flag). Ebert, however, knew that things were not quite as desperate as they looked. Fortified by his midnight telephone pact with Groener, he set to work at once organizing a provisional government—a necessary preliminary to an armistice, among other things—to function until a constituent assembly could be elected. To wean the Independent Socialists away from their Communist wing, Ebert offered to share power with them. After a whole day, and part of a night of bitter haggling and of fierce alarms, he achieved his objective: formation of a provisional but full and legal government, able to speak in the name of the new German republic. At 2:15 A.M. on November 11, Erzberger announced the good tidings to the Allied armistice representative at Rethondes, and the final talks got under way. (Up to that moment Erzberger had no way of telling whether or not he represented a German authority empowered to accept the Allied terms. The French were even more confused about what was happening in Berlin, and at one point Erzberger had to explain that a telegram ending with the words, THE IMPERIAL CHANCELLOR SCHLUSS, did not indicate the emergence of a new revolutionary leader in the German capital since "*schluss*" was merely German telegraphese for "stop.") Three hours and five minutes later the armistice agreement ending the greatest war in human history up to that time was formally signed.

The delirium of joy with which the news was greeted in Paris, London, and throughout the United States was only feebly echoed in Berlin, still reverberating from the crash of the monarchy. For the Germans the stillness over trenches was drowned out by the roar of revolutionary mobs in the streets. The cease-fire in the West heralded the imminent outbreak of civil war at home.

CHAPTER 18

The Fall of the House of Habsburg

AT dusk on November 11, 1918, while joy-intoxicated crowds, celebrating the death of war and the birth of hope, cheered, sang, embraced in Times Square, on the Champs-Elysées, in Piccadilly, two cars slid past the ragged sentinels of the newly founded Austrian People's Militia on duty at the back entrance of Schoenbrunn Palace. Though driven by trusted chauffeurs of the Imperial Court, the machines themselves were ordinary Vienna taxicabs. A rather ugly-looking demonstration of workers from the nearby Florisdorf steel works was beginning at the main gates of the palace, and the two drivers had been sent out to borrow the cabs so as to avoid attracting undesirable attention to their eminent passengers: a tired-looking young couple with a gaggle of unusually subdued blond children. Karl, Emperor of Austria, King of Hungary, his wife, the Empress Zita, and five little Archdukes and Archduchesses, accompanied by as much hastily packed baggage as the cabs would hold, were on their unobtrusive way to exile. Their destination was the chilly—and temporary—haven of Eckartsau Castle, a bare fifteen miles out of town but situated in a corner of the Burgenland which at that time was Hungarian soil.

Revolution had broken out in Vienna, fanned by news of the upheaval in Germany. Though Karl had obligingly relinquished the reins of government—his former ministers at the moment were sitting side by side with their socialist successors in the Royal-Imperial ministries, initiating them by easy stages into their new responsibilities, and no doubt exchanging with them bleak little Viennese jokes about the situation—the mood of the hungry masses in the city was dangerously unstable. It had seemed advisable from every viewpoint for the deposed monarch and his family to leave town at once, and without attracting too much attention.

To the superficial eye the flight of the last Habsburg Emperor from the capital of his ancestors lacks drama, despite its air of urgency, and Karl himself seems a pathetic rather than a tragic figure. As with many of the other decisive moments in the 600-year history of the dynasty it was not immediately clear exactly what this one had decided. Though Karl was in fact leaving for good, and was never to recover even one of the several crowns he had been forced to abandon, he did not realize the finality of the occasion. It was not, after all, the first time a Habsburg had been chased out of Vienna by revolution: there was the precedent of 1848 to suggest that his return might eventually be possible. Karl, in resigning his functions, had carefully avoided abdicating his rights. Technically he was still the reigning King of Hungary and though he had ceased to reign as Emperor, he would have found it difficult at the time—as would anyone else— to trace the precise frontiers of the empire that he had just renounced. The death throes of the Dual Monarchy could hardly be less ambiguous or embroiled than its whole juridical status had been. The fuzziness of the situation, the atmosphere of somehow inconclusive conclusion that surrounded it, was accentuated by the timing of the Imperial Family's departure. A day or two earlier it could have had more solemnity. A few hours later it might have seemed a heroic escape. Poor Karl bungled his exit as he had failed nearly everything else in his brief reign.

It is hard to make high tragedy out of misfortunes so like the messiness of everyday life, but underneath the surface flatness or incoherence of events, the collapse of the Habsburg dynasty was authentically tragic, not only because of its ultimate historical consequences, but even in a muted, Viennese way, for its very style. Karl had inherited the Habsburg tradition of defeat, and though it was not in him to manage anything brilliantly, not even a disaster, he upheld that tradition with honor and dignity. If the story lacks one kind of drama it combines in a strange, rather compelling fashion an almost Greek sense of inevitable doom with a harrowing feeling of unnecessary catastrophe. One is reminded of an airplane that gets out of control in landing, brushes a series of minor obstacles, and scatters bits of flaming wreckage for a mile before the final, almost anti-climactic crash. Karl was the hapless pilot, wrestling bravely and ineffectually up to the last fraction of a second with inexorable fate and his own blunders. His failure is curiously moving to the sensitized present-day intelligence. Karl was not a monster like Abdul Hamid, or a kind of defective like Nicholas, or a self-impostor like Wilhelm. Except for being more well-meaning than most of us normally are, and bearing himself a bit better in misfortune than we usually manage to do, and acting, perhaps, a shade less effectively in an emergency, he could be any of us. The last heir to six centuries of grandeur and medievalism comes close to incarnating that wistful new folk-hero of the modern age: The Little Man in the grip of giant circum-stance. The Chaplinesque tragedy is worth recounting.

Karl, as we noted earlier, succeeded his great uncle, Francis Joseph, on November 21, 1916. The old gentleman had attended to the business of dying with his usual simple dignity. Stricken with pneumonia, he had been persuaded to leave his desk early on the evening before, but he had left instructions to be called at the usual time in the morning. By then he was dead. His only friend, Katharina Schratt, was not present: he had wanted to spare her the sight of his sickness. She was escorted to the narrow iron cot next morning by Karl, aged twenty-nine, and a "good fellow" as his great uncle liked to call him. When a week later—after Francis Joseph had lain in state, for vigils and Masses such as nowadays only accompany the burial of a Pope—the young Emperor led the funeral procession through Vienna, some witnesses thought they detected a renewed attachment to the dynasty on the part of the hungry, war-weary Viennese public. The old Emperor had not been seen for so long, he had become almost a myth. But here was a modest young man, looking boyish in field-gray, his head bared, and between him and the slim figure of his wife, entirely draped in black from head to toe, walked his son, Otto, in skirts, sash, white socks and golden ringlets—what the well-dressed four-year-old wore in those days. In a world fast disintegrating, it was a reassuring symbol of the bourgeois security which in fact Vienna and the Empire would never know again. The funeral itself was something else: the last great affirmation of the baroque tradition. While the body of the old ruler was being laid to rest, every hour was taking a terrible toll of young men, whose rotting corpses were being turned to mud on the battle fields of Verdun, of the Somme and on Isonzo, where the Austrians and Italians were locked for the ninth time in a great inconclusive battle. Few of the Viennese who lined the sidewalks can have failed to realize that it was their past grandeur they were seeing buried.

An American witness recorded the anachronistic pageantry which was enacted before the body was admitted to lie with its peers in the crypt of the Capuchin church. As the procession approached the crypt, a knight in armor stepped up and knocked on the closed gate. At this a monk in a cowl, appearing at a small window, queried, "Who knocks?"

"The body of his August Majesty, the Emperor of Austria and King of Hungary demands to be admitted for sepulture," came the answer.

"We know of no such person here," the monk replied. "Again I say, who knocks?"

Now the knight, bowing humbly, murmured, "A poor brother, a fellow being, seeks entrance for eternal rest."

"Enter" said the monk, and as he spoke, the gates creaked open and the pallbearers carried the heavy coffin into the gloom of the crypt.

Francis Joseph had died and been buried according to rules as old as the dynasty. But there were no rules ordained for the death of the dynasty itself and for the dissolution of the Empire it had ruled. The frail young man who was to play the last act did not know the lines—there were none—and his voice never rose above the *Goetterdaemmerung* din.

Karl was the son of the notorious Otto, the "handsomest Archduke," who died in 1906 of too much high living. He had become heir apparent after the death of his uncle, Francis Ferdinand, whose children were debarred from the succession. His education, presided over by a doting mother— Otto had little taste for family life—and Jesuit priests, was exacting but of mediocre content, as was usual for the sons of reigning families. Young Karl did, however, end up by attending the University of Prague where he became conscious, as his predecessors never had been, of the aspirations of the minorities, but without being given an insight into the complicated puzzle of governing them. Karl spent the two first war years in various garrison towns, and in command of an army corps on the Italian front, where he endeared himself to his men by his simplicity.

As a Habsburg Emperor, or in fact as any kind of Habsburg, Karl was a curious anomaly. Perhaps the most up-to-date and enlightened member of his family in his political and social outlook since the times of the benevolent despot Joseph II—Karl, unlike his predecessor kept three telephones on his desk and loved to drive fast cars—he was from many viewpoints the most medieval in personality. Though his virtues were bourgeois rather than heroic in their expression, he recalls, at moments, such heroes of pious legend as St. Louis and Edward the Confessor. (His own family despite its sometimes austere clericalism seems to have produced no ruler of comparable saintliness.) Earnest and still capable of juvenile enthusiasms, overflowing with trust in his fellow men, he disliked the worldly cynics of the old court, who no doubt poked fun at his sometimes naive do-goodism.

Karl not only had strong religious convictions: he tried to express them, with a literalness which often disconcerted his entourage, both in private life and in state policy. Abstaining from alcohol could be viewed as a harmless eccentricity; refusing to condone the wartime bombing of enemy cities and the destruction of art treasures seemed to many a dangerous aberration.

Karl was, in fact, a sworn enemy to every form of violence, legal or otherwise; he considered it un-Christian. Once when he was talking in a relaxed mood with Count Tamas von Erdody, a childhood friend, and a member of his military staff, the latter playfully boasted about how perfectly he could imitate the Imperial signature. Karl laughed goodhumoredly, but then his face suddenly turned grave and with more than his usual earnestness he begged Erdody never to use his unorthodox talent to sign a death warrant in the Emperor's name. On another occasion, in connection with the secret mission of the Bourbon-Parma princes, Erdody reported having been obliged to knock a spy downstairs. "Oh, I hope the poor fellow did not break his neck," the Emperor exclaimed. Late one night in February 1918, while Karl was traveling to Budapest, a telegram reached the Imperial train begging clemency for four mutineers who were to be shot in the morning. The head of Karl's military cabinet did not see fit to disturb his master's sleep for such trivialities and the execution took place as scheduled. When the Emperor woke up and learned about the telegram he was furious at his aide. "You should have called me," he said sternly. "I am a man like any other."

All too frequently, Karl's efforts to inject Christian idealism into politics failed for lack of resolution. He was easily discouraged, and also far too easily swayed by his entourage, though he was neither as weak as the Czar nor as unstable as the Kaiser.

Zita, whom Karl married in 1911, helped to strengthen his sense of purpose, though her judgment was often less good than his. She was an active, energetic woman, frankly eager to have an influence upon state policy, and no doubt a bit bossy at times. Just as her husband was stronger in character than Nicholas, Zita seems to have been healthier and saner than Alexandra. She also had less time on her hands for meddling. Between 1911 and 1921 she presented the dynasty with eight children, and was scrupulous in fulfilling all her maternal duties. Politically, she was a good deal more reactionary than her husband. Whereas Karl had adopted as his own the doctrine of a federalized empire which the boldest members of Francis Ferdinand's private brain trust had urged upon the late heir shortly before his assassination, Zita, according to some of her critics, thought of the projected federation as a constellation of duchies and kingdoms, each to be ruled by a Bourbon-Parma prince. Karl himself, despite the democratic manners and the liberal outlook which caused one enthusiastic parliamentarian to describe him as "a People's Emperor," was no parlor pink. He believed in the Habsburg mission. It was primarily to save the dynasty that he wanted to liberalize the Empire.

By the time Karl took office, however, the centrifugal forces tearing at the fabric of the Dual Monarchy had become irreversible. At the beginning of the war, Count Stuergkh, the Prime Minister, had prorogued Parliament ("Parliaments are only a means to an end, where they fail, other means must be employed," he had said). In October 1916, in the face of Stuergkh's obstinate refusal to rescind the decree, a young socialist who was destined later to play a notable role in the Second Internationale, Friedrich Adler, son of the Social Democrat leader Viktor Adler, shot him dead while he was lunching, as usual, at the fashionable Meisl and Schadn restaurant.

Karl showed his desire for liberal reform by reconvening Parliament in the spring of 1917. It immediately became a public platform for the minorities' claims to independence.

Under Count Stuergkh's regime of "silence and compression," the rot eating away the foundations of the Empire had made fast progress. Before 1914 the minorities as a whole had aspired to nothing more than equality with the dominant races in the Empire: the Germans and the Magyars. But the Habsburg Germans, fighting shoulder to shoulder with their brethren of the Kaiser's Germany, were in no mood for concessions, and the Hungarians held the inexpugnable position of guardians of the Empire's larder. The minorities, which, added up, outnumbered the politically dominant German and Magyar groups by 10 millions, had been turned by wartime repression from grumbling but loyal subjects into plotting dissidents.

In the face of nationalist movements whose avowed minimal aim was now complete independence, Karl's dreams of a federal monarchy were not merely tinged with unreality, but were based on a complete fiction. In fact, Karl had nothing to offer. He had let himself be trapped by the Hungarian Prime Minister, Count Tisza, into going to Budapest for Coronation as King of Hungary (a ceremony which Francis Joseph had avoided). There he had sworn to respect the Hungarian constitution and "to preserve the integrity of the lands of the crown of St. Stephen." This barred him not only from championing the rights of those minorities oppressed by the Magyars, but even from respecting, as he had promised when he took office, the ancient constitution of Bohemia whose lands were partially under Hungarian domination.

There is a coronation portrait of Karl, Zita, and the Archduke Otto which shows them sitting stiffly on the gilded chairs deplorably typical of royal palaces the world over. Karl's headpiece, the crown of St. Stephen, is too big for him, and he holds the scepter as awkwardly as a school boy King Arthur. Zita's neck is stiff from the weight of the gold edifice, surmounted by a cross which presses down on her black hair. Little curly-haired Otto looks like a circus prince, with a huge aigrette topping the ermine toque worn above the ermine-lined cloak. They all look pathetically like children dressed up for a charade.

How grim and ineffectual the charade was as long as they were tied to Hungary on the one side, to Germany on the other, both Karl and Zita realized. Karl's secret negotiations with the Allies to give his people the peace they yearned for, as we have seen, had come to nothing, and by the end of 1917 all the belligerents once more proclaimed their will to fight to the end for a just cause. In October seven German divisions were sent to reinforce the Austrians on the Isonzo front. It was felt in Berlin that a spectacular victory would be the best cure for Austrian despondency. The rout of the hated Italians at Caporetto—the background for one of the dramatic episodes in Hemingway's *A Farewell to Arms*—did help to raise Austrian morale, but it also tied Vienna more firmly to Berlin's apron strings. When in October the German government proclaimed, "Germany will never, no never, make any concessions on the subject of the Alsace-Lorraine," Austria's Foreign Minister, Count Czernin, echoed obediently, "We fight for Alsace-Lorraine just as the Germans fight for Trieste."

It was the hapless Count, who by inadvertently bringing to light the Sixte de Bourbon affair, involved the monarchy in a scandal which gave it the coup de grace. In the spring of 1918 things were looking better for Austria than they had in many months. Russia and Rumania had been knocked out of the war. Italy's army was crippled for the time being, and thanks to the "bread peace" of Brest-Litovsk, the exhausted civilians of the Central Powers could reasonably hope for better rations, if not better times. The great German spring offensive which was to give the Allies the death blow, had started in Picardy. Count Czernin, cocky from his appearance on the stage of Brest-Litovsk, thought that a little psychological warfare was in order. In a speech delivered to the municipality of Vienna on April 2, he asserted that he had quite recently rejected a French offer of negotiations, because the proposed terms insisted on the return of Alsace-Lorraine. (Czernin was referring to new secret conversations in Switzerland between Austrian and French agents, which seem to have been originated by Austria.) This rash statement was to cheer the home team, by giving the impression that France was looking for a way out of the war, despite Clemenceau's loudly proclaimed policy of fighting on to total victory.

The "Tiger's" reply was short, brutal, and immediately reported by the press: "Count Czernin is lying." But Czernin would not leave well enough alone and engaged a spirited controversy with Clemenceau. He was skating on razor-thin ice, for although he had, a year ago, approved the Sixte de Bourbon mission, he had, it will be recalled, known nothing of the Emperor's autographed letter to Poincaré, and Karl failed to warn him of its existence in time. Not only that, but no sooner had the existence of such a letter been rumored in Paris, than Karl sent a telegram to the Kaiser denying its authenticity. At this Clemenceau, whose strongest virtue was not patience, had a facsimile published, for all to see.

The affair was one of those complex and futile imbroglios that are sometimes more decisive than great battles or solemn acts of policy. It also contains the essential essence of Karl's personal tragedy. In originally launching the peace negotiations behind his ally's back he had jesuitically sacrificed one moral duty to another, accepted shabby means to a noble end. He had set peace above honor. But his compromise with expediency had not been a total surrender to it. He had stopped short of the brink of outright falsehood. With the telegram to Wilhelm he threw himself right over it. His keen personal sense of honor and his unworldly conscience, inherited from some medieval ancestor, must have wrestled in anguish, with the cynical traditions of Metternichian diplomacy. Metternich won; for once St. Louis would have proved a sounder adviser.

The Emperor of Austria stood exposed to the world as a liar. In those days Europe, even in its death throes, was not hardened to such violations of the gentleman's code. Ambassadors prevaricated as a matter of course. Premiers falsified, and, like Bethmann-Holliveg, sometimes treated solemn covenants as scraps of paper. Monarchs themselves quibbled and cheated on occasion. But they did not put their signatures to a formal lie—least of all in writing to a brother monarch. The publication of Karl's telegram to the Kaiser was not only a mortal wound to his personal prestige as a ruler; it somehow tarnished the fading magic that still surrounded the Habsburg throne itself, the only remaining link between the peoples of the Empire. Perhaps the gravest link in the chain of disasters forged by Czernin's inno-cent blunder (he lost his job for it, of course, but was recompensed with the Grand Cross, set in diamonds, of the Crown of St. Stephen) was that Karl had to take the road to Canossa with respect to the Prussian allies whom he more than ever loathed and feared. Canossa in this case was the German Headquarters at Spa where Karl went in May. As one authority puts it, the price of his pardon was "the closest military, political and economic union which the two empires had hitherto concluded." Karl had lost his last pos-sibility of independent action.

In the face of this development the last die-hard Habsburg apologists in the Allied camp were silenced. The policy of preserving the Dual Monarchy as a counterweight to Germany, seemed now indefensible and Benes' cry of "Destroy Austria" became Allied policy. Events within the crumbling Em-pire both reflected and sustained the Entente's decision. The Emperor and his successive governments were no longer able to cope with the open hos-tility of the minorities. The pandemonium in the Vienna Parliament where the deputies representing the various nationalities aired their claims with increasing violence surpassed anything seen before. In July 1918 a Czech deputy declared to the House: "We regard Austria as a centuries' old crime against humanity . . . It is our highest national duty to betray Austria whenever and wherever we can. We shall hate Austria, we shall fight against her, and God willing, we shall in the end smash her to pieces." On Octo-ber 1 another Czech deputy, Stanek, declared that although his people had not shed a drop of blood willingly for the Central Powers, they had gladly made every sacrifice to bring about the imminent Allied victory. "The day of judgment is at hand," he shouted. His voice was covered by applause from some benches, shouts from others, the banging of desk lids. Cries of "Treason" from the German Austrians were encountered with a volley of briefcases and inkpots from the nationalities.

Separatism and defeatism steadily mounted as the hopes of spring faded and the outlook for the Central Powers darkened. The turn of the tide on the Western Front coincided with the flood of the Allied offensive up through the Balkans, originally launched from Salonika by the multi-national expeditionary force under France's General Franchet d'Esperey. Austria's share of the economic loot from Brest-Litovsk proved insufficient to compensate for the tightening grip of the Allied blockade.

By the late summer of 1918 the Dual Monarchy had curdled not only into rival nationalisms but also into a multitude of separate and hostile economic islands. Hungary withheld its wheat from the rest of the empire; each province and district similarly hoarded its meager stocks. Living conditions became intolerable in the big cities, especially in Vienna. The pressure of public opinion for bread and peace became irresistible.

On October 4, the Austrian government had joined the Germans in appealing to President Wilson for an armistice, based on the Fourteen Points, and on October 6, without waiting for an answer, the Emperor Karl in a last ineffectual effort to preserve some role for the dynasty in the new scheme of things issued a manifesto reorganizing the non-Hungarian part of the monarchy into a federal state with complete self-government for the subject nationalities. The clause excepting the Hungarian territories from the reform had been forced on the Emperor by the Hungarian Prime Minister with the usual threats to cut off food supplies in case of non-compliance, and it effectively invalidated whatever effect the Manifesto might have had on the dissident nationalities and on President Wilson's hoped-for good will.

(The Hungarian ruling class remained absolutely incapable of approaching the minorities problem from any other angle than the predatory Magyar one. When before issuing the Manifesto Karl had attempted to win the Hungarians to his point of view he sent Count Tisza, the Hungarian Prime Minister from 1913 to June 1917, to seek some modus vivendi with Hungary's South Slavs. The fiery, bearded Count had become so exasperated with his mission that on reaching Sarajevo he snarled at the dignitaries who had exposed their grievances, "It may be that we shall go under. But we shall grind you to pieces before we do.")

The Committee set up to put the provisions of the Manifesto into effect, was boycotted by the Czechs; the Southern Slavs walked out; the Germans would not commit themselves, the Ukrainians rejected the plan; the Poles were elsewhere, and the Italian minority did not consider it applied to them. The population in general viewed the Manifesto as an admission of defeat, and the imperial bureaucracy, feeling the ground sinking away under its feet, was demoralized. Instead of shoring up the Empire's tottering house of cards, the Manifesto proved to be an instrument of its collapse: the diets authorized under the new federal organization turned out to be ready-made Parliaments for the fine new states, which, within less than a month were to rise from the ruins of the old Dual Monarchy.

President Wilson's answer to the Emperor's peace plea was received on October 21. It was described by the new Foreign Minister, Count Burian, as "a bombshell which rent the frame of the monarchy apart." The Fourteen Points had demanded no more than the "freest opportunity of autonomous development" for the minorities, a demand which had been met by the Emperor's Manifesto. But in his latest note the American President, who, in the meantime had recognized the Czechoslovak National Council as a de facto government, stated that he was no longer at liberty to accept a mere autonomy for the Czechoslovak and Yugoslav peoples as a basis for peace. He insisted that they, and not he, "shall be the judges of what action on the part of the Austro-Hungarian Government will satisfy their aspirations." This note, and the rapidly approaching armies of General Franchet d'Esperey precipitated the chain reaction of revolutions which now separated the monarchy into its component parts and swept away the supranational imperial authority and its bureaucracy.

The Czechs were the first to break loose. In the summer of 1918 the Allied governments had recognized Czechoslovakia as a co-belligerent. On October 18 Masaryk had solemnly proclaimed Czechoslovak independence in Washington, and flown the new blue-red-white flag from his house. He had wanted to forestall the effects of Karl's Manifesto and to influence the American President favorably. The proclamation was, according to his own words, "cast in a form calculated to remind the Americans of their own Declaration of Independence."

The reminder had proved effective. President Wilson's note in effect warned the Emperor Karl that acceptance of Czech independence was the price of peace—part of the price. In the feeble hope that the Czechs themselves might be induced to retain some link, however nominal, with the Habsburg throne, Karl communicated the terms of the American note to the leaders of the legal Czech nationalist parties in the Empire and authorized them to leave for Geneva to confer with Benes, now the Foreign Minister of the Czechoslovak Provisional Government abroad.

Any chance of a compromise that would keep Czechoslovakia within the Empire was swept away by the direct impact of Wilson's note on the Czech masses when its content was officially released for publication in Prague on October 28. The crowds who had been waiting feverishly for the latest news in front of the offices of the newspaper *Narodni Politika* on Vencenclas Square, burst into wild cheers as the full implications of the note became apparent, and soon the streets were full of citizens happily pulling down Habsburg emblems from tobacco shops and public buildings. Carried away by these demonstrations of popular enthusiasm, the Prague National Committee decided to take over the administration. Those were hungry times and the first building they occupied was understandably the Corn Exchange, housing the country's rationing authorities. There was no resistance from the Austrian officials. On orders from Vienna, the military governor withdrew the Magyar troops who had been patrolling the streets, and the Austrian bureaucrats resignedly packed their bags. By evening, when the citizens of Prague saw the men of their beloved, national gymnastic clubs, the Sokols, keep order in the streets, they knew that independence had really come. Two days later the Slovak National Council pronounced itself in favor of unity with the Czech provinces of Bohemia, Moravia, and Silesia. (The Slovaks under Hungarian rule only joined the Republic after their former masters were driven out in 1920. So did the province of Sub-Carpathian Ruthenia for which a semi-autonomous status was provided in the constitution.) On November 14 a National Assembly, in its first session, declared the Habsburg Dynasty deprived of all its rights to the Bohemian lands, proclaimed a Republic and elected Thomas G. Masaryk its first President.

The South Slav peoples of the Empire were the next to secede. They had fought for their independence under particularly difficult conditions. Theirs was the first jab at the Habsburg Goliath and it had brought their champion, Serbia, four years of death and destruction. Although within four months of the Austrian attack in August 1914 the Serbs had thrown General Potiorek and his armies back over the border, they succumbed in 1915 to a typhus epidemic which claimed the lives of 300,000 and to a concerted attack of the Germans, Austrians, and Bulgars. In the winter of 1915–1916 what was left of the Serbian Army, together with the whole government, the Regent, Prince Alexander, and his invalid father King Peter (who had to be evacuated in an ox cart) withdrew themselves across the mountains of Albania and Para Montenegro to the Adriatic coast. The survivors of one of the most harrowing retreats in history were picked up by allied warships and transported to the island of Corfu. It was there that emigré leaders of the Empire's South Slavs met the exiled royal Serbian government, and on July 20, 1917, signed a common declaration affirming the unity of Serbs, Croats, and Slovenes and their intention to form a constitutional, democratic and parliamentary monarchy under the Karageorgevic dynasty.

On October 6 a National Council of Serbs, Croats, and Slovenes was set up in Zagreb, the chief city of the Dual Monarchy's South Slavs. Into its hands the governor of Croatia, on instructions from Karl, surrendered the executive power on October 29. The National Council declared for union with Serbia and severed all connections with the "ex-Hungarian and Austrian territories." On December 4 the kingdom of Serbs, Croats, and Slovenes, thereafter known as Yugoslavia, was proclaimed under the regency of Prince Alexander, later King Alexander I. The union of the South

Slavs under Serbian leadership, for which the conspirators of Sarajevo had plotted and died, was thus achieved. Princip, Cabrinovic, and Grabez, whose age had saved them from execution at the time, had all succumbed to tuberculosis and died in prison during the war. Their bodies were brought back to Sarajevo in 1920 and buried in the local cemetery alongside the bodies of their accomplices who had paid with their lives after the trial. The two schoolboys sentenced to prison terms were released after the collapse of the Dual Monarchy.[1]

Even the Dual Monarchy's Polish minority defected. It will be recalled that in the eighteenth century, Hohenzollern, Habsburg, and Romanov greed had partitioned Poland and wiped its name off the map. The Austrian share was the smallest and the Poles enjoyed a favored position in the Dual Monarchy; the numerical strength of Polish deputies in the Vienna parliament was such that no government could be formed without them. Most Poles regarded the Germans and the Russians as their real oppressors; there was little animosity toward Austria. After the Treaty of Brest-Litovsk and the Russian Revolution, the Polish deputies in the Reichsrat shifted to the opposition. On October 15 they informed the House that they now no longer considered themselves subjects of the Dual Monarchy, but citizens of the reborn Poland. The pianist, Ignace Paderewski, heading the emigré Polish National Committee in Paris, proved to be as able a propagandist for Poland in the United States as Masaryk had been for Czechoslovakia, and it was largely due to him that Wilson's Thirteenth Point demanded the creation after the war of an independent Poland with free access to the sea. At the end of October Austrian troops began withdrawing from Galicia. On November 14, 1918, Pilsudski who had been released from German imprisonment by the Social Democrat Revolution, took power in Warsaw. The various and often rival Polish independence movements eventually merged, and in January 1919, Paderewski as premier formed a coalition government while Pilsudski became President.

Thus even before the revolution in Vienna which was to cost Karl the throne, the Habsburg dynasty had been abandoned by all the minorities over which it had ruled. (In addition to those who joined Czechoslovakia, Poland, and Yugoslavia, the province of Transylvania joined Rumania, and the Italian-populated territories were at last redeemed by the mother country.) There remained the core of the Empire: the two master-nations, Austria and Hungary.

To Karl, and all those who put the survival of the supranational Habsburg Dynasty above that of the Empire, there remained a nominal hope. Austria-Hungary, even stripped down to its basic components, was a viable

---

[1] One, Cubrilovic, was eventually to become minister of forestry in the Tito government, and the other Popovic curator of the Ethnographic Department of the Sarajevo Museum.

and fair-sized power. In theory there was no overriding reason why it should not continue to accept and sustain the monarchy. In practice, too many factors were adverse: the winds of Wilsonism that were sweeping Europe, the accumulation of Karl's own errors, the social unrest born of hunger, the demoralization of impending defeat, the loss of prestige—and even of an essential raison d'être—as the outlying province of the Empire, began to fall away. And above all, perhaps the sheer momentum of fission. The final debacle of the monarchy was the culmination of a revolutionary chain reaction in the Magyar-German central nucleus of the Empire, triggered in part by the splitting off of great fragments from the Slavic periphery. Whereas the national revolutions in the subject nations were largely peaceful transfers of power from a collapsing authority, merely formalizing local secessions that had already taken place in fact, the disintegration of the Empire's core inevitably released explosive forces. It was simultaneously social, political, and national: a royal, royal-imperial, royal-and-imperial dissolution. It began almost at the same moment in the two Habsburg capitals and at the front.

On October 24 the Allies launched a great offensive on the Italian front along the Piave. For two days the Austro-Hungarian Army, sustained by tradition and training, fought back, although its soldiers were in rags, famished and plagued by malaria and Spanish influenza. "At the front, the Empire seems to live on in the all-nation-embracing unity of the army," wrote the Socialist, Otto Bauer, at the time. Yet it is precisely in the army and in the barracks that the Austrian revolution originated. And the ones to mutiny first were not the regiments of industrial workers, or those incorporating prisoners released by the Russians, but the stanchest, smartest, most dashing of the imperial troops: the Hungarians.

Two days after the start of the Allied offensive, the commander of the Hungarian divisions reported that as a regiment had paraded before him with the usual precision, one man stepped from the ranks, saluted smartly, and informed him that the unit would refuse to take up its positions. When orders were given for the man's arrest, the regiment called out as if with one voice, "We won't allow it," still standing at attention. Questioned separately the men swore that they would fight on to their last breath—but on their own borders. Since the Hungarian parliament had called for the return of its troops several days before, there was no alternative but to send them home, along with the other Hungarian divisions to whom the movement had spread. It is natural that the men called up to replace the Magyar, whose singing, cheering, homeward-bound regiments they often crossed as they moved up to the front, should not resist the epidemic for long. Under the impact of defeat and retreat the morale of the hard core of the army, the trusted loyal Tirolians of the famed Edelweiss Division, once commanded by Karl himself, broke too, and the soldiers headed for home, to defend their farms and families against the unknown. The individual and collective defective from the front spread confusion throughout both halves of the monarchy.

Meanwhile a queer kind of revolutionary tumult broke out in Budapest. Since the days of Kossuth, Magyar nationalism had been schizophrenically split between nostalgia for the heroic enthusiasms of the struggle against Austrian oppression and a fanatic determination to continue oppressing the subject races in Hungary. (A somewhat similar ambivalence is discernible today in South African nationalism and among other once colonized colonialists.) Wilsonism and the strains of defeat brought nostalgia to the top. The more fashionable it became to be a national minority, the more convinced Magyars became that is what they were themselves. As long as it was possible to resist the national liberation movement among their subject peoples, they did so by every ruthless means; when resistance ceased to be possible, they threw themselves into the movement, like prison guards joining a jailbreak. Apart from the sheer emotional contagion, a number of the less obfuscated Magyar landowners came to the conclusion that the best way to save what could be saved out of the general wreckage was to turn democratic—in their hearts they had always felt that all magnates were born free and equal—and espouse the triumphant Wilsonian doctrine of self-determination (which would in fact have saved Hungary many a cruel amputation if the victors had applied it honestly).

The leader of the Magyar Wilsonians was an aristocrat turned radical reformer, Count Michael Karoli. While it would be an exaggeration to say that the Count's fellow magnates were powerfully attracted by his ideals, they had foresightedly refrained from hanging him to one of their wagon tongues when they might have done so, and now they began to perceive dimly that the heretic in their midst might some day prove useful. Karoli's potential usefulness seemed all the greater at a moment when General Franchet d'Esperey's army was nearing the Hungarian frontier because he was notoriously pro-French. He had been interned in France on the outbreak of war in 1914 but had been subsequently released, so it was said, on the understanding that after return home he would work for the speedy end of the war.

Hungary's secession from the Empire started amid scenes of violence. On October 24, in Budapest, a revolutionary mob broke into the vast turreted, cupola-surmounted, venetian-gothic Parliament Building on the banks of the Danube and swarming past the racks where the deputies used to park their cigars before entering the chamber, they burst into the gilt-paneled hemicycle. Under the huge painting of Francis Joseph's coronation an incredible turmoil broke out, which only subsided when Prime Minister Wekerle submitted his resignation.

The resultant period of incipient chaos gave Karoli his cue. He announced the formation, under his chairmanship, of a Hungarian National Council, dedicated to separation from Austria, universal suffrage, land reform, and immediate peace. Despite the dread words "land reform," most of the magnates stood aside and let Karoli organize his seditious council realizing it offered their best hope of survival. In parliament Karoli openly proclaimed himself a friend of France. (Franchet d'Esperey unfortunately was not impressed; on November 8 he imposed on Hungary stringent armistice terms under which the national forces had to evacuate all southeast Hungary.)

In an effort to sanction what he could not prevent, Karl, King of Hungary still, appointed Karoli Prime Minister by telephone from Vienna on October 31. That same night Count Stephen Tisza, Karoli's chief opponent, was done to death by assassins who broke into his home. Karoli took his oath of allegiance to the King, but popular demonstrations which had increased in intensity after the streets of Budapest started filling with soldiers back from the front, forced him to rescind it a few days later. "We want a Prime Minister by revolution, not by royal decree," Karoli's Socialist supporters explained. Feelings against the Austrians and the Germans ran high with the workers and peasants who had suffered most from the war. An Austrian paper reported on November 3 that German troops who had had to cross Hungary on their way back from the front had arrived at the frontier station completely naked, their clothing, including their underwear, having been stripped from them on the way.

The ultimate—and fatal—paradox in the breakup of the Habsburg Empire was the belated discovery of the Austrian people, that is essentially the dominant German ethnic group in what remained of Austria, that they too were a submerged (and perhaps oppressed) nationality. For 600 years they had been too busy helping a supranational dynasty run a multi-national Empire to develop a nationalism of their own. Nationalism, as the Austrians had come into contact with it up to October 1918, had seemed an infantile disorder contracted at a certain stage of their evolution by most national minorities. Now, it came to the Austrians with a sudden sense of shock, they themselves had been a minority all along, without realizing it. They were just as entitled as anyone else to exercise the right of self-determination, about which the American President spoke so eloquently, and which their own good Emperor Karl had promised to all the nationalities in his Empire. Basing their action on the Emperor's Manifesto of October 16, the deputies of the Austrian Reichstrat set themselves up as one of the "national diets" provided for in the document, under the designation "Provisional National Assembly of the Independent German-Austrian State." To solemnize their newly found nationhood or perhaps independence, the Assembly men on October 30 met in the historic house on the Herrengasse where the Revolution of 1848 (Vienna Chapter) had been launched and under the sedate, frockcoated leadership of the politicians who headed the country's three major parties, appointed a Council to administer the new state. It would have been a secession, if there had been an Empire left to secede from, but it was not explicitly a revolt against the Habsburg Dynasty. One of the major parties, the Christian-Socialists, explicitly wanted to keep the Habsburgs as the rulers of a constitutional national monarchy. The Social-Democrats in principle wanted a republic, but as Stalin had jeeringly predicted before the war, many of them still had a strong sentimental attachment to the dynasty which they had so long served in the role of loyal opposition. One Socialist deputy proposed as a way out of the dilemma a republic with the ex-Emperor Karl as its first president. In addition to leaving the form of the new Austrian state to be determined by future developments, the Assembly also neglected to fix its geographical boundaries. "We cannot collect taxes," complained the new Socialist Chancellor, Karl Renner, "until we establish where they are collectable."

While waiting for the situation—or its own mind—to clear, the new government refrained from ousting the Emperor's last Imperial cabinet headed by Dr. Heinrich Lammasch, his former tutor. For three weeks the freshly appointed socialist secretaries sat side by side in the former *Kaiserlich-Koeniglich* ministries with the Imperial ministers, learning the rudiments of administration.

The old Imperial authority did not resist the new order. "My only wish is that everything shall be liquidated peaceably," Karl had confided to an intimate. The Renner government felt that the question of what to do with the dynasty did not rest solely with Austria. Events were fast approaching a decisive crisis. On October 27 Karl, urgently pressed by his desperate General Staff, sued for an armistice in the field. It was signed with the Allied Powers on November 3. Confusion as to the date and the hour caused the Austrians to lay down their arms before the Italians. . . . "The news of the armistice was received with relief by all of us," wrote prisoner Kurt von Schuschnigg. "Then there was the rounding up of prisoners, something quite incomprehensible to us all, for we had assumed the armistice to be a fact . . . We were under order to move on in marching kit to the bridge over the Tagliamento at Dignano, and when we got near to it, Scots infantry unexpectedly ordered us to disarm . . . When in distress we sought an explanation for this, the story got around that the Emperor and the Government had purposely tricked us by prematurely announcing an armistice in order to prevent the troops from returning home." The bungled armistice caused some 100,000 unsuspecting Austrians to fall into Italian captivity. Most of the others headed for home, by whatever conveyance they could squeeze into, leaving their weapons behind. Trampling over their officers, they seized control of the railway stations, crowded on the roofs of trains when they could no longer get into the carriages. The Vienna *Neue Freie Presse* of November 7 reported that "within the last few days the bodies of 297 soldiers have been found in the tunnels of the Southern Railway." As all the railway networks of the Empire converged on Vienna, thousands of soldiers poured into the city, many of them, especially those belonging to the subject nationalities, bent on plunder. Some 600,000 workers, released by the war industries, hungry and in rags, were also abroad. The prisoners-of-war camps outside Vienna were no longer adequately guarded. Fear of a mass breakout of prisoners added to the increasingly hysterical atmosphere of the capital, where more and more soldiers were tearing the imperial insignia from their uniforms, and often from that of their officers.

The specter of a proletarian march on Schoenbrunn, where the Imperial family were living, loomed larger and larger in the minds of elderly professors of the Lammasch ministry. Their last cabinet session had led to the dispirited wrangling over the advisability of recommending abdication or waiting for deposition. Up to that moment, the powerful Christian Social and German National parties clung to the idea of a constitutional monarchy, and Austrian politicians in general were too well versed in the art of diplomatic give and take to underestimate the possible usefulness of the Crown in negotiations with the Allies. But on November 10 the flight of the Kaiser Wilhelm and the establishment of a Social Democratic Republic in Germany became known, and the leaders of the Austrian State Government, fearing the contagion of revolution, warned the Emperor's ministers that the situation might become uncontrollable unless abdication were announced.

On Sunday morning November 10, at about the time when ex-Kaiser Wilhelm was being admitted as a refugee in Holland, Mass was being celebrated in the royal chapel in Schoenbrunn. As the organ rendered Haydn's *Gott Erhalte* amid the stifled sobs of the congregation, tearful, furtive glances converged on the gray and tired-looking young man kneeling on Francis Joseph's *prie-dieu*. It was Karl's last appearance in public. On Monday his ministers showed up early at the palace. Literally wringing their hands, they begged him to follow the Archbishop of Vienna's advice and sign at least a provisional abdication. "At once, your Majesty, at once," the elderly Prime Minister kept repeating nervously.

Karl never took an important decision without consulting Zita. He did so now. She looked at the proposed abdication document and flew into a rage. "A king can never abdicate," she said. "He can only be deposed. I would rather die with you here, then Otto would succeed us, and if he were deposed there will always be enough Habsburgs left."

The paper which the Emperor was about to sign was in fact not an abdication, as Minister Lammasch pointed out to the Empress when she had been calmed down. And there was really no alternative; the exhausted country could not afford civil war, he added. Karl signed.

The gist of his renunciation was stated in the proclamation which he issued before leaving on the same evening: "Still, as ever, filled with unchanging love toward all my peoples, I will not oppose my person as an obstacle to their free development. I recognize in advance the decision which German Austria will take on its future form of State. The people have assumed the government through its representatives. I renounce my share in the affairs of State."

(Karl never abdicated in his own name, nor did he renounce his dynastic rights. His son Otto still claims the throne.)

Karl was reluctant to leave and he knew he had nothing to fear from Renner's tame Socialists now that he had stepped down. The authority of the new regime was precarious, however; the hastily organized People's Militia was not either yet effective or wholly dependable. Minor clashes and disorders of various kinds often instigated by returned Austrian prisoners of war who had been Bolshevised in Russia, kept breaking out in the hungry city. The revolutionary fever in Vienna rose steadily throughout the day, foreshadowing the violent convulsion that lay ahead. By the end of the afternoon, with the Florisdorf steel workers marching on the palace, the Imperial Family no longer felt—or were—secure. Sorrowfully Karl yielded to Erdody's entreaties and allowed him to send out for the taxis while a few valises were quickly stuffed with valuables and necessities. Before going into exile, however, Karl insisted on one last funereal little ceremony. First he went with Zita and the children into the chapel and prayed. Then all the members of his entourage and the palace retainers who were to remain in Vienna—a few were scheduled to follow him into exile—assembled in the great reception room of the palace and Karl meticulously shook hands with them, one after the other, saying a few words to each in his direct, unpretentious way. Perhaps it was not such a bad exit after all.

A hundred-gun salute heralded the birth of the Austrian Republic on the next day, November 12. It was an uneasy birth. Many Viennese, as always finely tuned to overtones of irony, must have smiled sadly at Chancellor Renner's peroration: "Today democracy has become the fundamental law of the entire world, and we cannot do otherwise, we do not wish to do otherwise, we must not do otherwise than keep abreast of the methods of modern civilisation." As the crowds cheered in the Ringstrasse, there was an inexplicable delay in the hoisting of the red and white flag of the Austrian republic. A small Communist mob, attempting to storm the Parliament Building, had seized the emblem and tried to tear the white strip out of it before being dispersed. The attendant turmoil caused two deaths. There was no cheering for independence.

The Austrians, who had lived at the core of a state of 50,000,000 inhabitants extending over most of Central Europe, did not for a minute imagine that German-Austria, a geographical tadpole with Vienna as a head, could survive on its own. Moreover the outbreak of the democratic revolution in Germany had for the time being almost swept away the new-found Austrian sense of nationhood (it was only to revive, hesitantly, over the years after many trials). The Austrian Social-Democrats, who dominated the new regime in Vienna, felt particularly close to German comrades. Consequently, while Article 1 of the basic law defining the form of the state which the Provisional Assembly had finally voted after much soul-searching and confusion, formally made it a republic. Article 2 read: "German Austria is an integral part of the German Republic." In casting off the last shreds of Imperial sovereignty, the Austrian deputies had merely intended to lay the administrative foundations for a rapid merger of the former Habsburg home-farm with a reborn democratic Germany. They had created a nation without meaning to. Thus irony remained, after all, the supreme writ of the Habsburg Empire, even in death. The ultimately disastrous implications in this particular bit of irony, when it was given permanent sanction by the Allied refusal to permit the *Anschluss* (union) between Austria and Germany, will be examined later. For the present we need only note that the proclamation of the Austrian Republic for all practical purposes rang down the curtain on the last act of the Habsburg tragedy.

There remained (save for two pathetic, foredoomed restoration attempts much later) only a kind of formalistic epilogue before the stage went dark for ever. It was enacted the next day, November 13, at Eckartsau, where Karl and Zita were coping with the grim but humdrum problem of feeding and heating their family. A delegation sent from Budapest by Karoli, who was soon to prove the Kerensky of the Hungarian revolution, arrived with instructions that Karl give up his remaining crown, that of Hungary. The ex-Emperor received the Hungarian revolutionaries with the same friendly, dignified courtesy that he had displayed toward the Austrian ones and acquiesced at once to their demand—subject to essentially the one reservation that he had insisted upon in Vienna. He would not formally abdicate the Habsburg birthright in Hungary any more than in Austria, but he renounced all share in its government. That was sufficient for the Budapest delegates and the cryptoabdication was signed on the spot—the same spot virtually—where 650 years earlier Karl's ancestor Rudolph of Habsburg had defeated the Bohemians on the plains near Eckartsau and thus started the dynasty on its road to glory.

"No ruler has experienced a fate so ill as that which befell the Emperor Charles," wrote one of his republican successors, former Chancellor Kurt von Schuschnigg, whose own fate was soon to take a tragic turn. "Whether he was a great monarch, was wisely advised at all times, did the right thing always, is not the question here. To recognize that he was thoroughly good, brave, and honest and a true Austrian who wanted the best and in misfortune bore himself more worthily than many other men would have done is to assert the truth—and this truth has been suppressed far too long."

It is harder to write an equally succinct and equally fair epitaph on the Habsburg Dynasty and the Habsburg Empire as twentieth-century institutions.

"Perhaps the fairest judgement on the old Austrian Empire," writes one of its more clear-headed present day apologists, the British journalist Gordon Shepherd (*Austrian Odyssey*), "is that it lived both before and after its day. . . . The Austrian Empire and with it the Austrians, were international too early and national too late. For the outrageous state-patriotism under which her component states were founded in 1918 became passé almost as soon as it had triumphed . . . It is arguable that had Austria-Hungary survived the First World War by truce or victory, the Second would never have occurred. And it is conceivable that in this case the Austrian Empire, like the British would eventually have struck its own bargain with time."

The trouble is that Austria-Hungary could not possibly have survived the war, once it had to be fought to the bitter end, and that it was its own earlier failure to strike a bargain with time which more than anything else had unleashed the fatal war. Perhaps in reading the Habsburg chronicle it is enough to recognize that history, like most human experience, is essentially tragic. The same observation applies to the Wilsonian attempt to build a new world upon the wreckage of the old one. The real superiority of the Habsburgs—if they had one—over the men who were called upon to liquidate their heritage is that the splendor of their role never caused them to forget the true nature of the drama in which they were playing. They had conspicuously what the peacemakers of Versailles most lacked—a sense of tragedy.

CHAPTER 19

The Time of Troubles

THE Old World that Winston Churchill had found so fair in its sunset glory was a grim spectacle as night settled over its ruins. It was not only the battlefields that lay ravaged, but the order of society and the minds of men. The shock of defeat or revolution, and the abrupt disappearance of traditional symbols of authority helped to create almost overnight, a generation of political—if not plain—psychopaths. Adolf Hitler who was to embody their infernal archetype, was recuperating from temporary blindness caused by poison gas in the fourth Battle of Ypres when the chaplain attached to his hospital brought him the news that the war was lost, the Kaiser in flight, and the Imperial crown abolished. "Everything went black before my eyes again," Hitler later wrote, "and I staggered and stumbled my way back to the dormitory, flung myself upon my cot and buried my burning head in the blanket and pillow." As we know today, demons stood guard over his despair.

The anarchy that followed the overthrow of the three dynastic empires which had been the chief pillars of the old order in Europe, was by no means solely moral and emotional, however. The fallen monarchies had much to answer for—starting with the war—but in their day they had nonetheless fulfilled a necessary function. To the very end they had managed to dam up, and thus to keep under some control, a centuries-old mass of group-hatreds, fears, and greeds. The collapse of the great supranational —or at least supraparochial—authorities and the dissolution of long-accepted Imperial bonds released upon Europe a fearsome flood of conflicting national ambitions, of inflamed minority particularisms, of historic (sometimes almost prehistoric) irredentisms, of irreconcilable social aspirations and of rival political fanaticisms. A merciless triangular struggle began between Wilsonian nationalism, Bolshevism, and a disoriented but all-the-more reactionary monarchism, increasingly prone to seek renewal in a return to the tribal roots of autocracy. By the time the Peace Conference, faced with the giant task of liquidating the Old World's heritage, held its first meeting in Paris on January 18, 1919, Europe east of the Rhine, and parts of Asia, were a seething welter of civil and local wars. In some areas this bloody chaos, multiplied by hunger and plague to a medieval pitch of horror, lasted for nearly four years after the Armistice bugle had sounded in the clearing at Rethondes.

The continuing upheavals, spreading from Europe to the Near East and deep into the heart of Asia, became inextricably embroiled with the work of peacemaking. They both compounded the difficulties of the Allied statesmen, gathered in Paris to draw the blueprint for a new world order, and were aggravated by the blunders or inequities that the statesmen committed. All the subsequent misfortunes of Europe did not stem from the Treaty of Versailles, as it became fashionable for a while to maintain, but Versailles was only the first of the postwar settlements (the last one, the Treaty of Lausanne, was not signed until July 1923) and apart from the formal diplomatic instruments there were the day-to-day administrative or strategic decisions, sometimes irreparable ones, taken by the Allied representatives in Paris, sitting as a kind of soviet of victors. (The worst decision, perhaps, was the inhuman one to continue the blockade of the starving enemy until the first peace treaty was signed.) The interaction between the disorders begot of injustice imposed from above, and the injustices inherent in the disorders that sprang up spontaneously from below, fertilized the new seeding of dragon's teeth whose harvest our own generation was to reap some twenty years later. In this sense it can be said that World War II began in the troubled aftermath of World War I. That story, of course, lies beyond our present scope. Once the immense importance of the prolonged, tormented interregnum between general war and general peace—roughly from November 1918 to December 1922—has been underscored, it is enough to take note of a few broad trends and decisive events of the period that bear directly upon the last phase of dynastic Europe: the phase of liquidation.

The dominant pattern of the time was one of revolution and counterrevolution. As in Russia a year earlier, the democratic revolutions in Central Europe at the end of 1918 quickly led to Communist-led attempts to establish left-wing dictatorships, and these in turn to a revival, usually in a more virulent form, of the most reactionary forces associated with the fallen monarchies. Germany, Austria, and Hungary in particular served as battlegrounds to the opposed extremists. The Communist movements in these countries had authentic local roots, but the contagion of the Bolshevik example in Russia, spread in the main by returning prisoners of war, and the direct instigation of revolutionary agitators sent abroad by the Soviet government expressly to raise the European workers against their new bourgeois and democratic governments, were major factors. To a much greater degree than is generally realized, 1919 was a kind of dress rehearsal for 1945; there was even an ambitious—and nearly successful—attempt by Lenin to use the bayonets of the Red Army, as Stalin was to do a generation later, for imposing Bolshevism throughout Eastern and Central Europe. In final analysis much of the turmoil in Europe during the era of the peace settlements was simply the Russian civil war moving west.

At the time the German Army surrendered to the Allies in France, the Russian civil war had been raging for nearly a year. The apocalyptic character of the struggle, so vividly depicted in Boris Pasternak's *Dr. Zhivago* was perhaps mainly due to the anarchy prevailing throughout much of the Russian countryside, behind the fluid and ill-defined military fronts. Bands of guerrillas, irregulars, adventurers, and plain bandits added their depredations or savageries to the systematized terror—illustrated, for example, by the massacre of the Romanovs—of the opposing Red and White forces. The war, however, had become a big war and the main adverse armies were becoming increasingly professional.

The Whites (using the term to include all organized anti-Bolshevik forces from pale pink socialists or Green peasants to the most unregenerate monarchists) were generally weak in effectives but they were well supplied by the Allies with military equipment and at times were stiffened by foreign combat units. (In the course of the Russian civil war American, British, French, German, Greek, Serbian, Czech, Polish, and Japanese forces intervened more or less aggressively to support the White cause.) In the summer of 1918 the Whites almost succeeded in overthrowing the Reds, and would probably have done so if the Germans had not put substantial support behind the tottering Bolshevik dictatorship. In each of the next two years, the White armies under different leaders and in conjunction with various foreign intervention forces, again came dramatically close to final victory. (Their ultimate failure was due mainly to lack of co-ordination among the anti-Bolshevik factions in Russia, and to lack of agreement among the Allies as to when, where, and how far to back them.)

On the Communist side, the stress of civil war not only hardened the already ruthless Bolshevik personality and sharpened Bolshevik hostility toward the whole bourgeois world—viewed, with some justification, as a snarling pack of Imperialist interventionists—but tempered the newly formed Red Army into a formidable tool of power. The Red Army was largely Trotsky's creation. He had built it into an efficient fighting machine by means that were sometimes unorthodox in Marxist terms. "Do you know how many former Czarist officers are fighting in our army?" Trotsky once asked Lenin after the latter had expressed some mild concern in this regard.

"No," Lenin answered.

"Thirty thousand," Trotsky said. (The true figure was nearer to forty thousand.)

Trotsky also relied heavily on a sort of half-ideological, half-mercenary foreign legion composed mainly of Letts, Magyars, (former prisoners of war), and Chinese. Those professional or semiprofessional elements gave the needed stiffening to the enthusiastic but inexperienced young workers and peasants who made up the bulk of his forces. His own energy, tactical judgment, and courage supplied the other essential elements of victory. For months on end he virtually lived in his famous armored train, rushing from one threatened front to another, sometimes personally leading a crucial attack or standing under fire to rally the defence.

Hardly had the White offensive of 1918 been beaten back, when the Germans began to withdraw from Russian, or former Russian territories occupied under the terms of Brest-Litovsk. The Bolshevik forces rushed into the vacuum, upsetting the local nationalist regimes that had been supported by the Germans, and reclaiming the "liberated" territory for the USSR. The Allies hastily dispatched military help to Poland and to the surviving anti-Communist forces in the western Ukraine. A particularly confused situation developed in the Baltic territories, between Allied intervention forces, a freewheeling White Russian Army moving on Petrograd, German irregular bands and local patriots who regarded all the others as invaders. A Soviet attempt to reconquer Finland for the Revolution was checked by the Finnish nationalists with unofficial German military help.

The Red tide ebbed in 1919, when a White counteroffensive nearly captured Petrograd, and menaced Moscow. In 1920 the Soviets were again put in jeopardy by a two-pronged threat from the Crimean Army of General Peter Wrangel, the last and ablest of all the White leaders, and from a French-aided Polish Army sweeping down from the north. (The Poles, having wiped out their local Communists, were primarily fighting a national war of territorial conquest.)

It was the Red Army's successful counterattack to break the threatened encirclement that almost opened the gates of Central Europe to Communism. First, Wrangel was thrown back into the Crimea and blocked there (he was finally obliged to evacuate the remnants of his army by sea in November 1920). Then the Red armies, commanded by a former Czarist officer who had embraced Communism, General Mikhail Tukhachevski, turned on the overconfident Poles. Tukhachevski, who was later to be one of Stalin's most prominent victims, was the author of a new strategic doctrine: Revolution from without, in other words using the Red Army to carry Communism across Europe as Napoleon's armies had carried the principles of the French Revolution. The war with Poland gave him a chance to try out his theory; the ease with which he shattered the Polish armies, and the speed of his advance into Poland seemed to demonstrate its validity.

With French guidance and material help, the Poles at last succeeded in stopping the Russian offensive on the Vistula, before Warsaw, on August 14, 1920. The date deserves to be remembered in the West. "If Poland had been Sovietized," Lenin later declared, "the whole international system established by the victory over Germany would have crumbled. France would have had no buffer to protect Germany from Soviet Russia."

The buffer that Lenin had in mind was, of course, a pro-Western and anti-Communist Poland. He was probably wrong in supposing that the French in those days were primarily thinking of saving Germany from Communism in establishing the Polish buffer, but it is quite possible that he was right in arguing that if the buffer were destroyed Germany in her exhausted condition would become an easy prey to Communist pressures and infiltration, and the new Allied hegemony in Europe would vanish. Here, however, we are overrunning our story; it was not only because Tukhachevski was halted before Warsaw that Europe was saved from Bolshevization, but because Lenin had already failed a year or two earlier in his attempts to export the revolution to Central Europe by political and conspiratorial means. Or to be more exact, because the limited revolutionary bridgeheads he had thus succeeded in creating had already been wiped out by 1920. We must therefore turn back to 1918 to pick up the threads of this intrigue.

Thanks to the earlier encouragements of Soviet Ambassador Joffe, the left-wing German Socialists assembled in the Spartacus League under the leadership of Karl Liebknecht and Rosa Luxemburg were already ideological allies of Russian Bolshevism by the time the Kaiser was overthrown. As previously related, they had played a prominent role in Berlin's November revolution and they were bitter because Chancellor Ebert and his moderate Socialists had at the last moment prevented it from turning out like the Russian one. They were filled with venemous hatred of the bourgeois democratic republic and of the Eberts, Scheidemanns, and other "traitors" who, in creating it, had sold the workers' revolution down the river. They were ready to rise against the new German government whenever they felt they had the slightest chance of success; on the basis of their doctrinaire interpretation of the Marxist theory they felt confident that the chance would soon come.

The leading Bolshevik strategists had followed the progress of the German revolution from Moscow as best they could, and with passionate eagerness—Germany as the homeland of Karl Marx had a peculiar prestige and importance in the minds of all European socialists in those days. The Bolsheviks were no less doctrinaire than the German Spartacists and even more convinced that the moment was at hand when the workers of the world would throw off their chains and join hands with their Russian comrades for the final triumph of the revolutionary cause. It was in this conviction that Lenin and Trotsky had ventured on the desperate gamble of insurrection and dictatorship in Russia. If their estimate of the world situation had been wrong, their gamble, according to the orthodox Marxist view, was doomed to failure; a successful socialist revolution was not possible in one country alone, it was thought, because international capitalism would unite to suppress it. For a while, in the black early days of the civil war, it had seemed that this was exactly what was happening to Soviet Russia. Now it was clear that history, as usual, was proving those who considered themselves her favorite sons to be right. Only a small push was needed, and Germany was the place to give it.

To supply the push, Lenin sent the former Austrian-Polish journalist, Karl Radek, his wartime watchdog in the Parvus kennel, to Berlin, with secret instructions to organize and launch the German Communist revolution. He was to supply Liebknecht with financial help, technical advice and eventually with arms. He was also to insist on welding the somewhat loose-knit Spartacists into a disciplined Communist party on the conspiratorial Russian model. The new German Communist Party (KPD) came into being on December 30, 1918.

While the Red Army swept ahead through the Baltic territories toward the border of East Prussia, setting up Soviet puppet regimes as it advanced, workers' and soldiers' soviets began to spring up in the north German cities and street fighting became almost a daily occurrence in the capital.

Two days before Christmas a detachment of sailors who had occupied the royal stables near the Kaiser's palace ever since they had arrived from Kiel on November 8, incensed at having their pay stopped, and egged on by the Spartacists (as the Communists were still called), marched to the Chancellery and occupied it. They cut all the telephone wires except one: the secret line which connected Chancellor Ebert's desk with General Groener's headquarters. The sorely pressed Chancellor rang for help. By the time the troops sent by Groener showed up, the sailors had left, taking a Socialist deputy along as a hostage. An attempt to dislodge them from the stables next day resulted in a pitched battle. Although the army brought up artillery, and suffered considerable casualties, the well-armed and determined squatters remained in possession. (Their departure was later negotiated by the government, at the cost of considerable sums in back pay.)

It was a victory for the Communists, but one that spelled their doom. Badly rattled by the bloody events of Christmas Eve, Ebert was now ready to accept help from any quarter. Strong words from army headquarters about the desirability of getting rid of the Spartacists, the soldiers' and workers' soviets, perhaps even of ridding the government of its left-wing

Socialist members, suddenly held a conviction they had never held before. Force must be met with force, he decided, and he summoned to the post of Minister of National Defence, the Republic's strong man, Gustav Noske, who had earned the High Command's respect for his handling of the Kiel revolt. A former butcher, who had come to politics via the Trade Unions, Noske had become the Social Democratic party's expert on military affairs. He had none of Ebert's middle-class prejudice against spilling blood: "Someone has to be the blood-hound," he said. He was perfectly willing to wipe out the Communists, but with what?

The regular army was exhausted and demoralized. The men were no more willing to fight a civil war for the Socialist government than they had been for the Kaiser. "Home to Mother for Christmas" was uppermost in their minds, and the only way to avoid mass desertion had been to send them on leave. Only a few hundred men were still garrisoned in Berlin. But in the fight against the extreme left, Ebert and Noske had more allies than they knew. On January 8 both gentlemen were invited by an officer of the Staff to visit a military camp near Berlin where they were shown a secretly equipped and trained force of four thousand men, whose existence came as a complete surprise to them. These volunteers, who, in the words of a young major of the General Staff named Kurt von Schleicher, "knew no soldiers' soviets, only their rifles and their captains," were the first of many Free Corps which sprang up all over Germany. As in the Thirty Years' War, these private armies swore exclusive allegiance to the officer who not only commanded and trained them, but equipped them as well. Noske who had been a noncommissioned officer during the war, was naively delighted with what he saw. "Don't worry, everything is going to be all right now," he said to Ebert. (The Free Corps movement rapidly spread to the Baltic and Polish fronts where whole regiments refused to comply with the armistice terms; men and weapons remained at the call of their leaders and swelled the number of private armies. These irregulars fought with equal ferocity against the Bolsheviks and against the anti-Communist Poles who were seeping into German Silesia.)

Not two months had passed since the general rout of the German conservatives, time enough for them to size up the Ebert government as only pale-pink. The officials of the former Imperial administration, whom the Provisional Government, in the absence of trained replacements, had begged to remain at their posts in the ministries, in the Reichsbank, in the Law Courts, began to breathe freely and to plan for a regime more to their liking. The malcontents and the die-hards in the army started plotting secretly against a government which their Supreme Command was supporting overtly. Six weeks after the armistice two clandestine officers' associations "for the protection of the former *Fuehrer class*" were functioning. Before long General Ludendorff was back in Berlin—he had secretly slipped out of the country, wearing dark glasses, after the armistice—receiving mysterious visitors in a separate wing of the Hotel Adlon. As the government tried to steer the country through general elections to a constituent assembly, the signs of impending civil war grew ominous. At night handbills with "Kill the Jews, Kill Liebknecht," appeared on the walls; by day the streets were filled with the sound and fury of Communist demonstrations.

The Communist leaders were desperate. The revolution had slipped from the hands of the proletariat, the Officer Corps was back in the saddle, and the masses were turning elsewhere for leadership. A congress of delegates from the workers' and soldiers' soviets of Germany had voted in favor of convening the Assembly in spite of Communist obstruction, and elections were set for January 19, 1919. It was necessary to stage a trial of strength before then.

On January 6, 1919, openly encouraged by Radek, Communist shock troops in armored cars attempted to storm the Chancellery, while more than 100,000 supporters and sympathizers milled around in Unter den Linden. Other detachments occupied the Brandenburger Tor, the government printing offices, the railway stations and a number of barracks. Three hundred Communists headed by a sailor invaded the War Office. Liebknecht proclaimed a provisional government, and for three days the Reds held Berlin in their power. Noske counterattacked on January 9 with regular troops and volunteers from the Free Corps armed with howitzers and machine guns. On January 11 some 3000 veteran infantrymen entered the Wilhelmstrasse, and by January 15, Berlin was once more in the hands of the government. Repression was ruthless and earned the Defense Minister the nickname of "Moerder Noske" ("Murder Noske"). The two Communist leaders, Karl Liebknecht and Rosa Luxemburg, were arrested in the suburbs, by officers of the Guard Cavalry Division, and brought back to divisional headquarters at the Hotel Eden in Berlin. The officers dragged the elderly Rosa Luxemburg—a frail gray-haired idealist, despite her flamboyant nickname, "Red Rosa," and her extremist convictions—into the Tiergarten, where, after severe mishandling, she was finished off with revolver shots and thrown into the Landwehr Canal. Karl Liebknecht was shot "while attempting to escape." The sordid pattern of things to come was taking shape.

Although leaderless, the Communists fought on. The events which took place in Germany between January and May 1919 have been likened to those which put an end to the Paris Commune in the spring of 1871. At the government's command, formations of loyal troops and volunteers ruthlessly beat down the proletarian revolution. Wherever Communist rule still flickered, the army counterattacked. Germans killed Germans with savage abandon. "No pardon is given," a soldier of the Free Corps wrote his family. "We shoot even the wounded. The enthusiasm is great, almost unbelievable."

On February 6 the National Assembly convened to draft a new democratic constitution, not in Berlin, where the Communists were still too strong, but in the little Thuringian town of Weimar, under the auspices of Goethe and the protection of General Maerker's "Jaeger" (Hunters), one of the Free Corps legitimized by the Provisional Government. A Communist attempt to march on Weimar and disperse the assembly (the January elections had confirmed the resurgence of the right and heralded a comeback of the middle class) was scotched, but railway strikes interfered sporadically with communications between Weimar and the rest of Germany.

In March savage fighting broke out once again in Berlin. The temper of the working class had been dangerously inflamed by a renewed propaganda effort of the Russians, who still hoped that Germany would be the world revolutions' first conquest, by the catastrophic food situation (the Allied blockade was still on), and by the army's harsh repressive measures. Between the general strike which gripped the capital on March 3, and Noske's reconquest of the eastern suburbs on March 14, machine guns, artillery, and plain brutal murder by both sides claimed 1200 dead and 10,000 wounded. When the "bloody week of Berlin" was over, the city's workers were not only leaderless, but deprived of the considerable arsenal with which wholesale desertions from the army in the months since the armistice had provided them.

Munich was the next theater of civil war. A Soviet Republic of Bavaria, which proclaimed its intention of uniting with Russia and Hungary, was established on April 7, after six weeks of confusion following on the death of Kurt Eisner, the left-wing idealist who had led the November revolution in Munich. His championship of Bavarian rights and his disclosures about German war guilt had made him public enemy number one of the nationalists. On February 21 he was shot and killed in the street by a young nobleman, Count Arco Valley. (On the same day a Social-Democrat member of the Eisner government was murdered by a Communist.) The disorders that followed forced the Bavarian cabinet to flee Munich, and the city was taken over by the workers' and soldiers' soviets. A sailor from Kiel and a group of Communist activists, directed by a Bolshevik agent from Moscow, established a regime of terror, while the People's Commissars of the new Soviet Republic indulged in eccentricities of their own. One Dr. Tipp, who directed Foreign Affairs, declared war on Switzerland and Wurttemberg. "The dogs refused a loan of 60 locomotives," he explained. "I am certain that we will conquer them."

On May 1 after a full-scale military campaign ordered by Noske, Munich was occupied by government forces. The mangled bodies of the hostages left behind at the Luitpold Gymnasium by the retreating Communists were promptly and amply avenged by the Reichswehr and Free Corps formations, aided by local vigilantes. In the heady, reeking jungle of political anarchy then prevalent in Munich, anyone could become, if not a leader of men, at least an executioner or a spy. It was in this swamp of terror and desolation that Hitler's political career was spawned. He came to Munich early in 1919 after a short term as a guard in a prison camp and became an informer for the Army Commission entrusted with ferreting out accomplices of the Red atrocities. It was as an undercover agent for the army that he first encountered a small political group, the German Labor Party (the word "Labor" warranted a closer look, his superiors thought) which was to become the instrument of his rise to power.

By May 1919, six months after the end of the war, the back of the proletarian revolution had been broken, but Ebert's government found it more and more difficult to distinguish friend from foe. To the men of the extreme left the government was made up of "Social-traitors" who had done the German masses out of the proletarian revolution that was to usher in a brave new world. To the nationalists on the other hand, they were the "November Criminals" whose Judeo-Marxist plots had stabbed unvanquished Germany in the back. The new constitution had not yet been adopted and the Weimar constituent assembly was still sitting when the Allies presented Germany with the bill for the war. The terms of the treaty of Versailles, published in Berlin on May 7, came to the Germans as a punch below the belt. How they reacted we shall see further on.

Throughout Austria, and particularly in Vienna where dirty papers littered the grass plots around the statues and boarded-up windows could not keep out the cold during the long, grim winter of 1918–1919, the Communist offensive against the democratic regime followed the same general pattern as in Germany. It was less aggressively led, however, and never achieved the substantial measure of working-class support that it had in Germany. The Austrian Communists, inspired by Moscow but without the assistance of an inspired agitator like Radek, started before the end of 1918 to organize fighting squads of so-called Red Guards, recruited from army deserters and jobless factory workers, and usually trained by returned prisoners of war who had been Bolshevized in Russia. Street fighting occurred sporadically throughout the winter in Vienna, and in June 1919 the Communists attempted a full-scale *putsch* against the government. Unlike the German Socialists, the Austrian ones—just as moderate but more firmly attached to their principles—who controlled the Renner government refused help from the right-wing private armies that were beginning to spring up in Austria too, and faced the Communist insurrectionary threat with only the forces that the state legally commanded: the Vienna municipal police and the new *Volkswehr* (People's Militia). The former, still directed by the one-time Imperial Police-President, Schober, had remained loyal and efficient; the latter at least was loyal (though containing many former officers of the Imperial Army, the militia was run by committee, like the Russian Army in Kerensky's day). After a brief, sharp fight in the streets of the capital, the Communists were put to flight and the democratic Socialist government remained master of the state—at least nominally. The real ruler in Vienna was hunger, and the constant riots or clashes that disturbed the peace of the republic in its first year were stirred up more often by food shortages than by politics.

Volkswehr detachments repeatedly clashed with vigilante committees of property owners when, on government orders, they searched private homes, farms, hotels and even convents and monasteries for stores of hoarded food. The militia could not always prevent plundering, and occasionally the temptation to join in was too strong. In February 1919, an orderly deputation of workers walking through the streets of Linz on their way to government headquarters to protest the shortage of milk and meat were suddenly turned into ravenous looters by the example of half-grown boys raiding a restaurant for food. The orgy of plundering spread to nearly all the shops and hotels in town. In April 1919, hunger riots occurred in Vienna, in the course of which some police horses were also casualties. "The demonstrators," the Socialist leader Otto Bauer recalls, "threw themselves upon the fallen horses of the police, tore out pieces of flesh from the still warm bodies of the dead animals and carried them home as delicacies which had not been enjoyed for a long time."

In Hungary, as in Germany and as in Austria, the regime bred of defeat was faced with an explosion of the social forces pent up during the war, and again the Soviet government in Moscow intervened to activate the process, hoping thereby to promote the general European revolution on which it believed its own security depended. Count Michael Karoli, a gentleman and a parlor-pink, was no match for the situation, although he showed his appreciation of Hungary's most pressing problem by distributing his own estates to his peasants. But the Hungarians, who had fought on every far-flung front of the Dual Monarchy, while enjoying relative prosperity at home, were now faced with a multiple invasion of their historic lands. Karoli had disarmed the soldiers of the returning armies, to emphasize his pacific intentions, and to scatter their revolutionary elements. Helplessly he saw the southern areas of Hungary taken over by the Yugoslavs, a Rumanian army enter Transylvania, and Czech troops move into Slovakia. In March 1919 the Allied representative in Budapest ordered the Hungarian troops to withdraw even deeper into purely Magyar territory, and indicated that the new military demarcation line would form the future political frontier of the young republic. This was too much for Count Karoli, who was even more of a nationalist than he was a democrat. He resigned and so opened the flood gates to the social revolution which had been brewing for so long under the pressure of impenitent feudalism, aggravated, in the last four years, by shameless war-profiteering.

Bolshevism ruled Hungary for the next five months. Its leader, a Jewish journalist named Bela Kun, had been captured during the war by the Russians who trained him, equipped him with false papers and funds and returned him to Hungary as one of their best agents. His broad Tartar face and shaved skull, his uninhibited demagogy and his savage brutality made him seem the Red scourge personified. But at first he was supported not only by the Social Democrats, but by many bourgeois and military circles in the hope that Soviet Russia would help Hungary to regain its lost territories. Relations were established with Moscow and with the Soviet Republic in Munich, but the foreign help so often announced by Bela Kun never materialized. The confiscations of land, burning of country seats, mass arrests, arbitrary trials, and executions which marked Bela Kun's short dictatorship were in part chalked up to the Allies, whose unreasonable demands had delivered Hungary to Bolshevism. "It serves the Entente right," became a conversational leitmotiv.

Sir Harold Nicolson, then a young diplomat serving on the British peace delegation in Paris, who accompanied General Smuts to Budapest in April 1919, as a member of an international commission, describes a tragic counterfeit tea party for the benefit of the visitors at the former Budapest Ritz, the Hotel Hungaria. Nicolson was amazed to find the lobby full of aristocratic-looking Hungarians sipping lemonade to the strains of a gypsy orchestra and it was some time before he realized that there was something unnatural about the scene. "It suddenly dawns upon me," he recorded in his diary, "that each single table is absolutely silent. Not a word do they address to each other as they sip their lemonade. If one looks up suddenly one catches countless frightened eyes, and at the back of these eyes a mutely passionate appeal . . . this ghastly silence continues under the wail of the violins and under the gaze of the sentries guarding every exit. It is quite clear that all these huddles of silent people have been let out of prison for the afternoon."

It was with his military ventures that Bela Kun delivered the coup de grace to the country and to his own regime. Formed with the help of officers from the Imperial Army, his Red legions attacked the Czechs and the Rumanians. Their initial successes were short-lived; in July 1919 the Rumanians counterattacked and occupied Budapest. Moscow, busy with its own civil war, remained aloof. (A year later it might have been a different story.) Bela Kun and his cronies fled to Vienna. After repeated objurgations by the Allies, the Rumanians were finally persuaded to withdraw in November. They left with everything movable.

After their departure a counter-revolutionary army, commanded by the former Admiral of the Dual Monarchy's fleet, Miklos von Nagybanya Horthy, entered Budapest and proceeded to string Bela Kun's supporters from lampposts, to massacre Jews wholesale and, in general, to impose a regime of White terror which had nothing to learn from the preceding Red excesses. Finally, in January 1920, at the behest of the Allies, elections for a Constituent Assembly were held under secret suffrage. The resulting Assembly showed a monarchist majority, as the left parties had boycotted the elections in protest against White exactions, and it immediately abolished all legislation passed by the Karoli and Bela Kun governments. Hungary reverted to the status of a kingdom, with Horthy named as regent. It remained, however, a kingdom without a king, ruled by an admiral without a navy.

The Hungarian elections not only demonstrated the vigor of the anti-Communist trend that was now dominant again in Central Europe—particularly in agricultural regions—but also marked the first unmistakable ebbing of the tide of republicanism that had set in throughout the Continent with the fall of the Russian monarchy in 1917. Naturally the ex-Emperor Karl, who had never formally abandoned his royal titles, tried to exploit the situation. Leaving his safe and comfortable exile in Switzerland (the Austrian government had finally expelled him and confiscated all his property in March 1919) he twice managed to slip back into Hungary to claim his vacant throne. On the second and more dramatic of the two occasions, in October 1921, he landed from a small private airplane, accompanied by the pregnant Zita, in the Burgenland, at that time a contested border area, where Hungarian terrorists were trying to block the province's cession to Austria. It was a modern, mechanized, little-man's version of the Young Pretender's return.

As usual, Karl had been poorly advised. The failure of his earlier attempt had at least temporarily hardened anti-Habsburg sentiment in the country. Horthy, a singularly unromantic type of royalist, refused to recognize Karl as the nation's rightful sovereign. Instead he sent a regiment to put a swift end to the pathetic and slightly shoddy escapade. There was no Danubian Culloden; it was more like the police breaking up an exurban cocktail party that had got out of hand. Karl's local partisans dropped their shotguns and scattered; Karl and Zita were captured and permanently exiled from Hungary. The Hungarian parliament thereupon formally deprived the Habsburgs of all their dynastic rights in Hungary (somehow nobody had got around to doing it before) and restored to the people their ancient privilege of electing the king of their choice.

Several factors besides Karl's chronically unhappy touch and Horthy's reluctance to give up his job foredoomed a Habsburg restoration in Hungary. One was the international situation. In all the successor states of the Empire the Habsburgs, including poor Karl, had come in retrospective to seem fearsome tyrants, nine feet tall. A restoration of the dynasty anywhere in the lands over which it had once ruled was a recurrent nightmare in Prague, in Bucharest and in Belgrade. If Karl had been allowed to install himself again on the Hungarian throne it might have brought on Allied military intervention; even his feeble attempt provoked a mobilization on the part of Hungary's neighbors. (To forestall further Danubian crises, Karl, on British insistence, was exiled to the island of Madeira, where, forsaken by all but Zita and his children he died on April 1, 1922, of tuberculosis and despair.)

That was not the whole story, however. Karl was too kind, too Christian, and too civilized to succeed in crystallizing the anti-democratic reaction in Europe. The day of kings was over not because despotism was out of date but because harsher and more efficient patterns of despotism were beginning to emerge. Above all, the old dynasties were discredited in the eyes of their former subjects because they had been so international, even when they were not, like the Habsburgs, explicitly supranational. As a democratic credo, Wilsonism might be ebbing, but the tide of nationalism that the Fourteen Points had helped to set in motion was running stronger than ever in Europe, and the strongest perhaps in the former Habsburg Empire.

The Russian civil war had been the master-conflict in Europe, but it had by no means been the only one. The war between Poland and Russia was as much a national as an ideological combat, and the struggles in the Baltic states had been to some degree wars of national liberation waged by the emerging Latvian, Lithuanian, and Esthonian nationalisms. Early in 1919 the Poles and the Czechs had clashed violently over the disputed territory of Teschen in southeastern Silesia. Two years later an undeclared but fair-sized war was fought between Germany and Poland over their respective conflicting claims to Silesia. Yugoslavia and Italy were passionately disputing the Dalmatian coast. In 1920 a fierce three-year struggle that was partly a democratic revolution against the last shreds of Ottoman rule, partly a war of national independence, and partly an anticolonialist rising, broke out on the rugged Anatolian plateau of Asiatic Turkey. Like the other local wars of the period, but on a more dramatic scale, the fighting in Turkey marked the failure of the peacemakers—or world makers—in Paris to wind up the succession of the fallen dynasties without (in President Wilson's words) "introducing new, or perpetuating old, elements of discord and antagonism." How and why the failure occurred, and what it meant to the world, is the last chapter, by no means the least tragic one, in our story.

CHAPTER 20

The Doomed Peace

ANYONE who witnessed—if only on a television screen—
the San Francisco conference of 1945 which gave birth to
the United Nations, should have no difficulty in reviving upon the screen
of his imagination the atmosphere in which the Paris Peace Conference of
1919 began its work. There was the same exhilarating feeling of making a
new start, the same flush of hope for the future of humanity, the same
idealistic dedication to the cause of man, the same robust faith in the ability
of experts, if given a free hand by rulers and peoples, to untangle the strands
of destiny woven by millennia of human folly, misery and delinquency.
There was, however, one substantial difference. In 1919 this particular constellation of optimisms had never before taken shape in the public mind;
consequently it had never led to disillusionment. The idealism of the Paris
peacemakers was thus in certain respects more fervent and more fragile
than that of the San Francisco world-builders. Sir Harold Nicolson has
superbly recaptured the dawn mood of the earlier era in his *Peacemaking*
(written in 1919), the best human document on the Conference, and one
of the great political confessions of our times.

Contrasting the outlook of his generation with that of the cynical peacemakers who at the Congress of Vienna had labored to rebuild a monarchic
Europe shattered by war and revolution, Nicolson recalls his personal reflections on the train journey to Paris, early in January 1919, to take up his
Conference duties.

"I felt as the train approached St. Denis, that I knew exactly what mis-
takes had been committed by the misguided, the reactionary, the after all
pathetic aristocrats who had represented Great Britain in 1814.

"They had worked in secret. We on the other hand were committed to 'open covenants openly arrived at' . . . the peoples of the world would share in our every gesture of negotiations.

"At Vienna again, they had believed in the doctrine of 'compensations' . . . We believed in nationalism, we believed in the self determination of peoples. 'Peoples and provinces', so ran the four Principles of our Prophet [Woodrow Wilson], shall not be bartered about from sovereignty to sovereignty as if they were but chattels or pawns in the game . . .

"Nor was this all. We were journeying to Paris, not merely to liquidate the war, but to found a new order in Europe. We were preparing not peace only, but Eternal Peace. There was about us the halo of some divine mission. . . ."

With the exception of Wilson, the official delegates to the Conference (there were 70 of them representing 27 Allied powers) were not quite so starry-eyed. In fact, to the youthful Nicolson and his peers it seemed that most of them were interested in little but the loot—and they usually lacked the detailed knowledge of European geography and history which enabled the young experts to chart the frontiers of utopia with unerring fingers. Not only did the delegation leaders look blank at the mention of such recondite items as the Ipek Circumscription, the Strumitza Enclave or the Sanjak of Alexandretta, but Lloyd George once scandalized the specialists by publicly admitting that he had never heard of Teschen.

The attitude of the general public throughout Europe seems to have been somewhat mixed. The thrill of hope was felt to some degree almost everywhere; after the long night of officialized murder and oppression there was a deep, universal hunger among the peoples not only for peace, but for justice and fraternity. But the hatreds and the fears that the wartime propaganda machines had so recklessly propagated were still reverberating in the minds of victors and vanquished alike. They were sharpened by the age-old tradition of plundering and enslaving the conquered foe. If there was one position upon which idealists and cynics, experts and laymen, winners and losers tended to agree, it was to blame all of Europe's sufferings and disasters upon the fallen despotisms. War had been the sinister fruit of autocratic tyranny, injustice, and corruption. The Peace of Paris was to be at once the triumph and the validation of democratic internationalism.

The foremost standard bearer of the new creed was, of course, Woodrow Wilson himself, "our Prophet," as Nicolson called him. With his high-button black shoes, his drably impeccable clothes, his professorial pince-nez, his large, stern Covenanter's head, his unhealthy pallor and those distressing teeth, suggestive of a carnivorous horse, Wilson, then sixty-three, was neither a glamorous nor a winning figure. He looked less like a prophet than like a fashionable surgeon, one of those professional courts of last appeal who put in a brief, impersonal appearance at the bedsides of dying millionaires and confirm the diagnosis. The contrast with the dashing young Czar Alexander at the Congress of Vienna could hardly be more extreme, yet Wilson dominated the Conference of Paris, both politically and ideologically, to a far greater extent than Alexander had dominated the diplomatic ballet in Vienna. The President, disregarding the warnings of his soundest advisers, had insisted on personally heading the United States delegation. He had arrived in December and before the opening of the Conference had made a triumphant tour of the Allied capitals in the West. Everywhere enormous crowds had turned out to cheer him. His leadership of the Conference at first seemed unchallenged. In addition to the prestige of the Nobel Prize for Peace, awarded him in 1919, he had the strongest army in the world (because it was the only untired one), the food that starving Europe needed, the gold which could save it from bankruptcy. He also had the Faith.

The essence of Wilsonism is expressed in three basic texts: The Fourteen Points of January 8, 1918; the Four Principles of February 11, 1918; and the Five Particulars of September 27, 1918. The first two, at least, are in the main admirable documents: realistic, as well as high-minded, in the context of the day. (The Five Particulars besides being more controversial, apply primarily to the founding of the League of Nations.) As a blueprint for clearing away the wreckage of the old order in Europe and for laying the durable foundations of a new one, they hardly merit the scorn that has often been heaped upon them since. Many of their stipulations are still valid today, in fact are more pertinent than ever. It is worth rereading them.

The Fourteen Points are summarized as follows:

(1) Open covenants of peace, openly arrived at, after which there shall be no private international understandings of any kind, but diplomacy shall proceed always frankly and in the public view.

(2) Absolute freedom of navigation upon the seas, outside territorial waters, alike in peace and war . . .

(3) The removal, so far as possible, of all economic barriers . . .

(4) Adequate guaranties given and taken that national armaments will be reduced to the lowest point consistent with domestic safety.

(5) Free, open-minded, and absolutely impartial adjustment of all colonial claims, based upon a strict observance of the principle that in determining all such questions of sovereignty the interests of the populations concerned must have equal weight with the equitable claims of the Government whose title is to be determined.

(6) The evacuation of all Russian territory . . . Russia to be given unhampered and unembarrassed opportunity for the independent determination of her own political development and national policy. Russia to be

welcome and more than welcome in the League of Nations under institutions of her own choosing and to be given every form of assistance.

(7) Belgium to be evacuated and restored.

(8) France to be evacuated, the invaded portions restored and Alsace-Lorraine returned to her.

(9) A readjustment of the frontiers of Italy should be effected along clearly recognizable lines of nationality.

(10) The peoples of Austria-Hungary . . . to be accorded the freest opportunity for autonomous development. (*N.B. This point was subsequently modified to provide for complete independence in lieu of autonomy.*)

(11) Rumania, Serbia, and Montenegro to be evacuated, occupied territories to be restored! Serbia to be given free access to the sea.

(12) Turkish portions of Ottoman Empire to be assured a secure sovereignty. Subject nationalities to be assured security and absolutely unmolested opportunity of autonomous development. Freedom of the straits to be guaranteed.

(13) An independent Polish State to be erected which should include territories inhabited by indisputably Polish populations, which should be assured a free and secure access to the sea.

(14) A general association of nations to be formed under specific covenants for the purpose of affording mutual guarantees of political independence and territorial integrity to great and small States alike.

The Four Principles, summarized, are:

(1) Each part of the final settlement must be based upon the essential justice of that particular case.

(2) Peoples and provinces must not be bartered about from sovereignty to sovereignty as if they were chattels or pawns in a game.

(3) Every territorial settlement must be in the interests of the populations concerned; and not as a part of any mere adjustment or compromise of claims among rival states.

(4) All well-defined national elements shall be accorded the utmost satisfaction that can be accorded them without introducing new, or perpetuating old, elements of discord and antagonism.

What amounted to a fifth principle was contained in the statement with which Wilson prefaced the Four: that the eventual peace treaty should contain 'no annexations, no contributions, no punitive damages.'

If there was any serious weakness in the theoretical premises of Wilsonism as set forth in the Fourteen Points and in the Four Principles, it lay in their slightly naive faith in "open diplomacy" and in their implicit assumption that the chief vice of the Old World diplomacy had been its secrecy, rather than its irresponsibility. The very setting and work patterns of the Conference reflected this curious misreading of contemporary history. The plenary sessions of the Conference were held in the Clock Room of the Quai d'Orsay whose crystal chandeliers, gilt chairs, and damask hangings not only evoked the trappings of the prewar diplomacy but served as a pointed reminder of one of its most discreditable episodes: the unholy collusion between democratic France and Czarist Russia which had helped to make war inevitable. Moreover, the way the three chief Conference leaders—Wilson, Clemenceau, and Lloyd George—went about the task of putting the world to rights sometimes recalled the unhappy experiments in personal diplomacy of "Willy" and "Nicky"; indeed there were moments when it seemed disquietingly reminiscent of the monarchs at the Congress of Vienna bartering their pawns and chattels (and in the end producing a less iniquitous, more workmanlike peace than the Peace of Paris). Of Clemenceau, then seventy-eight, and looking, in Nicolson's words, like a gorilla of yellow ivory, with his bushy white eyebrows and drooping Tartar mustache, it has been said that he had one illusion, France, and one disillusion, mankind, including Frenchmen. Lloyd George, with his great white mane, his boundless energy and his Welsh emotionalism was less realistic but more versatile; no statesman ever made—and unmade—such momentous decisions with such lightning rapidity. "A man it was impossible not to admire, almost impossible not to love, barely possible not to forgive," as his son wrote of him. Nicolson sketches an unforgettable vignette of the three Conference leaders crouched over a big map spread out on the floor of the President's study, gaily dismembering the Ottoman Empire ("Turkey to be driven out of Europe and Armenia . . . Greece to have the Smyrna Zone . . . Italy to get a mandate over South Asia Minor . . . France to get the rest").

The anecdote illustrates the two logically antithetical but practically complementary attitudes in the minds of the Conference leaders which were mainly responsible for turning Europe's hope into gall and vinegar. One was the failure to realize—or the refusal to admit—that the old dynastic empires, for all their wickedness and oppressions, had assured the more or less peaceful co-existence of ethnic groups whom history and geography had doomed to live together, and that in so doing they had fulfilled a vital function, particularly from the economic viewpoint. Among the Allied leaders only Masaryk and Benes appear to have understood clearly that some Wilsonian substitute for the supranational sovereignty of the Habsburgs was needed in Central Europe. (Unfortunately their formula, a Slav-dominated *Mittel Europa,* had other drawbacks.) The other fatal error was simply to disregard the general tenets of Wilsonism—especially the vital caveat in the Fourth Principle against "introducing . . . new elements of discord and antagonism"—when dealing with particular cases.

After the debacle in Paris the legend developed in the United States that it was the greed, the cynicism and the duplicity of our European allies, triumphing over the unworldly New World idealism of the American delegates which had corrupted the peace. The legend conforms to the long-established American stereotype of native gullibility and European rascality, but overlooks the fact that in final analysis, the chief betrayer of Wilsonism was Wilson himself. Some authorities blame his advisers, or his political adversaries at home; others stress Wilson's own failings: his narrow-mindedness, his intellectual arrogance, his self-righteousness, his partisanship, and his curious mixture of indecision and doctrinaire rigidity. As Colonel House put it: "when the President stepped down from his lofty pedestal and wrangled with the representatives of other states upon equal terms, he became as common clay."

Lloyd George, who felt closer to Wilson than any of the leading Allied statesmen did, and Winston Churchill, who could not stand him, have recorded similarly ambivalent judgments of his personality. "Wilson," Lloyd George wrote in his memoirs of the conference, "was the most clear-cut specimen of duality that I have ever met. The two human beings of which he was constituted never merged or mixed . . . The gold was sterling and the clay was honest marl, and they were both visible to the naked eye. He was the most extraordinary compound I have ever encountered of the noble visionary, the implacable and unscrupulous partisan, the exalted idealist and the man of rather petty personal rancours." To Churchill it was the Jekyll-and-Hyde contrast between Wilson as an international idealist and Wilson as a Democratic party boss that was the most striking, and most fatal. "His [Wilson's] gaze," Churchill wrote in *The World Crisis*, "was fixed with equal earnestness upon the destiny of mankind and the fortunes of his party candidates. Peace and goodwill among all nations abroad, but no truck with the Republican party at home. That was his ticket and that was his ruin, and the ruin of much else as well."

The fact is that Wilson's "betrayal"—as Nicolson's memoir of the Peace Conference brings out with special clarity—was a deliberate choice between the two aspects of Wilsonism. In a series of backroom deals with his Conference partners—"little arrangements" which departed from the spirit of the Metternichian era only in their lack of moderation—the President repeatedly sacrificed the Fourteen Points (not to mention the Four Principles) in return for acceptance of the Covenant of the League of Nations. Wilson had not invented the League, a synthesis of various proposals going back to the sixteenth century, and was not even primarily responsible for drafting the Covenant, for which British and French experts had already made preparatory studies before America entered the war, but he attached greater importance to the proposed organization than most of his European partners did, he championed it more passionately than anyone else, and he had a more radical conception of its role. Whatever his faults as an

international statesman, the American President was one of the great political prophets of our century, or of any century; his dream was as tran-
scendent in its way as Lenin's. Wilson envisaged the League as something
fairly close to a real world government—one of his "Five Particulars" concerning it goes so far as to forbid all alliances, or even economic combina-
tions among its members—and no doubt he reasoned that its authority
would be adequate to protect the legitimate interests of the new minorities
that the peacemakers were so recklessly bringing into being. What did it
matter if new injustices were introduced into the map of Europe—and even
some old ones perpetuated—so long as that infallible machine for manu-
facturing justice, the League of Nations, was created? Surely some small
compromise with evil was permissible if the instrumentality of godliness
were thereby to be forged. That was the fallacy. One of several reasons
why the League eventually failed is that it had been built not upon the rock
of justice but upon the shifting sands of theocratic expediency.

Disillusionment began to spread long before the Conference had completed its work. The attempt to substitute open for secret diplomacy merely
seemed to combine the vices of both systems without preserving the virtues
of either. If some of the territorial bargains that were struck behind closed
doors were unedifying, the quasi-public rows between delegations were no
less so. Wilson clashed repeatedly with Clemenceau—the old Tiger had his
claws into the Saar Basin and the Rhineland and it took bitter struggles to
pry them loose—and even more violently with the Italian delegates, Prime
Minister Vittorio Emanuele Orlando and Foreign Minister Sidney Sonnino.
The secret Treaty of London (April 1915), had made exorbitant promises
to Italy: the south Tyrol, northern Dalmatia, most of the Dalmatian islands
and the Greek-populated Dodecanese islands, among other things. Naturally the Italian claims were contested on all sides, particularly by the
new-born Yugoslav state. Since the French and the British could not repu-
diate their pledge to their wartime ally, it fell on Wilson to deny Italy the
prize for which nearly half a million Italians had given their lives. The
Italian government—and a considerable part of Italian public opinion—
reacted with Mediterranean explosiveness. Orlando and Sonnino walked
out of the Conference. Finally a lame compromise was patched up which,
while largely negating the Wilsonian principle of self-determination, gave
satisfaction to none of the contending parties, least of all to the Italians.

(Italy had come late to nationhood and had only developed imperial
ambitions after all the richest colonial plunder had already been pocketed
by her more advanced rivals. Hence, despite the intellectual maturity or
sophistication of the Italian elite classes in most other respects, Italian
nationalism reflected the tormented romanticism of delayed adolescence.
The irresponsible opportunism of Italian foreign policy had been a factor
in setting the stage for World War I—a much more significant factor than it

has been possible to indicate within the limited scope of the present work—and was destined to play an even more destructive role in helping to bring on World War II. At Versailles as afterward, the leaders of the older Western nations oscillated between failing to take the basic Italian predicament seriously enough, and being too impressed by the operatics of Italian diplomacy.)

Even worse than the territorial injustices or absurdities that were finally embodied in the peace treaties—though they were bad enough—was the punitive spirit that crept into them, especially into the German treaty. "No punitive damages," Wilson had stipulated, but the real mood of the Conference, sedulously built up by irresponsible demagogues in the victor countries, was much better expressed by the famous pledge of Sir Eric Geddes, a cabinet colleague of Lloyd George, during the British electoral campaign of December 1918:

"I will squeeze her [Germany] until you can hear the pips squeak."

The final draft of the treaty obliged the German signatories to acknowledge their country's sole responsibility for causing the war—perhaps the worst outrage against history ever committed by civilized governments. It called for turning over the Kaiser and other German leaders for trial as war criminals, and required Germany to make good all civilian damage suffered by the Allies during the war. Pending determination of the amount—it was eventually fixed at the astronomic sum of $32,000,000,000—she was to pay a $5,000,000,000 installment by May 1921. The "war guilt" clause and the monstrous reparations bill probably contributed more than any other factors to the subsequent rise of Hitler.

The disarmament clauses of the treaty, while less unreasonable, were nearly as galling to German national pride. The new republican army was limited to 100,000 men; heavy equipment including war planes, was banned; the navy was restricted to six warships and was allowed no submarines. The Allies were authorized to occupy the Rhineland for fifteen years (longer if necessary) and the right bank of the Rhine was to be a demilitarized zone some thirty miles wide. German rivers were to be internationalized and the Kiel Canal was opened to all nations.

Up to the arrival of the German peace delegation on April 29, there had been no discussion between the Allies and their erstwhile adversary as to the terms of the projected treaty. Count Brockdorff-Rantzau, who as Foreign Minister headed the German delegation, was a stiff-necked aristocrat of ancient lineage. ("In our family," he had once remarked, "we consider the Bourbons as bastard Rantzaus.") He had been warned about what to expect, but had preferred not to believe the warnings. His sense of shock was reflected in his official comments on the Allied terms, formulated during a brief meeting of victors and vanquished at the Hotel Trianon in

Versailles. "We know the force of the hatred which confronts us here," said Brockdorff-Rantzau, reading in a choking voice from his memorandum, "and we have heard the passionate demand that the victors should both make us pay as vanquished and punish us as guilty. We are required to admit that we alone are guilty; such an admission on my lips would be a lie." The German reply was a dignified, sober, and in certain respects a moving statement, but Lloyd George who felt that some of its points were justly taken, recalls that its effect was ruined in the minds of the Allied representatives because Rantzau had remained seated while reading it, whereas Clemenceau in opening the meeting as Chairman of the Conference, had stood up. Rantzau's gesture was taken as a deliberate piece of Prussian arrogance. "The effect on President Wilson's mind was to close it with a snap," Lloyd George recorded. "He turned to me and said 'Isn't it just like them?' "

The Germans in general had no insight into the bitterness which the ruins of war and the submarine atrocities had left in the minds of their enemies. Nor were they fully aware of how complete their own defeat had been. It was not realized that the armistice had been the last resort in a desperate military situation, and that its necessity had been urged on the government by the High Command itself. The average German believed the armistice to have been a matter of military convenience, which would lead for the benefit of all to the just peace promised by Wilson. Now that they had got rid of the Kaiser, muzzled the revolution and written themselves a constitution which was a model of democracy, the German people expected Germany to be admitted as a member in good standing to the reborn society of nations. The new international system seemed particularly attractive to a generation of Germans brought up in the dread of encirclement. In the words of the historian Ludwig Dehio, President Wilson's gospel promised them "a release from their constrictions by means of the peaceful neutralization of the old, suffocating system, and so a miraculous solution to the whole German problem."

Revelation of the treaty's terms provoked a nation-wide outburst of fury and despair in Germany. The sense of injustice that they aroused in German minds was intensified by the humiliating treatment accorded the German peace delegates, isolated behind cage-like barriers at Versailles. For a few weeks civil war was forgotten and Chancellor Philip Scheidemann's cry, "May the hand wither which signs such a treaty," found an echo in every German breast. In meetings held all over the country, angry voices demanded that Germany withhold its signature from the "Diktat" of Versailles. The government realized that the cost was a resumption of hostilities. The Allies, the French in particular, were in no mood for dalliance. They had shown their hand by instigating a short-lived independent Rhineland Republic on June 1, 1919 (thus discrediting a genuine separatist movement in that province). The Allied blockade was still in force and the German people were on the verge of starvation. The German Supreme Command reluctantly informed the government that a resumption of the war was out of the question. On June 24 the German cabinet complied with an Allied ultimatum, a few hours before it ran out, and notified Clemenceau of its unconditional acceptance of the peace terms.

The peace with Germany was signed on June 28, 1919, at Versailles, thus becoming, for history, the Treaty of Versailles. The ceremony took place in the great, splendid, garish Hall of Mirrors of the Royal Palace, that almost Pharaonic monument to the megalomania of Louis XIV, whose remembered grandeur to this day quickens even the most republican of French pulses. Clemenceau, republican to the marrow and chauvinist to the fingertips, presided at the head of the huge horseshoe table, with Wilson on his right and Lloyd George on his left. It was his apotheosis, the Day of the Tiger. The formidable old man whose relentless will had driven a faltering nation to victory—and who had repeatedly lashed the fellow delegates at the Conference with the scorn of his savage self-honesties—had known prison and exile as a *Communard* in his youth, but it was the German siege of Paris in 1871 that he chiefly remembered. The ceremonial session of the Conference at Versailles was Clemenceau's revenge for the humiliation inflicted on France when Bismarck had proclaimed the German Empire in that same Hall of Mirrors almost half a century earlier; the treaty itself embodied his almost obsessive determination that Germany should never be strong enough to invade France again. While the peace guns outside the palace thundered a salute, and the cheering of the crowds could be heard in the distance, the two German plenipotentiaries, Dr. Mueller and Dr. Bell, pale and wooden-faced in their distress, signed their names to the long document that in the minds of the German people would irrevocably link the nascent German democracy with a day of national shame.

"Yes," Nicolson heard Clemenceau reply, with tears of emotion in his bleary old eyes, to the congratulations of one of his colleagues, "it is a beautiful day." Not all of those who had witnessed it agreed. "It was not unlike when in olden times, the conqueror dragged the conquered at his chariot wheels," writes Colonel House, the least doctrinaire and most sagacious of the American delegates. "To bed, sick of life," is the last notation on the historic day in Nicolson's Conference diary.

Save for the "war-guilt" clause and the unrealistic reparations claim— only a fraction of which was ever paid—the German treaty was less harsh than subsequent propaganda campaigns pictured it. It was a tragic error, however, that the same diplomatic instrument which penalized Germany for having lost the war also served to bring the League of Nations into being, and thus become the cornerstone of postwar order in Europe. The situation was in no way improved by the other settlements—all of them prepared by the Paris Conference—that were piled on top of it. The Austrian Peace Treaty, signed at St. Germain (near Paris) on September 10, 1919; the treaty with Bulgaria, signed at Neuilly (a suburb of the French capital) on November 27, 1919; the Hungarian treaty signed at the Trianon Palace in Versailles on June 4, 1920; and the Treaty of Sèvres with Turkey, carving up the Ottoman Empire, signed on August 20, 1920, but superseded later—for reasons that will shortly be related—by the milder treaty of Lausanne.

The new Europe was largely the work of the Paris Peace Conference—slightly modified by subsequent local plebiscites carried out under the terms of the various treaties—but certain of the national frontiers in eastern and northeastern Europe were based on other settlements. Some stemmed indirectly from the Treaty of Brest-Litovsk, others took shape during the chaos of the Russian civil war. (Soviet Russia had not been invited to the Paris Conference though some former Russian territories were disposed of there.) Altogether nine new independent states (three of which have since ceased to exist) came into being in Europe. They were Finland, Latvia, Lithuania, Esthonia—former territories of the Czarist Empire which had proclaimed their independence—resurrected Poland, composed of territory recovered from the Russian, German and Austro-Hungarian Empires—Czechoslovakia, Yugoslavia, Austria, and Hungary, these last two for the first time in centuries separate and fully soveriegn. Three countries that had figured on the map of prewar Europe had entirely disappeared; the Dual Monarchy, Serbia, and Montenegro; the last two had, of course, been integrated into the new Yugoslavia under the reign of the Karageorgevic dynasty, the Serbian ruling house. (The changes which took place in the map of Asia Minor will be dealt with separately.)

As the result of war and revolution Russia lost Finland, the Baltic provinces, her former Polish provinces—along with some Ukrainian territory—and Bessarabia (annexed by Rumania).

Germany was stripped of all her colonies by the Treaty of Versailles—they were divided among France, the British Commonwealth, Belgium and Japan—returned Alsace-Lorraine to France, temporarily surrendered the rich coal fields of the Saar Basin to French administration, gave up the Walloon cantons of Eupen and Malmedy to Belgium, and returned northern Schleswig to Denmark. Her heaviest losses were in the East. In addition to the former Polish provinces of the Empire she had to hand over to Poland a sizable and disputed piece of Silesia, along with a corridor to the Baltic—peopled in the majority by Poles—which divided East Prussia from the rest of the German Republic. The ancient Hanseatic city of Danzig, almost wholly German in population, was detached from Germany and became a free port under international administration (the other Hanseatic town of Memel eventually went to Lithuania). In time the questions of Danzig and of the Polish Corridor were to furnish Hitler the pretext for launching World War II.

Bulgaria was deprived of her former foothold on the Aegean coast and gave up substantial portions of her territory to Greece and Rumania. (Rumania, proportionately one of the biggest gainers from the peace settlements, also obtained Hungarian Transylvania.) Italy acquired south Tyrol, the Trentino, and the great Adriatic port of Trieste at the expense of Austria, and the Dodecanese islands at the expense of Turkey, but had to give up—in rage and mortification—most of her claims on the Dalmatian islands and Albania.

Austria and Hungary proved to be the chief victims of the peace settlements, the latter losing 192,000 out of 283,000 kilometres of territory, and 10,649,416 out of its former population of 18,264,533. Apart from the predominantly Slavic territories of the old Empire which had declared their independence and recombined to form Yugoslavia, Poland, and Czechoslovakia, huge German or Magyar minorities were lost to the Empire's successor states, to Italy and to Rumania. Some 3,000,000 Magyars were alienated from their homeland. The figure helps to explain the almost demoniac violence of Hungarian irredentism, expressed in the fiery slogan *Nem Nem Soha* (No, No, Never) between the two wars. Despite the protests of Austria and the understandable qualms of Wilson, 3,000,000 Austrian Germans were transferred to Czechoslovakia and more than 250,000 to Italy (in the south Tyrol) by the peace treaties.

Next to unscrambling an egg, it is true, the hardest task one can set oneself in Central and Eastern Europe, is to draw national borders that coincide even approximately with the ethnic and linguistic frontiers. Even if President Wilson had succeeded in upholding self-determination in every disputed case, the postwar successors to the prewar empires would inevitably have included sizable national minorities within their frontiers. The Danubian basin and the Balkans form a jumbled racial mosaic, and nothing save genocide or mass exodus can change its erratic pattern. In several cases, however, the diplomats in Paris had ended by virtually throwing self-determination out the window and by basing the new frontiers on the old criteria of strategic convenience or feudal inheritance. The Czechoslovak republic, to a large extent a twentieth-century resurrection of the medieval kingdom of Bohemia, was perhaps the extreme example. In 1921 its total population of 13,374,364 included 745,431 Magyars and 3,123,568 Germans—chiefly the so-called Sudeten Germans who were later to play a role in the international crisis that ultimately led to a new world war—as against 8,760,937 Czechs and Slovaks.

The rights enjoyed by the new minorities in Eastern and Central Europe varied from one group and from one state to another. The Sudeten Germans of Czechoslovakia were fairly well treated but were chronically discontented; exactly the same could have been said of the Czechs in the Dual Monarchy. The Hungarians in Rumania and Yugoslavia were often treated as the Slavs had been treated in the old Hungary; naturally they were indignant and vindictive. On the whole racial minorities probably fared a little better—though only a little better—than in the prewar empires.

Even graver was the resulting economic dislocation. In this respect, too, Austria suffered the most. The Habsburg Empire had been a common market of some 50,000,000 customers; its successors started putting up customs barriers against one another almost as soon as they had hoisted their respective national flags. Austria, with her population of 6,500,000—more than a third of it concentrated in the former Imperial capital, "a swollen head atop a dwarfed and shrunken body" as John Gunther put it—was not a viable economic unit in the fiercely nationalistic postwar Europe. The Austrians were well aware of the problem, and as we have seen, wanted to join with the new German Republic. The peace treaties, however, forbade the *Anschluss* by decision of the victor powers, fearful of any increment to Germany. Austria was condemned to an independence that her citizens dreaded.

To counterbalance this long list of blunders, betrayals, and injustices, the Allied peacemakers could boast of one unquestionable achievement: the establishment in Geneva on January 10, 1920, of the League of Nations, the first parliament of man in human history. In the long view, and as a stage in mankind's fumbling, stumbling progress toward one world, the creation of the League may some day be looked back upon as the most important outgrowth of the Paris Peace Conference, or even of the First World War. The institution's immediate capabilities for rectifying the errors and making good the deficiencies of the peace treaties, however, would hardly have been adequate to the task even if Soviet Russia and the United States had joined it from the start. As it was, Russia held aloof, and on March 19, 1920, the United States Senate refused to ratify the Treaty of Versailles, thereby automatically rejecting the league. (On the same day the Senate likewise threw out a security alliance with France and Britain.) It was a blow from which Europe—and in fact the whole world—never fully recovered.

As always in human affairs, the motivations of the "little group of wilful men" (as Wilson had dubbed his congressional opponents upon an earlier occasion) who blocked America's entrance into the League were muddled and complex. To a generation of American politicians, brought up on the Monroe Doctrine and still isolationist at heart, the whole concept of the League was formidable if not appalling. It represented not an evolution of the embryonic world-consciousness that was stirring in America as elsewhere, but a revolutionary leap into the future. The League Covenant, let us remember, was a far more audacious document in the political climate of 1919 than the Charter of the United Nations seemed in 1945. Indeed, from certain viewpoints, the League was a bolder experiment in internationalism than the UN is even today. The surprising thing in retrospect is that the United States Senate, and American public opinion, were willing to consider at all ratifying a commitment that was at once so futuristic and so momentous. What finally torpedoed the League, however, was less the spectre of world government than the fatal linkage between the territorial and punitive provisions of the Treaty of Versailles and the Covenant of the League. Many American liberals joined with the die-hard isolationists in rejecting what they viewed as an instrument for perpetuating injustice and oppression. Above all, perhaps, there was that petty sectarianism of Wilson's which impeded him in seeking bi-partisan support from the Republican leaders, a number of whom had been originally strong supporters of the League, or at least of some kind of international organization. In Washington as in Paris, it was Wilson, the party boss, who undid Wilson, the world prophet. The fact remains that his repudiation by the representatives of the American people was an irresponsible act which, in addition to crippling the League at the outset, simultaneously encouraged those European elements who were plotting to overthrow the peace settlements by violence and exasperated those who were determined to maintain them indefinitely by force. Nothing else that happened between the two great world conflicts did more to make the second one inevitable. To the traumatisms of war and revolution was added the traumatism of the maimed peace. It was these three unhealed wounds of history which chancred the political, social, and cultural institutions of the new European order that lasted from 1919 to 1939.

The Weimar Constitution was proclaimed in Germany on August 11, 1919. Because it had been born in the turmoil of frustrated revolt that accompanied Germany's ratification of the Treaty of Versailles (July 7, 1919) and because it had been fathered by the democratic leaders who, however reluctantly, had bowed to the *Diktat,* the Weimar republic became the foremost butt of the nationalist extremists who had hitherto devoted their savage energies largely to fighting the Communists or to contesting Polish encroachments in the East. Few German nationalists had ever cherished the democratic ideal; now it became the target of their hate. To liberate Germany from the chains of Versailles, as one of the Free Corps veterans explained to an American correspondent, Sigrid Schultz, it was necessary to save German men from becoming "democratic weaklings."

"What, in your opinion, is a democratic weakling?" Miss Schultz asked.

"Why, any German," was the scornful answer, "who forgets that his sole duty is to fight for greater Germany."

It was not Adolf Hitler who spoke thus, nor any of the gutter barbarians who would soon be flocking to his Swastika standard, but a cultivated young Prussian of good family, the writer Ernst von Salomon. Though soon to be involved in the demential assassination of the Jewish politician-industrialist Walter Rathenau (as great a nationalist as his murderers). Von Salomon was neither a thug nor an incurable fanatic. He was merely one of thousands of basically decent young Germans brought up in the worship of Kaiser and country and temporarily transformed into criminal lunatics under the shock of multiple disillusionments. The last, mad rear-guard action of the traditionalist Prussia to which von Salomon belonged was the so-called Kapp *putsch* of March 1920 aimed at overthrowing the republic and eventually restoring the monarchy.

Led by General Freiherr Walther von Luettwitz, a dapper, aristocratic officer of the old school, the Erhardt Brigade, one of the Free Corps which the Allied Control Commission had ordered disbanded (it was also the one to which von Salomon belonged), rose against the government in Berlin on March 13, 1920. To the strains of military bands, and carrying the old Imperial colors, the rebels marched to the Brandenburger Tor, where they were received by General Ludendorff, the master mind behind the plot. An hour earlier, in the pre-dawn gloom, the members of the government had fled Berlin by car, after proclaiming a general strike.

The High Command of the new Reichswehr refused to lift a finger in defense of the republic on the grounds that soldiers who had so recently fought shoulder to shoulder could not be expected to fire at one another. The *putsch* collapsed after three days under the weight of its own ineptitude, and as a result of the general strike. Its nominal leader, a German-American named Wolfgang Kapp, who had taken over the Chancellery, dressed in top hat and spats, fled in a taxi wearing an old brown hat pulled over his eyes. Ludendorff moved his conspiratorial headquarters to Munich. The government returned, and in the interest of national reconciliation, the Erhardt Brigade was allowed to march out of the city in military formation. Sigrid Schultz, watching its departure from a window of the Hotel Adlon recalls that "as the rearguard rounded the corner from Wilhelmstrasse to Unter den Linden, they raised their rifles and without hesitation fired point blank into the hundreds of unarmed civilians on the sidewalks. As a result of that action, which took in time only a few minutes, the Adlon lobby was filled with the dead and the wounded."

The failure of the Kapp *putsch* was a defeat for the old-fashioned monarchist nationalism of the *junkers* but it was not a real victory for German democracy. The center for agitation against the republic and against the *diktat* of Versailles shifted to Munich and leadership of the nationalist movement increasingly fell from the hands of the Prussian generals and colonels into those of the Austrian-born ex-corporal Hitler, and of his party comrade, the homosexual soldier-of-fortune Captain Ernst Roehm. In March 1924 Hitler reorganized his German Workers' Party on the basis of a new, more radical program and the next month he renamed it the National-Socialist German Workers' Party. Soon its members were also sporting a new arm band designed by their *Fuehrer:* Red, with a spiderlike black cross on a white field. The nickname Nazi, and the Swastika emblem had been born. Germany—and the world—were not to remain safe for democracy very long.

German National Socialism was among other things a kind of neurotic reaction to military defeat, to the Kaiser's desertion, to the injustices of Versailles and to the fear of Communism. Its vocabulary and mythology were drawn largely from the Pan-German propaganda of the Wilhelmine era, and from the ravings of the Austrian and Russian anti-Semites. What it possessed in the way of a coherent totalitarian doctrine was inspired to a large degree by Italian fascism, whose chief and principal theoretician, ex-Sergeant Benito Mussolini, had been the first demagogue in the West to launch a successful mass-movement based on the rehabilitation of autocracy dressed up as the leader-principle, decorated with various populist or socialist trimmings, and associated with ultranationalism. As in Germany, the bitterness engendered in Italy by the peace settlements and by the fear of Bolshevism had created conditions that favored a right-wing assault simultaneously against Wilsonian democracy and against the traditional leadership of Church and Throne. Mussolini, a larger and more tragic figure than is sometimes realized, had created his first *Fascio di Combattimento* in March 1919. In October 1922—after three years of social conflict and political instability which his black-shirted Fascists had done their best to aggravate—he ordered (but prudently refrained from joining) the so-called March on Rome by 100,000 of his followers, some of them armed. The gigantic bluff succeeded and King Victor Emmanuel III—to his subsequent regret—named the former Socialist editor Premier of Italy. Next month King and Parliament made him a temporary grant of dictatorial powers to "restore order." For a while Mussolini preserved the semblance of constitutionalism (a constitutionalism laced with castor oil for those who tried to exercise the right of opposition) but bit by bit he consolidated his power and completed the edifice of an ideologically ambitious new form of tyranny. Before long visitors to Italy would see the megalomaniac slogan *IL DUCE HA SEMPRE RAGIONE* (The Duce Is Always Right) painted in huge letters on the walls of palaces and the face of cliffs. As demagogic perversions of the democratic ideal, both German and Italian fascism were reflections of its impact on the European masses but they also reflected the nostalgia for a vanished paternalism that the monarchies had supplied. The phoenix of autocracy, in vulgar, gaudy, new feathers, was risen from the ashes of war.

A new autocracy, or at least a new autocrat, was already rising from the ruins of Abdul Hamid's empire. A queer situation had developed in the Ottoman capital at the end of the war. Defeat, partial or complete, had brought down Nicholas II, Wilhelm II, and the Emperor Karl; it set Sultan Mehmet VI, the nephew of Abdul Hamid, more firmly on his throne. All during the war the real master of the Ottoman Empire had been the former Young Turk leader Enver Pasha. The Sultan, Mehmet V, whom the Young Turks had installed when they deposed Abdul Hamid, had been a mere figurehead. His successor, the Crown Prince Vahdetten, had only been allowed to mount the throne upon Mehmet's death in 1918 because for forty years he had managed to make everyone believe he was a spineless simpleton. In reality Mehmet VI was made of the same stuff as his late uncle (Abdul Hamid had died peacefully in the arms of a faithful *kadine* only a few months earlier); he had the same cunning, the same lust for power, and the same cowardice. When Turkey had to sue for peace Enver departed—to a new career of wild adventure and eventual death on a nameless battlefield in Central Asia—and Mehmet recovered some of the authority he had been pining and scheming for. He knew that the victorious Entente Powers would rather deal with a tame sultan than with a demo-cratic—and chauvinistic—Young Turk general, and he rightly calculated that Allied support would keep him on the throne as long as he behaved like a pliant vassal. In time the Allies would start quarreling among them-selves—particularly if Mehmet practiced a little gentle well-poisoning, as his uncle had so often done—and then he would be free. From the viewpoint of preserving and even modestly restoring, the privileges of the dynasty, it was by no means an unrealistic policy. To almost anyone who had not been brought up in a harem, however, it might have seemed an intolerably humiliating one to execute.

Since the armistice treaty of Mudros, October 30, 1918 by which the Turkish forces had lain down their arms, Constantinople had been under slightly veiled military occupation by the Allies, with the British as the dominant occupation power. On February 8, 1919, the veil was torn. Gen-eral Franchet d'Esperey, mounted on a white horse given him by the local Greek community, rode into the Ottoman capital at the head of a detach-ment of newly disembarked French troops. It was a pointed and ironic allu-sion to the triumphant entry of Mehmet II in 1453. Among the Turks who witnessed with tight lips and burning eyes this premeditated affront to their national pride was Mustapha Kemal. The former young Turk of the Young Turks, now a general, had perhaps, the most brilliant war record in the Turkish army; it was chiefly thanks to him that the Allied landing at Gal-lipoli had failed. He was, of course, already hard at work again at his prewar avocation: political conspiracy.

In April 1919 the Sultan's government sent Kemal into polite exile by appointing him inspector general of the Turkish forces in the remote wilds of eastern Anatolia. Just before his departure from Constantinople he learned that two Greek divisions had landed at Smyrna on the Aegean coast of Turkey, and some Italian forces at Adalia, farther south, in an initial step toward the execution of the Allied plan for dismembering the Ottoman Empire. (Other features of the plan included an independent Armenia, independent Arab kingdoms, a British protectorate in Palestine and a French protectorate in Syria.) Landing in May at the Black Sea port of Samsun, Kemal according to one of his Turkish biographers, Irfan Orga, "stretched his arms to the wide sky over Anatolia and burst into the saddest yet most stirring of Turkish marches."

Whether or not the anecdote is more than a pious scrap of Kemalist hagiography, it symbolizes the spirit in which Kemal launched his revolution. The blue-eyed Salonika-born officer of Albanian—and possibly Jewish —descent was putting Europe behind him and returning both physically and emotionally to the Asian homeland of his distant Turanian ancestors. And he meant to make the whole world—or at least the Greeks, the French, and the British—tremble. Kemalism, as it gradually took shape from the example and teaching of its founder, had some affinities with Italian fascism and German National Socialism; it contained nationalist, militarist, socialist, and even racist elements. Though intensely authoritarian it was not permeated, however, with the obsessive hatred of democracy that afflicted Hitler and Mussolini—possibly because Kemal's Weimar was not a democratic regime but an anachronistic Sultan and a comprador government of pashas cowering at the feet of the Allies.

"Is it not sad," Kemal complained many years later when his attention was called to a foreign newspaper article comparing him with Mussolini, "that I should stand beside that mountain of complacency; that hyena in jackboots who could destroy the innocent Abyssinian savage without a moment's regret . . ." Essentially—though the word had not yet come into fashion—Kemalism was an anti-colonialist movement animating a war of national independence: the forerunner and the inspiration of the nationalist revolutions that have since thrown off the Western yoke throughout the Moslem world. Hence its irresistible dynamism.

The formal launching of the Kemalist revolution dates from the Resolution of Sivas (a town east of Ankara) on June 19, 1919, which proclaimed the government in Constantinople to be under foreign control and demanded the convocation of a representative congress in Anatolia. The rapid growth of the movement forced a change of government in Constantinople and the calling of elections, in which the Kemalists won a sweeping victory. The newly elected nationalist deputies met in Ankara and voted what amounted to a Turkish declaration of independence. When the Allies retaliated by occupying the public buildings in the Sultan's capital, by ordering the dissolution of parliament and by arresting and deporting a number of nationalist leaders, the Kemalist members of parliament who were still at large fled to Ankara. There, on April 23, 1920, they organized themselves in a Grand National Assembly, repudiated the authority of the puppet government in Constantinople and elected Kemal president of the republic.

We have become so used to seeing the triumph of nationalist movements in colonial or semi-colonial areas that it is hard at this distance to recognize the almost epic temper of the Kemalist revolution or to appreciate the extraordinary quality of Kemal's leadership. Turkish nationalism was an immense force, but in 1920 it was still inchoate and almost dormant. The Young Turks were nationalists of a sort, but despite their nickname, not explicitly Turkish ones, and under Enver's regime the whole reform movement had badly run to seed. Kemal rekindled the revolutionary idealism of 1908 and identified its goals exclusively with the interests of the Turkish people, as distinguished from those of the empire. He constantly talked about saving the Turkish nation from destruction but at the time many of his listeners did not fully realize that such a nation existed. It was in listening to Kemal that they became Turks. The transformation was rarely immediate or painless. Kemal often had great difficulty in convincing his brother officers that loyalty to this new, still slightly hazy ideal, the Turkish nation or people, should take precedence over the soldierly oath of loyalty they had sworn to the Sultan. He had perhaps even greater difficulty in convincing the poverty-stricken, illiterate, and war-weary Anatolian peasant that the time had already come to take the field again in what seemed an almost hopeless cause.

To an imaginative and aggressive soldier, the cause, of course, did not look hopeless, but it certainly involved a perilous fight against heavy odds. Though Kemal's military genius was a big factor in the final victory, the real secret of his leadership lay elsewhere. Like Lenin he had the charisma of efficacity, and his dour yet vibrant personality incarnated Turkish nationalism much as Lenin's incarnated the Bolshevik revolution. Kemal's identification with history was so total, however, that it ceased to be entirely lucid; he was utterly swallowed up by the cause he led. Even his failings became de-humanized in the process. The fleeting snatches of personal life that he allowed himself were squandered in wild and sordid debauchery, as if to underscore the worthlessness of every thought or feeling that could not be dedicated to the national renascence. Kemal's single-mindedness, it is true, was to a considerable extent forced on him by the struggle for survival in the early years of the Turkish revolution.

Mehmet VI, once again following the example of Abdul Hamid, sent teams of fanatic Moslem agitators into Anatolia to stir up all the reactionary elements of the countryside against Kemal, so that he had a civil war on his hands, in addition to all the others. The Allies simultaneously incited the Armenians and other minorities to rise against him. Then the Greek forces, in considerable strength, but with notable rashness, started to march on Ankara from the coast. For more than two years there was bitter, confused fighting throughout Asiatic Turkey. Gradually, stolidly, ruthlessly Kemal wiped out the counterrevolutionaries, crushed the rebellious minorities, and forced back the foreign invaders. The Greek retreat became a rout, then a mass exodus of the native Christian population. Ghastly atrocities were committed on both sides; women raped and crucified, old men clubbed to death, children impaled on bayonets, villages wantonly burned, wells systematically poisoned. In September 1922 the last Greek troops and refugees were evacuated by sea from Smyrna. Whatever could not be carried away was destroyed to prevent it falling into the hands of the hated Turk; everything including the pack animals used in the evacuation. The waterside scene at Smyrna left an indelible imprint on the mind of Ernest Hemingway, who covered the Greek-Turkish war as a newspaper correspondent; some years later it was to inspire one of his classic vignettes: "All those mules with their forelegs broken pushed over in the shallow water. It was all a pleasant business. My word, yes, a most pleasant business." Kemal was also impressed by Smyrna, but it was the huge fires that broke out in the wake of the evacuation which captured his imagination.

"This fire is a symbol," he told an awe-struck group of officers, as Kemal's French biographer, Benoist-Mechin, relates the scene. "It means that our country at last is freed of traitors and profiteers. Henceforth, Turkey, liberated and purified, belongs only to the Turks."

For three days, says Benoist-Mechin, Kemal let the fire burn, without the least attempt to bring it under control.

The Allies evacuated Constantinople in August 1923, taking the puppet Sultan with them. The Turkish republic was formally proclaimed—in Ankara, not in the old Ottoman capital—on October 29. Mehmet VI was stripped of all his temporal powers, though a nephew was briefly tolerated in succession as Caliph of Islam, the dimming Shadow of God on Earth. Kemal was honored with the ancient title of Gazi (Destroyer of the Infidels) —a somewhat ironic honor, since he was an atheist—and elected president. Five months later he abolished the Caliphate, the religious office of the Sultan, and banished all members of the Osmanli House from Turkish soil, thus writing a legal finis to the history of the Ottoman Dynasty. This iconoclastic gesture marked the beginning of the most drastic revolution from above carried out anywhere since the days of Peter the Great in Russia.

Peter had taken the beards off his *boyars:* Kemal in his determination to make Turkey a great modern power, took the traditional red fez off the heads of his pashas. Once, in fact, he slapped the face of the Egyptian minister for appearing at a diplomatic function in the forbidden headgear. His methods of obtaining compliance with his orders from his own constituents were even more drastic. "Beside him," wrote John Gunther, "Hitler is a milksop, Mussolini a perfumed dandy." Unlike the other neo-autocrats, however, Kemal established his dictatorship not for the sake of power but for the sake of his people. Having suppressed all his opponents, he eventually took the unprecedented step of creating an opposition by decree; thus democracy was at least nominally restored in Turkey. One of Kemal's reforms was to impose Western-style surnames. For himself he chose the surname Attaturk—Father of the Turks. He had thoroughly earned it both in his public and in his private careers.

With the end of the fighting between the new Turkey and the Allies the last stages of the liquidation of the former Ottoman Empire could be carried out, and the postwar frontiers of the Near East could be established. Some revisions were effected in the Treaty of Sèvres, but a number of changes based on it had already been put into effect. Turkey kept Constantinople and eastern Thrace, remaining as before astride the straits. She also kept the coastline of Asia Minor, along with the Anatolian plateau and the mountains of Armenia. On the other hand she recognized the annexation of Cyprus by Britain—which had long been installed on the island—and ceded the Dodecanese to Italy. The Arabs—who had been recruited in 1915 as guerrilla allies of the British by Lawrence of Arabia, the most romantic of the political warriors—got their freedom, or at least the southern and dusty side of it. The fertile Arab lands, and those known at the time to possess oil reserves, went under temporary mandates to the French and the British. The French, after a brief war with their reluctant wards, got what are today the republics of Syria and Lebanon, to the unhealable despair of Lawrence who had promised Damascus, the palm-girdled and many-mosqued to his desert friends. The British took Mesopotamia and Palestine. The Arabs thought they had been promised the latter territory as well as Syria, but conflicting arrangements had been entered into with the Zionist organizations to establish a Jewish national home in the Holy Land—one of those little political warfare arrangements originally intended to mobilize Western Jewry in support of the Allied cause and to undermine the loyalty of the Kaiser's Jewish subjects. Co-existence of Jews and Arabs in the same territory under British mandate seemed to be the best way out of an awkward situation, and at the time it probably was, though the decision planted the seeds of bitter and dangerous conflict in the future.

Gradually the roar of clashing mobs and the sound of gunfire died out in Europe, though new attempts at Communist insurrection or Fascist *putsch* flared up sporadically throughout the early twenties. The physical scars of war and revolution began to heal; the political, economic, and social wounds remained open. The fall of the despotic—or at least traditionally authoritarian—monarchies in Central, Eastern, and Southeastern Europe had not perceptibly enhanced the personal liberties of their former subjects. Dictatorships of one sort or another prevailed throughout most of the vast area. (Masaryk's Czechoslovakia was a happy exception.) Various factors mitigated to some degree their harshness. In the new Russian despotism there was at least the hope that present sacrifices would lead to future well being. In the successor states of the Habsburg Empire people had the satisfaction of being mishandled by policemen of their own blood, faith or social class; to some this was a real step forward; others, like many Croat subjects of the new Yugoslav kingdom, found it a dubious consolation. There was unquestionably more equality in the New Europe than there had been in the old, but some individuals and groups were still a great deal more equal than others. And, as the Swiss historian J. R. von Salis remarks, the antagonisms between rulers and ruled, between the new haves and the new—or not so new—have-nots stood forth more starkly than before the war. "In every case," von Salis writes, "it appeared that hallowed traditions and relations of mutual respect between governments and governed no longer existed, and that no new political legitimacy, no morally binding new order had appeared to provide guidance for collectivities and individuals in their relations to the state."

Much the same could be said of the relations between states—despite the League of Nations—as von Salis goes on to demonstrate. Wilson—and later Aristide Briand—tried to translate into political reality the new dream of brotherhood of peoples that writers like Romain Rolland and H. G. Wells had helped to popularize in the West, as Maxim Gorky and the more idealistic Soviet intellectuals of the first revolutionary generation had attempted to do in the East. But the dream splintered against an older political myth, the nationalist myth, which, as von Salis says, "proved to be more powerful and more durable than the idea of collective security propagated by the League of Nations"—so much so in fact that in time the League itself became to a large extent a rostrum for nationalist propaganda. (The developing Soviet doctrine of world revolution, not by persuasion and example but by subversion and aggression, was also ultimately deadly to the Wilsonian ideal.)

The economic aftermath of war and of peacemaking gave the final turn of the screw to the woebegone survivors of the prewar European civilization that had been based on the vanished monarchies. Virtually all of the former belligerent powers except the USSR, which had other problems, suffered to some degree from monetary inflation and the resultant depreciation of currency in the early 1920s. Austria and Germany were hit hardest, especially the latter.

In Austria, where runaway inflation started before Germany, but never reached the same monstrous proportions, a weird kind of "tourist season"

flourished for some time: it was cheaper for a man on the dole in England
to live in a luxury hotel in Austria than in a tenement at home. Bavarians
poured across the frontier into Salzburg by the thousands, buying clothes,
drugs, having their teeth fixed, or just mailing their letters at a saving.
Eventually stringent customs controls were established on the border and
smuggling was confined to the quarts of beer which a Bavarian could carry
home in his stomach. "Every night," recalls the writer Stefan Zweig, who
lived in Salzburg at the time, "the station was a veritable pandemonium of
drunken, bawling, belching humanity; some of them, helpless from over-
indulgence, had to be carried to the train on hand-trucks, and then, with
bacchanalian yelling and singing, they were transported back to their own
country." But the Austrians had their revenge when the krone was stabilized
and the mark plunged below it in value; the stampede across the border was
repeated, but this time in the opposite direction.

"This beer war between two inflations remains one of my oddest memories," wrote Zweig, "because it was a precise reflection, in grotesque and
graphic miniature, of the whole insane character of those years."

The German mark had already lost one-fourth of its value during the
war. The strain of reparations payments—about one-eighth of the national
income annually—contributed to its dizzy postwar decline. (To keep one's
perspective, however, it is worth recalling that later on, after Germany had
been freed of reparation payments by an international moratorium and
had defaulted on her foreign debt, Hitler's military budget ate up one-sixth
of the national income.) In November 1921 the mark could be changed at
200 to the dollar. By November 1923 the rate had climbed to four billion
marks for a dollar. At the peak of the inflation the price of one copy of a
daily newspaper rose to 200,000,000,000 marks. An ordinary postage
stamp cost twelve billion marks.

Insurance policies, savings deposits, and government bonds became almost worthless. Those who had practiced thrift and prudence and the lifelong self-restraint upon which they are based were turned into paupers.
Those who had gambled and squandered and borrowed beyond their
means often grew rich overnight. The purely economic blow that inflation
struck at the German—and to a lesser degree at the European bourgeoisie—
was murderous. The moral and psychological shock was even graver. With
their faith in the value of money—and in the traditional virtues associated
with moneymaking—destroyed, the middle classes lost a great part of their
trust not only in government, but in society, in God, in the basic decencies
of life itself. The psychic wound was all the more grievous because it followed so closely upon the shock inflicted by the downfall of the traditional
symbols of authority. And it was infected with a deadly fear: the new poor
of the German middle classes might or might not actually starve—some very
nearly did so—but they felt themselves threatened with a slow suffocation

of their self-respect through the social demotion to pauper or at best proletarian status. It is hardly surprising that they turned savage and gave Hitler
the mass following he needed to convert his lunatic-fringe movement into
a revolutionary menace.

Except in Russia the aristocracy suffered much less than the bourgeoisie from the economic consequences of war and revolution. Traditionally
much of their wealth was in land, which did not depreciate as much during
inflation—if it was heavily mortgaged there was a real benefit—and they had
not been brought up, as the middle classes had, to equate solvability and
respectability, or to regard accrual of worldly goods as the reward and
proof of pious living. The crumbling of the monarchies which it had been
their hereditary function to serve deprived them, however, of their social
raison d'être. Some nobles continued to serve society in their traditional
professional roles as officers or diplomats—they were no longer in much
demand as ministers or governors—but their opportunities for such service
were far fewer than they had been before the war, especially in the new nations of which they had formerly constituted the alien ruling class. Some
courageously accepted proletarian or even menial status like the Russian
taxi drivers, night-club doormen, and headwaiters in postwar Paris; others
went into business. A great many, however, drifted into more or less camouflaged parisitism, and like all social parasites speedily degenerated.
The once strictly guarded frontier between Society, where it still lingered on
in the old monarchic capitals, and cafe society gradually became blurred.
"In the early twenties," the Duke of Windsor recalls in his memoirs, *A
King's Story*, "the forces of change had not yet thrust so deeply into the texture of British society as to have obliterated much of the old elegance. . . .
During the so-called London season the West End was an almost continuous ball from midnight until dawn . . . the evening could always be saved
by recourse to one or another of the gay nightclubs, which had then become
so fashionable and almost respectable."

Among the deposed ruling houses it was the Habsburgs who, as might
be expected, best maintained the traditions of the Old World. Karl's son,
Archduke Otto, was brought up by his mother, the ex-Empress Zita, in the
expectation that he would one day return to the throne of his ancestors. Up
to 1938 the chances for a monarchist restoration, at least in Austria, seemed
fair, and though they have since faded Otto has taken care to manage both
his public and his private life in a manner befitting a possible future monarch. Several of the Hohenzollerns were less fastidious, or less fortunate,
though for a while the chances of restoration seemed even better in Germany than in Austria. Wilhelm lived in decent, if inglorious retirement
(the Dutch government had naturally refused to extradite him for trial by
the Allies after World War I) to his death in 1941, but the postwar career
of the former Crown Prince Friedrich Wilhelm was not particularly edify-

ing from any viewpoint. A pillar of international cafe society and a one-time supporter of Hitler, he died in 1951.

Legend is already beginning to depict the early 1920s as a time of hectic gaiety and of creative ferment. They were, it is true, the age of flaming youth, of the flapper, of the Charleston and—in America—of the raccoon coat and the hip flask; of Hemingway and Sinclair Lewis and F. Scott Fitzgerald; of D. H. Lawrence and James Joyce and the Surrealist Manifesto. The gradual shrinking of the frontiers of female modesty that had already been noticeable before the war picked up velocity. As currency fell, skirts steadily rose; in 1919 they were six inches from the ground; by 1925, when stabilization was at last attained, they had reached the knee.

Accompanying this vestimentary emancipation was a movement of revolt, particularly among young people, against every conventional restraint of mind or body. The American flapper, typified on the silent screen by the flaming-haired Clara Bow, was a timid conformist beside her European sister, coming of age amid the shattered idols of the fallen empires. "They [the postwar generation in Central Europe] revolted against every legitimated form for the pleasure of revolting," recalls Stefan Zweig, "even against the order of nature, against the eternal polarity of the sexes . . . homosexuality and lesbianism became the fashion, not from any inner instinct but by way of protest against the traditional and normal expressions of love. . . . The general impulse to radical and revolutionary excess manifested itself in art, too, of course . . . the comprehensible element in everything was proscribed, melody in music, resemblance in portraits, intelligibility in language. How wild, anarchic and unreal were those years . . ."

They were indeed unreal years, and though they were wild enough, they were seldom as gay as those of us who are now middle-aged like to recall them. Underneath the hectic sensation-seeking was a spiritual and emotional numbness. In the horror of war, in the shock of revolution, in the disillusionment of peace, Europeans had lost the naive faith in progress which had sustained their fathers and their grandfathers. Technical progress would no doubt continue but the belief that it would contribute to man's betterment was shattered beyond repair. The brightening morning of the air age—aviation had naturally made giant strides thanks to the war—did not lift men's hearts, at least in Europe, nor did the dawn of the radio age. (The first U.S. broadcasting station opened in East Pittsburgh in 1920.) "How strange it is," said G. K. Chesterton, "that mankind should have invented a machine for speaking to the whole world at precisely the moment when no man has anything to say." A few men did have something to say: Spengler in history for example, Hemingway, Aldous Huxley, Evelyn Waugh in literature, but it was not exactly a cheerful message. Even more depressing than Spengler's theme of the inevitable decline of Western civilization was that of the postwar degradation of personal relationships to which Hemingway, for all his chest beating and violence, was one of the most sensitive witnesses. Lady Brett's Montparnasse was a sad place. Post-war Vienna, a kind of dry Venice, emptied by the ebb tide of history, was even sadder. But Berlin, the hectic Babylon of the jazz age, was the saddest of all.

"I have a pretty thorough knowledge of history," Zweig writes again, speaking of Berlin in the 1920s, "but never to my recollection has it produced such madness in such gigantic proportions . . . What we had in Austria was just a mild and shy prologue to this witches' sabbath . . . Even the Rome of Suetonius had never known such orgies as the pervert balls at Berlin . . . But the most revolting thing about this pathetic eroticism was its spuriousness . . . Whoever lived through these apocalyptic months, these years, disgusted and embittered, sensed the coming of a counter-blow, a horrible reaction."

The reaction to which Zweig referred was, of course, Hitler's rise to power and subsequent bid for world hegemony. In reality, however, the Nazi-fascist revolution was to prove not so much an archaistic swingback of the pendulum after the revolt against traditional values, as a further and extreme symptom of their breakdown. Underlying all the sound and the fury of the early postwar years, becoming even more evident as they gradually died down, was a repetition on a more disastrous scale of the same generalized failure of leadership that, as we have noted again and again, had been such a conspicuous factor in the destruction of the old Europe. The political, spiritual, and social bankruptcy of the new power elites who succeeded the monarchs, the aristocrats and the old-fashioned bourgeois dynasties was in many respects more spectacular than their predecessors' had been. This time, however, the eclipse of leadership was not localized in one continent or limited to any particular class of society. The geographical New World, once it had repudiated Wilsonism, could contribute nothing to the redressment of the Old; in terms of the problems that confronted it, the America of Warren Gamaliel Harding and of Calvin Coolidge soon demonstrated that it was scarcely less anachronistic than the Austria-Hungary of Francis Joseph had been. Neither the shift of the European locus of power and prestige from the former Central Empires to the Western democracies, nor the replacement of the traditional ruling classes within the fallen monarchies by less obsolescent social elements gave the Occidental world as a whole sounder or more forward-looking direction than it had had before. Baldwin and Benes were to repeat the blunders of Aehrenthal and Grey; Stalin's foreign policy was to be as fatally incoherent as that of Nicholas. To an even greater degree than before 1914 the acceleration of change in every field was making collective or even individual adjustment to it increasingly difficult. History itself had become a runaway locomotive.

In the moral turmoil of postwar Europe, amid the rubble of the fallen hierarchies, under the darkening skies of the new, more terrible storm that was approaching, one symbol of man's hope stood out, and still stands to-day: The strange, moving new kind of monument which the recently belligerent nations put up to honor the memory of their war dead. The Tomb of the Unknown Soldier in Arlington National Cemetery, the Cenotaph of the Unknown Warrior in London, the nameless marble slab and the ritual flame under Napoleon's Arc de Triomphe reflect something more than a contemporary trend in funerary architecture or pageantry. Every society, after every war, has honored its slain heroes, but ours is the first to choose an anonymous hero; fifty years earlier the very words might have seemed a contradiction in terms.

The cult of the Unknown Soldier, however superficial it may be, can scarcely be imagined in the Austria-Hungary of Francis Joseph, in the Russia of Nicholas II, in the Kaiser's Germany. It took a new kind of war and a new way of thinking and feeling about war to make the concept meaningful or the symbol moving. A deep social change of some kind, perhaps a historic mutation, underlies the symbolism. Perhaps it is merely because ours is a faceless, mass society that we can choose a nameless hero.

But perhaps, instead, the ambiguous tombs are not simply monuments to the commonness of the Common Man, the conqueror of emperors and aristocrats, but shrines to his humanity. Perhaps they mark a minute yet significant evolution in the pattern of our minds, a broadening rather than merely a leveling, a new perception, however clouded, of the human condition and of the dignity that attaches to it, everywhere and always, in even the most pitiable and in even the most sordid of circumstances. There are other probable indications of such an evolution in individual attitudes accompanying the modest progress that has been achieved after two world wars in creating embryonic institutions of world co-operation. Perhaps now that the lesser tribal glories have faded it is easier for us to recognize our membership in the great tribe of man. The changes are at once so deep and so subtle that we cannot yet be certain they have really occurred, but it seems probable that they have, and we can therefore reasonably invoke at least one positive theme to close this story of the decline and fall and rebirth of despotism, of blind leaders and deluded masses, of old wrongs perpetuated and of new ones imposed, of revolution leading to war and war leading to revolutions, of peace still-born, of hopes once more aroused and again betrayed, of vast regressions, of one small, halting step forward. The advance may seem a feeble one to counterbalance so much tragic relapse, but the same no doubt could have been said of nearly every step that has been taken in man's long, slow, faltering progress upward from the primordial slime.

Bibliography

GENERAL.

The following works have been especially valuable in providing general background for the whole period of European history covered by my book or for substantial parts of it, and have been cited or otherwise drawn upon in the preparation of numerous chapters:

THE ORIGINS OF THE WAR OF 1914, Luigi Albertini, Oxford University Press, London, 1953.

LA CRISE EUROPEENNE ET LA PREMIERE GUERRE MONDIAL, Pierre Renouvin, Presses Universitaires de France, 1948.

WELTGESCHICHTE DER NEUSTEN ZEIT, J. R. von Salis, Orell Fussli, Zurich.

CHAPTER 1.

The works most frequently drawn on for the history of the Habsburg Monarchy and the biography of Francis Joseph and Francis Ferdinand are:

Taylor, A. J. P.: THE HABSBURG MONARCHY 1809–1918, Hamish Hamilton, London.

Redlich, Joseph: EMPEROR FRANCIS JOSEPH OF AUSTRIA, Macmillan, London, 1929.

Ernst, Otto, Dr.: FRANZ-JOSEPH AS REVEALED BY HIS LETTERS, Frederick H. Stokes Company, New York.

Tschuppik, Karl: FRANZ-JOSEPH, Hellerau, 1928.

von Margutti, Albert Freiherr: VOM ALTEN KAISER, Leipzig, Vienna, 1921.

Ketterl, Eugen: EMPEROR FRANCIS JOSEPH: AN INTIMATE STUDY, Skeffington and Son Limited, London.

Bagger, Eugene: FRANCIS JOSEPH, EMPEROR OF AUSTRIA: KING OF HUNGARY, G. P. Putnam's Sons, New York, London.

Other books consulted are:

Shepherd, Gordon: THE AUSTRIAN ODYSSEY, London, 1957.

Schuschnigg, Kurt von: FAREWELL AUSTRIA, Castle and Company, London, 1936.

Harding, Bertita: THE GOLDEN FLEECE: THE STORY OF FRANZ-JOSEPH AND ELIZABETH OF AUSTRIA, Bobbs-Merrill Company, Indianapolis.

The material for the Sarajevo episode is based mainly on:

Mousset, Albert: UN DRAME HISTORIQUE, L'ATTENTAT DE SARAJEVO, DOCUMENTS INEDITS ET TEXTE INTEGRALE DES STENOGRAMES DU PROCES, Payot, Paris, 1930.
Seton-Watson, R. W.: SARAJEVO, Hutchinson & Company, London, 1926.

and on a series of articles;

Taylor, A. J. P.: HOW A WORLD WAR BEGAN, *The Observer,* London, November 1958.

Further books used include:

Remak, Joachim: SARAJEVO, Criterion Books Inc., New York, 1959.
West, Rebecca: BLACK LAMB AND GREY FALCON, Viking Press, New York.

CHAPTER 2.

The evocation of pre-1914 Europe was derived from a number of books. Only those most frequently quoted and referred to are listed below. The three following range over most of Europe:

Zweig, Stefan: THE WORLD OF YESTERDAY, Castle, London, 1949.
Laver, James: EDWARDIAN PARADE, Edward Hulton, 1958.
Cowles, Virginia: EDWARD VII AND HIS CIRCLE, Hamish Hamilton, London.

For England:

Churchill, Sir Winston: THE WORLD CRISIS, Charles Scribner's Sons, New York, 1928.
George, David Lloyd: WAR MEMORIES, Little, Brown, Boston.
Asquith, Margot: AUTOBIOGRAPHY, Penguin.
Cooper, Diana: THE RAINBOW COMES AND GOES, Rupert Hart Davis, London, 1958.

For France:

Guilleminault, Gilbert: LA BELLE EPOQUE, Denoel, Paris, 1957.
Mauduit, Jean: MAXIM'S, Editions du Rocher, Monaco, 1958.
Glyn, Anthony: ELINOR GLYN, Hutchinson, London.
Tabouis, Geneviève: THEY CALLED ME CASSANDRA, Charles Scribner's Sons, New York, 1942.

For Germany:

Prince Bernhard von Bulow: MEMOIRS, Little, Brown, Boston, 1931–2.

Ludwig, Emil: WILHELM HOHENZOLLERN: THE LAST OF THE KAISERS, G. P. Putnam's Sons, New York, 1926.

Kuèrenberg, Joachim von: THE KAISER, Simon and Schuster, 1955.

For Vienna:

Trotsky, Leon: MY LIFE, Butterworth, London, 1930.

Hitler, Adolf: MEIN KAMPF, Reynal and Hitchcock, New York.

Freud, Ernst L.: THE LETTERS OF SIGMUND FREUD 1873–1939, Hogarth Press, London, 1960.

Freud, Martin: SIGMUND FREUD: MAN AND FATHER, Vanguard Press, New York, 1958.

Sperber, Manes: LE TALON D'ACHILLE, Calmann Levy, Paris.

Jenks, William: VIENNA AND THE YOUNG HITLER, Columbia University Press, New York.

Hamilton, Lord Frederic: THE VANISHED POMPS OF YESTERDAY, Doubleday Doran, New York.

Schierbrand, Wolf von: AUSTRIA-HUNGARY: POLYGLOT EMPIRE, Frederick H. Stokes Company, New York, 1917.

Sedgwyck, Henry Dwight: VIENNA: THE BIOGRAPHY OF A BYGONE CITY, Bobbs-Merrill Company, Indianapolis.

CHAPTER 3.

The material for the Bjorkoe episode is based mainly on the detailed accounts of it given by Emil Ludwig in WILHELM HOHENZOLLERN *and Karl F. Nowak in* GERMANY'S ROAD TO RUIN, *Macmillan, New York, 1932, and on the analysis of the encounter and of its implications given by Albertini.*

Sidelights on the repercussions in Russia of the meeting have been provided by A. Savinsky's RECOLLECTIONS OF A RUSSIAN DIPLOMAT, *Maurice Paleologue,* UN GRAND TOURNANT DE LA POLITIQUE MONDIALE 1904–1906, *Plon, 1935 and Maurice Bompard,* MON AMBASSADE EN RUSSIE 1903–1908, *Paris, 1935.*

CHAPTER 4.

General studies cited or drawn upon as background sources:

Pares, Sir Bernard: HISTORY OF RUSSIA, London, 1937.

———: THE FALL OF THE RUSSIAN MONARCHY, London, 1939.

(*the main sources on the history of the dynasty and the reign of Nicholas II*).

Florinsky, Michael F.: THE END OF THE RUSSIAN EMPIRE, Yale University Press, 1931.

Seton-Watson, Hugh: THE DECLINE OF IMPERIAL RUSSIA, Frederick A. Praeger, New York, 1960.

Charques, Richard: THE TWILIGHT OF IMPERIAL RUSSIA, Phoenix, London, 1958.

Trotsky, Leon: THE RUSSIAN REVOLUTION, Simon and Schuster, New York, 1936.

Wolfe, Bertram: THREE WHO MADE A REVOLUTION, New York, 1948.

Shub, David: LENIN, Doubleday, New York, 1949.
Almedingen, E. M.: THE EMPRESS ALEXANDRA, Hutchinson, London, 1961.
Moorhead, Alan: THE RUSSIAN REVOLUTION, Harper & Brothers, New York, 1958.

Memoirs and contemporary documents cited or drawn upon:

Paleologue, Maurice: LA RUSSIE DES TSARS, Plon, Paris, 1921.
Alexandra, Empress of Russia: THE LETTERS OF THE TSARITZA TO THE TSAR, Duckworth, London, 1923.
Nicholas II, Emperor of Russia: THE LETTERS OF THE TSAR TO THE TSARITZA, Bodley Head, London, 1929.
Nicholas II: JOURNAL INTIME, Payot, Paris.
Nicholas II: LETTERS OF TSAR NICHOLAS AND EMPRESS MARIE, London, 1937.
Wilhelm II, Emperor of Germany: CORRESPONDENCE ENTRE GUILLAUME II AND NICHOLAS II, Plon, Paris.
Weber-Bauler, Leon: FROM ORIENT TO OCCIDENT, Oxford University Press, New York, 1941.
Prince Bernhard von Bulow: MEMOIRS 1849–1919, Little, Brown, Boston.
Mossolov, A. A.: AT THE COURT OF THE LAST TSAR, London, 1935.
Nicholas II: THE SECRET LETTERS OF TSAR NICHOLAS, London, 1938.

Other works consulted:

Buchanan, Sir George: MY MISSION TO RUSSIA, London, 1923.
Spiridovich, A., General: LES DERNIERES ANNEES DE LA COUR DE TSARKOE SELO, Paris, 1928.
Guerassimov, General: TSARISME ET TERRORISME, Paris, 1928.
Troyat, Henri: LA VIE QUOTIDIENNE EN RUSSIE AU TEMPS DU DERNIER TSAR, Paris, 1959.

CHAPTER 5.

For an insight into the nature of the Habsburg Monarchy:

Taylor, A. J. P.: THE HABSBURG MONARCHY 1809–1918, Hamish Hamilton, London,

proved invaluable.

Other basic sources include the ones listed in the bibliography of Chapter 1. Additional books consulted were:

Kuerenberg, Joachim von: A WOMAN OF VIENNA, Cassel, London.
Anet, Claude: THE LOVE AND TRAGEDY OF A CROWN PRINCE, Hutchinson, London.

A novel, cited in the text, that brings imperial Vienna to life with special vividness is:

Musil, Robert: THE MAN WITHOUT QUALITIES, London, 1953.

CHAPTER 6.

Ottoman History and Institutions:

Davis, Wm. Stearns: A SHORT HISTORY OF THE NEAR EAST, University of Minnesota.

Grousset, Rene: L'EMPIRE DES STEPPES, Paris, 1939.

Lyber, A. H.: THE GOVERNMENT OF THE OTTOMAN EMPIRE IN THE TIME OF SULEIMAN THE MAGNIFICENT.

Penzer, Norman Mosely: THE HAREM, Harrap, London, 1936.

Toynbee, Arnold: A STUDY OF HISTORY (Vol. III), Oxford University Press.

Reign of Abdul Hamid and the Young Turk Revolution:

Haslip, Joan: THE SULTAN, Cassell, London, 1958. (This recent, popular but well-documented biography of Abdul Hamid has provided valuable background for the chapter and is cited in the text.)

Young, George: CONSTANTINOPLE, London, 1926.

Yeats-Brown, Francis: THE GOLDEN HORN, London, 1932.

Mears, E. G.: MODERN TURKEY, New York, 1924.

Benoist-Mechin: MUSTAPHA KEMAL: LE LOUP ET LE LEOPARD, Paris, 1954.

Orga, Irfan: PHOENIX ASCENDANT: THE RISE OF MODERN TURKEY, London, 1958.

Ottoman Foreign Relations:

Graves, P. P.: THE QUESTION OF THE STRAITS, London, 1931.

Howard, Harry N.: THE PARTITION OF TURKEY 1913–1923, University of Oklahoma.

CHAPTER 7.

The general sources listed, Albertini and Renouvin in particular, supply the basic material for this chapter along with A. J. P. Taylor's HABSBURG MONARCHY. *The Austrian angle is derived from:*

Hotzendorf, Conrad von: AUS MEINER DIENSTZEIT (1906–1918).

Redlich, Joseph: FRANCIS JOSEPH.

Molden, Berthold: ALOIS GRAF AEHRENTHAL SECHS JAHRE AUSSER POLITIK OSTERREICH UNGARNS, Deutsche Verlag's Austalt, Stuttgart, 1917.

Musulin, Freiherr von: DAS HAUS AM BALLHAUSPLATZ, Verlag fur Kullurpolitik, Munchen, 1924.

The German reactions are taken from Emil Ludwig op. cit., Nowak op. cit. and von Bulow's MEMOIRS.

A Russian view of the protagonists is to be found in:

Savinsky, A.: RECOLLECTIONS OF A RUSSIAN DIPLOMAT

and in his article in the February 1931 issue of Le Monde Slave "L'Entrevue de Buchlau."

Paleologue, Maurice: UN GRAND TOURNANT DE LA POLITIQUE MONDIALE 1904–1906 (cited in Chapter 3), and GUILLAUME II ET NICOLAS II, Plon, 1935.

CHAPTER 8.

Historical Background on Germany and the Hohenzollerns:

Taylor, A. J. P.: THE COURSE OF GERMAN HISTORY, Hamish Hamilton, 1935.

Meissner, Erich: A CONFUSION OF FACES, Faber and Faber, London.

Vermeil, Edmond: L'ALLEMAGNE CONTEMPORAINE, Aubier, Editions Montaigne, 1952.

Dehio, Ludwig: GERMANY AND WORLD POLITICS IN THE TWENTIETH CENTURY, Chatto and Windus, London, 1959.

Raphael, G.: KRUPP ET THYSSEN (Les Belles Lettres 1923).

Albertini: op. cit.

Renouvin: op. cit.

Biographical material on Kaiser Wilhelm:

Ludwig, Emil: op. cit.

Kuerenberg: op. cit.

Nowak: op. cit.

Muret, Maurice: GUILLAUME II, Paris.

Baumont, Maurice: L'AFFAIRE EULENBURG ET LES ORIGINES DE LA GUERRE MONDIALE, Payot, Paris, 1933.

Muller, Georg Alexander von, Admiral: REGIERTE DER KAISER?, Musterschmidt, Verlag, Frankfurt, 1959.

Cowles, Virginia: op. cit.

Topham, Anne: MEMORIES OF THE KAISER'S COURT, Dodd, Mead, New York, 1914.

Wheeler-Bennett, John: HINDENBURG: THE WOODEN TITAN, Macmillan, London.

On Labor Opposition:

Rosmer, A.: ZIMMERWALD, Paris, 1936.

CHAPTER 9.

In addition to the sources and studies listed under Chapter 1, particularly Sir Bernard Pares' THE FALL OF THE RUSSIAN MONARCHY, *extensive use was made in this chapter of* INTERROGATORIES: LA CHUTE REGIME TSARISTE, *Payot, Paris, 1927, a French translation, prefaced by Basil Maklakov, of selected verbatim reports of hearings before the Extraordinary Commission appointed by the Provisional Government in March 1917 to investigate the acts of the Czarist regime. Citations in this and subsequent chapters, translated by the author, are from this work. Limited use has also been made of the full Russian collection* PADENIE TSARKAVO REGIMA, *Moscow, 1925, 7 vol. Other works consulted include M. V. Rodzianko,* THE REIGN OF RASPUTIN, *London, 1929, V. N. Kokovzev,* OUT OF MY PAST, *London, 1923, and S. U. Witte,* MEMOIRS, *Paris, 1921.*

CHAPTER 10.

Redl Case and Austro-Russian "Dry War":

Seton-Watson, R. W. SARAJEVO, A STUDY IN THE ORIGINS OF THE GREAT WAR, London, 1926.
Redlich, Joseph: EMPEROR FRANCIS JOSEPH OF AUSTRIA, op. cit.
Fonroy, J.: LA BATAILLE DES SERVICES SECRETS, Paris, 1958.

Lenin and the Bolsheviks:

In addition to the sources listed under Chapter 1 the following works were consulted for this section:

Krupskaya, N.: MEMOIRES OF LENIN, London, 1942.
Freville, Jean: INESSA ARMAND, Paris, 1957.
SOUVENIRS SUR LENINE, Editions Sociales, Paris.
Charles, Pierre: LA VIE DE LENINE, Paris.
Souvarine, Boris: STALINE, APERCU HISTORIQUE DU BOLCHEVISME, Plon, Paris, 1937. (*The account of Kamo's career is largely based on Souvarine's.*)
Krassin, Lyubov: LEONID KRASSIN, HIS LIFE AND WORK, 1929.

Okhrana activities in Russia and abroad:

In addition to the sources previously cited, especially the French edition of the 1917 hearings of the investigating committee, INTERROGATOIRES, *the following works were utilized in writing this section:*

Laporte, Maurice: L'HISTOIRE DE L'OKHRANA, Paris, 1935.
Agafonov, V. K.: ZAGRANICHNAIA OKHRANKA, Moscow, 1919.
Heilbut, Ivan: LES VRAIS SAGES DE SION, Paris, 1937.

Franco-Russian Diplomatic Intrigues:

The main source utilized was UN LIVRE NOIR *with a preface by Rene Marchand, Librairie du Travail, Paris, (3 vol. collection of documents translated from the Czarist diplomatic archives released after 1918 by the Soviet government). Other sources consulted or drawn upon include:*

Albertini: op. cit.
Poincaré, Raymond: MEMOIRS, Doubleday, New York, 1926.
Sazonov, Sergei: FATEFUL YEARS, New York, 1928.

Black Hand Conspiracy:

This section is based mainly on Albertini, (cited in the text) and on the French edition of the Sarajevo trial proceedings, (op. cit. Chapter 1), but SARAJEVO *by Joachim Remak, Criterion, New York, 1959, likewise proved most helpful in summarizing and analyzing the most recent documentation available on the background of the Sarajevo crime, and use was also made of Seton-Watson, op. cit.*

CHAPTER 11.

The basic sources for this chapter are Albertini, Bernadotte E. Schmitt, THE COMING OF THE WAR, *New York, 1930, J. R. von Salis, op. cit. Maurice Paleologue's* AN AMBASSADOR'S MEMOIRS, *London and New York, 1923–25 and Emil Ludwig's* WILHELM HOHENZOLLERN.

The account of Francis Ferdinand's funeral and Francis Joseph's reaction to the murder are based on:

Seton-Watson, R. W.: SARAJEVO, op. cit.
Tschuppik, Karl: op. cit.
Margutti: op. cit.
Remak, Joachim: op. cit.
Redlich, Joseph: op. cit.
Hotzendorf, Conrad von: op. cit.

The portrait of Berchtold and the account of the German pressure on Vienna are derived from Albertini, Schmitt, and Salis, as is the account of the Potsdam lunch, with additional details from Kuerenberg's THE KAISER, op. cit. and A. J. P. Taylor's articles "How a World War Began" in the *Observer*, November 1958.

The deceptive calm of July 1914:

Lady Oxford THE AUTOBIOGRAPHY OF MARGOT ASQUITH, *Sir George Buchanan, op. cit., Geneviève Tabouis* THEY CALLED ME CASSANDRA, *op. cit., Karl Krause's* DIE LEZTEN TAGE DER MENSCHHEIT, *and* ELINOR GLYN, *op. cit.*

The elaboration of the Austrian ultimatum and its presentation in Belgrade are derived from Bernadotte Schmitt, J. R. von Salis, Albertini, whose account of Hartwig's death is closely followed here.

For the succession of events on July 27, the guiding thread is Albertini. For the theme of irresponsibility and the chain reaction of mobilizations: A. J. P. Taylor, THE COURSE OF GERMAN HISTORY, *Erich Meissner,* A CONFUSION OF FACES, *op. cit., and Bernadotte E. Schmitt, op. cit.*

For Russian reactions, and the Russian mobilization: Maurice Paleologue's AN AMBASSADOR'S MEMOIRS, *and his* GUILLAUME II ET NICOLAS II. *The scene between Sazonov and the Czar, and Pourtales' delivery of the German declaration of war are from the former, the scene in the Czar's bedroom is from the latter.*

Two French sources for the final events leading up to war are Abel Ferry's LES CARNETS SECRETS (1914–1918), *Bernard Grasset, Paris, 1957, and Marcelle Auclair,* LA VIE DE JEAN JAURES, *Le Seuil, Paris, 1954.*

Other books consulted:

Schierbrand, Wolf von: op. cit.
Ambassador James W. Gerard: MY FOUR YEARS IN GERMANY, New York, Doran, 1917.

von Bulow's Memoirs: op. cit.
Kuerenberg, Joachim von: THE KAISER, op. cit.
Ludwig, Emil: JULY '14, G. P. Putnam's Sons, New York, 1929.
Musulin: DAS HAUS AM BALLHAUSPLATZ, op. cit.

CHAPTER 12.

Basic Sources:

Renouvin: op. cit.
Churchill, Winston: THE WORLD CRISIS, op. cit.
von Salis: op. cit.

Anecdotes and Quotations:

Graves, Robert: "What Was That War Like, Sir," *Observer*, London, November
    9, 1958.
Seeger, Alan: LETTERS AND DIARIES, Charles Scribner's Sons, New York, 1917.
Sassoon, Siegfred: THE POEMS OF SIEGFRED SASSOON, Heinemann, London, 1938.
Read, Douglas: INSANITY FAIR, Jonathan Cape, London.
Hitler, Adolph: MEIN KAMPF, op. cit.
Thoumin, Charles: LA GRANDE GUERRE, Paris, 1916.
Wharton, Edith: FIGHTING FRANCE, Charles Scribner's Sons, New York, 1916.
Cameron, James: *1914*, Rinehart, London.
Ferry, Abel: LES CARNETS SECRETS D'ABEL FERRY, Grasset, Paris.
Muret, Maurice: GUILLAUME II, Paris.
The Crown Prince of Germany: MEMOIRS, Charles Scribner's Sons, New York.

CHAPTER 13.

This chapter generally follows the accounts of Pares, THE FALL OF THE RUS-
SIAN MONARCHY, *Maurice Paleologue,* AN AMBASSADOR'S MEMOIRS, *London and
New York, 1923–25, and Sir George Buchanan,* MY MISSION TO RUSSIA, *Little,
Brown, Boston, 1923 and draws primarily for citations upon* INTERROGATOIRES
(Payot) and THE LETTERS OF THE TSARITZA TO THE TSAR *(Duckworth). Cita-
tions have also been drawn from* OUT OF MY LIFE, *by Field Marshal Paul von
Hindenburg, Harper & Brothers, New York, from Trotsky's* HISTORY OF THE
RUSSIAN REVOLUTION, *and from* RUSSIA LEAVES THE WAR, *by George Kennan,
Faber & Faber, London. Other works consulted include Sir R. H. Bruce Lock-
hart,* BRITISH AGENT, *G. P. Putnam's Sons, New York and London, William
Henry Chamberlain,* THE RUSSIAN REVOLUTION, *Macmillan, 1935, Sergei Sa-
zonov,* FATEFUL YEARS: 1909–16, *Stokes, New York, 1928.*

CHAPTER 14.

*Among, or in addition to, the major sources already mentioned, this chapter
makes use particularly of Trotsky's* HISTORY OF THE RUSSIAN REVOLUTION, *Pares'*
DOWNFALL OF THE RUSSIAN MONARCHY, *the depositions before the Provisional*

Government's investigating committee taken mainly from the abridged French translation edited by Maklakov, THE LETTERS OF THE TSARITZA TO THE TSAR, THE LETTERS OF THE TSAR TO THE TSARITZA, THE SECRET LETTERS OF TSAR NICHOLAS, THE RUSSIAN REVOLUTION *by N. N. Sukhanov, edited and translated by Joel Carmichael, Oxford University Press, 1955,* THE CATASTROPHE, *by Alexander Kerensky, New York and London, 1927,* MEMOIRS, *by P. N. Milyukov, New York, 1955. The citation from* L'ILLUSTRATION *is taken from the excellent three-volume French anthology,* LA GRANDE GUERRE *by Richard Thoumin, Julliard, Paris, 1960.*

CHAPTER 15.

Peace Negotiations:

Renouvin: op. cit.
de Bourbon-Parme, Sixtus: L'OFFRE DE PAIX SEPAREE DE L'AUTRICHE, Paris, 1920.
Harding, Bertita: IMPERIAL TWILIGHT: THE STORY OF KARL AND ZITA OF HUNGARY, Bobbs-Merrill, Indianapolis.
Lloyd George, David: op. cit.
Szemere, P. und Czech, E.: DIE MEMOIREN DES GRAFEN TAMAS VON ERDODY, Amalthea, Wien, 1931.

Propaganda in World War I:

Lasswell, Harold: PROPAGANDA TECHNIQUE IN THE WORLD WAR.
Lumley, Frederick E.: THE PROPAGANDA MENACE, New York, 1933.
Taylor, Edmond: THE STRATEGY OF TERROR, Boston, 1940.
Creel, George: HOW WE ADVERTISED AMERICA, New York, 1920.

Allied Use of National Minorities:

Benes, Eduard: MY WAR MEMORIES, Allen Unwin, London, 1928.
Masaryk, Tomas Garrigue: THE MAKING OF A STATE, Frederick A. Stokes, New York, 1927.

Germany's Wartime Relations with the Bolsheviks:

This section draws heavily on the German diplomatic archives translated and edited, with notes, by Z. A. B. Zeman, Oxford, 1958. In addition to the documents themselves, Dr. Zeman's preface and notes have furnished valuable guidance. Other sources include Alan Moorhead's THE RUSSIAN REVOLUTION *(op. cit. Chapter 1),* RUSSIA LEAVES THE WAR, *by George Kennan (op. cit. Chapter 13), Leonard Schapiro's* HISTORY OF THE RUSSIAN COMMUNIST PARTY, *London, 1960, and N. Rutych's* LE PARTI COMMUNISTE AU POUVOIR, *Paris, 1960. The incident at the Finland Station is taken from Sukhanov (op. cit. Chapter 14). Also referred to were articles of Paul Oberg in* NEUE ZURCHER ZEITUNG, *December 21, 1957.*

CHAPTER 16.

Imprisonment and execution of the Imperial Family:

Along with sources mentioned in previous chapters—particularly Sokoloff's ENQUETE JUDICIAIRE *(op. cit. Chapter 14)—the following works were drawn upon:*

Gilliard, Pierre: LE DESTIN TRAGIQUE DE NICOLAS II ET DE SA FAMILLE, Payot, Paris.
Kerensky, A. F.: THE MURDER OF THE ROMANOVS, London, 1935.

The Bolshevik Rise to Power and the November Revolution:

In addition to works previously mentioned, notably Trotsky's HISTORY OF THE RUSSIAN REVOLUTION, *London 1932–1933, and Sukhanov, (op. cit.), the following were drawn upon for this section:*

Reed, John: TEN DAYS THAT SHOOK THE WORLD, New York, 1919.
Rutych, N.: op. cit.
Rauch, Georg von: A HISTORY OF SOVIET RUSSIA, Frederick A. Praeger, Inc. New York, 1958.
Wilson, Edmond: TO THE FINLAND STATION, New York.

Brest-Litovsk and the Civil War:

In addition to the works by Rauch, Rutych, Schapiro, Zeman, Souvarine, and Kennan, previously mentioned, the following were used in this section:

Wheeler-Bennett, John: BREST-LITOVSK: THE FORGOTTEN PEACE, Macmillan, London.
Rosmer, Alfred: MOSCOU SOUS LENINE, Paris, 1953.
———: LE MOVEMENT OUVRIER PENDANT LA GUERRE, (op. cit.).
Brubacker, Fritz: SOCIALISME ET LIBERTE, Neuchatel, 1955.
Serge, Victor: DESTIN D'UNE REVOLUTION, Paris, 1937.
Lockhart, Bruce: op. cit.

CHAPTER 17.

Accounts of Military Collapse and Kaiser's Abdication:

Baumont, Maurice: L'ABDICATION DE GUILLAUME II, Paris, 1930.
Wheeler-Bennett, John: HINDENBURG, op. cit.
Ludwig, Emil: op. cit.
Crown Prince's Memoirs (previously cited).
Prince Max von Baden: MEMOIRS, London, 1928.
Muller, Georg von, Admiral: op. cit.

For the German Revolution:

Lutz, Ralph Haswell: THE GERMAN REVOLUTION, Stanford University, 1922.
von Salis: op. cit.
Wheeler-Bennett, John: THE NEMESIS OF POWER, op. cit.

Strobel, Heinrich: THE GERMAN REVOLUTION AND AFTER, Jarrolds, London.
Schultz, Sigrid: GERMANY WILL TRY IT AGAIN, op. cit.
Wheeler-Bennett, John: BREST-LITOVSK, op. cit.

CHAPTER 18.

Austrian Military and Political Collapse:

Strong, David: AUSTRIA 1918–1919, Stanford University.
Taylor, A. J. P.: THE HABSBURG MONARCHY, op. cit.
Schuschnigg, Kurt von: FAREWELL TO AUSTRIA, op. cit.
von Salis, J. R.: op. cit.
Benes, Eduard: op. cit.
Renouvin: op. cit.
Horstenau, Glaise: DIE KATASTROPHE.
Redlich, Joseph: SCHICKSALSJAHRE OSTERREICHS.
Shepherd, Gordon: op. cit.
Bauer, Otto: THE AUSTRIAN REVOLUTION, Vienna.
The description of Francis Joseph's funeral is from Wolf von Schierbrand, op. cit.

Biographical details on Karl:

Polzer-Hoditz: KAISER KARL: AUS DER GEHEIMMAPPE SEINES KABINETSCHEFS, Amalthea, Zurich, 1929.
Szemere, P. und Czech, E.: DIE MEMOIREN DES GRAFEN TAMAS VON ERDODY, op. cit.
Harding, Bertita: IMPERIAL TWILIGHT, op. cit.

The Epilogue for the Sixte de Bourbon Affair:

The sources are given in Chapter 15.

Birth of Successor States:

Masaryk: THE MAKING OF A STATE (as previously cited).
Fodor, M. W.: SOUTH OF HITLER, George Allen & Unwin Ltd., London.
Macartney, C. A.: HUNGARY AND HER SUCCESSORS: THE TREATY OF TRIANON AND ITS CONSEQUENCES 1919–1937, O.U.P., 1937.

CHAPTER 19.

Over-all Source:

von Salis: op. cit.

Russian Civil War:

Trotsky: HISTORY OF THE RUSSIAN REVOLUTION, op. cit. STALIN, op. cit.

German Revolution:

Wheeler-Bennett, John: BREST-LITOVSK, op. cit.
Lutz, Ralph Haswell: GERMAN REVOLUTION, op. cit.
Schultz, Sigrid: op. cit.
Shirer, William: op. cit.
Wheeler-Bennett, John: THE NEMESIS OF POWER, op. cit.

For Austria and Hungary:

Strong, David: op. cit.
Bauer, Otto: op. cit.
Nicolson, Harold, Sir: PEACEMAKING, op. cit.
Harding, Bertita: IMPERIAL TWILIGHT, op. cit.

CHAPTER 20.

The Paris Peace Conference and its Consequences:

Nicolson: op. cit.
Lloyd George, David: WAR MEMOIRS, op cit.
House, Edward M.: INTIMATE PAPERS OF COLONEL HOUSE, Boston.
von Salis, J. R.: op. cit.
Churchill, Winston: op. cit.
Lansing, Robert: WAR MEMORIES OF ROBERT LANSING, SECRETARY OF STATE,
    New York, 1935.
Creel, George: op. cit.
Gunther, John: INSIDE EUROPE, Harper & Brothers, New York, 1936.
Poincaré, Raymond: op. cit.
Zweig, Stefan: op. cit.

The Rise of Hitler:

Shirer, William: THE RISE AND FALL OF THE THIRD REICH, Simon and Schuster,
    New York, 1960.
Schultz, Sigrid: op. cit.
Wheeler-Bennett, John: THE NEMESIS OF POWER, op. cit.
von Salomon, Ernst: THE QUESTIONNAIRE.

The Rise of Mussolini:

Mussolini, Benito: MY AUTOBIOGRAPHY, London, 1928.
Borgese, G. A.: GOLIATH: THE MARCH OF FASCISM, 1937.

The Kemalist Revolution:

Benoist-Mechin: op. cit.
Orga, Irfan: op. cit.
Gunther, John: op. cit.
Howard, Harry N.: op. cit.
Hemingway, Ernest: IN OUR TIME, op. cit.
Lawrence, T. E.: SEVEN PILLARS OF WISDOM, London, 1936.
Marlowe, John: THE SEAT OF PILATE, London, 1959.

Index